Fourth
Edition

THE PRACTICE OF PUBLIC RELATIONS

Fraser P. Seitel

Senior Vice President
Director of Public Affairs
The Chase Manhattan Bank

Macmillan Publishing Company
NEW YORK
Collier Macmillan Canada
TORONTO
Maxwell Macmillan International
NEW YORK   OXFORD   SINGAPORE   SYDNEY

To my mommy, who loans me money

Published by
Macmillan Publishing Company
866 Third Avenue, New York, New York 10022

Collier Macmillan Canada, Inc.
Suite 200
1200 Eglinton Avenue, E.
Don Mills, Ontario M3C 3N1

This book was set in Meridien and Univers.

Administrative Editor: Pamela Kusma
Developmental Editor: Dwayne Martin
Production Coordinator: Constantina Geldis
Art Coordinator: Raydelle Clement
Cover Designer: Cathy Watterson
Text Designer: Cynthia Brunk
Photo Editor: Gail L. Meese

Library of Congress Catalog Card Number: 88-62551
International Standard Book Number: 0-675-21092-5
Printed in the United States of America
  1   2   3   4   5   6   7   8   9—92   91

Cover Photo: Computer-generated art © PHOTOTAKE,
C. J. Hoffman

Credits: Part One: Photo by Kevin Fitzsimons/Merrill
Publishing; Part Two: Photo courtesy of Riverside
Hospital, Columbus, Ohio; Part Three: Photo by Gail
Meese/Merrill Publishing; Part Four: Photo courtesy of
Harworth, Inc., Holland, Michigan. Four-color insert: p.
1.: *Meet the Bank* courtesy of Custom Comic Services by
Michael D. Benton and R. Scott Deschaine, Distributed
by the Personal Economics Program of the American
Bankers Association; courtesy of The Chase Manhattan
Bank; courtesy of Anaglifics® system/3DMark, Inc. p. 2:
Courtesy of Noranda Inc. p. 3: Courtesy of The Chase
Manhattan Bank and courtesy of Hamilton College/
photo by William Ray. p. 4: Courtesy of The Potato
Board in Denver; courtesy of Thompson Printing; and
courtesy of Tassani Public Relations. p. 5: Courtesy of
Concerned American Indian Parents, The National
Conference of Christians and Jews, and Martin/Williams
Advertising; courtesy of National Rainbow Coalition;
and courtesy of Coffey Communications. *Senior Edition* is
a copyrighted and trademarked publication of Coffey
Communications, Inc., 190 W. Dayton St., Edmonds,
WA 98020-7207. p. 6: Courtesy of Pizza Hut; courtesy
of New York Racing Association, Inc. p. 7: Courtesy of
CPC/Best Foods and the Howard Marlboro Group;
courtesy of Toys for Adults; and courtesy of Days Inns of
America. p. 8: Courtesy of Vote America Foundation and
Grey Advertising; Videowall system designed by
Christian Jara, Christian Jara Associates, New York.
Article on p. xiii from Elizabeth M. Fowler, ''Careers:
New Stress on Public Affairs, *New York Times*, 28 April
1987, D31. Copyright © 1987 by The New York Times
Company. Reprinted by permission.

Foreword

The profession of public relations has never had more dignity than it possesses today. Once confused with the word *publicity*, it is now seen as a process that is a vital function of management. The public relations practitioner once operated at the lowest management levels. Today, it is a wise company that includes the public relations professional in the inner circle of top management.

Each year, I see new opportunities opening for students who have had solid training in the principles, practice, and ethics of public relations. Each year, I see increasing respect for the profession.

Virtually every business today operates within the view of the public eye. The well-being of stockholders, employers, and customers is tied to policies formulated, tested, and disseminated by public relations professionals.

Fraser P. Seitel brings to the study of public relations the practice of public relations at the highest levels. As senior vice president and director of public affairs at Chase Manhattan Bank, he is a decision maker in his own company and a first-hand observer of the results of public relations practice in major corporations with which the banking business is associated.

Like many of the students who will be reading this text, Mr. Seitel had his undergraduate education in communications. He holds two master's degrees—one an MBA. His experience as a classroom teacher encouraged him to balance the theoretical principles in the book with up-to-date cases, a number of which have not yet run their course and are still to be found on today's front pages.

The Practice of Public Relations has been a popular text through three editions. Now, in this fourth edition, Mr. Seitel has added new chapters on ethics, research, the law, and the concept of public relations as a total management function. It is the best of both possible worlds when the author of a text like this is not only a fine public relations practitioner, but a top corporate executive as well.

In my opinion, the principles, insights, and cases in *The Practice of Public Relations* will benefit communications students, business administration students, and a wide range of executives in both corporate and nonprofit organizations.

Ralph L. Lowenstein, Dean
College of Journalism and Communications
University of Florida

As senior vice president and director of public affairs for Chase Manhattan Bank, Fraser P. Seitel manages a staff of 50 professionals in the traditional areas of public relations work: community affairs, consumer relations, employee communications, financial communications, media relations, philanthropic activities, speech and article writing, and whatever else his management sees fit to hand him.

A Chase Manhattan veteran for almost two decades and a former Hill and Knowlton account executive, Mr. Seitel has supplemented his professional public relations career with steady teaching assignments at Fairleigh Dickinson University, Pace University, New York's Professional Development Institute, Chicago's Ragan Report Workshops, and Colorado's Estes Park Institute. After studying and examining many texts in public relations, he concluded that none of them "was exactly right." Therefore, in 1980 he wrote the first edition of *The Practice of Public Relations* "to give students a feel for how stimulating this field really is." In addition to being educational, his book is written in an engaging, conversational style that introduces students to the excitement, challenge, and uniqueness of public relations work.

Preface

Public relations is among the world's most exciting professions. It is constantly changing and is at the center of the action—from Russia's *glasnost* to the NASA *Challenger* disaster to the Cabbage Patch doll phenomenon to the Bhopal tragedy. Public relations decisions affect the credibility—indeed, the viability—of every organization.

It would be a real shame, therefore, to introduce someone to such a fascinating field with a boring book. This fourth edition of *The Practice of Public Relations* may be a lot of things, but it is not boring.

The focus of this book is on the practical nature of public relations work: communicating, writing, and solving problems. The knowledge provided here is meant to be used.

This book is designed to ensure that students fully understand how public relations theory relates to public relations practice. The field's philosophical underpinnings are aligned with practical examples, providing solid support for the concepts that are essential to public relations.

On the philosophical side, chapter 5 on ethics and chapter 6 on research offer comprehensive discussion of two of the most prominent issues in the field today. Chapter 22 introduces another increasingly important issue in public relations practice, the law.

On the practical side, 60 case studies confront the reader with the most complex public relations conundrums of our time—Watergate, South Africa, Tylenol, Suzuki's Samurai, Beech-Nut's baby juice, and more. A full-color section explores the vast arsenal of promotional weaponry available to the public relations practitioner.

Like the third edition, this text is supplemented with 23 question-and-answer interviews of the most well-known public relations professionals—from a public relations patriarch to the field's most famous current practitioner to the chief spokesman for the president of the United States. The insights of each add much to this volume.

Finally, features titled "Between the Lines" complement the essential elements in the text with readable, provocative examples, stretching from the marketing of basketball superstar Michael Jordan to Asher Edelman's college course in Questionable Ethics to the sad fall from grace of White House public relations professional Larry Speakes.

In an age dominated by the technology of the computer, public relations remains a brutally practical, intensely personal profession. In that spirit, the fourth edition of this book is designed to be a most enticing, useful, and user-friendly introduction to the immensely challenging practice of public relations.

Acknowledgments

This textbook is getting to be a lot of fun to update. The reason is that the practice of public relations never stands still. There's always something exciting going on that deserves comment. So when George Bush and Dan Rather stage a shouting match on national TV or when government leaders are caught with their hands in the cookie jar or when a beer company confronts rumors of urine in the brew—it receives comment here. What a great outlet!

Then, too, this text now has enough of a following that persuading willing and well-known experts in the field to be interviewed is getting easier. In this edition, I was delighted that Harold Burson, Barbara Toffler, Herb Schmertz, Marlin Fitzwater, Myron Kandel, and all the others were happy to help out. Their views add another dimension to the book.

I'm also most grateful, as always, to the crack support staff that helped turn out this fourth edition. Yolanda Rhymer, who looks forward to these new editions as much as she does a visit to her dentist, remained by my side as word-processor-in-chief. Michele Colletta, an administrative expert, was largely responsible for updating and refining the Suggested Readings that follow each chapter. Laura Johnson, Dorothy Barnes, and Sau-Woon Ma also provided valuable administrative support.

Keith McDavid, a designer of uncommon acumen despite his strange accent, once again masterminded the full-color section, which adds spice to this volume. The unquestionable hero, though, of this new edition has been my good friend and devoted counselor, Dr. Joe Snyder, the guiding light behind the ethics and legal chapters that dis-

tinguish this edition. Joe's seminal contribution clearly earns him the MVP award—Most Valuable Participant—for this fourth edition.

I am also indebted to colleagues at leading universities, whose constructive critiques of the other editions helped make this fourth edition an all-around better book: E. Brody, Memphis State University; John S. Detweiler, University of Florida; Jim Eiseman, University of Louisville; Sandy Grossbart, University of Nebraska; Marjorie Nadler, Miami University; Sharon Smith, Middle Tennessee State University; Robert Wilson, Franklin University; Paul Brennan, Nassau Community College; Carol L. Hills, Boston University; George Laposky, Miami-Dade Community College; Mack Palmer, University of Oklahoma; Judy VanSlyke Turk, Louisiana State University; Roger B. Wadsworth, Miami-Dade Community College; James E. Grunig, University of Maryland; Robert T. Reilly, University of Nebraska at Omaha; Kenneth Rowe, Arizona State University; Dennis L. Wilcox, San Jose State University; and Albert Walker, Northern Illinois University. In addition to these academic leaders, I thank the public relations teachers whose insightful suggestions aided this edition: Stanley E. Smith, Arizona State University; Dr. Jan Quarles, University of Georgia; Pamela J. Creedon, Ohio State University; Joel P. Bowman, Western Michigan University; Thomas H. Bivins, University of Oregon; Joseph T. Nolan, University of North Florida; Frankie A. Hammond, University of Florida; Bruce Joffe, George Mason University; and Marjorie Nadler, Miami University.

Finally, I am once again most grateful for the moral support provided me by four individuals of enormous generosity and encouragement. First, A. Wright Elliott, executive vice president of communications at Chase, remains a strong supporter and friend. Second, third, and fourth, Rosemary, Raina, and David Seitel remain the best.

Thank you, one and all.

Contents

New Stress On Public Affairs

BY ELIZABETH M. FOWLER

The public affairs departments of corporations are taking on new importance. They now embrace what used to be called public relations and government relations.

In recent years public relations personnel were among the first to be slashed in company staff reductions. Now there are indications that top managers are putting a new emphasis on public relations, with additional stress on relationships with communities and government entities.

For example, in reducing its public relations staff recently, the Olin Corporation "uncoupled state from Federal Government relations and assigned its manager responsibility for public relations as well," said Seymour Lusterman, a senior research expert for the Conference Board.

Olin also established a public affairs department, he said.

The board, a nonprofit business research organization, has just published a study called "The Organization and Staffing of Corporate Public Affairs."

There are other indications of a new emphasis on more effective public relations. Larry Speakes, former White House press spokesman for President Reagan, now serves as vice president for communications for Merrill Lynch, at a time when the image of the financial community has been tarnished by insider trading charges and other scandals at some Wall Street firms.

Merrill Lynch's training director, Madeline A. Weinstein, also a vice president, said recently that Mr. Speakes had asked that a segment on dealing with the press be included in training programs. The firm annually trains 1,750 new brokers, who are now called financial consultants instead of account executives, indicating their broader activities.

Merrill Lynch's current roster of 11,000 financial consultants around the country often have close contact with the public, the press, community organizations, and state and local governments, all of which require knowledgeable handling.

Egon Zehnder International Inc., one of the largest management recruiting firms, recently issued a survey of corporate public affairs at leading companies. It found that many top corporate officials were worried about their relationship with the press, and therefore the public, and wanted to improve their image.

One result is that the executives have been easing their traditional "no comment" approach when asked questions. They tended to agree that they would need "to be better able to communicate with the press in the future."

"There has been an idea around that companies have cut back on public relations staffs," Mr. Lusterman said last week, adding that the Conference Board survey he wrote indicated that, to the contrary, a number of companies were increasing their public affairs activities and upgrading the importance of that department within the company. He acknowledged that some companies did not respond to the survey because of current or planned staff reductions.

The Conference Board study indicates that senior public affairs officers whose responsibilities include government relations tend to be well educated—50 percent have bachelor's degrees, 24 percent master's degrees and 20 percent law degrees.

They tend to be middle-aged, with 17 percent 45 to 49 years of age and 59 percent older.

More than half of the top public affairs managers report directly to the chief executive, one indication of the importance given to such jobs.

Perhaps one problem for those working in public affairs is that the field spans a wide variety of specialties within a company—investor relations, employee communications (handbooks, newsletters), public information, relations with the community and with the Federal and local governments, media relations, and "issues management."

The last category might include specialists on minority problems and investment in South Africa, for example. In some companies there is a new part of the public affairs function—international public relations.

For public relations personnel with a broad knowledge, there might be good jobs in certain industries, according to Mr. Lusterman's study. He found that those companies increasing staffs included financial institutions, wholesale and retail trade concerns, and utilities. Those making the largest cuts in public affairs staffs, he said, were transportation companies and durable goods concerns.

PART ONE

The Basics

What Is Public Relations?

In the words of new wave rocker Buster Poindexter, aka David Johansen, as we head into the 1990s public relations "is hot, hot, hot."

- Former president of the United States Ronald Reagan, "the great communicator," was admired for his public relations skill as much as for any other quality. His Soviet counterpart, Mikhail Gorbachev, has been every bit Reagan's communications equal. In fact, Gorby's crowning achievement is *glasnost*, a public relations program to enhance the USSR in the eyes of the world.
- In the United States, the practice of public relations is estimated to be a several billion dollar business, with upwards of 550,000 practitioners.
- Almost 200 colleges and universities offer a public relations sequence or degree program. Many more offer public relations courses. In the vast majority of college journalism programs, public relations sequences rank first or second in enrollment.
- By the end of the century, public relations is predicted to experience phenomenal growth, accounting for as many as one million jobs and thereby more than tripling the number of such jobs over the next decade.[1]

By every measure the numbers are growing, as is the role and influence of public relations in our society. The U.S. government has 9,000 communications workers employed by the United States Information Agency alone. Another 1,000 communications specialists work in the Department of Defense. The 50 largest public relations agencies do upwards of one-half billion dollars in fee income annually.[2] Indicative of salary trends for communications executives, one public relations man in 1988 left his $640,000-per-year job at Mobil Oil to make even more money on his own.[3]

Yes, indeed, public relations is hot, hot, hot.

The field's strength stems from its roots, "a democratic society where people have freedom to debate and to make decisions—in the community, the marketplace, the home, the workplace and the voting booth. Private and public organizations depend on good relations with groups and individuals whose opinions, decisions and actions affect their vitality and survival."[4]

So pervasive has the influence of public relations become in our society that some even fear it as a pernicious force; they worry about "the power of public relations to exercise a kind of thought control over the American public."[5]

All of this is quite remarkable when you consider that only a decade earlier public relations was still a maligned and misunderstood art form, more renowned for the three martini lunch than for just about anything else.

How times have changed. As columnist George Will puts it, in an age "of skimmed surfaces, of facile confidence that reality is whatever can be seen and taped and reported,"[6] the practice of public relations has acquired newfound respect. Indeed, in an era of unrelenting questioning by the media and the public, an organization must be not only sensitive to but also highly considerate of its many publics.

A primary vehicle through which an organization shows its public sensitivity and consideration is its public relations professionals. Accordingly, the practice of public relations has shed its old misconceptions, acquired new responsibilities, and inherited an increasing amount of power, prestige, and pay in the 1980s.[7] The striking metamorphosis of public relations from a misunderstood trade to a respected profession will likely continue into the 1990s.

On the other hand, along with its new stature, the practice of public relations is still faced with unprecedented pressure.

- The very name *public relations* is being challenged by such euphemisms as *public affairs, corporate communications, public information,* and a variety of others.
- As public relations positions take on greater credibility, the competition to attain them becomes more intense. Today, the profession finds itself vulnerable to encroachment by people without public relations backgrounds, such as lawyers, marketers, and general managers of every stripe.
- Educational institutions, which have recognized the need to practice public relations intensively, have nonetheless been slow to recognize the need to teach it. This omission is particularly true in university business schools.
- Even though organizations throughout society desperately need professionals of general interests and broad-reaching ideas in sensitive public relations jobs, there is a continuing trend toward specialization in the field.
- The field is still plagued by misrepresentations of what it's all about. More often than not, the public's perception is that public relations is aimed *at* them not *for* them; they see themselves as the object of public relations, not the beneficiaries.[8]

The public relations profession is buffeted by countervailing pressures. It has earned the respect of management yet must still fight for its identity with the general public. It has earned acceptance in most organizations yet must fight for its rightful role in society. It is blessed with unlimited opportunities in the years ahead, yet its very survival is threatened by encroachment from out-siders.

Few other professions are subject to as continuous a current of contro-versy as is the practice of public relations. In any event, it is irrefutable that public relations today, in a comparatively short time and despite a number of handicaps, has evolved from a fringe function to a basic element of society. It has indeed entered its Golden Age.

OVERVIEW OF PUBLIC RELATIONS

Public relations affects almost everyone who has contact with other human beings. All of us, in one way or another, practice public relations daily. For an organization, every phone call, every letter, every face-to-face encounter is a public relations event.

To be sure, public relations is not yet a profession like law, accounting, and medicine, in which practitioners are trained, licensed, and supervised. Nothing prevents someone with little or no formal training from hanging out a shingle as a public relations specialist. Such frauds embarrass professionals in the field and, thankfully, are becoming harder and harder to find.

Over the last decade, public relations has steadily built its reputation, in-creased its prominence, and earned respect across a wide span of society. As today's institutions strive to understand more clearly the forces of change, adapt their activities to new pressures and aspirations, and listen and commu-nicate more effectively, public relations becomes more important. Institutions rely on their practitioners to help win public support and trust, without which they will be rendered powerless.

As the field increases in prominence, it grows in professional stature. The International Association of Business Communicators, a broad-based group that started with an internal communications focus, has 10,000 members. The Public Relations Society of America, with a national membership of almost 14,000, has accredited about one-third of its members through a standardized examination. The society has also investigated legal licensing—similar to that of the accounting and legal professions—for public relations practitioners.

The society's main objective is to increase the field's professionalism. It has a code of standards (see appendix A), which dwells heavily on a practi-tioner's ethical responsibilities. The society also provides additional opportuni-ties in specialized areas of practice: association, corporation, counseling, edu-cational institutions, educators, financial institutions, government, health, investor relations, and utilities. These sections have their own publications, seminars, and programs.

Thousands of practitioners are former newspaper and broadcast reporters, magazine writers, journalism school graduates, advertising agency alumni, and lawyers. Increasingly, practitioners are graduates of college public relations courses.

In an attempt to understand what public relations is and what it can and cannot accomplish, here are a few approaches toward defining public relations.

Marlin Fitzwater

I n January 1987 Marlin Fitzwater was appointed White House spokesman to succeed Larry Speakes. As assistant to the president for press relations, Fitzwater was largely credited with setting a new standard of professionalism and fairness for press relations during President Ronald Reagan's most trying period in office. Although Fitzwater has been a government public relations professional for more than 20 years, perhaps his most difficult public relations challenge was to help restore a measure of credibility to an administration rocked by the Iran-contra affair. By all accounts, he handled this task splendidly.

What is the primary mission of the president's press secretary?
The press secretary speaks for the president and the administration in terms of explaining decisions and issues to the American people.

What is the greatest challenge to the president's press secretary?
The greatest challenge is to accurately and in a timely manner reflect the president's views on the issues before the government. The

APPROACHES TO A DEFINITION

First, public relations is not

- The $10 million basketball center glad-handing the local businessmen at the cigar company's annual luncheon
- The sultry screen actress seductively caressing the after-shave lotion to the clicks of photographers' shutters
- The fast-talking hustler eagerly touting his contacts to a prospective client
- A defrocked evangelist (Jim Bakker), a former baseball slugger arrested for drug possession (Joe Pepitone), or the madam of a reopened bordello (Las Vegas Sheri)

Yet all of these and worse have, from time to time, been mistaken as part of the practice of public relations. As *PR Reporter,* one of the industry's leading

press secretary must measure his value in terms of how honestly and accurately he portrays the position and the ideas of the president.

How close was your access to President Reagan?
Access was not an issue. President Reagan was in constant and close communication with all of his senior staff, certainly including the press secretary.

What's your view on whether a press secretary should create quotes for the president?
The press secretary should reflect the president's thinking and disseminate the president's quotes. He should not create them.

What was your most trying time as the president's press secretary?
Representing the president in daily press briefings during the six to eight months of the Iran-contra investigations. The challenge was to preserve the dignity of the office of the president while at the same time defending the president's policies and programs in the face of a skeptical press.

What is the caliber and attitude of the journalists with whom you dealt at the White House?

The White House press corps represents the highest quality journalists in America. They are inquisitive, smart, relentless, and insightful.

How objective are they?
The White House press corps reports with considerable objectivity. However, some of them have definite points of view. But these points of view are normally an important aspect of their reporting and are sanctioned, if not encouraged, by their organizations.

What was the most rewarding aspect of your job?
Working with President Reagan and being a part of the president's decision-making process.

What advice would you give to public relations practitioners of the future?
Don't forget the basics. We are in the midst of a technology explosion in terms of information dissemination, but the basic principles of information collection are the same. Don't lose sight of honesty, accuracy, and sensitivity as you utilize the new technology.

publications, put it (only slightly tongue-in-cheek), "Exconvicts, child molesters, political fixers, call girls and their procurers, gambling casino bouncers, and a variety of glad-handing front men have been described as 'public relations counselors.' "[9]

A similar thought was expressed by John Sattler, former director of public relations at Ford: "Public relations is an easy and all-encompassing label to hang on people and events. Like cosmetics, it can be thought to cover all types of imperfections and blemishes. It was bound to attract varying levels of capability and competence and motives . . . and has its share of 'schlock' operators."[10]

Although all organizations have, by their existence, some kind of public relations, not all enjoy good public relations. That's what this book is all about—good public relations, the kind you must work at.

Whereas marketing and sales have as their primary objective selling an organization's products, public relations attempts to sell the organization itself. Central to its concern is the public interest.

Advertising also generally aims to sell products through paid means. Good public relations, on the other hand, cannot be bought; it must be earned. The credibility derived from sound public relations work may far exceed that gained through paid advertising.

Product publicity, although one aspect of public relations, is more closely aligned with advertising. In general, the elements of the marketing mix—advertising, product promotion, sales, publicity, and the like—may be but a small part of public relations. As Louis B. Lundborg, former chairman of Bank America, pointed out, "If the person who advises top management on the public implications of company policies and decisions . . . can be influenced by pressures from advertising or marketing forces, he is worthless to management as a PR counselor."[11]

The earliest college teachers of public relations exhorted students to

> learn new ways of using knowledge you already have—a different viewpoint, as if you moved to one side and looked at everything from unfamiliar angles. Project yourself into the minds of people you are trying to reach, and see things the way they do. Use everything you've learned elsewhere—English, economics, sociology, science, history—you name it.[12]

Several decades later, it is still widely thought that a broad background is essential to effectively manage public issues. Although specific definitions of public relations may differ, most who practice it agree that good public relations requires a firm base of theoretical knowledge, a strong sense of judgment, solid communication skills, and, most of all, an uncompromising attitude of professionalism.

Searching for a Single Definition

What, then, is public relations? A lot of people seem to have a pretty good idea, but few seem to agree. American historian Robert Heilbroner describes the field as "a brotherhood of some 100,000, whose common bond is its profession and whose common woe is that no two of them can ever quite agree on what that profession is."[13]

Basically, Heilbroner is right, although there have been a great many efforts over the years to come up with a suitable public relations definition. Perhaps the first recorded definition was found in the Bible: "To do good, and communicate, forget not."[14]

In 1923 Edward Bernays described the function of his fledgling public relations counseling business as one of providing "information given to the public, persuasion directed at the public to modify attitudes and actions, and efforts to integrate attitudes and actions of an institution with its publics and of publics with those of that institution."[15]

In 1939 in an article entitled "The Public Be Not Damned," *Fortune* magazine said, "Public relations is the label used to describe, at one and the same time, techniques and objectives" and "the conduct of individual businesses, as organizations of people banded together in an effort to make a living for themselves and a profit for investors."[16]

In 1944 the *Dictionary of Sociology* defined the field as "the body of theory and technique utilized in adjusting the relationships of a subject with its publics. These theories and techniques represent applications of sociology, social psychology, economics, and political science, as well as of the special skills of journalists, artists, organizational experts, advertising men, etc., to the specific problems involved in this field of activity."[17]

However, as late as 1960, *Webster's Dictionary* showed little understanding when it defined public relations as "relations with the general public through publicity; those functions of a corporation, organization, branch of military service, etc., concerned with informing the public of its activities, policies, etc., and attempting to create favorable public opinion."

Today, although a generally accepted definition of *public relations* still eludes practitioners, substantial headway toward a clearer understanding of the field is being made. One of the most ambitious searches for a universal definition was commissioned in 1975 by the Foundation for Public Relations Research and Education. Sixty-five public relations leaders participated in the study, which analyzed 472 different definitions and offered the following 88-word sentence:

> Public relations is a distinctive management function which helps establish and maintain mutual lines of communications, understanding, acceptance, and cooperation between an organization and its publics; involves the management of problems or issues; helps management to keep informed on and responsive to public opinion; defines and emphasizes the responsibility of management to serve the public interest; helps management keep abreast of and effectively utilize change, serving as an early warning system to help anticipate trends; and uses research and sound and ethical communication techniques as its principal tools.[18]

Another definition emerged from an assembly of public relations associations in 1978.

> Public relations practice is the art and social science of analyzing trends, predicting their consequences, counseling organization leaders, and implementing planned programs of action which will serve both the organization's and the public's interest.[19]

In 1980 the Task Force on the Stature and Role of Public Relations, chartered by the Public Relations Society of America, offered two definitions that project a perspective of the field at the highest policy-making level and encompass all its functions and specialities.

■ Public relations helps an organization and its publics adapt mutually to each other.
■ Public relations is an organization's efforts to win the cooperation of groups of people.[20]

Communications counselor L. L. L. Golden suggested that more people would understand the field if the term *relations with the public* were used to describe it.[21] Even though it is unlikely that a generally accepted definition of public relations will soon—or perhaps ever—be agreed upon, the attempts mentioned here provide some idea of the scope of the practice.

R-A-C-E Formula

Communications professor John Marston suggested that *public relations* be defined in terms of four specific functions: (1) research, (2) action, (3) communication, and (4) evaluation.[22] Applying the R-A-C-E approach involves researching attitudes on a particular issue, identifying action programs of the organization that speak to that issue, communicating those programs to gain understanding and acceptance, and evaluating the effect of the communication efforts on the public.

This formula is similar to one of the most repeated definitions of *public relations,* developed by *Public Relations News,* a leading newsletter for practitioners.

> Public relations is the management function which evaluates public attitudes, identifies the policies and procedures of an individual or an organization with the public interest, and plans and executes a program of action to earn public understanding and acceptance.[23]

The key word in this definition is *management.* Although most practitioners believe the field is close to the top of the policy-making pyramid, some think the word *management* is not part of a definition. For example, the Public Relations Society of America did not include it for simplicity reasons. That group's definition called public relations "the function that maintains an organization's relationships with society in a way that most effectively achieves the organization's goals."[24]

Underlying these definitions is an unstated word—*performance.* Without proper performance, good public relations is impossible. Stated another way, performance must precede publicity. Or in the less grandiose terminology of public relations professor Mack Palmer, "First lay the egg, then cackle."

Modern Shorthand Definitions

Other attempts to define the field have been less esoteric but no less germane. For the British Institute of Public Relations, "public relations is a deliberate, planned, and sustained effort to establish and maintain mutual understanding between an organization and its publics." For *Fortune* magazine "public relations is good performance today publicly appreciated because it is adequately communicated."

To one counselor "public relations is communicating truth—good works well told." To others it's

- "Persuasive communication designed to influence specific publics"
- "The winning of public acceptance by acceptable performance"
- "Doing good and getting credit for it"
- "*Performance* plus *Recognition*"

And then there's Murray, the cabdriver, who opined on the way to LaGuardia airport in late 1988 that "public relations is proper propaganda and common sense properly disseminated." Not bad, Murray.

How will this book define the practice of public relations? We'll agree with Professor James Grunig that *"public relations is the management of communications between an organization and its publics."*

The fact that few can agree on a precise definition of public relations should neither confuse nor overwhelm students in the field. The more we try to define it, the more we understand the scope of the practice. That no one can agree on a definition shows that public relations is a continually evolving profession.[25]

INTERPRETING MANAGEMENT TO THE PUBLIC

Public relations practitioners are basically interpreters. On the one hand, they must interpret the philosophies, policies, programs, and practices of their management to the public; on the other hand, they must translate the attitudes of the public to their management.

To accomplish these tasks accurately and truthfully, practitioners must gain attention, understanding, acceptance, and, ultimately, action from target publics. But first they have to know what management is thinking. Lewis A. Lapham, former vice-chairman of Banker's Trust Company, admitted that he'd learned "in tears and sweat, if not in blood, that public relations philosophy, inspiration, and action must flow from the top."[26]

Good public relations can't be practiced in a vacuum. No matter what the size of the organization, a public relations department is only as good as its access to management. For example, it's useless for a senator's press secretary to explain the reasoning of an important decision without first finding out what the senator had in mind. So, too, an organization's public relations staff is impotent without firsthand knowledge of the reasons for management's decisions and the rationale for organizational policy. As Lapham put it, "No matter how skillful the public relations techniques and technicians, they simply cannot succeed if top management is unaware of or sidesteps its responsibilities in describing its place in the community and in defining its objectives."[27]

The Railroaded Railroad

The Grand Northern Railroad couldn't get a break. In the summer came the floods. In the winter came the snow. In between came the cows mistaking the GN tracks for grazing land. For the 50,000 commuters who depended on the Grand Northern to get them to and from work each day, it meant perpetual and massive delays. The GN—or as it was derisively labeled by its riders, the Grand Nuisance—was a laughingstock.

One afternoon, Grand Northern's president decided to take action. He called a press conference. "From now on," he told the skeptical journalists, "this railroad will run on time every time. We will make a concerted effort to improve all phases of our customer service. You're going to see a real change in this railroad." He went on to announce a special program that would award bonuses to staff members demonstrating superior service to customers.

The next morning, sixteen miles from its destination, in the middle of an expansive open field miles from civilization, the GN Mainliner—pride of the GN fleet—sputtered miserably, coughed one last puff of steam, and collapsed with a groan, leaving hundreds of irate commuters to ponder their morning headline: "Grand Northern Promises 'Real Change' for Passengers."

QUESTIONS

1. How would you evaluate Grand Northern's public relations strategy?
2. In retrospect, what would you have counseled relative to the timing, content, and advisability of the press conference?
3. Having suffered this setback, what would you suggest as the firm's subsequent public relations approach?

The public relations department can counsel management. It can advise management. It can even exhort management to action. But management must call the shot on organizational policy. Practitioners must fully understand the whys and wherefores of policy and communicate the ideas accurately and candidly to the public. Anything less can lead to major problems.

INTERPRETING THE PUBLIC TO MANAGEMENT

The flip side of the coin is interpreting the public to management. Simply stated, this task means finding out what the public really thinks about the firm and letting management know. Regrettably, corporate history is filled with examples of public relations departments failing to anticipate the true sentiments of the public.

For example, in 1962 U.S. Steel produced a credible argument that a rise in steel prices was in the public's best long-term interest. That decision, however, was ill-timed and denounced by three government agencies and many national leaders. President Kennedy condemned the company's move as a blatant act of "contempt for 185 million Americans." Thereafter both the company and the industry were subject to scornful broadsides from all quarters.

In another incident several years later, General Motors paid little attention to an unknown consumer activist named Ralph Nader, who spread the message that GM's Corvair was unsafe at any speed. When Nader's assault began to be believed, the automaker assigned private detectives to trail him. In short order, General Motors was forced to acknowledge its act of paranoia, and the Corvair was eventually sacked at great loss to the company.

In the mid-1970s, as both the price of gasoline and oil company profits rose rapidly, Mobil infuriated a suspicious public by purchasing Marcor, parent of the Montgomery Ward department store chain, instead of spending its earnings on new oil exploration and development.

Government leaders, too, sometimes incorrectly interpret the public's sentiments. Late in his presidency, Jimmy Carter tried to enlist public support for his flagging economic program with a nationally televised address that discussed America's "malaise" and the need to get the nation moving again. Carter's speech backfired, it was generally agreed, because many Americans resented the notion that they and their country were languishing. The Carter malaise speech was later used to great advantage by Ronald Reagan in his successful bid for the presidency in 1980.

These examples indicate that organizations are often insensitive to the public's concerns. As Joseph T. Nolan, veteran public relations teacher and practitioner, has put it,

> Nobody has a larger stake in our economic system—or a larger say in our society—than U.S. business. Whether that system and that society continue to work to the satisfaction of business will depend, ultimately, on how successfully individual businesses demonstrate that they can work for the good of everybody.[28]

THE PUBLICS OF PUBLIC RELATIONS

The term *public relations* is really a misnomer. *Publics relations* or *relations with the publics* would be more to the point. Practitioners must communicate with many different publics—not just the general public—each having its own special needs and requiring different types of communications. Often, the lines that divide these publics are thin, and the potential overlap is significant. Therefore, priorities, according to organizational needs, must always be reconciled (Figure 1–1).

Technological change, in particular, has brought greater interdependence among people and organizations, and there is growing concern in organiza-

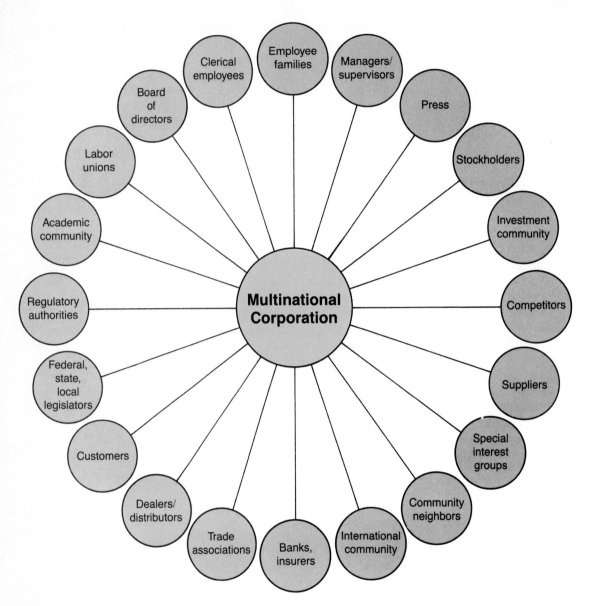

FIGURE 1–1   Twenty key publics of a typical multinational corporation. (Art by Lou Braun)

tions today about managing extensive webs of interrelationships. Indeed, managers have become interrelationship conscious.

Internally, managers must deal directly with various levels of subordinates, as well as with cross-relationships that arise when subordinates interact with one another. Externally, managers must deal with a system that includes government regulatory agencies, labor unions, subcontractors, consumer groups, and many other independent—but often related—organizations. The public relations challenge in all of this is to effectively manage the communications between managers and the various publics with whom they interrelate.

Definitions differ on precisely what constitutes a public. One definition suggests that a public arises when a group of people (1) face a similar indeterminate situation; (2) recognize what is indeterminate and problematic in that situation; and (3) organize to do something about the problem.[29] This framework can be used to define three stages in the evolution of publics.

1. **Latent publics**—when a group is in an indeterminate situation but does not recognize the situation as a problem. For example, in the early 1980s the vast majority of airline employees for such companies as Braniff, Laker, Continental, and World probably had little idea that the combination of airline deregulation and rising energy prices might have negative consequences for them. They quickly got the message, however, when all four companies began to totter and fall toward the brink of bankruptcy.
2. **Aware publics**—when the group recognizes the problem.
3. **Active publics**—when the group organizes to do something about the problem.[30]

This three-stage approach to defining publics may help practitioners design communications strategies to respond to each level of the evolutionary process.

Publics may also be classified into several overlapping categories.

1. **Internal and external**   Internal publics are inside the organization: supervisors, clerks, managers, stockholders, and the board of directors. External publics are those not directly connected with the organization: the press, government, educators, customers, the community, and suppliers.
2. **Primary, secondary, and marginal**   Primary publics can most help—or hinder—the organization's efforts. Secondary publics are less important, and marginal publics are the least important of all. For example, members of the Federal Reserve Board of Governors, who regulate banks, would be the primary public for a bank awaiting a regulatory ruling, whereas legislators and the general public would be secondary.
3. **Traditional and future**   Employees and current customers are traditional publics; students and potential customers are future ones. No organization can afford to become complacent in dealing with its changing publics. Today a firm's publics range from women to minorities to senior citizens to homosexuals. Each might be important to the future success of the organization.
4. **Proponents, opponents, and uncommitted**   An institution must deal differently with those who support it and those who oppose it. For supporters, communications that reinforce beliefs may be in order. But changing the opinions of skeptics calls for strong, persuasive communications. Often, particularly in politics, the uncommitted public is crucial. Many a campaign has been decided because the swing vote was won over by one of the candidates.

The typical organization is faced with a myriad of critical publics with whom it must communicate daily. It must be sensitive to their needs and concerns, communicating with each in a timely and effective manner. Although management must always speak with one voice, its inflection, delivery, and emphasis should be sensitive to each public.

THE ESSENCE OF PUBLIC RELATIONS

Ethics, truth, credibility—these values are what good public relations is all about. Cover-up, distortion, and subterfuge are the antitheses of good public relations.

Much more than customers for their products, managers today desperately need constituents for their beliefs and values. In the 1990s the role of public relations will be much more to guide management in framing its ideas and making its commitments. The counsel that management will need must come from advisors who understand public attitudes, public moods, public needs, and public aspirations.[31]

That public relations professionals will provide the needed counsel is indisputable for many reasons.

- The growth of people's influence all over the world makes essential the role of public relations as a detector, interpreter, and communicator.
- The growing diversity of people and their interests demands greater sophistication and skill to deal with it.
- Growing specialization in all fields is increasing the need for broader understanding and professional communications skills.
- The decline in writing skills in society increases the need for those who have such skills.
- There is a growing number of media and voices using the channels of communication.
- Technology and the spread of knowledge have increasingly made the world the province of public relations.
- Finally, the tendency for leaders of organizations to look inward creates a pressing need for those able to provide outside viewpoints and reach outside groups to earn goodwill for their organizations.[32]

Winning this elusive goodwill takes time and effort. Credibility can't be won overnight, nor can it be bought. If management policies aren't in the public's best interest, no amount of public relations can obscure that reality. Public relations is not effective as a temporary, defensive measure to compensate for management misjudgment. If management errs seriously, the best—and only—public relations advice must be to get the story out immediately.

If public relations has come of age as a serious and substantive profession, does that mean the end of the slick-talking image merchant? Hardly. People will always be interested in finding an angle or sneaking one by in the flimflammiest traditions of P. T. Barnum. But clearly the profession is growing more sophisticated, with many practitioners thinking of their work in the same vein as counselor Emanuel Goldberg.

> Public relations today is not product publicity, lavish trips or gifts to the media at Christmas, or a smile at the teller's window. It's a very deep kind of private and public service. It conceives themes and programs, advises management on thorny issues, deals constructively with a wide variety of oft-conflicting publics . . . writes capably and imaginatively, surveys attitudes, promotes good community, race and employee relations, plans for emergencies, creates radio and television programs, gets into publishing and films and slides and exhibits, adapts to similar tasks overseas, meets with analysts, brokers, and money managers, collaborates in marketing and advertising campaigns, and on and on and on.[33]

In today's information society, the presence of public relations has never been more pervasive. Nor has its power been more potent as the demands increase to communicate effectively. No matter what it's called, the practice of public relations is here to stay. As counselor Philip Lesly has put it, "Whether the references are favorable, unfavorable or neutral, the significant fact is that the field has been growing rapidly in public awareness."[34]

No matter how you define it then, public relations has become part of our common language, and its practice is essential in the conduct of our relationships.

NOTES

1. John V. Pavlik, *Public Relations: What Research Tells Us* (Newbury Park, CA: Sage Publications, 1987): 85.
2. Jack O'Dwyer, *O'Dwyer's Directory of Public Relations Firms 1987* (New York: J.R. O'Dwyer Co., 1987): 7.
3. Paula Span, "Chronicles of the PR Warrior," *The Washington Post*, 28 April 1988, C1.
4. "The Design for Undergraduate Public Relations Education," a study co-sponsored by the public relations division of the Association for Education and Journalism and Mass Communication, the Public Relations Society of America, and the educators' section of PRSA, 1987, 1.
5. Jeff Blyskal and Marie Blyskal, *PR: How the Public Relations Industry Writes the News* (New York: William Morrow and Company, 1985): 61.
6. George F. Will, "Well, I Don't Love You E.T.," *Newsweek*, 19 July 1982, 76.
7. Robert K. Gray, "Public Relations," *Washington Journalism Review* (January/February 1980): 43.
8. Philip Lesly, "Report and Recommendation: Task Force on Stature and Role of Public Relations," *Public Relations Journal* (March 1981): 32.
9. *PR Reporter* 15, no. 16 (17 April 1972): 1.
10. John E. Sattler, remarks at a seminar of the Public Relations Society of America, Dearborn, MI, 1 April 1976.
11. Louis B. Lundborg, "Executive Survival Kit," *Industry Week*, 14 April 1980, 12.

12. Berton J. Ballard, lecture at San Jose State University, San Jose, CA, 1948. Cited in Pearce Davies, "Twenty-Five Years Old and Still Growing," *Public Relations Journal* (October 1977): 22–23.

13. Cited in Scott M. Cutlip and Allen H. Center, *Effective Public Relations*, 6th ed. (Englewood Cliffs, NJ: Prentice-Hall, 1985): 5.

14. Heb. 13:16.

15. Edward L. Bernays, *Crystallizing Public Opinion* (New York: Liveright Publishing Corp., 1961): LV.

16. "The Public Be Not Damned," *Fortune*, 1 March 1939, 83.

17. Pratt Henry Fairchild, ed., *Dictionary of Sociology* (New York: Philosophical Library, 1944).

18. Rex F. Harlow, "Building a Public Relations Definition," *Public Relations Review* 2, no. 4 (Winter 1976): 36.

19. First World Assembly of Public Relations Associations, Mexico City, Mexico, 1978.

20. Lesly, "Report and Recommendation," 30.

21. L. L. L. Golden, *Only by Public Consent* (New York: Hawthorn Books, 1968).

22. John E. Marston, *The Nature of Public Relations* (New York: McGraw-Hill, 1963): 161.

23. Denny Griswold, *Public Relations News*, International Public Relations Weekly for Executives, 127 East 80th Street, New York, NY 10021.

24. C. Thomas Wilck, "Toward a Definition of Public Relations," *Public Relations Journal* (December 1977): 26.

25. Counselor John Cook provides an irreverant and insightful analysis of the various definitions, myths, and premises of public relations in "PR Without the BS," *Public Relations Quarterly* (Spring 1974): 6–25.

26. Cited in John F. Budd, Jr., *An Executive's Primer on Public Relations* (Philadelphia: Chilton, 1969): xii.

27. Ibid.

28. Joseph T. Nolan, "Protect Your Public Image with Performance," *Harvard Business Review* (March/April 1975): 142.

29. John Dewey, *The Public and Its Problems* (Chicago: Swallow Press, 1927).

30. James E. Grunig, "Defining Publics in Public Relations: The Case of a Suburban Hospital," *Journalism Quarterly* (Spring 1978): 109.

31. Robert Cushman, Chairman, Norton Company, remarks to the New England Chapter of the Public Relations Society of America, Worcester, MA, 27 February 1980.

32. Lesly, "Report and Recommendation," 17.

33. Emanuel Goldberg, "Public Relations: Before and After Watergate," *Congressional Record* 120, no. 177 (17 December 1974): 40591.

34. "Never Mind How Field Defines Itself: Power Brokers, Public Think 'PR' Pandemic," *PR Reporter* (4 January 1988): 6.

Armstrong, Richard A. "Public Affairs vs. Public Relations." *Public Relations Quarterly* (Fall 1981): 26.

Awad, Joseph. *The Power of Public Relations.* New York: Praeger, 1985.

Baxter, Bill L. "Education for Corporate Public Relations." *Public Relations Review* (Spring 1985): 38–41. This article, based on a survey by the Public Relations Society of America, indicates that public relations courses stress journalism and general writing skills.

Bernays, Edward L. *Crystallizing Public Opinion,* LV–LVI. New York: Liveright Publishing Corp., 1961.

Black, Sam, and Melvin L. Sharpe. *Practical Public Relations.* Englewood Cliffs, NJ: Prentice-Hall, 1983.

Brody, E. W. *The Business of Public Relations.* New York: Praeger, 1987.

Brough, B. *Publicity and Public Relations Guide for Business.* Sunnyvale, CA: Oasis Press, 1985.

Canfield, Bertrand R., and H. Frazier Moore. *Public Relations: Principles, Cases and Problems.* 6th ed. Homewood, IL: Richard D. Irwin, 1973.

Cantor, Bill. *Experts in Action: Inside Public Relations.* White Plains, NY: Longman, 1984.

Center, Allen H., and Frank E. Walsh. *Public Relations Practices: Case Studies.* 2d ed. Englewood Cliffs, NJ: Prentice-Hall, 1985.

Cole, Robert S. *The Practical Handbook of Public Relations.* Englewood Cliffs, NJ: Prentice-Hall, 1981.

Cook, John. "PR Without the BS." *Public Relations Quarterly* (Spring 1975): 6–25.

Cutlip, Scott M., Allen H. Center, and Glen M. Broom. *Effective Public Relations.* 6th ed. Englewood Cliffs, NJ: Prentice-Hall, 1985.

Dilenschneider, Robert L., and Dan J. Forrestal. *Dartnell Public Relations Handbook.* 3d ed. Chicago: Dartnell Publishing Co., 1987.

Harlow, Rex F. "Building a Public Relations Definition." *Public Relations Review* 2, no. 4 (Winter 1976): 34–41.

Hill, John W. *The Making of a Public Relations Man,* 131–143. New York: David McKay, 1963.

Kadon, Ann, and John Kadon. *Successful Public Relations Techniques.* Scottsdale, AZ: Modern Schools, 1976.

Lesly, Philip. *Bonanzas and Fool's Gold Treasures and Dross from the Nuggetizing of Our Lives.* Chicago: Acclaim Communications (P.O. Box 81085), 1987.

———. "Report and Recommendations: Task Force on Stature and Role of Public Relations." *Public Relations Journal* (March 1980): 21–44. This presents an overview analysis of the entire public relations profession and indications of the likely course it might take in the years ahead.

———. "The Stature and Role of Public Relations." *Public Relations Journal* (January 1981): 14–17. A blue-ribbon task force analysis of the future of the profession.

———, ed. *Public Relations Handbook.* 2d ed. Englewood Cliffs, NJ: Prentice-Hall, 1978. Included are chapters on problems that plague nonprofit organizations, trade associations, schools and universities, newspapers, and other groups. This manual also offers valuable information on numerous communication techniques.

Margulies, Walter P. "Back to Fundamentals." *Public Relations Journal* (April 1982): 50–51.

Marston, John E. *Modern Public Relations.* New York: McGraw-Hill, 1979.

"The New Public Relations." *Public Relations Journal* (January 1981): 29–33.

SUGGESTED READINGS

Newsom, Douglas A. "Realities, Questions and Challenges for Public Relations Education." *Public Relations Journal* (March 1984): 15.

Newsom, Doug, and **Alan Scott.** *This is PR: The Realities of Public Relations.* Belmont, CA: Wadsworth, 1984.

Nolte, Lawrence W. *Fundamentals of Public Relations.* 2d ed. New York: Pergamon Press, 1979.

Nolte, Lawrence W., and **Dennis L. Wilcos.** *Effective Publicity: How to Reach the Public.* New York: John Wiley and Sons, 1984.

Norris, James. *Public Relations.* Englewood Cliffs, NJ: Prentice-Hall, 1984.

Olasky, Marvin N. "Roots of Modern Public Relations: The Bernays Doctrine." *Public Relations Quarterly* (March 1985): 25–27. The author suggests that the beginning of modern public relations was the so-called Bernays doctrine that posited the notion that communication, done skillfully, could effectively "engineer public consent" to bring about social goals.

Randall, Craig. "Hype Springs Eternal." *United Inflight Magazine* (November 1985): 48–51, 130–148.

Read, Nat B., Jr. "Laws of Public Relations." *Public Relations Journal* (May 1982): 20.

Reilly, Robert T. *Public Relations in Action.* Englewood Cliffs, NJ: Prentice-Hall, 1987.

Simon, Raymond. *Public Relations: Concepts and Practice.* Columbus, OH: Grid, 1976.

———. *Public Relations: Concepts and Practice.* New York: Macmillan, 1984.

———. *Public Relations Management: Casebook.* Columbus, OH: Publishing Horizons, 1986.

———. *Publicity and Public Relations Worktext.* 4th ed. Columbus, OH: Grid, 1978.

Stephenson, Howard. *Handbook of Public Relations.* 2d ed. New York: McGraw-Hill, 1971.

Stevens, Art. *The Persuasion Explosion.* Washington, DC: Acropolis Books, 1985.

Sullivan, Michael. *Management Audit for Public Relations Firms.* Doylestown, PA: Sullivan Associates (P.O. Box 229), 1987.

Voros, Gerald J., and **Paul Alvarez.** *What Happens in Public Relations.* New York: American Management Associations, 1981.

Watergate

I felt sure that it was just a public relations problem that only needed a public relations solution.

—Richard M. Nixon*

In 1972 Richard Nixon was elected president of the United States in a landslide. His opponent, Senator George McGovern, won only Massachusetts and the District of Columbia.

Two years later, on August 8, 1974, Nixon resigned in disgrace and humiliation. His administration had been tarnished by illegal wiretapping, illegal surveillance, burglary, and unlawful use of the law. The president and his men were toppled by the most profound political scandal in the nation's history, which grew out of a series of break-ins at the Democratic national headquarters in a Washington, DC, building named Watergate.

One notion raised in the aftermath of Watergate was that the president and his advisors were too concerned about public relations, about covering up the facts, and that this concern led to their downfall. This castigation of public relations for its supposed role in Watergate is ironic. For had Nixon or his aides been able to comprehend the broad ramifications and deal with them straightforwardly, they might have been judged with more compassion and spared their severe and precipitous fall. (Although the field of public relations took the heat for the Watergate scandal, most of Nixon's key public relations advisors came from the field of advertising.)

As excerpts from transcripts indicate, neither the president nor his advisors knew much about good public relations. By ignoring virtually every elementary public relations principle, they destroyed any chance of many Americans understanding and forgiving them for their misjudgments.

Here are six of the more onerous miscalculations from the Watergate saga.

1. In late 1972, while rumors abounded that the administration was corrupt, the White House remained silent. As the president concluded in a conversation with top aides H. R. Haldeman and John Dean, "We take a few shots and it will be over. Don't worry." Evidently, Nixon felt the public would grow tired of the perpetual pounding on Watergate—therefore his strategy, "Hang tough and ignore it."

2. The spotlight on Watergate intensified, and the media refused to let up. Nixon ordered Dean to prepare an enemies list of journalists and others who opposed the administration, saying, "I want the most comprehensive notes on all those who tried to do us in." Evidently, Nixon felt that going directly after particular individuals would stifle their efforts. This step, according to Dean, was to use "available federal machinery to screw our political enemies."

3. In early 1973 the Senate's investigation dominated national news. The president and his aides were invited to testify, but they declined on the grounds of executive privilege.

4. Like *executive privilege*, the term *national security* also received an extensive workout during the Watergate period. In March 1973 the president discussed with Haldeman and Dean the break-in at the office

---

*Richard Nixon, *RN: The Memoirs of Richard Nixon* (New York: Grosset & Dunlap, 1978), 773.

of the psychiatrist of Daniel Ellsberg, an administration enemy who had leaked secret Pentagon papers to the *New York Times*. Dean suggested that the break-in be defended as national security. The president agreed, saying, "We had to get information for national security grounds. We had to do it on a confidential basis. Neither [the FBI nor the CIA] could be trusted." Several years later, both Dean and Haldeman were imprisoned, primarily because of their roles in the break-in.

5. In October 1973 Nixon had had enough of Archibald Cox, the special prosecutor he appointed to get to the bottom of the Watergate case. When Cox persisted in trying to secure the release of the president's confidential tapes, Nixon ordered Attorney General Elliot Richardson to fire him. Richardson refused and resigned. Deputy Attorney General William Ruckelshaus, the next in line, also refused and was fired. Finally, Solicitor General Robert Bork, the third person in line, fired Cox. In one fell swoop, Nixon's Saturday Night Massacre became a new cause célèbre, and the Watergate fires were reignited.

6. The president's relations with the media steadily deteriorated. About a major report by Dean on Watergate, Nixon told an aide, "We've got to keep our eye on the Dean thing—just give them some of it, not all of it . . . just take the heat."

Facing an audience of several hundred newspaper editors in November 1973, the president rambled, "In all of my years of public life, I have never obstructed justice. And I think too that I could say that in my years of public life, that I welcome this kind of examination, because people have got to know whether or not their president is a crook. Well, I am not a crook."

Later on, the president instructed Press Secretary Ronald Ziegler in responding to substantive press queries: "Just get out there and act like your usual cocky, confident self."**

QUESTIONS

1. How sound was the early White House public relations strategy to hang tough in the midst of media flak?
2. Why didn't Watergate go away?
3. Why was the compilation of an enemies list a mistake?
4. Did the enemies list serve any purpose for Nixon?
5. Was invoking executive privilege justified in the administration's refusal to appear before the Senate Watergate Committee?
6. What were the public relations consequences of invoking executive privilege?
7. How would you have interpreted the Saturday Night Massacre if you were an objective observer?
8. What public relations/credibility problems might have been caused by the break-in at the office of Ellsberg's psychiatrist and the subsequent national security explanation defending it?
9. How would you assess Nixon's media relations philosophy?
10. If you had been Nixon's public relations counselor, what would you have recommended upon learning the full story about Watergate?

Helpful hint for answering the questions: British statesman Edmund Burke once said, "It is not what a lawyer tells me I may do, but what humanity, reason, and justice tell me I ought to do."

**This case is adapted from one of the more significant analyses of Watergate as a study in public relations: Joseph T. Nolan, "Watergate: A Case Study in How Not to Handle Public Relations," *Public Relations Quarterly* (Summer 1975): 23–26. It is reprinted by permission. Also see Gladys Engel Lang and Kurt Lang, "Polling on Watergate: The Battle for Public Opinion," *Public Opinion Quarterly* 44: 530–547.

The Evolution of
Public Relations

The practice of public relations has been shaped by several underlying and pervasive trends in our complex, industrialized society. Three fundamental trends, in particular, are directly related to the evolution of public relations: (1) the growth of big institutions; (2) the increasing incidence of change, conflict, and confrontation in society; and (3) the heightened awareness of people everywhere as a result of more sophisticated communications technology.

■ The bigness of today's society has played a significant role in the development of public relations. The days of the mom and pop grocery store, the tiny community college, and the small local bank are rapidly disappearing. In their places have emerged supermarket chains and 24-hour-a-day 7-Elevens, statewide community college systems with populous branches in several cities, and the beginnings of multibank, multistate banking networks. As institutions have grown larger, as the U.S. population has burgeoned to nearly 241 million, and as people have had to deal increasingly with bureaucracy, so too have institutions themselves refined their methods of communicating with their publics. Specifically, the public relations profession has evolved to interpret these large institutions to the publics they serve.
■ The increasing incidence of change, conflict, and confrontation in society is yet another reason for the evolution of public relations. Women's rights and affirmative action, consumerism and environmental awareness, labor-management disputes, and the unhappiness of the general public with large institutions have all contributed materially to the need for more and better communications and the existence of more and better communicators.

Then, too, the rapidity of societal change has added to the necessity for professional public relations. Today, nothing stands still for long. The credibility of organizations is challenged constantly, and their role in society can change instantly. Our expectations of an organization's responsibilities are ever-changing. And the emerging technologies of the computer age—robotics, genetic engineering, telecommunications, and the rest—put added pressure on an organization to continually adapt not only its communicated messages but its methods of communicating as well.

■ A final factor in the development of public relations has been the heightened awareness of people everywhere. First came the invention of the printing press. Later it was the pervasiveness of mass communications: the print media, radio, and television. Then it was the development of cable, satellite, videotape, video discs, video typewriters, portable cameras, word processors, and all the other communications technologies that have helped fragment audiences and deliver Marshall McLuhan's "global village." All have contributed to the necessity in today's society to better understand and manage the communications process.

ANCIENT BEGINNINGS

Although we think of public relations as a 20th century phenomenon, its roots are ancient. Leaders in virtually every great society throughout history understood the importance of influencing public opinion through persuasion. For example, the Iraqis of 1800 B.C. hammered out their messages on stone tablets so that farmers could learn the latest techniques of harvesting, sowing, and irrigating.[1] The more food the farmers grew, the better the citizenry ate and the wealthier the country became—a good example of planned persuasion to reach a specific public for a particular purpose, in other words, public relations.

Later on, the Greeks put a high premium on communication skills. The best speakers, in fact, were generally elected to leadership positions. Occasionally, aspiring Greek politicians enlisted the aid of Sophists (individuals renowned for both their reasoning and their rhetoric) to help fight verbal battles. Sophists would gather in the amphitheaters of the day and extol the virtues of particular political candidates. Often, their arguments convinced the voters to elect those candidates. Thus, the Sophists set the stage for today's lobbyists, who attempt to influence legislation through effective communication techniques.

The Romans, particularly Julius Caesar, were also masters of persuasive techniques. When faced with an upcoming battle, Caesar would rally public support through assorted publications and staged events. Similarly, during World War I a special U.S. public information committee, the Creel Committee, was formed to channel the patriotic sentiments of Americans in support of the U.S. role in the war. Stealing a page from Caesar, the committee's massive verbal and written communications effort was successful in marshaling national pride behind the war effort. According to a young member of the Creel Committee, Edward L. Bernays (later considered by many as the father of public relations), "This was the first time in our history that information was used as a weapon of war."[2]

Even the Catholic church had a hand in the beginnings of public relations. In the 1600s, under the leadership of Pope Gregory XV, the church established a college of propaganda to "help propagate the faith." In those days the term *propaganda* did not have a negative connotation; the church simply wanted to inform the public about the advantages of Catholicism.

EARLY AMERICAN EXPERIENCE

The American public relations experience dates back to our founding as a republic. Influencing public opinion, managing communications, persuading individuals at the highest levels—all were at the core of the American Revolution. The colonists tried to persuade King George III that they should be accorded the same rights as Englishmen. "Taxation without representation is tyranny!" became their public relations slogan to galvanize fellow countrymen.

When King George refused to accede to the colonists' demands, they combined the weaponry of sword and pen. Samuel Adams, for one, organized committees of correspondence as a kind of revolutionary Associated Press to speedily disseminate anti-British information throughout the colonies. He also staged events to build up revolutionary fervor, like the Boston Tea Party, where colonists masqueraded as Indians, boarded British ships in Boston Harbor, and pitched chests of imported tea overboard—as impressive a media event as has ever been recorded, sans television. When several Boston dockhands were shot by the enemy, Adams publicized the event as the Boston Massacre, and the people were persuaded.

Thomas Paine, another early practitioner of public relations, wrote periodic pamphlets that urged the colonists to band together. In one issue of *Common Sense*, Paine wrote poetically, "These are the times that try men's souls. The summer soldier and the sunshine patriot will, in this crisis, shrink from the service of their country." The people listened, were persuaded, and took action—testifying to the power of early American public relations.

LATER AMERICAN EXPERIENCE

The creation of the most important document in our nation's history, the Constitution, also owed much to public relations. Federalists, who supported the Constitution, fought tooth and nail with Anti-Federalists, who opposed it. Their battle was waged in newspaper articles, pamphlets, and other forms of persuasion, in an attempt to influence public opinion. To advocate ratification of the Constitution, political leaders like Alexander Hamilton, James Madison, and John Jay banded together, under the pseudonym Publius, to author letters in leading newspapers. Today, those letters are bound in a document called *The Federalist Papers* and are still used in the interpretation of the Constitution.

After ratification the Constitutional debate continued, particularly over the document's apparent failure to protect individual liberties against government encroachment. Hailed as the Father of the Constitution, Madison framed the Bill of Rights in 1791, which ultimately became the first ten amendments to the Constitution. Fittingly, the first of those amendments safeguarded,

Edward L. Bernays

E dward L. Bernays is a public relations patriarch. In 1923 he wrote the seminal book on the subject, *Crystallizing Public Opinion*, which laid down the principles, practices, and ethics of the profession. In that same year, at New York University, he taught the first college course in public relations. A nephew of Sigmund Freud, Bernays pioneered the application of the social sciences to public relations. In partnership with his late wife, he has advised presidents of the United States, industrial leaders, and legendary figures—from Enrico Caruso to Eleanor Roosevelt. Indeed, Edward Bernays himself is a legend in the field of public relations.

When you taught the first public relations class, did you ever envision the profession growing to its present stature?

I gave the first course in public relations after *Crystallizing Public Opinion* was published in 1923. I decided that one way to give the term *counsel on public relations* status was to lecture at a university on the principles, practices, and ethics of the new profession. New York University was willing to accept my offer to do so. But I never envisioned at that time that the profession would spread throughout the United States and then throughout the free world.

What were the objectives of that first public relations course?

The objectives were to give status to the new profession. Many people still believed the term *counsel on public relations* was a euphemism for publicity man, press agent, flack. Even H. L. Mencken in his book on the American language ranked it such. But in his *Supplement to the American Language* published some years later, he changed his viewpoint and used my definition of the term.

What are the most significant factors that have led to the rise in public relations practice?

The most significant factor is the rise in people power and its recognition by leaders. Theodore Roosevelt helped bring this about with his Square Deal. Woodrow Wilson helped with his New Freedom, and so did Franklin Delano Roosevelt with his New Deal. And this tradition was continued as time went on.

Do you have any gripes with the way public relations is practiced today?

I certainly do. The meanings of words in the United States have the stability of soap bubbles. Unless words are defined as to their meaning by law, as in the case of professions—for instance, law, medicine, architecture—they are in the public domain. Anyone can use them. Recently, I received a letter from a model agency offering to supply me with a "public relations representative" for my next trade fair at which we might exhibit our client's products. Today, any plumber or car salesman or unethical character can call himself or herself a public relations practitioner. Many who call themselves public relations practitioners have no education, training, or knowledge of what the field is. And the public equally has little understanding of the meaning of the two words. Until licensing and registration are introduced, this will continue to be the situation.

What pleases you most about current public relations practice?

What pleases me most is that there are, indeed, practitioners who regard their activity as a profession, an art applied to a science, in which the public interest, and not pecuniary motivation, is the primary consideration; and also that outstanding leaders in society are grasping the meaning and significance of the activity.

What's the most significant problem that confronts the field?

The most significant problem confronting the field is this matter of definition by the state of what public relations is and does—defining it, registering and licensing practitioners through a board of examiners chosen from the field, and developing economic sanctions for those who break the code of ethics.

How would you compare the caliber of today's public relations practitioner with that of the practitioner of the past?

The practitioner today has more education in his subject. But unfortunately, education for public relations varies with the institution where it is being conducted. This is due to the lack of a standard definition. Many institutions of higher learning think public relations activity consists of skillful writing of press releases and teach their students accordingly. This is, of course, not true. Public relations activity is applied social science.

Where do you think public relations will be twenty years from now?

It is difficult to appraise where public relations will be twenty years from now. I don't like the tendency of advertising agencies gobbling up large public relations organizations. That is like surgical instrument manufacturers gobbling up surgical medical colleges or law book publishers gobbling up law colleges. However, if licensing and registration take place, then the profession is assured a long lifetime as long as democracy itself.

among other things, the practice of public relations: "Congress shall make no law respecting an establishment of religion, or prohibiting the free exercise thereof; or abridging the freedom of speech, or of the press, or the rights of the people peaceably to assemble, and to petition the government for a redress of grievances." In other words, people were given the right to speak up for what they believed in and the freedom to try to influence the opinions of others. Thus was ratified the practice of public relations.[3]

Into the 1800s

The practice of public relations continued to percolate in the 19th century. Among the more prominent—yet negative—antecedents of modern public relations that took hold in the 1800s was press agentry. Two of the more well-known—some would say notorious—practitioners of this art were Amos Kendall and Phineas T. Barnum.

In 1829 President Andrew Jackson selected Kendall, a writer and editor living in Kentucky, to serve in his administration. Within weeks Kendall became a member of Old Hickory's "kitchen cabinet" and eventually became one of Jackson's most influential assistants.

Kendall performed just about every White House public relations task. He wrote speeches, state papers, and messages and turned out press releases. He even conducted basic opinion polls. Although Kendall is generally credited with being the first authentic presidential press secretary, his functions and role went far beyond that.

Among Kendall's most successful ventures in Jackson's behalf was the development of the administration's own newspaper, the *Globe*. Although it was not uncommon for the governing administration to publish its own national house organ, Kendall's deft editorial touch refined the process to increase its effectiveness. Kendall would pen a Jackson news release, distribute it for publication to a local newspaper, and then reprint the press clipping in the *Globe* to underscore Jackson's nationwide popularity. Indeed, that popularity continued unabated throughout Jackson's years in office, with much of the credit going to the president's public relations advisor.*

Most public relations professionals would rather not talk about Phineas T. Barnum as an industry pioneer. Barnum was a huckster—pure and simple. His end was to make money, and his means included publicity. He remained undaunted even when the facts sometimes got in the way of his promotional ideas. "The public be fooled" might well have been his motto.

Like him or not, Barnum was a master publicist. In the 1800s, as owner of a major circus, Barnum generated article after article for his traveling show.

---

*Kendall was most decidedly not cut from the same swath as today's neat, trim, buttoned-down press secretaries. On the contrary, Jackson's man was described as "a puny, sickly looking man with a weak voice, a wheezing cough, narrow and stooping shoulders, a sallow complexion, silvery hair in his prime, slovenly dress, and a seedy appearance" (Fred F. Endres, "Public Relations in the Jackson White House," *Public Relations Review* 2, no. 3 [Fall 1976]: 5–12).

He purposely gave his star performers short names—for instance, Tom Thumb, the midget, and Jenny Lind, the singer—so that they could easily fit into the headlines of narrow newspaper columns. Barnum also staged bizarre events, such as the legal marriage of the fat lady to the thin man, to drum up free newspaper exposure. And although today's practitioners scoff at Barnum's methods, some press agents still practice his techniques. Nonetheless, when today's public relations professionals bemoan the specter of shysters and hucksters that still overhangs their field, they inevitably place the blame squarely on the fertile mind and silver tongue of Phineas T. Barnum.

Emergence of the Robber Barons

The American Industrial Revolution ushered in many things at the turn of the century, not the least of which was the growth of public relations. The 20th century began with small mills and shops, which served as the hub of the frontier economy, giving way to massive factories. Country hamlets, which had been the centers of commerce and trade, were replaced by sprawling cities. Limited transportation and communications facilities became nationwide rail-road lines and communications wires. Big business took over, and the businessman was king.

The men who ran America's industries—and without exception they were all male—seemed more concerned with making a profit than with improving the lot of their fellow citizens. Railroad owners such as William Vanderbilt, bankers such as J. P. Morgan, oil magnates such as John D. Rockefeller, and steel impresarios such as Henry Clay Frick—each ruled the fortunes of thousands of others. Typical of the reputation acquired by this group of industrialists was the famous—or perhaps apocryphal—response of Vanderbilt when questioned about the public's reaction to his closing of the New York Central Railroad: "The public be damned!"

Little wonder that Americans cursed Vanderbilt and his ilk as robber barons who cared little for the rest of society. Although most who depended on these industrialists for their livelihood felt powerless to rebel, the seeds of discontent were being sprinkled liberally throughout the culture. It was just a matter of time before the robber barons would get their comeuppance.

Enter the Muckrakers

When the ax fell on the robber barons, it came in the form of criticism from a feisty group of journalists dubbed muckrakers. The muck that these reporters and editors "raked" was dredged from the scandalous operations of America's business enterprises. Upton Sinclair's novel *The Jungle* attacked the deplorable conditions of the meat-packing industry. Ida Tarbell's *History of Standard Oil* stripped away the public facade of the nation's leading petroleum firm. Magazines such as *McClure's* struck out systematically at one industry after another. The captains of industry, so used to getting their own way and having to answer to no one, were wrenched from their environment of peaceful passivity and rolled out on the public carpet to answer for their sins. Journalistic shock stories soon led to a wave of sentiment for legislative reform.

As journalists and the public became more anxious, the government got more involved. Congress began passing laws telling business leaders what they could and couldn't do. Trust busting then became the order of the day. Conflicts between employers and employees began to break out, and newly organized labor unions rose to the fore. The socialist and Communist movements began to take off. Ironically, it was ''a period when free enterprise reached a peak in American history, and yet at that very climax, the tide of public opinion was swelling up against business freedom, primarily because of the breakdown in communications between the businessman and the public.''[4]

For a time, these men of inordinate wealth and power found themselves limited in their ability to defend themselves and their activities against the tidal wave of public condemnation. They simply did not know how to get through to the public effectively. To tell their side of the story, the business barons first tried using the lure of advertising to silence journalistic critics; they tried to buy off critics by paying for ads in their papers. It didn't work. Next, they paid publicity people, or press agents, to present the companies' positions. Often, these hired guns painted over the real problems and presented their client's view in the best possible light. The public saw through this approach.

Clearly, another tack had to be discovered to get the public to at least consider the business point of view. Business leaders were realizing that a corporation might have capital, labor, and natural resources, yet be doomed to fail if it lacked intelligent management, particularly in the area of influencing public opinion. The best way to influence public opinion, as it turned out, was through the vehicles of honesty and candor. Such simple truths were the keys to the accomplishments of American history's first successful public relations counselor, Ivy Lee.

IVY LEE: THE REAL FATHER OF MODERN PUBLIC RELATIONS

Ivy Ledbetter Lee was a former Wall Street newspaper reporter who plunged into publicity work in 1903. Lee believed in neither Barnum's the-public-be-fooled approach nor Vanderbilt's the-public-be-damned philosophy. To Lee the key to business acceptance and understanding was that the public be informed. Lee firmly believed that the only way business could answer its critics convincingly was to present its side honestly, accurately, and forcefully. Instead of merely appeasing the public, Lee thought a company should strive to earn public confidence and good will. Sometimes, this task meant looking further for mutual solutions. Other times, it even meant admitting that the company was wrong.* Hired by the anthracite coal industry in 1906, Lee set forth his beliefs in a Declaration of Principles to newspaper editors.

> This is not a secret press bureau. All our work is done in the open. We aim to supply news. This is not an advertising agency; if you think any of our matter ought properly to go to your business office, do not use it. Our matter is accurate. Further details on any subject treated will be supplied promptly, and any editor will be assisted most cheerfully in verifying any statement of fact . . . . In brief, our plan is frankly and openly, on behalf of business concerns and public institutions, to supply to the press and public of the United States prompt and accurate information concerning subjects which it is of value and interest to the public to know about.[6]

In 1914 John D. Rockefeller, Jr., who headed one of the most maligned and misunderstood of America's wealthy families, hired Lee. As Lee biographer Ray Eldon Hiebert pointed out, Lee did less to change the Rockefellers' policies than to give them a public hearing.[7] For example, when the family was censured scathingly for its role in breaking up a strike at the Rockefeller-owned Colorado Fuel and Iron Company, the family hired a labor relations expert (at Lee's recommendation) to determine the causes of an incident that had led to several deaths. The end result of this effort was the formation of a joint labor-management board to mediate all workers' grievances on wages, hours, and working conditions. When the chairman of the Colorado company balked at the plan, John, Jr., (again on Lee's advice) personally toured the mines, listened to the miners' complaints, and even danced with the miners' wives at a social function. By the end of his visit, Rockefeller was not only a hero to the miners, but also a new man to the public. Years later, John, Jr., admitted that the public relations outcome of the Colorado strike "was one of the most important things that ever happened to the Rockefeller family."[8]

In working for the Rockefellers, Lee tried to "humanize" them, to feature them in real-life situations, such as playing golf, attending church, and celebrating birthdays. Simply, Lee's goal was to translate the Rockefellers into terms that every individual could understand and appreciate. Years later, despite their critics, the family came to be known as one of the nation's outstanding sources of philanthropic support.

Lee's contributions to the development of public relations went beyond his work with the Rockefellers. He urged the American Tobacco Company, for example, to initiate a profit-sharing plan. He advised the Pennsylvania Railroad to beautify its stations. He educated the American public about ocean travel to

---

*Lee's dramatic influence on the standards of the emerging profession is obvious in an observation made in 1963 by Earl Newsom, prominent public relations counsel, who told a colleague, "The whole activity of which you and I are a part can probably be said to have had its beginning when Ivy Lee persuaded the directors of the Pennsylvania Railroad that the press should be given the facts on all railway accidents—even though the facts might place the blame on the railroad itself.[5]

overcome the negative impressions of the *Titanic* and *Lusitania* disasters. In addition, he was instrumental in working with Admiral Richard Byrd and aviator Charles Lindbergh to combat the public's fear of flying.

Ironically, even Ivy Lee could not escape the glare of public criticism. In the late 1920s Lee was asked to serve as advisor to the parent company of the German Dye Trust, which, as it turned out, was an agent for the policies of Adolf Hitler. When Lee realized the nature of Hitler's intentions, he advised the Dye Trust cartel to work to alter Hitler's ill-conceived policies of restricting religious and press freedom. For his involvement with the Dye Trust, Lee was branded a traitor and dubbed "Poison Ivy" by members of Congress investigating un-American activities. The smears against him in the press rivaled the most vicious against the robber barons.

Despite his unfortunate involvement with the Dye Trust, Ivy Lee is recognized as the individual who brought honesty and candor to public relations. Lee, more than anyone before him, lifted the field from a questionable pursuit (that is, seeking positive publicity at any cost) to a professional discipline designed to win public confidence and trust through communications based on candor and truth.

THE GROWTH OF MODERN PUBLIC RELATIONS

Ivy Lee, in effect, opened the gate. After he helped establish the idea that firms had a responsibility to inform their publics, the practice began to grow in every sector of American society.

Government

During World War I, as earlier noted, President Woodrow Wilson established the Creel Committee under journalist George Creel. It proved to be an effective force, mobilizing public opinion in support of the war effort and stimulating the sale of war bonds through Liberty Loan publicity drives. Not only did the war effort get a boost, but so did the field of public relations.

During World War II the public relations field received an even bigger boost. With the Creel Committee as its precursor, the Office of War Information (OWI) was established to convey the message of the United States at home and abroad. Under the directorship of Elmer Davis, a veteran journalist, the OWI laid the foundations for the United States Information Agency as the voice of America around the world.

World War II also saw a flurry of activity to sell war bonds, boost the morale of those at home, spur production in the nation's factories and offices, and, in general, support America's war effort as intensively as possible. By virtually every measure, this full-court public relations offensive was an unquestioned success.

The proliferation of public relations officers in World War II led to a growth in the number of practitioners during the peacetime that followed. This was probably a good thing, especially in light of the feisty, combative attitude of President Harry Truman toward many of the country's largest institutions. For example, in a memorable address over radio and television on April 8, 1952, President Truman announced that, as a result of a union wage dispute, "the government would take over the steel plants." The seizure of the steel mills touched off a series of historical events that reached into Congress and the Supreme Court and stimulated a massive public relations campaign, the likes of which had rarely been seen outside the government.[9] The steel conflict between the president and big business was the first of many such battles that have marked the government-business relationship over the years.

Counseling

The nation's first public relations firm, the Publicity Bureau, was founded in Boston in 1900, specializing in general press agentry. The first Washington, DC, agency was begun in 1902 by William Wolff Smith, former correspondent for the *New York Sun* and the *Cincinnati Inquirer*. Two years later Ivy Lee joined with George Parker to begin a public relations agency that was later dissolved. Lee reestablished the agency in New York in 1919 and brought in T. J. Ross as a partner. The T. J. Ross agency remains today the nation's oldest public relations counseling firm.

John W. Hill entered public relations in 1927 after a dozen years as a journalist. Together with William Knowlton, Hill founded Hill and Knowlton, Inc., in Cleveland. Hill soon moved east, and Knowlton dropped out of the firm. However, the agency quickly became one of the largest public relations operations in the world, with 1,050 employees in 20 countries and 20 U.S. cities. Hill stayed active in the firm for half a century and mused about the field's beginnings.

> In 1927, public relations was just in its infancy. Think of the contrast of the present with fifty years ago. Less than a handful of counseling firms anywhere in the world and barely a handful of practitioners tucked away and lost in the offices of a very few large corporations—far removed from the executive suite.[10]

In addition to Hill, the Creel Committee associate chairman, Carl Byoir, launched his own public relations counseling firm in 1930. Ironically, 56 years later, Byoir's firm, Carl Byoir & Associates, merged with Hill and Knowlton to become the largest public relations company in the world.

Besides Byoir and Hill, Earl Newsom and Pendleton Dudley also founded early firms. Newsom, who began Newsom & Company in 1935, generally limited his public relations practice to counseling companies like Ford, General Motors, and Jersey Standard. In his otherwise critical treatment of public relations, *The Image Merchants*, author Irwin Ross paid tribute to Newsom's success.

> The goal of a good many public relations men is someday to attain the lonely eminence of Earl Newsom. His fees are high; his clients include some of the most august names in the corporate roster; and his work involves pure "consultation."[11]

P. T. Barnum Revisited: The Days of Super Hype

Although most public relations professionals disagree with the publicity-seeking antics attributed to P. T. Barnum, publicity for publicity's sake is still very
much in vogue, especially in the numerous national photo magazines. In a
return to the kind of media hype that Barnum made famous over 100 years
ago, today's magazine journalists occasionally sacrifice everything—including
objectivity and news judgment—to land a story about a hot personality or a
hot project.

This is especially true in the case of the movie industry, where personality
journalism—also labeled *disposable journalism*—reigns supreme. For example,
in the summer of 1982, with America mired in a nagging recession, Hollywood
launched a gaggle of escapist movies, built around exotic personalities, to take
the country's mind off its economic problems. Hollywood publicists had a field
day as personality-oriented magazines, such as *People* and *Us,* and news magazines, such as *Time* and *Newsweek,* made a mad dash to pick up on the summer movie mania.

In the first month of their runs, largely because of the lavish magazine
publicity they received, many of the summer films did spectacularly. *Conan, the
Barbarian* grossed $33 million; *Star Trek II* grossed $51 million; *Rocky III*
grossed $56 million; and *E. T.,* the blockbuster of all time, grossed $87 million
in its first month in movie theaters.

The success of these movies was quickly followed by dolls, video games,
magazines, coloring books, lunch boxes, and assorted other merchandising
spin-offs. By the late 1980s the personality cult had reached the airwaves, with
network programs like "Entertainment Tonight" and "Life-styles of the Rich
and Famous" spawning local facsimiles that seemed a lot more palatable than
viewing programs on economic and societal dilemmas.

As *Newsweek* cultural affairs editor Charles Michener summarized the
craze, "There's a great deal of public apathy toward news. The line is growing
very blurred between news and entertainment. It's big business, and agents
and PR people are now in the position of playing magazines off against each
other in ways that they never could before. It obviously has to do with people
seeking escape."

Dudley, like Newsom, got started early and remained in public relations until
his death in 1966 at age 90. Dudley's firm later became Dudley-Anderson-
Yutzy, one of the most admired agencies for introducing innovative techniques
to win public approval.

Another early counselor, Harold Burson, emphasized marketing-oriented public relations, "primarily concerned with helping clients sell their goods and services, maintain a favorable market for their stock, and foster harmonious relations with employees."[12] Today, Burson-Marsteller ranks as one of the world's largest public relations agencies.

Corporations

Problems in the perception of corporations and their leaders dissipated in the United States in the wake of World War II. Public opinion polls of that period ranked business in an esteemed position. People were back at work, and business was back in style.

Smarter companies—General Electric, General Motors, American Telephone & Telegraph (AT&T), for example—worked hard to preserve their good names through both words and actions. Arthur W. Page became AT&T's first public relations vice president in 1927. Page was a pacesetter, helping to manage AT&T's reputation as a prudent and proper corporate citizen. Indeed, Page's five principles of successful corporate public relations are as relevant now as they were in the 1930s.

1. To make sure management thoughtfully analyzes its overall relation to the public
2. To create a system for informing all employees about the firm's general policies and practices
3. To create a system giving contact employees (those having direct dealings with the public) the knowledge needed to be reasonable and polite to the public
4. To create a system drawing employee and public questions and criticism back up through the organization to management
5. To ensure frankness in telling the public about the company's actions[13]

Paul Garrett was another who felt the need to be responsive to the public's wishes. A former news reporter, he became the first director of public relations for General Motors in 1931. Garrett once reportedly explained that the essence of his job was to convince the public that the powerful auto company deserved trust, that is, "to make a billion-dollar company seem small."

Education

One public relations pioneer who began as a publicist in 1913 was Edward L. Bernays, nephew of Sigmund Freud and author of the landmark book *Crystallizing Public Opinion* (see page 26). Bernays was a true public relations scholar, teaching the first course in public relations in 1923. Bernays's seminal writings in the field were among the first to disassociate public relations from press agentry or publicity work. As Bernays wrote later,

> At first we called our activity "publicity direction." We intended to give advice to clients on how to direct their actions to get public visibility for them. But within a year we changed the service and its name to "counsel on public relations." We recognized that all actions of a client that impinged on the public needed counsel. Public visibility of a client for one action might be vitiated by another action not in the public interest.[14]

Historian Eric Goldman credited Bernays with "[moving] along with the most advanced trends in the public relations field, thinking with, around, and ahead of them."[15]

Other leading public relations educators included Milton Fairman, a Chicago news reporter and corporate public relations practitioner who later served as president of the Foundation for Public Relations Research and Education; Rex F. Harlow, who formed the American Council on Public Relations in 1939 and later presided over its merger with the Public Relations Society of America (PRSA) in 1947; and W. Howard Chase, a founding member of the PRSA, who advocated that public relations professionals should concern themselves with public issues management rather than with more narrow communications problems.

PUBLIC RELATIONS COMES OF AGE

As noted earlier in this chapter, public relations really came of age as a result of the confluence of three general factors in our society: (1) the growth of large institutions and their sense of responsibility to the public; (2) the increased changes, conflicts, and confrontations among interest groups in society; and (3) the heightened awareness of people everywhere brought about by increasingly sophisticated communications technology.

Growth of Large Institutions

Ironically, the public relations profession received perhaps its most major forward thrust when business confidence suffered its most severe setback. The economic and social upheaval caused by the Great Depression of the 1930s provided the impetus for corporations to seek public support by telling their stories. Public relations departments sprang up in scores of major companies, among them Bendix, Borden, Eastman Kodak, Eli Lilly, Ford, General Motors, Standard Oil, Pan American, and U.S. Steel. The role that public relations played in helping regain post-Depression public trust in big business helped project the field into the relatively strong position it enjoyed during World War II.

Again, the Truman years marked a challenging period for public relations practitioners. That era was characterized by controls on information in the name of national security, Communist scares, and a general antagonism between government and big business. Nonetheless, as big business became more

Terrorism in the Satellite Era

Nowhere has new communications technology been more striking than in its use as a persuasive tool in the politics of war in the 1980s—particularly by terrorists. Using the 1979 capture of American embassy employees as the linchpin, Iranian militants in Tehran launched a massive, long-distance, nonstop media campaign to convince the world of their nation's mistreatment at the hands of the shah. Angry mobs of Iranian fanatics were beamed live and in blazing color to millions of Western homes on a nightly basis—only serving to infuriate viewers and further strain anti-Iranian feelings.

In the summer of 1982, hopelessly surrounded in the suburbs of West Beirut, Lebanon, by the Israeli army, Palestinian Liberation Organization Chief Yasir Arafat also tried to use the world media to slip out of his predicament. When a U.S. congressional delegation with an accompanying television camera crew visited him, Arafat signed a document in his bunker—in full view of the television cameras—ostensibly recognizing Israel's right to exist. Within an hour of Arafat's televised encounter with the congressmen, authoritative Palestinians in the West rushed to clarify that what their leader really meant in signing the document was that "Israel would be recognized when we get an independent Palestinian state."

Three years later, when Palestinian gunmen hijacked a TWA jetliner, murdered an American passenger, and terrorized all aboard, they also gleefully posed for international television with a gun at the head of the plane's pilot. Indeed, by the late 1980s, manipulation of the world's media had become a disturbing and increasingly more important objective of terrorists who would stop at nothing—including cold-blooded murder—to gain control of the airwaves.

and more cognizant of the vulnerable public role it played in American society, so too did corporate managers become increasingly aware of the important role that could be played by skillful public relations practitioners.

Change, Conflict, and Confrontation

Disenchantment with big institutions reached a head in the 1960s. The conflicts during the early part of the decade between private economic institutions—especially large corporations—and various disenfranchised elements of society arose from long-standing grievances. As one commentator put it, "Their rebellion was born out of the desperation of those who had nothing to lose. Issues were seen as black or white, groups as villainous and virtuous, causes as holy or satanic, and leaders as saints or charlatans."[16]

The social and political consternation of the 1960s dramatically affected many areas, including the practice of public relations. The Vietnam War fractured society. In addition, people began talking about the environment, the rights of minorities and consumers, and, once again, the ills perpetrated by big business. Assassinations of civil rights leaders, political heroes, and even the president of the United States—all magnified by the omnipresence of television—caused the American public to demand answers to society's ills.

Ralph Nader began to look pointedly at the inadequacies of the automobile industry. Women, long denied equal rights in the workplace and elsewhere, began to mobilize into activist groups, such as the National Organization of Women (NOW). Environmentalists, worried about threats to the land and water by business expansion, began to support groups such as the Sierra Club. Minorities—particularly blacks and Hispanics—began to petition and protest for their rights through such groups as the Congress on Racial Equality, the National Association for the Advancement of Colored People (NAACP), and the Student Nonviolent Coordinating Committee. Homosexuals, senior citizens, birth control advocates, and social activists of every kind began to challenge the legitimacy of large institutions. Not since the days of the robber barons had large institutions so desperately needed professional communications help.

Heightened Public Awareness

The 1970s brought a partial resolution of the problems that afflicted society in the 1960s. Many of these solutions came through the government in the form of affirmative action guidelines, senior citizen supports, consumer and environmental protection acts and agencies, aids to education, and a myriad of other laws and statutes.

As for society's large institutions—particularly big business—they began to clearly recognize their responsibilities as social creatures. Business began to contribute to charities. Managers began to consider community relations a first-line responsibility. The general policy of corporations confronting their adversaries was abandoned. In its place most large companies adopted a policy of conciliation and compromise.

This new policy of social responsibility became corporate gospel in the 1970s and has continued through the 1980s. Corporations have come to realize that their reputations are a valuable asset, to be protected, conserved, defended, nurtured, and enhanced at all times. In truth, institutions in the 1980s have had little choice but to get along with their publics. Largely because of the increasingly more sophisticated communications technology, the public at large is more aware and better informed than in any previous period.

For example, by 1989, 90 million American homes had television, with another 45 million wired for cable. The potential of two-way communications systems through cable, satellite, computer, and video disc technologies promises to further revolutionize the information transmission and receiving process. As a result, publics have become much more segmented, specialized, and sophisticated. Public relations professionals have had to discard many of the traditional methods used to reach and influence these publics. With companies facing the new reality of instant communication through desktop video display terminals, instant file and retrieval through centralized data banks, and comprehensive management information systems, the public relations challenge for the 1990s has become significant indeed.

PUBLIC RELATIONS EDUCATION

As the practice of public relations has developed, so too has the growth of public relations education. In 1951, 12 schools offered major programs in public relations. Four years later there were 28, with 66 other schools offering some instruction in the subject. By 1964, more than 40 colleges and universities offered major programs or sequences in public relations, and another 280 institutions provided some classroom work in the field.

By 1970 there were about 100 schools offering concentrated work in public relations, with nearly 300 others offering at least one course dealing with the profession. By 1980 there were 18,000 students enrolled in public relations degree programs. Public relations graduate enrollments at that time stood at around 4,000 students—nearly double the entire student enrollment in public relations degree programs 10 years earlier. In the 1990s, more than 200 universities will offer sequences in public relations study.

Even though discussion has continued about where public relations education should appropriately be housed—in journalism, business, or liberal arts—the profession's role as an academic pursuit has continued to gain strength. Indeed, the largest jump in the history of public relations enrollments took place between 1975 and 1980, when the number of undergraduates in public relations courses doubled and the number of graduate students in public relations rose by two-thirds.[17]

PUBLIC RELATIONS TODAY

Today, public relations is big business.

- Hundreds of thousands of practitioners work in public relations in the United States alone.
- The Public Relations Society of America, organized in 1947, boasts a growing membership of 14,000 in more than ninety chapters nationwide.
- The Public Relations Student Society of America, formed in 1968 to facilitate communications between students interested in the field and public relations professionals, has 5,000 student members at 151 colleges and universities.
- More than 3,000 U.S. companies have public relations departments.
- More than 1,400 public relations agencies exist in the United States, some billing millions of dollars per year.

- More than 500 trade associations have public relations departments.
- Top communications executives at major companies and agencies draw salaries in six figures.
- Boston University's Graduate School of Public Communication is devoted primarily to instruction in public relations activities.
- At the University of Florida, public relations education has passed the half-century mark.

The scope of modern public relations practice is vast. Press relations, employee communications, public relations counseling and research, local community relations, audiovisual communications, contributions, and numerous other diverse activities fall under the public relations umbrella. Because of this broad range of functions, many public relations practitioners today seem preoccupied with the proper title for their calling—public relations, external affairs, corporate communications, public affairs, corporate relations, ad infinitum. They argue that the range of activities involved offers no hope that people will understand what the pursuit involves unless an umbrella term is used.[18]

Practitioners also worry that as public relations becomes more prominent, its function and those who purportedly practice it are subject to increasingly intense public scrutiny.

- When former White House aides Michael Deaver and Lyn Nofziger were indicted for illegal lobbying violations in 1987, the public relations business was tarred by association.
- Public relations was skewered again when former White House press secretary Larry Speakes admitted in 1988 that he made up presidential quotes.
- In the same year, when the chief communications executive of Mobil Oil, Herb Schmertz, left his $640,000-per-year job, it was also national news.
- And in 1988 when Attorney General Ed Meese fired the Justice Department's respected chief spokesman, Terry Eastland, conservative and liberal observers alike called for Meese's resignation.

Clearly, the public relations field today—whatever it is called and by whomever it is practiced—is in the spotlight. With upwards of 550,000 people in the United States practicing public relations in some form, the field has solidly entrenched itself as an important, influential, and professional component of our society.[19]

1. Scott M. Cutlip, Allen H. Center, and Glen M. Broom, *Effective Public Relations*, 6th ed. (Englewood Cliffs, NJ: Prentice-Hall, 1985), 23.
2. Edward L. Bernays, speech at the University of Florida Public Relations Symposium, Gainesville, FL, 1 February 1984.
3. Harold Burson, speech at Utica College of Syracuse University, Utica, NY, 5 March 1987.
4. Ray Eldon Hiebert, *Courtier to the Crowd: The Story of Ivy L. Lee and the Development of Public Relations* (Ames: Iowa State University Press, 1966).
5. Rex Harlow, "A Public Relations Historian Recalls the First Days," *Public Relations Review* (Summer 1981): 39–40.
6. Cited in Sherman Morse, "An Awakening in Wall Street," *American Magazine* 62 (September 1906): 460.
7. Hiebert, *The Story of Ivy L. Lee.*
8. Cited in Alvin Moscow, *The Rockefeller Inheritance* (Garden City, NY: Doubleday, 1977), 23.
9. John W. Hill, *The Making of a Public Relations Man* (New York: David McKay, 1963), 69.
10. John W. Hill, "The Future of Public Relations," speech delivered at the Seventh Public Relations World Congress, Boston, MA, 14 August 1976.
11. Irwin Ross, *The Image Merchants* (Garden City, NY: Doubleday, 1959), 85.
12. Burson, Utica College speech.
13. Cited in Noel L. Griese, "The Employee Communications Philosophy of Arthur W. Page," *Public Relations Quarterly* (Winter 1977): 8–12.
14. Edward L. Bernays, "Bernays' 62 Years in Public Relations," *Public Relations Quarterly* (Fall 1981): 8.
15. David L. Lewis, "The Outstanding PR Professionals," *Public Relations Journal* (October 1970): 84.
16. S. Prakash Sethi, "Business and Social Challenge," *Public Relations Journal* (September 1981): 30.
17. Albert Walker, "End of Decade Survey Shows Academic Growth in Public Relations," *Public Relations Review* (Summer 1982): 46–60.
18. "Diverse Titles Splinter Image of Field: Report of PRSA's Special Committee on Terminology," *Public Relations Reporter* (20 April 1987): Tips & Tactics.
19. Robert Kendall, "Public Relations Employment: Huge Growth Projected," *Public Relations Review* (Fall 1984): 23.

NOTES

SUGGESTED READINGS

Bernays, Edward L. "Bernays' 62 Years in Public Relations." *Public Relations Quarterly* (Fall 1981): 8.

——. *Crystallizing Public Opinion,* XLVIII–LVI. New York: Liveright Publishing Corp., 1961.

——. *The Later Years: PR Insights, 1956–1958.* Rhinebeck, NY: H & M (44 W. Market St., P.O. Box 311), 1987.

Black, Sam. *Public Relations in the 1980s.* Elmsford, NY: Pergamon Press, 1980.

Burson, Harold. "A Decent Respect to the Opinions of Mankind." Speech delivered at the Raymond Simon Institute for Public Relations. New York: Burson-Marsteller (866 Third Ave.), 5 March 1987. This speech highlights public relations activities that have influenced the United States from colonial times to the present day.

Dennis, Lloyd B. "The 'Promises, Promises' Era Is Turning," *Public Relations Quarterly* (Winter 1981–82): 13–17. This lists important trends concerning social responsibility during the rest of this decade.

Dunn, S. W. *Public Relations: A Contemporary Approach.* Homewood, IL: Richard D. Irwin, 1986.

Friedman, William H. "Public Relations and the Sense of History." *Public Relations Quarterly* (Summer 1981): 26–27.

Harlow, Rex. "A Public Relations Historian Recalls the First Days." *Public Relations Review* (Summer 1981): 33–42. Harlow's years of experience in the field and his detailed recollection of personalities and events have enabled him to recreate the excitement of the first days of public relations.

Hill, John W. *The Making of the Public Relations Man.* New York: David McKay, 1963.

Irwin, James W. "Four Decades of Public Relations." *Public Relations Quarterly* 12 (Spring 1967): 21–28.

Olasky, Marvin H. "A Reappraisal of 19th Century Public Relations." *Public Relations Review* (Spring 1985): 3–11. The author calls for a return to the voluntarism and spirit of public enthusiasm that characterized public relations in the 19th century.

Phillips, Charles. *Secrets of Successful Public Relations.* Englewood Cliffs, NJ: Prentice-Hall, 1986.

Poppe, Fred. *50 Rules to Keep a Client Happy.* New York: Harper & Row, 1987.

PR Reporter (P.O. Box 600, Exeter, NH 03833–0600). Weekly.

Public Relations Career Directory. Hawthorne, NJ: Career Press (62 Beverly Rd., P.O. Box 34), 1987.

Public Relations Journal (PRSA, 33 Irving Place, New York, NY 10003). Monthly.

Public Relations News (127 E. 80 St., New York, NY 10021). Weekly.

Public Relations Quarterly (P.O. Box 311, Rhinebeck, NY 12572).

Public Relations Review (10606 Mantz Rd., Silver Spring, MD 20903).

Rogers, Henry. *One-Hat Solution: Strategy for Creative Middle Management.* New York: St. Martin's Press, 1986.

Ross, R. D. *Management of Public Relations.* Melbourne, FL: Krieger, 1984.

Sethi, S. Prakash. "Business and Social Challenge." *Public Relations Journal* (September 1981): 30–31, 34. This overview looks at the evolving relationship between business and society during the last two decades.

Stephenson, Howard. *Handbook of Public Relations.* 2d ed. New York: McGraw-Hill, 1971.

Walker, Albert. "End of Decade Survey Shows Academic Growth in Public Relations." *Public Relations Review* (Summer 1982): 46–60.

Coke Are It

For 99 years the Coca-Cola Company—with a product that had become more American than apple pie—knew only the sweet taste of success. Then midway through 1985, because of a colossal management misjudgment based primarily on faulty research, disaster struck. In late April Coke's hard-driving chairman, Roberto Goizueta, announced that the company would scrap the original, 99-year-old secret formula for Coca-Cola. Amid great fanfare Goizueta introduced the new Coke with its "smoother, rounder, yet bolder—more harmonious flavor."

The reason for Coke's decision to retire the old formula was that its primary product was losing its market share to arch-competitor Pepsi-Cola and the youth-oriented "Pepsi generation" promotional campaigns. Coke needed to increase its appeal to the young, so it decided to sweeten the old recipe, bringing it closer to Pepsi.

Despite subsequent criticism to the contrary, Coca-Cola did not move precipitously to change the formula. In fact, it moved cautiously, relying on extensive research to see whether the switch made sense. Specifically, the company spent about $4 million over 4½ years to taste-test the new soda pop on nearly 200,000 consumers. Tests took many forms. Some were blind tests without the emotion-laden brand name attached to them. Others posed such questions as, "What if this were a new Coke taste?"

The company learned from all this testing that more people liked the new, sweeter formula than liked the old. This was good news to Coke, which had consistently lost out to Pepsi in head-to-head taste tests over the years. However, Coke neglected in its research to disclose to interviewees that the product they were sipping would ultimately replace their old favorite entirely. And this, as it turned out, was a tragic research oversight.

Immediately after Goizueta's announcement, Coke launched a multimillion dollar advertising campaign to introduce the new

Coke. In the first month after its introduction, new Coke showed every sign of fulfilling the chairman's declaration that the decision was "one of the easiest we ever made." Indeed, shipments to Coke bottlers during that May rose by the highest percentage in five years. New Coke was tried by a record number of people for any product, and more than three-quarters of those who tried it indicated they would eagerly buy it again.

Then, without warning, the roof caved in. Articles began appearing across the country about the angry old Coke loyalists who wanted original Coke returned. Coca-Cola headquarters was flooded with thousands of angry phone calls and sacks of nasty mail. Bottlers, Coke's front-line contact with consumers, began to feel the heat, and a petition was circulated among bottlers demanding the return of the old formula.

Coca-Cola management turned again to research to find out what was going on.

- When they polled 900 consumers about which Coke they liked better, 60 percent said old and only 30 percent said new.
- When they followed up with a survey of another 5,000 consumers, the results only further confirmed the bad news.
- When they held smaller, focus-group sessions to observe how consumers thought the company should deal with the problem, they kept getting the same answer: "Bring back old Coke."

So, in early July, three months after the introduction of new Coke, an embarrassed Coca-Cola president Donald Keough announced that the company was bringing back its old formula, now dubbed Classic Coke. New Coke, the company said, would be marketed separately to see whether it could or couldn't survive. At his press conference Keough read from complaint letters comparing the switch in formulas to "burning the flag" and "God making the grass purple." Said Keough, "All of the time and money and skill that we poured into consumer research could not reveal the depth of feeling for the original taste of Coca-Cola."

Others agreed. One researcher told *Fortune* magazine, "Taste tests don't take into account the emotional tie-in with the old brand, which is all wrapped up with people's childhoods. Now that consumers are drinking out of cans labeled 'new' Coke, naturally there is an emotional backlash."*

In September, two months after its public chastening, the Coca-Cola Company, without any fanfare, began its new television advertising campaign with the slogan "We've got a taste for you." "Coke is it" would be the Coca-Cola theme no more.

QUESTIONS

1. In terms of attaining a younger image, what alternatives did the Coca-Cola Company have besides changing the original formula?
2. How could new Coke have been introduced more quietly?
3. Ultimately, why did the research backfire that indicated consumers would enjoy new Coke?
4. How do you explain the research phenomenon that 94 percent of those who hadn't tried new Coke preferred the old?
5. What does this case indicate about the vulnerability of research findings?

---

*Among the most comprehensive analyses of the new Coke saga are Ann E. B. Fisher, "Coke's Brand-Loyalty Lesson," *Fortune*, 5 August 1985, 44–46; John Koten and Scott Kilman, "How Coke's Decision to Offer 2 Colas Undid Four and a Half Years of Planning," *Wall Street Journal*, 15 July 1985, 1; and Eric Gelman, "Hey America, Coke Are It!" *Newsweek*, 22 July 1985, 40–42.

3

Managing for Public Relations

A s the world heads into the 1990s, public relations, like most other organizational pursuits, must compete for its survival in an atmosphere of rising manpower costs, shrinking markets, and volatile public opinion. Management is insisting that public relations be run as a management process. Like other management processes, professional public relations work emanates from clear strategies and bottom-line objectives, which flow into specific tactics, each with its own discrete budget, timetable, and allocation of resources. Stated another way, public relations today is much more a planned, persuasive social/managerial science than it is a knee-jerk, damage-control reaction to sudden flare-ups.

On the organizational level, as public relations has enhanced its overall stature, it has been brought increasingly into the general management structure of institutions. Indeed, the public relations function works most effectively when it reports directly to top management.

On the individual level, public relations practitioners are increasingly expected to have mastered a wide variety of technical communications skills, such as writing, editing, placement of articles, production of printed materials, and video programming. At the same time, by virtue of their relatively recent integration into the general management process, public relations professionals are expected to be fluent in management theory and technique. In other words, public relations practitioners themselves must be, in every sense of the word, managers.

JUST WHAT IS IT YOU DO EXACTLY?

Sometimes it's tough to define exactly what the job of public relations is. It's not that practitioners don't know what they do, but rather that they have trouble categorizing it. For example, chances are good that public relations people have been involved somewhere along the line in these ventures:

- Newspaper interview
- Press conference
- Annual report
- Speech by a politician or community leader
- School official leading a community service drive
- Security analyst presentation by top executives
- Educational television program funded by a business firm
- Institution's facilities brochure
- Groundbreaking, topping out, or grand opening ceremony
- Corporate contribution to a minority enterprise
- College blood drive to benefit a local hospital
- Charity dinner
- Companywide graphics program that changes the look of packaging, stationery, signs, publications, and the firm's image

This list covers just the obvious. Far more subtle is the constant counseling of management by public relations people on issues of policy that affect an organization's publics. In sum, whenever communications, key publics, and questions of public policy come together, a good public relations staff or agency will be involved in devising and implementing appropriate strategies.

SCOPE OF THE PRACTICE

The duties and responsibilities of public relations practitioners are as diverse as the publics with whom different institutions deal. For example, here is a partial list of potential public relations duties.

1. **Reaching the employees** through a variety of internal means, including newsletters, television, and meetings. Traditionally, this role has emphasized news-oriented communications rather than benefits-oriented ones, which are usually the province of personnel departments.
2. **Coordinating relationships with the print and electronic media,** which includes arranging and monitoring press interviews, writing news releases and related press materials, organizing press conferences, and answering media inquiries and requests. A good deal of media relations work is spent attempting to gain favorable news coverage for the firm.
3. **Coordinating activities with legislators** on local, state, and federal levels. This includes legislative research activities and public policy formation.
4. **Orchestrating interaction with the community,** perhaps including open houses, tours, and employee volunteer efforts designed to reflect the supportive nature of the organization to the community.
5. **Managing relations with the investment community,** including the firm's present and potential stockholders. This task emphasizes personal contact with securities analysts, institutional investors, and private investors.

6. **Supporting activities with customers and potential customers,** with activities ranging from hard-sell product promotion activities to "soft" consumer advisory services.

7. **Coordinating the institution's printed voice to its publics** through reprints of speeches, annual reports, quarterly statements, and product and company brochures.

8. **Coordinating relationships with outside specialty groups,** such as suppliers, educators, students, nonprofit organizations, and competitors.

9. **Managing the institutional—or nonproduct—advertising image,** as well as being called on increasingly to assist in the management of more traditional product advertising.

10. **Coordinating the graphic and photographic services** of the organization. To do this task well requires knowledge of typography, layout, and art.

11. **Conducting opinion research,** which involves assisting in the public policy formation process through the coordination and interpretation of attitudinal studies of key publics.

12. **Managing the gift-giving apparatus,** which ordinarily consists of screening and evaluating philanthropic proposals and allocating the organization's available resources.

13. **Coordinating special events,** including travel for company management, corporate celebrations and exhibits, dinners, ground-breakings, and grand openings.

14. **Management counseling,** which involves advising administrators on alternative options and recommended choices in light of public responsibilities.

REPORTING TO TOP MANAGEMENT

In many organizations today, public relations is accorded a prominent role in management decision making. Frequently, the public relations director reports directly to top management—generally to the chief executive officer. The reason for this is simple. If public relations is to be the interpreter of management, then it must know what management is thinking at any moment on virtually every public issue. If public relations is made subordinate to any other discipline—marketing, advertising, legal, administration, whatever—then its independence, credibility, and ultimately, value as an objective management counselor will be sacrificed.

Whereas marketing and advertising groups must, by definition, be advocates for their specific products, the public relations department has no such mandated allegiance. Public relations, rightfully, should be the corporate conscience. An organization's public relations professionals should enjoy enough autonomy to tell it to management "like it is," as sportscaster Howard Cosell might put it. If an idea doesn't make sense, if a product is flawed, if the general

Harold Burson

Harold Burson is chairman of Burson-Marsteller, a worldwide public relations firm with 2,100 employees and 40 offices in 21 countries. He was chief executive officer of Burson-Marsteller from its founding in 1953 until January 1988. Burson is a legendary public relations practitioner and lecturer, the recipient of virtually every major honor awarded by the profession.

How has the business of public relations changed over time?
Public relations has, over time, become more relevant as a management function for all manner of institutions, public and private sector, profit and not-for-profit. CEOs increasingly recognize the need to communi-

cate to achieve their organizational objectives. Similarly, they have come to recognize public relations as a necessary component in the decision-making process. This has enhanced the role of public relations both internally and for independent consultants.

Why should an organization hire a public relations firm?
The public relations function can be divided into two principal classes of activity: the strategic and the implementing. Public relations firms play a major role on behalf of clients in both areas. In the realm of the strategic, a public relations firm brings to a client an independent perspective based on broad organizational experience with a wide spectrum of clients and problems. The public relations firm is not encumbered with the many internal considerations that frequently enter into the corporate or institutional decision-making process. In implementing programs, the public relations firm has a broad range of resources, both functional and geographic, that can be brought to bear on a client's problem. Furthermore, the public relations firm can usually be held to more specific accountability—both in terms of results and costs.

What constitutes the ideal public relations man or woman?
Public relations today covers so broad a range of activity that it is difficult to establish a set of specifications for all the kinds of people wearing the public relations mantle. Generally, I feel four primary characteristics apply to just about every successful public relations person I know.

1. They're smart—bright, intelligent people; quick studies. They ask the right questions. They have that unique ability to establish credibility almost on sight.
2. They know how to get along with people. They work well with their bosses, their peers, their subordinates. They work well with their clients and with third parties like the press and suppliers. They are emotionally stable—even (especially) under pressure. They use the pronoun *we* more than *I*.
3. They are motivated, and part of that motivation involves an ability to develop creative solutions. No one needs to tell them what to do next; instinctively, they know. They don't fear starting with a blank sheet of paper—to them the blank sheet of paper equates with challenge and opportunity.
4. They can write; they can articulate their thoughts in a persuasive manner.

What are the primary attributes you look for in a subordinate?

Presumably, this pertains to character traits. If so, it's difficult to avoid those textbook traits present on any list. But so be it! Here are some of those that mean the most to me.

- **Integrity**—not only if he/she can be trusted with the cash box. Perhaps most important, can that person be trusted to be totally truthful and open in reporting the negative as well as the positive—and in a timely fashion? Is he/she willing to say, "I don't know the answer," and ask for help?
- **A strong work ethic**—those in higher management (and we at Burson-Marsteller like to think all our hires are capable of

higher management) set the pace for those who work for and with them. I prefer a fast pace with high productivity.
- **Be a team player**—in building an organization, we have developed our share of stars, even superstars. But those achieving that distinction have invariably reached it because they got help from others along the way. We say we are a sharing organization. Team players willingly share and welcome receiving help.
- **Commitment**—to Burson-Marsteller and to our clients alike. An early associate of mine once said, "When my client gets stuck with an ice pick, I bleed." Clients are quick to sense that kind of commitment, and so do those who work alongside that kind of person.
- **A willingness to take responsibility**—someone who both seeks the rewards and accepts the penalties for being in charge.

How do ethics apply to the public relations function?

In a single word, pervasively. Ethical behavior is at the root of what we do as public relations professionals. We approach our calling with a commitment to serve the public interest, knowing full well that the public interest lacks a universal definition and knowing that one person's view of the public interest differs markedly from that of another. We must therefore be consistent in our personal definition of the public interest and be prepared to speak up for those actions we take in carrying out our mission.

institutional wisdom is wrong, it is the duty of the public relations professional to challenge the consensus.

This is not to say that advertising, marketing, and all other disciplines shouldn't enjoy a close partnership with public relations. Clearly, they must. All disciplines must work to maintain their own independence while building long-term, mutually beneficial relationships for the good of the organization. However, public relations should never shirk its overriding responsibility to enhance the organization's credibility by ensuring that corporate actions are in the public interest.

MANAGEMENT THEORY OF PUBLIC RELATIONS

In recent years public relations has developed its own theoretical framework as a management system. In particular, the work of communications professors James Grunig and Todd Hunt has done much to advance this development.[1] Grunig and Hunt suggest that public relations managers perform what organizational theorists call a boundary role; they function at the edge of an organization as a liaison between the organization and its external and internal publics. In other words, public relations managers have one foot inside the organization and one outside. Often, this unique position is not only lonely but also precarious.

As boundary managers, public relations people support their colleagues by helping them communicate across organizational lines both within and outside the organization. In this way public relations professionals also become systems managers, knowledgeable of and able to deal with the complex relationships inherent in the organization.

- They must consider the relationship of the organization to its environment— the ties that unite business managers and operations support staff, for example, and the conflicts that separate them.
- They must work within organizational confines to develop innovative solutions to organizational problems. By definition, public relations managers deal in a different environment from that of their organizational colleagues. The amorphous world of perceptions, attitudes, and public opinion, in which public relations managers dwell, is alien to the more empirical, quantitative, concrete domain of other business managers. Public relations managers, therefore, must be innovative, not only in proposing communications solutions, but also in making them understandable and acceptable to colleagues.
- They must think strategically. Public relations managers must demonstrate their knowledge of the organization's mission, objectives, and strategies. Their solutions must answer the real needs of the organization. They must reflect the big picture. Business managers will care little that the company's name was mentioned in the morning paper unless they can recognize the strategic rationale for the reference.

■ Public relations managers must also be willing to measure their results. They must state clearly what they want to accomplish, systematically set out to accomplish it, and measure their success. This means using such accepted business school techniques as management by objectives (MBO), management by objectives and results (MOR), and program evaluation and research technique (PERT).

■ Finally, as Grunig and Hunt point out, in managing an organization's public relations system, practitioners must demonstrate a comfort with the various elements of the organization itself: (1) functions, the real jobs of organizational components; (2) structure, the organizational hierarchy of individuals and positions; (3) processes, the formal decision-making rules and procedures the organization follows; and (4) feedback, the formal and informal evaluative mechanisms of the organization.[2]

Such a theoretical overview is important to consider in properly situating the practice of public relations as a management system within an organization (Figure 3–1).

PLANNING FOR PUBLIC RELATIONS

Like research, planning in public relations is essential not only to know where a particular campaign is headed, but also to win the support of top management. Indeed, one of the most frequent complaints about public relations is that it is too much a seat-of-the-pants activity, impossible to plan and difficult to measure. Clearly, planning in public relations must be given greater shrift. With proper planning, public relations professionals can indeed defend and account for their actions.

Before organizing for public relations work, practitioners must consider objectives and strategies, planning and budgets, and research and evaluation. The broad environment in which the organization operates must dictate overall business objectives. These, in turn, dictate specific public relations objectives and strategies. And once these have been defined, the task of organizing for a public relations program should flow naturally.

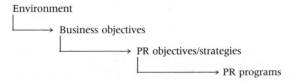

Setting objectives, formulating strategies, and planning are essential if the public relations function is to be considered of equal stature with other organizational components. Planning requires thinking. Planning a short-term public relations program to promote a new service may require less thought and time than planning a longer-term campaign to win support for a public policy issue. However, in each case, the public relations plan must include clear-cut objectives to achieve organizational goals, strategies to reach those objectives,

General Statement of Mission

CHASE

October 1984

The Chase is a broad-based international banking institution that provides a wide range of financial and finance-related services to quality customers, in selected markets, throughout the world. Consistent with this core mission, Chase will be a leading lender for sound, productive investment and for the financing of industry, commerce and individuals.

In all its activities, the Bank is committed to providing services only of the highest quality. In so doing, we expect to earn a return on our assets and our stockholders' investment at a level equal to or better than the other leaders in the U.S. banking industry.

The triple requirement that the Bank's activities be of high quality, productive purpose and competitive profitability will cause Chase to be selective in the services rendered. The requirement that our clientele also represent quality tiers of the markets we serve will cause Chase to be selective in choosing which customers we will serve.

Chase recognizes the unique value of its history and of its franchise. We will not allow this franchise to be weakened; nor do we intend to alter our basic business thrust. However, we recognize the potential for significant change in the financial system both in the U.S. and in important locations overseas — changes that will enlarge not only the scope of permissible services but the geographic breadth in which they may be offered. It is our intent to prepare for such change, to promote such change, and to offer expanded services as permitted by law and as are consistent with our mission and our capabilities. Our commitment to grow and expand while keeping faith with our banking tradition and our quality standards will nourish our ability to change in a planned, focused manner. Given this focus, our people will produce the types of change and growth we need.

Chase will be a leader within our industry, within the private enterprise system, and in those markets and communities we choose to serve. We intend to be recognized and respected by our many publics for . . . knowledge-ability . . . professionalism . . . quality of service . . . the high ethical character of our staff . . . undisputed technical ability . . . the financial strength of our corporation, and — most importantly — for the highest level of integrity in the conduct of our affairs.

Thus, dedication to the achievement of excellence in everything we do will continue The Chase's heritage as a unique institution. This demands that we seek the highest level of quality in: selecting, developing and managing our people; marketing our products and services; servicing our customers, and anticipating and responding to the changing needs of the communities in which we do business. ∎

FIGURE 3–1 In managing the public relations function, the organization's overriding mission, such as the one above, must always be considered first before planning a public relations program. (Courtesy of Chase Manhattan Bank)

tactics to implement the strategies, and measurement to determine whether the tactics worked.

Often the enemy of public relations planning is time, of which public relations people have precious little. By the very nature of their job, they are on call to management, frequently drafted to serve as "fire fighters" in any number of crisis situations.

- A wildcat strike breaks out in a steel plant, and public relations is asked by the press for details.
- A stockholder launches a sudden proxy fight, and public relations is asked for management's reaction.
- A branch office is held up by armed robbers, and public relations is called to report on how much they got.

Such activities may be exciting, but they don't do much for long-range planning. Indeed, if a conscious effort isn't made, planning and objective-setting time can easily get lost. Priorities for the perpetual fire fighter have a short-term orientation, with most days spent squelching brush fires and doing little else. Fire fighting may solve immediate dilemmas, but it won't do much to advance the institution or its public relations function. Thoughtful planning is critical, and good public relations professionals clearly understand this fact.

The fire-fighting aspects of many public relations jobs have caused practitioners to master the art of contingency planning. The contingency approach borrows from systems theory and enables public relations managers, first, to anticipate the major internal and external factors with which they must deal and, second, to plan in a contingency sense to cope with these environmental demands. The point is that public relations professionals must have the flexibility to respond quickly to changes in the environment. Although practitioners can't predict to the moment when the strike or the proxy fight or the robbery will occur, they can—and should—be prepared for just such a contingency.

MANAGING BY PUBLIC RELATIONS OBJECTIVES

An organization's goals must define what its public relations goals will be, and the only good goals are ones that can be measured. Public relations objectives and the strategies that flow from them, just like those in other business areas, must be results-oriented. As the old baseball pitcher Johnny Sain used to say, "Nobody wants to hear about the labor pains, but everyone wants to see the baby."

So, too, must public relations people think strategically. Strategies are the most crucial decisions of a public relations campaign. They answer the general question, "How will we manage our resources to achieve our goals?" The specific answers then become the public relations tactics used to implement the strategies. Ideally, strategies and tactics should profit from pretesting.

Harried Harry

Harry Detweiler runs the public information unit of the state commerce department. Harry purposely left last Thursday wide open to plot the department's objectives and strategies for next year. At 9:10 A.M. his secretary buzzed for his reaction to the previous night's basketball championship. He chatted about it for a few minutes, hung up, and went back to planning. At 9:30 the commissioner called and asked whether he'd mind getting back to an outside consultant who had just called. Harry got right on it. He promised to send the consultant the requested materials, hung up, and then searched for and found the information. He buzzed his secretary to make sure it got delivered to the consultant.

At 10:15 *Business Week* called to find out how the department viewed the regional economy. Harry thought of farming out the request to one of his subordinates but decided instead to personally call a department economist with the query. While he was talking to the economist, both the *Wall Street Journal* and an environmentalist left messages for call backs.

The *Journal* wanted an item for its Business Bulletin column on the state's health insurance plan. It took Harry a while to track down the right person to answer the question. The environmentalist's call was a bit tricky, dealing with the department's reduction in air purification requirements for new plants. Harry tried to answer the question as best he could and advised the caller to seek further clarification from the state environmental commissioner.

By 11:30 Harry was off the phone and ready to order lunch at his desk when Vince Ripkoon, his supervisor, invited him out to eat. Harry accepted. By 2:15 Harry was back in the office to discover five call-back slips and the news that his secretary had scheduled an afternoon meeting with several transportation department staff members interested in starting an interagency house organ. "Planning," Harry sighed dejectedly as he packed up his materials, "is impossible in a madhouse like this."

QUESTIONS

1. Is Harry right about not having time to plan?
2. What's wrong with his approach to planning?
3. What might he have done with the various phone calls he received?
4. Should he have interrupted the planning process to talk to the press, the environmentalist, and the transportation department staff people?
5. If you were Harry's boss, on what criteria might you base your review of his accomplishments?

As for objectives, good ones stand up to the following questions:

- Do they clearly describe the end result expected?
- Are they understandable to everyone in the organization?
- Do they list a firm completion date?
- Are they realistic, attainable, and measurable?
- Are they consistent with management's objectives?[3]

Increasingly, public relations professionals are managing by objectives, adopting MBO techniques to help quantify the value of public relations in an organization. The two questions most frequently asked by general managers of public relations practitioners are "How can we measure public relations results?" and "How do we know whether the public relations program is making progress?" Management by objectives can provide public relations professionals with a powerful source of feedback. MBO ties public relations results to management's predetermined objectives. Even though procedures for implementing MBO programs differ, most programs share four points.

1. Specification of the organization's goals with objective measures of the organization's performance
2. Conferences between a superior and a subordinate to agree on achievable goals
3. Agreement between the superior and the subordinate on objectives consistent with the organization's goals
4. Periodic reviews by the superior and the subordinate to assess progress toward achieving the goals

Again, the key is to tie public relations goals to the goals of the organization and then to manage progress toward achieving those goals. The goals themselves should be clearly defined and specific, practical and attainable, and measurable.

The key to using MBO effectively in public relations work can be broken down into seven critical steps.[4]

1. Defining the nature and mission of the work
2. Determining key result areas in terms of time, effort, and personnel
3. Identifying measurable factors on which objectives can be set
4. Setting objectives/determining results to be achieved
5. Preparing tactical plans to achieve specific objectives, including
   - Programming to establish a sequence of actions to follow
   - Scheduling to set time requirements for each step
   - Budgeting to assign the resources required to reach the goals
   - Fixing individual accountability for the accomplishment of the objectives
   - Reviewing and reconciling through a testing procedure to track progress
6. Establishing rules and regulations to follow
7. Establishing procedures to handle the work

Avoiding the Great Retainer Rip-Off

Sometimes organizations that employ public relations agencies may be confused about exactly what they are paying for. Some experts argue, in fact, that many corporations are getting ripped off by agencies plucking monthly fees out of the air and billing them in a lump sum back to the client with no charges broken out or activities accounted for.*

Basically, public relations agencies price their services in four ways.

1. **The hourly charge**   This is a clean deal for the client. The meter runs while work is performed; it's flipped off when work stops. Law firms bill their clients this way.
2. **The project basis**   This works well for organizations with predictable needs—an annual report, a speech, a press conference, an analyst meeting, or whatever. This is a one-time, one-shot deal, and the client and the firm agree, in advance, on the cost.
3. **The fee-plus approach**   This provides an income floor for the agency, based on an anticipated number of staff hours to be required. Above that, an hourly fee is levied. This approach allows the client the flexibility of adjusting activity levels as events dictate without being burned financially.
4. **The retainer**   This is the great imponderable—a fee paid at the beginning of each month, regardless of agency activity, to cover the assumed manpower costs plus a reasonable profit to the consultancy for performing public relations services. Such fees can range from $1,000 per month at smaller agencies all the way up to $10,000 and more at larger ones. That's more than $100,000 per year for public relations counsel, and it doesn't include out-of-pocket expenses, which generally are passed on to the client with a 15 to 20 percent markup. No wonder some clients have begun to cry "Rip off" as they pay steadily escalating retainers—essentially on faith.

*Chris Barnett, "Avoiding the Great Retainer Rip-Off in Public Relations," *San Jose Business Journal,* 18 November 1985.

By applying MBO techniques to public relations work, the function becomes not only more measurable but also more meaningful in the eyes of business management.

BUDGETING FOR PUBLIC RELATIONS

Like any other business activity, public relations programs must be bolstered with sound budgets and principles of cost control. After identifying objectives and strategies, the public relations practitioner must detail the particular tactics that will help deliver those objectives. At that point the practitioner should also begin to estimate costs. The key to budgeting may lie in performing these two steps: (1) estimating the extent of the resources—both manpower and purchases—needed to accomplish each activity; and (2) estimating the cost and availability of those resources.[5] With this information in hand, the development of a budget and monthly cash flow for a public relations program becomes easier. Such data also provide the milestones necessary to audit program costs on a routine basis and to make adjustments well in advance of budget crises.

Most public relations programs operate on limited budgets. Therefore, whenever possible, adaptable programs—ones that can be readily recycled and redesigned to meet changing needs—should be considered. For example, television, magazine, and newspaper advertising generally is too expensive for most public relations budgets. On the other hand, special events, personalized literature, direct mail, personal contacts, and promotional displays are the kinds of inexpensive communications vehicles that can be easily duplicated.[6]

Budgeting in public relations is, by definition, somewhat arbitrary. For example, if you need to budget for a recruiting brochure, you must first decide how many copies, colors, and pages are needed and how elaborate you want the document to be. A brochure can be produced for $2,500 as well as $10,000. But the difference in quality between a $.50-per-copy document and a $2-per-copy one is substantial. Estimates for material costs should be sought from several suppliers before settling on a specific budget. In addition, public relations budgets should be reasonable—ordinarily a fraction of advertising budgets—and flexible enough to withstand mid-course corrections.

Most public relations agencies treat client costs in a manner similar to that used by legal, accounting, and management consulting firms: the client pays only for services rendered, often against an established monthly minimum for staff time. Time records are kept by every employee—from chairperson to mail clerk—on a daily basis to be sure that agency clients know exactly what they are paying for.

PREPARING THE PUBLIC RELATIONS CAMPAIGN PLAN

The public relations campaign puts all of the aspects of public relations planning—objectives, strategies, research, tactics, and evaluation—into one cohesive whole. The plan specifies a series of "whats" to be done and "hows" to get them done—whatever is necessary to reach the objectives.

The skeleton of a typical public relations campaign plan resembles the following:

1. **Backgrounding the problem** This is the so-called situation analysis, background, or case statement that specifies the major aims of the campaign. It can be a general statement that refers to audiences, known research, the organization's positions, history, and the obstacles faced in

reaching the desired goal. A public relations planner should divide the overriding goal into several subordinate objectives, which are the "whats" to be accomplished.

2. **Preparing a proposal**   The second leg of the campaign plan sketches broad approaches to solve the problem at hand. It outlines the strategies, the "hows," and the public relations tools to be used to fulfill the objectives. The elements of the public relations proposal may vary depending on subject matter but generally include the following:

- *Situational analysis*—description of the challenge as it currently exists, including background on how the situation reached its present state
- *Scope of assignment*—description of the nature of the assignment—what the public relations program will attempt to do
- *Target audiences*—specific targets identified and apportioned into manageable groups
- *Research methods*—specific research approach to be used
- *Key messages*—specific selected appeals: What do we want to tell our audiences? How do we want them to feel about us? What do we want them to do?
- *Communications vehicles*—tactical communications devices to be used
- *Project team*—key players who will participate in the program
- *Timing and fees*—a timetable with proposed costs identified

The specific elements of any proposal depend on the unique nature of the program itself. When an outside supplier submits a proposal, additional elements—such as cancellation clauses, confidentiality of work, and references—should also be included.

3. **Activating the plan**   The third stage of a campaign plan details operating tactics. It may also contain a time chart, specifying when each action will take place. Specific activities are defined, people are assigned to them, and deadlines are established. This stage forms the guts of the campaign plan.

4. **Evaluating the campaign**   To find out whether the plan worked, evaluation methods should be spelled out here. Pretesting and posttesting of audience attitudes, quantitative analysis of event attendance, content analysis of media success, surveys, sales figures, staff reports, letters to management, feedback from others—the specific method of evaluative testing is up to the practitioner. But the inclusion of a mechanism for evaluation is imperative.[7]

A public relations campaign plan should always be spelled out—in writing—so that planners can keep track of progress and management can assess results. And although planning in public relations is important and should be taken more seriously than it presently is by public relations professionals, the caveat of the management gurus of the mid-1980s, Thomas Peters and Robert Waterman, must always be considered: "The problem is that the planning becomes an end in itself."[8] In public relations this occurrence cannot be allowed. No matter how important planning may be, public relations is assessed principally in terms of its action, performance, and practice.

The Perfect Public Relations Manager

In a speech on February 27, 1980, Robert Cushman, chairman and chief executive officer of the Norton Company of Worcester, MA, laid out nine requisites for perfect public relations managers.*

1. They should be students of public attitudes and perceptions, who understand that communications is not just what you say, but also what others hear.
2. They must understand a variety of different publics and the things that make them tick—from security analysts to hard hats, from state senators to Mexican Americans.
3. They must have ideologies, yes—but with enough flexibility and empathy to understand conflicting views and the role of trade-offs.
4. They must be honest, open, and accessible.
5. They must hold a deep interest in what's going on in the world; they should be concerned about Iran, Afghanistan, an election, energy, inflation, education, tax reform, the capital problems of business, new economic philosophies, and new trends in art, music, and public tastes. In short, they should be Renaissance people.
6. They must have ideas and be responsive to the ideas of others.
7. They must be good writers.
8. They must be in touch with the real world and protect senior managers from insulating themselves from what is happening out there.
9. Most of all, they must talk straight to members of management. We don't want to be patronized. We don't want sycophants. We want advisors who will advocate, debate, and defend their thinking and proposals.[11]

*Robert Cushman, speech before the New England Chapter of the Public Relations Society of America, 27 February 1980.

ORGANIZING THE PUBLIC RELATIONS DEPARTMENT

Once an organization has analyzed its environment, established its objectives, set up measurement standards, and thought about appropriate programs and budgets, it is ready to organize a public relations department. Departments range from one-person operations to firms such as that of General Motors, with a staff of more than 200 persons (half professionals and half support staff) responsible for relations with the press, investors, civic groups, employees, and governments around the world. Oil companies, such as Mobil and Exxon, and banks, such as Chase and Citibank, have departments well in excess of 100 staff members.

Typically, most departments begin as small operations and grow as the business environment changes. For example, the increasing importance of public relations with investors, employees, and minority groups has created new areas for department expansion. As an exhaustive study by the Conference Board pointed out, there is no one best way to organize for public or external relations.[9] Some firms use decentralized organizational structures, with public relations reporting to a communications professional, public affairs reporting to a legal professional, and investor relations reporting to the head accountant. In other companies the public relations or communications function is organized centrally, under one executive who is responsible for dealing with many of the firm's key publics.

In government, public relations professionals typically report directly to department heads. In universities the public relations function is frequently coupled with fund-raising and development activities. In hospitals public relations is typically tied to the marketing function.

As for the names of the departments in which public relations is housed, organizations use a wide variety of names for the function. Ironically, the trend in the 1980s seems to be away from use of the traditional term *public relations* and toward *corporate communications*. In one comprehensive analysis about 30 percent of the organizations surveyed still used *public relations*, whereas *corporate communications* or just plain *communications* was used by nearly 20 percent. About 8 percent used *public affairs,* and another 8 percent used *advertising/ public relations*. Among the other titles in use were *corporate relations* and *public information*.[10]

ORGANIZING FOR COMMUNICATIONS AT CHASE MANHATTAN BANK

A typical organization for communications activity can be found at New York's Chase Manhattan Bank (Figure 3–2). Chase is a multinational financial services company with more than 40,000 employees in more than 2,000 locations worldwide. The bank's communications activities are managed by the Corporate Communications Group, with a staff of more than 100 professionals. That staff is headed by an executive vice president/director, who reports directly to the chairman of the board and chief executive officer and indirectly to the bank's president and chief operating officer. Thus, by the very nature of these reporting relationships, the communications director is plugged in to most major corporate decisions.

Chase's Corporate Communications Group is divided into several individual components, responsible for distinct communications activities.

1. **Public affairs** is responsible for communications with the bank's internal and external publics through the media, internal periodicals, management speeches, and shareholder publications such as the annual and quarterly reports. This division is also responsible for supervising the bank's com-

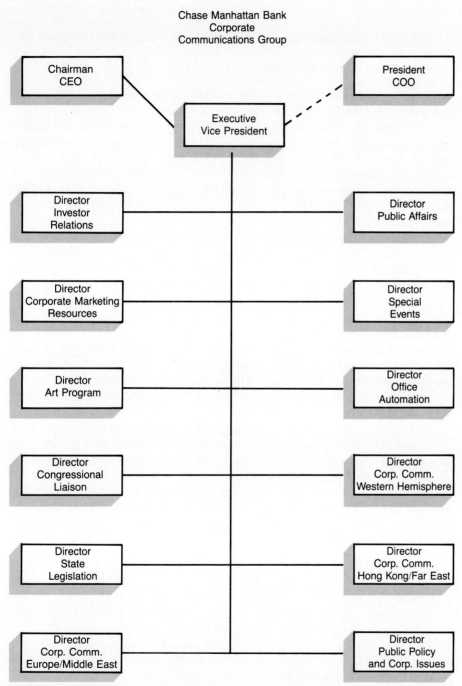

FIGURE 3–2 Chase Manhattan Bank's communications operation is headquartered in the Corporate Communications Group, composed of more than 100 professionals who perform a variety of discrete functions. (Art by Cal Austin)

YOU MAKE
THE CALL

Planning the GE Plant Closing

Public relations planning must follow general organizational planning. Sometimes, as the saying goes, "It just don't work that way."

On April 16, 1985, the *Virginian-Pilot* newspaper published a page-one story stating that because of "poor sales and increased foreign competition, the General Electric Company might halt production of televisions and close its Suffolk, VA, manufacturing plant, eliminating 1,800 jobs." While GE spokesmen vociferously denied the speculation, the article quoted industry analysts and GE employees who suggested that the closing of the 19-year-old plant was "just a matter of time."

General Electric immediately cried foul and demanded a meeting with *Virginian-Pilot* editors. They complained that the newspaper's information came from unnamed sources—employees who might have misunderstood what they had been told by management in private meetings at the factory. They complained that the story allowed a perception that company executives had, in effect, "already made the decision to close the plant." This allegation, they argued, could significantly hurt GE's business.

In an internal memo distributed to its plant employees after the newspaper story, the company wrote: "The article regarding the Consumer Electronics Business Operations is unfortunate in that many employees are perceiving it as an announcement. In fact, no announcements have been made. No decisions have been reached."

Meanwhile, the *Virginian-Pilot* made two declarations: (1) it stood by its story, and (2) it invited GE's general manager to be interviewed to clarify the situation. The general manager declined, and the company remained silent.

In June GE announced it would reduce its Suffolk workforce by 295 employees, adding, "Further cuts might be necessary." In October the company announced that it was closing the Suffolk plant, eliminating all remaining jobs.

QUESTIONS

1. Assuming the company had a good idea in April that the Suffolk plant might soon be closed, how would you characterize its public relations planning for this eventuality?
2. What public relations options did the company have during the seven-month period of speculation? How did the firm handle this period?
3. Do you think the *Virginian-Pilot* handled the story responsibly?
4. In a public relations sense, how else might the company have planned for the eventual closing of its plant?

This case is based largely on Gerald P. Merrell, "Speculation on Plant Closing Leaves GE Angry, Silent," *Media Institute Forum* (Fall 1985): 1–6, 7.

munity relations, consumer affairs, and philanthropic giving program, through which 2 percent of Chase's after-tax profits is contributed annually to hundreds of charities of every kind. Finally, the division maintains Chase's archives, where important historical records are housed.

2. **Investor relations** is responsible for contact with securities analysts and investors. This division is headed by an investment professional comfortable with the jargon and workings of Wall Street.

3. **Corporate marketing resources** coordinates the bank's advertising in its many markets. Often, the division serves as a consultant to line-marketing departments, who control their own advertising budgets. In addition to responsibilities for market research and planning, the unit manages the bank's relationships with its advertising agencies.

4. **Congressional liaison** is the bank's lobbying and policy formulating arm. This unit includes the bank's three registered Washington lobbyists as well as a research staff to assist in policy development.

5. **Special events** coordinates the bank's presentation at conferences, conventions, and seminars. External events personnel are experts in scheduling, planning, and design and are responsible for ensuring that Chase's presentation on the road is tastefully executed.

6. **The state legislation unit** is responsible for the bank's role in Albany, New York's state capital, as well as in other states around the country. This function becomes particularly important in the 1980s as banks like Chase are granted the privilege of expanding their activities across state lines.

7. **Office automation** enables the Corporate Communications Group to stay on the cutting edge of new communications technology, such as word processing and electronic mail. At Chase, fittingly, the communications group serves as the bank's guinea pig in experimenting with the latest technology to deliver information.

8. **The bank's art program** consists of more than $8 million of art, purchased to enhance Chase's premises around the world. This unit is staffed by a group of experienced fine arts professionals, who perform a unique and important role for a financial institution.

9. **Public policy and corporate issues** has primary responsibility to keep the bank abreast of emerging public issues. Through a pervasive issues contact network within the bank, this unit counsels senior management on breaking legislative developments.

10. **International communications** employs representatives in major markets overseas. These officers report directly to New York communications personnel so that the bank can present a unified and cohesive appearance around the world.

ORGANIZING THE PUBLIC RELATIONS AGENCY

The biggest difference between an external agency and an internal department is perspective. The former is outside looking in; the latter is inside looking out (often for itself, quite literally). Sometimes the use of an agency is necessary to escape the tunnel vision syndrome that afflicts some firms, in which a detached viewpoint is desperately needed. An agency unfettered by internal corporate politics might be better trusted to present management with an objective reading of the concerns of its publics.

An agency has the added advantage of not being taken for granted by a firm's management. Unfortunately, management sometimes has a greater regard for an outside specialist than for an inside one. This attitude frequently defies logic but is nonetheless often true. Generally, if management is paying (sometimes quite handsomely) for outside counsel, it tends to listen carefully to the advice.

Agencies may also fit certain unique needs of an organization. A company may need a technically complex speech, a specially targeted consumer program, or a particularly pointed financial relations project. Such needs may be filled quickly and professionally by outside counsel.

Public relations counsel is, by definition, a highly personalized service. A counselor's prescription for a client depends primarily on what the counselor thinks a client needs and how that assessment fits the client's own perception of those needs. Often, an outsider's fresh point of view is helpful in focusing a client on particular problems and opportunities and on how best to conquer or capitalize on them.

On the other hand, since outside agencies are just that—outside—they are often unfamiliar with details affecting the situation of particular companies and with the idiosyncrasies of company management. The good external counselor must constantly work to overcome this barrier. The best client-agency relationships are those with free-flowing communications between internal and external public relations groups so that both resources are kept informed about corporate policies, strategies, and tactics. A well-oiled, complementary department/agency relationship can result in a more positive communications approach for an organization.

Organizing for Public Relations at Hill and Knowlton

Hill and Knowlton (H&K) is not your typical public relations agency. Although the majority of agencies are small shops with several counselors, H&K serves more than 1,000 clients in the United States, Canada, Europe, Asia, Australia, and Latin America. H&K even has a public relations office in Beijing, People's Republic of China.

Headquartered in New York City, H&K has grown from a two-man operation with one client to a 1,050–staff member operation of almost $70 million in income. In August 1986 H&K reinforced its role as the world's largest public relations agency by acquiring the third largest agency, Carl Byoir & Associates.

H&K is one of a number of public relations agencies to merge with advertising agencies, having been acquired by J. Walter Thompson (JWT) in

1980. Although today a wholly owned Thompson subsidiary, H&K is still relatively autonomous in serving its diverse client list.

The agency is organized into a variety of specialty areas, ranging from the "plain vanilla" public relations services of media relations, financial relations counseling, editorial services, and research and information to some of the most exotic functions, such as merger and acquisitions/takeover communications, sports development, agricultural business communications, interview, speech and confrontation training, and even a unit that specializes in public relations work for lawyers. Figure 3–3 offers just a taste of the H&K specialty menu.

WHAT'S IT PAY?

Without question the communications function has increased in importance and clout. Top communications professionals in many large corporations today draw compensation packages well into six figures. Entry-level jobs for writers and editors generally fall into the $15,000-$25,000 range. Managers of public relations units, press relations, consumer relations, financial communications, and the like may earn anywhere from $20,000 to $100,000. Public relations directors may range in salary from $30,000 to upwards of $200,000 (Table 3–1, p. 67). Public relations agency salaries may be a bit higher in some cases than corporate staff salaries since account executives are on the line earning income for the firm (Table 3–2, p. 68). But job security in an agency is usually less than that offered by a corporation.

WHAT MANNER OF MAN/WOMAN?

What kind of individual does it take to become a competent public relations professional? New York counselor Art Stevens speculated that in most people's minds, a PR man—and presumably PR woman—would appear something like this:

> A man steps into a phone booth and says the magic words *corporate image*. Suddenly there is a flash of typewriter ribbon, and he becomes "PR Man"—a wide smile fixed on his face. His fingers flex in anticipation of countless handshakes; his mind forms strings of pleasant, glib words; his amino acids brace themselves for the four martinis that he must down during the traditional three-hour lunch.
>
> His looks take on the appearance of Tony Curtis in *Sweet Smell of Success*. There's also a touch of Jack Lemmon in *Days of Wine and Roses*. Beads of perspiration form on his brow as he anticipates the excitement and satisfaction of conning the world. No one knows precisely what he does and how he does it, but he conveys glamour and intrigue.[11]

If only that glamour and intrigue were true! Regrettably, most practitioners would moan, "It simply ain't so."

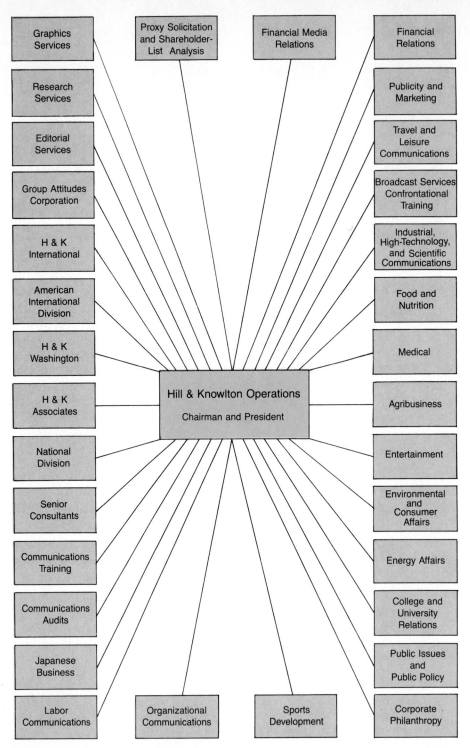

FIGURE 3-3 Hill and Knowlton, a subsidiary of the JWT Group and one of the largest public relations agencies in the world, is compartmentalized into a diverse cross-section of specialty areas. (Art by Candida Alvarez)

TABLE 3–1 Comparison of 1987 and 1986 median salaries of public relations/public affairs practitioners in the United States and Canada, by type of organization.

Type of Organization	Median Salary 1987	Median Salary 1986	Salary Range	Median Salary Change*
All U.S. organizations	$45,000	$42,000	$15,000–180,000	$5,000
All Canadian organizations†	40,000	44,500	17,000–120,000	3,250
PR firms	48,000	50,000	15,000–180,000	3,000
Advertising agencies (PR section)	41,000	40,500	18,000–121,000	6,000
Other consulting	45,000	42,000	24,500–100,000	5,000
Banks	45,000	44,000	19,800–160,000	2,000
Insurance companies	45,000	46,500	18,500–120,000	5,000
Other financial service org'ns	48,000	47,000	18,750–150,000	8,000
Consumer product companies	59,000	41,500	25,000–140,000	6,000
Industrials	56,000	53,250	18,000–150,000	2,000
Conglomerates	‡	46,850	‡	‡
Travel/Tourism	29,000	NA	19,500–118,000	4,000
Transportation	‡	53,500	30,000– 65,000	‡
Utilities	50,675	54,250	26,500–127,000	8,675
Health care: Hospital	36,000	38,000	20,000–160,000	2,100
Health care: Other	40,500	NA	22,000– 56,000	500
Education: Administration	40,000	33,680	20,000– 80,000	4,300
Education: Academic	31,750	NA	20,000– 57,000	1,750
Trade/Professional associations	41,000	40,000	20,000–120,000	3,000
Social services/Nonprofit	30,000	30,510	17,500–126,000	1,800
Government: Federal	43,000	41,000	17,000– 63,000	4,250
State	32,500	30,000	20,800– 60,000	(500)
Local	38,450	38,805	23,300– 86,000	(250)

SOURCE: *PR Reporter* (14 September 1987): 2.

NOTES: (1) 4,339 questionnaires were mailed to a random sample of PRSA and CPRS members and *prr* subscribers (to represent practitioners who are not members of these organizations); 916 valid questionnaires were returned, or 21%. (2) "Median Salary" and "Median Salary Increase" are the points on the scale above which—and correspondingly below which—50% of respondents fall. (3) Salaries by type of organization are for the United States only.

*Calculated on the difference between 1987 median salaries and the median of "last year's salary" as reported by 1987 respondents.

†For consistency Canadian respondents were asked to state salaries in U.S. dollars.

‡Sample size is too small to compute median.

In order to make it, a public relations practitioner ought to possess a set of specific, technical skills as well as an appreciation of the proper attitudinal approach to the job. On the technical side these six skills are important:

1. **Knowledge of the field**—an understanding of the underpinnings of public relations, culture and history, and philosophy and social psychology

TABLE 3-2 Fifty largest U.S. public relations operations, independent and ad agency affiliated, for the year ending December 31, 1987.

Public Relations Operation	1987 Fee Income	Employees	Fee Income % Change
1. Hill and Knowlton (A)	114,500,000	1,600	+14.3
2. Burson-Marsteller* (A)	110,000,000	1,868	
3. Shandwick	65,400,000	982	
4. Ogilvy & Mather PR Group (A)	38,457,000	738	
5. Rowland Company Worldwide (A)	28,077,000	439	
6. Daniel J. Edelman	25,153,527	362	+20.0
7. Manning, Selvage & Lee (A)	23,614,000	322	+9.3
8. Fleishman-Hillard	23,361,986	335	+27.2
9. Doremus Porter Novelli (A)	22,670,241	290	+8.8
10. Ketchum Public Relations (A)	21,011,000	275	+23.5
11. Golin/Harris Communications (A)	19,002,000	308	+9.4
12. Creamer Dickson Basford (A)	18,000,000	250	
13. Regis McKenna	14,500,000	174	+14.5
14. Ruder Finn & Rotman*	—	270	
15. GreyCom (A)	10,954,000	219	+167.0
16. Robinson, Lake, Lerer & Montgomery (A)	10,900,000	109	+42.0
17. Howard J. Rubenstein*	—	120	
18. Cohn & Wolfe* (A)	—	94	
19. Financial Relations Board	7,404,487	88	+28.1
20. Dorf & Stanton Communications	6,337,075	118	+20.9
21. Robert Marston and Assocs.*	—	65	
22. Mona Meyer & McGrath	5,190,719	70	+17.0
23. Ayer Public Relations* (A)		33	
24. The Softness Group	4,388,614	56	+81.5
25. Gibbs & Soell	4,253,917	56	+27.0
26. The Kamber Group	4,083,000	70	-6.0
27. Anthony M. Franco*	—	66	

2. **Communications knowledge**—an understanding of the media and the ways in which they work, of communications research, and, most importantly, of the writing process

3. **Knowledge of what's going on around you**—an understanding of the current events and factors that influence society: literature, language, politics, economics, and all the rest—from the Polisarios in Morocco to the politics in Manila; from West Germany to West Beirut; from Geraldine Ferraro to Louis Farakhan; from Bryant Gumbel to Boy George. A public relations professional must be, in the truest sense, a Renaissance man or woman.

4. **Business knowledge**—an understanding of how business works, a bottom-line orientation, and a knowledge of one's company and industry

Public Relations Operation	1987 Fee Income	Employees	Fee Income % Change
28. Hill, Holliday, Connors, Cosmopulus (A)........	3,602,600	30+	+3.0
29. Mallory Factor.................................	3,580,000	46	+16.0
30. E. Bruce Harrison Co...........................	3,279,038	41	+32.3
31. Aaron D. Cushman and Assocs.*...............	3,000,000	60	
32. Earle Palmer Brown PR* (A)....................	3,000,000	35	
33. Lobsenz-Stevens...............................	2,972,000	43	+25.0
34. Creswell, Munsell, Fultz & Zirbel (A)...........	2,964,939	33	+26.5
35. Ficom International............................	2,804,000	62	+40.0
36. Hank Meyer Associates	2,703,804	29	
37. KCS&A..	2,700,000	30	
38. Madeline de Vries.............................	2,637,179	35	+44.4
39. Clarke & Co.* (A).............................	2,500,000	36	
40. Makovsky & Co	2,500,000	35	+27.0
41. Public Communications........................	2,444,026	34	+4.7
42. The Rockey Co.................................	2,401,903	40	+19.6
43. Cone Communications	2,370,386	52	+55.4
44. Gelman & Gray (A)	2,323,300	25	
45. Hi-Tech Public Relations.......................	2,246,488	24	+30.9
46. Geltzer & Co	2,229,650	33	
47. Edward Howard & Co	2,109,693	30	−1.1
48. Charles Ryan Assocs. (A).......................	2,099,469	54	+3.0
49. Watt, Roop & Co	2,053,378	23	+1.6
50. Dye, Van Mol, Lawrence & Ericson	2,045,543	44	+6.0

SOURCE: Reprinted by permission from *O'Dwyer's Directory of PR Firms,* New York: J. R. O'Dwyer Co., 1988.

(A) Identifies ad agency relationship.

*Denotes incomplete substantiation of figures.

5. **Knowledge of bureaucracy**—an understanding of how to get things done in a bureaucratic organization, how to use and gain power for the best advantage, and how to maneuver in a politically charged environment

6. **Management knowledge**—an understanding of how public policy is shaped and an appreciation of the various pressures on and responsibilities of senior managers

In terms of attitude, public relations professionals ought to possess the following four characteristics:

1. **Communications orientation**—a bias toward disclosing rather than withholding information. Public relations professionals should *want* to commu-

nicate with the public. They should practice the belief that the public has a right to know.

2. **Advocacy**—a desire to be advocates for their employers. Public relations people must stand up for what their employers stand for. Although they should never distort, lie, or hide facts, occasionally it may be in an organization's best interest to avoid comment on certain issues. If practitioners don't believe in the integrity and credibility of their employers, their most honorable course is to quit.

3. **Counseling orientation**—a compelling desire to advise senior managers. As noted, top executives are used to dealing in tangibles, such as balance sheets, costs per thousand, and cash flows. Public relations practitioners understand the intangibles, such as public opinion, media influence, and communications messages. Practitioners must be willing to support their beliefs—often in opposition to lawyers or personnel executives. They must even be willing to disagree with management at times. Far from being yes men, public relations practitioners must have the gumption to counsel no.

4. **Personal confidence**—a strong sense of honesty and ethics, a willingness to take risks, and, not unimportantly, a sense of humor. Public relations professionals must have the courage of their convictions and the personal confidence to represent proudly a curious—yet critical—role in any organization.

In recent years many more women have joined the public relations ranks. Women now account for just under half of all practitioners but still earn substantially less than men. For example, the median salary of public relations professionals, according to one survey, was $50,812 for men but only $35,500 for women.[12] In addition, the number of minority public relations professionals has not grown substantially over the years, which is a problem the field must confront.

However, despite its demographic idiosyncrasies, public relations takes neither a false smile nor a glad hand. Rather it takes solid communications, human relations, judgment, and learning skills. It also takes professionalism and, most important, hard work.

1. James E. Grunig and Todd Hunt, *Managing Public Relations* (New York: Holt, Rinehart and Winston, 1984): 89–97.
2. Ibid.
3. Richard H. Truitt, "Wanted: Hard-Headed Objectives," *Public Relations Journal* (August 1969): 12, 13.
4. George L. Morrisey, *Management by Objectives and Results for Business and Industry,* 2d ed. (Reading, MA: Addison-Wesley Publishing Co., 1977): 9.
5. Jack Tucker, "Budgeting and Cost Control: Are You a Businessman or a Riverboat Gambler?" *Public Relations Journal* (March 1981): 15.
6. Donald T. Mogavero, "When the Funds Come Tumbling Down," *Public Relations Journal* (October 1981): 13.
7. Anthony Fulginiti, "How to Prepare a Public Relations Plan," *Communication Briefings* (May 1985): 8a, b.
8. Thomas J. Peters and Robert H. Waterman, Jr., *In Search of Excellence* (New York: Harper & Row, 1982): 40.
9. "Managing Corporate External Relations: Changing Perspectives and Responses," Report 679, New York: Conference Board, 1976.
10. Jack O'Dwyer, *O'Dwyer's Directory of Corporate Communications* (New York: J. R. O'Dwyer Co., 1985): 2.
11. Art Stevens, "Public Relations: The Image of the Imagemaker," *AMA Management Review* (November 1971): 2–10.
12. "23rd Annual Survey of the Profession, Part 1: Salaries and Demographics," *PR Reporter* (14 September 1987): 6.

Block, Edward M. "Strategic Communications: Practicing What We Preach." Speech at PRSA Annual Convention. New York: Burson-Marsteller (866 Third Ave.), 8 November 1987.

Burger, Chester. "So You Want to Start Your Own Business." *Public Relations Journal* (August 1981): 20–22.

Burson, Harold. *What Works for Me.* New York: Random House, 1987.

Careers in Public Relations. New York: PRSA (33 Irving Place).

Chase, Howard. "The Corporate Imperative Management of Profit and Policy." *Public Relations Quarterly* (Spring 1982): 25–29. The new organizational design described here is intended to bring order, logic, control, effectiveness, and economy to the twin responsibilities of corporate management—profit and public policy.

Cluff, Susan. "The Changing Face of Corporate Communication." *Communication World* (IABC, 870 Market St., San Francisco, CA 94102) (May 1987): 27–31.

Curry, Talmer E., Jr., and **Deanne N. Haerer.** "Flexi-Time: Is It for You?" *Public Relations Journal* (March 1981): 54–57.

Fraser, Bruce W. "How to Be a Freelance Public Relations Professional . . . and Survive." Tips & Tactics, a supplement of *PR Reporter* 25, no. 9 (22 June 1987). Author discusses the pros and cons of freelancing.

"Guidelines for Public Relations Professionals." *Public Relations Journal* (January 1981): 33.

Grunig, James E., and **Todd Hunt.** *Managing Public Relations.* Orlando, FL: Holt, Rinehart & Winston, 1984.

Jackson, Patrick. "Tomorrow's Public Relations." *Public Relations Journal* (March 1985): 24–25. By raising our sights, embracing research, and learning without end, today's practitioners will be able to meet the future world challenges, Jackson advises.

Jensen, Alan W. "The Status of Public Relations in Major U.S. Banks." *Public Relations Review* (Summer 1983): 53–64. From a survey of 645 bankers, Jensen concluded that bank public relations departments tend to be less independent and are more likely to be adjuncts of other divisions of the institution, usually marketing.

Kirban, Lloyd. "Showing What We Do Makes a Difference." *Public Relations Quarterly* (Fall 1983): 22–27.

"Monsanto Decentralizes & Downsizes Without Losing on Public Affairs." New York: Business International (One Dag Hammarskjold Plaza), 19 October 1987.

National Directory of Corporate Public Affairs. Washington, DC: Columbia Books (1350 New York Ave., NW).

Peters, Thomas J., and Robert H. Waterman, Jr. *In Search of Excellence*. New York: Harper & Row, 1982.

Safire, Bill. *The Relations Explosion*. New York: Macmillan, 1963.

"Twenty-First Annual Survey of the Profession." *PR Reporter* (30 September 1985): 1–6.

Theahan, Frederick C. "New Professionals: A Profile." *Public Relations Journal* (March 1984): 26–29. A survey of recent graduates provides the average starting salaries by district, the percentage actually starting in the field, and the source of their first full-time job.

Theus, Kathryn T. "Gender Shifts in Journalism and Public Relations." *Public Relations Review* (Spring 1985): 42–50. This article discusses the increased female enrollment in journalism and communications schools, which graduate classes of up to 60 percent women.

Tucker, Jack. "Budgeting and Cost Control: Are You a Businessman or a Riverboat Gambler?" *Public Relations Journal* (March 1981): 14–17. Effective public relations programs cannot be developed without a budget or implemented without controls.

Wright, Donald K. "Accreditation's Effects on Professionalism." *Public Relations Review* (Spring 1981): 48–61. The author attempts to chart the professionalism of public relations by comparing practitioners' rankings of occupational values with criteria associated with the concept of professionalism.

The Loquacious Bank Economist

New City's Gonzo National Bank was the largest bank in the world in terms of total assets and deposits. Many of its deposits emanated from foreign customers, including foreign multinational companies and foreign banks. Indeed, the Japanese were among the most important and most prosperous of all Gonzo customers.

One August the United States began putting strong pressure on the Japanese to revalue the yen; as a result, Japanese goods would cost more to purchase than those of American competitors. In America more dollars would have to be paid out to purchase Japanese imports. Therefore, a revaluation upward of the Japanese yen would be deleterious to the Japanese economy while stimulating the American economy.

On the evening of September 15, after several weeks of intense American pressure, the Japanese reluctantly announced that they would revalue the yen. At Gonzo National, management internally welcomed the Japanese announcement, interpreting it as a boon to the sagging U.S. economy. They agreed, however, that no public statement would be made for fear the bank's good Japanese clients would consider such a statement to be rubbing salt in the wound. They further agreed that the bank's public relations department would respond to the Japanese announcement with a simple "No comment."

At 8:00 A.M. on September 16, after the Japanese announcement, vacationing Gonzo National economist H. John Hollingsworth was at home eating breakfast when the telephone rang. He answered it, and on the line was his next door neighbor Lawrence Shields, international business editor of the Associated Press wire service. Shields was interested in knowing what Hollingsworth thought of last night's Japanese announcement.

"What do I think of it?" Hollingsworth replied. "Why, I think it's great. A change in the yen rate was a key part needed to make the U.S. plan work. It's a victory for America."

Shields thanked his neighbor for the information and hung up. Hollingsworth went back to his morning coffee. Fifteen minutes later a bulletin went out over the 4,000 Associated Press news wires at newspapers and brokerage houses throughout the world. It read:

AP, NEW CITY, 8:15 A.M.—Gonzo National Bank calls Japanese revaluation announcement a great victory for America. Economist H. John Hollingsworth of New City's 80-billion-dollar Gonzo National Bank today said yesterday's decision by the Japanese government to revalue the yen was "a key part needed to make the United States plan work. It's a victory for America."

Within six minutes John T. Knoll, public relations director for Gonzo National, received a call from the bank's president. The president told him that the Dow Jones ticker machine in his office had just carried an item reporting that Gonzo National had called the Japanese revaluation "a great victory for the

U.S." The president asked Knoll to come up to his office immediately.

At 8:24 A.M. Knoll and the president began to weigh the consequences of the inadvertent announcement. The president pointed out that the Japanese had "hundreds of millions of dollars of deposits in our bank." He said he personally was friendly with the American representatives of Mitsubishi Bank, the Bank of Tokyo, and several other large Japanese banks with offices in New City. "When these fellows see that statement," he said, "they'll be livid." The president suggested to Knoll that the Japanese were proud people and that the revaluation was something they felt forced into.

"Revaluation was understandably unpopular among Japanese business leaders," the president said, "and now it looks like Gonzo National is rubbing it in. We've got real trouble," he concluded.

As the president chronicled customer relations and real business problems that the announcement had evoked, Knoll began contemplating the media ramifications. The newspapers, he thought, would see the announcement on the wire, and tomorrow morning's headlines could be frightening. Indeed, even if Gonzo's Japanese customers didn't see the story on the news wires in their offices, they would still probably read about the announcement in tomorrow's newspapers. Obviously, thoughtful action had to be taken quickly.

"John," the president said solemnly, "it's 8:30. At 8:45 I'd like to see you back here with a plan for our reaction to this mess. As I see it, we've got public relations considerations with respect to media reaction on one hand and Japanese customer reaction on the other. Failure to handle either effectively will cost us an enormous amount of business. Go back to your office and think about it. I'll see you in fifteen minutes."

QUESTIONS

1. What recommendation would you make to the president about Gonzo National's public response to the initial statement? Would you issue another statement? Why or why not? If you issued another statement, what would it say? From whom would it come? When would it be issued? To whom would it be issued?
2. What recommendation would you make to the president about Gonzo National's contacting Japanese clients? Would you attempt to contact them? Why or why not? If you would contact them, how should it be done? When should it be done? What should be said? Who should say it?

The Court of Public Opinion

4

Public opinion is an elusive and fragile commodity. It is difficult to move most people toward a strong opinion on anything. It is even harder to move them away from an opinion once they reach it. The heart of public relations still lies in the public opinion process; it is concerned with how public opinion is formed and how it is influenced by communication. This chapter discusses attitude formation and change and public opinion creation and persuasion.

For public relations professionals, the concept of public opinion—and its power—must be understood and confronted. Indeed, meaningful public relations practice can be undertaken only after the bases for and nuances of public opinion are understood. Public relations work then attempts to influence public opinion, the attitudes that support it, and the actions taken on its behalf.

For an organization the ultimate reflection of public opinion lies in its so-called corporate image, the overall impression that it conveys to its publics. Obviously, every individual views every organization differently. However, one overriding goal of public relations professionals is to convince the vast majority to view their organization in a favorable light. Clearly, this effort revolves around the proper—and profitable—performance of the organization. But it also has much to do with an organization's understanding of and influence on public opinion.

DEFINING PUBLIC OPINION

Public relations educator Walt Seifert insists that "the United States Supreme Court is not the highest in our land. Our highest court is the Court of Public Opinion, which meets every hour."[1] He has a point. Public opinion is highly influential in our society. Favorable public opinion can help elect a political candidate, sell a consumer product, or raise the price of a corporate stock. Unfavorable public opinion, on the other hand, can be the kiss of death for an individual, a product, or an institution.

Public opinion, like *public relations*, is not easily defined. Newspaper columnist Joseph Kraft called public opinion "the unknown god to which moderns burn incense." Edward Bernays called it "a term describing an ill-defined, mercurial, and changeable group of individual judgments."[2] And Princeton professor Harwood Childs, after coming up with no less than forty different yet viable definitions, concluded with a definition by Herman C. Boyle: "*Public opinion* is not the name of something but the classification of a number of somethings."[3]

Splitting public opinion into its two components, *public* and *opinion*, is perhaps the best way to understand the concept. Simply defined, *public* signifies a group of people who share a common interest in a specific subject—stockholders, for example, or employees or community residents. Each group is concerned with a common issue—the price of the stock, the wages of the company, or the building of a new plant.

An opinion is the expression of an attitude on a particular topic. When attitudes become strong enough, they surface in the form of opinions. When opinions become strong enough, they lead to verbal or behavioral actions.

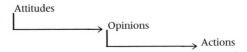

A corporate executive and an environmentalist from the Sierra Club might differ dramatically in their attitudes about the relative importance of pollution control and continued industrial production. Their respective opinions on a piece of environmental legislation might also differ radically. In turn, how their organizations respond to that legislation—by picketing, petitioning, or lobbying—might also differ.

DEFINING ATTITUDES

If an opinion is an expression of an attitude on a particular topic, what then is an attitude? Unfortunately, that is not an easy question to answer. It had been generally assumed that attitudes were predispositions to think a certain way about a certain topic. But recent research has indicated that attitudes may more likely be evaluations that people make about specific problems or issues. These conclusions are not necessarily connected to any broad attitude.[4] For example, an individual might favor a company's response to one issue but disagree vehemently with its response to another. Thus, that individual's attitude may differ from issue to issue.

Attitudes are based on a number of characteristics.

1. **Personal**—the physical and emotional ingredients of an individual, including size, age, and social status.
2. **Cultural**—the environment and life-style of a particular geographic area, such as Japan versus the United States or rural America versus urban Amer-

ica. National political candidates often tailor messages to appeal to the particular cultural complexions of specific regions of the country.

3. **Educational**—the level and quality of a person's education. To appeal to the increased number of college graduates in the United States today, public communication has become more sophisticated.

4. **Familial**—people's roots. Children acquire their parents' tastes, biases, political partisanships, and a host of other characteristics. Even though some pediatricians insist that children pick up most of their knowledge in the earliest years, few would deny the family's strong role in helping mold attitudes.

5. **Religious**—a system of beliefs about God or the supernatural. Religion is making a comeback. In the 1960s many young people turned away from formal religion. In the 1980s even with several evangelical scandals, religious fervor reemerged. From followers of traditional Christianity and Judaism to disciples of Hare Krishna and the Reverend Sun Yung Moon to believers in the various fundamentalist sects of the Bible Belt, religion is back, with its influence on attitudes.

6. **Social class**—position within society. As people's social status changes, so do their attitudes. For example, college students unconcerned with making a living may dramatically change their attitudes about such concepts as big government, big business, wealth, and prosperity after entering the job market.

7. **Race**—ethnic origin, which today increasingly helps shape people's attitudes. The history of blacks and whites in America has been a stormy one, with peaceful coexistence often frustrated. Nonetheless, minorities in our society, as a group, continue to improve their standard of living. And in so doing, blacks, Chicanos, Puerto Ricans, and others have retained distinct racial pride in and allegiance to their cultural heritage.

These characteristics help influence the formation of attitudes. So, too, do other factors such as experience, economic class, and political and organizational memberships. Again, recent research has indicated that attitudes and behaviors are situational—influenced by specific issues in specific situations. Nonetheless, when others with similar attitudes reach similar opinions, a consensus, or public opinion, is born.

TYPES OF ATTITUDES

Strictly speaking, attitudes are positive, negative, or nonexistent. A person is for something, against it, or couldn't care less. Studies show that most people don't care much one way or the other. For any one issue, a small percentage of people express strong support, and another small percentage express strong opposition. The vast majority are right smack in the middle—passive, neutral, indifferent. Former Vice President Spiro T. Agnew called them "the silent majority." In many instances—political campaigns being a prime example—this

Herb Schmertz

Herb Schmertz is principal of the Schmertz Company, a communications consulting firm begun in 1988. He was formerly vice president of public affairs at Mobil Oil Corporation and a director of Mobil Corporation and Mobil Oil. In his years at Mobil, Schmertz earned the distinction of being perhaps the best-known public relations professional in the United States. Under his guidance Mobil developed a reputation as the nation's most outspoken corporation. His book, *Goodbye to the Low Profile: The Art of Creative Confrontation,* describes the theory and practice behind that reputation. He also is co-author of the novel *Takeover.*

Why was Mobil so outspoken in its views?
The answer is twofold. First, Mobil was committed to dialogue. A pluralistic society demands vigorous competition in the marketplace of ideas. We believed that nobody speaks for any business better than the business itself.

Second, we believed that companies, like individuals, have distinct personalities. Our personality included a sensitivity to the environment in which we operated. The ultimate survival of any single institution in our society is closely linked to the strength and vitality of all our free institutions—our universities, our free press, our churches, and our cultural groups. Mobil's top management obviously supported participation in the marketplace of ideas and our concern for the world around us. Without management's support, none of our programs would have worked.

How successful do you think you were in this approach?
We knew that 100 percent support for our views and philosophies could not be achieved. We risked rebuttal and perhaps at-

silent majority holds the key to success because they are most readily influenced by a communicator's message.

It's hard to change the mind of a person who is staunchly opposed to a particular issue or individual. Likewise, it's easy to reinforce the support of a person who is wholeheartedly in favor of an issue or an individual. Social scientist Leon Festinger discussed this concept when he talked about cognitive

tack by those who had a vested political interest in opposing us. However, by participating in the debate over political and economic issues, we broadened the spectrum of facts, views, opinions, and philosophy available for our publics to consider in making decisions.

What's your opinion of the media?
The nature of television operating under the tyranny of the 25-second bite [limit] makes it inherently less fair and less accurate than print media. Newspapers have the space to develop complicated ideas, accept letters to the editor, print corrections, and even accept advocacy advertising. Yet I believe the media in general tend toward sensationalism, to reporting gossip and recriminations, without thoroughly exposing the political motivations that give rise to them.

Do you think Mobil's program had an impact on the media?
Yes, indeed—a very good impact. When I left Mobil, I received some surprisingly favorable reviews from the media. Even the most cynical reporters had to admit we made good copy. I think it was healthy for journalism to have someone attacking the media. We contributed to positive changes in media procedures, such as reduced use of anonymous sources, better trained reporters, and better prepared reporters. We even helped, I think, develop a larger market for business and economic news than was ever the case before.

What should be the proper relationship between the media and business?
The current adversarial relationship between business and the media serves no purpose. If a relationship of mutual trust were to develop, the press would undoubtedly have better access to businessmen, and the result would be a better informed American public.

The basic purpose of journalism should be to inform, and information can best be solicited from the business community in an atmosphere free of cat-and-mouse games. Journalists have to rediscover the objectivity that used to be their stock and trade and free themselves of the I-make-the-news-I-report syndrome.

What's your view of the state of the public relations profession today?
Public relations is in a state of substantial change as a new breed of management takes over American industry. The most successful managements will use public relations much more as a business tool than ever before—for marketing, for protecting the company from the acts of others that may damage shareholders, for achieving intellectual superiority over the competition, for merchandising top management to the firm's most important publics, and for enhancing employee morale.

dissonance, saying that individuals tend to avoid information that is dissonant or opposed to their own points of view, and they tend to seek out information that is consonant, or in support of their own attitudes.[5] In other words, one who regularly reads the liberal *Village Voice* probably wouldn't read the conservative *National Review,* and vice versa. In effect, this example is cognitive dissonance in action.

As Festinger's theory intimates, the people whose attitudes can be influenced most readily are those who have not yet made up their minds. In politics, as noted in chapter 1, this group is often referred to as the swing vote. Many elections have been won or lost on last-minute appeals to these politically undecided voters. In addition, it is possible to introduce information that may cause dissonance in the mind of a receiver.

Understanding this theory and its potential for influencing the silent majority is extremely important for the public relations practitioner, whose objective is to win support through clear, thoughtful, and persuasive communication. Moving a person from a latent state of attitude formation to a more aware state and finally to an active one becomes a matter of motivation.

SOURCES OF MOTIVATION

People are motivated by different factors, and no two people are apt to respond exactly the same way to the same set of circumstances. Each of us is motivated by different drives and needs.

The most famous delineator of what motivates people was Dr. Abraham Maslow, whose hierarchy of needs helps define the origins of motivation, which, in turn, help explain attitudes and public opinion. Maslow postulated a five-level hierarchy.

1. The lowest order of needs was the physiological needs, encompassing a person's biological demands—food and water, sleep, health, bodily needs, exercise and rest, and sex.
2. A second level was that of safety needs, including security, protection, comfort and peace, and orderly surroundings.
3. A third level was that of love needs, such as acceptance, belonging, love and affection, and membership in a group.
4. A fourth level was that of esteem, the need for recognition and prestige, confidence and leadership opportunities, competence and strength, intelligence and success.
5. The highest order of needs was one of self-actualization, or simply becoming what one is capable of becoming. Self-actualization involves self-fulfillment and achieving a goal for the purpose of challenge and accomplishment.

According to Maslow, the needs at all five levels compose the fundamental motivating factors for any individual or public.

POWER OF PERSUASION

Perhaps the most essential element in influencing public opinion is the principle of persuasion. Persuading is the goal of the vast majority of public relations programs. Persuasion theory has myriad explanations and interpretations. Ba-

Capitulating to Public Opinion

Sometimes riding out the half-truths, falsehoods, and innuendos that confuse the public is no easy task—especially when the name of your well-known diet product is the same as that of a deadly disease. Jeffrey Martin, Inc., the distributor of Ayds appetite-suppressant candy, faced just that issue when AIDS (acquired immune deficiency syndrome) began attracting public attention in the early 1980s.

Company officials took the controversy in stride. In 1986 Ayds launched a $5 million advertising campaign with the tag line "A lot of will power in every little piece." Said the company's executive vice president, "Consumers are smart enough to tell the difference between a disease and a diet product. The product has been around for 45 years. Let the disease change its name."

Alas, the diet candy blinked first. In mid-1987, with more than 21,000 reported deaths from AIDS, the new owners of Ayds candy, Dep Corporation, were having second thoughts about their new acquisition's name. Said the Dep chairman, "Obviously with a name like Ayds, we'll have to do something."

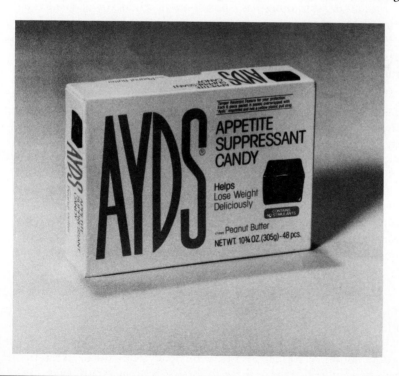

sically, persuasion means getting another person to do something through advice, reasoning, or just plain arm-twisting. Books have been written on the enormous power of advertising as a persuasive medium. More recently, public relations, too, has been given credit for leading a persuasion explosion in the 1980s.[6]

Researchers in recent years have questioned whether we really can be persuaded—particularly through the mass media. In the late 1940s and 1950s, evidence mounted that such communication rarely has a persuasive effect. Most evidence came from voting studies and studies of information flow from the media to individuals, as researched by Elihu Katz and Paul Lazarsfeld. The studies of Carl Hovland and his colleagues at Yale University also demonstrated that the credibility of a source exercised a prime influence on the persuasiveness of the message being delivered.

Social scientists and communications scholars take issue with the view of many public relations practitioners that a story on network news or the front page of the *New York Times* has a tremendous persuasive effect. Scholars argue that the media have a limited effect on persuasion—doing more to reinforce existing attitudes than to persuade toward a new belief. There is little doubt, however, that the persuasiveness of a message can be increased when it arouses or is accompanied by a high level of personal involvement. In other words, an individual who cares about something and is in fundamental agreement with an organization's basic position will tend to be persuaded by a message supporting that view.

Following this belief is the persuasion theory of Michael Ray—the hierarchies of effects.[7] According to this theory, there are at least three basic orderings of knowledge, attitude, and behavior relative to persuasion.

1. When personal involvement is low and little difference exists between behavioral alternatives, knowledge changes are likely to lead directly to behavioral changes.
2. When personal involvement is high but behavioral alternatives are indistinguishable, behavioral change is likely to be followed by attitudinal change, similar to Festinger's cognitive dissonance approach.
3. When personal involvement is high and clear differences exist among alternatives, people act in a more rational manner. First, they learn about the issue. Second, they evaluate the alternatives. Then they act in a manner consistent with their attitudes and knowledge.

The application of Ray's hierarchy to public relations rests in the ability of a practitioner to personally involve a target in an organization, issue, or idea and then to argue rationally for a particular alternative.

To these complex theories of persuasion is added the simpler, yet no less profound notion of former Secretary of State Dean Rusk: "One of the best ways to persuade others is to listen to them." No matter how one characterizes persuasion, the goal of most communications programs is, in fact, to influence a receiver to take a desired action.

INFLUENCING PUBLIC OPINION

Conducted wisely, public relations can influence public opinion. A thoughtful campaign can crystallize attitudes, reinforce beliefs, and occasionally change minds. But the process can't be approached haphazardly. First, the opinions to be changed or modified must be identified and understood. Second, the target publics must be clear. Finally, the practitioner must have in sharp focus the objectives that influence particular publics and opinions.

Dr. G. Edward Pendray, a former editor of *Public Relations Journal,* offered the following nine maxims in dealing with public opinion:[8]

1. **The better they know you, the more they'll like you—provided you deserve it**. Organizations often feel that their poor image stems from a general lack of knowledge of their activities. Becoming better known means that liabilities as well as assets will be highlighted. So a firm that seeks the limelight must also accept the attendant responsibility.
2. **Change yourself; it's easier than changing the public.** The public will never change its thinking about you unless you, on your own, reform any questionable policies and practices.
3. **Speak the language of action.** If you want to be listened to, support your words with actions. Words alone are hollow.
4. **Weary not in well-doing.** Public opinion takes time to develop. Don't give up good programs if they don't meet with immediate public recognition. Give it time to build.
5. **Truth rides out the storm; half-truth and falsehood blow away.** Always base public relations programs on truth. There simply is no substitute.
6. **Put your heart where your money is.** Money alone can't buy favorable public opinion. Back up your money with personal participation. The public will get the message.
7. **You may like cake, but you can fish better with worms**. You must tell your story in terms of the public's needs, not your own. If you have an abstract idea to get across, bait the hook with human interest, not self-interest.
8. **People interest people most.** People want to hear about other people; they're less interested in a firm. Express things in terms of human interest.
9. **Watch that log—it may be a crocodile**. Clever or easy solutions rarely work. Before taking any public stand, an organization must thoroughly examine all the ramifications.

Thoughtfully applying these rules before embarking on a campaign to influence public opinion can pay off in long-lasting benefits. Alternatively, ignoring these rules can cause decisive setbacks in the court of public opinion.

YOU MAKE THE CALL

When Hutton Talks . . .

By 1985 E. F. Hutton & Company had become the fifth largest retail brokerage house in the United States, with revenues approaching $3 billion. Its advertising slogan—"When E. F. Hutton talks, people listen"—was well known. But midway through that year, people began listening to Hutton in a way the firm found most embarrassing. In May Hutton pleaded guilty to 2,000 felony counts resulting from an illegal check overdraft scheme that involved approximately 100 of its nearly 400 branches nationwide from 1980 to 1982. The firm agreed to pay $2.75 million in fines and set up an $8 million fund to reimburse the banks.

The Justice Department did not bring charges against individuals. It said that only two mid-level individuals could be charged in a criminal sense and that the plea agreement was preferable because it established new law in cash management and sent a strong signal to other corporations. The media and a congressional subcommittee, however, sharply criticized Hutton and the Justice Department, saying that top executives should have been punished. Cartoonists and headline writers around the country had a field day with Hutton's slogan; one of many parodies read, "When E. F. Hutton talks, it says 'Guilty'."

In a move to settle the matter, Hutton retained former Attorney General Griffin Bell, who led a team of fourteen lawyers in a summer-long investigation into individual wrongdoing. As a result of the inquiry, three senior executives resigned or retired, six branch managers were fined $25,000 each, and three regional executives were suspended for thirty days without pay. These actions stilled some of the criticism, but negative publicity continued for months as Hutton reached settlements with state and federal regulatory bodies. Connecticut, for example, held public hearings and ultimately fined the company $350,000.

Under siege, Hutton conducted an extensive internal and external information program to present its positions to employees, clients, and the media. It suspended advertising briefly but did not abandon its 15-year-old slogan. In July the company ran the ad shown here in several papers to help boost employee morale; and in the fall it launched a new national TV advertising campaign using Olympic athletes to personify the quest for excellence.

QUESTIONS

1. If you were Hutton's public relations director, what steps would you take to assess the damage?
2. Should Hutton have retained its advertising slogan in the wake of its well-publicized problems?
3. What measures might you adopt to resurrect Hutton's corporate image?

E.F. Hutton Talks...

"Thank you."

That's the most important thing we can say to our 17,500 employees and our thousands of customers and clients. The loyalty and support of our clients and the commitment to excellence and integrity of our employees is what built our reputation over 81 years and what has seen us through the trying times of these past few weeks. You are the best.

To those in government and industry who look on with concern, we simply say, if you judge us on our merits, we are confident of your conclusions.

We will continue to meet the investment needs of our clients in more than 500 local communities and we are proud to say "When E.F. Hutton Talks, People Listen."

Sincerely,

Robert Fomon

Robert Fomon
Chairman and
Chief Executive Officer

(Courtesy of E. F. Hutton)

POLISHING THE CORPORATE IMAGE

Most organizations today and the people who manage them are extremely sensitive about the way they are perceived by their critical publics. In one nationwide survey of 100 top executives, more than half considered it "very important to maintain a good public image."[9] As a result, some corporate managements today are reluctant to stick their collective necks out. As former General Motors executive John DeLorean described the executive thinking at his alma mater, "General Motors management feels that the corporation simply draws the lion's share of criticism. The best way to reduce this inevitable criticism, as top management sees it, is to keep a low, faceless profile."[10] Ironically, in the case of General Motors, the company was one of the first U.S. corporations to adopt a high-profile, industrial statesman approach to public affairs.* Indeed, few firms today can afford to keep a low profile.

Consider the following:

- Procter & Gamble voluntarily recalled and permanently removed from the market its successful Rely tampons when it was suspected that they contained carcinogenic agents.
- McDonald's reluctantly went public to defuse a quickly spreading rumor that ground worms were among the tasty ingredients in its patented hamburger.
- J. P. Stevens, the nation's second largest textile manufacturer, reluctantly agreed to reconsider its labor practices when a group of activists successfully focused national media attention on the firm's treatment of its employees.
- New York City judges—smarting from attacks on their efficiency, integrity, and judgment—hired a public relations firm to improve their sagging image.
- Several of the nation's largest banks went public in opposition to the apartheid policies of the South African government after considering the merits of arguments raised by church groups about lending money to South Africa.

Most organizations today understand clearly that it takes a great deal of time to build a favorable image for a corporation but only one slip to create a negative public impression. In other words, the corporate image is a fragile commodity. Yet most firms also believe that a positive corporate image is essential for continued long-term success.

As Ray D'Argenio, the former communications director of United Technologies, put it, "Corporate communications can't create a corporate character. A company already has a character, which communications can reinforce."[11] United Technologies distinguished itself largely through an aggressive and unique advertising campaign that dared to be different. "We didn't seek to dissolve into the mainstream of companies," says D'Argenio. "Rather, we wanted to be distinct." So successful was the United Technologies advertising campaign that few readers needed the corporate logo to remind them that the

---

*Also ironically, John DeLorean was arrested—and subsequently acquitted—in a 1983 blaze of publicity for attempted cocaine smuggling.

Love That Sara Lee Underwear

Talk about clarifying the corporate image . . . In 1985 Consolidated Foods Corporation learned that 98 percent of 800 people surveyed were aware of the products of its subsidiary Sara Lee. At the same time the company was unhappy that its own Consolidated Foods name didn't give consumers and investors an accurate picture of the broad range of the company's products, from foods to vacuum cleaners to underwear.

So . . . dismissing several alternative names recommended by consultants and defying all logic, corporation executives decided to rename the firm to take advantage of the high recognition level of the subsidiary responsible for only 8 percent of its products. Thus, the Sara Lee Corporation was born, complete with a line of underwear. As Yogi Berra said when they told him the people of Dublin had just elected a Jewish mayor, "Only in America!"

SARA LEE CORPORATION

company was the sponsor of a simple yet novel series on subjects ranging from creativity to proper language to the importance of the individual in society (Figure 4–1).

Even though every employee in an organization plays a part in shaping a firm's public image, the public relations department is technically responsible. A practitioner must realize that image—a function of a company's mission, objectives, people, and performance—must be based on fact.

DISCOVERING THE CORPORATE IMAGE

Helping an organization discover its own special and distinct corporate image is an important function of the public relations practitioner. In the process the practitioner must ask the following basic questions:

- **What is the firm's present corporate image?** How does the public perceive the company? Does this perception differ from that of management? Often research turns up significant discrepancies. For example, one computer company, which prided itself on its frequent communication with Wall Street analysts, was surprised to learn that it was perceived by analysts as pushy.

Brighten Your Corner

Have you
noticed the
great difference
between the
people you
meet?
Some are as
sunshiny as
a handful of
forget-me-nots.
Others come on
like frozen mackerel.
A cheery, comforting
nurse can
help make a
hospital stay
bearable.
An upbeat secretary
makes visitors
glad they came
to see you.
Every corner of the
world has its clouds,
gripes, complainers,
and pains in the
neck—because many
people have
yet to
learn that
honey works better
than vinegar.
You're in control
of *your* small
corner of the
world.
Brighten it. . .
You *can*.

FIGURE 4–1 Although many companies attempted to construct a differentiable corporate image through advertising, few succeeded as well as United Technologies, which kept its messages succinct, savvy, and sparkling. (Courtesy of United Technologies Corporation, Hartford, CT)

In another example a food chain that considered its new menu to be up-to-date discovered that everyone under forty still thought of the firm as old and stodgy. One public utility, active in community affairs, was amazed to discover that few in the community appreciated the full extent of the firm's public service activities.

■ **What corporate image does the firm want?** An organization can't be all things to all people. One department store might decide, for instance, that its market is the upper middle class. Another store might shoot for an even more elite market. Still another might wish to project the image of a discount merchant, servicing the less well-to-do. Before an organization can take action in achieving a new corporate image, it must first decide the specific kind of image it wants to attain (Figure 4–2).

■ **How do the company's various entities—products and/or services—affect the image of the company? Does this vary by audience?** Many times, a company's divisions, subsidiaries, or products have a completely different image from that of the rest of the firm. Often this is a good idea, but sometimes it isn't. If a firm wants to be looked on as a consistently high-class/high-quality operation, a profitable yet low-class/low-quality area within that corporation might be detrimental to the overall corporate image. This is the kind of tough issue with which an organization must grapple if it wishes to convey a cohesive corporate image among all of its parts. Then, too, different audiences associated with different elements of an organization may perceive the firm's image to be completely different. Often, this is exactly what the organization wants.

■ **What must a firm do to win a new corporate image?** Often, the process starts with changing the internal culture. The company's procedures might need revision. Product lines might require reexamination. If the firm truly wishes to change, corporate philosophies might have to be adjusted. Sometimes the very name of the company needs to be changed to shed an old image and don a new one.

The Corporate Image at Mobil Oil

The serious energy shortages of the mid-1970s and the subsequent skyrocketing oil prices created a ground swell of negative public opinion directed toward the nation's largest oil companies. A traditionally closed-mouthed group, the oil companies were momentarily caught off guard by the barrage of media accusations. Each of the so-called seven sisters chose a different manner of responding to the criticism. Some opened up their side of the story to the public. Others began massive defensive advertising. Still others began sponsoring public affairs programs on television.

Mobil Oil did all of these things and much, much more; it came out swinging in every direction (Figure 4–3). First, it sponsored a series of feisty ads on the opposite-editorial (op-ed) pages of major newspapers, offering its own opinions about energy, the need to accumulate capital in society, and the

The Corporate Signature

Our signature is an arrangement of our mark and logotype. It is considered as one design element in any layout or application situation. A complete corporate signature must be used whenever identification is necessary. Each authorized arrangement has an established relationship between the mark and logotype. This relationship is not to be altered or changed in any way.

Preferred form
for vertical format

Preferred form
for horizontal format

Alternate form
for horizontal format

FIGURE 4–2 The key to a corporate image that gets through to people is a combination of simplicity, unity, and balance. These excerpts from the corporate identity manual of David's lemonade, the creation of Fulton + Partners, Inc., are examples of a clear corporate image. (Courtesy of Sanders Printing Corporation)

FIGURE 4–3 Among the arrows in Mobil Oil's public relations quiver were these op-ed advertisements, which noted weekly the company's viewpoint on matters from national energy policy to the importance of profits in society; Observations columns, which editorialized on economic and energy-related issues; cartoons, which mainly poked fun at bureaucrats; and sponsorship of public affairs television programs, a more soft-sell approach. (Copyright © Mobil Oil Corporation. Reprinted by permission.)

role of business in general. It then sent key executives to cities around the country to appear on more than 100 talk shows, news broadcasts, and radio call-in programs to explain its side of the energy crisis. Mobil Oil also sponsored a series of energy-related cartoons for newspapers, and it created and placed a series of editorial columns, called Observations, again discussing the implications of the energy situation. In addition, it channeled millions of dollars into the sponsorship of public affairs programs such as "Masterpiece Theatre" on the public broadcasting network.

Mobil's corporate image offensive was unprecedented. As *Fortune* magazine somewhat dourly admitted, "Few organizations of any kind can rival Mobil in the artfulness and sophistication with which it presses its opinions, whether it is advocating a national energy policy, resisting congressional proposals to end vertical integration in the oil industry, or championing the cause of mass transit."[12]

The cornerstone of Mobil's public relations thrust was its op-ed advertising campaign. Ironically, the ads rarely mentioned the company's service stations or its products. Rather, they emphasized corporate issues: the free enterprise system, energy conservation, and the importance of profits. Mobil's clear intent in sponsoring this kind of bold, aggressive, full-scale campaign was to speak out in defense of its interests, the interests of the oil industry, and its perception of the national interest.

Whenever Mobil found itself misinterpreted in a media story, it lashed back. In fact, so infuriated was the company with an item in the *Wall Street Journal* in 1984 that it decided to boycott the newspaper by not giving it any more corporate news. Said Mobil public affairs director Herb Schmertz, "We concluded that the situation couldn't get worse. We did it for our own self-respect." Schmertz added, "We believe in leading, not following, taking the initiative and abandoning the low-profile policy. In a word—confrontation."[13]

To back up his words, Schmertz wrote a book, *Goodbye to the Low Profile*. In 1988 he quit his $640,000-per-year job and took his confrontational philosophy on the road as a consultant. And Mobil headed into the 1990s, perhaps a little less willing to stick out its corporate neck but nonetheless continuing to sport a healthy—make that robust—$30 million public affairs budget.

BEWARE THE TRAPS OF PUBLIC OPINION

Analyzing public opinion is not as easy as it looks. Once a company wins favorable public opinion for a product or an idea, the trick is to maintain it. The worst thing to do is sit back and bask in the glory of a positive public image—that's a quick route to image deterioration.

Public opinion is changeable, and in assessing it, communicators are susceptible to a number of subtle yet lethal traps.

■ **Cast in stone** This fallacy assumes that just because public opinion is well established on a certain issue, it isn't likely to change. Not true. Consider an

The Name Game: A New Look for the Corporate Image

Walter P. Margulies, president of Lippincott and Margulies, probably said it best: "The nostalgic and the quaint have no place in the world of corporate identity."* Margulies should know. Together with a handful of other design consultants, he has helped a growing number of U.S. corporations change their names, their trademarks, and their communications looks in order to keep up with a changing society. Corporate identity consultants have become lucrative components in the communications agency marketplace. In 1986 alone, 1,382 organizations changed names, including 686 because of acquisitions or mergers.

Sometimes such corporate identity consultants point out obvious incongruities between a firm's traditional logo and its more recent activities. For example, RCA was advised to get rid of its fox terrier mascot, Nipper, in light of its involvement with advanced missile technology and the space program (Figure A). Curiously, the company first adopted and then rejected the advice, choosing to restore in 1978 its famous trademark. *(Continued, pp. 94–95)*

The new Nipper

FIGURE A

issue such as women's liberation. In the early 1960s people laughed at the handful of women raising a ruckus about equal rights, equal pay, and equal treatment. By the early 1970s women's liberation pervaded every sector of our culture, and nobody laughed. In the space of a decade, public opinion about the importance of this issue had shifted substantially.

■ **Gut reaction** This fallacy assumes that if management feels in its corporate gut that the public will feel strongly in a certain direction, then that must be

More often, the consultants suggest a new graphics approach, adopted in the case of U.S. Steel Corporation after three years of planning, testing, market research, and self-analysis. Ironically, in 1986 U.S. Steel not only changed its logo again, but also changed its name—to USX Corporation—when it diversified into other areas. The *X* represents the company's symbol on the New York

FIGURE B Corporate logos provide instant identification. These corporate logos are so identifiable that one glance tells what companies they are: the Chase Manhattan Bank octagon, the Blue Shield snake, the Prudential rock, and the Hartford deer. U.S. Steel spent millions of dollars to develop its modern trademark, USS, then switched to USX. Xerox's problem is that its name and logo are so widely used that it must fight a continual battle to have the name treated as a proper adjective with a capital *X* rather than a verb with a lowercase *x*.

the way to go. *Be careful.* Some managements are so cut off from the real world that their knee-jerk reactions to issues often turn out to be more jerk than anything else. One former auto company executive, perhaps overstating the case, described the problem this way: ''There's no forward response to what the public wants today. It's gotten to be a total insulation from the realities of the world.'' Certainly, management's instincts in dealing with the

Stock Exchange. Figure B shows various company logos, including U.S. Steel and the new USX logo.

The circumstances surrounding name changes vary greatly.

- UAL, Inc., the old United Airlines, was more than an airline, and its chairman reasoned that by changing the firm's name, its stock price would improve. So in 1987, UAL's name was changed to the computer-generated Allegis. But the chairman spent so much time on the new name and so little on anything else that, along with the new moniker, the board voted for a new chairman as well.
- United Aircraft, a traditional supplier of flight products, had expanded into other industrial and commercial spheres such as electric power generation and transmission, laser technology, and marine propulsion. Consequently, it decided to become United Technologies Corporation to more accurately reflect its new identity.
- Perhaps the granddaddy of all corporate identity programs was the $110 million name change undertaken by the Standard Oil Company of New Jersey to become Exxon on all its signs, stationery, and pumps.

Why do firms go to the trouble of changing their names? There is no one answer. Some do it because of a change in their product mix; others do it because they want their name and logo to more accurately convey their idea of the firm's image. (However, it is difficult to understand why a company would adopt a name reminiscent of alphabet soup—for example, the MBPXL Corporation.) Some adopt new names to keep up with the times. Still others do it because it just seems to make sense; as one executive of New York's First National City Bank put it when his company changed its name, "Everybody calls us Citibank anyway, so we thought we might as well make it official."

---

*Cited in Stewart Alter, "Margulies Advises Companies to Start Modern," *ANNY* (13 August 1976), 15.

---

public may be questionable at times. Generally, gut-reaction judgments should be avoided in assessing public opinion.
- **General public** There may well be a public at large, but there's no such thing as the general public. Even the smallest public can be subdivided. No two people are alike, and messages to influence public opinion should be as pointed as possible rather than scattershot. Sometimes individuals may qual-

ify as members of publics on both sides of an issue. In weighing the pros
and cons of lower speed limits, for example, many people are both drivers
and pedestrians. So categorizing them into one general group can be a mistake.

- **Words move mountains** Perhaps they do, sometimes; but public opinion
is usually influenced more by events than by words. For example, in 1979
nuclear power foes lacked a solid political base until an accident at Pennsylvania's Three Mile Island plant rallied public sentiment against the proponents of nuclear power.
- **Brother's keeper** It's true that most people will rise up indignantly if a
fellow citizen has been wronged. But they'll get a lot more indignant if they
feel they themselves have been wronged. In other words, self-interest often
sparks public opinion. An organization wishing to influence public opinion
might be well advised to ask initially, "What's in this for the people whose
opinion we're trying to influence?"

ONE STEP AHEAD OF PUBLIC OPINION

Influencing public opinion remains at the heart of professional public relations
work. Perhaps the key to realizing this objective is anticipating or keeping
ahead of trends in our society. Anticipating trends is no easy task. But in the
latter part of the 1980s trend watching developed into a veritable cottage industry. One self-styled prognosticator riding the crest of trend analysis was
John Naisbitt, whose book *Megatrends* claimed to predict the new directions
that would revolutionize American lives at the turn of the century. Among
them,

- Shift to an information society
- Shift toward a world economy
- Shift from short-term profits to long-range planning
- Shift toward networking as a way to solve common problems
- Shift toward greater individual voices in actions and policies
- Shift toward self-reliance
- Shift toward new technology in all aspects of society[14]

Some might argue that there is nothing very revolutionary in these megatrends (and they might well be right). Nonetheless, such trends deserve to be
scrutinized, analyzed, and evaluated by organizations in order to deal more
effectively with the future.

As public relations counselor Philip Lesly has pointed out, "The real
problems faced by business today are in the outside world of intangibles and
public attitudes."[15] To keep ahead of these intangibles, these public attitudes,
and these kernels of future public opinion, managements will turn increasingly
to professional public relations practitioners for guidance.

1. Walt Seifert, "Our Highest Court: Public Opinion," *Public Relations Journal* (December 1977): 24.
2. Cited in Edward L. Bernays, *Crystallizing Public Opinion* (New York: Liveright Publishing Corp., 1961), 61.
3. Cited in Harwood L. Childs, *Public Opinion: Nature, Formation, and Role* (Princeton, NJ: Van Nostrand, 1965), 15.
4. James E. Grunig and Todd Hunt, *Managing Public Relations* (New York: Holt, Rinehart & Winston, 1984), 130.
5. Leon A. Festinger, *A Theory of Cognitive Dissonance* (New York: Harper & Row, 1957), 163.
6. Art Stevens, *The Persuasion Explosion* (Washington, DC: Acropolis Books, 1985), 9.
7. John V. Pavlik, *Public Relations: What Research Tells Us* (Newbury Park, CA: Sage Publications, 1987), 74.
8. G. Edward Pendray, "PR Folklore," *Public Relations Journal* (October 1970): 20.
9. "Image Is a Priority to 53% of Executives Surveyed," *Wall Street Journal*, 23 July 1981.
10. J. Patrick Wright, *On a Clear Day You Can See General Motors* (New York: Avon Books, 1980), 279.
11. Ray D'Argenio, speech at the Communications Executive of the Year Luncheon, sponsored by Corpcom Services, 10 December 1981.
12. Irwin Ross, "Public Relations Isn't Kid-Glove Stuff at Mobil," *Fortune* (September 1976): 106.
13. "Herb Schmertz—Campaign Manager," *Memo*, Public Relations Society of America–New York Chapter, February 1985.
14. John Naisbitt, *Megatrends* (New York: Warner Books, 1982), 12.
15. Philip Lesly, "How the Future Will Shape Public Relations—and Vice Versa," *Public Relations Quarterly* (Winter 1981–82): 7.

NOTES

Baer, Daniel H., "Selling Management on Public Relations Research." *Public Relations Quarterly* (Fall 1983): 9–11.
Bennett, Amanda. "What Went Wrong: Experts Look at the Sudden Upheaval at Allegis." *Wall Street Journal* (24 June 1987): 29.
Bernays, Edward L. "Public Dissatisfaction with Institutions," *Public Relations Quarterly* (Summer 1981): 15.
Cantril, Hadley. *Gauging Public Opinion*. 1947. Reprint. Port Washington, NY: Kennikat Press, 1971.
"Corporate Image Check List." *Public Relations Journal* (April 1982): 50. A listing of key questions for the professional communicator creates an ongoing communications strategy for an organization.
Fink, S. *Crisis Management: Planning for the Inevitable*. New York: AMACOM (135 W. 50th St.), 1986.
Finn, David. "Thoughts and Images," *Public Relations Journal* (May 1984): 12–15.
Gollner, Andrew. *Social Change and Corporate Strategy: The Expanding Role of Public Affairs*. Stamford, CT: IAP (105 Old Long Ridge Road), 1984.
Gray, James G., Jr. *Managing the Corporate Image: The Key to Public Trust*. Westport, CT: Quorum Books, 1986.

SUGGESTED READINGS

Idea Bank for Annual Reports. New York: Corporate Shareholder Press (271 Madison Ave.), 1987.

Irvine, Robert B. *When You Are the Headline: Managing a News Story*. Homewood, IL: Dow Jones-Irwin, 1987.

Johnston, David C-H. "Communicating Your Social Role." *Public Relations Journal* (December 1981): 18–19. This compares a company's social role and its economic mission.

Leff, Suzanne. "10 Dos and Don'ts of Naming." *Public Relations Journal* (December 1987): 37, 38. This checklist gives guidelines for coining memorable company or product names for effective promotion.

Lerbinger, Otto. *Managing Corporate Crises: Strategies for Executives*. Boston: Barrington Press (P.O. Box 291, Boston University Station), 1986.

Lesly, Philip. "How the Future Will Shape Public Relations—and Vice Versa." *Public Relations Quarterly* (Winter 1981–82): 4–8.

————. *Overcoming Opposition: A Survival Manual for Executives*. Englewood Cliffs, NJ: Prentice-Hall, 1984.

Lippmann, Walter. *Public Opinion*. New York: Harcourt Brace & Co., 1922. Reprint. New York: Macmillan, 1965. This remains a classic.

Margulies, Walter P. "Back to Fundamentals," *Public Relations Journal* (April 1982): 50–51. The public relations professional has the primary responsibility for vigilance over the corporation's image.

Masel-Walters, Lynne. "Working with the Press: Strategies for the '80s," *Public Relations Quarterly* (Fall 1984): 24–27. This article explains the best ways to communicate with the press; positive attitude, not panicking, speaking on the record and developing a communications policy are among those suggested.

Meyers, Gerald. *When It Hits the Fan*. Boston: Houghton Mifflin, 1986.

Nager, Norman and **Richard Truitt**. *Strategic Public Relations Counseling*. White Plains, NY: Longman, 1987.

Naisbitt, John. *Megatrends*. New York: Warner Books, 1982.

Nolan, Joseph T. "Protect Your Public Image with Performance." *Harvard Business Review* (March/April 1975): 135–42.

Nowling, J. R. "The Professional's Way," *Public Relations Quarterly* (Winter 1981–82): 21–22.

O'Neill, Harry W. "How Opinion Surveys Can Help Public Relations Strategy." *Public Relations Review* (Summer 1984): 3–12.

Pinsdorf, M. *Communicating When Your Company Is Under Siege*. Lexington, MA: Lexington Books, 1986.

The Tragedy of Love Canal

A heartless corporation dumped toxic chemicals in Love Canal, then walked away from the problem, leaving behind a neighborhood full of victims.
—Advertisement for *Reason* magazine in the *Washington Monthly*, June 1982

You're about to be untricked. If you believe that the guilty party in the Love Canal tragedy is the Hooker Chemical & Plastics Corporation . . . then you've been snookered.
—*Reason*, February 1981, p. 17

In the public's mind Love Canal was a tragedy, pure and simple. The story began as a community relations dilemma and gradually mushroomed into a national public relations nightmare, which dramatically influenced public opinion about chemical wastes and waste sites. Here, in some detail, is the chronology of the complex events of Love Canal.

1910	Visionary John Love digs Love Canal to create electricity, but project is abandoned in light of a better, competitive project, Niagara Falls.
Early 1940s	Hooker Chemical, an industrial company with no consumer franchise, buys Love Canal as a potential site to dispose of wastes from its Niagara Falls plant.
1942	Hooker completes the legal transactions to commence dumping what ultimately amounts to approximately 21,800 tons of company waste into Love Canal.
1942–1951	Following standard operating procedures, Hooker dumps its

chemical wastes into the canal, covering the waste with layers of clay. Other wastes besides those from Hooker are also dumped into the canal. In light of the soil characteristics of the area as well as the sparse population surrounding the canal, it constituted an excellent dumping ground for the chemicals.

1952	Niagara Falls Board of Education insists that Hooker sell the land adjacent to the canal to construct a school.
1953	Hooker, under pressure, sells the property to the board for $1. The school board agrees to assume all risk and liability. Hooker engineers advise the board that the clay cap encasing the dump site must not be disturbed. However, the board allows a highway to be built over the southern tip of the site, leases some of the land for development, and allows the soil to be removed for landfill. Finally, the school board votes to construct a school next to the canal. As part of this project, foundations are dug for homes, risking penetration of the canal's clay cover.
1954	In removing 3,000 cubic yards of fill from Love Canal, an architect reports hitting "a soft spot in the ground, which turned out to be a drain-filled

ditch trench, which gave off a strong chemical odor." Upon further investigation, the excavator makes contact with a pit filled with chemicals. He immediately stops work.

1955–1957 The new school building adjacent to the Love Canal opens its doors to 500 students. Meanwhile, thousands of cubic yards of soil are moved from the top of the canal in order to grade the surrounding area. Among the only modifications is the movement of the location of the kindergarten playground so as not to interfere with chemical deposits.

1957 Hooker publicly—and strongly—warns the community, through local newspaper ads, about the potential dangers of Love Canal. Nonetheless, sewers are dug at the canal, penetrating the clay cover for the first time. The Hooker warnings are quickly forgotten.

1958 Children, playing on the landfill area of Love Canal, contract chemical burns from exposed residues on the surface of the canal. Hooker warns the school board again.

1968 The New York State Department of Transportation rips into the canal at the southwestern end during construction of a new expressway.

1976 Niagara Falls experiences record rains that pour into the by-now opened Love Canal, forcing large quantities of chemicals up and out into the community. Such lethal chemicals as toluene, leachate, and 3-4-5-T, or Agent Orange, are liberally dumped into neighborhood basements. People begin to become increasingly concerned about the dangers of Love Canal. Hooker proposes to pay one-third of an estimated $850,000 cleanup bill, but the city fails to come up with the balance, and the plan is aborted. The U.S. Congress passes the Resources Conservation and Recovery Act, the first cradle-to-grave tracking system for hazardous waste.

1978 Reporter Michael Brown begins reporting on problems at Love Canal in the *Niagara Gazette*. The Love Canal Home Owners Association is formed to bring attention to the chemical waste problems. The association alleges that area children have contracted birth defects because of the chemical wastes of Love Canal. Governor Hugh Carey, running for reelection, seizes the issue and vows that the state of New York will buy the 85 to 90 homes in the Love Canal area and evacuate all residents to hotels until the Love Canal problem can be resolved.

1979   After observing a general policy of silence on the advice of legal counsel, Hooker decides to become more public. Up until now, Hooker has shunned the limelight, perhaps believing that it had no legal liability for Love Canal–related problems and therefore had no responsibility to go public. However, with the name Love Canal now synonymous with images of poisoned water, deformed babies, and negative public opinion toward chemical dumping, the company decides to change its tune. Hooker decides to allow its president to be interviewed by reporter Mike Wallace on the CBS network show "60 Minutes." Although the interview lasts two hours, in the 8½ minutes that make the air the president is barbecued. After the show Hooker cries foul and prepares its own 15-minute rebuttal tape.

1980   In April the state of New York files a $365 million lawsuit against Occidental Petroleum, Hooker Chemical Company, and Hooker Chemical & Plastics Corporation, accusing them of responsibility for the Love Canal problems. On May 17 the Environmental Protection Agency (EPA) holds a press conference to release the results of a preliminary genetic study showing chromosome damage in 11 of 36 Love Canal residents tested. The private laboratory that performed the tests for the EPA acknowledges that the preliminary findings are not definitive. On May 21 President Carter declares a state of emergency in the Love Canal area, paving the way for the evacuation of up to 710 families.

1982   The EPA issues a definitive report on Love Canal, concluding that Hooker had effectively contained the central dump site and that in terms of toxic chemicals, the zone around Love Canal was as habitable as the rest of the Niagara Falls area.

1988   A federal judge rules that Occidental Chemical Corporation, successor to Hooker, is liable for the cost—estimated at more than $250 million—of cleaning up the Love Canal landfill. "It is beyond dispute that the company's disposal practices were at least partially responsible for the release, or a threatened release, of the chemicals from the Love Canal landfill," the judge said. The company says it is "disappointed by the ruling."

In an editorial the *New York Times* summarized that after years of "incomplete, misleading, or erroneous scientific information," the residents of Love Canal—and indeed, the public at large—"have paid a heavy price for the confusion." The editorial concluded, "The first lesson of Love Canal turns out to be very much like that of Three Mile Island: Such complex situations must be handled, above all, with credibility."

Rightly or wrongly—and Hooker argued strongly that its overriding concern throughout was "protection of the public against a recognized potential hazard"—the term *Love Canal* passed into common usage as a symbol of corporate indifference to the hazards of chemical wastes, much as *Watergate* became a generic term for government corruption. With most of the public now acutely aware of the dangers—real or perceived—in disposing of hazardous wastes, the tragedy of Love Canal clearly took its toll on public opinion.*

QUESTIONS

1. How would you rate Hooker's handling of Love Canal? Did reality jibe with perception?
2. What do you think Love Canal did for the reputation of Hooker Chemical?

3. Would the company have been wise to expand on its 1976 proposal to pay one-third of the cleanup bill for Love Canal?
4. If you had been Hooker's management in the late 1970s, would you have heeded legal advice to maintain a low profile in the face of criticism about Love Canal?
5. Would you have recommended that Hooker come out of its low-profile closet by agreeing to the "60 Minutes" interview?
6. Did the fact that Hooker was not a retail company and had no trade name to trade on help or hinder it in dealing publicly with Love Canal?
7. Does it surprise you that in the spring of 1982 Hooker's parent decided to change the company's name from the Hooker Chemical Company to the Occidental Chemical Company? Why not?

---

*For further information on the Love Canal case, consult Eric Zuesse, "Love Canal: The Truth Seeps Out," *Reason* (February 1981): 16–33; "Notoriety Makes Love Canal a Symbol Which Hooker Treats as a Local Issue; Classic Case of Legal Facts vs. Public Feeling," *PR Reporter* 23, no. 35, 8 September 1980, 1; "The War of Words at Love Canal," *New York Times*, 17 July 1982, 18; and A. J. Carter, "Niagara Families Battle Illness," *Newsday*, 30 April 1979.

Ethics

Ethical dilemmas are all around us. In every sector of our society, major institutions are sending out mixed signals about the value of moral conduct. Part of the problem is that ethical issues often tend to be complicated and unclear.

- The Pentagon, Congress, and several of the nation's largest defense contractors are rocked by a front-page federal inquiry into bribery and fraud charges against certain of their members and employees.
- Hertz Corporation overcharges consumers and insurers $13 million for repairs to damaged rental cars.
- Ocean Spray Cranberries, Inc. is indicted by a federal grand jury for pollution in Middleboro, MA.
- Beech-Nut Company is found guilty of secretly diluting apple juice for babies.
- Presidential aides Michael Deaver and Lyn Nofziger, both communications professionals, are convicted of government ethics violations regarding lobbying.
- The president of the Public Relations Society of America is forced to resign when it is revealed that he has profited from an insider trading scheme.

There may be no obvious solution that is right or that does not cause some harm. Ethical guidelines are just that—guidelines. They don't necessarily provide right answers, just educated guesses. And reasonable people can and do disagree about what is moral, ethical, and right in a given situation.

Nonetheless, when previously respected business, government, and religious leaders, as well as other members of society, are exposed as cheaters, con artists, and even crooks, those who would look up to and be influenced by such people are correctly appalled. Little wonder then that societal pressure in the area of ethics has never been more intense. In public relations no issue is more critical than ethics—of both the practice and the practitioner.

In 1959 public relations counselor David Finn wrote,

Ethics is, unfortunately, a bad word to use when executives are sitting around a table struggling with practical problems of the day. Any public relations man who has ever had the experience of counseling his client to do something because it is "ethical" knows this to be true. It is considered a foreign, if not embarrassingly naive, word. Most businessmen react positively to such phrases as "better from a long-range point of view," "sounder business policy," or even "good public relations" than to the idea of doing something because it is "more ethical."[1]

Although Finn may have been right in 1959, today his view is not accurate. In politics the revelations of Watergate and Iran-contra; in business, Wall Street insider trading and overseas bribery scandals; in government, outbreaks of kickbacks on the local, state, and national level; and a host of other notorious incidents have focused society in general and the public relations profession in particular on the subject of ethics.

The bigness of most institutions in the 1990s—companies, schools, hospitals, associations, news organizations, and even professions like public relations—immediately makes them suspect. All have become concerned about their individual cultures—the values, ideals, principles, and aspirations that underlie their credibility and viability. As the internal conscience of many organizations, the public relations department has become a focal point for the institutionalization of ethical conduct. Increasingly, management has turned to public relations officers to lead the internal ethical charge, to be the keeper of the organizational ethic.

ETHICS IN SOCIETY

What exactly are *ethics*? Roughly translated, an individual's or organization's ethics come down to the standards that are followed in relationships with others—the real integrity of the individual or organization.

Public relations people, in particular, must be ethical. They can't assume that ethics are strictly personal choices without relevance or related methodology for resolving moral quandaries. Rather, as the Code of Professional Standards of the Public Relations Society of America states (appendix A), practitioners must be scrupulously honest and trustworthy, acting at all times in the public interest, which, by definition, also represents the best interests of individual organizations. Indeed, if the ultimate goal of the public relations professional is to enhance public trust of an organization, then only the highest ethical conduct is acceptable.

Many have commented on the importance of a high sense of ethics in society.

■ Legendary sportswriter Grantland Rice once said, "When the one great scorer comes to write against your name, he marks not that you won or lost, but how you played the game."

- The equally legendary but more contemporary football coach Joe Paterno has said, "Winning is important, but it isn't everything."
- Another legend in another field, public relations counselor Joe Snyder, has rejected the idea that anyone in society today can remain "value neutral."

Snyder and many others in public relations have called into question the standards and values practiced by many today in a society that often demonstrates a low regard for ethics.

- Faced with dwindling resources, increased competition, and rising threats of acquisition by unfriendly suitors, businesses have, in alarming numbers, been exposed in their sacrifice of the ethical for the expedient. Clearly this was the case in the summer of 1988, when several of the nation's largest defense contractors were investigated for bribery and fraud involving government military contracts.
- Government ethics have become debatable. When executive branch officials at the highest levels of the Reagan administration, from Budget Director David Stockman to White House Press Secretary Larry Speakes (see box on pp. 110–111) to Presidential Chief of Staff Donald Regan, author kiss-and-tell memoirs that reap publishing windfalls at the expense of the president they served, are they really doing it because of the public's right to know? Even more serious, President Reagan's one-time national security advisor, John Poindexter, and his assistant Oliver North admit to lying to the Congress about details of Iranscam—an Iran-Nicaragua connection to skirt U.S. law.

  In the legislative branch House of Representatives leaders—including the highest ranking official, Speaker Jim Wright—are paraded before the House Ethics Committee for improperly intervening for constituents, accepting abnormally high royalties from supporters, and generally bending the rules. In the Senate one member, Joe Biden, is revealed to have borrowed— some would say plagiarized—unattributed quotations and even life experiences from Robert Kennedy and a British official, Neil Kinnock. Another member, Gary Hart, is forced to give up his presidential bid in the wake of a bitterly embarrassing sex scandal.
- In journalism a Pulitzer Prize is won by a *Washington Post* reporter, Janet Cooke, whose heartrending description of an impoverished young drug addict turns out to be a total fabrication.
- In the ministry so-called televangelists, like Jim Bakker and Jimmy Swaggart, are called to task for their hypocritical "sins of the flesh."
- Even the United Transportation Union in New York City is exposed as a front for the Philip Morris cigarette company; the union's Open Letter advertising campaign against a proposed smoking ban on commuter trains turns out to be clandestinely written and paid for by Philip Morris.

Ethical violations are certainly not new in society: the 1919 Black Sox scandal in baseball, the 1950s salad oil scandal in business, and numerous government scandals over the years are cases in point. Nonetheless, people

Barbara Ley Toffler

Barbara Ley Toffler is one of the nation's most well-known authorities on the subject of ethics. A founding partner of Resources for Responsible Management in Boston, Toffler is on the faculty of the Graduate School of Business Administration at Harvard University, where she has taught organizational behavior and human resource management. She lectures on the subject of ethics and is the author of *Tough Choices: Managers Talk Ethics*, published in 1986.

Are there any absolutes in dealing with ethics?

In the United States one has to start with the Judeo-Christian tradition. We believe that truth-telling is an absolute. But unfortunately life today is a complicated exercise. For instance, what if telling the truth is harmful to someone else's sense of self-esteem? In most situations we're faced with competing claims—loyalty to an organization *vs.* responsibility to the public, for example. Sometimes fulfilling one claim means having to compromise another. I dislike the negative implications of the term *situational ethics,* but, in reality, that's what usually applies.

What is the state of ethics in business?
Private industry clearly is struggling with ethical issues. Many companies are paying serious attention to creating an ethical environment in their firms and encouraging employees to act with integrity. I'm not certain that all of the firms engaged in these activities are truly committed to resolving the tough ethical problems that face them. However, the smart companies are those that take ethics seriously and realize that ethics can't be tacked on. It must be integrated into business goals, business practices, and the way that employees conduct themselves.

How do you solve an ethical problem in an organization?
First, you've got to talk to the key people, those who run the organization. Next, you must meet with other groups and elicit their views on issues and problems in the organization. Then you must consider the environment in which the organization operates and what issues loom on the horizon. Then, like a doctor, you've got to diagnose the company

and its problems so that you can both suggest preventive medicine and design and implement responses to existing conditions. Such a study of ethics in an organization isn't at all "glitzy" and doesn't necessarily make good press. It takes intensive and extensive commitment throughout the organization, and most of all, it takes a lot of hard work.

What is the state of ethics in government?
I wouldn't say the public sector is less ethical than others. But one of the most fascinating things I've noticed is that the public sector managers with whom I've dealt don't tend to think about ethics in terms of their own behavior. Rather, they think first about the constituencies they serve. A private sector manager, by contrast, focuses first on his or her behavior and is therefore more self-reflective. The reason that public sector people run into more difficulty in this area is not that they are less ethical, but rather they often don't know where to look.

What is the state of ethics in religion?
People who do pastoral counseling today struggle terribly with ethics and probably have the most difficulty in dealing successfully with ethical problems in complex situations. As professionals of religion, they feel obligated to enact that which is absolutely ethical. The stresses of dealing in a complex world make this particular charge difficult, if not impossible. A theologian might say, "I don't like any of the choices, so I won't decide." Well, often neither do we like our choices, but we *must* make a decision. A manager must always decide and act. And therein lies the ethical dilemma.

What is the state of ethics in public relations?
Public relations people have as difficult a job as anyone in society. Their role is to manage all of the boundaries between the organization and the outside world and within the organization itself. Consequently they struggle mightily with difficult ethical problems all the time. If anything, they tend to err on the side of loyalty to and protection of the organization, which is their primary charge. Is that unethical? Again, it all depends.

How does one begin to act ethically?
First, spend time thinking about how others view the world. One critical word in ethics is *respect*. In fact, the Golden Rule falls a bit short. What it should say is, "Do unto others as you would have them do unto you—*if you were they*." It takes empathy and understanding to settle conflicts. Another key word is *competence*. A manager can't be ethical unless he or she is also competent. Frankly, a great deal of unethical behavior in our society is attributable to incompetent people. Finally, because most ethical situations involve competing claims and complex situations where people can't simply apply what they believe, acting ethically also demands imagination. In public relations, when you consider a complicated situation where you must defend the organization, act fairly with respect to the public, and explain your actions to the press, you must have the imagination to think through various scenarios to arrive at positive solutions. By imagination I don't mean creating stories to cover things up. Rather I mean using an active, creative imagination to arrive at positive solutions that are also ethical.

today are legitimately concerned about the increasing incidence of ethical violations in a seemingly value-free, self-indulgent society. Nowhere is the push for higher ethical standards more pronounced than in the areas of business, journalism, and public relations.

ETHICS IN BUSINESS

For many people today, regrettably, the term *business ethics* is an oxymoron. Its mere mention stimulates thoughts of unscrupulous financiers like Ivan Boesky illegally raking in millions of dollars with insider stock tips or of companies like Rockwell International being indicted by a federal grand jury for defrauding the U.S. Air Force.

Fraud, price-gouging, runaway pollution—all these allegations have made headlines in recent years. And American business, perhaps the most ethical business system in the world, has been shocked—so much so that in 1987 the former Securities and Exchange Commission chairman John Shad donated $30 million to begin a program at Harvard Business School to make the study of ethics an integral part of the curriculum.

Mr. Shad is not alone. Fearing public and government retribution, companies have taken action to

- develop ethical codes and credos in the form of handbooks, policy statements, and guidelines
- conduct training sessions, preferably by line managers, on ethical conduct

- create ethics committees that report to top management or the board of directors
- provide toll-free numbers or other means for employees to blow the whistle on ethics violators
- conduct surveys to ensure ethical compliance
- demonstrate enforcement by punishing ethics violators[2]

In one significant 1988 study, a leading business group, the Business Roundtable, pointed out the "crucial role of the chief executive officer and top managers in establishing a strong commitment to ethical conduct and in providing constant leadership in tending and reviewing the values of the organization."[3] The Roundtable study debunked the myth that there is an inherent contradiction between ethics and profits. On the contrary, it emphasized that there is a strong relationship between acting ethically, maintaining a good reputation for fair and honest business, and making money.

Another 1988 study of key business leaders, conducted by the accounting firm Touche Ross, corroborated the notion that a majority of business leaders—63 percent—"believe that a business enterprise actually 'strengthens' its competitive position by maintaining high ethical standards." Only 14 percent said that a company with high ethical standards was a "weaker competitor."[4] The

Touche Ross research of more than 1,000 business leaders also turned up other interesting findings about the current state of business ethics.

- Intense concentration on short-term earnings is a major threat to American business ethics today. Respondents ranked this threat almost equal to that posed by decay in cultural and social institutions.
- Respondents ranked the United States as having higher standards of business ethics than any other country, noting high standards also in the United Kingdom, Canada, Switzerland, and Germany.
- Among industries respondents ranked commercial banking; utilities; and drugs, pharmaceuticals, and cosmetics as the three most ethical.
- Among all professions respondents ranked the clergy, teachers, engineers, and accountants as the four most ethical.[5]

One business problem that leads to ethical abuses is the murkiness of the law, from insider-trading regulations to the laws that govern access to personal records via computers. An activity that is legal is not necessarily ethical. Regrettably, the wave of ethics violations in business has stimulated a rash of so-called white-collar crime, such as stealing company secrets and equipment. The power of computers has exacerbated the problem. And if business is not quick to reverse this trend, an antibusiness backlash is sure to follow.

In response, a more positive peer pressure among business leaders and companies is emerging. When Niels Hoyvald of Beech-Nut Nutrition Corporation was found guilty in 1988 of 351 counts of violating the Food, Drug and Cosmetic Act—his company misrepresented as pure apple juice a product it distributed to babies—Hoyvald's lawyers came up with a unique proposition to spare him from a prison sentence. Specifically, said his lawyer, Brendan V. Sullivan (who also served as Oliver North's attorney), let Mr. Hoyvald teach ethics to business students: "Business students undoubtedly hear this principle regularly in their ethics classes. But the impact of the message would be far clearer coming from Niels Hoyvald, whose career has been shattered because he did not heed it, than it could ever be coming from a textbook or a professor."

CORPORATE CODES OF CONDUCT

In addition to corporate executives becoming ethics teachers, another manifestation of the increased attention to corporate ethics is the growth of internal codes of conduct. Codes of ethics, standards of conduct, and similar statements of corporate policies and values have proliferated in recent years. In 1964 a Conference Board study found such documents in 40 percent of surveyed companies. By 1979 the number had increased to 73 percent of Fortune 1000 companies, with more than 90 percent of the largest firms having adopted written codes.

The reasons corporations have adopted such codes vary from company to company.

<table>
<tr><td>BETWEEN
THE LINES</td></tr>
</table>

Larry Speakes No More

The sad saga of former White House press secretary Larry Speakes is as pointed an example of an ethical dilemma as any in recent public relations history. By all accounts Speakes served President Ronald Reagan as an able and respected spokesperson. His credo seemed to be to tell the truth, no matter what. Indeed, Speakes was interviewed for the third edition of *The Practice of Public Relations* shortly after leaving the White House and offered the following observations:*

What's the biggest problem of the president's press secretary?
It is impossible to identify something as the "biggest" problem. One of the greatest frustrations of the job was the fact that most reporters automatically assumed the government was lying. This was the aftermath of Watergate, but it was inappropriately and unfairly applied to the Reagan administration. We told the truth; I was always a bit disadvantaged when I was forced to convince people I was doing so.

What's the overriding objective of the president's chief spokesman?
My overriding objective as the president's chief spokesman was to tell the truth.

What advice would you give to the public relations practitioners of the future?
I would advise practitioners two things: (1) tell the truth, and (2) understand that journalists have a job to do and be as considerate of their professional needs as you expect them to be of yours.

Such words would come back to haunt the former press secretary. In mid-1988, having become communications director of Merrill Lynch, Speakes revealed in his book *Speaking Out* that he had manufactured quotes and had attributed them to President Reagan. For example, when Reagan and Soviet leader Mikhail Gorbachev held their historic first meeting in Geneva in 1985, according to Speakes White House officials found Mr. Gorbachev to be a master at handling the press "while Reagan was very tentative and stilted." Consequently, Speakes told reporters that the president had said, "There is much that divides us, but I believe the world breathes easier because we are talking together," and the quote was widely reported by American news organizations even though the president hadn't really said it. In his book Speakes conceded in retrospect that it was "clearly wrong to take such liberties" even though the president would not have disavowed the words—until Speakes's book came out, that is.

In a ringing denunciation Larry Speakes's successor at the White House, Marlin Fitzwater, characterized his predecessor's actions as a "damn outrage."

---

*Fraser P. Seitel, *The Practice of Public Relations*, 3d ed. (Columbus, OH: Merrill Publishing Company, 1987), 137.

Merrill Lynch wasn't particularly happy either, reportedly alarmed that Speakes's admissions might tarnish its new ad campaign, "A Tradition of Trust." Two weeks after his book's publication, Speakes resigned from his Merrill Lynch job.

And the lesson in all of this? Frankly, despite the self-righteous indignation of the media, the lesson isn't at all clear. Like it or not, public relations people do indeed fabricate statements for their employers—it goes with the territory. And if such statements are approved by employers in advance, ethical questions are less pertinent. However, public relations people rarely announce or even acknowledge that they have authored such statements. Ironically then, in violating the confidence of the president by retrospectively telling the truth about the bogus quotes, Larry Speakes may have committed his most costly misstep.

■ **To increase public confidence**   The scandals concerning overseas bribery and domestic political campaign contributions during the 1970s led to a decline of public trust and confidence in business. Many firms responded with written codes of ethics.

■ **To stem the tide of regulation**   As public confidence declined, government regulation of business increased. Some estimated the cost to society of compliance with regulations at $100 billion per year. Corporate codes of conduct, it was hoped, would serve as a self-regulation mechanism.

■ **To improve internal operations**   As companies became larger and more decentralized, management needed consistent standards of conduct to assure that employees were meeting the business objectives of the company in a legal and ethical manner.

■ **To respond to transgressions**   Frequently when a company itself was caught in the web of unethical behavior, it responded with its own code of ethics. For example, the McCormick Company instituted an ethics plan after it was revealed that its grocery products division had inflated sales and earnings figures, which ultimately required the company to restate its earnings for the years between 1977 and 1981.[6]

Ralph Waldo Emerson once wrote that "an organization is the lengthened shadow of a man." By the latter part of the 1980s, many corporate executives realized that just as an individual has certain responsibilities as a citizen, so, too, does a corporate citizen have responsibilities to the society in which it is privileged to operate (Figure 5–1).

The challenge of institutionalizing ethics by shaping a specific code of conduct for an organization is a difficult one. The specific elements depend on the particular values, heritage, and objectives of the corporation itself (Figure 5–2). According to former Chase Manhattan chairman David Rockefeller, four fundamental cornerstones of ethical behavior must be present in any organization.

1. Honesty and candor in all activity
2. Integrity in the use of corporate resources
3. Avoidance of conflict of interest
4. Fairness in dealings with all[7]

Well-drawn, enforceable codes of ethics also generally contain five broad areas of commentary.

1. **Statement of corporate philosophy**   Frequently embodied in a letter from the chief executive, this statement is a preface to the principles, guidelines, and rules that make up the code of conduct.
2. **Broadly stated principles**   In many codes a company states its commitment to such values as honesty, fairness, and responsibility.
3. **Guidelines for decision making**   Companies often develop guidelines in the most sensitive areas, such as outside investments, payments to govern-

Our Guiding Principles

Over our long history we have evolved standards and values guiding the management of the company that comprise an unwritten creed. These beliefs are central to conducting our affairs responsibly in fulfilling our obligations to shareowners, employees, customers and the communities in which we work.

Two contemporary developments suggest that a more formal statement of the company's principles is in order. One, the substantial increase in the size and geographic breadth of the company, and, two, the growing interest of the public in the ethical practices and social commitments of business. To be responsive to these new needs, our Board of Directors two years ago approved a written declaration of the canons that have guided this company's operations for so many years.

Since these are not static rules to be filed, but active principles to be practiced, they have recently been reviewed and again endorsed.

Implicit in the responsible conduct of the affairs of the company is one fundamental consideration — our consistent compliance with all pertinent laws, regulations and ethical standards.

These principles are personal and important to us. Obviously, they are not unique. We share many of them with other responsible and successful members of the business community.

We set forth these guiding principles looking ahead to continued growth for our company, improvement in the quality of life of our people and continued constructive relationships with the communities closest to us.

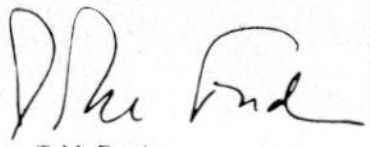

T M Ford
Chairman and President

FIGURE 5–1   The principles enumerated here by the chief executive of the Emhart Corporation represent the obligations the company believes it has to its corporate community. (Courtesy of Emhart Corporation)

ment officials, transmission of confidential information, and acceptance of gifts from clients.

4. **Prohibited conduct and affirmative duties**   Many codes impose affirmative duties, such as requiring employees to report suspected code violations and disclose possible conflicts of interest.

5. **Illustrations and case studies**   Many times, a corporation includes brief case studies of conduct that is discouraged or desired under the code. These not only serve to clarify and make concrete the intent of the code but also become the basis for discussion of ethical conflicts and duties in the course of management training and executive development.

FIGURE 5–2 Corporate codes of conduct in a variety of sizes, shapes, and comprehensiveness proliferated in the latter part of the 1980s.

CORPORATE SOCIAL RESPONSIBILITY

Closely related to the ethical conduct of an organization is its social responsibility, which has been defined as a social norm. This norm holds that any social institution, including the smallest family unit and the largest corporation, is responsible for the behavior of its members and may be held accountable for their misdeeds.[8]

In the late 1960s, when this idea was just emerging, initial responses were of the knee-jerk variety. A firm that was threatened by increasing legal or activist pressures and harassment would ordinarily change its policies in a hurry. Today, however, organizations and their social responsibility programs are much more sophisticated. As one practitioner put it, "Social responsibility today is treated just like any other management discipline—you analyze the issues, evaluate performance, set priorities, allocate resources to those priorities, and implement programs that deal with issues within the constraints of your resources."[9]

Many companies have created special committees to set the agenda and target the objectives. The primary concerns of the Corporate Responsibility Committee of Chase Manhattan Bank are illustrative.

1. To continue Chase's leadership in equal opportunity employment, both at home and abroad
2. To foster a broader and healthier economic base in New York City and other areas served by the bank
3. To encourage housing and community development facilities
4. To improve the physical and cultural environment of the bank's community
5. To initiate comprehensive international social responsibility programs

Social responsibility touches practically every level of organizational activity, from marketing to hiring, from training to work standards. A partial list of social responsibility categories might include the following:

■ **Product lines**—dangerous products, product performance and standards, packaging, and environmental impact
■ **Marketing practices**—sales practices, consumer complaint policies, advertising content, and fair pricing
■ **Employee services**—training, counseling and placement services, transfer procedures, and educational allowances
■ **Corporate philanthropy**—contribution performance, encouragement of employee participation in social projects, and community development activities
■ **Environmental activities**—pollution control projects, adherence to federal standards, and evaluation procedures of new packages and products
■ **External relations**—support of minority enterprises, investment practices, and government relations
■ **Employment of minorities and women**—current hiring policies, advancement policies, specialized career counseling, and opportunities for special minorities such as the physically handicapped
■ **Employee safety and health**—work environment policies, accident safeguards, and food and medical facilities

More often than not, organizations today have incorporated social responsibility into the mainstream of organization practice. Most firms recognize that social responsibility, far from being an add-on program, must be a corporate way of life. For example, Levi Strauss, Xerox, IBM, and others encourage employees to take time off to participate in community projects. Xerox employees have built wheelchair ramps for handicapped persons in Detroit, cleared land and built picnic tables in a park near Houston, and served as juvenile probation officers in St. Louis. Leaves for such projects may range from a month to a year to several years.[10]

The $100,000 Lesson Plan

In 1987, when the Columbia Business School asked Asher B. Edelman, an expert on corporate takeovers, to teach a course on corporate raiding, Dean John C. Burton thought students would gain some valuable lessons. Exactly how valuable he was soon to learn. As a final exam, Mr. Edelman offered a finder's fee of $100,000 to the student who could identify a corporate takeover candidate that the professor would actually decide to buy.

When the *New York Times* and others publicized the $100,000 student assignment, Dean Burton rescinded the offer. "We felt that the linkage between direct economic incentive and what goes on in the classroom—especially an incentive of this magnitude—would bias the academic environment," Dean Burton said. Mr. Edelman did not agree, citing "a violation of the integrity of the classroom, of my right to teach after I was hired, and of the student's right to learn."

Reaction to Dean Burton's squelching of the deal was generally applauded. Said the publisher of Columbia's campus newspaper, "Business school professors should teach students how to be ethical and how to be good managers, not how to be millionaires." Most periodicals and other business school leaders also applauded Dean Burton's action. But there was at least one disgruntled group—Professor Edelman's students. In a poll taken by the professor after the dean's declaration, only one of 14 students backed the dean. The rest saw nothing wrong with the incentive. Said one, "When money is introduced, your energy is channeled into areas where it ordinarily wouldn't be. With $100,000 you have to ask, 'Can I afford *not* to concentrate on that?'"*

*Also see Leslie Wayne, "Columbia Gives 'F' to a $100,000 Lesson Plan," *New York Times,* 14 October 1987, A1,D6; Nancy J. Perry, "Edelman's Art of Reward," *Fortune,* 9 November 1987, 159; Barbara Kantrowitz and Tessa Namuth, "A $100,000 Question Stirs Up Columbia," *Newsweek,* 26 October 1987, 76.

Little wonder that business rose up in unified opposition in 1977 to the suggestion by Commerce Secretary Juanita Kreps that the government establish a Social Performance Index to assess the efforts of individual companies in such areas as environmental controls, affirmative action, minority purchasing, resolution of consumer complaints, and product testing. To many executives, "The scheme constituted a public scorecard that would put corporations in competition with each other for public favor, with the Commerce Department acting as referee."[11] To many business people, already sold on the importance of social responsibility, such a government scorecard was just not necessary.

ETHICS IN GOVERNMENT

Politics has never enjoyed an unblemished reputation. But in the campaigns of 1988, the so-called sleaze factor in government reached a new low. The ethical problems of the Reagan administration were well documented—from the secret Iran-contra negotiations of National Security Advisor John Poindexter and Colonel Oliver North to the lobbying violations of the presidential assistants Lyn Nofziger and Mike Deaver to the continuing ethical cloud overhanging Attorney General Ed Meese. Indeed, it was ironic that President Reagan, seemingly so trusted by his countrymen, had an administration so suspect.

On Capitol Hill the sleaze factor was strictly bipartisan. The Democratic speaker of the house, Jim Wright, reportedly intervened for former Egyptian President Anwar Sadat on behalf of a business friend seeking oil rights in Egypt and intervened similarly at the Interior Department to influence the award of gas leases to a company in which Wright had a $15,000 investment. Wright also received an unheard-of royalty of 55 percent on sales of an alleged book of his thoughts, published by a wealthy, long-time supporter.

On the Republican side in 1985, five days after New York Senator Alfonse D'Amato introduced a securities bill favorable to junk (deep discount) bond dealers, he received $500 donations from 36 executives of the largest junk bond house, Drexel Burnham Lambert. The good senator described the gifts as "absolutely coincidental." That same year, when Indiana Senator Dan Quayle tried to repeal an amendment requiring military contractors to report on their labor costs, he received $92,000 from the defense industry. Any connection? "Ridiculous," said Quayle, who later ran into additional ethical problems as George Bush's vice presidential running mate. And although few Kansas farmers grow tobacco, Kansas Senator Robert Dole fought hard to save a 1985 tobacco subsidy program. The next year five tobacco companies contributed $13,400 to Dole's reelection campaign. Dole pooh-poohed any link.

The sleaze factor in government is, of course, nothing new. In 1976, when the shah of Iran was petitioning Congress for financial aid, the wife of influential New York Senator Jacob Javits was drawing down $500,000 from Iran as a public relations representative for the country. However, society today seems increasingly less willing to tolerate such violations from those whose livelihood depends on public trust. In the 1990s it is likely that ethics in government will become an even more important issue as fed-up voters insist on representatives who are honest, trustworthy, and clean.

ETHICS IN JOURNALISM

The Society of Professional Journalists, Sigma Delta Chi, is quite explicit on the subject of ethics (Figure 5–3).

> Journalists at all times will show respect for the dignity, privacy, rights and well-being of people encountered in the course of gathering and presenting the news.

THE SOCIETY OF PROFESSIONAL JOURNALISTS,
SIGMA DELTA CHI

Code of Ethics

THE SOCIETY of Professional Journalists, Sigma Delta Chi believes the duty of journalists is to serve the truth.

WE BELIEVE the agencies of mass communication are carriers of public discussion and information, acting on their Constitutional mandate and freedom to learn and report the facts.

WE BELIEVE in public enlightenment as the forerunner of justice, and in our Constitutional role to seek the truth as part of the public's right to know the truth.

WE BELIEVE those responsibilities carry obligations that require journalists to perform with intelligence, objectivity, accuracy and fairness.

To these ends, we declare acceptance of the standards of practice here set forth:

RESPONSIBILITY:

The public's right to know of events of public importance and interest is the overriding mission of the mass media. The purpose of distributing news and enlightened opinion is to serve the general welfare. Journalists who use their professional status as representatives of the public for selfish or other unworthy motives violate a high trust.

FREEDOM OF THE PRESS:

Freedom of the press is to be guarded as an inalienable right of people in a free society. It carries with it the freedom and the responsibility to discuss, question and challenge actions and utterances of our government and of our public and private institutions. Journalists uphold the right to speak unpopular opinions and the privilege to agree with the majority.

ETHICS:

Journalists must be free of obligation to any interest other than the public's right to know the truth.

1. Gifts, favors, free travel, special treatment or privileges can compromise the integrity of journalists and their employers. Nothing of value should be accepted.

2. Secondary employment, political involvement, holding public office and service in community organizations should be avoided if it compromises the integrity of journalists and their employers. Journalists and their employers should conduct their personal lives in a manner which protects them from conflict of interest, real or apparent. Their responsibilities to the public are paramount. That is the nature of their profession.

3. So-called news communications from private sources should not be published or broadcast without substantiation of their claims to news value.

4. Journalists will seek news that serves the public interest, despite the obstacles. They will make constant efforts to assure that the public's business is conducted in public and that public records are open to public inspection.

5. Journalists acknowledge the newsman's ethic of protecting confidential sources of information.

ACCURACY AND OBJECTIVITY:

Good faith with the public is the foundation of all worthy journalism.

1. Truth is our ultimate goal.

2. Objectivity in reporting the news is another goal, which serves as the mark of an experienced professional. It is a standard of performance toward which we strive. We honor those who achieve it.

3. There is no excuse for inaccuracies or lack of thoroughness.

4. Newspaper headlines should be fully warranted by the contents of the articles they accompany. Photographs and telecasts should give an accurate picture of an event and not highlight a minor incident out of context.

5. Sound practice makes clear distinction between news reports and expressions of opinion. News reports should be free of opinion or bias and represent all sides of an issue.

6. Partisanship in editorial comment which knowingly departs from the truth violates the spirit of American journalism.

7. Journalists recognize their responsibility for offering informed analysis, comment and editorial opinion on public events and issues. They accept the obligation to present such material by individuals whose competence, experience and judgment qualify them for it.

8. Special articles or presentations devoted to advocacy or the writer's own conclusions and interpretations should be labeled as such.

FAIR PLAY:

Journalists at all times will show respect for the dignity, privacy, rights and well-being of people encountered in the course of gathering and presenting the news.

1. The news media should not communicate unofficial charges affecting reputation or moral character without giving the accused a chance to reply.

2. The news media must guard against invading a person's right to privacy.

3. The media should not pander to morbid curiosity about details of vice and crime.

4. It is the duty of news media to make prompt and complete correction of their errors.

5. Journalists should be accountable to the public for their reports and the public should be encouraged to voice its grievances against the media. Open dialogue with our readers, viewers and listeners should be fostered.

PLEDGE:

Journalists should actively censure and try to prevent violations of these standards, and they should encourage their observance by all newspeople. Adherence to this code of ethics is intended to preserve the bond of mutual trust and respect between American journalists and the American people.

FIGURE 5–3 The Society of Professional Journalists, Sigma Delta Chi, has elaborated in some detail on the ethical guidelines that should govern reporters and editors.

1. The news media should not communicate unofficial charges affecting reputation or moral character without giving the accused a chance to reply.
2. The news media must guard against invading a person's right to privacy.
3. The media should not pander to morbid curiosity about details of vice and crime.

And so on.

Unfortunately, what is in the code often doesn't reflect what appears in print or on the air. More often than not, journalistic judgments run smack into ethical principles.

- In 1984, when presidential candidate Jesse Jackson held a background breakfast with some reporters, his words were supposed to be unattributable to him in print. One attendee, Milton Coleman of the *Washington Post,* later told a colleague that the candidate had referred to Jews as "Hymie" and to New York as "Hymietown." Although Coleman never used the material in the *Post,* his colleague did. And Jackson's relations with the Jewish community suffered irreparably.
- That same year, when Senator Gary Hart became the Democratic front-runner for the presidential nomination, *Miami Herald* reporters staked out his Washington home long enough to notice that an attractive blond visitor came in one day and didn't leave until early the next. The resulting scandal cost Hart not only the nomination but also the remainder of his political career. *Miami Herald* executives argued that surreptitiously trailing Hart was ethical since the public had a right to know.
- When Pennsylvania's treasurer, R. Budd Dwyer, shocked a 1987 press conference by putting a pistol in his mouth and firing, some editors, albeit a minority, used a series of photos (Figure 5–4) that graphically depicted Dwyer's suicide.
- In 1988, when a Steele County, Minnesota, woman's description of a bloody fight between two men was broadcast over the police radio band, she begged an *Owatonna People's Press* reporter not to use her name. She feared reprisal from either or both of the men. The next day's story reported her name, address, and an account of what she had seen. The following day one of the men was found stabbed to death, and the other was arrested not far from the woman's home.

These examples—all of questionable ethics—illustrate the difficulty of living up to journalistic codes of ethics. A journalist's job is to get the story. Often that means trampling over the personal privacy and trust of the subject.

Many times the ethical decisions faced by journalists are subtle ones. For example, a journalist quoting an anonymous source in a news story runs up against an ethical dilemma; most of the time such sources have a bias toward the issue on which they are commenting—an anonymous Democrat talking about a Republican program, a competitor talking about a rival firm's product, or a securities analyst talking about a favorite or a despised stock. Clearly, journalists and editors can't be totally objective, but they should always strive

FIGURE 5–4 A series of three Associated Press photographs shows Pennsylvania treasurer R. Budd Dwyer motioning to reporters, putting a pistol in his mouth, and actually firing the shot that claimed his life. The first picture in the series is shown here; however, the other two are so graphic that ethical standards—not to mention good taste—precluded their presentation in this text. (Courtesy AP/Wide World Photos)

to be fair. And that involves being aware of the biases and hidden agendas of news sources and understanding the ethical questions raised by quoting such sources.

To monitor ethical problems, so-called news councils have been established from time to time with lukewarm support among journalists. Only one state news council exists, in Minnesota. And a national news council died from lack of interest. More successful have been the ombudsman columns at leading newspapers, which discuss their own papers' news stories that may fall short ethically.

In less complicated times, such news councils and ombudsmen weren't necessary. Journalists of old knew a good deal about the extramarital romances of presidents Roosevelt, Eisenhower, Kennedy, and Johnson, but little was reported. Later on, some journalists accused those who withheld such information of keeping the public in the dark about news bearing on the character of important leaders. The accusation may be accurate, but the fact remains that journalists of that day exercised considerable self-restraint. To this day, there are some tabloids that dote on gossip and scandal and restrain nothing. More respected news organizations ruminate daily about the ethical implications of printing this or reporting that.

The point is that a sense of ethics helps an individual make moral decisions. And journalists have to make their decisions with speed and certainty. They can't usually afford to say maybe, and they can never say, "We'll have time to get back to this when the dust settles." Their decisions must meet a deadline. And usually, the principles, values, and ideals that get reported depend largely on the individual doing the reporting.

For the public relations practitioner, who more often than not is on the other end of the story, an appreciation of the problems associated with journalistic ethics must always be kept in mind. Despite clear professional codes, journalistic ethics often rely on the personal makeup of the journalist. Therefore, the cardinal rule for a public relations person dealing with a journalist is: If you don't want something repeated in print, don't say it to anyone, especially a reporter.

ETHICS IN PUBLIC RELATIONS

In light of numerous misconceptions about what the practice of public relations is or isn't, it is imperative that practitioners emulate the highest standards of personal and professional ethics. Within an organization, public relations practitioners must be the standard bearers of corporate ethical initiatives. By the same token, public relations consultants must always counsel their clients in an ethical direction—toward accuracy and candor and away from lying and hiding the truth.

The Public Relations Society of America has been a leader in the effort to foster a strong sense of ethics among its membership. Its Code of Professional Standards is a model in the attempt to promulgate high standards of public

YOU MAKE THE CALL

Where Lies Loyalty?

Often the ethical path a person chooses is clouded by such murky areas as loyalties, obligations, and judgments. As a case in point, Dan Dripman, financial editor of *Newark Magazine,* stayed friendly with Wally Bokstoski even after Bokstoski left the paper's financial desk to become public relations director of Poobah Industries.

At Poobah, Bokstoski developed a healthy respect for Poobah's wealthy and well-known chairman, Clark Poobah, whose family was continually making news. One day Dripman called Bokstoski to say that he had in his possession Chairman Poobah's personal investment holdings, which had been leaked to him by someone at Poobah Industries. Dripman told his former colleague that he wouldn't use the material unless Bokstoski told his boss. Dripman said that as long as they continued to trust each other "I won't run anything without giving your boss ample time to respond to a story."

Taking Dripman at his word, Bokstoski said nothing about the reporter's information. A month later, with Poobah Industries' declining earnings featured prominently in the news, Dripman called his buddy and said that he planned to use the purloined Poobah material the following week. He asked Bokstoski to set up an interview with the chairman to discuss his investment holdings.

When Chairman Poobah got Bokstoski's call, the first question he asked was, "When did you know of this?"

Bokstoski replied truthfully, "I learned of it four weeks ago, but Dripman promised not to run anything until we got our chance to respond."

Poobah was dumbfounded. "Why didn't you tell me at the time? We might have been able to secure a legal injunction against publication of stolen property."

Bokstoski had no response. And a month later, after publication of Dripman's embarrassing revelations, Bokstoski had no job.

QUESTIONS

1. Had you been Bokstoski, when would you have notified Chairman Poobah about the Dripman material?
2. What mistake did Bokstoski make?
3. How ethical was Dripman's behavior?
4. Why do you think Bokstoski lost his job?
5. To what extent was bad judgment at issue here rather than ethical improprieties?

service and ethical conduct. In recent years the PRSA code has been tested on a variety of issues, ranging from noncompetition agreements with the employees of a public relations firm, to the protection of public relations campaign proposals to prospective clients, to paying employees and consultants finder's fees to obtain new accounts.

In 1987 a study by the Foundation for Public Relations Research and Education covering the years 1950 to 1985 revealed a strong adherence in the field to the ethical code originally adopted in 1950. During that period of time 168 issues and complaints were registered and investigated. Articles of the code most frequently cited were these:

- A member shall deal fairly with clients or employers, past, present, and potential, with fellow practitioners and the general public.
- A member shall adhere to truth and accuracy and to generally accepted standards of good taste.
- A member shall conduct his or her professional life in accord with the public interest.
- A member shall not intentionally communicate false or misleading information and is obligated to use care to avoid communication of false or misleading information.
- A member shall not engage in any practice that tends to corrupt the channels of communication or the processes of government.

The foundation concluded that the code, with its enforcement provisions, is a good one: "It has been, can be, and will be improved. It is a vibrant, living document that depends, as our future and that of public relations depends, on constant understanding and application by the society's members."[12]

Ironically, in 1986 the president of the Public Relations Society of America, Anthony M. Franco, abruptly resigned after signing an SEC consent decree following charges of insider trading violations. Even more ironic, Franco said in his defense, "I had legal advice but no outside public relations counsel, which I should have gotten."[13]

Although the Franco case embarrassed the public relations field, the Public Relations Society didn't shrink from the ethical challenge in subsequent years. When Speakes had his fabricated quotes problem in 1988, PRSA President Dwayne Summar was quick to renounce that conduct as "inconsistent with the Public Relations Society of America's Code of Standards for the Practice of Public Relations." Summar went on to point out that Speakes didn't join PRSA until after he left his position as the president's chief spokesman. "In becoming a member, he pledged to uphold the code," Summar said.[14] At the World Congress of Public Relations in Melbourne, Australia, that same year, Summar reported that the PRSA was organizing a common code of ethics, which could be adopted by public relations associations around the world. One such code of ethics was that adopted by the International Association of Business Communicators (Figure 5–5).

IABC CODE OF ETHICS

The IABC Code of Ethics has been developed to provide IABC members and other communication professionals with guidelines of professional behavior and standards of ethical practice. The Code will be reviewed and revised as necessary by the Ethics Committee and the Executive Board.

Any IABC member who wishes advice and guidance regarding its interpretation and/or application may write or phone IABC headquarters. Questions will be routed to the Executive Board member responsible for the Code.

Communication and Information Dissemination

1. Communication professionals will uphold the credibility and dignity of their profession by encouraging the practice of honest, candid and timely communication.

The highest standards of professionalism will be upheld in all communication. Communicators should encourage frequent communication and messages that are honest in their content, candid, accurate and appropriate to the needs of the organization and its audiences.

2. Professional communicators will not use any information that has been generated or appropriately acquired by a business for another business without permission. Further, communicators should attempt to identify the source of information to be used.

When one is changing employers, information developed at the previous position will not be used without permission from that employer. Acts of plagiarism and copyright infringement are illegal acts; material in the public domain should have its source attributed, if possible. If an organization grants permission to use its information and requests public acknowledgment, it will be made in a place appropriate to the material used. The material will be used only for the purpose for which permission was granted.

Standards of Conduct

3. Communication professionals will abide by the spirit and letter of all laws and regulations governing their professional activities.

All international, national and local laws and regulations must be observed, with particular attention to those pertaining to communication, such as copyright law. Industry and organizational regulations will also be observed.

4. Communication professionals will not condone any illegal or unethical act related to their professional activity, their organization and its business or the public environment in which it operates.

It is the personal responsibility of professional communicators to act honestly, fairly and with integrity at all times in all professional activities. Looking the other way while others act illegally tacitly condones such acts whether or not the communicator has committed them. The communicator should speak with the individual involved, his or her supervisor or appropriate authorities – depending on the context of the situation and one's own ethical judgment.

Confidentiality/Disclosure

5. Communication professionals will respect the confidentiality and right-to-privacy of all individuals, employers, clients and customers.

Communicators must determine the ethical balance between right-to-privacy and need-to-know. Unless the situation involves illegal or grossly unethical acts, confidences should be maintained. If there is a conflict between right-to-privacy and need-to-know, a communicator should first talk with the source and negotiate the need for the information to be communicated.

6. Communication professionals will not use any confidential information gained as a result of professional activity for personal benefit or for that of others.

Confidential information can be used to give inside advantage to stock transactions, gain favors from outsiders, assist a competing company for whom one is going to work, assist companies in developing a marketing advantage, achieve a publishing advantage or otherwise act to the detriment of an organization. Such information must remain confidential during and after one's employment period.

Professionalism

7. Communication professionals should uphold IABC's standards for ethical conduct in all professional activity, and should use IABC and its designation of accreditation (ABC) only for purposes that are authorized and fairly represent the organization and its professional standards.

IABC recognizes the need for professional integrity within any organization, including the association. Members should acknowledge that their actions reflect on themselves, their organizations and their profession.

Printed with the assistance of the Mead Corporation and Brown & Kroger Printing, Dayton, OH

FIGURE 5–5 The International Association of Business Communicators adopted these seven tenets to guide the professional behavior of its members.

An ethical flap related to the Speakes revelation involved Harold Burson, chairman of Burson-Marsteller, whose interview in a Melbourne, Australia, daily following the Speakes affair was headlined "It Is Not Unethical to Conceal the Truth." Said Burson in a letter to the paper's editor, the principle to be followed in any "bad news situation is to disclose as quickly as possible the facts at hand, especially those that are adverse to the client." But, he continued, "there are instances where the public relations representative cannot or should not reveal immediately everything known about a given developing story." Such instances, he explained, include releasing names of accident casualties before informing families of the victims and disclosing negotiating strategies in a takeover/merger situation or during labor negotiations. He said that withholding such information is "neither untruthful, unprofessional, nor counter to the public interest."[15]

The final analysis, in public relations as in life, comes down to the ethics of the individual. If a practitioner is dishonest, if he or she steals clients or strains the truth in the practice of professional duties, the entire profession of public relations suffers the consequences. Unethical practitioners do still exist, but their numbers have shrunk considerably over the years. Today, the field is dominated by professionals who take seriously not only their skill, but also their responsibility to operate at the highest level of ethical conduct.

ETHICAL ISSUES GOING FORWARD

The success of public relations in the 1990s and beyond will depend to a large degree on how the field responds to the issue of ethical conduct. Public relations professionals must have credibility in order to practice. They must be respected by the various publics with whom they interact. To be credible and to achieve respect, public relations professionals must be ethical. It is that simple.

The media, too, are confronting significant ethical questions. In this post-Watergate era of journalism, reporting the facts sometimes is less important than finding a hook that is controversial. Television journalism, in particular, has been confronted with disturbing ethical dilemmas. Today, when hostages are seized or terrorists spring to power, more often than not television journalists rush headlong to broadcast as much of the story as quickly as possible. Often in recent years this rush has nurtured terrorist purposes. Television reached perhaps its lowest ebb in the summer of 1985 when a TWA commercial aircraft was hijacked in the Middle East and "the hostages' survival was the terrorists' admission ticket for on-going access to the media—and world opinion."[16] Media excesses, particularly regarding terrorist actions, have brought into question Edward R. Murrow's warning that terrorists not be permitted to "shoot their way onto our air."[17]

To be sure, it's difficult—for the media or anyone else—to act ethically when working with unethical mandates. For the public relations profession in general and individual public relations practitioners in particular, credibility in the years ahead depends on how scrupulously they observe and apply ethical principles in everything they do.

FIGURE 5–6 The outbreak of ethical transgressions caused *Harper's Magazine* editors in 1987 to commission leading ad agencies to "do their thing" with the seven deadly sins themselves. Let's hear it for gluttony! (Copyright © 1987 by *Harper's Magazine*. All rights reserved. Reprinted from the November issue by special permission.)

The Public Relations Insider

Kelly Craft is a public relations consultant whose life has changed radically recently. His wife just gave birth to their third child, and they purchased a four-bedroom house in an exclusive suburb to accommodate the growing family. With new bills weighing heavily on his mind, Kelly has seemed subdued at the office in contrast to his normally flamboyant style.

Returning from lunch one afternoon, Kelly overheard an elevator conversation involving two officers from the bank in the building. They were discussing a request from Apex Industries for a $200 million credit to finance an acquisition. They speculated that the takeover target was Schultz Investment, a multinational real estate development firm. Both Apex and Schultz were clients of Craft's public relations firm.

Back in the office, Kelly called his associate on the Apex account and discovered that Apex had, indeed, requested a large line of credit. He then called his associate handling the Schultz account, who indicated that Schultz would be interested in being acquired for the right price. The associate added that Schultz had just broken off talks with IBM about being acquired, and he cautioned Craft not to mention that the IBM talks had in fact broken off.

Craft immediately contemplated investing his $4,000 tax return in Schultz Investment shares in the hope of realizing a quick profit. With such a profit he could replace his roof and have his new house painted. He also realized, however, that his plans might be viewed as trading on inside information. On the other hand, since neither company was a customer of his—only of his firm—he felt his investment was based purely on his own research and was therefore allowable.

Kelly invested his $4,000 immediately in shares of Schultz Investment. Two weeks later, Apex announced that it would acquire Schultz Investment. The shares of Schultz went up four dollars, and Craft sold his stock, realizing a $1,600 profit.

Feeling elated, Craft told the whole story to his friend and colleague Sam Sauerball. Sauerball's initial reaction was enthusiastic. But then it occurred to him that Kelly's success resulted from trading on insider information—a clear violation of the firm's code of ethics. Furthermore, Sauerball thought that the code required him to report Kelly's infraction, an especially difficult proposition in light of their friendship.

Further complicating his predicament was Sauerball's realization that Kelly was an immensely popular individual in the company and that public relations counselors heard all kinds of rumors all the time and certainly were permitted to invest in stocks. So where should the line be drawn?

QUESTIONS

1. If you were Sauerball, where would you draw the line?
2. Would you have done what Craft did?

NOTES

1. David Finn, "Struggle for Ethics in Public Relations," *Harvard Business Review* 12 (January–February 1959): 9.
2. John A. Byrne, "Businesses Are Signing Up for Ethics 101," *Business Week,* 15 February 1988, 56–57.
3. "An Overview of a Landmark Roundtable Study of Corporate Ethics," *Roundtable Report* (February 1988): 1.
4. "Ethics in American Business," Touche Ross, January 1988.
5. Ibid.
6. Brian Sullam, "Ethics Codes Becoming Standard for Business," *Baltimore Sun,* 27 March 1983.
7. David Rockefeller, address at Boy Scouts of America Greater New York Council's Distinguished Citizens Award Dinner, New York, 23 June 1977.
8. Donald K. Wright, "Social Responsibility and Public Relations: A Multi-Step Theory," *Public Relations Review* (Fall 1976): 25.
9. Interview with Andrew R. Baer, former manager of public relations for the Equitable Life Assurance Society, 21 January 1979.
10. "On the Job," *Money* (November 1974): 28.
11. Carlton E. Spitzer, "Should Government Audit Corporate Responsibility?" *Public Relations Review* (Summer 1981): 14.
12. Public Relations Society of America, study of ethical files, 1950–85, Foundation for Public Relations Research and Education, 17 April 1987.
13. "Franco Speaks Publicly for First Time About His Case," *PR Reporter* (13 April 1987): 2.
14. Public Relations Society of America, news release, 15 April 1988.
15. *Public Relations News* (16 May 1988): 2.
16. "Some Ethical Questions," address by David C. Venz, director of corporate communications for Transworld Airlines, before the Society of American Travel Writers, New York, 7 September 1985.
17. Ibid.

Behrman, Jack N. *Discourses on Ethics and Business*. Boston, MA: Oelgeschlager, Gunn & Hain, 1981.

Biddle, Wayne. "Ethics According to General Dynamics." *New York Times*, 16 August 1985, A12.

Bishop, Nancy. "New Ethics Policies Spell Out Worker No-No's." *Dallas Morning News*, 12 February 1985.

Bowman, James S. "The Management of Ethics: Codes of Conduct in Organizations." *Public Personnel Management Journal* 10, no. 1 (1981): 59–66.

Cimons, Marlene. "U.S. Business Finds Profit in Its Ethics." *Los Angeles Times*, 27 November 1982, 1.

Code of Ethics and Standards of Professional Practice. New York: Association of Management Consulting Firms (230 Park Ave.).

Corporate Ethics: A Prime Business Asset. New York: Business Roundtable (200 Park Ave.), February 1988. Members of TBR supplied information to develop this report on policy and practice in company conduct.

Cressey, Donald R., and Charles A. Moore. "Managerial Values and Corporate Codes of Ethics." *California Management Review* 25, no. 4 (Summer 1983): 53–77.

Cross, Robert. "Corporate Conscience: Putting Big Business on Its Best Behavior." *Chicago Tribune*, 3 January 1985, section 2, p. 1.

Drucker, Peter F. "What Is 'Business Ethics'?" *The Public Interest* (Spring 1981).

Ethics in American Business. New York: Touche Ross (1633 Broadway), January 1988. This report on ethical behavior is based on a poll of key business leaders.

Foster, Lawrence G. "The Johnson & Johnson Credo and the Tylenol Crisis." *New Jersey Bell Journal* 6 (Spring 1983): 1–7.

Foundation for Public Relations (310 Madison Ave., New York, NY 10017). The foundation issued a report on an ethics and standards study conducted by PRSA in 1987 to determine adherence to PRSA's code.

Gibbons, Edward F. "Business Ethics: Making a Corporate Code of Ethics Work." Bentley College, *Proceedings of the First National Conference on Business Ethics* (March 1981): 88–90.

Goldman, Alan H. *The Moral Foundations of Professional Ethics*. Totowa, NJ: Rowman & Littlefield, 1980.

Goodpaster, Kenneth E., and John B. Matthews. "Can a Corporation Have a Conscience?" *Harvard Business Review* (January-February 1982): 132–41.

Implementation and Enforcement of Codes of Ethics in Corporations and Associations. Survey conducted for the Ethics Resource Center by Opinion Research Corporation, Princeton, NJ, 1980.

McCoy, Bowen H. "The Parable of the Sadhu." *Harvard Business Review* (September-October 1983): 103–108.

Miller, William H. "Business' New Link: Ethics and the Bottomline." *Industry Week* (29 October 1984): 49–53.

Moeller, Clark. "Corporate Codes of Ethics: A Key to Economic Freedom." *Management Review* 69 (September 1980): 60–62.

"An Overview of a Landmark Roundtable Study of Corporate Ethics." *Roundtable Report*. New York: Business Roundtable (200 Park Ave.).

SUGGESTED READINGS

Posner, Ari. "The Culture of Plagiarism." *New Republic* (18 April 1988): 19–24.

"PR Groups Combine on Code of Ethics." *Jack O'Dwyer's Newsletter*. New York: J. R. O'Dwyer Co. (271 Madison Ave.), 18 May 1988.

Seibert, Donald V. "Time to Revive a Commitment to Ethics." *New York Times,* 25 December 1983, F2.

Sevareid, Eric. "Ethics and the Media." *Across the Board*. New York: Conference Board (845 Third Ave.), May 1988, pp. 12, 13.

Singer, Claude. "The Political Morality of Lending to Nonfriendly Nations." *Bankers Magazine* (November/December 1982): 20–24.

Sullam, Brian. "Ethics Codes Becoming Standard for Business." *Baltimore Sun,* 27 March 1983.

Weaver, Paul H. *The Suicidal Corporation*. New York: Simon & Schuster, 1988. A former Ford Motor Company public affairs staffer says that Ford is not the place to be entirely honest with one's publics.

Weber, James. "Institutionalizing Ethics into the Corporation." *MSU Business Topics* 29, no. 2 (1981): 47–52.

White, Bernard J., and Ruth B. Montgomery. "Corporate Codes of Conduct." *California Management Review* 23, no. 2 (Winter 1980): 80–87.

The Xerox Policy on Business Ethics. Stamford, CT: Xerox Corporation (P.O. Box 1600).

The Bank's South Africa Policy

To: Barrie Clem, Bigge Bank Public Affairs Director
From: I. M. DeLaw, Chairman of the Board
Re: South Africa Policy

My office has just learned that next Tuesday, the day of our annual shareholders' meeting, a group of community activists, politicians, religious leaders, and Harvard University students will convene on the plaza surrounding headquarters to demonstrate against our involvement in South Africa. The group refers to itself as Foes of Apartheid Policy, or simply FAP.

Basically, FAP is attacking us because of our current policy with respect to South Africa. They are demanding that we do the following:

- Immediately cease lending money to the government of South Africa, its parastatal institutions, Namibia, or the Homelands
- Immediately cease lending money to the private sector in South Africa
- Close down our office in Johannesburg and fire the 20 staff members working there
- Publicly excoriate the policy of apartheid

As you know, for the last 30 years our bank has loaned money to the government of South Africa. Last year, we barely broke even on these loans. However, we made $10 million on loans to the private sector in South Africa. As you also know, we regularly contribute to South African nonprofit institutions, including $400,000 over the years to institutions active in educational, community development, and legal efforts—all of which help nonwhites.

Our bank has also been a signer of the Sullivan Principles, the generally accepted criterion for measuring corporate behavior in South Africa. We also have felt that lending to firms in South Africa who support black employment is in everyone's best interests. And 6 of our 20 Johannesburg staffers are nonwhite.

Nonetheless, we've got a real problem here. For one thing, the city council has proposed a bill prohibiting the city from depositing funds in banks that make loans to the South African government and its agencies. As you know, we do a *lot* of business with the city.

Furthermore, I understand that Columbia University, Fairleigh Dickinson University, and Purdue University, among others, all have decided to divest themselves of stock holdings in banks that loan to the government of South Africa. As you know, these universities have a goodly number of Bigge Bank shares.

With these FAPs running around, we'll clearly need to respond at the annual meeting with answers to their most pressing questions.

I need your help. We don't have much time. Please be back to me shortly on how we should handle these hot potatoes.

Thank you and Godspeed.

I. M. D.

QUESTIONS

1. If you were Clem, would you suggest that the bank continue lending to the government of South Africa and related institutions?
2. Should the bank continue lending to the private sector in South Africa?
3. Should the bank remove its Johannesburg office?
4. What should be the bank's South Africa policy?

Research

6

I n the 1980s the Sperry Corporation advertised a basic strength in a unique and most effective manner. "We listen" was the company's simple yet profound theme (Figure 6–1). Public relations professionals, too, have begun to listen—both inside and outside their organizations. Indeed, the element of listening has become an increasingly important part of the public relations practitioner's job.

Another name for listening in public relations work is *research*, particularly the kind that involves public opinions, attitudes, and reactions to the policies and practices of an organization. Research has become essential in the practice of modern public relations. Instinct, intuition, and "gut-feelings" all remain important in the conduct of public relations work; but management today demands more—measurement, analysis, and evaluation at every stage of the public relations process. In an era of scarce resources, management wants facts and statistics from public relations professionals to show that their efforts contribute not only to overall organizational effectiveness but also to the bottom line. Why should we introduce a new employee newspaper? What should it say and cost? How will we know it's working? Questions like these must be answered through research.

Research should be applied in public relations work both at the initial stage, prior to planning a campaign, and at the final stage to evaluate a program's effectiveness. Early research helps to determine the current situation, prevalent attitudes, and difficulties that the program is up against. Later research examines the program's success, along with what else still needs to be done. Research at both points in the process is critical.

Even though research does not necessarily provide unequivocal proof of a program's effectiveness, it does allow a means for public relations professionals to support their own intuition. It's little wonder, then, that the idea of measuring public relations work has steadily gained acceptance.[1]

FIGURE 6-1 At Sperry the theme for the 1980s was "We listen." (Courtesy of Sperry Corporation)

WHAT IS RESEARCH?

Research is the systematic collection and interpretation of information to increase understanding[2] (Figure 6–2). Most people associate public relations with *conveying* information, and although that association is accurate, research must be the obligatory first step in any project. A firm must acquire enough accurate, relevant data about its publics, products, and programs to answer these kinds of questions:

- How can we identify and define our constituent groups?
- How does this knowledge relate to the design of our messages?
- How does it relate to the design of our programs?
- How does it relate to the media we use to convey our messages?
- How does it relate to the schedule we adopt in using our media?
- How does it relate to the ultimate implementation tactics of our program?

It's a difficult task to delve into the minds of others, whose backgrounds and points of view may be quite different from one's own, with the purpose of understanding why they think as they do. Research skills are partly intuitive,

FIGURE 6–2 An early research effort, albeit a futile one, was the return of the biblical scouts sent by Moses to reconnoiter the land of Canaan. They disagreed in their reports, and the Israelites believed the gloomier versions. This failure to correctly interpret the data caused them to wander another 40 years in the wilderness. (An even earlier research effort was Noah's sending the dove to search for dry ground.) (Courtesy of Trout & Ries)

partly an outgrowth of individual temperament, and partly a function of acquired knowledge. There is nothing mystifying about them. Although we tend
to think of research in terms of impersonal test scores, interviews, or questionnaires, they are only a small part of the process. The real challenge lies in using
research—knowing when to do what, with whom, and for what purpose.[3]

TYPES OF PUBLIC RELATIONS RESEARCH

In general, research is conducted to do three things: (1) describe a process,
situation, or phenomenon; (2) explain why something is happening, what its
causes are, and what effect it will have; and (3) predict what probably will
happen if we do or don't take action. Most research in public relations is either
theoretical or applied. Applied research solves practical problems; theoretical
research aids understanding of a public relations process.

Applied Research

In public relations work applied research can be either strategic or evaluative.
Both applications are designed to answer specific practical questions.

- **Strategic research** is used primarily in program development, to determine
  program objectives, develop message strategies, or establish benchmarks. It
  often examines the tools and techniques of public relations. For example, a
  firm that wants to know how employees rate its candor in internal publications would first conduct strategic research to find out where it stands.
- **Evaluative research,** sometimes called summative research, is conducted
  primarily to determine whether a public relations program has accomplished
  its goals and objectives. For example, if changes are made in the internal
  communications program to increase candor, evaluative research can determine whether the goals have been met. Formative research, a variant of
  evaluation, can be applied during a program to monitor progress and indicate where modifications might make sense.

Theoretical Research

Theoretical research is more abstract and conceptual than applied research. It
helps build theories in public relations work in areas such as why people communicate, how public opinion is formed, and how a public is created. Knowledge of theoretical research is important as a framework for persuasion and a
base for understanding why people do what they do.

Some knowledge of theoretical research in public relations and mass
communications is essential for practitioners to understand the limitations of
communication as a persuasive tool. Attitude and behavior change have been
the traditional goals in public relations programs, yet theoretical research indicates that such goals may be difficult or impossible to achieve through per-

suasive efforts. According to such research, other factors are always getting in the way.

Researchers in the 1980s found that communication is most persuasive when it comes from multiple sources of high credibility. Credibility itself is a multidimensional concept that includes trustworthiness, expertise, and power. Others have found that a message generally is more effective when it is simple because it is easier to understand, localize, and make personally relevant. According to still other research, the persuasiveness of a message can be increased when it arouses or is accompanied by a high level of personal involvement in the issue at hand. The point here is that knowledge of theoretical research can help practitioners not only understand the basis of applied research findings but also temper management expectations of attitude and behavioral change resulting from public relations programs.

In public relations, then, research may be applied to determine, in advance of a communications program, the attitudes and beliefs of a public. It can be used to monitor the performance of a public relations program in process. And it can be used as an evaluative mechanism to determine a program's progress, success, and suggested modifications. When limited information is available, public relations research can also help clarify issues. For example, attitudes are often fuzzy, and people may say they like something without being specific about the particular characteristics they admire. Research can probe deeper to determine the specifics. Frequently, research may also confirm assumptions about public opinion. Intuition may be accurate, but research corroborates the validity of the public relations program.

METHODS OF PUBLIC RELATIONS RESEARCH

Observation is the foundation of modern social science. Scientists, social psychologists, and anthropologists make observations, develop theories, and, hopefully, increase understanding of human behavior. Public relations research, too, is founded on observation. The three primary forms of public relations research are methods, mostly indirect, of observing human behavior.

- **Surveys** are designed to reveal attitudes and opinions—what people think about certain subjects.
- **Communication audits** are often designed to reveal disparities between real and perceived communications between management and target audiences. Management may make certain assumptions about its methods, media, materials, and messages, whereas its targets may confirm or refute those assumptions.
- **Unobtrusive measures**—such as fact finding, content analysis, and readability studies—enable the study of a subject or object without involving the researcher or the research as an intruder.

Each method of public relations research offers specific benefits and should be understood and used by the modern practitioner.

Tyrus C. Ragland

T yrus C. Ragland founded Message Factors, Inc., a marketing research firm, in 1967. He has developed a variety of proprietary market research services—Strength and Weakness Analysis, Value Perception Test™, TIPS™ (The Information Prioritizing System), Communication Strategy Research, Quality of Service Analysis, and Copy Check. Message Factors has offices in Memphis, Cincinnati, Atlanta, Denver, and Tampa, with 350 clients in 30 states.

How important is research in public relations?
Market research is important to public relations in the following ways:

- Knowing what to say—for example, a manufacturing client found that the public thought the steam coming out of one of its smokestacks was pollution.
- Knowing what not to say—some subjects, particularly those that are emotionally charged, cannot be addressed effectively, regardless of the company's desire to tell its side of the story.
- Knowing who to say it to—that is, which publics most need communication on a particular subject. However, public relations practitioners must be careful of demographic analysis where differences are due more to the way younger, older, better educated, lesser educated, male, female, etc. people respond than to real divergence in opinion.

Can you really measure public relations success?
Yes, and there are several ways to do it. First, companies are moving toward the concept of answering the important question, "How are we getting business?" They want to know the impact of all they do, public relations included, and which efforts contribute most to their success.

We know from tracking public opinion for more than 20 years that banks often do not get much credit for their community involvement from the public. However, geographical markets are very different in this respect. Some don't expect it at all, whereas in one market a bank's continued sponsorship of a public concert series proved to be the most effective communication effort we have ever tested.

What can a practitioner expect to derive from research?
One of the most important things is learning when *not* to respond. Years ago, when utility rates were increasing rapidly and utilities were political footballs, a populist governor regularly attacked one of our clients. By the time the company could respond, they were several attacks behind. We began a continuous tracking study to see if the public was really paying attention. The answer was no. When it removed itself from the battlefield, the power company improved its image by not being seen as involved in public spats anymore.

It's also important to know what *not* to talk about. Another utility story: during times of rapidly rising utility rates, it made sense to utilities to tell their story about utility economics. The problem was this issue infuriated the public, no matter how it was communicated. A no-win situation.

What is the future of research in public relations?
The key change will be the same as for the market research field overall—more emphasis on clarity, knowing what answers to questions mean when you get them back. For example, if 50 percent of the public thinks a company is a "good corporate citizen," how

should we respond to that statistic? It may be a good, bad, or indifferent showing. Without benchmarks we don't know. However, if we know that similar companies score 70 percent, we know 50 percent is not so good.

Also, there is a known demographic predisposition to respond in certain ways. For example, younger people tend to be more questioning and critical. Thus, different benchmarks are needed for their opinions versus those of older people. Similarly, geographic areas of the country differ. Even within a state we have found significant differences among urban neighborhoods, suburbs, small towns, and rural areas. Without benchmarks for each of these areas, responses cannot be properly interpreted.

This is particularly important for ego-intensive subjects. Here, the relative, not the absolute, answer is what really counts. People logically reject the idea that they are influenced by advertising, buy products for prestige, etc. Only benchmarks can tell us how significant such answers are. The opposite side of this coin is rationalization. People tend to give us "motherhood" (overstated) answers to things that sound logical for them to do/believe. The benchmark also helps us get this type of answer in perspective.

Inexpensive computers and databases have made the extensive use of benchmarks possible. This improves the value of research because we will not only know the statistics, but will also know what they mean.

SURVEYS

▬▬▬▬▬

Survey research is one of the most frequently used research methods in public relations. Surveys can be applied to broad societal issues, such as determining public opinion about a political candidate, or to the most minute organizational problem, such as whether shareholders like the quarterly report. Surveys come in two types.

1. **Descriptive surveys** offer a snapshot of a current situation or condition. They are the research equivalent of a balance sheet—capturing reality at a specific point in time. A typical public opinion poll is a prime example.
2. **Explanatory surveys,** on the other hand, are concerned with cause and effect. Their purpose is to help explain why a current situation or condition exists and to offer explanations for opinions and attitudes. Frequently, such explanatory or analytical surveys are designed to answer the question why. Why are our philanthropic dollars not being appreciated in the community? Why are employees not believing management messages? Why is our credibility being questioned?

Surveys generally consist of four elements: (1) the sample, (2) the questionnaire, (3) the interview, and (4) the analysis of results. (Direct mail surveys, of course, eliminate the interview step.) Because survey research is so critical in public relations, we will examine each survey element in some detail.

The Sample

The sample, or selected target group, must be representative of the total public whose views are sought. Once a survey population has been determined, a researcher must select the appropriate sample or group of respondents from whom to collect information. Sampling is tricky. A researcher must be aware of the hidden pitfalls in choosing a representative sample, not the least of which is the perishable nature of most data. Survey findings are rapidly outdated because of population mobility and changes in the political and socioeconomic environment. Consequently, sampling should be completed quickly.

Two approaches are used in obtaining a sample: probability sampling and nonprobability sampling. The former is more scientific; the latter, more informal.

Probability Sampling   In probability sampling each member of a population has a known chance of being selected. Probability sampling is based on a mathematical criterion that allows generalizations from the sample to be made to the total population. There are four types of probability samples.

1. **Simple random sampling** gives all members of the population an equal chance of being selected. First, all members of the population are identified, and then as many subjects as are needed are randomly selected—usually with the help of a computer. Election polling uses a random approach; al-

Pay Attention To What I Do, Not What I Say

Public relations professionals must always keep in mind that, as most research has shown, attitudes are not a reliable predictor of behavior. In other words, people often talk one way but act another.*

- Ask American adults whether they're satisfied with their jobs, and 88 percent will answer yes. But only 30 percent of those adults expect to have the same job in five years. Another 31 percent of them plan to quit their jobs, and 25 percent don't know where they will be working in five years.
- A whopping 76 percent of American adults vow they exercise regularly, and 33 percent will tell you that they exercise strenuously three or more times a week. But when those self-proclaimed fitness fans waddle over to the scales, the truth comes out. Fully 59 percent of all U.S. adults—about 105 million people—are overweight.
- Another 65 percent of adults claim they are making a real effort to eat more brussels sprouts and cauliflower; 59 percent try hard to eat enough fiber; 56 percent claim they avoid eating too much fat; 57 percent say they are cutting down on salt; and 46 percent steer clear of high-cholesterol foods. But the number of adults who would like to see more all-you-can-eat specials in restaurants increased from 30 to 37 percent during the past decade. By contrast, the number who want more dieter's specials declined from 18 to 16 percent over the same period.

What's the point? People sometimes tell you what they think you want to hear rather than what they really believe. So be wary of even the most buttoned-up research.

*Joe Schwartz, "Do As I Say," *U.S. Demographics*, April 1988.

though millions of Americans vote, only a few thousand are ever polled on their election preferences. The Nielson national television sample, for example, consists of 1,700 homes out of 90 million TV households. The Census Bureau uses a sample of 60,000 to 75,000 out of 90 million households to obtain estimates of employment and other population characteristics.

How large should a random sample be? The answer depends on a number of factors, one of which is the size of the population. In addition, the more similar the population elements are in regard to the characteristics being studied, the smaller the sample required. In most random samples the following population-to-sample ratios apply, with a five percent margin of error:[4]

Population	Sample
1,000	278
2,000	322
3,000	341
5,000	355
10,000	370
50,000	381
100,000	383
500,000	383
Infinity	384

Random sampling owes its accuracy to the laws of probability, which are best explained by the example of a barrel filled with 10,000 marbles, 5,000 green ones and 5,000 red ones. If a blindfolded person selects a certain number of marbles from the barrel—say 400—the laws of probability suggest that the most frequently drawn combination will be 200 red and 200 green. These laws further conjecture that with certain margins of error (discussed on p. 153 under "Analysis") a very few marbles can represent the whole barrel, which can correspond to any size—city, state, or nation.

2. **Systematic sampling** is closely related to simple random sampling, but it uses a random starting point in the sample list. From then on, the researcher selects every nth person in the list. Since each member of the population does not have an equal probability of being selected, this type of sampling is less reliable than simple random sampling. It is also cheaper and easier to perform.

3. **Stratified sampling** is used to survey different segments or strata of the population. For example, if an organization wants to determine the relationship between years of service and attitudes toward the company, it may stratify the sample to ensure that the breakdown of respondents accurately reflects the population makeup. In other words, if more than half of the employees have been with the company more than 10 years, more than half of those polled should also reflect that level of service. By stratifying the sample, the organization's objective can be achieved.

4. **Cluster sampling** involves first breaking the population down into small heterogeneous subsets, or clusters, and then selecting the potential sample from the individual clusters or groups. A cluster may often be defined as a geographic area, such as an election district.

Nonprobability Sampling   Nonprobability samples come in two types, the convenience sample and the purposive sample.

1. **Convenience samples** are relatively unstructured, rather unsystematic, and designed to elicit ideas and points of view. Journalists use convenience samples when they conduct man-on-the-street interviews. The most common type of convenience sample in public relations research is the focus group.

Focus groups generally consist of 8 to 12 people with a moderator encouraging in-depth discussion of a specific topic. Focus groups generate concepts and ideas rather than validate hypotheses.

2. **Purposive sampling**—often called quota sampling—permits a researcher to choose subjects on the basis of certain characteristics. For example, the attitudes of a certain number of women, men, blacks, whites, rich, or poor may need to be known. Quotas are imposed in proportion to each group's percentage of the population. The advantage of quota sampling is that it increases homogeneity of a sample population, thus enhancing the validity of a study. However, it is hard to classify interviewees by one or two discrete demographic characteristics. For example, a particular interviewee may be black, Catholic, female, under 25, and a member of a labor union all at the same time, making the lines of demographic demarcation pretty blurry.

The Questionnaire

Before creating a questionnaire, it's wise to talk informally with the type of people the study is designed to reach. These talks should yield insights into how target publics think. In addition, because everybody today receives questionnaires, researchers should follow these tips in their design process.

1. Keep it short, probably under 20 questions. It's terrific if the questionnaire can be answered in five minutes.
2. Use structured, not open-ended questions. People would rather check a box or circle a number than write an essay. But leave room at the bottom for general comments or "Other." Also, start with simpler, nonthreatening questions before getting to the more difficult, sensitive ones. This approach will build respondent trust as well as commitment to finishing the questionnaire.
3. Measure intensity of feelings. Let respondents check "very satisfied," "satisfied," "dissatisfied," or "very dissatisfied," rather than "yes" or "no." One popular approach is the semantic differential technique in Figure 6–3.
4. Don't use fancy words or words that have more than one meaning. If you must use big words, make the context clear.
5. Don't ask loaded questions. "Is management doing all it can to communicate with you?" is a terrible question. The answer is always "no."
6. Don't ask double-barreled questions. "Would you like management meetings once a month, or are bimonthly meetings enough?" is another terrible question.
7. Pretest. Send your questionnaire to a few colleagues, and listen to their suggestions.
8. Attach a letter explaining how important the respondents' answers are, and let recipients know they will remain anonymous. Respondents will

Dictaphone   **Stowe**

FIGURE 6–3 In questionnaires one common device to measure intensity of feelings is the semantic differential technique, which gives respondents a scale of choices from the worst to the best. These semantic differential scales for portable dictating equipment and for ski lodges are typical. (Courtesy of Trout & Ries)

feel better if they think the study is significant and their identities are protected. Also, specify how and where the data will be used.

9. Hand-stamp the envelopes—preferably with unique commemorative stamps. Metering an envelope indicates assembly-line research, and researchers have found that the more expensive the postage, the higher the response rate. People like to feel special.

10. Follow up your first mailing. Send a reminder postcard three days after the original questionnaire. Then wait a few weeks and send a second questionnaire, just in case they've lost the first.

11. Send out more questionnaires than you think necessary. The major weakness of most mail surveys is the unmeasurable error introduced by nonresponders. You're shooting for a 50 percent response rate; anything less tends to be suspect.

12. Enclose a reward. There's nothing like a token gift of merchandise or money—a $2 bill works beautifully—to make a recipient feel guilty for not returning a questionnaire.[5]

Figure 6–4 illustrates an internal survey using a questionnaire with a simple rating format. Appendix B gives an example of a more elaborate questionnaire.

The Chase Manhattan Bank, N.A.
1 Chase Manhattan Plaza
New York, New York 10015

CHASE

May 11, 1977

TO ALL STAFF MEMBERS

We are currently in the midst of revitalizing our corporate internal
communications programs and practices. At this point, however, to
move forward and to do the job right, we need some information from
you.

To begin with, we need to know what you think about the various corporate internal communications programs already in place. We also
need to know what kinds of information you need to keep in tune with
Chase and its overall directions. And, finally, we need to know
what information you feel is necessary if you are to do the best
possible job in fulfilling your particular responsibilities.

The ideal way to get this information would be to talk with each of
you directly, but this is obviously unrealistic. But we can speak
with many of you indirectly through the survey that we are conducting.

We are extremely interested in having your opinion on this critical
matter, and therefore urge you to take the time to give us serious,
thoughtful answers to the questions that are attached.

We are firmly committed to establishing a vital internal communications program which is responsive to your information needs. You
can be sure that we'll be listening to what you have to say.

Sincerely,

1. **In general, would you say that the information Chase gives its employees keeps you:**

   1) Very well informed
   2) Reasonably well informed
   3) Somewhat informed
   4) Not too well informed
   5) Not informed at all

2. **Generally, when Chase gives information to employees, how do you feel about it?**

   1) Always believe it
   2) Usually believe it
   3) Believe it about half the time
   4) Seldom believe it
   5) Never believe it

3. **Overall, how would you rate the timeliness of the information you receive about the bank and your job?**

   1) Very good
   2) Good
   3) So-So
   4) Poor
   5) Very poor

Please rate the *importance* of each of the following as a *source of information.*

	VERY IMPOR-TANT	IMPOR-TANT	SOME-WHAT IMPOR-TANT	NOT TOO IMPOR-TANT	NOT AT ALL IMPOR-TANT	NEVER RECEIVED INFORMATION FROM THIS SOURCE
4. Your Supervisor	1	2	3	4	5	9
5. Chase Manhattan News	1	2	3	4	5	9
6. Staff Bulletin	1	2	3	4	5	9
7. Benefits News	1	2	3	4	5	9
8. Recorded Message Service	1	2	3	4	5	9
9. Annual Report	1	2	3	4	5	9
10. Chase Quarterly	1	2	3	4	5	9
11. Bulletin Boards	1	2	3	4	5	9
12. Consumer Sense	1	2	3	4	5	9
13. Benefits Booklets	1	2	3	4	5	9
14. Orientation	1	2	3	4	5	9
15. Other Chase Employees (The grapevine)	1	2	3	4	5	9

Have you any comments on your answers to questions 4-15? Include suggestions for improvement in any of the above
sources of information. PLEASE **WRITE IN SPACE PROVIDED BELOW.**

FIGURE 6-4 In the area of internal communications and morale, companies constantly devise questionnaires to seek employee opinions about current communications channels. This figure shows the introduction to and first portion of a survey distributed to a random sampling of Chase Manhattan Bank employees. (Courtesy of
Chase Manhattan Bank)

BETWEEN
THE LINES

Of Computers, Word Processors, and Databases: The Brave New World of Public Relations Research

Public relations, like most other fields, is rapidly approaching the day when a practitioner will research an article, speech, or news release in the comfort of home or office, with instant access to worldwide databases, including those of the organization's computerized files, universities, research organizations, and governments. Up-to-date information will be available on almost any subject. Where once it took weeks to complete a research project, soon that same project will be completed in minutes, with the docile assistance of a computer terminal.

The day is rapidly approaching when the vast majority of public relations researchers will gather their material, write their articles, correct their syntax and grammar, switch paragraphs, add or delete sentences, and produce perfect, finished, original copy without typewriters, typewriter paper, ribbons, carbon paper, correction fluid, or dirty hands. The day of the computer, word processor, and database is upon us. And public relations research will reap the benefits.

Already, most offices are moving toward word processing automation to handle information. Word processing equipment has reduced many legal, business, and medical costs, for example, by automatically producing frequently used forms and standard letters from memory units. In public relations work manuscripts and releases can be produced on the keyboard/cathode ray tube (CRT) unit, easily edited, and printed out as many times as desired through the equipment's memory.

Instead of reproducing manuscripts only on paper, word processing equipment permits their reproduction also on magnetic tapes or discs, known variously as floppy discs or data discs, which already are accepted by many wire services.

Particularly important for public relations research are online databases, which store vast quantities of information on current or historical subjects. Some of the major information service vendors available to public relations practitioners are described here.[9]

BRS Information Technologies
1200 Route 7
Latham, NY 12110
800–833–4707
800–553–5566 (in New York)

For over a decade, this service has supplied a large number of databases, with primary emphasis on medical, engineering, educational, and business-oriented information. Price structure varies according to the type of service selected. The Open Access Plan has an annual password fee of $75, a $35 per connect-hour charge, a telecommunications charge of about $9, and a database royalty fee of up to $70 an hour.

DIALOG Information Services, Inc.
Lockheed Corporation
3460 Hillview Avenue
Palo Alto, CA 94304
800–334–2564

DIALOG was started as a commercial venture in 1972 by the Lockheed Corporation. It is one of the largest online services, offering more than 250 databases that range from business and economics to science and technology. DIALOG charges no subscription fees but has a wide variation in connect-hour cost. Each database has a set hourly cost, ranging from $15 to $175. DIALOG is available 24 hours a day, seven a days a week.

Dow Jones News/Retrieval Service
P.O. Box 300
Princeton, NJ 08540
609–452–2000

This is a part of Dow Jones and Company, publisher of the *Wall Street Journal*. More than 25 databases are offered, primarily relating to business and economics, financial and investment services, and general news and information. The *Wall Street Journal* is available in summary form as well as in its entirety. Costs start with a subscription fee of $49.95 for companies and $29.95 for individuals. There is also a $12 annual service fee. After this, fees are set at $.90 per minute for prime time and $.20 per minute for nonprime time. The service is available 22 hours each day.

DIALCOM Services, Inc.
1109 Spring Street
Silver Spring, MD 20910
800–435–7342

DIALCOM, begun in 1970, was bought in 1986 by British Telecom. It offers gateways to databases such as UPI, the Official Airline Guide, and the Bureau of National Affairs. It also offers gateway services to other online vendors, which enable customers to access databases offered on Dow Jones/Retrieval Service, BRS, DIALOG, and the Source. Fee structure is based on the number of hours used, not databases accessed. Costs for accessing the gateway services are based on the rates charged by other vendors. The service operates 24 hours a day, seven days a week.

Facts on File
460 Park Avenue, South
New York, NY 10016
212–683–2244

Facts on File summarizes information daily from leading U.S. and foreign periodicals, the publications of Commerce Clearing House, Congressional Quarterly, Congressional Record, State Department Bulletin, presidential documents, and official press releases. Subject areas are as diverse as the news of the day. Annual subscription fee is $440.

NewsNet, Inc.
945 Haverford Road
Bryn Mawr, PA 19010
800–345–1301

NewsNet was started in 1982 by Independent Publications. It offers primarily newsletters and wire services. There are more than 200 specialized business newsletters and wire services, covering more than 35 industries, including telecommunications, publishing, broadcasting, electronics and computers, energy, investment, accounting, and taxation. Prices range from $24 to more than $100 an hour, depending on the newsletter being accessed. There is also a monthly minimum charge of $15. NewsNet is available 24 hours each day.

LEXIS and NEXIS
Mead Data Central
9333 Springboro Pike
P.O. Box 933
Dayton, OH 45401
800–227–4908

LEXIS and NEXIS are two of the information services provided by this division of Mead Corporation. LEXIS is a legal information database containing full-text documents from federal cases, case law from the United States and parts of Europe, state and federal regulations, and other legal records. NEXIS is a full-text database containing 160 major newspapers, magazines, and newsletters. In 1988 a group of media in the NEXIS databank was organized as the Advertising and Public Relations Library, including news wires and communications-oriented publications. Fee structure is complex, but the range of costs varies from $7 to $23 for the search and $30 per hour for connect charges. Both services are available 24 hours a day on weekdays and all weekend hours except from 10:00 P.M. Saturday to 6:00 A.M. Sunday.

ORBIT
SDC Information Services
2500 Colorado Avenue
Santa Monica, CA 90406
800–421–7229
800–352–6689

The System Development Corporation, a division of Burroughs Corporation, created ORBIT in 1972, enabling users to search for information in nearly 90 databases with more than 55 million citations. ORBIT covers several different subject areas, including business, chemistry, engineering, electronics, energy, government, life sciences, patents, social sciences, and industry-specific databases. Hourly charges are different for each database and range from $35 to $300 per hour. The service operates 24 hours a day during the week with fewer hours during the weekend.

The Source
Source Telecomputing Corporation
1616 Anderson Road
McLean, VA 22102
800–336–3366

The Source, owned by *Reader's Digest,* is an information service primarily for the home market. In addition to business-oriented databases and services, the Source is well-known for services that allow users to interact on line. Costs include a membership fee of $49.95 and a daytime charge of $.36 per minute, with a nighttime rate of $.14 per minute for most services. The Source is open 23 hours a day, seven days a week.

The Interview

Research interviews can provide a more personal, firsthand feel for public opinion. Interviews can be conducted in a number of ways, including face-to-face, telephone, mail, and drop-off techniques.

Face-to-Face or Personal Interviews This approach is considered the most reliable because it permits in-depth polling. Such interviews can be conducted one-to-one or through survey panels, often called idea juries or focus groups. These panels can be used, for example, to measure buying habits or the impact of public relations programs on a community or organizational group. They can also be used to assess general attitudes toward certain subjects, such as new products or advertising.

With the focus group technique a well-drilled moderator leads a group through a discussion of opinions on a particular product, organization, or idea. Participants represent the socioeconomic level desired by the research sponsor—from college students to office workers to millionaires. Almost always, focus group participants are paid for their efforts. Sessions are frequently videotaped and then analyzed, often in preparation for more formal, more specific research questionnaires.

Focus groups should be organized with the following guidelines in mind:

1. **Define objectives and audience.** The more tightly you define your goals and your target audience, the more likely you are to gather relevant information. In other words, don't conduct a focus group with friends and family members, hoping to get a quick and inexpensive read. Nothing of value will result.
2. **Recruit your groups.** Recruiting participants takes several weeks, depending on the difficulty of contacting the target audience. Contact is usually made by phone, with a series of questions to weed out those who don't fit specifications, competitors' employees, and members of the news media (to keep the focus group from becoming a news story). "Professional" participants who have participated in a group in the past year should also be screened out; they may be more interested in the money than in helping you find what you're looking for.
3. **Choose the right moderator.** Staff people who may be magnificent conversationalists are not necessarily the best focus group moderators. The gift of gab is not enough. Professional moderators know how to establish rapport quickly, how and when to probe beyond the obvious, how to draw comments from reluctant participants, how to keep a group on task, and how to interpret results validly.
4. **Conduct enough focus groups.** One or two focus groups are usually not enough. Four to six are better to uncover the full range of relevant ideas and opinions. Regardless of the number of groups, however, you must resist the temptation to add up responses; that practice gives the focus group more analytical worth than it deserves.

5. **Use a discussion guide.** This is a basic outline of what you want to investigate. It will lead the moderator through the discussion and keep the group on track.
6. **Choose proper facilities.** The discussion room should be comfortable, with participants sitting around a table that affords observers a good view of all members. Closed-circuit TV and two-way mirrors may be used for observers, but participants should always be told when they are being observed.
7. **Keep a tight rein on observers.** Observers should rarely be in the same room with participants; the two groups should ordinarily be separated. Observers should view the proceedings seriously; this is not "dinner and a show."
8. **Consider using outside help.** Setting up focus groups can be time-consuming and complicated. Often the best advice is to hire a firm recommended by the American Marketing Association or the Marketing Research Association so that the process, the moderator, and the evaluation can be done as professionally as possible.[6]

Telephone Interviews   In contrast to personal interviews, telephone interviews suffer from a high refusal rate. Many people just don't want to be bothered. Such interviews may also introduce an upper-income bias because lower-income earners may lack telephones. However, the increasing use of unlisted numbers by upper-income people may serve to mitigate this bias. Telephone interviews must be carefully scripted so that interviewers know precisely what to ask, regardless of a respondent's answer. Calls should be made at less busy times of the day, such as early morning or later afternoon (Figure 6–5).

   With both telephone and face-to-face interviews, it is important to establish rapport with the interview subject. It may make sense to begin the interview with nonthreatening questions, saving the tougher, more controversial ones—on income level or race, for example—until last. Another approach is to depersonalize the research by explaining that others have devised the survey and that the interviewer's job is simply to ask the questions.

Mail Interviews   These constitute the least expensive approach, but they often suffer from low response rates. You are aiming for a 50 percent response rate. Frequently, those who return mail questionnaires are people with strong biases either in favor of or, usually, in opposition to the subject at hand. As noted, one way to generate a higher response from mail interviews is through the use of self-addressed, stamped envelopes or enclosed incentives, such as dollar bills or free gifts.

Drop-Off Interviews   This approach combines face-to-face and mail interview techniques. An interviewer personally drops off a questionnaire at a household, usually after conducting a face-to-face interview. Because the interviewer has already established some rapport with the interviewee, the rate of return with this technique is considerably higher than it is for straight mail interviews.

GUIDELINE RESEARCH CORPORATION
3 West 35th Street
New York, NY 10001

Job #C30-046
August, 1986

5-1

INTERNAL PUBLICATION SURVEY
- Screener -

SEX: (6)   LOCATION:
Male 1
Female 2   (7,8)

DIVISION: (9)
DOMESTIC:
Corporate Industries 1
Domestic Inst. Banking 2
International (NY) 3
Investment (Capital Mkts.) . 4
Tradings & Security 5
INTERNATIONAL
Asia 6
Europe 7
Latin America/Canada 8

RESPONDENT'S NAME:
TELEPHONE #: (   )
INTERVIEWER: DATE:

| ASK TO SPEAK WITH PERSON ON LIST. |

A. Hello, my name is _____ from Guideline Research Corporation, an independent market research firm in New York City. I would like to speak with (NAME OF PERSON ON LIST). (IF PERSON NO LONGER AT THAT NUMBER, TRY TO GET CONNECTED TO NEW NUMBER.)

TERMINATE Q. A: RESPONDENT NO LONGER AT THIS NUMBER ----- 1 2 3 4 5 6 7 8 9 (10)

B. (IF QUESTIONED BY SECRETARY ABOUT THE NATURE OF THE CALL, SAY:)
My company has been asked by Chase to conduct a survey among various bank officers throughout the world and (NAME OF OFFICER) has been selected as part of the study. (ONLY IF ASKED, SAY:) If you wish you can verify this by calling Mr. Fraser Seitel (Sy-Tell), head of Public Affairs and Internal Communications at 212-552-4503.

TERMINATE Q. B: RESPONDENT NOT AVAILABLE ----- 1 2 3 4 5 6 7 8 9 (11)

C. (IF LISTED RESPONDENT IS REACHED, SAY:)
Hello, my name is _____ from Guideline Research firm in New York City. We have been asked by Chase to conduct a survey to get reactions to various employee publications. Your name has been randomly selected from a list of bank officers throughout the world. It will only take 15 minutes of your time and your cooperation will help Chase improve the quality of the information you receive in these publications.

(IF RESPONDENT REFUSES TO BE INTERVIEWED, TERMINATE AND TALLY BELOW.)

TERMINATE Q. C: REFUSED ----- 1 2 3 4 5 6 7 8 9 (12)

-2-

D. First, when thinking about publications that Chase publishes for its employees, which ones come to mind? (DO NOT READ LIST. RECORD "FIRST," AND THEN "ALL OTHER" MENTIONS APPROPRIATELY UNDER Q. D BELOW.) Any others?

(ASK Q. E FOR EACH PUBLICATION NOT MENTIONED IN Q. D. START AT X'D PUBLICATION OR FIRST PUBLICATION FOLLOWING THE "X".)

E. Have you ever heard of (FIRST PUBLICATION)? (RECORD UNDER Q. E BELOW.)

(IF "GLOBAL BANKER" NOT MENTIONED IN Q. D OR Q. E, TERMINATE, ERASE AND RECORD BELOW.)

TERMINATE Q. D/E: NOT AWARE ----- 1 2 3 4 5 6 7 8 9 (13)

F. (ASK Q. F ONLY OF PRE-LISTED PUBLICATIONS THAT WERE MENTIONED IN Q. D OR Q. E.) And, do you receive (FIRST PUBLICATION IN Q. D/Q.E)? (RECORD UNDER Q. F BELOW)

G. (ASK Q. G FOR EACH PRE-LISTED PUBLICATION MENTIONED IN Q. D OR Q. E.) Have you ever read an issue of (FIRST PUBLICATION)? (REPEAT FOR EACH PRE-LISTED PUBLICATION IN Q. D OR Q. E. RECORD UNDER Q. G BELOW.)

H. (ASK Q. H FOR EACH PRE-LISTED PUBLICATION MENTIONED IN Q. G.) Thinking about (FIRST PUBLICATION), how would you rate it overall on a scale of "1" to "5," with "5" meaning you like it very much and "1" meaning you don't like it at all. (REPEAT FOR EACH RESPONSE IN Q. G. RECORD RESPONSE UNDER Q. H BELOW.)

	Q.D UNAIDED AWARENESS		Q.E Aided Awareness	Q.F RECEIVE			Q.G Ever Read	Q.H Overall Rating
START HERE:	First Mention (14)	All Others (15)	(16)	Yes	No	Don't Know	(22)	
Chase Asia News	1	1	1	1 . 2 . 3 (17)			1	(23)
Chase Business	2	2	2	1 . 2 . 3 (18)			2	(24)
Chase Directions	3	3	3	1 . 2 . 3 (19)			3	(25)
Financial Outlook	4	4	4	1 . 2 . 3 (20)			4	(26)
Global Banker	5	5	5	1 . 2 . 3 (21)			5	(27)
Other (SPECIFY)	0	0						
	0	0						

I. (IF "GLOBAL BANKER" NOT MENTIONED IN Q. G, ASK Q. I. OTHERWISE, SKIP TO INSTRUCTIONS AFTER Q. I.) What would you say are some of the reasons why you have not read Global Banker? (PROBE FULLY)

28-
29-
30-
31-
32-

• IF "GLOBAL BANKER" NOT READ IN Q. G, SKIP TO Q. 8 ON MAIN QUESTIONNAIRE. SAVE QUESTIONNAIRE. THIS DOES NOT COUNT TOWARDS COMPLETION QUOTA.
• IF "GLOBAL BANKER" READ IN Q. G, GO TO MAIN QUESTIONNAIRE -- Q. 1.

TERMINATE: QUALIFIED/REFUSED ----- 1 2 3 4 5 6 7 8 9 (33)

FIGURE 6-5 Telephone interviewers must be guided by this kind of prepared script to ensure that appropriate responses are achieved for the whole questionnaire. (Courtesy of Guideline Research Corporation)

Analysis

After selecting the sample, drawing up the questionnaire, and interviewing the respondents, the researcher must analyze the findings. Often a great deal of analysis is required to produce meaningful recommendations.

The objective of every sample is to come up with results that are valid and reliable. A margin of error explains how far off the prediction may be. A sample may be large enough to fairly represent the larger universe; yet depending on the margin of sampling error, the results of the research may not be statistically significant. That is, the differences or distinctions detected by the survey may not be sizable enough to offset the margin of error. Thus, the margin of error must always be determined.

This concept is particularly critical in political polling, where pollsters are quick to acknowledge that their results may accurately represent the larger universe—but normally with a 2 or 3 percent margin of error. Thus, the results could be as much as 3 percent more or less for a certain candidate. Consequently, a pollster who says a candidate will win with 51 percent of the vote really means that the candidate could win with as much as 54 percent or lose with as little as 48 percent of the vote.

Political polls are fraught with problems. They cannot scientifically predict outcomes. Rather, they freeze attitudes at a certain point in time, and people's attitudes obviously change with the tide of events. Perhaps the most notorious political poll was that of the *Literary Digest* in 1936, which used a telephone polling technique to predict that Alf Landon would be the nation's next president. Landon thereupon suffered one of the worst drubbings in American electoral history at the hands of Franklin Roosevelt. It was probably of little solace to the *Literary Digest* that most of its telephone respondents, many of whom were Republicans wealthy enough to afford phones, did vote for Landon.

The point here is that in analyzing results, problems of validity, reliability, and levels of statistical significance associated with margins of error must be considered before recommendations based on survey data are offered.

COMMUNICATION AUDITS

The second primary method in public relations research is the communication audit, which frequently evaluates how an organization is doing with respect to a particular constituent group. Communication audits are typically used to analyze the standing of a company with its employees or community neighbors, assess the readership of routine communication vehicles such as annual reports and news releases, or examine an organization's performance as a corporate citizen. Communication audits often provide benchmarks against which future public relations programs can be applied and measured.

More recently, communication audits have been used to provide information on how to solve

BANZAI HOSPITAL AUDIT
January 5, 1990

GUIDELINES
1. All interviews are confidential. Assure those you interview that their statements will be held in confidence so that the source of their remarks will not be identifiable.
2. Copy all of your interview notes within 24 hours after each interview is completed, to protect against possible loss of your notes.
3. Use an informal interview style, referring to the question sheets as little as possible. Have the questions in mind before the interview so that they can come up during conversation.
4. Type up your notes, using direct quotes as much as possible.

INTERVIEW CATEGORIES
Board members
Executive staff
Medical staff
Volunteers
Community leaders
Residents and tenants

Families of residents and tenants
Financial supporters
Business leaders
News media
General public

BANZAI COMMUNICATION AUDIT
Board members
1. How did you become involved with Banzai?
2. How do you perceive your role with Banzai? Are your assignments and responsibilities clear?
3. What are the strengths of Banzai today? weaknesses?
4. If it was in your power to do so, what would you change about Banzai?
Medical staff
1. How would you describe your relationship with the institution?
2. Is communications a factor in your relationship? How? Is there a need for improvement? What suggestions do you have?
3. How do you think the institution is perceived in the community? Why? Any suggestions for community programs that should be undertaken?
4. Do you believe this institution provides adequate patient information?
Volunteers
1. How do you get information about what is happening in the institution? What are your best sources? Do you think you get enough information? If not, what else would you like to know?
2. Is there an effective way for you to communicate upward? Do you take advantage of it? What type of information do you pass along?
3. How do you think the institution is perceived in the community? Why?
Community leaders
1. What do you know about the institution?
2. What are your sources of information? Which do you consider the most reliable?
3. How do you value the institution? Does the community perceive the institution in the same light?
4. What recommendations do you have that would help the institution respond to community needs?

BUDGET
The audit will take approximately 120 days. Budget will be kept to the lowest possible figure but will be in the $12,000 to $15,000 range for professional services and about $5,000 for out-of-pocket expenses.

PROCEDURE
A preliminary audit report will be prepared following completion of the interviews. This draft will be reviewed with appropriate members of Banzai staff to uncover possible misconceptions, misinterpretations, or errors. A final audit report will follow in 15 days.

- bottlenecked information flows
- uneven communication workloads
- employees working at cross-purposes
- hidden information within an organization that is not being used, to the detriment of the institution
- conflicting or nonexisting notions about what the organization is and does[7]

The most effective communication audits start with a researcher who (1) is familiar with the public to be studied, (2) generally understands the attitudes of the target public toward the organization, (3) recognizes the issues of concern to the target public, and (4) understands the relative power of the target public vis-à-vis other publics (Figure 6–6).

UNOBTRUSIVE METHODS

Of the various unobtrusive methods of data collection available to public relations researchers, probably the most widely used is simple fact finding. Facts are the bricks and mortar of public relations work; no action can be taken unless the facts are known, and the fact finding process is continuous.

Each organization must keep a fact file of the most essential data with which it is involved. For example, such items as key organization statistics, publications, management biographies and photos, press clippings, media lists, competitive literature, pending legislation, organizational charters and by-laws—all should be kept on file and updated. Even better, computerized listings of such facts offer easier access when research is called for in these areas.

Another unobtrusive method is content analysis, the primary purpose of which is to describe a message or set of messages. For example, an organization with news releases that are used frequently by local newspapers can't be certain, without research, whether the image conveyed by its releases is that which the organization seeks. By analyzing the news coverage, the firm can get a much clearer idea of the effectiveness of its communications. Such content analysis might be organized along the following specific criteria:

- **Frequency of coverage**   How many releases were used?
- **Placement within the paper**   Did releases appear more frequently on page 1 or 71?
- **People reached**   What was the circulation of the publications in which the releases appeared?
- **Messages conveyed**   Did the releases used express the goals of the organization, or were they simply informational in content?

FIGURE 6–6   A typical communication audit will gather subjective information on how an organization is perceived by its major constituencies, to determine what communications systems are being used, which are the most effective, and whether the information being transmitted is regarded as sufficient by recipients.

- **Editing of releases** How much did the newspaper edit the copy submitted? Were desired meanings materially changed?
- **Attitude conveyed** Was the reference positive, negative, or neutral to the organization?

Another unobtrusive method, the readability study, helps a communicator determine whether messages are written at the right educational level for the audience. Typical measures include the Flesch Formula, the FOG Index, and the SMOG Index—all based on the concept that the greater the number of syllables in a passage, the more difficult and less readable the text.[8]

Clearly, there is nothing particularly mysterious or difficult about unobtrusive methods of research. Such methods are relatively simple to apply, yet they are essential in arriving at appropriate modifications for an ongoing public relations program.

EVALUATIVE RESEARCH

No matter what type of public relations research is used, results of the research and the research project itself should always be evaluated. In evaluating after-the-fact, researchers can learn how to improve future efforts. Were the target audiences surveyed the right ones? Were the research assumptions applied to those audiences correct? Were questions from research tools left unanswered?

Research results can be evaluated in a number of ways. Perhaps the most common in public relations is a seat-of-the-pants evaluation, where anecdotal observation and practitioner judgment are used to estimate the effectiveness of the public relations program. Such evaluation might be based on feedback from members of a key public, personal media contacts, or colleagues, but the practitioner alone evaluates the success of the program with subjective observation.

More scientific evaluation results from public relations opinion polls and surveys and fact finding research, such as content analysis, where the numerical tabulation of results is evaluated and often combined with seat-of-the-pants observation. One of the most effective evaluative techniques to determine the success of a program is to pretest target audiences prior to the implementation of the public relations program and then posttest after the program's completion. A comparison of the results of the two tests enables a more scientific assessment of the program's success.

The evaluation of most public relations research is by no means foolproof. One 1986 study revealed that few public relations research efforts satisfied generally accepted criteria for establishing causality: (1) time ordering—implementation of the campaign before changes are observed, (2) correlation—relationship between campaign objectives and observed changes, and (3) parsimoniousness—an economical research design that rules out all alternative explanations (in other words, being sure the public relations campaign caused the change).[10]

USING OUTSIDE RESEARCH HELP

Despite its occasional rough spots, public relations research has made substantial gains in recent years in quantifying the results of public relations activities. Counseling firms—such as Hill and Knowlton, Ketchum Public Relations, and Doremus Porter Novelli—have even organized separate departments to conduct attitude and opinion surveys as well as other types of research projects.

Ketchum, for example, has devised a computer-based measurement system that evaluates public relations results on both a quantitative and qualitative basis. The Ketchum system focuses on the differences in placement of publicity, that is, where in a periodical publicity has a better chance of being noticed. Although the Ketchum system cannot predict attitudinal or behavioral change, it nonetheless is a step forward in providing practitioners with a mechanism to assess the extent to which their publicity has been seen.

It often makes sense to use outside counsel for research assistance. In evaluating the performance of outside consultants, practitioners should ask the following questions:[11]

1. From what population is the sample drawn, and is it the right population?
2. Are random sampling techniques used?
3. Is the sample size adequate?
4. Has the researcher specified the margin of error?
5. If data are broken into subcategories, are the margins of error for each category specified, and are they adequate?
6. Is the method of contact—telephone, mail, or personal interview—justified?
7. Are interviewers professionally trained?
8. Is the timing of interviews right; have results been contaminated by external events?
9. Are the survey questions precise, objective, and clear?
10. Does the researcher have a vested interest in the survey results? For example, when Pete Dawkins ran for the U.S. Senate in New Jersey in 1988, he sent out a questionnaire that asked voters to answer yes or no on the following "objective" survey questions concerning the two candidates:
    - Can you cite one specific accomplishment made by Frank Lautenberg since he became our U.S. Senator?
    - Were you aware that Frank Lautenberg has voted to increase taxes 12 times?
    - Were you aware that Frank Lautenberg voted for a pay increase for senators less than six months after he was elected?
    - Pete Dawkins was in the top of his West Point class, a Heisman Trophy winner, a Rhodes Scholar, earned a Master's and Ph.D. from Princeton, and became the youngest general in the U.S. Army, followed by success in the world of business. Do you feel Pete Dawkins has the leadership we need for New Jersey in the U.S. Senate?

YOU MAKE THE CALL

The Cuyhoda County Questionnaire

Patty Kay is director of public information for Cuyhoda County. In anticipation of the county's attempt to attract industry from other parts of the region, Kay plans an attitude survey of Cuyhoda County residents to reveal the benefits they see in living in the county. She hopes to discover the qualities that make Cuyhoda County attractive to most people, as well as any unattractive qualities that may annoy residents.

Here's her survey.

1. Do you enjoy living in Cuyhoda County?
   (Very much, considerably, not at all)
2. What is the most attractive quality about the county?
   (Schools, transportation access, recreation)
3. What is the most unattractive quality of the county?
   (Crime, climate, racial mix)
4. On the whole, how would you rate Cuyhoda County as a place to work?
   (Excellent, good, poor)
5. How important to you is continued industrial development in the county?
   (Very important, not very important, no opinion)
6. On a scale of 1 to 5, how would you rate your enthusiasm toward Cuyhoda County?
   (1, 2, 3, 4, 5)
7. If you were asked to list the major benefit that a new resident could expect by moving to Cuyhoda County, what would it be?

Thank you.

QUESTIONS

1. Do you think Kay will be able to derive meaningful results from the data she collects?
2. How would you rate her questions in terms of specificity?
3. Will each question evoke only one answer?
4. What problems are raised by the format of the questionnaire? by the wording of the questions? by the choice of language?

Often before turning to outside consultants, the best first step is to determine whether research has already been done on your topic. Because research assistance is expensive, it makes little sense to reinvent the wheel. It is much wiser to piggyback on existing research.

FUTURE OF PUBLIC RELATIONS RESEARCH

Because today's management wants proof that public relations departments are worth what they're paid, research in the field will undoubtedly continue to increase in importance. To be sure, it has a ways to go. In the spring of 1988 Ketchum Public Relations conducted a comprehensive nationwide survey on public relations research, measurement, and evaluation among 253 public relations executives, counselors, and academicians. The results were revealing.

- First, 32 percent agreed strongly and 44 percent agreed somewhat that research is an essential component of the public relations planning, program development, and evaluation process. Only 24 percent disagreed.
- However, 93 percent said that "in actual fact, research is still talked about much more in public relations than it is actually being done." Of those interviewed, 54 percent agreed strongly with that statement.
- Only 57 percent thought it is possible to measure public relations outcome, impact, and effectiveness in precise terms; 43 percent believed it is not possible to measure public relations outcomes precisely.
- By a 71 percent-to-28 percent margin, respondents thought that most public relations research is for the planning of programs and activities, rather than for measuring and evaluating public relations effectiveness.

The intelligent use of research represents a technology for both defining problems and evaluating solutions. The day of the seat-of-the-pants practitioner is over. Even though intuitive judgment remains a coveted and important skill, management must see measurable results. As the editor of *Public Relations Journal* put it,

> The pressure is on. Public relations results and effectiveness will either measure up under searching examination by vigilant and cost-conscious managements, or the profession will languish in a melange of press agentry, publicity, and promotion.[12]

Nonetheless, informed managements recognize that public relations may never reach a point where its results can be fully quantified. Management confidence is still a prerequisite for active and unencumbered programs. However, such confidence can only be enhanced as practitioners become more adept in using research.

NOTES

1. Ray Chapman, "Measurement: It Is Alive and Well in Chicago," *Public Relations Journal* (May 1982): 28.
2. John V. Pavlik, *Public Relations: What Research Tells Us* (Newbury Park, CA: Sage Publications, 1987), 16.
3. Robert Van Riper, "The Uses of Research in Public Relations," *Public Relations Journal* (February 1976): 18.
4. Walter K. Lindenmann, "Opinion Research: How It Works; How to Use It," *Public Relations Journal* (January 1977): 13.
5. Walter K. Lindenmann, *Attitude and Opinion Research: Why You Need It/How To Do It*, 3d ed. (Washington, DC: Council for Advancement and Support of Education, 1983), 35–38.
6. David L. Nasser, "How to Run a Focus Group," *Public Relations Journal* (March 1988): 33–34.
7. Seymour Hamilton, "Selling the CEO on a Communication Audit," *IABC Communication World* (May 1988): 33.
8. Pavlik, *What Research Tells Us*, 39.
9. Kalman B. Druck, Merton Fiur, and Don Bates, *New Technology in Public Relations* (New York: Foundation for Public Relations Research and Education, 1987), 15–20.
10. Pavlik, *What Research Tells Us*, 68.
11. Michael Ryan, "Ten Criteria for Getting Good Research," *Public Relations Journal* (July 1983): 18–19.
12. Leo J. Northart, "Editor's Notebook," *Public Relations Journal* (July 1979): 8.

SUGGESTED READINGS

Abrahamson, Mark. *Social Research Methods*. Englewood Cliffs, NJ: Prentice-Hall, 1983.

Attitude and Opinion Research: Why You Need It/How to Do It. 3d ed. Washington, DC: Case (11 DuPont Circle).

Awards, Honors, Prizes. Detroit, MI: Gale Research Co. (Book Tower).

Babbie, Earl R. *The Practice of Social Research*. 4th ed. Belmont, CA: Wadsworth, 1986.

Beiswinger, George L. "Database Update." *Public Relations Journal* (March 1982): 37–39.

Blackstrom, Charles H., and Gerald Hursh-Cesar. *Survey Research*. 2d ed. New York: Wiley, 1981.

Brownstone, D. M. *Where to Find Business Information: A Worldwide Guide for Everyone Who Needs the Answers to Business Questions*. New York: John Wiley & Sons.

Chapman, Ray. "Measurement: It Is Alive and Well In Chicago," *Public Relations Journal* (May 1982): 28–29. A survey of PRSA chapter members reveals broad support for measuring the effectiveness of public relations programs and the use of a variety of tools.

Dillman, Don A. *Mail and Telephone Surveys: The Total Design Method*. New York: Wiley, 1978.

Druck, Kalman B., Merton Fiur, and Don Bates. *New Technology in Public Relations*. New York: Foundation for Public Relations Research and Education, 1987.

Erdos, Paul L. *Professional Mail Surveys*. New York: McGraw-Hill, 1970.

Finn, Peter. "Demystifying Public Relations." *Public Relations Journal* (May 1982): 12–17.

———. "How PR Can Use Research." *Public Relations Journal* (May 1982): 12ff.

FORTUNE 500 Directory (250 W. 49th St., New York, NY 10019).

The Foundation Directory. New York: The Foundation Center (79 5th Ave.), 1988.

Frey, J. H. *Survey Research by Telephone*. Beverly Hills, CA: Russell Sage Foundation, 1983.

Hamilton, Seymour. "Selling the CEO on a Communication Audit." *Communication World* (IABC, 870 Market St., San Francisco, CA 94102). (May 1988): 33, 34.

Hill, Don. "In Search of Excellence." *Public Relations Journal* (May 1982): 36–37.

How to Find Business Intelligence in Washington. Washington, DC: Washington Researchers Publishing Co., 1988.

"Importance of Polls in Public Relations," *Social Science Monitor* (February 1983): 1ff.

International Directory of Special Events & Festivals. Chicago, IL: Special Events Reports (213 W. Institute Place).

Investor Relations Almanac/Resource Directory. New York: Corporate Shareholder Press (271 Madison Ave.).

Jeffcoat, A. E. "A Touch of Amazement." *Public Relations Journal* (May 1981): 34–36.

Katz, Elaine Falk. "Measuring the Measurers." *Public Relations Journal* (May 1982): 30–31, 33.

Kopec, Joseph A. "The Communication Audit." *Public Relations Journal* (May 1982): 24–27.

Krippendorff, Klaus. *Content Analysis: An Introduction to Its Methodology*. Beverly Hills, CA: Russell Sage Foundation, 1980.

Leffingwell, Roy J. "Flying by the Seat of Our Pants." *Public Relations Quarterly* (Summer 1981): 25.

———. "Recognizing There Is a Problem." *Public Relations Quarterly* (Spring 1981): 29.

———. "Social Science Research Findings Could Save Us a Great Deal of Money." *Public Relations Quarterly* (Winter 1981–82): 30.

Lindenmann, Walter. *Attitude and Opinion Research: Why You Need It/How to Do It*. Washington, DC: Council for Advancement and Support of Education, 1983.

———. "Polls: Are We Taking Them Too Literally?" *Public Relations Journal* (May 1981): 21–23. Practitioners rely heavily on polls, which could lead to some wrong answers and, even worse, some fatal conclusions.

Makower, J., and A. Green, eds. *Instant Information*. Englewood Cliffs, NJ: Prentice-Hall, 1987.

Nagel, Gerald S.. "Finding a Better Way to Spend Your Time." *Public Relations Journal* (May 1982): 18–20. Content analysis is an easy, do-it-yourself way to increase effectiveness and quality of work.

———. "How to Conduct Basic Research." *Public Relations Journal* (May 1981): 26–29. This step-by-step procedure tells how to conduct a do-it-yourself survey.

Nasser, David L. "How to Run a Focus Group." *Public Relations Journal* (March 1988): 33, 34.

Newsletter on Newsletters (P.O. Box 311, Rhinebeck, NY 12572). Weekly.

Palshaw, John L. "Full Service Research." Pebble Beach, CA: Palshaw Measurement (P.O. Box 1439), September/October 1987.

———. "The Planning of Research." Pebble Beach, CA: Palshaw Measurement (P.O. Box 1439), November/December 1987. The author points out those items that must be considered to make a research plan work.

Pavlik, John. *Public Relations: What Research Tells Us*. Newbury Park, CA: Sage Publications, 1987.

Professional's Guide to Public Relations Services. New York: R. Weiner (888 7th Ave.), 1985.

Public Interest Profiles (250 activist groups). Washington DC: Foundation for Public Affairs (1255 23rd St., NW).

Reardon, Kathleen Kelly. "The ABCs of Research." *Public Relations Journal* (May 1981): 21–23.

Robinson, Edward J. *Public Relations and Survey Research*. New York: Appleton-Century-Crofts, 1969.

Smith, Rea W. "25 Years of Shoring Up the Profession." *Public Relations Journal* (May 1981): 38–40.

Strenski, James B. "New Concerns for Measurement." *Public Relations Journal* (May 1981): 16–17.

———. "Techniques for Measuring Public Relations Effectiveness." *Public Relations Quarterly* (Spring 1982): 21–24.

Television & Cable Factbook. 2 vols. Washington, DC: TV Digest (1836 Jefferson Place, NW).

Toth, Elizabeth L. "Broadening Research in Public Affairs." *Public Relations Review* (Summer 1986): 27–36.

Researching a Position for Alan Louis General

The administrator at Alan Louis General Hospital confronted a problem that he hoped research could help solve. Alan Louis General, although a good hospital, was smaller than most of Houston's other hospitals and less well known. In its area alone it competed with 20 other medical facilities. Alan Louis needed a "position" that it could call unique to attract patients to fill its beds.

For a long time the Alan Louis administrator, Sven Rapcorn, had believed in the principle that truth will out. Build a better mousetrap, and the world will beat a path to your door. Erect a better hospital, and your beds will forevermore be 98 percent filled. Unfortunately, Rapcorn learned, the real world seldom recognizes truth at first blush.

In the real world, more often than not, perception will triumph. And because people act on perceptions, those perceptions become reality. Successful positioning, Rapcorn learned, is based on recognizing and dealing with people's perceptions. And so Rapcorn set out with research to build on existing perceptions about Alan Louis General.

In the first step Rapcorn talked to his own doctors and trustees to gather data about their perceptions, not only of Alan Louis General but also of other hospitals in the community. From this data gathering, pictures of each major competitor began to emerge. For example, the University Health Center had something for everybody—exotic care, specialized care, and basic, bread-and-butter care. Houston General was a huge, well-respected hospital, whose reputation was so good that only a major tragedy could

shake its standing in the community. Mercy Hospital was known for its trauma center. And so on. As for Alan Louis itself, doctors and trustees said that it was a great place to work, that excellent care was provided, and that the nursing staff was particularly friendly and good. The one problem, everyone agreed, was that "nobody knows about us."

The second step in Rapcorn's research project was to test attributes important in health care. Respondents were asked to rank eight factors in order of importance and tell Rapcorn and his staff how each of the surveyed hospitals rated on those factors. The research instrument used a semantic differential scale of 1 to 10, with 1 the worst and 10 the best possible score. Questionnaires were sent to two groups: 1,000 area residents and 500 former Alan Louis patients.

The third step in the research was to tabulate results. Among area residents responding, the eight attributes were ranked accordingly:

1. Surgical care—9.23
2. Medical equipment—9.20
3. Cardiac care—9.16
4. Emergency services—8.96
5. Range of medical services—8.63
6. Friendly nurses—8.62
7. Moderate costs—8.59
8. Location—7.94

After the attributes were ranked, the hospitals in the survey were ranked for each attribute. On advanced surgical care, the most important feature to area residents, Houston General ranked first, with University

Health Center a close second. Alan Louis was far down on the list. The same was true on virtually every other attribute. Indeed, on nursing care, an area in which its staff thought Alan Louis excelled, the hospital came in dead last in the minds of area residents. Rapcorn was not surprised. The largest hospitals in town scored well on most attributes; Alan Louis trailed the pack.

However, the ranking of hospital scores according to former Alan Louis patients revealed an entirely different story. On surgical care, for example, although Houston General still ranked first, Alan Louis came in a close second. And its scores improved similarly on all other attributes. In fact, in nursing care, where Alan Louis came in last on the survey of area residents, among former patients its score was higher than that of any other hospital. It also ranked first in terms of convenient location and second in terms of costs, range of services, and emergency care.

The fourth step in Rapcorn's research project was to draw some conclusions. He concluded three things.

1. Houston General was still Number 1 in terms of area hospitals.
2. Alan Louis ranked at or near the top on most attributes, according to those who actually experienced care there.
3. Former Alan Louis patients rated the hospital significantly better than the general public did.

In other words, thought Rapcorn, most of those who try Alan Louis like Alan Louis.

The great need was to convince more people to try the hospital.

But how could this be accomplished with a hospital? Other marketers generate trial by sending free samples in the mail, offering cents-off coupons, holding free demonstrations, and the like. Hospitals are more limited in this area. Rapcorn's challenge was to launch a communications campaign to convince prospects to see other area hospitals in a different, less favorable light and/or to give people a specific reason to think about trying Alan Louis. In other words, he needed to come up with a communications strategy that clearly differentiated Alan Louis—admittedly among the smallest hospitals in the area—from the bigger, less personal hospitals in town. Rapcorn was confident that the data he had gathered from the research project was all he needed to come up with a winning idea.

QUESTIONS

1. What kind of communications program would you launch to accomplish Rapcorn's objectives?
2. What would be the cornerstone—the theme—of your communications program?
3. What would be the specific elements of your program?
4. In launching the program, what specific steps would you follow—both inside and outside the hospital—to build support?

Communication: The Backbone of Public Relations

he public relations practitioner is a professional communicator. Above all others in an organization, the practitioner must know how to communicate. And this knowledge sets the public relations professional apart from the others.

Fundamentally, communication is a process of exchanging information, imparting ideas, and making oneself understood by others. It also, importantly, includes understanding others in return. Indeed, understanding is critical to the communications process. If one person sends a message to another, who disregards or misunderstands it, then communication hasn't taken place. But if the idea received is the one intended, then communication has been accomplished. Thus, a boss who sends subordinates mountains of memos isn't necessarily communicating with them. If the idea received is not the one intended, then the sender has done little more than convert personal thoughts to words—and there they lie.

Although all of us are endowed with some capacity for communicating, the public relations practitioner must be better than most. Indeed, the effectiveness of public relations professionals is determined by their own ability to communicate and to counsel others on how to communicate. Before public relations practitioners can earn the respect of management and become trusted advisors, they must demonstrate a mastery of many communications skills— writing, speaking, listening, promoting, and counseling. Just as the controller is expected to be an adept accountant and the legal counsel is expected to be an accomplished lawyer, so, too, is the public relations professional expected to be an expert communicator.

This ability to communicate is the key to success in public relations, although expertise in management and marketing also contributes. Consequently, it's essential that practitioners understand the theory behind interpersonal communications, that is, how people communicate.

Frankie A. Hammond

Frankie Hammond is associate professor of public relations in the College of Journalism and Communications at the University of Florida, where she has taught since 1974. During a five-year period as di-rector of development and placement for the college, Professor Hammond helped more than 1,000 graduates launch their professional careers in public relations, advertising, journalism, and broadcasting. A former reporter and editor, Professor Hammond has also served as acting associate chairman for the University of Florida's Department of Advertising and Public Relations.

What changes have you noticed among public relations students since you first started teaching?
As a group, today's students appear more ambitious than many of the students in my classes during the mid-1970s. Most are goal-oriented, dedicated, and eager to join the work force.

What advice do you give your students who want to become public relations practitioners?
Write. Rewrite. Then write some more. Sharpen your problem-solving capabilities. Get as much practical experience as you can in school and during summers. Join the Public Relations Student Society of America. Take advantage of every opportunity to improve yourself and your abilities.

Why should a student be interested in a career in public relations?

THE S-E-M-D-R APPROACH

Many books have been written on the subject of communication theory. Theoretical explanations of how people communicate vary as much as do the definitions of public relations itself. In its most basic sense, communication commences with a source, who sends a message through a medium to a receiver.

Although there are numerous models of communication, one of the most fundamental is the S-M-R approach. This model suggests that the communication process begins with the source, who issues a message to a receiver, who then decides what action to take, if any, relative to the communication. This

Public relations is such a multifaceted endeavor that any individual with a sharp, inquiring mind should be interested in it. The opportunities for personal and professional growth offer a lifetime of interesting work, interesting people, and a lot of fun.

How easy is it to get a job in the field?
Solid writing ability, common sense, and good judgment are always in demand. There are many entry-level spots for well-rounded, energetic, and skilled new graduates. But the lethargic need not apply.

What distinguishes a good public relations practitioner?
Judgment and ethics, backed by communications skills and a familiarity with the social and behavioral forces that make people tick. An understanding of the public relations process and how it impacts on and is impacted by society is a must. The ability to view problems as opportunities and a good sense of humor are also important.

What is the most significant challenge confronting public relations today?
The constant change in the environment in which public relations operates, and therefore the constant change in its practice, is undoubtedly the most significant challenge today. The successful practitioner must adapt to meet the alterations and variations or become an anachronism.

If you had your career to start over again, what would you do?
Basically, I would do what I have done. I have had a variety of interesting experiences as the result of a willingness to take advantage of opportunities and new directions as they came up. It's added a broader perspective to my thinking. But it would be nice to have this life plus one or two more to do all the things that sound interesting and fun.

What will the state of public relations be like in the year 2000?
Virtually every organization will have a public relations effort. It will be impossible to survive without it. The need for and appreciation of public relations will increase as the field continues to shift away from sheer communications toward counseling and advising. The number of practitioners in top-level jobs will increase by the turn of the century, with more and more CEOs named from the ranks of practitioners.

element of receiver action, or feedback, underscores that good communication always involves dialogue between two or more parties.

The S-M-R model has been modified to include additional elements: (1) an encoding stage, in which the source's original message is translated and conveyed to the receiver; and (2) a decoding stage, in which the receiver interprets the encoded message and takes action. This evolution from the traditional model has resulted in the S-E-M-D-R method, which illustrates graphically the role of the public relations function in modern communications; both the encoding and the decoding stages are of critical importance in communicating any public relations message.

The Source

The source of a message is the central person or organization doing the communicating. The source could be a politician giving a campaign speech, a school announcing curriculum changes, or even, as one superior court judge in Seattle ruled, a topless go-go dancer in the midst of gyrating.*

Although the source usually knows how it wants the message to be received, there is no guarantee that it will be understood that way by the receiver. In many cases—a public speech, for example—the speaker is relatively limited in the ability to influence the interpretation of the message. Gestures, voice tone, and volume can be used to add special importance to certain remarks, but whether the audience understands what is intended may ultimately depend on other factors, particularly the encoder.

The Encoder

What the source wants to relate must be translated from an idea in the mind to a communication. In the case of a campaign speech, a politician's original message may be subject to translation or reinterpretation by at least three independent encoders.

1. The politician may consult a speech writer to help put ideas into words on paper. Speech writers become encoders in first attempting to clearly understand the politician's message and then effectively translating that message into language that an audience will understand and, hopefully, accept.
2. Once the speech is written, it may be further encoded into a news release. In this situation, the encoder—perhaps a different individual from the speech writer—selects what seem to be the most salient points of the speech and provides them to media editors in a fairly brief format.
3. A news editor may take the news release and retranslate it before reporting it to the voters, the ultimate audience of the politician's message.

Thus, the original message in the mind of the politician has been massaged three separate times before it ever reaches the intended receivers. Each time, in all likelihood, the particular encoder has added new subjective shadings to the politician's original message. The very act of encoding depends largely on the encoder's own personal experience.

Words/Semantics   Words are among our most personal and potent weapons. Words can soothe us, bother us, or infuriate us. They can bring us together or drive us apart. They can even cause us to kill or be killed. Words mean different things to different people, depending on their backgrounds, oc-

---

*According to the judge, topless go-go dancing is protected by the First Amendment because it is a way of communicating. "I don't have to like the message to say that she has a right to convey the message," the judge ruled in dismissing charges against a topless dancer ("Dancing to the First Amendment," *Forbes*, 15 September 1972, 23).

cupations, education, or geographic locations. What one word means to you might be dramatically different from what that same word means to your neighbor. The study of what words really mean is called semantics, and the science of semantics is a peculiar one indeed.

Words are perpetually changing in our language. What's in today is out tomorrow. What a word denotes according to the dictionary may be thoroughly dissimilar to what it connotes in its more emotional or visceral sense. Even the simplest words—*liberal, conservative, profits, consumer activists*—can spark semantic skyrockets. Many times, without knowledge of the territory, the semantics of words may make no sense. Take the word *cool*. In American vernacular a person who is cool is good. A person who is "not so hot" is bad. So *cool* is the opposite of "not so hot." But wait a minute; "not so hot" must also be the opposite of *hot*. Therefore, in a strange and convoluted way, cool must equal hot.

Even more confusing is the language used by various special publics in society, which seems foreign to the uninitiated.

- To a computer analyst a bit and a bomb and a chip are commonplace. The rest of us might have a hard time discerning that a bit is the smallest binary number, a bomb is a piece of computer equipment that ceases to function, and a chip is a tiny wafer of silicon or an equally tiny complete circuit.
- To a human resources manager a 401(k) is a salary deferral plan. A Gantt chart is a bar chart used in project planning and scheduling. And COBRA, of course, is the Consolidated Omnibus Budget Reconciliation Act of 1986, covering employers of 20 or more who offer group health plans.
- And then there are teenagers, whose vocabularies defy description. Sure, *they* know what they're talking about; but do the rest of us have any idea that *fresh* means cool, *dweeb* means nerd, *gleek* means spitting, *deaf* means the same thing as *fresh*, and *biter* is another name for *gleek*?

Finally, there are the dozen words—important for communicators to know—that, according to Yale University, are the most persuasive in the English language: *discovery, easy, new, proven, guarantee, health, love, money, results, safety, save,* and *you*.

The point here is that the words used in the encoding stage have a significant influence on the message conveyed to the ultimate receiver. Thus, the source must depend greatly on the ability of the encoder to accurately understand and effectively translate the true message—with all its semantic complications—to the receiver.

The Message

Once an encoder has taken in the source's ideas and translated them into terms a receiver can understand, the ideas are then transmitted in the form of a message. The message may be carried in a variety of communications media: speeches, newspapers, news releases, press conferences, broadcast reports, and

Chantilly Laced

The Chantilly National Bank and Trust Company was not only a well-known bank in Chantilly, Ohio, but it was also the most prominent financial institution in the entire Midwest. For many years Chantilly's earnings steadily improved, until the Ohio bank had become fully competitive with its rivals on the East and West Coasts. The reputation of Chantilly's management was impeccable. Its people were coveted by other institutions. Its systems, controls, policies, and programs were the envy of the banking industry.

Chantilly's communications approach was equally laudable; its philosophy was one of proactive communications. It regularly held briefings with the media and securities analysts. Its management gave frequent speeches and held leadership positions in industry associations. Management also took strong public positions on industry issues. Chantilly was active politically and was known for its outspokenness in standing up for what it believed in.

That's why in the summer of 1988, it came as a shock to most industry analysts when Chantilly National Bank began experiencing problems.

- First, a front-page article in the *Wall Street Journal* suggested that Chantilly's loan portfolio was in rocky shape. The article pointed out that a number of prominent credits in the Chantilly portfolio were experiencing rough times.
- The *Journal* article was followed by a number of major corporate bankruptcies, each of which seemed to announce Chantilly Bank as a primary lender.
- The coup de grâce occurred in the fall of 1988. A small, Texas bank, known widely for its hip-shooting policies on energy-related loans, declared bankruptcy. It was immediately revealed that a number of much larger banks had participated with the bankrupt Texas institution in lending to questionable energy companies. The most prominent bank among these larger lenders was Chantilly National Bank and Trust Company.

Weeks passed, Chantilly's stock plummeted, but still the bank shunned making a comprehensive public explanation. Instead, it chose to issue cryptic press statements on the earnings impact of its problems. Finally, four weeks after the crisis reached its apex, Chantilly did a communications about-face.

First, senior Chantilly officials flew to New York City to meet with securities analysts in an effort to restore confidence in the bank. At the meeting, which was off limits to the media, the bank discussed specific problem loans in depth. This disclosure was unprecedented in the banking industry. Most financial institutions firmly refuse to discuss particular details of proprietary customer relationships. In this instance, however, Chantilly had sought and received customer approval before doing so.

The next day, back in Ohio, the bank's chairman conducted a wide open press conference, reiterating in detail what the analysts had been told the day before about the bank's problem loans. The immediate impact of the public relations turnaround was positive. The bank's stock, for the first time in a month, experienced a slight increase. One journalist reported that the bank had taken "the extraordinary step of inviting in a handful of reporters and revealing the skeletons of decimated corporations in its closets in an unusual exhibition of candor aimed at restoring its stature in the financial community."

However, despite the excruciating lengths to which Chantilly had gone in detailing specific problem loans, in the days following the press conference, new corporate bankruptcy petitions were filed in which Chantilly was named as a creditor. When asked why the bank had not revealed its problems earlier, Chantilly's chairman cited an Ohio privacy law that, according to legal counsel, "prevented the bank from making such disclosures."

As a macabre postscript (as if things weren't bad enough), in the midst of Chantilly's loan problems the windows on the bank's new San Francisco office tower blew out in a freak storm, injuring pedestrians and causing a furor on the coast. Concluded a harried Chantilly public relations officer, "Who would ever believe this?"

QUESTIONS

1. How would you rate the way Chantilly handled its communications in the face of its problems?
2. Had you been Chantilly's public relations director, what communications course would you have recommended that management take?
3. Do you agree with the timing of the analyst meeting and press conference to disclose Chantilly's problem loans?
4. What about the specific loan problems disclosed at the meetings? From what you know, do you think this was enough disclosure? too much?
5. Again, if you were Chantilly's public relations director, how would you have responded to the suggestion by the bank's legal counsel that Ohio privacy law prevented you from comprehensively discussing your problems?
6. Now that the public relations damage has been done, what communications posture do you think the bank should adopt for the future?

face-to-face meetings. Communications theorists differ on what exactly constitutes the message, but here are three of the more popular explanations.

1. **The content is the message.** According to this theory, which is far and
   away the most popular, the content of a communication—what it says—
   constitutes its message. According to this view, the real importance of a
   communication—the message—lies in the meaning of an article or in the
   intent of a speech. Neither the medium through which the message is being
   communicated nor the individual doing the communicating is as important
   as the content.

2. **The medium is the message.** Other communications theorists—the late
   Canadian professor Marshall McLuhan being the best known—argue that
   the content of a communication is not the message at all. According to
   McLuhan, the content is less important than the vehicle of communication.

   McLuhan's argument stemmed largely from the fact that many people
today watch television. He said that television is a "cool" medium; that is,
someone can derive meaning from a TV message without working too hard.
On the other hand, reading involves hard work to fully grasp an idea; thus,
newspapers, magazines, and books are "hot" media. Furthermore, Mc-
Luhan argued, a television viewer can easily become part of that which is
being viewed. In other words, the television program becomes the message,
and the viewer becomes part of the content of that message. Indeed, the
steady barrage of TV film on the fighting in Vietnam in the 1960s and Lebanon in the 1980s probably influenced public opinion about those wars.
These nightly broadcasts became, for many viewers, antiwar messages.

   One direct outgrowth of this medium-is-the-message theory was the
mid-1970s development of the friendly-team style of local television news
reporting. Often called the eyewitness approach, this format encouraged interaction among TV newscasters in order to involve viewers as part of the
news team family. McLuhan believed that the spread of this format
throughout the country was an example of local media serving "as service
environments that envelop the entire life of man and society in totally new
conditions."[1] Although many have scoffed at McLuhan's somewhat mysti-
cal approach to communications, many politicians have taken the professor's words to heart.

   The medium of television has become particularly important to the
president of the United States. John F. Kennedy literally won the presidential election on the strength of his TV debate performance against Richard
Nixon. President Gerald Ford, although not particularly well known for his
public speaking presence, rehearsed assiduously for TV appearances and
performed well. President Jimmy Carter also took pains with his TV image,
occasionally dressing casually—in cardigan sweaters rather than dark
suits—to subtly convey a message of confidence, informality, and the antithesis of the imperial presidency.

   In recent years the best use of television to its maximum advantage
for the White House was made by Ronald Reagan. Clearly, he had the most

Are You Sure It Means What You Think It Means?

Words can get you in a lot of trouble. Public relations professionals, who deal on a daily basis with the arcane province of semantics, must be aware of and sensitive to the potential explosiveness of words and phrases. The following random list of culturally biased phrases is a case in point. How many of these can you adequately define? Are you sure?

- Over the hill
- Cool your jets
- Catch-22
- Out of the blue
- Go for it
- Stonewall it
- A "10"
- We blew it
- A boo-boo
- Get it together

- Jive turkey
- Shot full of holes
- Flipped out
- Circular file
- Deep six it
- Put it on the back burner
- The bottom fell out
- Wasted
- Workhorse
- Taking care of business (TCBing)

experience in the medium, having begun as a movie actor and later becoming a media spokesman for General Electric. Just how good Reagan was on television was underscored in his debates with 1984 Democratic candidate Walter Mondale; Reagan revealed himself as a witty, articulate, unflappable performer. During his term President Reagan used television to boost virtually every important administration program, from budget cuts to strategic defense to relations with the Soviets. In 1985 the president literally bypassed the 3,000 reporters at the United States–Soviet summit in Geneva to personally critique the meeting before a televised session of Congress. "Maybe it's the old broadcaster in me," Reagan told the American people, "but I decided to file my own report directly to you." In 1988 Reagan wowed the Soviet people with a bravura performance in Russia at the fourth summit, including an eloquent speech at Moscow University and meetings with refuseniks and other dissidents—all of which was played back to the United States on TV.

President Reagan's overwhelmingly effective use of the TV medium was as good an indication as any that future presidential aspirants and officeholders at all levels will continue to regard TV as the primary vehicle for communicating their messages.

3. **The person is the message.** Still other theorists argue that it is neither the content nor the medium that is the message, but rather the speaker. For example, Hitler was a master of persuasion. His minister of propaganda,

BETWEEN THE LINES

Are You Sure You Saw What You Thought You Saw?

First, read the sentence that follows:

FINISHED FILES ARE THE RESULT OF YEARS OF SCIENTIFIC STUDY COMBINED WITH THE EXPERIENCE OF MANY YEARS.

Now, count the *F*s in the sentence. Count them only once, and do not go back and count them again.

QUESTION
How many *F*s are there?

ANSWER
There are six *F*s. However, because the capital *F* in *OF* sounds like a capital *V*, it seems to disappear. Most people perceive only three *F*s in the sentence. Our conditioned, habitual patterns (mental blocks) restrict us from being as alert as we should be. Frequently, we fail to perceive things as they really are.

Josef Goebbels, used to say, "Any man who thinks he can persuade, can persuade." Hitler practiced this self-fulfilling communications prophecy to the hilt. Feeding on the perceived desires of the German people, Hitler was concerned much less with the content of his remarks than with their delivery. His maniacal rantings and frantic gestures seized public sentiment and sent friendly crowds into a frenzy. In every way Hitler himself was the primary message of his communications.

Today, in a similar vein, we often refer to a leader's charisma. Frequently, the charismatic appeal of a political leader may be more important than what that individual says. President John F. Kennedy, for example, could move an audience by the very inflection of his words. Jesse Jackson can bring a group to its feet, merely by shaking a fist or raising the pitch of his voice.

Often, people cannot distinguish between the words and the person who speaks them. The words, the face, the body, the eyes, the attitude, the timing, the wit, the presence—all form a composite that, as a whole, influences the listener. As communications consultant Roger Ailes has put it, it comes down to the like factor in communication. Ailes points out that some candidates get votes just because people like them. "They forget that you're short, or you're fat, or you're bald . . . they say 'I like that guy.' "[2] In such cases the source of the communication becomes every bit as important as the message itself.

The Decoder

After a message has been transmitted, it must be decoded by a receiver before action can be taken. This stage is like the encoding stage in that the receiver takes in the message and translates it into his own common terms. Obviously, language again plays a critical role. The decoder must fully understand the message before acting on it; if the message is unclear or the decoder is unsure of its intent, there's probably little chance that the action taken by the receiver will be the action desired by the source. Messages must be in common terms.

A good example of the problem of uncommon terms is the following fictitious exchange between the Bureau of Standards of the U.S. Department of Commerce and a New York plumber. The plumber had written the bureau to say that she had found hydrochloric acid to be a good drain cleaner and to ask whether the acid was harmless for this purpose.

Washington replied, "The efficacy of hydrochloric acid is indisputable, but the chlorine residue is incompatible with metallic permanence."

The plumber, unfamiliar with scientific terminology, replied that she was mighty glad that the bureau agreed with her.

The bureau answered with a note of alarm: "We cannot assume responsibility for the production of toxic and noxious residues with hydrochloric acid and suggest that you use an alternate procedure."

The plumber replied that she was happy that the bureau still agreed with her.

The bureau finally exploded: "Don't use hydrochloric acid, you jackass. It eats the hell out of your pipes."[3]

Perception

How a receiver decodes a message depends greatly on that person's own perception. How an individual looks at and comprehends a message is a key to effective communications (Figure 7–1). Remember that everyone is biased; no two people perceive a message identically. Personal biases are nurtured by many factors, including stereotypes, symbols, semantics, peer group pressures, and—especially in today's culture—the media.

Stereotypes   Everyone lives in a world of stereotypical figures. Ivy Leaguers, Midwesterners, feminists, bankers, politicians, PR types, and thousands of other characterizations cause people to think of certain specific images. Public figures, for example, are typecast regularly. The dumb blonde, the bigoted blue-collar worker, and the shifty used car salesman are the kinds of stereotypes our society—particularly television—perpetuates.

Consider the plight of the poor businessman. As syndicated cartoonist Charles Saxon wrote, "The big problem for cartoonists is that most businessmen don't fall into comfortable stereotypes."[4] Nonetheless, cartoonists are obligated to come up with stereotypes. Therefore, the ubiquitous businessman

What do you see: Fish or fowl?

FIGURE 7–1 Often what we see may not be what others see. (Hint: there are both white fish and black fowl.) (Courtesy of Trout & Ries)

caricature is middle-aged, looks like he might be posing for a portrait in *Fortune*, rarely relaxes his facial features, and, in general, looks overblown and pompous.

Like it or not, most of us are victims of such stereotypes. For example, research indicates that a lecture delivered by a person wearing glasses will be perceived as "significantly more believable" than the same lecture delivered before the same audience by the same lecturer without glasses. The stereotyped impression of people with glasses is that they are more trustworthy and more believable.

Symbols The clenched fist salute, the swastika, and the thumbs up sign all leave distinct impressions with most people. Marshaled properly, symbols can be used as effective persuasive elements. The Statue of Liberty, the Red Cross, the Star of David, and many other symbols have been used traditionally for positive persuasion. Indeed, in the Falkland Islands invasion by Argentina in 1982, England used the symbol of its queen—and the honor of the crown—to stimulate public sentiment behind the war effort to win the islands back. Later that same year, a disgruntled antinuclear activist tried to hold the Washington

Monument hostage as a symbol of a threatened nation. In the Mideast in the mid-1980s, Shiite fundamentalists burned the American flag as a symbol of the American "satan."

Semantics   Public relations professionals make their living largely by knowing how to use words to effectively communicate desired meanings. Occasionally, this is tricky, since the same words may hold contrasting meanings for different people. Especially vulnerable are popular and politically sensitive phrases such as "capital punishment," "law and order," "liberal politician," "right winger," and on and on until you reach the point where the Oakridge Mall in San Jose, California, demanded that the gourmet hamburger restaurant on its premises, with a logo depicting a smiling hamburger with a monacle and top hat, either change its "suggestive name" or leave the mall. The restaurant's name? Elegant Buns.

In the 1990s the label *terrorist,* a misnomer that the media have bestowed on those who hijack planes and blow up airport terminals, may play right into the hands of those who attack innocent civilians. Since behavioral science studies show that such people seek the aura of power, calling them terrorists concedes that they are, in fact, achieving their aims. One semanticist argued that such criminals should be called condemned barbarians or savages, rather than terming "a puny misfit as a great terrorist."[5]

Semantics must be handled with extreme care because language and the meanings of words change constantly. Good communicators always consider the consequences of the words they plan to use *before* using them.

Peer Groups   In one famous study, students were asked to point out, in progression, the shortest of three lines.

A _____

B _____

C _____

Although Line B is obviously the shortest, each student in the class except one was told in advance to answer that Line C was the shortest. The object of the test was to see whether the one student would agree with his peers. Results generally indicated that, to a statistically significant degree, all students, including the uncoached one, chose C. Peer pressure prevails.

Media   The power of the media—particularly as an agenda setter or reinforcement mechanism—is also substantial. A common complaint among lawyers is that their clients cannot receive fair trials because of pretrial publicity leading to preconceived verdicts among potential jurors who read newspapers and watch television.

In one famous case in North Carolina, Army officer Jeffrey MacDonald was put on trial in 1970 for the savage killing of his wife and two children. The officer claimed that he was innocent and that a band of hippies had stabbed him and killed his family. State newspapers publicized the case extensively, running photographs of the soldier and commentary about the circumstances of the murders. Neither the soldier nor his lawyer would talk to the press. A random telephone survey, taken a week before the trial, indicated that most people thought the soldier was guilty. Several weeks later, however, the Army dropped murder charges against him when it couldn't make a case. Ironically, nine years later the man was convicted of those murders, subsequently released, and then found guilty on appeal. In 1985 MacDonald's story was the subject of a scathing book and a television docu-drama, "Fatal Vision," after which subsequent appeals were flatly rejected.

The point remains that people often base perceptions on what they read or hear without bothering to dig further to elicit the facts of the situation. Although appearances are sometimes revealing, they are often deceiving.

The Receiver

You really aren't communicating unless someone is at the other end to hear and understand what you're saying. This situation is analogous to the old mystery of the falling tree in the forest: does it make a noise when it hits the ground if there's no one there to hear it? Regardless of the answer, communication doesn't take place if a message doesn't reach the intended receivers and exert the desired effect on those receivers.[6]

Sometimes, even though the message reaches the correct receivers, their perceptions of that message are not what was intended, as in the following examples:

> When [the former addict] . . . was put in charge of an antidrug addiction program, [he] . . . commented . . . "The first thing that impressed me . . . was that people were talking about things I didn't understand. *Values*—that's what you get when you go to Macy's; *principles*—those are the guys in schools; *conviction*—that's what you get when you go in front of a judge."

> When it was first offered, only four girls enrolled in a special female weight lifting course at the University of California. The following semester, the instructor changed the course name from Weight Lifting to Weight Training for Figure Control. A short time later, 200 women had enrolled in the course.[7]

Even if a communication is understood clearly, there is no guarantee that the motivated action will be the desired one. In fact, a message may trigger several different effects.

1. **It may change attitudes.** This result, however, is very tough to accomplish and rarely happens.
2. **It may crystallize attitudes.** This outcome is much more common. Often a message will influence receivers to take actions they might already have been thinking about taking but needed an extra push to accomplish. For example, a receiver might want to contribute to a certain charity, but seeing

The Erring Encoder

To swing the election, Representative Rankle desperately needed the votes of the Booneville Urban League chapter. "It's up to you, Herby," Rankle confided to his chief speech writer, Herbert Mertz, "to make sure we get the key points across in my speech tonight, to let 'em know I'm up to speed on the issues—particularly campaign contributors and busing." On the former issue, Rankle was well aware of rumors that his campaign was subsidized by several underworld figures. On the latter issue, Rankle knew that the recent burning of a school bus had created an enormous amount of tension among Urban League members.

"Make it clear, Herby, that I am against revealing the names of campaign contributors because I believe in protecting an individual's right to privacy, and I don't intend to focus the spotlight of public attention on those who have contributed to my campaign. I wouldn't like it if I were they, and I know they wouldn't either. As far as busing, let 'em know that I know the debate is a hot one, but that I simply will not accept the old, pat answers. I intend to seek revolutionary solutions on this issue of heated debate."

"I understand perfectly, Congressman," Mertz smiled. "Just leave the writing to me."

Regrettably for Rankle, that's exactly what he did. It took only a few sentences to convince the audience that Rankle was either crooked, stupid, insensitive, or a combination of all three. Here's how his speech began: "I intend tonight, ladies and gentlemen, to address two subjects that I know are on your minds—campaign contributors and busing. On the former, I believe quite strongly that a candidate should never disclose the names of his campaign contributors. I know my contributors well, and I know that such disclosure would frankly embarrass them. Were I in their position, I have no doubt that I, too, would be embarrassed.

"Let me be equally frank on school busing—indeed, another burning issue in our community. Neither I nor my running mates will sit by when others call for the old pat solutions. We will fight their every move. In a word, my colleagues and I are revolting! Tonight, I intend to prove it."

QUESTIONS

1. Where did Mertz go wrong in encoding the message?
2. Might Mertz have believed his encoding was correct?
3. How many faux pas did Rankle commit in his remarks? Might they be enough to cost him the election?
4. Had you been Mertz, what would you have done differently in encoding the speech?

a child's photo on a contribution canister might crystallize the attitude sufficiently to trigger action.

3. **It might create a wedge of doubt.** Communication can sometimes force receivers to modify their points of view. A persuasive message can cause receivers to question their original thinking on an issue.

4. **It may do nothing.** Often, communication results in no action at all. When the American Cancer Society waged an all-out effort to cut into cigarette sales, the net impact of the communication campaign was hardly significant.

Feedback

Feedback is critical to the process. A communicator must get feedback from a receiver to know what messages are or are not getting through and how to structure future communications. Occasionally, feedback is ignored by professional communicators, but this is always a mistake.

Whether the objectives of a communication have been met can often be assessed by such things as the amount of sales, number of letters, or number of votes obtained. If individuals take no action after receiving a communication, feedback must still be sought. In certain cases, although receivers have taken no discernible action, they may have understood and even passed on the message to other individuals. This person-to-person relay of received messages creates a two-step flow of communications: (1) vertically from a particular source and (2) horizontally from interpersonal contact. The targeting of opinion leaders as primary receivers is based on the hope that they will distribute received messages horizontally within their own communities.

In any event, it's always a sound investment to research how many people saw or heard a message, how many agreed with it, how many acted on it, and what action they took. Without measurement an organization is communicating blindly.

PUBLIC RELATIONS PERSUASION

As discussed in chapter 4, the goal of most public relations messages is persuasion rather than simple information. In most cases, after a public relations problem has been researched and a strategy conceived, an action phase of communication commences, generally designed to persuade. Again, such persuasion should be ethical, rather than relying on scare tactics or appealing to hateful notions.

Public relations practitioners should be familiar with the variety of communication approaches available, from interpersonal to small group to mass audience. The media available for such communications are myriad—everything from interpersonal speech to visual aids to skywriting. In recent years, innovations—electronic technology, electronic mail, electronic conferencing, desktop publishing, and the like—have speeded public relations messages.

Whaaat?

Extra credit for anyone who can decode the following sentence:

> We respectfully petition, request, and entreat that due and adequate provision be made, this day and the date herein after subscribed, for the satisfying of this petitioner's nutritional requirements and for the organizing of such methods as may be deemed necessary and proper to assure the reception by and for said petitioner of such quantities of baked products as shall, in the judgment of the aforesaid petitioner, constitute a sufficient supply thereof.*

Whaaat?

---

*Give us this day our daily bread.

The ultimate communication is influenced by many factors: emotional reactions, superstitions, physical conditions, prejudices, indifference to the message, and numerous others. A smart communicator must be aware of the common mistakes that people make when they communicate.

- **Failing to listen well**   Most people are poor listeners. If you're doing more than half the talking when you're in a meeting with others, then you should improve your listening skills. Listeners should be active.
- **Failing to use the "you" approach**   People are interested in what's in it for them, not what you or the organization desires. A "you" approach communicates to the recipient that the speaker cares about the recipient's needs.
- **Sending the wrong nonverbal signals**   Experts say that 65 percent of a message is conveyed nonverbally in face-to-face communication. People look for such things as body position and movement, gestures, facial expression, eye contact, silence, use of space and time, and so on.
- **Failing to write to be understood**   Many people write to *im*press, not to *ex*press. They use long, pompous words in the mistaken belief that such words add dignity and strength to their messages. They don't.
- **Lacking knowledge of audiences**   Communicators must relate their messages to the specific characteristics, needs, and interests of their audiences. They should know such things as educational levels and occupations, beliefs and attitudes, group loyalties and norms, and the disposition of the audience—friendly, hostile, or indifferent.
- **Failing to realize that communication is a two-way process**   Many think communication is finished when information is imparted. They fail to consider that communication involves getting feedback and evaluating it.

■ **Failing to observe common courtesies** If communicators come across as impersonal or rude, their ability to communicate with people will suffer. On the other hand, if they are respectful of others and treat them courteously, their audiences will listen to what is said. More importantly, they are apt to understand and appreciate the message.[8]

There really is no trick to effective communication. Other than some facility with techniques, hard work and common sense are the basic guiding principles. Naturally, communication must follow performance; organizations must back up what they say with action. Slick brochures, engaging speeches, intelligent articles, and a good press may capture the public's attention; but in the final analysis the only way to obtain continued public support is through proper performance.

NOTES

1. Marshall McLuhan, "Sharing the News, Friendly Teamness; Teeming Friendliness," brochure, McLuhan Associates and American Broadcasting Companies, 1971.
2. "The 'Like Factor' in Communications," *Executive Communications* (February 1988): 1.
3. Bertram R. Canfield and H. Frazier Moore, *Public Relations Principles: Cases and Problems* (Homewood, IL: Richard D. Irwin, 1973), 67, 68.
4. Charles Saxon, "How to Draw a Businessman," *New York Times*, 28 March 1982, 2F.
5. "Semantics Power," *PR Reporter* (4 April 1988): 4.
6. H. Zane Robins (vice president and general manager of Burson-Marsteller Associates), remarks at a meeting of the American Management Association, Chicago, IL, 20 January 1969.
7. John E. Cook, "Communication Criteria: Necessary and Effective," *Public Relations Journal* (January 1974): 31.
8. Frank Grazian, "Common Mistakes People Make When They Communicate," *Communication Briefings* (August 1987): 8A, B.

Asimov, Isaac. "The Electronic Revolution," *Public Relations Quarterly* (Spring 1982): 4–5.

Baldrige, L. *Complete Guide to Executive Manners.* New York: Rawson Associates, 1985.

Bleecker, Samuel E., and **Thomas V. Lento.** "Public Relations in a Wired Society." *Public Relations Quarterly* (Spring 1982): 6–12.

Brush, Douglas P. "The New Technology." *Public Relations Journal* (February 1981): 10–13.

Budd, John F., Jr. "Credibility vs. 'Con.' " *Public Relations Quarterly* (Spring 1982): 13–14.

Burger, Chester. "The Edge of the Communications Revolution." *Public Relations Review* (Summer 1981): 3–12. Included are predictions of how new communications technology will change corporate America.

Coyle, Lee. "RSVP: The Ohio Bell Approach." *Public Relations Journal* (February 1981): 24.

Crable, Richard, and **Steven Vibbert.** *Public Relations as Communication Management.* Edina, MN: Burgess International Group, 1986.

Degen, C. *Understanding & Using Video: Guide for the Organizational Communicator.* White Plains, NY: Longman, 1985.

Forney, T. Michael. "The New Communication Technology." *Public Relations Journal* (March 1982): 20–23.

Fraser, Edith A. "Association Public Relations: The State of the Art." *Public Relations Journal* (October 1981): 18–21, 30. This description focuses on several important trends occurring in the use of communications in the 1980s and their effect on public relations.

"Glossary of Common Acronyms and Terms of Modern Human Resource Management." Orangeburg, NY: Implementation Support Associates (100 Dutch Hill Road).

Goodman, Ronald, and **Richard S. Ruch.** "In the Image of the CEO." *Public Relations Journal* (February 1981): 14–19.

Grazian, Frank. "Common Mistakes People Make When They Communicate." Blackwood, NJ: Communication Briefings (806 Westminster Blvd.), August 1987. To help people identify areas that could be improved, the author brings some serious communication errors to light. This sheet is a "must read."

Hakensen, David. "Creativity In a 'High-Tech' Mode." *Public Relations Journal* (March 1982): 29.

Hecht, Andrea Platt. "How to Bring Middle Management into the Communication Process." *Public Relations Journal* (October 1981): 16.

Hilton, J. *Straight Talk About Videoconferencing.* Englewood Cliffs, NJ: Prentice-Hall, 1986.

Johnston, David C. H. "Communicating Your Social Role." *Public Relations Journal* (December 1981): 18.

Kopee, Joseph A. "The Communication Audit." *Public Relations Journal* (May 1982): 24–27. This article describes a communication audit: what it does, how to do it, what it costs, and why it should be an essential part of internal and external communication plans and programs.

SUGGESTED READINGS

McCallister, Linda. "The Interpersonal Side of Internal Communications." *Public Relations Journal* (February 1981): 20–23. Most organizations monitor their formal communications, but little attention is given to person-to-person relationships. Here, the communications professional is given tips on how to improve internal communications.

"The New Public Relations." *Public Relations Journal* (January 1981): 29–33.

Personal Image Consultants. New York: Editorial Service (96 State St.).

Prestanski, Harry. "Human Information Processing in the Development and Implementation of Public Relations Programs." *Public Relations Quarterly* (Summer 1981): 16–20.

Ragan Report (Ragan Communications, 407 S. Dearborn, Chicago, IL 60605). Weekly.

Redding, C. *Corporate Manager's Guide to Better Communications*. Glenview, IL: Scott, Foresman & Co., 1984.

Robinson, Edward J. *Communication and Public Relations*. Columbus, OH: Merrill, 1966.

Severin, W., and **J. Tankard**. *Communication Theories, Origins, Methods, Uses*. White Plains, NY: Longman, 1987.

Stevens, Art. *The Persuasion Explosion*. Washington, DC: Acropolis Books, 1985.

Williams, Patrick R. "The New Technology and Its Implications for Organizational Communicators." *Public Relations Quarterly* (Spring 1982): 15–16.

The IUD Notice "Mumbo Jumbo"

For over a decade the A. H. Robins Company was plagued with health claims arising from its Dalkon Shield birth control device. The company began marketing the device in early 1971, only to be implicated three years later in the deaths of four women who had become pregnant while wearing the Dalkon Shield and suffered septic abortions from infection in the uterus. By June 1974 Robins had suspended distribution and sale of the Dalkon Shield, and by January 1975 the product was permanently removed from the market.

Nonetheless, the damage had been done. In 1979 a federal court awarded $6.8 million to a Colorado woman who charged that the use of a Dalkon Shield had caused a miscarriage that almost killed her. Late in 1980 Robins recommended to doctors that they recall all Dalkon Shields.

Late in 1984 Robins started an advertising campaign aimed at convincing women still wearing the device to have it removed. Claims paid by Robins and its insurers at the time amounted to more than $244 million in 7,600 suits involving the device. Midway through 1985 Robins set aside $615 million to settle legal claims from women who had used its Dalkon Shields. But in August, realizing its reserve fund would not be enough to pay the legal expenses for the now 15,500 suits and claims it faced, Robins filed for bankruptcy protection from its creditors.

Shortly thereafter, Robins proposed an international publicity and advertising campaign setting an end-of-the-year deadline for women wishing to file claims against the company. Robins worded its announcement in the following manner:

Any claims filed after December 30, 1985, shall be disallowed. Any person or entity that is required to file a proof of claim and that fails to do so by December 30, 1985, shall not be treated as a creditor for purposes of voting or distribution, and any claim of such person or entity shall be forever barred; provided, however, that a proof of claim for any claim against A. H. Robins, Incorporated, arising out of the rejection by A. H. Robins Company, Incorporated, of a voidable transfer as described in Bankruptcy Code Section 502(g) and 502(h), must be filed on or before the later of December 30, 1985, and 30 days after the entry of an order authorizing the rejection of the executory contract or unexpired lease, or 30 days after the entry of an order or judgment avoiding the transfer.

In October a federal judge ordered the company to simplify the notice because it was written in "legal mumbo jumbo" and not in plain English.

In January 1986 the company's revised, plain English advertising and publicity campaign began with a new claims deadline set for April 30, 1986 (Figure A). At the end of the year, the company faced more than 300,000 claims on behalf of women charging that the Dalkon Shield had caused infertility, involuntary abortions, pelvic disease, and, in some cases, death.

In December 1987 a federal judge said that A.H. Robins would have to set aside about $2.5 billion in its bankruptcy reorganization plan to compensate the women injured by the Dalkon Shield. The judge's estimate was more than double the sum Robins had projected at a hearing the prior month. The company said it would "try to meet the demands" that the judge had set.

IMPORTANT NOTICE
REGARDING THE
DALKON SHIELD INTRAUTERINE
BIRTH CONTROL DEVICE (IUD) AND
A. H. ROBINS COMPANY, INCORPORATED

On August 21, 1985, A. H. Robins Company, Incorporated, the maker of the Dalkon Shield, filed a case under Chapter 11 of the United States Bankruptcy Code.

If you: (a) may have been injured because you used the Dalkon Shield; or

(b) may have used the Dalkon Shield but have not as yet experienced an injury; or

(c) may have been injured because of another person's use of the Dalkon Shield

and if you wish to assert a claim against the A. H. Robins Company, Incorporated, the United States Bankruptcy Court for the Eastern District of Virginia must receive your claim in writing at the Clerk's office or at the address below **on or before April 30, 1986, or you will lose your right to make a claim.** Receipt of a simple statement containing your full name and complete mailing address and the fact that you are making a Dalkon Shield claim will register your claim.

Mail your statement with your full name and complete mailing address to:

Dalkon Shield
P. O. Box 444
Richmond, VA 23203
U.S.A.

Mail your claim promptly. Each claimant is required to file a separate claim. You do not need a lawyer to file a claim.

After your claim is registered, you will be sent a questionnaire with additional instructions. You must complete this questionnaire and return it or your claim may be disallowed. Claimants residing in the United States must return the questionnaire by June 30, 1986. Claimants residing outside the United States must return the questionnaire by July 30, 1986.

If you have already filed a claim with the United States Bankruptcy Court for the Eastern District of Virginia, do not file a second claim as your claim is already registered. You also will be sent a formal questionnaire with additional instructions with which you must comply.

An Important Health Warning To Women Using An IUD

If you are still using an intrauterine birth control device (IUD) inserted in the early to mid 1970s, this message is for you. Many women had an IUD called the Dalkon Shield inserted during that time. It is important that each Dalkon Shield be removed, since there is substantial medical opinion that its continued use may pose a serious personal health hazard. If you are still using a Dalkon Shield, A. H. Robins Company will pay your doctor or clinic to remove it.

A. H. Robins ceased distribution of the Dalkon Shield in 1974. Many claims have been made that the device causes health problems, including pelvic infections, that may result in serious injury or death. In 1980, A. H. Robins advised doctors to remove the Dalkon Shield from any woman still using it. In 1983, the U.S. Food and Drug Administration and other government agencies issued the same advice based on their concern about pelvic infections among Dalkon Shield users.

A. H. Robins will pay your doctor or clinic for any examination needed to find out if you are using the Dalkon Shield. If you are, A. H. Robins will pay the cost of having it removed.

The Dalkon Shield

WHAT TO DO

If you know you are using a Dalkon Shield IUD, or if you are using an IUD inserted in the early to mid 1970s and are unsure of the kind, call your doctor or health clinic for an appointment. Your call will be in confidence, and there will be no cost to you.

If you have further questions, please call A. H. Robins Company toll free. The number is **1-800-247-7220.** (In Virginia call collect **804-257-2015.**)

A·H·ROBINS
1407 Cummings Drive, Richmond, Virginia 23220

FIGURE A (Courtesy of A. H. Robins Co.)

QUESTIONS

1. Does it appear to you that Robins acted in good faith through the Dalkon Shield controversy?

2. Does the fact that Robins insisted that its product "posed no greater risk to its users than any other intrauterine device" change your answer to Question 1?

3. Do you think the judge was justified in making the company revise the wording of its deadline announcement?

4. How might you have worded the ultimate announcement?

For further information about the Dalkon Shield controversy, see Christopher Policano, "A. H. Robins and the Dalkon Shield," *Public Relations Journal* (March 1985): 17–21; Stuart Diamond, "Robins in Bankruptcy Filing Cites Dalkon Shield Claims," *New York Times,* 22 August 1985, 1; Francine Schwadel, "Robins and Plaintiffs Face Uncertain Future," *Wall Street Journal,* 23 August 1985, 4.

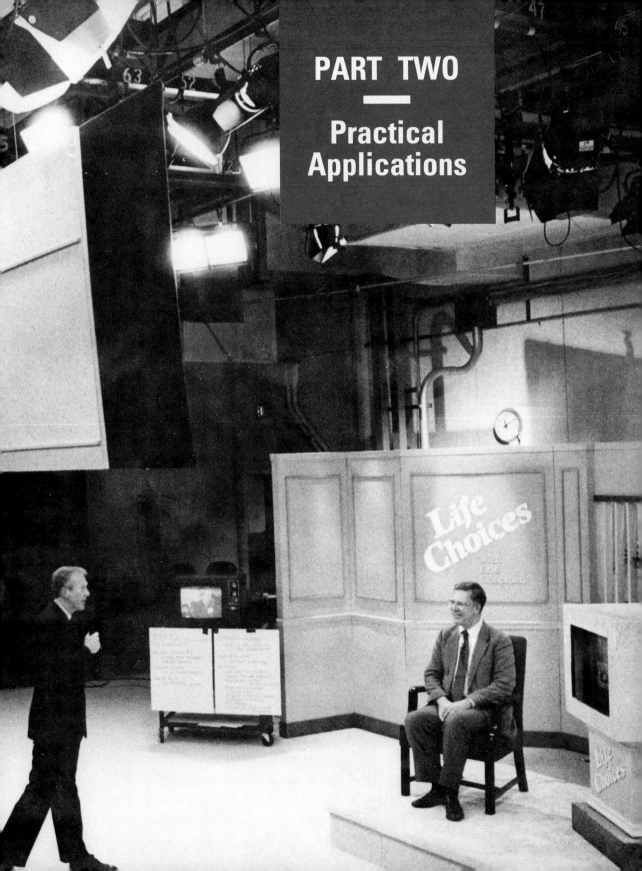

PART TWO

Practical Applications

8

Public Relations Writing Fundamentals

The ability to write easily, coherently, and quickly distinguishes the public relations professional from others in an organization. It's not that the skills of counseling and judgment aren't just as important; some experts argue that these skills are far more important than knowing how to write. Maybe. But not knowing how to write—how to express ideas on paper—may reduce the opportunities to ascend the public relations success ladder.

General managers usually come from finance, legal, engineering, or sales backgrounds, where writing is not stressed. But when they reach the top, they are expected to write articles, speeches, memos, and testimony. Here they need advisors, who are often their trusted public relations professionals.

What does it take to be a public relations writer? For one thing, it takes a good knowledge of the basics. Although practitioners probably write for a wider range of purposes and use a greater number of communications methods than do other writers, the principles remain the same, whether writing an annual report or a case history, an employee newsletter or a public speech. This chapter and the two that follow will explore the fundamentals of writing: (1) discussing public relations writing in general and news releases in particular; (2) reviewing writing for reading; and (3) discussing writing for listening.

WRITING FOR THE EYE AND THE EAR

Writing for a reader differs dramatically from writing for a listener. A reader has certain luxuries a listener does not have. For example, a reader can scan material, study printed words, dart ahead, and then review certain passages for better understanding. A reader can check up on a writer; if the facts are wrong, for instance, a reader can find out pretty easily. To be effective, writing for the eye must be able to withstand the most rigorous scrutiny.

On the other hand, a listener gets only one opportunity to hear and comprehend a message. If the message is missed the first time around, there's usually no second chance. This situation poses a special challenge for the writer—

to grab the listener quickly. A listener who tunes out early in a speech or a broadcast is difficult to draw back into the listening fold.

Public relations practitioners—and public relations students—should understand the differences between writing for the eye and the ear. Although it's unlikely that any beginning public relations professional would start by writing speeches, it's important to understand what constitutes a speech and how it's prepared and then be ready for the assignment when opportunity strikes. Because writing lies at the heart of the public relations equation, the more beginners know about writing, the better they will do. Any practitioner who doesn't know the basics of writing and doesn't know how to write is vulnerable and expendable.

WRITING FUNDAMENTALS

Few people are "born writers." Like any other discipline, writing takes patience and hard work. The more you write, the better you should become, provided you have mastered the basics. Writing fundamentals do not change significantly from one form to another.

What are the basics? According to counselor F. John Pessolano, the basics are part theory, part practice, and part common sense. Here's Pessolano's three-part formula for writers, from the novice to the novelist.

1. **The idea must precede the expression.** Think before writing. Few people can observe an event, immediately grasp its meaning, and sit down to compose several pages of sharp, incisive prose. Writing requires ideas, and ideas require thought. Ideas must satisfy four criteria.

   - They must relate to the reader.
   - They must engage the reader's attention.
   - They must concern the reader.
   - They must be in the reader's own self-interest.

   Sometimes ideas come quickly. At other times they don't come at all. But each new writing situation does not require a new idea. The trick in coming up with clever ideas lies more in borrowing old ones than in creating new ones. An old idea, refined to meet a specific communications objective, can be most effective. Stated another way, never underestimate the importance of maintaining good files.

2. **Don't be afraid of the draft.** After deciding on an idea and establishing the purpose of a communication, the writer should prepare a rough draft. It is a necessary and foolproof method for avoiding a mediocre and half-baked product.

   Writing, no matter how good, can usually be improved with a second look. The draft helps one organize ideas and plot their development before committing them to a written test. It often enhances writing clarity if you know where you will stop before you start. Organization should be logical;

it should lead a reader in a systematic way through the body of the text. Sometimes, especially on longer pieces, an outline should precede the draft.

3. **Simplify, clarify, aim.** In writing, the simpler the better. The more people who understand what you're trying to say, the better your chances for stimulating action. Shop talk, jargon, and "in" words should be avoided. Clear, normal English is all that's required to get an idea across. In practically every case what makes sense is the simple rather than the complex, the familiar rather than the unconventional, and the concrete rather than the abstract.

Clarity is another essential in writing. The key to clarity is tightness; that is, each word, each passage, each paragraph must belong. If a word is unnecessary, a passage redundant, a paragraph vague—get rid of it. Writing requires judicious editing; copy must always be reviewed with an eye toward cutting.

Finally, writing must be aimed at a particular audience. The writer must have the target group in mind and tailor the message to reach them. To win the minds and deeds of a specific audience, one must be willing to sacrifice the understanding of certain others. Writers, like companies, can't expect to be all things to all people.

Television journalist Bill Moyers offers this advice for good writing:

Strike in the active voice. Aim straight for the enemy: imprecision, ambiguity, and those high words that bear semblance of worth, not substance. Offer no quarter to the tired phrase or overworn idiom. Empty your knapsack of all adjectives, adverbs, and clauses that slow your stride and weaken your pace. Travel light. Remember the most memorable sentences in the English language are also the shortest: "The King is dead" and "Jesus wept."[1]

Flesch Readability Formula

Through a variety of writings, the late Dr. Rudolf Flesch staged a one-man battle against pomposity and murkiness in writing.* According to Flesch, anyone can become a writer. He suggests that people who write like they talk will be able to write better. In other words, if people were less inclined to obfuscate their writing with 25-cent words and more inclined to substitute simple words, then not only would communicators communicate better, but receivers would receive more clearly.

In responding to a letter, Flesch's approach in action would work like this: "Thanks for your suggestion, Tom. I'll mull it over and get back to you as soon as I can." The opposite of the Flesch approach would read like this: "Your suggestion has been received; and after careful consideration we shall report our findings to you." See the difference?

---

*Among the more significant of Flesch's books are *Say What You Mean, The Art of Plain Talk, The Art of Readable Writing,* and *How to Be Brief: An Index to Simple Writing.*

INTERVIEW

Robert A. Williams

Robert A. Williams is the public relations director of the Greater New York Councils of the Boy Scouts of America, the country's largest local boy scout unit. Previously, Williams was a writer and account executive with the public relations firms of Carl Byoir & Associates and Geltzer & Company. He also has had extensive experience as a newspaper reporter, having served as a by-lined contributor to the *New York Times* since 1972. His reporting and writing have earned him awards for journalistic excellence from a variety of press associations. Williams is also an adjunct associate professor of communica-

tions arts at St. John's University in New York, where he teaches public relations and journalism.

How important is writing in public relations?
Clear, concise writing is probably the most important tool of the public relations practitioner.

Words on paper continue to be the principal conduit by which a person transmits information to another person. We in the writing business use words to tug at the emotions: we can make readers laugh, cry, even march off to war. Crisp writing—words that dance off a page—should be at the head of everyone's list.

Are writers born or made?
The question reminds me of people I meet who squeal, "Oh, you're a *writer?* I just l-l-l-love to write, too!"

Don't we all. Plopping words on paper is easy. Everyone's a writer, right? But searching for the precise words to say the precise thing is the challenge.

I remember a cub reporter at a newspaper at which I worked. The initial stories he wrote were horrendous: half truths, not enough facts, sloppy construction. You name the shortcoming, his story contained it. But he continued to write. And editors continued to polish and restructure his work. Before long he developed into one of our best writers.

So you see, anyone born with an interest in writing can be made into a good writer.

How do you approach each writing assignment?
Now you're asking for my secrets. Okay, I'll come clean.

When I receive a writing assignment—whether it's for a news release, newspaper story, or magazine feature—the first thing I do is make sure my interviewing has brought me all the facts. Not *most* of the facts—*all* the facts. I keep talking to people until I'm satisfied I have accumulated the information I need to begin to write. Interviewing and research, you see, are essential parts of writing.

How would you assess the state of writing among public relations practitioners today?
Overall, it's poor. This is not to say that good writing doesn't exist in the public relations field. But the quality of most writing I see is embarrassingly inferior.

Many people entering our field really haven't mastered the basics. Not only can't Johnny read, he can't write correctly, either! This shortcoming hurts even more when people who are in the business of language and words, in fact, haven't mastered the craft. The answer? As I see it, our educational systems across the country—I'm talking grammar school, high school, and, yes, even college—have got to get back to basics.

Is the news release dead?
Is the nickel cigar history? Are high-buttoned shoes passé? Are the raccoon coat, straw hat, and swell expressions, such as "Oh voe dee doe doe," outdated on college campuses? Of course, they are!

But the news release, on the other hand, is as strong as ever!

In our society the written word remains the best way for us to transmit information. Sure, the methods may change—many of us now send information by computer instead of via a news release in an envelope—but everything still boils down to the written word. A news release is still the ideal way for a public relations practitioner to communicate with the media.

Incidentally, if you're wondering what "Oh voe dee doe doe" means, look it up—or ask your grandparents. They probably used the expression all the time.

What's the best advice you can give to practitioners just starting out?
First, read everything you can get your hands on: newspapers, magazines, books—even pulp novels. If you intend to be a wordsmith, you must understand the language inside out. Reading will help you develop your skills.

Next, go out and do it! The best way to learn how to write is to write. Over and over, day in and day out. There simply is no substitute. The more you write, the more you learn, and the easier it should become.

Finally, if you're not on the staff of your college newspaper, make tracks to the editor as soon as you finish reading this interview. Write as much as you can while you're in college. This will afford you a valuable opportunity to see what writing is all about, and to feel what it's like to be a writer.

The other day I came across some stories I wrote for my college newspaper. Boy, were they horrible! My lead on one piece must have run 150 words! But I still feel proud of the effort it took to put them together.

There are countless examples of how Flesch's simple dictum works.

- Few would remember William Shakespeare if he had written sentences like "Should I act upon the urgings that I feel or remain passive and thus cease to exist?" Shakespeare's writing has stood the test of centuries because of sentences such as "To be or not to be?"
- A scientist, prone to scientific jargon, might be tempted to write, "The biota exhibited a 100 percent mortality response." But, oh, how much easier and infinitely more understandable to write, "All the fish died."
- One of President Franklin D. Roosevelt's speech writers once wrote, "We are endeavoring to construct a more inclusive society." F.D.R. changed it to "We're going to make a country in which no one is left out."
- Even the most famous book of all, the Bible, opens with a simple sentence that could have been written by a 12-year-old: "In the beginning, God created the heaven and the earth."

Flesch gave seven suggestions for making writing more readable.

1. Use contractions, like *it's* or *doesn't*.
2. Leave out the word *that* whenever possible.
3. Use pronouns like *I, we, they,* and *you*.
4. When referring back to a noun, repeat the noun, or use a pronoun. Don't create eloquent substitutions.
5. Use brief, clear sentences.
6. Cover only one item per paragraph.
7. Use language the reader understands.

To Flesch the key to all good writing was getting to the point.

THE SECRET OF THE INVERTED PYRAMID

Newspaper writing is the Flesch formula in action. Reporters learn that words are precious and are not to be wasted. In their stories every word counts. If readers lose interest early, they're not likely to be around at the end of the story.

That's where the inverted pyramid comes in. Newspaper story form is the opposite of that for a novel or short story. Whereas the climax of a novel comes at the end, the climax of a newspaper story comes at the beginning. A novel's important facts are rolled out as the plot thickens, but the critical facts in a newspaper story appear at the start. In this way, if readers decide to leave a news article early, they have already gained the basic ideas.

Generally, the first tier, or lead, of the inverted pyramid is the first one or two paragraphs, which include the most important facts. From there, paragraphs are written in a descending order of importance, with progressively less important facts presented as the article continues—thus, the term *inverted pyramid*. (See Figure 8–1 for an exception to the pyramid style.)

The Flesch 60-Word Blacklist

In his book *Say What You Mean*, Rudolf Flesch expressed particular loathing for the following words, which, he contended, could easily be replaced by the words in parentheses.

1. advise (write)
2. affirmative (yes)
3. anticipate (expect)
4. appear (seem)
5. ascertain (find out)
6. assist (help)
7. complete (fill out)
8. comply (follow)
9. constitute (be)
10. cooperate (help)
11. deceased (dead)
12. deem (think)
13. desire (want)
14. determine (figure, find)
15. disclose (show)
16. effect (make)
17. elect (choose, pick)
18. endeavor (try)
19. ensue (follow)
20. execute (sign)
21. experience (have)
22. facilitate (make easy)
23. failed to (didn't)
24. forward (send)
25. furnish (send)
26. inasmuch as (since)
27. inconvenience (trouble)
28. indicate (say, show)
29. initial (first)
30. in lieu of (instead of)
31. insufficient (not enough)
32. in the event that (if)
33. locate (find)
34. negative (no)
35. obtain (get)
36. personnel (people)
37. pertaining to (of, about)
38. presently (now)
39. prior to (before)
40. prohibit (forbid)
41. pursuant to (under)
42. provide (give, say)
43. represent (be)
44. request (ask for)
45. require (need)
46. residence (home, address)
47. reveal (show)
48. review (check)
49. spouse (wife, husband)
50. state (say)
51. submit (give, send)
52. subsequent (later)
53. substantial (big, large, great)
54. sufficient (enough)
55. supply (send)
56. sustain (suffer)
57. terminate (end, stop)
58. thus (so, that way)
59. transpire (happen)
60. vehicle (car, truck)

Rudolf Flesch, "The 60-Word Blacklist" from *Say What You Mean*. Copyright © 1972 by Rudolf Flesch. Reprinted by permission of Harper & Row Publishers, p. 72.

Pullman Kellogg NEWS

A Member of the Wheelabrator-Frye Group
Three Greenway Plaza East, Houston, Texas 77046
Arthur L. Dowling, Vice President Advertising and Public Relations
(713) 960-2160

Contact: Ray Waters, Manager of Public Relations

For Release: UPON RECEIPT

CONTINUED COOPERATION IS KELLOGG'S CHRISTMAS PLEDGE

1980 comes to an end, and a new year is about to begin. It is a time to pause; to reflect on the past; to look to the future.

Pullman Kellogg began the year as a division of Pullman Incorporated. In November, Pullman Incorporated was merged into Wheelabrator-Frye, Inc. In 1981, it is planned that the M.W. Kellogg name -- a name synonymous with excellence throughout our industry, throughout the world -- be readopted.

In extending wishes for a joyous holiday season and a rewarding new year, Ray Waters, Kellogg's manager of public relations, reaffirmed his department's commitment to strive to reflect that excellence, saying the department will continue to attempt to provide media with information on Kellogg's worldwide activities honestly and speedily -- not only relating to material emanating originally from the department, but in responding to queries received.

"No public relations group can perform its job effectively without earning and retaining the confidence of the press corps," he said. "We will continue to work diligently to deserve that confidence.

"Peace, love and season's greetings to all."

- 30 -   #86 - 12/22/80

United Kingdom: Pullman Kellogg Limited, The Pullman Kellogg Building, Wembley (London), Middlesex HA9 0EE, Telephone (01) 903-8484
The Netherlands: Kellogg Continental B.V., De Boelelaan 873, Amsterdam, Telephone 020-42 99 55

The M.W. Kellogg Company NEWS

a subsidiary of Wheelabrator-Frye Inc.
Three Greenway Plaza East, Houston, Texas 77046
Arthur L. Dowling, Vice President Advertising and Public Relations
(713) 960-2160

Contact: Ray Waters, Manager of Public Relations

For Release: UPON RECEIPT

Houston, 23 December...Christmas sees an international company with its good name back again, operating under a new president from within a new parent organization, and looking forward to its first full year with the restored name of The M.W. Kellogg Company, under the direction of Robert W. Page, president and chief executive officer. Page had been president of Rust Engineering Inc. of Birmingham, another member company within the Wheelabrator-Frye organization. Wheelabrator-Frye Inc. acquired Pullman Incorporated late in 1980. With that acquisition, Kellogg became a member of the Wheelabrator group.

Ray Waters, public relations manager for the worldwide Kellogg group of companies, said today that 1981, a year of change, has served as a prologue to a decade of commitment to the enhancement of man's condition by the careful exploitation and utilization of his energy resources.

With that corporate commitment came the restatement of what Waters calls Kellogg's public relations credo -- to work with the diverse publics in the best manner possible; to cooperate to the best of his ability to serve their needs and the needs of Kellogg, its sister-companies and its parent organization; and to be as honest and open with those organizations as is humanly possible. He reiterated to the media his often stated belief: "No public relations department can be effective without earning the respect of its publics and without exhibiting, in return, respect for their needs for information and assistance.

"This effort will continue," he said, in extending the best wishes of the season to them.

- 30 -   #55-23 DECEMBER 1981

FIGURE 8-1 For several years Pullman Kellogg bent the rules of inverted pyramid style each Christmas season. The first release (left) was typical of the public relations manager's substitute Christmas card. In 1981, when Pullman changed its name to M. W. Kellogg, the company seized the occasion to combine some new, pertinent corporate information with its Christmas time tradition (right). (Courtesy of M. W. Kellogg Co.)

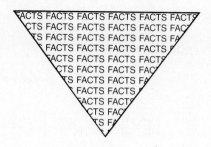

The lead is the most critical element, usually answering who, what, why, when, where, and occasionally how. For example, the following lead effectively answers most of the initial questions a reader might have about the subject of the news story.

> Rock Hudson, movie idol of millions, died yesterday in Hollywood after suffering from AIDS.

That sentence tells it all; it answers the critical questions and highlights the pertinent facts. It gets to the point quickly without a lot of extra words. In only 14 words it captures and communicates the essence of what the reader needs to know.

This same style of easy and straightforward writing forms the basis for the most fundamental and ubiquitous of all public relations tools—the news release.

THE NEWS RELEASE

The news release is a valuable but much maligned device. Most public relations professionals swear by it. Some newspaper editors swear about it. But everybody uses it to promote activities, communicate policies, and let the public know what an organization is up to. A news release may be written as the document of record to state an organization's official position—for example, in a court case or in announcing a price or rate increase. More frequently, however, releases have one overriding purpose: to influence a publication to write favorably about the material discussed. Each day, in fact, professionals send releases to editors in the hopes of stimulating favorable stories about their organizations.

Most of the time, news releases are not used verbatim. Rather, they may tip off editors to potential stories or serve as editorial reminders about coming stories. In both instances the news release forms the point of departure for an original newspaper or magazine story. Unfortunately, as one hardened newspaper editor put it, "Few (releases) are worth the paper they are printed on . . . particularly in this day of escalating paper costs."[2] Much of the editorial

PUBLIC AFFAIRS DEPARTMENT
277 Park Avenue, New York, N.Y. 10172

RELEASE
ON RECEIPT

Contact: Nicholas R. Iammartino
212-573-4131

BORDEN COMPLETES THREE SNACK ACQUISITIONS
Purchase of Sooner Snacks Marks Entry into U.K. Market

NEW YORK, April 7, 1988 -- Borden, Inc. (NYSE: BN) today announced the
completion of three acquisitions that strengthen its positions as a leader in
worldwide snacks, a strategic growth area that should contribute an estimated
$1.15 billion to Borden's projected 1988 sales of $7.3 billion. The
acquisitions, totaling about $88 million in estimated full-year sales, are:

o Sooner Snacks Limited, a major U.K. producer and marketer of potato

   chips and other snacks;

o Nuschelberg, a West German chain of retail bakeries; and

o The Crane potato chip brand name and other selected assets from

   Illinois Snack Foods, Inc.

"The Sooner Snacks purchase not only is the largest of the three, but
also marks our entry into the important U.K. snack market," said R. J.
Ventres, Borden chairman and chief executive officer. "We are already the
second-largest salty snack producer in the United States and the world. We
enhanced our international position just two months ago by acquiring Humpty
Dumpty Foods Ltd. in Canada, and we have snack units in Spain, Ecuador and
Malaysia as well.

"Nuschelberg adds to the number one position we hold in West Germany in
another type of snacks, namely, sweet baked snacks and specialty breads,"
Mr. Ventres continued. "That's a category with $6 billion per year in
national sales, more than a dozen times larger than salty snacks in Germany."

-more -

FIGURE 8–2 Borden's announcement easily qualifies as news. The company's first-paragraph reference to its position "as a leader in worldwide snacks" is an attempt to subtly publicize a message that Borden would like to see in print.

criticism of news releases revolves around the apparent shoddiness with which releases are planned and executed. In one survey of newspaper editors, six factors in particular goaded editors about news releases. They are arranged here in order of onerousness.

1. Information isn't localized.
2. Information isn't newsworthy.
3. Release contains too much advertising puffery.
4. Release is too long and cumbersome.
5. Release arrived too late to be useful.
6. Release was poorly written.[3]

Faced with paper shortages, spiraling production costs, shrinking news holes, and intense deadline pressures, editors simply don't have time to wade through masses of poorly written, self-serving pap. They're looking for news. According to most editors, most releases just don't contain much news. As one city editor, who claimed to receive hundreds of releases daily, scornfully put it,

> Most press releases are written for clients and not for reporters. The people who write them must know this, so I don't imagine they will be persuaded to change their practices, which they must feel serve a useful purpose. The fact that it is not a news purpose or even a public relations purpose is probably irrelevant to them. It keeps the fees or the paychecks coming.[4]

These editorial comments are instructive to public relations professionals as a reminder of what news release writing should be all about—releasing news. The writer's first question must be, "What in our announcement is newsworthy?" The most newsworthy facts must be extricated, segregated, and arrayed in the news release to interest the editor and, by extension, the publication's readers. At the same time, the release writer must keep in mind the particular message that the writer's employer would like to get across. Such allusions should never be blatant but rather subtle enough to qualify generally as part of the news (Figure 8–2).

Understandably, editors are proud people who don't readily admit to borrowing other people's ideas, particularly those of public relations people. Nevertheless, public relations ideas and releases are used regularly in most publications and serve as an integral part of newspaper content. If a release pierces the print barrier verbatim in a newspaper or magazine, the sponsor's message takes on the heightened stature associated with objective news reporting (Figure 8–3).

Format

The format of a news release is important. Since the release is designed to be used in print, it must be structured for easy use by an editor. Certain mechanical rules of thumb should be followed.

David Rockefeller Optimista Sobre Aumento Economía P.R.

(393)
EL DIARIO-LA PRENSA
NEW YORK, N.Y.
D. 90,000

APR 3 0 1978

David Rockefeller, presidente del Chase Manhattan Bank, citó como un ingrediente principal en la continuada recuperación económica de Puerto Rico, su habilidad para mantener la clase de clima comercial que continuará señalando la isla como un sitio que invita a la inversión exterior.

En un discurso ante la Cámara de Comercio de Puerto Rico en los Estados Unidos, el banquero neoyorquino señaló que eliminando cualquier error serio en la estrategia económica,

la economía de Puerto Rico deberá generalmente crecer paralelamente con la economía de los Estados Unidos.

Específicamente Rockefeller declaró que es razonable esperar que Puerto Rico aumente su economía alrededor de un 4%, durante los próximos cuatro años asumiendo que la de los Estados Unidos aumentará también de 4 a 4½ por ciento.

Rockefeller añadió que se sentía entusiasmado por los recientes desarrollos económicos positivos registrados en Puerto

Rico, entre los que señaló que el empleo está emergiendo de los bajos niveles de la recesión.

A tales efectos señaló que el total de empleados en la isla está aumentado en una tasa anual de alrededor del 4½ por ciento.

Dijo también que el gobierno puertorriqueño desarrolla un programa para consolidar la deuda pública a un corto término y además reducir sus planes de préstamos, así como los de pertenecientes a las corporaciones públicas.

The Journal of Commerce
NEW YORK, N. Y.
D. 25,820

APR 2 8 1978

Business Climate 'Aids' Puerto Rico

David Rockefeller, chairman of the Chase Manhattan Bank, Thursday cited as a key ingredient in Puerto Rico's continued economic recovery, its ability to maintain "the kind of business climate which will continue to stamp the island as an inviting location for external investment."

Addressing the Puerto Rico Chamber of Commerce in the United States, the New York banker said that "barring any serious mistakes in economic strategy, Puerto Rico's economy should generally grow in pace with the U.S. economy."

Specifically, Mr. Rockefeller said "it seems reasonable to expect Puerto Rico to grow at close to 4 percent" over the next four years, assuming U.S. growth of 4 to 4½ percent.

Mr. Rockefeller said he was "encouraged" by a number of positive recent economic developments in Puerto Rico, including.

Continued emphasis of the Government-Development Bank on sound and conservative practices of debt management.

"The government has now embarked on a program to consolidate short-term debt and reduce its own borrowing plans and those of its public corporations," Mr. Rockefeller said.

Employment seems to be re-emerging from the dismal levels of the recession.

Mr. Rockefeller said the total number of people employed on the island is increasing at an annual rate of about 4½ percent. Further, while unemployment in March was still high at 17 percent, "when you compare this with the level of 19 percent in February and 20 percent in December, it suggests real improvement."

(704)
SAN JUAN STAR
SAN JUAN, PUERTO RICO
D. 51,000 SUN. 83,000

APR 2 8 1978

4% growth in island's economy foreseen by David Rockefeller

NEW YORK (UPI) — David Rockefeller, chairman of the Chase Manhattan Bank, Thursday cited as a key ingredient in Puerto Rico's continued economic recovery the island's ability to maintain "the kind of business climate which will continue to stamp it as an inviting location for external investment."

Addressing the Puerto Rico Chamber of Commerce in the United States, the New York banker said that "barring any serious mistakes in economic strategy, Puerto Rico's economy should generally grow in pace with the U.S. economy."

Specifically, Rockefeller said "it seems reasonable to expect Puerto Rico to grow at close to 4 percent" over the next four years, assuming U.S. growth of 4 to 4½ percent.

Rockefeller said he was "encouraged" by a number of positive recent economic developments in Puerto Rico, including:

—Continued emphasis of the Government Development Bank on sound and conservative practices of debt management. "The government has now embarked on a program to consolidate short-term debt and reduce its own borrowing plans and

those of its public corporations," Rockefeller said.

—Employment seems to be re-emerging from the dismal levels of the recession. Rockefeller said the total number of people employed on the island is increasing at an annual rate of about 4½ percent.

Further, he said, while unemployment in March was still high at 17 percent, "when you compare this with the level of 19 percent in February and 20 percent in December, it suggests real improvement."

—Another area of encouragement is agriculture, where the government has begun to promote the development of import substitution crops such as rice and vegetables and the production of beef and poultry.

Rockefeller added that recent economic statistics in Puerto Rico's construction industry, which was hard hit by the recession, are also encouraging. However, he said, "the private sector is advancing at a much slower pace" than renewed construction activity in the public sector.

- **Spacing**   News releases should always be typed and double-spaced on one side only of 8½″ by 11″ paper. No editor wants to go rummaging through a handwritten release or a single-spaced, oversized piece of paper with typing on both sides.
- **Paper**   Inexpensive paper stock should be used. Reporters win Pulitzer Prizes with stories written on plain copy paper. Nothing irritates an editor more than seeing an expensively embossed news release while watching newspapers die from soaring newsprint costs.
- **Identification**   The name, address, and telephone number of the release writer should appear in the upper part of the release in case an editor wants further information. It's a good idea to list two names, with office and home telephone numbers.
- **Release date**   Releases should always be dated, either for immediate use or to be held until a certain later date, often referred to as an embargoed date. In this day of instant communication, however, newspapers frown on embargoes. And only in the most extreme cases—for example, proprietary or confidential medical or government data—will newspapers honor them. Frequently, a dateline is used on releases; it is the first line of the release and tells where the story originated.
- **Margins**   Margins should be wide enough for editors to write in, usually about 1 to 1½ inches.
- **Length**   A news release is not a book. It should be edited tightly so that it is no more than two pages long. Words and sentences should be kept short.
- **Paragraphs**   Paragraphs should also be short, no more than six lines at most. A single sentence can suffice as a paragraph. Because typographical composers may type exactly what they see in front of them, syllables should not be split from one line to the next. Likewise, paragraphs should be completed before a new page is begun, to ensure that a lost page in the news or composing rooms will not disrupt a particular thought in the release.
- **Slug lines**   Journalistic shorthand, or slug lines, should appear on a release—such things as "more" at the bottom of a page when the release continues to another page and "30" or "###" to denote the end of the release. Page numbers and one-word descriptions of the topic of the release should appear on each page for quick editorial recognition.
- **Headlines**   Headlines are optional. Often, headlines are avoided, and releases are begun one-third of the way down the page to allow editors to devise original headlines. Some practitioners prefer headlines to presell an editor on the gist of the news release that follows.
- **Proofreading**   Grammar, spelling, and typing must be perfect. Misspellings, grammatical errors, or typos are the quickest route to the editorial wastebasket.

FIGURE 8–3   Although editors don't like to admit it, sometimes news releases score with point-blank accuracy. In this case a news release was picked up verbatim by a wire service, translated into Spanish, and given wide circulation in the sponsor's target markets. (Courtesy of Chase Manhattan Bank)

■ **Timing** News release writers must be sensitive to editorial deadlines. Newspapers, magazines, and broadcast stations work under constant deadline pressure. A general interest release should arrive at an editor's desk a week to 10 days in advance of the paper's deadline. Since stale news is no news, a release arriving even just a little late may just as well never have been mailed.

To ensure that releases reach editors on time, many institutions either hand deliver them or have them delivered by a messenger service. Most large cities have messengers to move news, messages, and parcels around town in a hurry. The use of news wires is even faster than messenger delivery. Commercial services, such as PR News Wire and Business Wire, have offices around the country to distribute client news releases to media outlets on their own private wire. Such wires charge clients in return for running a complete news release. Most large cities are also served by direct-mail firms that can provide addresses by zip code. Such firms as Associated Release Service, Media Distribution Services, and PR Aids are expert in disseminating news releases accurately and quickly to the right publication.

Style

The style of a news release is almost as critical as its content. Sloppy style can break the back of any release and ruin its chances for publication. Style must also be flexible and evolve as language changes.

Those who think that capital letters, commas, and proper spelling are relatively insignificant concerns should note the price many companies pay for poor style, according to a leading designer of corporate annual reports.

> We have found that 25 to 50 percent of a company's last-minute changes—and charges—are due to tinkering with capitalization, punctuation, and other choices of style. We have also found that style varies from company to company and from year to year with no apparent reason, resulting in an unprofessional tone in too many annual reports.[5]

One element of style that has evolved over the years relates to sexism in writing. Dealing with gender has become more important for a writer and also more difficult. No matter how hard a writer tries to be even-handed in treating men and women in print, he—or she—is bound to offend someone. In the mid-1970s the Washington Press Club published guidelines for the elimination of sexual bias in the media. Among its highlights were these rules:

1. Terms referring to a specific gender should be avoided when an alternative term will do. Use *business executive* instead of *businessman* and *city council member* for *councilman*.
2. Where neither a gender-free term nor any term accurately designating gender is yet in common use, continue to employ the old terminology—for

example, *Yeoman* First Class Betty Jones or Mary Smith, a telephone company *lineman*.

3. No occupational designation should include a description of the person's gender unless the sex of the individual is pertinent to the story. For example, don't use *woman lawyer* or *male nurse*.

4. Avoid terms like *man made* for synthetic, *man-on-the-street* for ordinary citizen, *manpower* for workforce, *man and wife* for husband and wife, and *co-ed* for student.

Despite such attempts to eliminate sexism in writing style, satisfying everyone is a nearly impossible task for any writer.

Most public relations operations follow the style practiced by major newspapers and magazines, rather than that of book publishers. This news style is detailed in various guides published by such authorities as the Associated Press, United Press International, and the *New York Times*.

Because the press must constantly update its style to conform to changing societal concepts, news release style is subjective and everchanging. However, a particular firm's style must be consistent from one release to the next. The following are examples of typical style rules:

- **Capitalization**   Most leading publications use capital letters sparingly; so should you. Editors call this a down style, because only the most important words begin with capital letters.

- **Abbreviations**   Abbreviations present a many-faceted problem. For example, months, when used with dates, should be abbreviated, such as Sept. 2, 1987. But when the day of the month is not used, the month should be spelled out, such as September 1987. Days of the week, on the other hand, should never be abbreviated. In addition, first mention of organizations and agencies should be spelled out, with the abbreviation in parentheses after the name, such as Securities and Exchange Commission (SEC).

- **Numbers**   There are many guidelines for the spelling out of numbers, but a general rule is to spell out numbers up through nine and use figures for 10 and up. Yet figures are perfectly acceptable for such things as election returns, speeds and distances, percentages, temperatures, heights, ages, ratios, and sports scores.

- **Punctuation**   The primary purpose of punctuation is to clarify the writer's thoughts, ensure exact interpretation, and make reading and understanding quicker and easier. Less punctuation rather than more should be the goal. The following are just some of the punctuation marks a public relations practitioner must use appropriately.

  1. The colon introduces listings, tabulations, and statements and takes the place of an implied "for instance."

  2. The comma is used in a variety of circumstances, including before connecting words, between two words or figures that might otherwise be misunderstood, and before and after nonrestrictive clauses.

3. In general, exclamation points should be resisted in releases. They tend to be overkill!

4. The hyphen is often abused and should be used carefully. A single hyphen can change the meaning of a sentence completely. For example, "The six-foot man eating tuna was killed" means the man was eating tuna; it should probably be punctuated "The six-foot, man-eating tuna was killed."

5. Quoted matter is enclosed in double or single quotation marks. The double marks enclose the original quotation whereas the single marks enclose a quotation within a quotation.

■ **Spelling**   Many words, from *adviser* to *zucchini,* are commonly misspelled. The best way to avoid misspellings is to have a dictionary always within reach. When two spellings are given in a dictionary, the first spelling is always preferred.

These are just a few of the stylistic stumbling blocks that writers must consider. In the news release, style should never be taken lightly. The style, as much as any other part of the release, lets an editor know the kind of organization that issued the release and the competency of the professional who wrote it.

Content

The cardinal rule in release content is that the end product be newsworthy. The release must be of interest to an editor and readers. Issuing a release that has little chance of being used by a publication serves only to crush the credibility of the writer.

When a release is newsworthy and of potential interest to an editor, it must be written clearly and concisely, in proper newspaper style. It must get to the facts early and answer the six key questions. From there it must follow inverted pyramid structure to its conclusion. For example, the following is not a proper lead for a release:

> CLEVELAND, OHIO, MARCH 7, 1988—Chief Justice William Rehnquist will speak tomorrow in Cleveland. He will speak at 8 P.M. He will address the convention of the American Bar Association. His address will be a major one and will concern the topic of capital punishment.

Why would an editor discard this lead? In the first place, it does not get to the heart of the issue—the topic of the speech—until the very end. Second, it's wordy. If the editor decided to use it at all, he'd have to rewrite it. Here's what should have been submitted:

> Chief Justice William Rehnquist will deliver a major address on capital punishment at 8 P.M. tomorrow in Cleveland before the American Bar Association convention.

The Ten Commandments of News Releases

Once upon a time, a public relations sage offered the following ten commandments, which—alas—get broken from time to time.

1. **Thou shalt be selective with the releases thou sendest.** Don't waste your ammunition on stories that bore you. They'll bore others, too.
2. **Thou shalt not send multiple copies of the same release.** It causes confusion and wastes time, yet occasionally the *New York Times* has been known to run a release tossed out by one editor and salvaged by another.
3. **Thou shalt have contact names and phone numbers on all releases.** Reporters must be able to get in touch with someone who can clarify information and answer questions. Don't send out announcements if you don't intend to be there when reporters call.
4. **Thou shalt know deadlines.** It's a good idea to let reporters know what's coming. That way, if it's especially newsworthy, they can save space and won't be surprised when it arrives close to the deadline.
5. **Thou shalt follow up with a telephone call.** Don't assume that a reporter received an important release. Releases get overlooked. Messages get lost. And newsrooms don't have secretaries. Sometimes reporters miss significant releases, so it's all right to check up from time to time. But don't call needlessly.
6. **Thou shalt take no for an answer.** If, after having given it your best shot, the answer is no, forget it. Don't be offended, and don't take it personally.
7. **Thou shalt find out about standard criteria.** All periodicals follow guidelines for things like executive changes and company news briefs. You get to know these by reading the publication. And remember that requirements may change. No newspaper editor likes to know his paper isn't being read, especially by those looking for ink.
8. **Thou shalt know and respect the meaning of** *exclusive*. *Exclusive* means just that—giving a release to one publication at the expense of its competition. It does not mean giving it to two publications at the same time. Also, it does not mean giving the release to one television station and one newspaper. If reporters get burned, they tend to remember.
9. **Thou shalt not send releases to people who left the publication years ago.** Few things disturb an editor more than receiving mail addressed to a deceased predecessor.
10. **Thou shalt get to know reporters before needing one.** Even if a reporter doesn't use all your releases, it helps to get to know the person. Public relations people occasionally forget that reporters are people, too.

Even though the second sample cut the verbiage in half, the pertinent questions still got answered: who (Chief Justice William Rehnquist), what (a major address on capital punishment), where (Cleveland), when (tomorrow at 8 P.M.), and why (American Bar Association is holding a convention). In this case how is less important. But whether the reader chooses to proceed further into the release or not, the story's gist has been successfully communicated in the lead.

News releases can be written about almost anything, but three frequent subjects are product and institutional announcements, management changes, and management speeches.

THE ANNOUNCEMENT

Frequently, practitioners want to announce a new product or institutional development, such as construction plans, earnings, mergers, acquisitions, or company celebrations. The announcement release should have a catchy yet significant lead to stimulate an editor to capitalize on the practitioner's creative idea. The following are two examples:

> "Tennis whites," the traditional male court uniform, will yield to bright colors and fashion styling this spring as Jockey spearheads a new wave in tennis fashion with the introduction of a full line of tennis wear for men.

> The creation of the first manufacturing joint-venture company in Romania, involving a Romanian company and an American firm, was announced today by the Romanian Ministry of Machine Tools and Electro Techniques and Control Data Corporation.

Typically in an announcement release, after the lead identifies the significant aspects of the product or development, a spokesperson is quoted for additional product information. Editors appreciate the quotes because they then do not have to interview a company official.

> The new, lightweight plastic bottle for Coca-Cola began its national rollout today in Spartanburg, SC. This two-liter package is the nation's first metric plastic bottle for soft drinks.
>
> "We are very excited about this new package," said John H. Ogden, president, Coca-Cola U.S.A. "Our two-liter plastic bottle represents an important advancement. Its light weight, toughness, and environmental advantages offer a new standard of consumer benefits in soft drink packaging."

The subtle product "plug" included in this release is typical of such announcements. Clearly, the organization gains if the product's benefits are described in a news story. But editors are sensitive to product puffery, and the line between legitimate information and puffery is thin. One must always be sensitive to the needs and concerns of editors. A professional avoids letting the thin line of product information become a short plank of puffery.

YOU MAKE
THE CALL

Bungling the Bromo News Release

Bromo Corporation

CONTACT: Lance Ravenoo

Release date: Hold for Sept. 20, 1986

Bromo Company Announces Revolutionary Digital Clock

LINCOLN, SEPT. 21, 1986—Gromo Corporation today announced they would begin marketing immediately a revolutionary digital wristwatch, capable of withstanding more pressure than any other digital watch on the market.

The new watch, described by scientists as "an amazing piece of modern machinery," was produced in Bromo's Lincoln, Texas, plant. The watch was market-tested in the Lincoln, Nebraska, area and was universally applauded by test participants.

"I've never seen a watch absorb so much punishment," was the response of one participant.

According to Lance Ravenoo, Bromo's director of marketing, "We believe this watch will outpace any other timepiece on the market. It's capacity to withstand abuse is simply unvelievable."

The Bromo watch, which is also waterproof, comes in two styles: a "nautical" that retails for $37.50 and the "free spirit" which retails for $380.0.

QUESTIONS

1. If you were an editor, would you use the Bromo news release?
2. How many errors can you spot?

THE MANAGEMENT CHANGE

Newspapers are often interested in management changes, but editors frequently reject releases that have no local angle. For example, the editor of the Valdosta, Georgia, *Citizen* has little reason to use this announcement:

> NEW YORK, NY, SEPT. 5, 1988—Jeffrey O. Schultz has been named manager of the hosiery department at Bloomingdale's Paramus, NJ, store.

On the other hand, the same release, amended for local appeal, would almost certainly be used by the *Citizen*.

> NEW YORK, NY, SEPT. 5, 1988—Jeffrey O. Schultz, son of Mr. and Mrs. Siegfried Schultz of 221 Starting Lane, Valdosta, has been named manager of the hosiery department at Bloomingdale's Paramus, NJ, store.

Sometimes one must dig for the local angle. For example, suppose Mr. Schultz was born in Valdosta but went to school in Americus, Georgia. With this knowledge, the writer might prepare the following release, which would have appeal in the newspapers of both Georgia cities.

> NEW YORK, NY, SEPT. 5, 1988—Jeffrey O. Schultz, son of Mr. and Mrs. Sieg-fried Schultz of 221 Starting Lane, Valdosta, and a 1976 graduate of Americus High School, was named manager of the hosiery department of Bloomingdale's Paramus, NJ, store.

Penetrating local publications with the management change release is relatively easy once the local angle has been identified, but achieving publication in a national newspaper or magazine is much harder. The *Wall Street Journal,* for example, will not use a management change announcement unless the individual has attained a certain level of responsibility, usually corporate vice president or higher, in a major firm. In other words, if a release involves someone who has not attained senior executive status at a listed company, forget it, at least as far as the *Wall Street Journal* is concerned.

For national consumption it is the importance or uniqueness of the individual or company that should be emphasized. For example, an editor might not realize that the following management change is unique:

> WASHINGTON, DC, JUNE 6, 1988—Yolanda King of Sacramento, CA, today was promoted to the rank of admiral in the United States Navy.

However, the same release stands out clearly for its news value when the unique angle is played up.

> WASHINGTON, DC, JUNE 6, 1988—Yolanda King of Sacramento, CA, today was named the first woman admiral in the history of the United States Navy.

One can never go wrong being straightforward in a news release, but a local or unique angle to help sell the story to an editor should always be investigated.

THE MANAGEMENT SPEECH

Management speeches are another recurring source of news releases. The key to a speech news release is selecting the most significant portion of the talk for the lead. A good speech generally has a clear thesis, from which a lead naturally flows. Once the thesis is identified, the remainder of the release simply embellishes it.

> BOONEVILLE, MO, OCT. 18, 1988—Booneville Mining Company is "on the verge of having several very profitable years," Booneville Mining President Marsha Mulford said today.
>
> Addressing the Booneville Chamber of Commerce, the Missouri mining company executive cited two reasons for the positive projections: the company's

Promoting a President at Oswego U.

As public information director of Oswego University, you are advised that the university's board of trustees has selected the fifteenth president in the school's history. He is Wilson W. Waters, a 1952 graduate of Oswego, who has most recently served as the school's dean of students. In researching Waters's background, you uncover a few other interesting facts.

- He is 50 years old, married to the former Renee Siggerson of Yankton, South Dakota.
- He was born in Oswego and spent the first 21 years of his life there.
- He has a master's degree from Brown University and a Ph.D. from Harvard.
- He is 6'9", Jamaican, and played 15 years in the National Basketball Association.
- He had been dean of students at Oswego for 10 years.

Your assignment, according to the board, is to publicize the Waters announcement as extensively as possible in local and national media.

QUESTIONS

1. Are these facts sufficient to write a news release about the new Oswego president? What additional information would help?
2. From the data given, what angle would you pursue for local Oswego editorial consumption?
3. What would your lead be for national media consumption?
4. Are there any facts given that you wouldn't use in the release?

orders are at an all-time high, and its overseas facilities have "turned the corner" on profitability in the current year.

Normally, if the speech giver is not a famous person, the release should not begin with the speaker's name but with the substance of the remarks. If the speaker is a well-known individual, leading with a name is perfectly legitimate.

> Federal Reserve Chairman Alan Greenspan called today for a "new attitude toward business investment and capital formation."

The body copy of a speech release should follow directly from the lead. Often, the major points of the speech must be paraphrased and consolidated to conform to a two-page release. In any event, it is frequently a significant challenge to convert the essence of a management speech to news release form.

REVOLUTIONIZING PUBLIC RELATIONS WRITING

New technologies, particularly the computer, have truly revolutionized public relations writing. It used to be that a public relations writer would turn to the typewriter and start banging away. Today, with personal computers capable of desktop publishing, the days of the old-fashioned typewriter are numbered. Eventually, computers will be used in virtually all forms of design and production of printed and electronic materials, and public relations will be truly paperless. From one computer workstation a practitioner will produce publications through her word processor, give and receive messages, pick up her mail, and even view videotapes to monitor the media.

Although public relations writers aren't quite there yet, one technological innovation that is catching on rapidly is desktop publishing, which allows people with a personal computer to design and produce documents that look almost as though they have been professionally typeset. Begun in 1985, desktop publishing is starting to transform the world of internal communications. All it requires is a personal computer, a laser printer and software for word processing, charts or drawings if desired, and publishing applications such as layout. Getting started can cost as little as $2,000 if one relies on someone else's laser printer. The laser printer itself adds another $2,000.

Desktop publishing is still in its infancy. For the most part desktop published copy looks as if it came out of a computer—which, of course, it did. As the equipment associated with desktop publishing improves, so, too, will the quality of graphics and type. Also, as increasing numbers of practitioners wade into the desktop publishing pool, their output will continue to be refined and perfected. Increasingly, the new communications technology will change the way that public relations writers approach their tasks and complete their assignments.

THE IMPORTANCE OF EDITING

Editing is the all-important final touch for the public relations writer. In a news release a careful self-edit can save the deadliest prose. An editor must be judicious. Each word, phrase, sentence, and paragraph should be weighed carefully. Good editing will ''punch up'' dull passages and make them sparkle. For instance, ''The satellite flies across the sky'' is dead. But ''The satellite roars across the sky'' comes alive.

In the same context good editing will get rid of passive verbs. Invariably, this will produce shorter sentences. For example, ''The cherry tree was chopped down by George Washington'' is shorter and better as ''George Washington chopped down the cherry tree.''

A good editor must also be gutsy enough to use bold strokes—to chop, slice, and cut through unnecessary verbiage, bad grammar, misspellings, incorrect punctuation, poorly constructed sentences, misused words, mixed metaphors, non sequiturs, clichés, redundancies, circumlocutions, and jargon. Sentences like "She is the widow of the late Nelson Apfelbaum" and "The present incumbent is running for reelection" are intolerable to a good editor.

Probably the two most significant writing and editing supports for a practitioner are a good unabridged dictionary and a thesaurus. To these might be added *Bartlett's Familiar Quotations, World Almanac,* and an encyclopedia.

Editing should also concentrate on organizing copy. One release paragraph should flow naturally into the next. Transitions in writing are most important. Sometimes it just takes a single word to unite two adjoining paragraphs. Such is the case in the following example, which uses the word *size.*

> The machine works on a controlled mechanism, directed by a series of pulleys. It is much smaller than the normal motor, requiring less than half of a normal motor's components.
>
> Not only does the device differ in size from other motors, but it also differs in capacity.

Writing, like fine wine, should flow smoothly and stand up under the toughest scrutiny. Careful editing is a must.

NOTES

1. Bill Moyers, "Watch Your Language," *The Professional Communicator* (August-September 1985): 6.
2. Charles Honaker, "News Releases Revisited," *Public Relations Journal* (April 1981): 25.
3. Bill L. Baxter, "The News Release: An Idea Whose Time Has Gone?" *Public Relations Review* (Spring 1981): 30.
4. Charles Honaker, "News Releases Revisited," 25.
5. Corporate Annual Reports, "Guide to Business Writing Style" (New York: Corporate Annual Reports, 1975), p. 1. Available from 112 E. 31 St., New York, NY.

SUGGESTED READINGS

Ayer Press. *Ayer Public Relations and Publicity Stylebook.* Philadelphia, PA: Ayer Press, 1975. This book guides the publicist in copy preparation.
Baxter, Bill L. "The News Release: An Idea Whose Time Has Gone?" *Public Relations Review* (Spring 1981): 27–31. Professor Baxter recommends concrete steps public relations practitioners can take to bring releases up to a new standard.
Beach, M. *Getting It Printed: How to Work with Printers/Graphic Art Services.* Portland, OR: Coast to Coast Books (2934 N.E. 16th Ave.), 1986.
Blewett, Steve. "On Being a Pro: A House Organ Editor Speaks." *Public Relations Quarterly* (Summer 1981): 9–10.
Cohen, P. *A Public Relations Primer: Thinking and Writing.* Englewood Cliffs, NJ: Prentice-Hall, 1987.
"Diving into Desktop Publishing." San Francisco, CA: Gillian/Craig Associates (165 Eighth St., #301).
Editing the Organizational Publication. Chicago: Ragan Communications (407 S. Dearborn), 1984.

Erb, Lyle L. "Experts' Misuse of Language: Part One." *Public Relations Quarterly* (Spring 1982): 32.

———. "Writer's Notebook." *Public Relations Quarterly* (Spring 1981): 32.

———. "Writer's Notebook." *Public Relations Quarterly* (Winter 1981–82): 32.

Flesch, Rudolf. *The Art of Plain Talk*. Paperback ed. New York: Macmillan, 1962.

———. *Say What You Mean*. New York: Harper & Row, 1972.

Fowler, H. W. *A Dictionary of Modern English Usage*. Oxford, England: Oxford University Press, 1926.

Greaser, Constance U. "Writers, Editors and Computers." *Public Relations Journal* (March 1982): 26–28.

"Hacking Through the Paper Jungle." *Public Relations Journal* (August 1981): 26.

Hayakawa, Samuel I. *Writing Language in Thought and Action*. 4th ed. New York: Harcourt Brace Jovanovich, 1978.

———. *The Use and Misuse of Language*. New York: Fawcett, 1973.

Honaker, Charles. "News Releases Revisited." *Public Relations Journal* (April 1981): 25–27. Honaker explains why editors are repulsed by the steady and overwhelming flow of releases that are poorly written, fatuous, and without news value.

Jordon, Lewis, ed. *The New York Times Manual of Style and Usage*. New York: McGraw-Hill, 1977.

Meyer, H. *How to Write*. Washington, DC: Storm King Press (P.O. Box 3566), 1986.

Moyers, Bill, "Watch Your Language." *Professional Communicator* (August-September 1985): 4–6.

Newsom, Douglas, and Bob Carrell. *Public Relations Writing: Form and Style*. Belmont, CA: Wadsworth Publishing, 1986.

Publishing Newsletters. Rhinebeck NY: Newsletter Clearinghouse (P.O. Box 311).

Ruchti, Ulrich, and Norman Wasserman. "Public Companies Have to View Themselves as Publishers." *Public Relations Quarterly* (Winter 1983): 9–13.

Standard Periodical Directory. New York: Oxbridge Communications, 1988.

Strunk, W., and E. B. White. *Elements of Style*. New York: Macmillan, 1972.

Success in Newsletter Publishing & Hotline. Washington, DC: Newsletter Association (1341 G St., NW). Biweekly.

Tilden, Scott, Anthony Fulginiti, and Jack Gillespie. *Harnessing Desktop Publishing*. Pennington, NJ: Scott Tilden (4 W. Franklin Ave.), 1987.

Video Monitor (10606 Mantz Rd., Silver Spring, MD 20903). Monthly.

Walsh, Frank. *Public Relations Writer in the Computer Age*. Englewood Cliffs, NJ: Prentice-Hall, 1986.

The Raina News Release

Background: The Raina, Inc. carborundum plant in Blackrock, Iowa, has been under pressure in recent months to remedy its pollution problem. Raina's plant is the largest in Blackrock, and even though the company has spent $1.3 million on improving its pollution control equipment, black smoke still spews from the plant's smokestacks, and waste products are still allowed to filter into neighboring streams. The pressure on Raina has been intense of late.

- On September 7 Andrew Laskow, a private citizen, called to complain about the "noxious smoke" that was befouling the environment.
- On September 8 Mrs. Lizzy Ledger of the Blackrock Garden Club called to protest the "smoke problem" that was wreaking havoc on the zinnias and other flowers in the area.
- On September 9 Clarence "Smoky" Salmon, president of the Blackrock Rod and Gun Club, called to report that 700 people had signed a petition against the Raina plant's pollution of Zeus Creek.
- On September 10 WERS-radio editorialized that "the time has come to force area plants to act on solving pollution problems."
- On September 11 the Blackrock City Council announced plans to enact an air and water pollution ordinance for the city. The council invited as its first witness before the public hearing Leslie Sludge, manager of the Raina carborundum Blackrock plant.

News Release Data:

1. Leslie Sludge, manager of Raina's carborundum Blackrock plant, appeared at the Blackrock City Council hearing on September 11.
2. Sludge said Raina already has spent $1.3 million on a program to clean up pollution at its Blackrock plant.
3. Raina received 500 complaint calls in the past three months protesting its pollution conditions.
4. Sludge said Raina was "concerned about environmental problems, but profits are still what keeps our company running."
5. Sludge announced that the company had decided to commit another $2 million for pollution abatement facilities over the next three months.
6. Raina is the oldest plant in Blackrock and was built in 1900.
7. Raina's Blackrock plant employs 10,000 people, the largest single employer in Blackrock.
8. Raina originally scheduled its pollution abatement program for 1992 but speeded it up because of public pressure in recent months.
9. Sludge said that the new pollution abatement program would begin in October and that the company projected "real progress in terms of clean water and clean air" as early as June 1991.
10. In 1986 Raina, Inc. received a Presidential Award from the Environmental Protection Administration for its "concern for pollution abatement."
11. An internal Raina study indicated that

Blackrock was the "most pollutant-laden" of all Raina's plants nationwide.

12. Sludge formerly served as manager of Raina's Fetid Reservoir plant in Fetid Reservoir, New Hampshire. In two years as manager of Fetid Reservoir, Sludge was able to convert it from one of the most pollutant-laden plants in the system to the cleanest, as judged by the Environmental Protection Administration.

13. Sludge has been manager of Blackrock for two months.

14. Raina's new program will cost the company $2 million in all.

15. Raina will hire 100 extra workers especially for the pollution abatement program.

16. Sludge, 35, is married to the former Polly Usion of Wheeling, West Virginia.

17. Sludge is author of the book *Fly Fishing Made Easy*.

18. The bulk of the expense for the new pollution abatement program will be spent on two globe refractors, which purify waste destined to be deposited in surrounding waterways, and four hyperventilation systems, which remove noxious particles dispersed into the air from smokestacks.

19. Sludge said, "Raina, Inc. has decided to move ahead with this program at this time because of its long-standing responsibility for keeping the Blackrock environment clean and in response to growing community concern over achieving the objective."

20. Former Blackrock plant manager Fowler Aire was fired by the company in July for his "flagrant disregard for the environment."

21. Aire also was found to be diverting Raina funds from company projects to his own pockets. In all, Aire took close

to $10,000, for which the company was not reimbursed. At least part of the money was to be used for pollution control.

22. Aire, whose whereabouts are presently not known, is the brother of J. Derry Aire, Raina's vice president for finance.

23. Raina's Blackrock plant has also recently installed ramps and other special apparatus to assist handicapped employees. Presently, 100 handicapped workers are employed in the Raina Blackrock plant.

24. Raina's Blackrock plant started as a converted garage, manufacturing plate glass. Only 13 people worked in the plant at that time.

25. Today, the Blackrock plant employs 10,000, covers 14 acres of land, and is the largest single supplier of plate glass and commercial panes in the country.

26. The Blackrock plant was slated to be the subject of a critical report from the Private Environmental Stabilization Taskforce (PEST), a private environmental group. PEST's report, "The Foulers," was to discuss "the 10 largest manufacturing polluters in the nation."

27. Raina management has been aware of the PEST report for several months.

QUESTIONS

1. If you were assigned to draft a news release to accompany Sludge to the Blackrock City Council meeting on September 11, which items would you use in your lead (i.e., who, what, why, where, when, how)?

2. Which items would you avoid using in the news release?

3. If a reporter from the *Blackrock Bugle* called and wanted to know what happened to former Blackrock manager Fowler Aire, what would you tell him?

Writing for the Eye

9

Writing for reading was traditionally among the strongest areas for most public relations professionals. Most practitioners entered public relations through the field of print journalism. Accordingly, most practitioners had been schooled in the techniques of writing for the eye. Today, of course, a background in the print media is not particularly necessary to practice public relations work. Indeed, as noted, public relations professionals today gravitate into the field from a variety of backgrounds—law, television, general management, political science, and education. Nonetheless, demonstrating a facility for writing for reading continues to be a requirement for public relations work.

Although the news release is the most frequently used communications vehicle designed to be read, additional written tools are possible, each with its own purpose and style. This chapter will review the biography, the backgrounder, the feature story, the case history, the byliner, the memorandum, and the pitch letter. Each of these may stand alone as an individual communication. Often, however, several are combined as limited elements in a press kit (to be discussed later), which can provide editors with story ideas. The practitioner must know when each particular vehicle is appropriate.

THE BIOGRAPHY

Next to the news release, the most popular tool is the biography, often called the biographical summary or just plain bio. The bio recounts pertinent facts about a particular individual. Most organizations keep a file of bios covering all top officers. Major newspapers and wire services prepare standby bios on well-known people for immediate use on breaking news, such as sudden deaths.

Lyle L. Erb

Lyle L. Erb is a columnist for *Public Relations Quarterly*. He was in the newspaper business for 38 years. In addition, he edited *Seminar, A Quarterly Review for Journalists* for nine years, and he published *In Black and White*, the eclectic newsletter for those who write and edit for publication, for three years. Now retired, Erb is a consultant in Pacific Beach, California.

What is public relations?

> Public relations—the noble art of pulling the wool over the sheep's eyes so that the wolf appears to be a little lamb (see *Public Relations Counsel*).
> Public Relations Counsel—a wolf in sheep's clothing; sometimes found in Grandma's bed.
> —The Devil's Dictionary

Whatever else it may be, public relations is not a profession, except in the narrow sense that a great many people earn their livings from it. Rather, it is an art, a craft, a calling which, as pursued by the best of practitioners, seeks to communicate a corporate or personal image to the general public with factual accuracy, honest integrity, and incorruptible faith.

How would you assess the state of public relations writing today?
Deplorable. That is a generality, but in general accurately descriptive of most of the press releases, scripts, pitch letters, etc. that come to me for review.

What are the fundamentals you consider sacrosanct in writing?

Be brief. Use short words. Write short sentences, short paragraphs. Eschew obfuscation. Avoid clichés, slang, fad words. Shun hyperbole and circumlocution. Be direct—active, not passive. Have respect for the tools of our trade, the words we work with. Don't use words like *sacrosanct*.

Do you think anyone can master public relations writing skills?

No. (I assume you mean *everyone*.) Many college graduates today can't write a simple sentence. They are ignorant of basic rules of grammar. They can't spell. Yet some of them are successful public relations practitioners.

As a columnist, what kinds of pitch letters do you especially appreciate?

Those that DO NOT begin with danglers: "As a writer, I want you to know . . ."; "As an investor, there is an opportunity . . . ." For example, in this question, what does the phrase "as a columnist" modify?

What advice would you give a colleague who had to write a public relations feature and couldn't get started?

Do your research thoroughly. Decide what you want to say. Tell them you're going to say it. Say it. Tell them what you said.

What constitutes a good press kit?

A good one presents the facts—"Just the facts, ma'am"—about the product, service, or person. A bad one exaggerates, overemphasizes, intensifies, and is replete with italics, capital letters, and astounders!

How does one become a "good" writer?

By writing. Writing, revising, and rewriting. A good copy editor can improve almost anyone's writing. Good writing is not necessarily fine writing. As one sage put it, "When you think you have written an especially fine line, blot it out. It will do wonders for your style." Remember that facility is not felicity. "You write with ease to show your breeding, but easy writing's curst hard reading" (Thomas Moore's *Life of Sheridan*). The writing may be easy. It's the revising and rewriting that's hard work.

What constitutes good "public relations writing"?

There is no such thing as good "public relations writing," just as there is no such thing as good "journalistic writing" or say, good "legal writing." Good writing is good writing. Bad writing is what gave rise to such opprobrious terms as *journalese* and *legalese*. Good writing communicates. And that's what public relations is all about. (We are not speaking here of fiction or belles lettres.)

Straight Bios

The straight bio lists factual information in a straightforward fashion in a descending order of importance, with company-oriented facts preceding more personal details.

> David Rockefeller became chairman of the board of directors and chief executive officer of the Chase Manhattan Bank, N.A. in New York on March 1, 1969, and of the Chase Manhattan Corporation upon its formation on June 4, 1969.
>
> During his career with Chase Manhattan, Rockefeller gained a worldwide reputation as a leading banker and spokesman for the business community. He spearheaded the bank's expansion both internationally and throughout the metropolitan New York area and helped the bank play a significant role as a corporate citizen.
>
> Rockefeller joined the Chase National Bank as an assistant manager in the foreign department in 1946. He was appointed an assistant cashier in 1947, second vice president in 1948, and vice president in 1949.
>
> From 1950 to 1952 he was responsible for the supervision of Chase's business in Latin America, where, under his direction, new branches were opened in Cuba, Panama, and Puerto Rico, plus a representative office in Buenos Aires.

Narrative Bios

The narrative bio, on the other hand, is written in a breezier, more informal way. This style gives spark and vitality to the biography to make the individual come alive.

> David Rockefeller, who has been described as a man possessed of "a peculiar blend of enterprise, prudence, knowledge, and dedication," was born in Manhattan on June 12, 1915. His mother was the former Abby Aldrich, daughter of Senator Nelson Aldrich of Rhode Island. She had met John D. Rockefeller, Jr., the shy son of multimillionaire John D. Rockefeller, when he was an undergraduate at Brown University in Providence.
>
> John D. Rockefeller, Jr., was anxious that his children not be spoiled by the fortune his father had created and therefore put them on strict allowances. The household atmosphere was deeply religious, with one of the children reading the scriptures each morning before breakfast. Mrs. Rockefeller was an exceptional woman, with a strong interest in the arts. She and David were very close.
>
> Throughout David's academic career, he attended schools in which the Rockefeller family had an interest—either philanthropic, sentimental, or both. Abby and John D., Jr., had attended traditional private schools, but David and his three brothers were sent to Lincoln School, an experimental venture conducted by the Teachers College of Columbia to try out the progressive techniques of John Dewey.

Because of its personal tone, a good narrative bio is more difficult to write than the standard bio, which allows little room for embellishment.

Grepso the Clown Bio

As the public relations director for WAAH-TV, you are assigned to write both a straight bio and narrative bio on the station's ever-popular Grepso the Clown. Here are some key facts.

1. Grepso's real name is Howie Barmad. He is 45 and a former light-heavyweight boxing contender.
2. Grepso was born in Jersey City, New Jersey.
3. He joined WAAH 10 years ago as a newscaster, later worked as a weatherman, and 5 years ago became Grepso the Clown.
4. Grepso was educated at Harvard University, where he received a B.A. degree in philosophy and graduated magna cum laude.
5. He has been voted clown of the year for three years in a row as northeastern chairman of the United Cerebral Palsy Telethon.
6. Grepso lives in Basking Ridge, New Jersey. His hobbies include collecting tropical fish, snorkeling, and fingerpainting.

QUESTION

From the data given, how would you write a straight bio on Grepso? a narrative bio?

THE BACKGROUNDER

Background pieces, or backgrounders, generally provide additional information about the institution making an announcement (Figure 9–1). Backgrounders are usually longer and more general in content than the news release. For example, a two-page release announcing the merger of two organizations may not permit much description of the companies involved. A four- or five-page backgrounder provides editors with more depth on the makeup, activities, and history of the merging firms. Backgrounders are usually not used in their entirety by the media but rather are excerpted.

Subject matter dictates backgrounder style. Some backgrounders are written like a news release, in a snappy and factual manner. Others take a more descriptive and narrative form.

Example One: News Release Style

BACKGROUNDER—SWENSEN'S ICE CREAM COMPANY

The original Swensen's Ice Cream Shoppe was established in 1948 by Earle Swensen at the corner of Union and Hyde in San Francisco.

K mart Corporation News

Contact: Barbara Palazzolo
            Manager of Public
            Communications
            (313) 643-5200

FOR IMMEDIATE RELEASE

K MART TOUCHES COMMUNITY
THROUGH LOST CHILD PROGRAM

TROY, Mich., May 1, 1985 -- If K mart is successful in implementing its Lost Child Program, its services could help prevent the abduction of innocent children across the country. But while child safety is the ultimate objective of the company's nationwide public service program, even the most modest of figures indicate the battle will be uphill -- and long.

Flyers that feature the photographs of four missing children, as well as safety tips for parents and children, will be available free of charge to all K mart customers in displays at K mart stores, and also inserted into each photo processing order handled by K mart's more than 2,000 stores nationwide. The company processes more than 43 million bags of photographs annually.

Persons who may have information about a child pictured on a flyer will be instructed to phone the National Center for Missing and Exploited Children at its toll-free phone number (1-800-843-5678).

- more -

- 2 -

The program was proposed by Guardian Industries Photo Division, a supplier of photo processing to K mart. Guardian will provide all graphic services for the flyers. K mart will also help with the financing of the program and prepare and distribute the first seven million flyers to U.S. K mart stores. The flyers will be inserted into photo orders by each photo processor -- Guardian, American Photo, Colorcraft, Bicknell and Phototron. Photos will be changed every month. After the first seven million flyers are used, the individual photo processors will print and distribute flyers in their orders to K mart.

"The individual stores will be able to implement the program as it best suits their geographic area and business," K mart Vice Chairman Samuel G. Leftwich said. "We will then monitor the stores to get a feel for the local impact of the program.

"The program will begin at our store level. K mart managers will also be provided with speeches to address community groups as to the need of child safety education. In addition, we are looking to other avenues to help better educate children and parents about the seriousness of abductions.

"By using the flyers and other information, K mart will have the means to convey to the public information that could lead to the recovery of missing children," he added. "But the greatest service we can provide our communities is that of education."

- 0 -

FIGURE 9–1 This backgrounder supplements information in the sponsor's news release, which accompanied it. (Courtesy of K Mart Corporation)

In 1963 Mr. Swensen licensed the company's predecessor, See Us-Freeze, Inc., later known as United Outlets, Inc., to use Swensen's trade names, trade secrets, recipes, and methods of operation as the basis for Swensen's franchise system. The license agreement was modified in June 1975 and permits the company to use the licensed property and franchise Swensen's shops in all areas of the world except the city and county of San Francisco.

In February 1980 the company became a wholly owned subsidiary of Red River Resources, Inc., and its corporate headquarters was moved to Phoenix, Arizona.

Swensen's now has operations in 31 states and the District of Columbia as well as seven foreign countries.

Example Two: Descriptive, Narrative Style

BACKGROUNDER—SICKLE CELL DISEASE

The man was a West Indian black, a 20-year-old student in a professional school in Illinois. One day in 1904, he came to James B. Herrick, an eminent Chicago cardiologist, with symptoms Herrick had never seen before and could not find in the literature. The patient had shortness of breath, a disinclination for exercise, palpitation, jaundice, cough, dizziness, headache, leg ulcers, scars from old leg ulcers, many palpable lymph nodes, pale mucous membranes, muscular rheumatism, severe upper abdominal pain, dark urine, and anemia. Blood smears showed many odd-shaped cells, but what arrested the eye was the presence of numerous sickle-shaped cells.

Herrick kept the patient under observation for many years. He did not suspect that he was looking at a disease that afflicted millions of people, including thousands of blacks in America.

In devising a backgrounder, a writer enjoys unlimited latitude. As long as the piece catches the interest of the reader/editor, any style is permissible.

THE FEATURE

Closely related to the backgrounder is the feature story. Features in magazines or newspapers are the opposite of news items. They're often light and humorous, although some are serious. One of the foremost sources of feature writing is the *Wall Street Journal*. Each business day the *Journal*'s front page is dominated by three "leader" articles, most written in a time-tested feature writing style. Basically, the *Journal* system separates each story into three distinct parts, sometimes labeled the D-E-E system (description, explanation, evaluation).[1]

Description

The typical *Journal* story begins by describing an existing situation, often with a light touch, in such a way that readers relate it directly to their own environment.

Seated at student desks in a small room, prospective Delta Airline pilots pore over a battery of psychological tests.

"This is ridiculous," mutters one of the four applicants. "What do these tests have to do with whether I'll make a good pilot? What the hell does it matter whether I like to sing in the shower?"

It may matter a great deal.[2]

Explanation

The second part of the *Journal* feature explains how a situation, trend, or event came to be. It is often historical in nature, citing dates, places, and people from the past. It often relates how other factors (economic, sociopolitical, or environmental) may have come to bear on the topic.

Delta is among hundreds of U.S. concerns that are turning more to psychologists for guidance in deciding who gets what job. Through testing and interviews, psychologists help screen prospective employees and select promotion candidates—occasionally all the way up the corporate ladder. The trend isn't new.[3]

Evaluation

The final section of the *Journal* feature evaluates the meaning of what is contained in the first two parts. It often focuses on the future, frequently quoting sociologists, psychologists, or other experts on the meaning of the phenomenon discussed.

"We're not interested in exposing or destroying a man," says Melvin Reid, president of a management consulting firm that does psychological testing. "We're interested in coming to general conclusions that both employee and employer will find useful in selection and placement."[4]

In public relations the D-E-E approach often works in feature writing assignments (Figure 9–2).

THE CASE HISTORY

The case history is frequently used to tell about a customer's favorable use of a company's product or service. Generally, the case history writer works for the company whose product or service is involved. Magazines, particularly trade journals, often welcome case histories, contending that one person's experience may be instructive to another.

Case history articles generally follow a five-part formula.

1. They present a problem experienced by one company but applicable to many other firms.
2. They indicate how the dimensions of the problem were defined by the company using the product.

FINE *food & spirits*

May 6, 1985

Ken Fine
(201) 569-8999

TENAFLY "DAIRY QUEEN" SOLD TO OWNERS OF FINE FOOD & SPIRITS

The Tenafly "Dairy Queen", on the verge of being torn down for a retail-office building, has been rescued from the wrecking ball by its next-door neighbors.

The owners of Fine Food & Spirits, 14 Riveredge Road, have agreed to purchase the "Dairy Queen" from Ed and Beatrice Bugash, owners of the Tenafly landmark since 1960.

"We're delighted," said Mr. Bugash, who along with his wife have been fixtures in the ice cream store 12 hours a day, six months a year for the past 25 years.

"This store is a part of Tenafly -- an institution -- and we feel better now knowing the Fines will continue the tradition," said Mr. Bugash.

Ken Fine, co-owner of Fine Food & Spirits, said he and his partners bought the ice cream store as much for the community as they did for themselves. "We've grown up in Tenafly over the past 30 years, and the 'Dairy Queen' has always been a part of this community," said Mr. Fine.

- more -

FINE FOOD & SPIRITS 14 Riveredge Road, Tenafly, New Jersey 07670 (201) 569-8999

FINE FOOD & SPIRITS

- 2 -

"After school, after Little League -- we all had to rush to the 'Dairy Queen.' It was second nature," he added.

Mr. Fine and his associates began negotiating for the property after a proposed sale to Michael Goodman & Associates fell through, when the developers failed to obtain a variance from the Tenafly Planning Board to build a retail-office building on the site.

The new owners began operating the store last month and plan major enhancements in the months ahead. "First, we'll add benches, bike racks and shrubs to create a park-like environment for the family," Mr. Fine said. "Later on, we'll introduce coffee, bagels, rolls and donuts for morning commuters and business people. We'll also sell newspapers."

Mr. Fine said that additional plans call for expanding to a limited menu of light food to go -- hamburgers, hot dogs, chicken nuggets, old-fashioned French fries and the like. "We'll also be adding a cookie and penny candy store," Mr. Fine said.

"Our goal is to ensure that this store which has been a part of Tenafly for 30 years, continues as a community focal point for many years to come," said Mr. Fine.

\# \# \#

A late-inning save for the old Dairy Queen

By John H. Kuhn
Staff Writer

TENAFLY — A tradition is being saved at West Railroad Avenue and Riveredge Road.

While the planning board was considering the now-defunct plan for a two-story commercial building on the Dairy Queen property, youngsters in borough sports programs were asking parents and coaches where they would get their after-game treats if the DQ closed.

But Ken Fine, who owns Fine Foods and Spirits store, has allayed the youngsters' fears. He has bought the half-acre site and plans to continue and expand the business, he said in a recent interview.

The purchase will provide additional parking for Fine's other business, especially if he goes ahead with plans for a cafe restaurant on the second floor of his food-and-liquor store. "That's in the back of my mind," he said, "but not this year."

The Dairy Queen has been a fixture at the corner since it opened in 1954. "It's always been part of the fun of winning," one youngster said between bites from an oversize ice-cream cone."

Remarked a coach: "I'd save some money, but it wouldn't be the same for the kids with the DQ."

Mr. and Mrs. Ed Bugash, who operated the store from 1960 until recently, kept it open from spring until fall and closed the rest of the year. But Fine said he plans to operate it year-round, add a grill and a penny-candy section, and provide cookies and breads.

"There will be a small expansion," said Fine, who also plans to provide breakfast and to clean the area. "The outlook for business is good, and it will benefit the adjacent business."

"We've grown up in Tenafly over the past 30 years," he said, "and the Dairy Queen has always been a part of this community. After school, after Little League, we all had to rush to the DQ."

Said Bugash: "This store is a part of Tenafly — an institution — and we feel better now knowing it will continue the tradition."

Fine would not disclose what he paid for the property and business, but he said it was less than the $550,000 mentioned when the commercial developer was before the planning board. The board rejected the commercial plan because of a lack of off-street parking.

FIGURE 9–2 A news release, written in feature style, may provoke an editor to use material that might not otherwise merit news coverage. This feature release, which resulted in news coverage, is a case in point. (Newspaper article reprinted by permission from *The Record,* Hackensack, New Jersey)

3. They indicate the solution adopted.
4. They explain the advantages of the adopted solution.
5. They detail the user company's experience after adopting the solution.

Incorporating the D-E-E approach into the case history writing process may interest an editor in a particular product or service. Done skillfully, such a case history is soft sell at its best—beneficial to the company and interesting and informative to the editor and readers.

THE BYLINER

The bylined article, or byliner, is a story signed and ostensibly authored by an officer of a particular firm. Often, however, the byliner is ghostwritten by a public relations professional. In addition to carrying considerable prestige in certain publications, byliners allow corporate spokespeople to express their views without being subject to major reinterpretation by the publication.

Perhaps the major advantage of a byliner is that it positions executives as experts. The fact that an organization's officer has authored an informed article on a subject means that not only are the officer and the organization credible sources but also, by inference, that they are perhaps more highly regarded on the issues at hand than their competitors. Indeed, the ultimate audience exposed to a byliner may greatly exceed the circulation of the periodical in which the article appears. Organizations regularly use byliner reprints as direct mail pieces to further their image with key constituent groups. Such use of reprints is further discussed in chapter 11.

It is often a good idea for a writer to outline the byliner, noting at the outset the major points the author wishes to get across. Although most byliners are more formal than case histories and generally contain many facts and figures, they can still lend themselves to the D-E-E writing approach.

THE MEMORANDUM

Humorist Art Buchwald tells of the child who visited his father's office. When asked what his dad did, the son replied, "He sends pieces of paper to other people, and other people send pieces of paper to him." Most people who work know a great deal about memoranda. Inside many organizations the memo is the most popular form of communication. Memos are written for a multitude of purposes and adopt numerous forms. Even though almost everyone gets into the memo-writing act, writing memos correctly takes practice and hard work.

The key to writing good memos is clear thinking. Many memos reflect unclear thinking and are plagued by verbosity and fuzzy language. Inverted pyramid style is often a good way to compose a memo. More often, rewriting turns out to be the key. As professor Marvin Swift has put it,

Don't—Repeat—Don't Use "Do Not"

In writing for the eye, public relations practitioners should keep in mind that publications sometimes mistakenly drop out words in print. Invariably, the most important words are the ones dropped.

For example, the public relations officer of the labor union who issues the statement "We do not intend to strike," may have his quote appear in the next day's paper as "We do intend to strike"—the *not* having been inadvertently dropped by the paper. A slight yet significant change.

The remedy: Use contractions. It's pretty hard to drop out a significant word or distort the intended meaning when the statement is "We don't intend to strike."

Rewriting demands a real openmindedness and objectivity. It demands a willingness to cull verbiage so that ideas stand out clearly. And it demands a willingness to meet logical contradictions head-on and trace them to the premises that have created them. In short, it forces a writer to get up his courage and expose his thinking process to his own intelligence . . . . It demands that you put yourself through the wringer, intellectually and emotionally, to squeeze out the best you can offer.[5]

Public relations people, in particular, must write good memos. Frequently they must prepare long, internal white papers, position papers, or standby statements that are to clearly outline the firm's position. Such documents are used to respond to inquiries on sensitive subjects and can't be vague or subject to misinterpretation.

In general, the more textually taut a memo is, the less chance that it will fall prey to others in the organization who are prone to pounce on it. One rule of thumb for memo writing is to pretend to send the memo to yourself as a straight telegram at your own expense. Chances are, the less your telegram costs, the more effective the memo will be.

THE PITCH LETTER

The pitch letter is a sales letter, pure and simple. Its purpose is to interest an editor or reporter in a possible story, interview, or event. Figure 9–3 offers an example of two excellent pitch letters for the same product. Although letter styles run the gamut, the best are direct and to the point, while at the same time catchy and evocative. The lead, unlike that of a rambling personal letter, should hit the reader between the eyes.

IF you EVER WANT TO SEE the little NATIONAL LAMPOON aLive again IN YOUR CRUmmY MAILBOX, you KNOW WhAt you HAVE to DO!!!

you've BEEN WARNED.
DON'T PLAY CUTE.

National Lampoon

This Is Your Last Chance . . .

Say good-bye, sweetheart. This is it! You can kiss the $7.95 one-year subscription to the *National Lampoon* good-bye just as you've said *au revoir* and *harry verderchi* to the fifty-cent gallon of gas, the ten-cent cigar, and the twenty-cent bus ride.

The price is going up and we're giving you fair warning. We're not saying exactly how much we're going to charge for the new one-year subscription but — it's less than the gross national product of Yugoslavia and more than a rubdown in a midget massage parlor.

The reasons for the increase in price are numerous in addition to greed:

1. The cost of paper has skyrocketed. All right, let's examine that. What does it mean to a magazine operation? Well, our editors drink a lot of coffee and this means an increase in the price of coffee cups. They throw paper airplanes around the room while trying to think of funny things to say. Up your cost of paper airplanes by 50 percent.

2. The cost of typewriters has increased. This doesn't affect us since no one on our staff knows how to type.

3. The cost of manufacturing has increased. This means that our editor in chief will be paying more for his Mercedes-Benz this year, and that means more for you to kick in. Would you ask the editor in chief of the world's most widely read adult humor magazine to drive around in last year's Mercedes-Benz?

4. The price of grain is spiraling. (We don't know what that means, but it is an exact quote from the *Wall Street Journal* so it must be important.)

O.K., put this all together and it means — raise the subscription prices. No more $7.95. So, this is it. This is your last chance. From here on in, it's clipsville. You pay more.

If you really want to save, take out a two- or three-year subscription. The savings are so big that we actually lose money every time you or anyone else subscribes for two or three years. We do it only because our subscription manager is insecure and he wants to know that he'll have at least a handful of people around for a long time.

No more message. If you want the latest in yocks, mirth, and lovable satire, subscribe today and subscribe at these pre-inflation prices.

Sincerely,

Herbert Hoover
Subscription Manager

FIGURE 9-3 Pitch letters should be enticing, catchy, and evocative. Even though these examples from the subscription department of the *National Lampoon* magazine may not qualify as garden variety pitch letters, they certainly are enticing, catchy, and evocative. (Courtesy of *National Lampoon*)

For example, Father Bruce Ritter, the founder of Covenant House, a home for wayward children, began one letter this way:

> *Please* read what I have to tell you.
> Children are being sold.
> Their bodies and spirits are being corrupted.
> They are forced into a life of abuse and degradation.
> Where?
> India? Uganda? Peru?
> No!
> Right here in New York, the Big Apple, Fun City.
> Covenant House began as a response to the needs of these children of the streets. Will you join with me in helping to carry out this work?

Such unbridled, heart-tugging language is typical of a good, compassionate pitch letter.

Pitch letters that sell generally contain several key elements. First, they open with a grabber, an interesting statement that impels the reader to read on. Next, they explain why the editor and/or publication should be interested in the pitch, or invitation. Finally, they are personally written to specific people, rather than being addressed to ''editor'' (which is the journalistic equivalent of ''occupant'').

A variant of the pitch letter is the query letter, in which the practitioner asks an editor to consider an article on the company's or client's product. Normally, the query letter describes the product in some detail and invites the editor to respond if interested in pursuing the suggested story.

Pitch letter mechanics are similar to those of the release. Writing should be sharp and pointed. Whenever possible, length should be held to one page. Spelling of names, especially the editor's, should be perfect. Facts and statements in the letter should be carefully checked. Practitioners should remember that editors regularly receive many pitch letters. If an editor isn't interested in a pitch, don't badger. The trick is to capture in the letter the essence of a story that the editor can't pass up.

OTHER TOOLS

Other public relations tools, such as the round-up article, the fact sheet, and the Q & A, may be helpful in certain infrequent situations.

The Round-Up Article

Although many publications discourage publicity about a single company, they encourage articles that summarize, or round up, the experiences of several companies within an industry. These survey articles may be initiated by the publications themselves or at the suggestions of public relations people.

Weaker or smaller companies, in particular, can benefit from being included in a round-up story with stronger, larger adversaries. Thoroughly researching and drafting round-up articles is a good way to secure articles that mention the practitioner's firm in favorable association with top competitors. Wire services, in particular, are regular users of round-ups.

The Fact Sheet

Fact sheets are short documents that compactly profile an organization. They generally support the information in news releases and backgrounders. Editors find fact sheets helpful as a quick supply of resource material for articles.

Fact sheets are designed to provide an editor with a quick thumbnail sketch of an organization, individual, or event. For example, a typical one-page corporate fact sheet includes a brief description of the company and its product lines, the names of its top managers, its location, current sales figures, leading products, and a summary of its history. How is all this possible in a one-page sketch? Figure 9–4 shows how.

The Q & A

The question and answer form, or Q & A, often substitutes for or complements a fact sheet in conveying easy-to-follow information. In the Q & A the writer lists frequently asked questions about the subject and then provides appropriate answers. A skillfully written Q & A can often substitute for a personal interview between an editor and a company official.

PHOTOGRAPHIC SUPPORTS

Photos, if used properly, can enhance brochures, annual reports, or even news releases. Any practitioner involved with printed material should know the basics of photography. Although a detailed discussion of photographic terms and techniques falls beyond the scope of this book, public relations practitioners should be relatively conversant with photographic terminology and able to recognize the attributes that characterize good photos.

1. Photos should be "live," in real environments with believable people instead of studio shots of stilted models (Figure 9–5).
2. They should focus clearly on the issue, product, image, or person that the organization wishes to emphasize, without irrelevant, visually distracting clutter in the foreground or background.
3. They should be eye-catching, using angles creatively—overhead, below, to the side—to suggest movement on the part of the photographer.
4. They must express a viewpoint—an underlying message.

FOR IMMEDIATE RELEASE
AUGUST 13, 1987

FOR MORE INFORMATION CONTACT:
RICK LYKE
ERIC MOWER AND ASSOCIATES INC.
315/472-4703

QUICK FACTS ON THE C.F. HATHAWAY COMPANY

COMPANY: C.F. Hathaway is a division of Warnaco Inc. the $600 million apparel marketer. Warnaco's Menswear Group includes Hathaway, and lines from Christian Dior, Chaps by Ralph Lauren, Puritan, Pringle of Scotland and Thane. Other Warnaco apparel divisions include: Warner's and Olga intimate apparel, Geoffrey Beene, Hathaway for Women, White Stag Sportswear for women; and activewear by Speedo, Spalding, Jack Nicklaus and White Stag Skiwear.

MANAGEMENT: Richard Pressler is president and chief executive officer of C.F. Hathaway Co.

LOCATION: C.F. Hathaway Co. has corporate offices at 90 Park Avenue in New York and headquarter manufacturing facilities in Waterville, Maine. Hathaway apparel is sold worldwide through various licensing agreements.

SALES: C.F. Hathaway sales increased 22 percent nationwide in 1986, with a 38 percent increase in key brand markets during a year in which the dress shirt industry reported a flat performance.

PRODUCTS: C.F. Hathaway Company is famous for its dress shirts and is recognized, as well, for neckwear and sportswear.

LEADERSHIP: C.F. Hathaway Company is America's oldest manufacturer of dress shirts, with its roots dating back to 1837. The company is recognized for its many innovations in styling and manufacturing techniques.

#

A Division of **WARNACO** Inc.

FIGURE 9–4 In this fact sheet, the public relations counsel of C. F. Hathaway Company describes all that an editor needs to know about the firm—on one sheet of paper in a rapid-fire, straightforward manner. (Courtesy of C. F. Hathaway Company)

These kinds of shots are often difficult, especially for the novice photographer. It often makes sense, therefore, to hire a professional. Some organizations are fortunate to have photographers on staff. Others must hire freelancers who may charge upwards of $1,000 to $2,500 per day for annual report work.

Almost as important as the photograph itself is the coordination of photographic assignments. Practitioners should work closely with the photographer and the intended subject, notifying both well in advance of specific needs and dates. Too often, a photographer must wait—and charge for—a day or two just for a setup to be ready. Worse, photos taken in hasty setups may show safety hazards or outdated equipment, necessitating costly retouching or even reshooting. Finally, photographers may not understand the nuances behind a public relations photo without the counsel of the person who scheduled the

FIGURE 9–5 Occasionally, a specially conceived photo can attract extensive publicity. In 1959, when Chase Manhattan Bank was in the midst of constructing its downtown One Chase Manhattan Plaza headquarters, photographer Robert Mottar asked the hundreds of workers to freeze for a moment so that this picture could be recorded for posterity. It also was reported in many of New York City's daily newspapers, which acknowledged both the bank and its new location. (Courtesy of Chase Manhattan Bank)

shot. Consequently, planning for and following through on photographic assignments becomes a critical responsibility for practitioners.

Just as photos say something about the nature of an organization, so interesting graphic design suggests innovation and leadership. Annual report design, for example, is big business. Many firms, large and small, refuse to cut corners in the design of printed material. Charts, typography, photo captions, headlines—even paper stock—are important elements in conveying a corporate image. Today, expressing an institutional personality is such a critical and delicate challenge that outside assistance is generally considered a wise and necessary investment.

THE PRESS KIT

Press kits are often distributed to the media in conjunction with an announcement. Press kits incorporate several methods of communication, including graphics, for possible use by newspapers and magazines. A bare-bones press kit consists of a news release, backgrounder, and perhaps a photo. This kit may be all the media need to understand and portray an announcement. Other announcements might require a fact sheet or a Q&A. It is important to weigh carefully each item in the press kit. An editor does require a certain amount of information to understand a story but doesn't appreciate being overwhelmed by too much copy and too many photos. In making up a press kit, the ability to judge how much is enough becomes critical. Figure 9–6 shows the press kit used to unveil a statue marking the 25th anniversary of David Rockefeller on Wall Street.

In preparing a press kit, public relations practitioners must keep the following points in mind:

- Be sure information is accurate and thorough and answers the most fundamental questions a journalist may have.
- Provide sufficient background information to allow the editor to select a story angle from the materials prepared.
- Don't be too commercial. Offer balanced, objective information.
- Confine opinions and value judgments to quotes from credible sources.
- Never lie. It's tantamount to editorial suicide.
- Visually arresting graphics may mean the difference between finding the item in the next day's paper or in the same day's wastebasket.

THE STANDBY STATEMENT

Organizations sometimes take actions or make announcements that they know will lead to media inquiries or even public protests. In such cases firms prepare concise statements to clarify their positions, should they be called to explain. Such standby statements generally are defensive in nature. They should be

FIGURE 9–6 Although a press kit can have an unlimited number of materials, often a complete story can be told with just a few strategic documents. In this case a news release, fact sheet/backgrounder, and photograph tell the whole story. (Courtesy of Chase Manhattan Bank)

The Misleading Memo

To: Public Relations Department
From: Rita Rey, Public Relations Director

It has recently been brought to my attention that many of the press comments our organization has been receiving in the negative may stem from our policy of refusing all press interviews, regardless of the publication making the request.

Obviously, such negative stories do our company no good with its many publics and often present an unfair and misleading presentation as to our philosophy and approach. I wish therefore to inform all concerned—those who have refused interviews in the past and all others as well—that we will immediately change our policy to entertain all requests from the press and judge each on its merits.

If there are any questions about company policy on this matter, please contact me.

QUESTIONS

1. What's wrong with this memo?
2. How would you improve it?

brief and unambiguous so as not to raise more questions than they answer. Such events as executive firings, layoffs, price increases, or extraordinary losses are all subject to subsequent scrutiny by the media and are therefore proper candidates for standby statements.

TO WRITE OR NOT TO WRITE

Written methods of communication are often overused. Everyone from editors to corporate presidents complains about getting too much paper. So before the professional even thinks of putting thoughts on paper, the plan must be assessed and these questions answered:

1. **Will writing serve a practical purpose?** Have a use in mind for the communication before you write it. If you can't come up with a purpose, don't write.
2. **Is writing the most effective way to communicate?** Face-to-face or telephone communication may be better and more direct than writing. Writing

occasionally is used as an excuse for not calling or seeing someone in person. In most cases it's better to resolve a situation quickly, and there is no quicker method than going directly to the source.

Sometimes, too, the written word is lifeless. An audiovisual presentation to a training group, for example, may be more interesting and effective than a training manual. Again, the objective of the message dictates the form.

3. **What is the risk?** Writing is always risky. Just ask a lawyer. Retracting a printed comment is a lot harder than taking back an oral one. Before committing words to paper, carefully weigh the risks. In the early 1970s a confidential internal memo from an ITT lobbyist made its way into the hands of syndicated columnist Jack Anderson, who printed the memo verbatim. The memo concerned sensitive negotiations between ITT and the U.S. Justice Department. Once the secret document was published, ITT's reputation took a severe tumble. Should the memo have been written? No. Could ITT have avoided the scandal? Absolutely.

4. **Are the timing and the person doing the writing right?** Timing is extremely important in writing. A message, like a joke, can fall flat if the timing is off. Timing, of course, depends on the particular subject and the circumstances surrounding it. The question "Would it be better to wait?" should always be asked before writing. The person doing the writing is also important. A writer should always ask whether he or she is the most appropriate person to write. Perhaps the message is right, but someone at a different level or in a different position in the organization may be able to write it better.

The pen—or the typewriter—is a potent weapon. But like any weapon, writing must be used prudently and properly to achieve the desired objective.*

NOTES

1. Timothy Hubbard, "Anatomy of Excellence," *Columbia Journalism Review* (Fall 1968): 31–33.
2. John Koten, "Psychologists Play Bigger Corporate Role in Placing of Personnel," *Wall Street Journal*, 11 July 1978, 1. Reprinted by permission of Dow Jones & Co., Inc.
3. Ibid.
4. Ibid., p. 20.
5. Marvin H. Switt, "Clear Writing Means Clear Thinking Means . . . ," *Harvard Business Review* (January–February 1973): 62.

*For an interesting analysis of when to write and when not to write, see Dan J. Forrestal, "It's the Little Things That Count," *Public Relations Quarterly* (Summer 1974): 17–18.

Berrey, Lester V. *Roget's International Thesaurus*. 3d ed. New York: Thomas Y. Crowell, 1962.

Blythin, Evan, and Larry A. Samovar. *Communicating Effectively on Television*. Belmont, CA: Wadsworth Publishing, 1985.

Cable Hotline. New York: Larimi Communications (5 W. 37th St.). Monthly.

Dyer, Janet. " 'Predictable': The Watchword for 1980 Reports." *Public Relations Journal* (August 1981): 9. Annual report layouts for the 1980s seem to follow the same format time after time.

Fernald, James C. *Funk & Wagnalls Standard Handbook of Synonyms, Antonyms and Prepositions*. New York: Funk & Wagnalls, 1947.

Grabow, Bert G. "10 Laws of Report Production." *Public Relations Journal* (August 1981): 18–19. Grabow discusses the 10 uncodified laws of annual report production.

Honaker, Charles. "News Releases Revisited." *Public Relations Journal* (April 1981): 25–27.

"How to Write a Wrong." Long Beach, CA: American Association of Retired Persons (P.O. Box 2400). The objective here is to assist consumers in writing to-the-point complaint letters. Free.

Lustig, Theodore. "The Trade Show as Report Theme." *Public Relations Journal* (August 1981): 14–17.

G & C Merriam Co. *The Merriam-Webster Book of Word Histories*. Springfield, MA: G & C Merriam Co., 1976. This volume rejects certain accepted theories of meaning but presents many of interest. Under the *G's* alone you can learn the origin of *genius, gin, goon, gorgeous, gossip, gridiron,* and more.

———. *The Merriam-Webster Pocket Dictionary of Synonyms*. Springfield, MA: G & C Merriam Co., 1972. This is useful for careful attention to shades of meaning and for short examples of good usage by established writers.

———. *The Merriam-Webster Thesaurus*. Springfield, MA: G & C Merriam Co., 1978. More than 100,000 synonyms, antonyms, idiomatic equivalents, related words, and contrasted terms are included.

Miller, Martin, and Frank Pagani. "Upgrading Small Company Reports." *Public Relations Journal* (August 1981): 12–13.

Oxford University Press. *The Compact Edition of the Oxford English Dictionary*. Oxford, England: Oxford University Press, 1971.

Riblet, Carl, Jr. *The Solid Gold Copy Editor*. Tucson, AZ: Flacon, 1972.

Television & Cable Factbook. 2 vols. Washington, DC: TV Digest (1836 Jefferson Place, NW).

SUGGESTED READINGS

The Leather Pitch Letter

In January 1987 Dr. Jane Mellenkamph of the University of Idaho completed experimentation on a novel process through which genuine leather could be made water repellent. With this process, for the first time ever, leather could be washed with ordinary laundry soap and water. Dr. Mellenkamph immediately patented her leather-treating process and spread the word throughout the leather-tanning industry.

In June Samuel S. Sobelham, president of Associated Leather Tanners of Atlanta, purchased all rights to Dr. Mellenkamph's patent. Sobelham, a veteran in the industry, considered the Mellenkamph formula the most revolutionary breakthrough in history. Sobelham was convinced that glove manufacturers would fall all over each other to purchase his specially treated, water-resistant leather.

But Sobelham misjudged his market. For the next year he tried unsuccessfully to create an interest in the new product. "We've heard all these washable leather stories before," echoed most of the glove manufacturers. "There's no such thing as a washable leather; don't bother us" was the reply he heard most often.

By June 1988 Sobelham concluded it was useless to deal directly with manufacturers. He would have to go around them to the only group who could force glove manufacturers to act—the general public.

He turned to public relations counselor Ed Andrews to come up with a plan to inform the public about the new product. He explained to Andrews that this product was developed at the critical stage of the tanning process and exceeded any federal washability standards. Sobelham said there was no other product like it on the market. He said that the only reason glove manufacturers weren't yet interested in the product was that they frankly couldn't and didn't believe it.

Andrews returned to his small shop and considered his strategy to put the product on the map and convince glove manufacturers that public interest in and potential demand for the product were keen. Three days later he was back to Sobelham with the following plan. He thought that they could hold a press conference in the Grand Ballroom of New

York City's Plaza Hotel at noon on July 1. Rather than billing it as a traditional press conference, it would be a fashion show at which professional models would exhibit all kinds of expensive and nonexpensive gloves made of washable leather. The gloves themselves would run the gamut of textures, styles, and colors.

In addition to the gloves and models, the highlight of the conference would be a long table on which were crystal bowls filled with various materials—axle grease, chicken fat, chocolate ice cream, coffee, grape juice, etc. After exhibiting the gloves to the crowd, each model would dip the gloves in a different bowl and would then deposit them in one of two washing machines at the front of the room. The gloves would be washed and the results dramatically revealed to the crowd. This unique fashion show, Andrews reasoned, could provoke important headlines from the nation's influential fashion editors in attendance. With favorable stories from the fashion press, glove manufacturers around the country would be bidding for Associated Leather Tanners' patented process.

Sobelham reacted with one word to Andrews's idea, "Boffo!"

When Andrews returned to his own office, he realized that the fashion editors would have to be drawn to the fashion show through a pitch letter. He knew that each day, major fashion editors received 10 to 20 letters inviting them to various functions. Sometimes the pitch letter meant the difference between an important attendee and a no-show. Therefore, Andrews figured, his pitch letter had to be tight, catchy, and enticing—in other words, perfect. If the editors failed to show, the Ed Andrews public relations firm would be minus one client.

QUESTIONS

1. What are the essential facts that Andrews must get into his pitch letter?
2. If you were Andrews, would you send every editor the same pitch letter, or would particular editors get different versions?
3. If you were Andrews, what would you say in your pitch letter?

Writing for the Ear

10

Writing for listening involves the spoken word. A person who hears a speech, radio broadcast, or television announcement generally gets one crack at the message. There is rarely a second chance.

The key to writing for listening is to write as if you are speaking. Use simple, short sentences, active verbs, contractions, and one- and two-syllable words. Let phrases stand alone. Be brief.

This chapter will touch on the most widely used methods of communicating to be heard, including speeches, presentations, broadcast releases, public service announcements, and film scripts. As people read less and watch and listen more, writing for the ear becomes increasingly important for the public relations professional. Accordingly, where once public relations was dominated by print-oriented professionals, today, more and more practitioners enter the field with strong radio and television orientations.

THE SPEECH

Speech writing has become one of the most coveted public relations skills. Increasingly, speech writers have used their access to management to move up the organizational ladder. The prominence they enjoy is due largely to the importance top executives place on making speeches.* Today's executives are called on by government and special interest groups to defend their policies, justify their prices, and explain their practices to a much greater degree than ever before. In this environment a good speech writer becomes a valuable asset.

Most executives rely on public relations professionals to write their speeches and, in many cases, to contribute to the ideas for the speech. The work is demanding. According to Pittsburgh speech writer James G. Busse, a

---

*A poll commissioned by *PR Reporter* (vol. 20, no. 50, 19 December 1977, p. 2) found speech making to be the major public relations activity in which chief executives participated.

Richard F. Stockton

Richard F. Stockton is the senior advisor and coordinator of executive presentations for Exxon Corporation. He previously served as a senior speech writer for Chase Manhattan Bank, Morgan Guaranty Trust Company, and Citibank. Mr. Stockton's two decades of executive speech writing follow 10 years of dramatic writing for radio, stage, and network television.

How hard is it to write an executive speech?

Like a marriage, it flows along more smoothly when both parties work at it. A speech writer who has to function in isolation, as a mind reader, is less likely to get the message right the first time. But it can be done. The first draft of a speech is generally the easiest. Then you begin earning your keep.

How does one become a speech writer?
By infiltration. No one has ever been hired as a speech writer who wasn't already an employed speech writer. So a devious strategy is essential. Start with any job that requires writing, then drop hints and samples of your best writing wherever you can. Volunteer. Polish up some earlier speech that flopped. Offer to jot down a few ideas on some future speech—then submit the whole thing. Don't be shy. Don't give up. If you aren't fired as a nuisance, you may get a shot at it.

How does one approach the speech writing assignment?
Identify one or two—never more than three—main points about which the speaker has genuinely strong feelings and the listeners have a vested interest. Remember that a captive audience will be wholly dependent on your sense of fair play to spare them a tedious harangue or personal prejudices or a string of shopworn clichés. The audience needn't agree with the points made, so long as each one relates to their interests. If the executive doesn't share any interests with an audience, he shouldn't be there.

Is there a general format to most speeches?
Very general. A lively opening, a genial wrap-up, and no more than the above-mentioned three major points in between. If the framework gets more rigid than that, the audience will become aware of it and start following the format instead of the text. Public riots have been incited by speakers who announce that they have divided their speech into six themes with four subtopics each from which they will draw nine principles of action.

How liberally should a speech writer use humor?
Few audiences object to being entertained. In most cases, a bit of humor up front relaxes both the speaker and the audience. But it must amuse the speaker first. If the speaker has any qualms—get it out—quick! Peppering a text with lively anecdotes that the speaker is not comfortable with or not confident of putting across is a disservice to everyone.

How cognizant of the "spoken word" should a speech writer be?
There is no substitute for a good ear. Any spoken text that can't be grasped on the fly by a reasonably attentive listener is of little use. You can tidy up the grammar for publication, if it gets to that. If an audience once focuses on syntax, it can't focus on anything else. Executives are most effective when speaking in their own, comfortable, everyday vernacular.

Should a speech writer experiment with rhetorical flourishes?

Like all writers, speech writers must have a love of language and a passion for the spoken word. But like other passions, it needs restraining. If the second cleverest way of phrasing a point communicates it better, let the first one go—even if it's a line that Oscar Wilde would have envied. Planting a rhetorical landmine in an executive's text, as an experiment, has about the same practical appeal as playing Russian roulette.

How important is it to "know" the speaker?
Both the writer and the speaker will find the end-product more gratifying if it reflects not only the views but the personality of the speaker. Some speakers can inject their personal touch into a text with little studied effort in the final draft. Others can't and end up projecting a different persona from the platform than they display elsewhere. Audiences generally detect the difference and resent it. Most speakers learn from experience that the time spent in working directly with the speech writer is well invested.

Who are the best speech writers?
I have a theory, totally unprovable, that speech writers are people who always think of the perfect retort or the most telling way to drive home an argument after the party's over and everyone has gone home. If this happens to you, you may be a speech writer. You have only to improve your timing and supply those surefire, verbal dynamics to your speaker before the event.

writer must possess certain basic qualifications: "The ability to unite words and ideas skillfully and reasonably fast; a talent for getting along with top executives; an understanding of the realities of economics and business; a working knowledge of the world and its people; an inherent curiosity; a healthy respect for deadlines; the ability to write for oral presentation; good judgment in deciding what corporate managements should and shouldn't be saying; and the discretion to keep his mouth shut about his work."[1]

A speech possesses five overriding characteristics.

1. **It is designed to be heard, not read.** The mistake of writing for the eye instead of the ear is the most common trap of bad speeches. Speeches needn't be literary gems, but they ought to sound good.
2. **It uses concrete language.** The ear dislikes generalities. It responds to clear images. Ideas must be expressed sharply for the audience to get the point.
3. **It demands a positive response.** Every word, every passage, every phrase should evoke a response from the audience. The speech should possess a special vitality—and so, for that matter, should the speaker.
4. **It must have clear-cut objectives.** The speech and the speaker must have a point—a thesis. If there's no point, then it's not worth the speaker's or the audience's time to be there.
5. **It must be tailored to a specific audience.** An audience needs to feel that it is hearing something special. The most frequent complaint about organizational speeches is that they all seem interchangeable—they lack uniqueness. That's why speeches must be targeted to fit the needs of a specific audience.

Beyond these five principles and before putting words on paper, a speech writer must have a clear idea of the process—the route—to follow in developing the speech.

THE SPEECH-WRITING PROCESS

The speech-writing process breaks down into four components: (1) preparing; (2) interviewing; (3) researching; and (4) organizing and writing.

Preparing

One easy way to prepare for a speech is to follow a 4W checklist. In other words, answer the questions who, what, where, and when.

■ **Who**   The who represents two critical elements, the speaker and the audience. A writer should know all about the speaker: manner of speech, use of humor, reaction to an audience, background, and personality. It's almost impossible to write a speech for someone you don't know.

The writer should also know something about the audience. What does this audience think about this subject? What are its predispositions toward the subject and the speaker? What are the major points with which it might agree? The more familiar the writer is with the who of a speech, the easier the writing will be.

■ **What**   The what is the topic. The assigned subject must be clearly known and well defined by the writer before formal research is begun. If the writer fails to delineate the subject in advance, much of the research will be pointless.

■ **Where**   The where is the setting. A large hall requires a more formal talk than a roundtable forum. Often, the location of the speech—the city, state, or even a particular hall—bears historic or symbolic significance that can enhance a message.

■ **When**   The when is the time of the speech. People are more awake in the morning and get sleepier as the day progresses, so a dinner speech should be kept short. The when also refers to the time of year. A speech can always be linked to an upcoming holiday or special celebration.

Interviewing

Interviewing speakers in advance is essential. Without that chance the results can be dismal. A good interview with a speaker often means the difference between a strong speech and a poor one. Stated another way, the speech writer is only as good as his access to the speaker.

In the interview the speech writer gets some time—from as little as 15 minutes to over an hour—to observe the speaker firsthand and probe for the keys to the speech. The interview must accomplish at least three specific goals for the speech writer.

1. **Determine the object of the talk**   The object is different from the subject. The subject is the topic, but the object is the purpose of the speech—that is, what exactly the speaker wants the audience to do after she is finished speaking. Does she want them to storm City Hall? To love big business? To write their congressional representatives? The interviewer's essential question must be "What do you want to leave the audience with at the conclusion of your speech?" Once the speaker answers this question, the rest of the speech should fall into place.

2. **Determine the speaker's main points**   Normally, an audience can grasp only a few points during a speech. These points, which should flow directly from the object, become touchstones around which the rest of the speech is woven. Again, the writer must determine the three or four main points during the interview.

3. **Capture the speaker's characteristics**   Most of all during the interview, the writer must observe the speaker. How comfortable is she with humor? How informal or deliberate is she with words? What are her pet phrases

and expressions? The writer must file these observations away, recall them during the writing process, and factor them into the speech.

Researching

Like any writer, speech writers sometimes develop writer's block, the inability to come up with anything on paper. One way around writer's block is to adopt a formalized research procedure.

1. Dig into all literature, books, pamphlets, articles, speeches, and other writings on the speech subject. Prior speeches by the speaker are also important documents to research. A stocked file cabinet is often the speech writer's best friend.
2. Think about the subject. Bring personal thoughts to bear on the topic. Presumably, the speaker has already discussed the topic with the writer, so the writer can amplify the speaker's thoughts with his own.
3. Seek out the opinions of others on the topic. Perhaps the speaker isn't the most knowledgeable source within an organization about this specific subject. Economists, lawyers, accountants, doctors, and other technical experts may shed additional light on the topic. Outside sources, particularly politicians and business leaders, are often willing to share their ideas when requested.

Organizing and Writing

Once preparation, interviewing, and research have been completed, the fun part begins. Writing a speech becomes easier if, again, the speech is organized into its four essential elements: introduction, thesis, body, and conclusion.

Introduction   A speech introduction is a lot like handling a bar of soap in the shower: the first thing to do is get control. An introduction must grab the audience and hold its interest. An audience is alert at the beginning of a talk and is with the speaker. The writer's job is to make sure the audience stays there.

The speech writer must take full advantage of the early good nature of the audience by making the introduction snappy. Audience members need time to settle in their seats, and the speaker needs time to get his bearings on the podium. Often, the best way to win early trust and rapport with the audience is to ease into the speech with humor.

> I understand full well that a conference speaker should have one overriding priority: to make it short. Perhaps I'll steal a page from the eight-year-old who was told to write a brief biography of Benjamin Franklin. He wrote, "Benjamin Franklin was born in Boston. At an early age he moved to Philadelphia. As he walked down the street, a lady saw him and started laughing. He married the lady and discovered electricity!"

Thesis   The thesis is the object of the speech, its purpose or central idea. A good thesis statement lets an audience know in a simple sentence where a speech is going and how it will get there. For example, its purpose can be to persuade.

> The federal government must allow home football games to be televised.

Another thesis statement might be to reinforce or crystallize a belief.

> Sunday football viewing is among the most cherished of winter family home entertainments.

The purpose of yet another thesis statement might merely be to entertain.

> Football viewing in the living room can be a harrowing experience. Let me explain.

In each case the thesis statement lets the audience know early what the point of the speech will be and leads listeners to the desired conclusion. Many writers prefer to skip the thesis and hit the audience throughout the speech with the central idea in a three-part organization, commonly described as

- Tell 'em what you're gonna tell 'em.
- Tell 'em.
- Tell 'em what you told 'em.

Body   The speech body is just that—the general body of evidence that supports the three or four main points. Although facts, statistics, and figures are important elements, writers should always attempt to use comparisons or contrasts for easier audience understanding. For example, note the comparisons in the following two passages:

> It took 80 years for the telephone to be installed in 34 million American homes. It took 62 years for electrical wiring, 49 years for the automobile, and 47 years for the electric washing machine to arrive in that same number of homes. Television reached that saturation point in a mere 10 years.
>
> In a single week 272 million customers passed through the checkout counters of American supermarkets. That's equal to the combined populations of Spain, Mexico, Argentina, France, West Germany, Italy, Sweden, Switzerland, and Belgium.

Such comparisons dramatically hammer points home to a lazy audience.

Conclusion   The best advice on wrapping up a speech is to do it quickly. As the old Texas bromide goes, "If you haven't struck oil in the first 20 minutes, stop boring." Put another way, the conclusion must be blunt, short, and to the point. It may be a good idea to orally review the major points and thesis one last time and then stop. For example, the following quotation makes an excellent conclusion—short, but sweet.

In closing, it was Malcolm Muggeridge who said, "There is no such thing as darkness; only the failure to see." We in the business community are playing not to lose instead of playing to win. Let's play to win.

THE SPOKEN WORD

Since speeches are meant to be heard, the writer should take advantage of tools that emphasize the special qualities of the spoken word. Such devices can add vitality to a speech, transcending the content of the words themselves. Used skillfully, these devices can elevate a mediocre speech into a memorable one.

1. **Alliteration,** the repetition of initial sounds in words, was used in this famous description of the press in a speech given by former Vice President Spiro T. Agnew.

   Nattering nabobs of negativism.

2. **Antithesis** incorporates sharply opposed or contrasting ideas in the same passage. President Kennedy was famous for his savvy use of antithesis.

   Let us never negotiate out of fear, but let us never fear to negotiate . . . . Ask not what your country can do for you, ask what you can do for your country.

3. **Metonomy** substitutes one term for another closely associated one; it gives a passage more figurative life. For example, the following passage, without metonomy, is flat.

   Ladies and gentlemen, people of Rome, and all of you from the surrounding area, I'd like your attention for the next few moments.

   But note the difference when metonomy is used.

   Friends, Romans, countrymen, lend me your ears.

4. **Metaphor and simile** figuratively connect concepts having little literal connection, such as the use of the torch symbol in the following passage from President Kennedy.

   Let the word go forth, from this time and place, to friend and foe alike, that the torch has been passed to a new generation of Americans, born to this century and unwilling to witness or permit the slow undoing of those human rights to which we are committed today at home and around the world.

5. **Personification** gives life to animals, inanimate objects, or ideas, as in the following passage from William Hazlett.

   Prejudice is the child of ignorance.

6. **Repetition** is the use of the same words or phrases over and over again. For example, Churchill's use of the phrase "we shall" in the following:

Speech Writing Pays . . . and So Does Speech Giving

Not every practitioner wants to be a speech writer. Some can't take the dead-lines. Others shy away from the responsibility of creating 10 to 15 pages of prose out of a few ideas. But for many who do accept the challenge, speech writing pays, not only in prestige, but also in remuneration.

In government, experienced writers typically find themselves in the $35,000 to $50,000 pay range. In the corporate ranks the "scarcity of top cor-poration executive speech writers has pushed salaries into the $40,000 to $100,000 range." Indeed, large companies will frequently hire top freelance speech writers, who charge between $1,500 to $4,000 per speech.

One drawback of the executive speech writer is the frequent feeling of insecurity, brought about by management change. As one writer put it, "As an extension of the executive's mind and often being neither fish nor fowl with an organization, the position tends to have all the security of a point leader in an infantry platoon."* Nevertheless, speech writing has become a fine art, practiced by an increasing number of practitioners intent on winning greater management respect and earning more money.

So, too, has speech giving. Today, every management consultant, out-of-work politician, and retired military officer is out on the hustings delivering 20-minute messages for pay—sometimes great pay.

For example, former Central Intelligence Agency director Stansfield Turner charged $7,500 for a speech. Former broadcaster Eric Sevareid charged $10,000, whereas "Wall Street Week" moderator Louis Rukeyser and *New York Times* columnist and former public relations man William Safire chipped in at $17,000 for 20-minute talks. By the late 1980s, in fact, it seemed that just about every entrepreneurial capitalist had gotten into the speech-making act—including reborn ones like Russian defector Arkady Shevchenko, who charged $13,000 per speech. Why, even Robert Bork, the rejected Supreme Court nom-inee, drew $12,000 per speech, which no doubt helped nurse the wounds of his failure to be confirmed by the Senate.

All in all, nice work if you can get it.

*Jerry Tarver, "Washington Newspaper Reports on the Role of the Speech Writer," *The Effective Speech Writer's Newsletter* 4, no. 1 (June–July 1978): 2.

We shall fight on the beaches, we shall fight on the landing-grounds, we shall fight in the fields and in the streets, we shall fight in the hills. We shall never surrender . . .

Most of all, in using the spoken word, a writer must always understand fully the spoken words chosen in the speech. And the speaker must also understand the context and definition of the words used. One of the more embarrassing illustrations of this requirement was President John F. Kennedy's use of a German phrase while standing before the Berlin Wall. Agreeing with his speech writers that it would be appreciated to refer to himself as a symbolic citizen of Berlin, Kennedy proclaimed the immortal line: "Ich bin ein Berliner." What the president and his speech writers didn't know—but could easily have found out—was that Berlin citizens never refer to themselves as Berliners. They reserve that term for a favorite confection often munched at breakfast. Effectively, then, the president's words meant, "I am a jelly-filled doughnut."

Despite the hidden pitfalls, a public relations professional should not be reluctant to experiment with ear-oriented devices in creating speeches. These devices, after all, are the very essence of writing for listening.

Using Humor

Speech humor can be either a godsend or a curse. It's a tricky business. Humor in a speech should never be too ambitious, because the typical executive is not David Letterman. High comedy, rapid-fire jokes, and satire should be avoided at all costs. In general, speech humor must follow three rules.

1. **It must be relevant.** A speaker won't win support by rattling off unrelated jokes. Rather, humor must be an integral part of the talk, used to either underscore a point or introduce one. For example, the following illustration is a good way to introduce a speech about competitiveness and getting ahead.

   > When Woodrow Wilson was governor of New Jersey, a very ambitious young civil servant called him at his home at 3:30 one morning and said urgently, "Mr. Governor, I'm sorry to wake you, but your state auditor has just died and I'd like to know if I can take his place."
   >
   > Mr. Wilson thought that over for a moment and then replied, "Well, I guess it's all right with me, if it's all right with the undertaker!"

2. **It must be in good taste.** Topics such as sex, weight, age, race, and religion should ordinarily be avoided in a speech. People are just too touchy. If there is even the slightest chance that a joke might offend the audience, it should not be used. One safe target is the speaker herself. A speaker willing to poke fun at herself can generally win the admiration of the audience. For example, in assessing his team's chances, Oklahoma basketball coach Billy Tubbs said, "This year we plan to run and shoot. Next year we plan to run and score."

3. **It must be fresh.** Stale humor can sour an audience. A joke that goes over well for millions of people on network television would not be a good can-

Every Picture Tells a Story

As executive speech making has become more important, a plethora of counseling firms have sprung up to advise executive speakers on how to create and deliver winning speeches. Communispond, Inc. developed one of the most novel concepts. Because most executives are neither comfortable at a podium nor confident in their ability to perform before a large audience, Communispond came up with the concept of drawing pictures to replace formal written speeches. Essentially, after gathering all available evidence and support material and outlining in words what they want to cover, Communispond-trained executives are encouraged to draw pictures, called ideographs, to properly reflect the subject at hand. For example, a corporate speaker who wants to express the notion that the ship of American capitalism is being fired on by Socialist salvos around the world might sketch an ideograph similar to the one here.

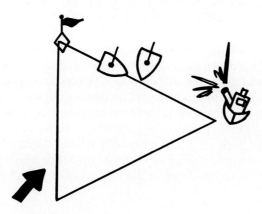

In this way Communispond-trained speakers are taught to use their nervousness to convey natural, human conviction. In other words, not constrained by lifeless written copy, an executive is free, as Communispond puts it, "to speak as well as you think."

Although not right for everyone, Communispond's unique approach, when mastered, allows for a much more extemporaneous and lively discourse than the average prepared text. Fortunately, however (at least as far as corporate speech writers are concerned), most executives still insist on the security blanket of a full-blown, written text.

didate for a subsequent speech because too many people have heard it. Speech writers must carefully select humor for its crispness. Some organizations subscribe to topical humor services to keep speakers current. Other institutions hire freelance joke writers for executive speeches. In each case speech writers try to avoid the fate of Samuel Johnson's English student, whose paper provoked the professor to respond:

> I found this report to be good and original. However, the part that was *good* was not original. And the part that was *original* was not good.

Humor is worth experimenting with. It can spark a dull speech. It can give credibility to an unsure speaker. But it's explosive, so handle it with care.

Tightening the Talk

Editing is the final responsibility of the speech writer. Like any other form of writing, the speech must be tight. After completing the draft, the writer should carefully review each sentence and word. One way to tell if a speech makes sense and moves smoothly is to recite it aloud and have someone listen to it. By obtaining advance audience reaction, a writer can present a final product with more assurance.

How long it takes to write a speech depends on the subject's complexity. Normally, a double-spaced page of speech type takes 2 to 2½ minutes to read. A 20-minute, major address may be 10 to 12 pages in length and take several days to write, exclusive of research and preparation time.

As a general rule, no speech should ever exceed 20 minutes. Most people will just not sit still these days for long addresses. So no audience will be upset at a speaker who gives a 20-minute speech when scheduled to speak for 40 minutes. Indeed, it's much better to leave the audience hungry for more rather than fed up after too much. Some of the most famous speeches in history were the shortest.

- General Douglas MacArthur, on leaving Corregidor, promised, "I shall return."
- Martin Luther King, Jr., leading a civil rights march in the South, proclaimed, "We shall overcome."
- General Dennis McAullife, on being ordered to surrender by the Nazis, defiantly replied, "Nuts!"

Now those are short—but memorable—speeches.

Embellishing the Speech

After a speech is written and approved, the skillful public relations practitioner will embellish it to help stimulate readership or republication. Having endured the arduous process of preparing a speech, the public relations professional has a responsibility to interest others in the talk. Ordinarily, the widest dissemination of an executive speech is through the public media. With many such speeches vying for editorial space, interesting an editor in using a speech is a difficult challenge. One device is to give the speech a provocative title: the title is the first thing an editor sees. Occasionally, a good title may influence an editor's decision to use excerpts of the speech in print.

Another device to disseminate executive speeches is a speaker's bureau. A speaker's bureau, generally established and managed by a firm's public relations group, is an office through which company speakers are recruited, assigned, and equipped with verbal ammunition. In other words, after willing speakers in the organization are located, the public relations department selects appropriate community forums, schedules the speakers, and prepares them with speeches. Often, a speech written for a top executive can be recycled through the speaker's bureau and used by many different speakers in various settings. Thus, the speaker's bureau can be an excellent community relations tool as well as speech dissemination device. However, setting up and maintaining a speaker's bureau entails a great deal of work and must be worth the investment in time.

The key to speech writing, just like any other kind of writing, is experience. With speech writing becoming a more competitive and sought-after pursuit among practitioners, it is difficult for an interested novice to break in. However, most political candidates or nonprofit community organizations are more than willing to allow beginners to try their hand at drafting speeches, generally for no compensation. For the budding writer such voluntarism is a good way to learn the ropes of speech writing. Few other activities in public relations offer as much fulfillment—both psychically and monetarily—as does speech writing.

MAKING AN EFFECTIVE PRESENTATION

A business presentation is different from a speech. A presentation generally is designed to sell a product, service, or idea. And everyone, somewhere along the line, must deliver a presentation. Like any other speaking device, making an effective presentation depends on following established guidelines. Here are 10 points worth pursuing prior to presenting.

1. **Get organized.** Before considering your presentation, consider the four *W*s of speech writing: Who are you addressing? What are you trying to say? Where and when should something happen?
2. **Get to the point.** Know your thesis. What are you trying to prove? What is the central purpose of your presentation?
3. **Be logical.** Organize the presentation with some logic in mind. Don't skip randomly from one thought to another. Lead from your objective to your strategies to the tactics you will use to achieve your goal.

4. **Write it out.** Don't wing it. If Johnny Carson and David Letterman write out their ad libs, so should you. Always have the words right in front of you.

5. **Anticipate the negatives.** Keep carping critics at bay. Anticipate their objections and defuse them by alluding yourself to vulnerabilities in the presentation.

6. **Speak, don't read.** Sound like you know the information. Practice before the performance. Make the presentation become a part of you. Reading suggests uncertainty. Speaking asserts assurance.

7. **Be understandable.** Speak with clarity and concreteness so that people understand you. If you want to make the sale, then you must be clear.

8. **Use wise graphics.** Audiovisual supports should do just that—support—the presentation. Graphics should be used more to tease than to provide full-blown information. And graphics shouldn't be crammed with too much information. This will detract from the overall impact of the presentation. Because there are so many audiovisual channels available to a presenter (see appendix D), it may be wise to seek professional help in devising compelling graphics for a presentation.

9. **Be convincing.** If you aren't enthusiastic about your presentation, no one else will be. Be animated. Be interesting. Be enthusiastic. Sound convinced that what you're presenting is an absolute necessity for the organization.

10. **STOP!** A short, buttoned-up presentation is much more effective than one that goes on and on. At his inaugural U.S. President William Henry Harrison delivered a two-hour, 6,000-word address into a biting wind on Pennsylvania Avenue. A month later, he died of pneumonia. The lesson: when you've said it all, sit down, and shut up.

One corporate leader who knows how to make an effective presentation is Chrysler chairman Lee Iacocca. So particular is Iacocca as a presenter that he leaves nothing to chance. For example, after many frustrating experiences with lecterns that were too small or too large or that included broken microphones, Iacocca ordered a special $5,000 lectern with special height and width features, a clock, microphones, extra media jacks, and a compressor for a cooling fan.[2] The lectern is covered with leather and prominently displays the Chrysler logo. And everywhere the chairman speaks, his lectern is sure to go.

RADIO AND TELEVISION WRITING

As many as two-thirds of the American people get their news from radio and television. Almost every American home has at least one TV set and several radios.

Indeed, there are more U.S. homes with television sets than with indoor plumbing. As a nation we have about 1,000 TV stations, 8,000 radio stations, four national TV networks, cable TV networks, and scores of national and regional radio networks. Radio is with us constantly, and TV, although not yet quite as mobile, seems almost as pervasive.

Unfortunately, TV and radio are the animals public relations people generally understand the least. For one thing, as noted earlier, many practitioners were trained in the print medium and feel more comfortable dealing with newspapers and magazines than with their electronic counterparts. Additionally, many believe that TV and radio provide limited publicity opportunities as compared to the larger news holes of the average daily newspaper.

Like it or not, TV and radio are extraordinarily powerful forces in our society. Practitioners can no longer opt to ignore them. The following discussion introduces writing vehicles that can be used in dealing with radio and TV broadcasters.

The Broadcast News Release

The principal document in reaching broadcast editors is the basic news release. Most public relations departments don't take the time to prepare special releases for broadcast use, but well they might, because broadcast style differs materially from written style. For example, although the following release might be fine for print use, it would have trouble in a broadcast context.

> GRAND FORKS, ND—The North Dakota National Bank today announced it was lowering its home mortgage lending rate to 12 percent from 12½ percent, effective immediately.
>
> Marcus D. Pickard, III, president and chief executive officer of North Dakota National Bank, said, "We are lowering the home mortgage rate because of increasing competitive pressures in the mortgage market and the trend of declining interest rates generally."
>
> Mr. Pickard added that this was the first reduction in the home mortgage rate in North Dakota in five years.

Fine for print, perhaps. But this translation would be a much better lead for broadcast.

> GRAND FORKS, ND—The home mortgage rate is coming down. North Dakota National Bank today announced it was lowering its home mortgage rate to 12 percent from 12½ percent, effective immediately.
>
> Bank President Marcus Pickard said the move was taken because of "competitive pressures and the trend of declining interest rates."
>
> This marks the first reduction in North Dakota's mortgage rate in five years.

This second release would be an ideal news item on a local TV or radio newscast. Normally, such an item lasts 10, 20, or 30 seconds, no more. Infrequently, an important item may take a minute to cover. Generally, in writing for broadcast, the shorter the better. Material must catch the listener early. The story should be told in the first two or three sentences, allowing the listener to tune out early. In other words, in most broadcast writing the inverted pyramid must be much more pointed to capture a listener's attention.

The following checklist may be helpful in writing for TV and radio.

1. **Use simple, declarative sentences.** The following sentence is awkward, overly dramatic, and unnatural.

> Turning the first spade of sod on the site of the new $3 million University Center today, Mayor Grumble hailed the Dexter University building program as a "great step forward for the state's finest university."

It would be better like this:

> Construction began today on the $3 million Dexter University Center. Mayor Grumble, on hand for the dedication, called the school's building program "a great step forward for the state's finest university."

2. **Numbers and statistics should be rounded off.** No one will remember this:

> The Ajax Company today announced year-end earnings of $999,765.

But they may remember this:

> The Ajax Company today announced year-end earnings of slightly under $1 million.

3. **Attribution should usually precede the quote.**

> Hospital administrator Christie Gardner says, "Winston Hospital will not bow to pressure."

4. **Try to avoid direct quotes.** Direct quotes often lead to long, clumsy sentence structure. Paraphrase instead.

5. **Personalize whenever possible.** The following is a good print lead but a poor broadcast one.

> The Bureau of Labor Statistics announced today that the cost of living has gone down another 2 percent in the last quarter.

Personalize it for broadcast.

> If you hadn't noticed, your grocery bill is coming down. That was the good news today from the Bureau of Labor Statistics, which announced that the cost of living has declined 2 percent for the quarter.

6. **Avoid extended description.** Middle initials, for example, or full corporate titles are unnecessary in the time-constrained environment of broadcast news. For instance, in print, write this:

> Marie M. Daniel, president and chief executive officer of Avorn Products, Inc.

The Bank Broadcast Release

Chase Manhattan Bank is one of the world's premier authorities on the energy industry. It employs a department of energy economists and is a leader in energy lending around the world. The bank is concerned with maintaining and enhancing its relationships with energy companies and regularly distributes information about the energy industry to the media. The following is a typical Chase print release about the energy industry.

NEW YORK, NY—Chase Manhattan Bank reported today that some of the abnormal factors influencing the net earnings of a group of representative petroleum companies "continued to play a major role in the first quarter of this year," resulting in gains of 43 percent in the United States and 167 percent in the rest of the world. However, the gains are likely to be short-lived, the bank said.

The bank's monthly publication, *The Petroleum Situation*, found that worldwide, the companies earned 111 percent more than the year-earlier period; however, "well over half of the worldwide increase in profits can be traced to accounting procedures involving inventories."

Chase energy economists explained that many importing nations require the companies to treat inventories on a first-in, first-out basis as well as carry very large inventories as a safety measure. "The petroleum companies are required to apply the cost of inventories acquired months earlier to their current revenue. Under this system, radical changes in the cost of inventories, either up or down, will have a major impact on profits," the bank said.

According to *The Petroleum Situation*, "That is exactly what happened in the first quarter of this year."

QUESTIONS

1. In writing for broadcast, what would be the most important messages that Chase would wish to convey?
2. What elements in this print release are inappropriate for broadcast use?
3. How would you translate this print release into appropriate broadcast form?

But in broadcast, say this:

Avorn Products President Marie Daniel

7. **Avoid hackneyed expressions and clichés.** Trite phrases should be avoided in all writing. But in broadcast such phrases are particularly annoying. Hackneyed jargon changes yearly, but these are typical shopworn expressions: "in the wake of," "passed away," "riot-torn," "scandal-ridden," "flatly denied," and "sharply rebuked."

Public relations people should aim for TV and radio more often and more releases should be written with the needs of broadcasters in mind. The skillfully written and placed broadcast release can often carry a more powerful potential for achieving results than an equivalent print release.

Public Service Announcements

The public service announcement, or PSA, is a TV or radio commercial, usually from 10 to 60 seconds long, that is broadcast at no cost to the sponsor. Nonprofit organizations, such as the Red Cross and United Way, are active users of PSAs. Commercial organizations, too, may take advantage of PSAs for their nonprofit activities, such as blood bank collections, voter registration drives, health testing, and the like. The spread of local cable television stations has expanded the opportunity for placing PSAs on the air. Nevertheless, radio PSAs are still far more widely used.

Unlike news releases, radio PSAs are generally written in advertising-copy style—punchy and pointed. The essential challenge in writing PSAs is to select the small amount of information to be used, discard extraneous information, and persuade the listener to take the desired action. The following is a typical 30-second PSA.

> The challenge of inflation has never been more serious than it is today.
> The need for strong national leadership has never been more pressing than it is today.
> Americans must tell their elected leaders to stop spending and regulating and start listening to the people.
> But they won't until *you* demand it.
> Until you demand that they stop overspending, stop crippling our economy with needless regulation, stop suffocating America with outrageous taxes.
> You can make a difference.
> This message brought to you by Hooter Valley National Bank.

Although PSAs may combine voices and sound effects for radio and film for television, the most frequently used type of PSA is the spot announcement designed to be read by station personnel or recorded by the sponsoring organization. The following 10-second PSA is an example.

> I'm Mario Andretti, and I've had some close shaves in my racing career. The National Safety Council tells us that 500 people will be killed on the highways this Memorial Day weekend. Be one of the safe ones: drive carefully and live.

In timing PSAs, it's best to read statements aloud to more accurately predict the length of time they will take on the air.

According to survey research, broadcasters use three primary criteria in determining which PSAs make the air: (1) sponsorship; (2) relevance of the message to the community; and (3) message design. In terms of sponsorship, the reputation of the sponsor for honesty and integrity is critical. As to the relevance of the message, urgent social problems, such as health and safety issues, and education and training concerns all rank high with broadcasters. In message design the more imaginative, original, and exciting the message, the better the chance of its getting free play on the air.[3]

Film Scripts

Film is another important medium for public relations people, especially for those working for national associations and large consumer products companies. Hundreds of firms sponsor films for schools and community groups. Most are professionally written and produced. For example, Modern Talking Picture Service, the nation's largest sponsored film distributor, handles films and collateral services for hundreds of clients.

Writing a film script demands linking audio and video messages. The writer must not overexplain the video but must add just enough dialogue to enhance the visual message. One common film script format is for video directions to be listed on the left side of a page and audio directions and dialogue on the right.

Although practitioners rarely get involved in writing film scripts, some do supervise commercial film companies commissioned to create a sponsored film. Obviously, familiarity with the medium helps greatly.

Video Newsclips

One of the most controversial and fast-growing public relations broadcast tools is the video newsclip—also called video news release or VNR—in which a practitioner packages a flim clip describing a news event involving an organization. VNRs have proliferated as a consequence of the growth in local news programming. Cities around the United States are running three or four half-hour newscasts a day. In the top 125 TV markets alone, there are 275 medical reporters, 155 business reporters, and 184 consumer reporters, all of whom have at least one weekly segment to fill. Much of the time, they need help.[4]

Generally produced by outside production services, VNRs run from 30 to 90 seconds and are designed to be incorporated into local TV newscasts. For example, tobacco and liquor firms have had success placing TV newsclips of auto races—with corporate identification neatly embedded in the passing race cars. In other cases the sponsoring agency may be a more integral part of the clip itself. For example, Toy Manufacturers of America produced a TV newsclip on how to choose a Christmas toy. The clip played before 103 million people throughout the nation. Brunswick Corporation created a clip demonstrating new equipment at a major bowling tournament. This clip also received wide

YOU MAKE THE CALL

The Shreveport Shriners' PSA

The Shreveport Blood Bank is approaching dangerously low levels and urgently needs to replenish its supply. The Shriners, in their traditional spirit of community service, have volunteered to organize a citywide blood drive. The Shriners will tour the city in five roving bloodmobiles. The drive will begin Monday, August 21, and end Sunday, August 27.

Each of Shreveport's three major radio stations has agreed to run PSAs on the blood drive. As the Shriners' public relations director, you have been asked to compose three different PSAs: 10-second, 30-second, and 60-second spots.

QUESTION

What would you say in the three PSAs for the blood drive?

play. Western Electric produced a clip that took a behind-the-scenes look at the company's massive communication complex for a national political convention.

The key in each of these cases and the key in every salable TV newsclip is the newsworthiness of the clip itself. In dealing with television, newsclips must be professionally produced, scripted, and edited. Such a clip may cost a sponsor between $3,000 and $6,000, including production and national distribution, depending on the number of stations covered. A successful TV clip should return a sponsor at least $5 of commercial air time for each $1 invested.[5]

VNRs are not for everyone. In general, an organization should consider producing a video news release when

- It is involved in a legitimate medical, scientific, or industrial breakthrough
- The video will clarify or provide a new perspective on issues in the news
- Visuals will help a news department provide its viewers with a better story
- The video can be used as background footage while a station's reporter discusses pertinent news copy
- The organization can provide unusual visuals that stations themselves can't get
- The VNR provides an interview segment that stations, again, can't get on their own.[6]

How does one create a VNR? First, the purpose of the video must be considered. Is there a need for it? Second, the time element must be factored in. How much time do we have? Third is the matter of money. How much do we have to spend on it? Fourth, any obstacles must be considered, such as contending with bad weather, unavailability of key people, and so on. After all of these elements are considered, a rough script should be drawn before approaching an outside production company so that key managers in the organization understand and agree on what the objective of the VNR will be.

Video news releases have triggered heated controversy in recent years. Shortly before Japanese Prime Minister Yasuhiro Nakasone met President Reagan in 1985, U.S. television viewers saw news reports showing American produce on its way to Japan's markets. The reports featured Mike Mansfield, the U.S. ambassador to Japan and a staunch opponent of import quotas, saying, "Japanese markets aren't as closed as we might think." What TV viewers weren't told was that parts or all of the news reports were produced for the government of Japan by a Washington public relations firm, which was later criticized by the Justice Department for failing to "label some of its electronic news releases as political propaganda."[7]

Many large TV stations will not use sponsored newsclips as a matter of principle, but some smaller stations swear by them. Said one Montana station owner, "We enjoy them. The folks who produce them are nice people, and they're too smart to try and mislead you."[8]

Despite their controversial nature, the fact remains that using such video newsclips may be a most effective and dramatic way to convey an organization's message to millions of people.

1. James G. Busse, "The Ghost in the Executive Suite," *TWA Ambassador Magazine* (June 1978): 43.
2. "Create Your Own Comfort," *Decker Communications Report* V, no. 9 (October 1984): 4.
3. R. Irwin Goodman, "Selecting Public Service Announcements for Television," *Public Relations Review* (Fall 1981): 26–28.
4. Richard Green and Denise Shapiro, "A Video News Release Primer," *Public Relations Quarterly* (Winter 1987–88): 10.
5. Hilliard A. Schendorf, "ABC's of TV News Film," *Public Relations Journal* (June 1977): 19.
6. Michael M. Klepper, "Do-It-Yourself Evening News," *IABC Communication World* (July/August 1987): 62–63.
7. "Public Relations Firms Offer 'News' to TV," *Wall Street Journal,* 2 April 1985, section 2, p. 1.
8. Herman M. Rosenthal, "Beware of News Clips Massaging Your Opinions," *TV Guide,* 21 April 1984, 6.

NOTES

SUGGESTED READINGS

Ailes, Roger, and Jon Kraushar. *You Are the Message*. Homewood, IL: Dow Jones-Irwin, 1988.

Associated Press. *Broadcast News Stylebook*. (Available from the author, 50 Rockefeller Plaza, New York, NY 10020.) Featured is a more generalized style than that of the UPI book with suggestions of methods and treatment for the preparation of news copy and information pertinent to AP broadcast wire operations.

Block, M. *Writing Broadcast News—Shorter, Sharper, Stronger*. Chicago, IL: Bonus Books, 1987.

Broadcasting Publications. *Broadcasting*. (Available from the author, 1735 DeSales St., NW, Washington, DC 20036; published weekly on Monday.) This basic news magazine for radio, television, and cable television industries reports all activities involved in the entire broadcasting field.

"A Common Sense Guide to Making Business Videos." (Available from Creative Marketing Corporation, 2875 S. 171 St., New Berlin, WI 53151–3511.) Anyone not familiar with business videos will benefit from this booklet, which zeros in on the planning needed to make a successful video.

Daily Variety. (Available from 1400 N. Cahuenga Blvd., Hollywood, CA 90028.) This trade paper for the entertainment industries is centered mainly in Los Angeles, with complete coverage of West Coast production activities; it includes reports from all world entertainment centers.

Detz, J. *How to Write and Give a Speech*. New York: St. Martin's Press, 1985.

Executive Speaker (P.O. Box 292437, Dayton, OH 45429). Newsletter.

Goodman, R. Irwin. "Selecting Public Service Announcements for Television." *Public Relations Review* (Fall 1981): 25–34. This gives insights into what information a station's public service director is looking for in deciding which PSA to air.

Green, Richard, and Denise Shapiro. "A Video News Release Primer." *Public Relations Quarterly* (Winter 1987–88): 10–13.

Hannaford, Peter. *Talking Back to the Media*. New York: Facts on File Publications, 1986.

Heinz, J. *Writing Effective Business Speeches*. (Available from the author, 233 E. Wacker, #3111, Chicago, IL 60601.) 1986.

"A Layperson's Guide to Satellite Broadcasting." *O'Dwyer's PR Services Report* (271 Madison Ave., New York, NY 10016) (December 1987): 4.

MacDonald, R. H. *Broadcast News Manual of Style*. White Plains, NY: Longman, 1987.

Martel, Myles. "Combating Speech Anxiety." *Public Relations Journal* (July 1981): 20–21. The tension-laden self-consciousness that hits most speakers can be alleviated with a proper attitude toward the five elements discussed in this article.

Novelli, William D. "You Can Produce Effective PSAs." *Public Relations Journal* (May 1982): 30–32.

Poriotis, Wesley. "Is There Life After Manuscript?" *Public Relations Journal* (July 1981): 22–23.

"Public Relations Firms Offer 'News' to TV," *Wall Street Journal* (2 April 1985): section 2, p. 1.

Robinson, James W. *Winning Them Over*. Rocklin, CA: Prima Publishing & Communications, 1987.

Rosenthal, Herman M. "Beware of News Clips Massaging Your Opinions." *TV Guide* (21 April 1984): 4–9.

Seitel, Fraser. *Writing an Effective Speech*. Chicago, IL: Bank Marketing Association, 1984.

Smith, Richard N. "How to Get Publicity Mileage from Your Speech." *Public Relations Journal* (July 1981): 21, 28.

Speechwriter's Newsletter. (Available from Ragan Communications, 407 S. Dearborn, Chicago, IL 60605.)

Stecki, Ed, and Frank Corrado. "How to Make a Video" (Part I). *Public Relations Journal* (February 1988): 33, 34.

Tarver, Jerry. "How to Put 'Good' Humor in Your Next Speech." *Public Relations Journal* (February 1975): 15–17.

United Press International. *Broadcast Stylebook.* (Available from the author, 220 E. 42nd Street, New York, NY 10017.) It's not a rule book, but it suggests methods and treatment for the proper preparation of news copy, with examples of wire copy and brief comments on correct and incorrect methods of news wire copy preparation. It's designed to help people write the kind of copy used by an announcer.

Variety. (Available from 154 W. 46th St., New York, NY; published weekly on Wednesday.) This paper publishes news, features, and commentary each week on every aspect of show business, with extensive reviews of productions around the world.

Illinois Power's Reply

In the 1980s no network news program rivaled the incredible impact of CBS-TV's "60 Minutes." Watched each Sunday night by nearly 40 million Americans, "60 Minutes" regularly ranked as one of the most popular programs in the nation and the show most feared by public relations practitioners. When "60 Minutes" came calling, scandal or at least significant problems couldn't be far away.

Such was the thinking at Illinois Power Company (IP) in Decatur, Illinois, in the fall of 1979, when "60 Minutes" sent reporter Harry Reasoner to find out why the company's Clinton nuclear reactor project was behind schedule and over budget.

What followed—the exchange between "60 Minutes" and Illinois Power—ranks as a classic confrontation in the annals of public relations. Because Illinois Power suspected that "60 Minutes" aimed to do a hatchet job, the company agreed to the interviews only if it, too, videotaped the "60 Minutes" filming on its premises. In other words, IP would videotape the videotapers; it would report on the reporters. Reasoner and his producer reluctantly agreed to the arrangement.

On November 25, 1979, "60 Minutes" broadcast a 16-minute segment on the Clinton plant, charging IP, as the company feared, with mismanagement, missed deadlines, and costly overruns that would be passed on to consumers. Viewers saw three former IP employees accuse the utility of making no effort to control costs, allowing slipshod internal reporting, and fabricating

estimates of construction completion timetables. One of the accusers was shown in silhouette with a distorted voice because, as reporter Reasoner intoned, "he fears retribution."

The day after the CBS story, IP's stock fell a full point on the New York Stock Exchange in the busiest trading day in the company's history. Rather than responding as most companies do—with bruised feelings, a scorched reputation, and feeble cries of "foul" to its stockholders—IP lashed back with barrels blazing. Within days of the broadcast, IP produced "60 Minutes/Our Reply," a 44-minute film incorporating the entire "60 Minutes" segment, punctuated by insertions and narrative presenting the company's rebuttal.

The rebuttal included videotape of CBS film footage not included in the program, much of which raised serious questions about the integrity of the material CBS used. The rebuttal also documented the backgrounds and possible motives of the three former employees CBS quoted, all of whom had been fired for questionable performance. One of the former employees, in fact, was the leader of the local antinuclear group opposing IP.

Initially, the reply tape was aired to a relatively small audience: the company's employees, customers, shareholders, and investors. But word traveled quickly that Illinois Power had produced a riveting, broadcast-quality production, so true to the "60 Minutes" format—ticking stopwatch and all—that it could easily be mistaken for the original itself. Within a year, close to 2,500 copies of the devastating rebuttal had been distributed to legislators, corporate executives, journalists, and others. Excerpts were broadcast on television stations throughout the nation, and the IP production became legendary. As the *Wall Street Journal* put it, "The program focuses new attention on news accuracy . . . . Although even a telling, polished, counter-program like Illinois Power's can't reach the masses of a national broadcast, the reply tape has proven effective in reaching a significant 'thinking' audience."*

Even CBS was impressed. The producer of the original "60 Minutes" segment called the rebuttal highly sophisticated, especially for a company that had first seemed to him to be a "down-home cracker barrel" outfit. The Illinois Power tape soon spawned imitators. Companies such as Chevron, Union Carbide, Commonwealth Edison, and many others began experimenting with defensive videotaping in dealing with television journalists.

Although "60 Minutes" admitted to some sloppiness in its reporting and to two minor factual inaccuracies, it essentially stood by its account. Complained CBS executive producer Don Hewitt, "We went in as a disinterested party and did a news report. They made a propaganda film for their side, using our reporting for their own purposes." Perhaps. But one irrefutable result of the dramatic confrontation between the huge national network and the tiny local utility was that the Illinois Power Company earned its

place in public relations history as the company that brought the mighty "60 Minutes" to its knees.

Three years after the Illinois Power confrontation, a *TV Guide* poll discovered that America's "most trusted television journalist" was Harry Reasoner. Evidently nobody asked Illinois Power.**

QUESTIONS

1. Do you agree with Illinois Power's original decision to let "60 Minutes" in despite the suspicion that the program would be a "hatchet job"? What might have happened if IP turned down the "60 Minutes" request?
2. If "60 Minutes" had turned down Illinois Power's request to videotape the Reasoner interviews, would you have still allowed the filming?
3. Presume Illinois Power didn't tape the "60 Minutes" filming on its premises. What other communications options might the company have pursued to rebut the "60 Minutes" accusations?
4. Do you think IP did better by allowing "60 Minutes" in to film or would they have been better off keeping CBS out?

---

*Sandy Graham, "Illinois Utility Sparks Widespread Interest with Its Videotape," *Wall Street Journal,* 12 April 1980, 23.

**For further information on the Illinois Power case, see *Punch, Counterpunch: "60 Minutes" vs. Illinois Power Company,* Washington, DC: Media Institute, 1981, and "Turning the Tables on '60 Minutes,'" *Columbia Journalism Review* (May/June 1980): 7–9.

Public Relations Marketing

11

I n the 1980s most companies realized that public relations could play an expanded role in marketing products. Marketing, literally defined, is the selling of a service or product—through pricing, distribution, and promotion. Public relations, literally defined, is the marketing of an organization. In many organizations today, particularly hospitals and nonprofit institutions, the selling of both individual services and the organization are inextricably interwined. Certainly public relations techniques can enhance the marketing process and must be considered in the marketing of any service, product, or organization, as a key element in the marketing plan.

In the past, marketers treated public relations as an ancillary part of the promotional element in the marketing mix. They were concerned primarily with making sure their products met the needs and desires of customers and were priced competitively, distributed widely, and promoted heavily through advertising and merchandising. Gradually, however, these traditional notions among marketers began to change for several reasons.

- Consumer protests about both product value and safety and government scrutiny of product demands began to shake historical views of marketing.
- Product recalls—from automobiles to tuna fish—generated recurring headlines.
- Ingredient scares began to occur regularly.
- Advertisers were asked to justify their messages in terms of social needs and civic responsibilities.
- Rumors about particular companies—from fast-food firms to pop rock manufacturers—spread in brushfire manner.
- General image problems of certain companies and industries—from oil to banking—were fanned by a continuous blaze of criticism in the media.

The net impact of all this was that, even though a company's products were still important, customers also began to consider a firm's policies and practices on everything from air and water pollution to minority hiring.

INTERVIEW

Art Stevens

Art Stevens is president of Lobsenz-Stevens, Inc., a leading public relations firm headquartered in New York City. Ever since he was named public relations director of Prentice-Hall at the age of 25, Stevens has contributed substantially to the public relations field. He is a frequent contributor to leading publications and author of *The Persuasion Explosion*, which deals with the role and influence of contemporary public relations practices. Stevens's background in corporate, financial, product, educational, marketing, and political public relations has earned him the highest distinction conferred on a public relations practitioner—the industry's Distinguished Service Award.

How important is public relations in the marketing mix?
Extremely important and not as well understood by many marketing people as one would think. There are more and more marketplace pressures on marketing people than ever before. Each product category has literally dozens of competing brand names which often cause confusion and indecision on the part of consumers. There is no limit to the brand name choices the consumer must make. Anything that helps project a brand name to greater top-of-mind awareness will help the product move off the shelf.

Enter public relations. Public relations offers the marketer various alternatives that other forms of marketing don't. Included among public relations' vast arsenal of marketing tools are publicity, "brandstanding" (a term I coined to refer to the increasing use of public relations special events), stunts, promotion, and many others. Public relations offers marketing people an economic way to reach millions of people at a cost that network television advertising can't touch.

How do you promote a client's product with public relations?
By finding ways to interest the media to include the product's name in articles. Nothing is more credible than third-party editorial endorsement of a product by the media.

Publicity is a highly productive communications technique because it successfully meets the following criteria:

- It delivers a message in a highly believable form. The reader accepts the message readily because it is recognized not as a sponsored message but rather as the viewpoint of the publication. This implied endorsement is extremely valuable when a campaign seeks to bring across a concept.
- It makes possible repetition of a message in many different ways. This is a vital factor in gaining acceptance for a new concept or product.
- It enables a message to be presented in detail and reaches audiences at an extremely low cost.
- It is especially productive when the client is engaged in interesting activities or products. Or, to express this as editors do, when a company's activities are newsworthy.

What's the proper role of publicity vis-à-vis advertising and marketing?
Publicity serves as a complementary tool to advertising, sales promotion, direct marketing, and other major marketing tools. It no longer serves as a stepchild but has taken its rightful place at the marketing table.

Publicity is a way to extend product reach and visibility in a way that the other marketing components cannot do. Publicity's role is to carry forth the same central themes that pervade the other marketing tools.

How does one secure publicity for a product?
First, determine the unique characteristics of a product, which truly distinguish it from the pack.

Next, conduct a media audit with target editors, writers, reporters, and broadcasters to determine which media have feature segments in the works that could include a discussion of your product and its benefits. Among the other techniques that can be used are identifying an authority who can be positioned as a product spokesperson on radio and television interviews; tying your product in with existing sports programs; creating a special event; and developing service articles for the media—articles that advise and educate the consumer.

What should the proper relationship be between a client and a public relations agency?
One of mutual trust, support, and confidence. The healthiest client-agency relationships I've ever seen are those where the client truly feels that the agency is part of the client family and is not pressured unmercifully to perform.

What are the advantages of using a public relations agency?
Objectivity and experience. An outside agency can bring a client insights, observations, and recommendations based on the agency's being at arm's distance to the client and outside the organization. Often a client will become mired in a particular situation and be simply too close to the forest to see the trees. It is in the category of objectivity that an agency's greatest contributions can be felt.

Beyond these social concerns, the effectiveness of advertising itself began to be questioned. The increased number of advertisements in newspapers and on the airwaves caused clutter and posed a significant burden on advertisers to make the public aware of their products. In the 1970s the trend toward shorter TV advertising spots contributed to three times as many products being advertised on TV as there were in the 1960s. In the 1980s the spread of cable added yet another multichanneled outlet for product advertising. Against this backdrop the potential of public relations as an added ingredient in the marketing mix became increasingly more credible.[1]

Indeed, marketing professor Philip Kotler has suggested that in addition to the traditional four *P*s of product, price, place, and promotion, two additional *P*s be added to define the marketing concept today: (1) political power and (2) public opinion formation through public relations. Said Kotler, "Marketers are always looking at economic factors and rational factors. They should examine the conflicts, the special-interest and pressure groups, the vested interests, the political realities, and create appeals in those arenas."[2]

THE MARKETING PLAN

For public relations to be effective as a tool in marketing, it must be introduced early in the marketing plan, rather than as an afterthought. The plan should carefully lay out the organization's objectives, strategies, and tactics for promoting and selling a product. Public relations may be used in the marketing plan to realize a number of objectives.

1. Helping a company and product name become better known
2. Helping introduce new or improved products
3. Helping increase a product's life cycle (i.e., complementing advertising and sales promotion with additional product information)
4. Seeking out new markets and broadening existing ones at reduced costs
5. Establishing an overall favorable image for the product and company

Basically, public relations can play a critical role in positioning a product appropriately in the market. A product's position is the image the product conveys in the public mind. For example, if the public truly believes that Colonel Sanders chicken is "finger licking good," then the firm's product positioning strategy has worked. When the public really believes that the folks at Allstate are "the good hands people" or that the group from Avis really does "try harder," that's effective product positioning. Companies spend millions of dollars trying to position their products in the public mind.

Public relations offers a practical and inexpensive device for conveying product messages and helping position a firm's products. About 8 of 10 new products fail to catch on, and the cost of these annual failures has been estimated in the billions of dollars. Public relations, then, should be involved early and integrated fully into the marketing plan. Whether in helping market a new product or enhancing the staying power of an old one, public relations can make a telling difference in product success.

PRODUCT PUBLICITY

In light of the difficulty today in raising advertising awareness above the noise of so many competitive messages, marketers are turning increasingly to product publicity as an important adjunct to advertising. Although the public is generally unaware of it, a great deal of what it knows and believes about a wide variety of products comes through press coverage. Articles in the newspaper's "living" section—describing the attributes of a brand of Burgundy or the advantages of down coats or enriched dog foods—often arise from product publicity information distributed by the manufacturer.[3]

Traditional product publicity—whether it introduces a new product or promotes a long-standing one—focuses on some feature of the product that appeals to the public. More recently, companies have begun to link products or brands to events or issues that help publicize the product while positioning it in the public mind. Such an approach has been dubbed by public relations counselor Art Stevens as brandstanding. Such tie-ins can range from the sponsorship of conferences and special-interest brochures to the presentation of contests and sporting events (Figure 11–1). To Stevens effective brandstanding must have the following characteristics:

1. The event or issue linked to a product must invite publicity (i.e., it must be newsworthy).
2. The people attracted must be users or potential users of the product.
3. There must be a meaningful or necessary link between the product and the event. In other words, tying the product to the event must make sense.
4. The link should be evident but not intrusive. The product must be subservient to the event or issue.
5. A concurrent program of promotion must support the effort. The event shouldn't just lie there without proper promotional backup.
6. Follow-up evaluation of results is important to see whether sponsorship of the event should continue.[4]

In an increasing number of cases, companies have found that by associating with a certain type of sponsorship—quality tennis, golf, or track and field events, for example—the firm's image is not only promoted but also enhanced.

Third-Party Endorsement

Perhaps more than anything else, the lure of third-party endorsement is the primary reason smart organizations value product publicity as much as they do advertising. Third-party endorsement refers to the tacit support given a product by a newspaper, magazine, or broadcaster who mentions the product as news. Advertising often is perceived as self-serving. People know that the advertiser not only created the message but also paid for it. Publicity, on the other hand, which appears in news columns, carries no such stigma. When a message is "sanctified by third-party editors, it is more persuasive than advertising messages, where the self-serving sponsor of the message is identified."[5]

What they did for love. *For the love of running—the triumph that follows the torment—a record 12,530 men and women finished the 1980 New York City Marathon. □ There's nothing like it in the world of distance running. The size of the field. The enthusiasm of the endless onlookers. The exhilarating scenes along the five-borough course. □ Manufacturers Hanover is pleased to be a major sponsor of the annual New York City Marathon, just one in a series of running events we sponsor around the world. Because we admire the pluck and perseverance that runners embody.* **MANUFACTURERS HANOVER**

FIGURE 11–1 Manufacturers Hanover Trust of New York City (Manny Hanny) is one bank that has clearly associated itself with sporting events. In addition to the New York City Marathon, which has become an institution in the international world of track and field, Manny Hanny regularly sponsors professional baseball, hockey, golf, and a variety of other athletic events. Why? Perhaps, as this ad suggests, the bank wishes to emulate the kind of pluck and perseverance that athletes embody. (This ad reprinted with the express permission of Manufacturers Hanover Trust)

Editors have become sensitive to mentioning product names in print. Some, in fact, have a policy of deleting brand or company identifications in news columns. Public relations counselors argue that such a policy does a disservice to readers, many of whom are influenced by what they read and may desire the particular products discussed. Counselors further argue that journalists who accept and print public relations material for its intrinsic value and then remove the source of the information give the reader or viewer the false impression that the journalist generated the facts, ideas, or photography.[6]

Equally reprehensible are the public relations practitioners who try to place sponsored features without disclosing promotional origins. In other words, some companies will distribute cartoons or stories—either directly or through mail order services—without identifying the sponsor of the material. Obviously, such a practice raises ethical questions. Understandably, editors do not soon forgive firms who sponsor such anonymous articles.

Most good marketers will use product publicity as an effective complement to advertising. They know that positive publicity adds credibility to advertisements. In rare cases marketers may forsake advertising entirely and plow all their funds, on a much more limited scale, into public relations.

RESPONDING TO PRODUCT CHALLENGES

Whereas third-party endorsements can help a product, the public specter of shoddy merchandise can cause irreparable product damage. When Ralph Nader publicly denounced the General Motors Corvair as being "unsafe at any speed," the media publicized the charges; several years later the Corvair was no more. Bon Vivant, a New Jersey soup maker, had its vichyssoise recalled by the Food and Drug Administration when a couple was stricken with botulism after sampling a can. The incident was duly reported in the media, and the company never recovered. Occasionally, products are faulty and deserve to be pilloried. At other times, criticism may be less justified. In any event, nine rules should be followed when a firm's products are attacked publicly.

1. **Don't ignore the criticism.** Unless an organization is very lucky, attacks on it or its products won't go away. A response will have to be made eventually. But always consider the source. Not every critic deserves to be taken seriously. Evaluate the credibility of the source before acting.
2. **Don't waste time.** A response is much better sooner than later. Get the facts quickly. Don't respond without knowing all the pertinent details. Then time the response to secure maximum impact.
3. **Don't use cosmetic surgery.** Negative criticism can't be turned around with short-term solutions. Move quickly to devise total solutions to alleviate the problem. Piecemeal solutions will only cause the product and the organization to "twist slowly, slowly" in the media.
4. **Don't overlook the consumer's viewpoint.** Sometimes a company that believes in its own integrity and the integrity of its products can be so sure

E.T.'s Favorite Candy

One of the most spectacular third-party endorsements of all time occurred in 1982, when Universal Pictures approached Hershey Foods Corporation for a promotional tie-in between Hershey's candy and the hero of a new Universal science fiction picture. Hershey, as it turned out, was Universal's second choice. Reportedly, the company's first choice, M&M/Mars, turned down the original offer to tie in its M&M candy. Hershey, however, accepted on behalf of its Reese's Pieces candy and, in a practice unheard of in Hollywood promotional deals, paid no money for the movie plug—so grateful were the film makers to land the candy company's endorsement.

The rest, of course, is history. The movie was *E.T., The Extra-Terrestrial*, the biggest box office draw in the history of moviedom. Early in the movie, the lovable but famished E.T. follows a trail of brown, yellow, and orange Reese's Pieces to the little boy who would become his friend and savior.

Two weeks after the film opened, Reese's Pieces' sales tripled. After the movie's first month in theaters, sales of Reese's Pieces were up 70 percent. Hershey, in fact, put up $1 million of promotional money, the largest public relations offensive for a single brand in Hershey history, to extol the virtues of "E.T.'s favorite candy."

Although the Hershey people were ecstatic over their adopted hero, they were unsure at first about the affiliation. As one executive put it, "Our major concern was what kind of creature was this going to be? Is this going to be an X-rated space creature?" Fortunately for Hershey, its vice president for new business development saw still photos from the unreleased film and concluded, "He was a strange-looking creature. But I told all our executives, 'You're gonna *love* him.' "* They did.

*Stephanie Mansfield, "Sweet Success: Reese's Cashes in on E.T.'s Candy Cravings," *Washington Post*, 14 July 1982, Bl.

that it is doing the right thing that it overlooks the most essential viewpoint—that of the consumer. This mistake can be fatal.

5. **Shoot for key publics.** Know who's most influential. Consumer reporters, consumer advocates, and politicians may be able to set the record straight if they are reached quickly and effectively. Direct approaches to these pivotal individuals may convert potential disasters into minor brush fires.

6. **Don't overlook the positives.** Although some contrition may be necessary, don't go overboard. The product may have many redeeming virtues and one specific flaw. If that can be corrected quickly and inexpensively enough, the product may rebound sharply. Don't spoil its chances by overconfessing.

(Courtesy of Hershey Foods Corp.)

7. **Involve top management.** Public relations spokespersons may not be enough to convince skeptical publics that a company intends to correct its product problem. A committed and concerned top manager speaking openly and honestly in the media about the company's corrective plans is a most persuasive method.

8. **Don't quote too many people.** In any product publicity crisis, the fewer spokespersons, the better. It's easier to stay organized and consistent in responses if only a few designated spokespersons express the company's official position.

9. **Think long-term.** Always consider the lasting impacts that a prolonged product publicity crisis will have on a company.

PUBLIC RELATIONS MARKETING ACTIVITIES

In addition to product publicity, a number of other public relations activities are regularly used to help market products. These activities include article reprints, trade show participation, the use of spokespersons, special events, and consumer-oriented appeals.

Article Reprints

Once an organization has received product publicity in a newspaper or magazine, it should market the publicity further to achieve maximum sales punch. Marketing can be done through article reprints aimed at that part of a target audience—wholesalers, retailers, or consumers—who might not have seen the original article. Reprints also help reinforce the reactions of those who read the original article.

As in any other public relations activity, reprints should be approached systematically, with the following ground rules in mind:

1. **Plan ahead,** especially if an article has major significance to the organization. Ideally, reprints should be ordered before the periodical goes to press so that customers can receive them shortly after the article hits the newsstands.
2. **Select target publics** and address the recipients by name and title. This strategy will ensure that the reprint reaches the most important audience.
3. **Pinpoint the reprint's significance** either through underlining pertinent information in the article, making marginal notes, or attaching a cover letter. In this way the target audience will readily understand.
4. **Integrate the reprint** with other similar articles and information on the same or related subjects. Often, several reprints can be combined into a single mailing piece. Also, reprints can be integrated into press kits and displays.

Trade Shows

Trade show participation enables an organization to display its products before important target audiences. The decision to participate should be looked at with the following factors in mind:

1. **Analyze the show carefully.** Make sure the audience is one that can't be reached effectively through other promotional materials, such as article reprints or local publicity. Also be sure the audience is essential to the sale of the product. For example, how responsible are the attendees for the actual purchase?
2. **Select a common theme.** Integrate public relations, publicity, advertising, and sales promotion. Unify all elements for the trade show and avoid, at all costs, any hint of interdepartmental rivalries.

3. **Make sure the products displayed are the right ones.** Decide well in advance exactly which products are the ones to be shown.
4. **Consider the trade books.** Often trade magazines run special features in conjunction with trade shows, and editors need photos and publicity material. Always know what special editions are coming up as well as their deadline schedules.
5. **Emphasize what's new.** Talk about the new model that's being displayed. Discuss the additional features, new uses, or recent performance data of the products displayed. Trade show exhibitions should reveal innovation, breakthrough, and newness.
6. **Consider local promotional efforts.** While in town during a trade show, an organization can enhance both the recognition of its product and the traffic at its booth by doing local promotions. This strategy means visiting trade magazine editors and local media people to stir up publicity for the product during the show.

Spokespersons

In recent years the use of spokespersons to promote products has increased. Spokespersons shouldn't disguise the fact that they are advocates for a particular product. Their purpose is to air their sponsor's viewpoint, which often means going to bat for a controversial product.

One example is the tobacco industry. In the early 1970s, with cigarette and cigar ads banned on television and radio, the Tobacco Institute, funded by the major tobacco companies, launched a far-reaching speakers campaign to get its story to the public. During the first three years of the campaign, tobacco speakers appeared in 350 cities in 48 states and received coverage on 1,300 television and radio shows and in almost 300 newspapers. William Kloepfer, Jr., public relations director for the Tobacco Institute, described the approach.

> We do not try to sell cigarettes or promote smoking. Our public relations objective is to bring a seemingly closed subject back to the level of controversy in the public's mind.
>
> We are not attempting to win the argument or make the public view smoking as harmless. We want the public to understand that there is a scientific controversy which has to be resolved by research—not propaganda.[7]

Spokespersons must be articulate, fast on their feet, and thoroughly knowledgeable about the subject. When these criteria are met, the use of spokespersons as a marketing tool can be most effective.

In the 1980s this approach was refined to encompass corporate chief executive officers (CEOs) as lead company spokespersons. For example, Frank Perdue, the CEO of a local New York chicken supplier, singlehandedly put his company on the map through advertising and publicity personal appearances. Soon, rent-a-car chairpersons, clothing designers, airline CEOs, and numerous others began appearing regularly to speak for their company's products or services.

By the late 1980s the concept of using celebrities to endorse products had spread beyond the pale. Actor Robert Young, in his Marcus Welby physician's coat, sold Sanka coffee. Ageless comedian Bob Hope endorsed Texaco. New wave comic Jay Leno spoke fondly of Doritos brand corn chips. But nowhere was spokesmanship bigger business than for athletes, some of whom are mini-conglomerates (Figure 11–2).

Especially picky in marketing their images are rock stars. Indeed, when Prince, the diminutive Minnesota rocker with the risque lyrics, was asked for his photo for use in a certain public relations textbook, the author received the following warning from the decidedly unrocklike law firm of Manatt, Phelps, Rothenberg & Tunney.

> Please be advised that our client does not desire to grant you permission to use any picture or likeness of him in connection with your textbook.*

So there.

Although celebrity spokesmanship is big business today, it is not without its peril. In the early 1980s actor Orson Welles was fired by the wine merchant Paul Masson because Welles was so compelling a personality that viewers remembered him but not the product. In the late 1980s another spirits manufacturer, the Seagrams Company, couldn't have been pleased when its flamboyant spokesman, actor Bruce Willis, admitted that he had a drinking problem. Willis's co-star in the hit TV show "Moonlighting," Cybill Shepherd, was also dropped as spokeswoman for the National Beef Council when she confessed that she personally shunned the product. Even though studies are inconclusive as to whether spokespersons really do assist sales of products, the proliferation of celebrity "pitchmen" is likely to continue unabated.

Special Events

Special public relations events also help to market products. This approach is designed to capture media attention by linking a firm's product with the event created. For example, when Senator William Proxmire wanted to find out

---

*Letter from Jody Graham of Manatt, Phelps, Rothenberg & Tunney, Los Angeles, CA, 10 May 1985.

FIGURE 11–2 Michael Jordan (top, left), the high-flying basketballer with the boyish grin and disarming graciousness, clearly has become king of the sports endorsement hill with Nike, Wilson Sporting Goods, and Chevrolet just the tip of the "Air Jordan" promotional iceberg. Close behind is another "All Everything"—Los Angeles Lakers superstar Earvin "Magic" Johnson (top, right). And footballers Jim McMahon (bottom, left) and William "The Refrigerator" Perry (bottom, right) of the Chicago Bears have also been big names on the endorsement trail. (Courtesy of ProServ, the Los Angeles Lakers, the Chicago Bears, and Drexel Burnham Lambert. Copyright © 1986.)

The Shoes of the Thunder Man

Getting celebrities to endorse products is an increasingly popular form of product promotion. Like everything else, getting John Madden to drink your beer or convincing Madonna to endorse your cosmetics costs money—sometimes, big money—upwards of $100,000 a year for top stars.

Occasionally, celebrities get confused over exactly what they are endorsing. Take the case of Darryl Dawkins, the immense professional basketball center affectionately dubbed Chocolate Thunder. In the spring of 1982, Dawkins signed a $50,000-a-year endorsement contract with Nike sneakers. In return for wearing Nike shoes when in uniform, Dawkins was promised a share in a royalty pool to which Nike contributed 10 to 20 cents for each pair of shoes sold. Dawkins was also promised a Nike bonus of $10,000 if he was voted the most valuable player in the National Basketball Association or if he finished first in league scoring or rebounding. Nike also supported the Dawkins sponsorship by printing 20,000 Chocolate Thunder posters.

In light of all this, it was understandable that Nike executives were just a bit dismayed when Dawkins showed up on the basketball court wearing shoes made by Pony Sports & Leisure. Nike promptly sued its errant charge for compensatory damages for the useless posters and punitive damages for fraud.

Actually, Nike was lucky. According to the company's general counsel, another athlete once wore shoes with one company's stripe on one side and another company's mark on the other and tried to collect from both. "When we caught him, he said that if he'd had any more room, he would have tried three."*

whether city workers were worth what the taxpayers paid them, he climbed aboard a New York City garbage truck and became a sanitation worker for a day—all in the spotlight of media cameras. When Parker Brothers sought continued recognition for its traditional Monopoly game, it borrowed a bank branch for a day and staged a real-life monopoly game—with real money. When Columbia Pictures introduced the movie *Close Encounters of the Third Kind*, it flew more than 300 reporters to Los Angeles and New York for special press screenings, at which the journalists were given leatherette bags and tape recorders labeled CE3K. The movie became a box-office sensation.

There are no particular rules for special events. They range from media extravaganzas to simple ground-breaking and open-house ceremonies. Figure 11–3 illustrates a ski tournament sponsored by Fleischmann's. Special events can be risky, however, especially when the party is held and no one from the media attends.

*Tamar Lewin, "Conflict over Endorsements," *New York Times,* 2 August 1982, D1,3.

In planning special events, public relations professionals are well advised to seek outside help, even though it usually doesn't come cheap. Practitioners can find just about any type of assistance by consulting local directories and industry source books, which are periodically updated to include an ever-changing variety of external services that support public relations work—from fund-raising to sky writing to blowing up balloons. Done sparingly and conceived thoughtfully, special events can significantly enhance the marketing of a product or institution.

Consumer-Oriented Public Relations

Public relations also helps market products through appeals to consumer demands. Sponsoring nutritional recipes, publishing consumer information advice, and lobbying for consumer-oriented legislation all help market a compa-

FIGURE 11–3 Fleischmann's Margarine sponsored a special national cross-country ski competition, where its name was prominently displayed on all of the competitors at the more than 40 ski touring centers and recreational facilities that hosted the competition. (Courtesy of Padilla, Speer, Beardsley, Inc.)

ny's products. If consumers believe a company is sincerely concerned about their welfare, their trust may translate into purchase decisions. Moreover, a company that voluntarily acts in the public interest, without being prodded by the government, can generally expect to receive a good deal more favorable publicity than a competitor forced to comply with regulations or legislation. Figure 11–4 shows consumer information provided by a large grocery store chain, General Foods Corporation.

MARKETING FOR THE ENTREPRENEUR

For the small entrepreneur starting out in business, public relations sophistication can be a great advantage. A small operation can effectively use public relations techniques to enhance the marketing of its products and itself. The key to using public relations techniques to market a small company is the same as it is in promoting a large company: before any public relations program can be considered, solid results must be achieved. In other words, performance must always precede publicity.

Before deciding on a public relations program, an entrepreneur should consider the following six questions:

Sane talk about fats, cholesterol and your heart

Should you cut back on <u>all</u> fats, saturated <u>and</u> unsaturated? Is there new thinking on cholesterol? Below is a new U.S. Dietary Guideline, with comment from General Foods.

Most Americans eat far too much fat, period.

The fat we should cut down on includes *all* fat…animal and vegetable, saturated and unsaturated. Some fats tend to increase our blood cholesterol, and too much fat of any kind can make us overweight.

Science is divided about the connection between the fats and cholesterol we eat, the cholesterol and triglycerides in our blood, and heart disease. The simple cause-and-effect relationships aren't as certain as we once thought.

U.S. health officials simply do not think you should gamble with too high an intake of fat and cholesterol while the debate over proof rages on.

As you study the Guideline below, remember there are no easy answers. And these underlying principles become even more important:

1. Select from a wide **variety** of foods in each basic food group to help avoid adding too much fat or cholesterol to your diet.

2. Use **moderation** when you eat foods known to be high in fat, or cholesterol.

3. As you change your eating habits, be sure to maintain a proper **balance** of nutrients. If you decide to cut down on fatty meats, for example, turn to other sources of protein, such as lean meats, fish, poultry, and dried beans.

Next: Sane talk about starch and fiber. To date, General Foods has reprinted three of the seven U.S. Dietary Guidelines and plans to reprint the remaining ones soon in this newspaper. The seven Guideline titles are:
  1. Eat a variety of foods.
  2. Maintain ideal weight.
  3. Avoid too much fat, saturated fat and cholesterol.
  4. Eat foods with adequate starch and fiber.
  5. Avoid too much sugar.
  6. Avoid too much sodium.
  7. If you drink alcohol, do so in moderation.

1 How much fat should you avoid?
There is no single answer, but most of us could afford to eat about one third less fat. It's high in calories, and being overweight increases risk of heart attack.

2 Should we cut down on all fat?
Yes!! Fat has 250 calories per ounce, twice the calories of carbohydrates or protein. The fats in nuts and olives are equal in calories to the fats in whole milk or ice cream. Margarine has just as many calories as butter. When you reduce fats, don't just avoid one type. Cut down across the board.

3 Are there special problems with saturated fats?
Foods high in animal fat are usually high in cholesterol. Many studies show that eating too much saturated fat can increase blood cholesterol and triglyceride levels for many people.

4 What is cholesterol and where does it come from?
Cholesterol is a fat-like substance that is a normal part of blood and all body tissue. It is essential for the synthesis of certain important hormones. There are several different forms of blood cholesterol. When too much is present in your bloodstream, it can contribute to the clogging of your arteries and increase your risk of heart attack. Some cholesterol is supplied by the food you eat, but your own liver produces it even if you have *no* cholesterol in your diet.

5 Can you eat a high-fat, high-cholesterol diet and still have normal blood cholesterol levels?
For some people the answer is yes, but it's not a license to steal. Have a doctor check the cholesterol and triglyceride levels in your blood annually.

6 Can you go on a low-fat, low-cholesterol diet and still have high blood cholesterol levels?
Yes. For some people, the body chemistry does not respond to these dietary

Note: Underlinings and numbers for editorial comment by General Foods.
© General Foods Corporation, 1980

changes. And there is evidence that, for some, the protein and carbohydrates in the diet can affect cholesterol and triglycerides in the blood. Nonetheless, a low-fat, low-cholesterol diet *will* help many people.

7 Why is there controversy over these recommendations?
There is genuine uncertainty about the relationship between diet and heart disease. Not all people react the same way. There is tremendous variation in the response of individuals to dietary fat and cholesterol. Another part of the controversy has an optimistic note: The rate of heart attacks has declined significantly in the last ten years.

8 How do you tell saturated from unsaturated fats?
Most saturated fat comes from animal sources and is hard like butter or cheese, or fat on meat. Most unsaturated fat is of vegetable origin and liquid, like corn oil. *But there are exceptions!* Many animal fats, such as pork and butter fat, also contain substantial amounts of unsaturated fats. And some vegetable oils like coconut or palm are actually saturated. When vegetable oil is hydrogenated, as in solid shortening or "regular" margarine, it becomes partially saturated.

9 What other common risk factors can affect your heart?
In addition to smoking and high blood pressure, there's stress. Heredity. Drinking too much. Not exercising. Overexertion. Being overweight. Or being a diabetic, to name a few.

10 Does the basic principle, "Eat a variety of foods," still stand when it comes to fats and cholesterol?
More than ever. Your body needs *some* fat. All saturated fat and cholesterol need not be eliminated, particularly if they come in a food rich in other nutrients, like milk or eggs.

11 Should you give up eggs, shrimp, liver?
No. Unless your doctor advises you that your blood cholesterol levels are too high, don't feel that you must totally avoid high-cholesterol foods like shellfish, organ meats and eggs. They can be plentiful sources of the protein and important vitamins and minerals you need. *Moderate.* Don't eliminate.

12 Do you need fat at all?
Most people would reject a diet without fat as unpalatable. And remember some fat is essential for a healthy body. It is better to cut down your use of fats, than to try to eliminate them totally.

13 Should you switch to polyunsaturates?
Scientists are reexamining the evidence. They're now less convinced that increased use of polyunsaturates is the most effective and safe way of lowering blood cholesterol. So moderate your intake of *all* fats.

General Foods urges you to study the U.S. Dietary Guidelines

FIGURE 11–4 General Foods complements its advertising with marketing promotion in the form of consumer-oriented product publicity and public relations programs. (Courtesy of General Foods Corporation)

YOU MAKE THE CALL

Marketing the Jordache Look

In the 1980s few companies could boast as successful a link between public relations and marketing as Jordache, the maker of what used to be called dungarees and today are called blue jeans. Jordache was the creation of Joe Nakash, who began in New York City in the late 1970s with $25 in his pocket, sleeping in the bus terminal by night, and sweeping floors by day.

After beginning several jeans stores in Brooklyn with his brothers, Ralph and Avi, Joe Nakash borrowed $300,000 to begin his own jeans manufacturing company. Using the first names of his brothers and himself and adding a *che* because it sounded French, Joe Nakash invented Jordache and with it the Jordache look. Then the fun started.

The Nakash brothers decided to blow their entire new business loan on promotion.

- They bought time on "60 Minutes" and ran an ad featuring a topless Lady Godiva and a young man wearing Jordache jeans. CBS objected strongly to the commercial, and Jordache achieved significant publicity from its rejection. Orders for Jordache jeans began to pour in.
- The brothers attracted additional publicity when they refused to make jeans larger than size 36 so that only the lean could wear them. Predictably, the Jordache ads provoked cries of "sexism" and "exploitation of women." Equally predictably, the company returned the volley, insisting loudly that their product connoted "vivaciousness and healthy attractiveness." The debate was great media copy.
- When the *New York Times* banned a Jordache ad of a topless couple because "the couple was smiling," the company reshot the ad with the models *not*

1. **What are our long-range goals and objectives?** A clear statement of mission helps an organization target its potential audiences. How many clients does it serve now? Does it want to grow? How fast? Is the mission complementary to the human services, educational, cultural, or arts activities in the community? What problems does the company hope to solve?
2. **What are our short-term goals?** Each short-term objective must be evaluated against the longer-range mission to avoid an appearance of jumping from one short-term goal to another.
3. **Who needs to know about us?** By clearly identifying the individuals or groups that need to know each particular objective, the entrepreneur can determine the appropriate channel of communication to reach that individual or group.

smiling. Jordache then publicly censured the *Times* for practicing its own brand of morality. More coverage resulted.

■ When rival firms began to counterfeit Jordache jeans, the Nakash brothers hired a legal and detective team to track them down and invited reporters to come along for the kill. This, too, got extensive coverage.

■ When a Jordache blimp crashed at takeoff, leaving the invited reporters with a nonevent, an ambulance delivered Jordache models to the press conference site and turned a fiasco into a party.

Even though such product publicity techniques may have smacked of the days of P.T. Barnum, the Nakash brothers didn't seem to mind. They seemed quite content with an image that had, in four years, parlayed brother Joe's original $25 into a $350 million, 8,000-employee business.

QUESTIONS

1. Why wouldn't the Jordache public relations/marketing strategy work for other companies?
2. Do you think the word-of-mouth publicity that the Jordache stunts provoked was helpful for the company's image?
3. Was the decision not to market jeans beyond size 36 a good one?
4. How would you rate the Jordache public relations thrust in terms of clearly positioning the company?

4. **What are we doing now?** The entrepreneur should first carefully audit communication efforts, from updating mailing lists to analyzing how key publics are regularly reached.
5. **What else can we do?** The entrepreneur should look inward to see whether there are programs on which to capitalize by publicly telling the firm's story.
6. **Do we have the money to do what we want?** Many entrepreneurs have limited budgets. Advertising costs money. So does postage. So does telemarketing. Therefore, a pivotal part of the entrepreneur's public relations role is to determine what the proposed program will cost and, if it exceeds available funds, either scale it back appropriately or work to obtain the necessary funds.

YOU MAKE THE CALL

The Birth of the Cabbage Patch Doll

They were soft. They were huggable. They were absolutely unique. And in the winter of 1983, they were the hottest thing to hit the toy market since the pet rock. They were the Cabbage Patch Kids, those adorable (or gruesome, depending on your point of view) dolls designed by a Georgia sculptor and adopted by their new owners.

In marketing the Cabbage Patch dolls, the Coleco Company relied on public relations to fan the fires of Cabbage Patch mania. Coleco hired Richard Wiener, Inc., public relations counsel, to promote the Cabbage Patch Kids. Wiener first hired a psychologist to study what made the doll so attractive to children. Among the strongest positive characteristics discovered was that the physical appearance of the dolls inspired a nurturing instinct in children. The adoption idea contributed to that instinct and was therefore good. A position paper on this finding was developed and placed in the Cabbage Patch Kids press kit distributed to the media. Additionally, a "Parenting Guide" was presented to each new Cabbage Patch Kid owner.

The rest of the public relations plan rolled out accordingly.

- In October a 15-city Cabbage Patch Kids spokesperson tour hit major television and radio news/talk shows in major markets.
- A mass adoption of Cabbage Patch Kids was staged in Boston, with children invited to the affair with the promise of a free doll.
- Cabbage Patch Kids press kits were mailed to major newspapers around the country. Capitalizing on the media's interest in technology, the public relations material pointed out that the computer-run manufacturing equipment minutely altered the facial features of each doll so that no two Cabbage Patch Kids were alike.
- Wire services were alerted to shortages in toy stores around the nation.
- Jane Pauley, the pregnant host of the "Today" show, was sent her own Cabbage Patch doll. Shortly thereafter, the Cabbage Patch Kids landed 5½ minutes on "Today." This, according to the Wiener agency, was the turning point. " 'Today' gave our story credibility through third-party endorsement . . . that far outweighs an advertisement."*
- In late November, in light of the tremendous Cabbage Patch crush at toy stores everywhere, Coleco announced it was pulling its advertising from television because it "couldn't get enough dolls into the stores."
- Finally, after donating numerous dolls for promotional giveaways to hospitals and other charities, the Wiener firm arranged to have First Lady Nancy Reagan present Cabbage Patch Kids to two Korean children who were in the United States for heart operations.

In the end everybody in the United States, parents and nonparents, knew about the Cabbage Patch Kids. Cabbage Patch mania was as stunning a victory for product publicity as any in the annals of modern marketing. And for Coleco, which declared bankruptcy in 1988, it was a once-in-a-lifetime success.

QUESTIONS

1. What was the risk to Coleco of promoting Cabbage Patch Kids as "available for adoption"?
2. What was the value of first securing and then publicizing the comments of psychologists on the adoption feature of the Cabbage Patch Kids?
3. If you were Coleco's public relations director, how would you answer critics who charged that the only reason the company pulled its Cabbage Patch advertising was to avoid legal liability?
4. Do you think the public relations–oriented marketing approach of the Cabbage Patch Kids would lead to as much as, more, or less recognition than that of other nationally advertised dolls that relied primarily on advertising?

*Jeff Blyskal and Marie Blyskal, *PR: How the Public Relations Industry Writes the News* (New York: William Morrow, 1985), 124.

If the entrepreneur decides that public relations support will be helpful and can be afforded, the following rules may help secure added recognition for a small firm.

- **Work to achieve visibility.** An entrepreneur in a small company can try to publicize the company through free publicity in the media. Local media are generally receptive to the announcement of a new firm, new officers, new products, and new locations of local business operations. An entrepreneur who takes the time to become familiar with local journalists may find a few willing to use the company's announcements.
- **Compose a facilities brochure.** No matter how small the firm, a brochure describing its products, prices, and philosophy is a good idea. A facilities brochure can serve as a calling card to potential customers. If done in a quality manner, such a brochure may suggest prestige and credibility, both vital attributes for any business.
- **Use direct-mail marketing.** Once a facilities brochure is created, it should be mailed to customers and prospects. In this context it is often wise to use an outside, professional mailing service and mailing list supplier. The facilities brochure should have a return response coupon or a postage-paid response card to facilitate customer inquiries.
- **Work at becoming known in the community.** Small businesspersons should be joiners. They should join the local Chamber of Commerce, Better Business Bureau, civic clubs such as Rotary and Kiwanis, Junior Achievement, or Big Brother/Big Sister. Achieving recognition in a community isn't difficult for someone willing to put in the work and the hours. For a businessperson in a small company, such active participation in community affairs can mean valuable business contacts.
- **Consider advertising.** Advertising for a small business can, of course, be tremendously helpful. However, it is not a necessity. Advertising is expensive and can prove wasteful if it is not used strategically. Advertising in the telephone classified directory is probably a good idea; so, too, is sticking to the local media. Print advertising for a small business should have some built-in mechanism, such as a coupon, to indicate reader response.

Most small entrepreneurs have limited means. Therefore, to increase reach and recognition in the marketplace, a wise entrepreneur will take advantage of public relations techniques to enhance marketing initiatives.

THE AGE OF PUBLIC RELATIONS MARKETING

Marketing professor Philip Kotler has said that the days of traditional product marketing may be giving way to a more subtle, social, or public relations marketing. According to Kotler, companies must deal with dwindling resources, inflation that continues to limit buying power, consumers who are becoming more sophisticated, environmental and quality-of-life considerations, and government control. With these worries companies may be just as concerned about staying in business as they are with maximizing sales.[8] In light of these changing societal characteristics, a new kind of radical marketing may develop.

1. **Quality of life**   Rather than being the "seller science," the purpose of marketing in the future may be to assist sellers in selling better, buyers in buying better, and governments in regulating better. Quality rather than quantity may become the most important variable in marketing goods and services.
2. **Interest orientation**   Rather than being needs-oriented, marketers in the future may be more interest-oriented. That is, they may serve the educational or social interest of consumers more than anything else.
3. **External decision making**   Rather than sellers freely setting prices and controlling marketing factors, external parties may be represented in the marketing decision-making process.
4. **Nonsegmentation**   Rather than varying their product offerings as they choose, marketers may be limited to offering less differentiation in styles, colors, and models.
5. **Restraint**   Rather than catering to all the wants of consumers, future marketers may have to concentrate on conserving resources and counteracting increased and unnecessary costs to customers.

Although radical marketing is not yet upon us and perhaps may never be, Kotler's thesis underscores the importance of marketers thinking beyond traditional notions of product, price, distribution, and promotion as the key elements in selling a product. More and more, managements of consumer product companies are inviting public relations input in the development of marketing programs. Brand and product promotion managers are increasingly recognizing that public relations programs can address specific marketing objectives with the same precision that advertising offers and with equal or better cost efficiency. Indeed, some predict that we are on the threshold of a major readjustment in marketing promotion.

By the end of the 1980s, in fact, cable TV and media proliferation may provide a communications base that not only will increase the importance of public relations in the marketing mix but also may well permit product public relations to become an equal partner to product brand advertising.

NOTES

1. Richard M. Detwiler, "Yes, Virginia, It's All True—What They Say About Third Party Endorsements," *Public Relations Journal* (May 1974): 10–11.
2. "Kotler: Rethink the Marketing Concept," *Marketing News,* 14 September 1984, 1.
3. Art Stevens, "Brandstanding: Long-Lived Product Promotion," *Harvard Business Review* (May-June 1981): 54.
4. Ibid.
5. Detwiler, "Yes, It's All True," 10–11.
6. Milton Williams, "Deleting Product Identification," *Editor & Publisher,* 26 June 1976, 33.
7. Cited in Nancie Gee, "Tobacco Speakers Roam U.S.," *Publicist,* (July/August 1977): 1.
8. Philip Kotler, "Marketing Management in an Era of Shortage," speech before the New York/New Jersey chapter of the American Marketing Association, Rutgers University, Newark, NJ, 10 November 1974.

SUGGESTED READINGS

Cooper, P. *Health Care Marketing: Issues/Trends.* Rockville, MD: Aspen, 1986.

Deran, Elizabeth. *Low Cost Marketing Strategies: Field-Tested Techniques for Tight Budgets.* New York: Praeger, 1987.

Goldman, J. *Public Relations in the Marketing Mix.* Lincolnwood, IL: Crain Books, 1985.

Greyser, Stephen A. "Changing Roles for Public Relations." *Public Relations Journal* (January 1981): 18–25.

Haley, R. *Developing Effective Communications Strategy: A Benefit Segmentation Approach.* New York: John Wiley & Sons, 1985.

Hauman, David J. *The Capital Campaign Handbook: How to Maximize Your Fund-Raising Campaign.* Washington, DC: Taft Group (5130 MacArthur Blvd., NW), 1987.

Health Care PR Handbook: Success Strategies for PR Pros in Health Care. New York: Madison Avenue Communications, 1987.

Levitt, Theodore. "Marketing Myopia." *Harvard Business Review* 53, no. 5 (September/October 1975): 26–48. Management's failure to analyze its markets and customers' needs could account for some degree of corporate decline.

Marketing Your Hospital: Strategy for Survival. Chicago, IL: AHA (P. O. Box 99376).

Mayall, Robert L. "Does Anybody Here Know How to Play This Game?" *Public Relations Journal* (June 1981): 33.

McKenna, Regis. *The Regis Touch: New Marketing Strategies for Uncertain Times.* Reading, MA: Addison-Wesley, 1986.

Miller, Irwin. *Health Care Survival Curve: Competition and Cooperation in the Marketplace.* Homewood, IL: Dow Jones-Irwin, 1984.

Miller, Peter G. *Media Marketing.* New York: Harper & Row, 1987.

Nickels, W. *Marketing Communication & Promotion.* New York: John Wiley & Sons, 1984.

Schwartz, Gerald. "Planning Product Publicity Pays Off." *Nation's Business.* New York: G.S. Schwartz & Co.

Smith, W. J. *The Art of Raising Money.* New York: AMACOM (135 W. 50th St.), 1985.

Snyder, Leonard. "An Anniversary Review of the Tylenol Crisis." *Public Relations Review* (Fall 1983): 24–34.

Special Events Report (213 W. Institute Pl., Chicago, IL 60610). 24 per year.

Sports Marketing News (1460 Post Rd., E, Westport, CT). Biweekly.

Stevens, Art. "What's New in Product Publicity?" *Public Relations Journal* (December 1981): 16–17. Brandstanding is one way that product publicity can address specific marketing objectives with the same precision that advertising offers and with equal or even better cost-efficiency.

Topor, R. *Marketing Higher Education.* Washington, DC: CASE (11 DuPont Circle), 1984.

Ulkman, Lisa. "The Role for Special Events." *Public Relations Journal* (June 1984): 21. This article discusses the importance of the $850 million special events industry and its creation of opportunities for two-way communication between consumer and sponsors.

Wiklund, Erik. *International Marketing Strategies: How to Build Market Share.* New York: McGraw-Hill, 1987.

Zufall, Dorothy L. "How to Adapt Marketing Strategies in Health-Care Public Relations." *Public Relations Journal* (October 1981): 14.

Rely Tampons

Procter & Gamble (P&G), one of the nation's most successful marketers, entered the $1 billion-a-year menstrual products industry in early 1980, when its Rely tampons went into national distribution. Rely, which the company had test-marketed since 1974, had drawn rave reviews. Indeed, said one industry analyst, "The consumer preference was one of the greatest they ever had for a new product."

Rely was an immediate success. The product won almost 20 percent of the U.S. market in less than six months. The key to P&G's success was superior product performance. Rely had improved absorbency, an important plus for the 50 million women who use tampons. Other tampon manufacturers soon added "thirsty fibers" to their products to compete with the P&G market blockbuster.

Little noticed by P&G and other manufacturers was a case reported in Colorado in 1978 of a sometimes-fatal disorder called toxic shock syndrome (TSS). On identification of the syndrome, the U.S. Center for Disease Control in Atlanta began to study this disease, which caused vomiting, diarrhea, plummeting blood pressure, rashes, fever, and occasionally death. In May 1980 the center reported an increase in the incidence of the disease, the primary victims being menstruating women. In June the center linked toxic shock with tampon use, although it said, "No particular brand of tampon is associated with unusually high risk."

Then, on September 18, 1980, the bottom fell out for P&G. On that day Rely tampons were singled out as resulting in "an increased risk," even though "cases of TSS have occurred with tampons produced by all five of the major U.S. tampon manufacturers," according to the center. Immediately, P&G executives met with officials of the Food and Drug Administration, which regulates tampons. On September 19 consumer groups publicly called for the recall of P&G's Rely brand.

Faced with a media disaster and fearing a product recall, P&G didn't hesitate. On September 23 it voluntarily took Rely off the market and agreed to launch a print and broadcast campaign urging women to return already-purchased tampons for a refund. Other super-absorbent tampons, however, remained on the market. To hasten scientific progress into TSS, P&G assigned a staff of in-house researchers to investigate the problem and then committed another $2 million to research TSS at 14 private institutions.

Despite its prompt handling of the Rely matter, P&G was served with 400 lawsuits from surviving victims and the next of kin of those who died from TSS after using Rely tampons. Additionally, the company took a $75 million write-off on its Rely business and was stuck with almost 900,000 cartons of Rely packages (which were ultimately used as an alternate heat source for the company's plants).

On the public relations side, however, the company was universally praised for voluntarily taking Rely off the market. Investors hailed the company for not allowing the Rely crisis to overwhelm it—for controlling the situation rather than having the TSS controversy control the company. Moreover, P&G was commended for not allowing the incident to interfere with the marketing of its many other successful products, such as Tide detergent, Crest toothpaste, and Folgers coffee. All functioned as usual during the crisis.

P&G's chairman, Edward Harness, promised his stockholders that the Rely debacle did not mean the end of P&G in the tampon business. Harness pointed out that Rely's introduction was the culmination of more than 20 years of P&G research. Also, importantly, he told the shareholders that the company absolutely believed, "There is no medical or scientific evidence of which we are aware that Rely is in any way defective or that any of its ingredients are harmful or contribute to the development of toxic shock syndrome." But, Harness concluded, the fact that the company's scientists believed Rely to be harmless was less important than P&G's long-held view "that the company and the company alone is responsible for the safety of our products. To sacrifice the principle could over the years ahead be a far greater cost than the monetary losses we face on the Rely brand."*

---

*For further information on the Rely tampon case, see Steve Byers, "Two Cases of How to Handle a Public Problem," *Milwaukee Journal,* 2 October 1980, 17; Nan Robertson, "Toxic Shock," *New York Times Magazine,* 19 September 1982, 32; Dean Rotbart and John A. Prestbo, "Killing a Product: Taking Rely Tampons Off Market Put Procter & Gamble Through a Week of Agonizing," *Wall Street Journal,* 3 November 1980, 1; Pamela Sherrid, "Tampons After the Shock Wave," *Fortune,* 10 August 1981, 114–129.

QUESTIONS

1. What might have happened if Procter & Gamble had publicly disputed the 1980 finding of the Center for Disease Control?
2. What other options did P&G have besides removing Rely from the market?
3. How badly do you think P&G's public image was tarnished by the Rely controversy and subsequent lawsuits?
4. Could there have been a potential spillover impact on other P&G products from negative public opinion?
5. Had you been the public relations director of one of the four other U.S. tampon manufacturers, what public relations response would you have recommended to your management in the wake of the P&G decision?

Helpful hint in answering questions: Reflecting on what advice he would give to companies that someday might find one of their products similarly caught up in a safety controversy, retired P&G Chairman Harness advised, "Keep the ball in your own court if you can. Do it right, before somebody does it wrong for you."

12

Public Relations Advertising

Despite what many general managers think, advertising is not the same as publicity. The basic difference is that advertising costs money—a lot of it—because you control what is said, when, where, and to whom. Publicity, which will be further discussed in chapter 13, is far less costly but also less controlled.

Traditionally, organizations have used advertising to sell products. Only occasionally—for example, the railroads and utilities in the 1920s—have firms used advertisements for purposes other than product promotion. In 1936 Warner & Swasey initiated an ad campaign that stressed the power of America as a nation and the importance of American business in the nation's future. After World War II, Warner & Swasey continued ads promoting the free enterprise system and opposing government regulation of business. This unique type of advertising—the marketing of an image rather than a product—became known variously as institutional advertising, image advertising, public service advertising, and public relations advertising.

Whereas promotional advertising was hard sell, public relations advertising was softer. Whereas promotional advertising talked about the particular virtues of using specific products, public relations advertising focused on the general image the company wanted to convey and the public issues it wanted to confront. Whereas promotional advertising sought purchasing action for its products, public relations advertising sought support for its positions.

Such ads typically were used to announce name changes, management changes, merger plans, or other information that promoted the company in general rather than its particular products. This kind of specialized advertising remained very much the exception rather than the rule until the 1970s.

ADVERTISING PRESSURES OF THE 1970s

In 1970, U.S. corporations spent a little more than $150 million to advertise images and issues. By 1974 the amount spent on such advertising increased to $220 million.[1] One reason for this tremendous growth can be summarized in

Steve Rivkin

Steve Rivkin is principal of Rivkin and Associates, a New York City-based market positioning counseling firm. Prior to this, he was executive vice president of Trout & Ries Marketing Consultants. Before joining that agency in 1974 as an account supervisor, Rivkin was assistant to the vice president of corporate affairs at IU International Corporation, a Philadelphia-based conglomerate, and had served as associate editor of *Iron Age Magazine*. He is a frequent speaker on advertising and marketing before business, association, and college audiences.

How do you define public relations?

Public relations is the art of doing good and making sure you get caught at it.

What do you mean by "positioning" a company?

Positioning a company means getting into the mind of your prospect with a single, memorable concept or set of ideas about that company. The basic approach of positioning is not to create something new and different, but rather to manipulate what's already there, to retie the connections that already exist.

How do you go about positioning an individual company or product?

Positioning a company is actually thinking in reverse. Instead of starting with you or your company, you start with the prospect.

Step 1 is to research how your company is perceived in the minds of whatever marketplace is important to you. (Perception is more important than reality.) Don't rely on what management says the company's perceived image is. Your audience's answer may be 180 degrees away.

Step 2 is to get some internal consensus on what position you ideally want to occupy. (If everybody wants to face a different direction, it's going to be a very difficult march.)

Wishing alone won't make it so. So Step 3 is to find out who's in the way of obtaining your desired position. (Maybe you'd like to be known as the world's largest maker of digital widgets. Unfortunately, your competitor is the Digital Widget Company and has five times your revenues and three times your awareness in the widget-buying community.)

Step 4 is money. Do you have enough money to make it happen? Communications is incredibly expensive today. It takes money to establish a position; it takes money to hold a position once you've established it.

Positioning is also a process that's cumulative. Step 5 is a willingness to hang in there with the same basic idea, year after year. Most successful companies rarely change a winning formula. (How many years have you seen those Marlboro men riding into the sunset? Crest has been fighting cavities for so long, they're into their second generation of kids.)

Finally, you should be sure that your carefully honed positioning strategy doesn't vanish in a cloud of confusion. Step 6 demands that everything you communicate matches your position. (There's nothing more counterproductive than a speech before a securities analysts group that contradicts the message in the same day's *Wall Street Journal* advertisement.)

As long as an organization's products are good, why should it worry about its corporate image?
It shouldn't have to. (But whoever said life was fair?) In a multinational, multiproduct, multimedia world, getting noticed is getting tougher. Companies are buying and selling companies at a dizzying rate. Does the reputation of a product or brand automatically transfer along with stock ownership? For most companies, a corporate audience is dif-

ferent from a product audience. (Your banker may not buy your motor oil, but your garage owner isn't going to lend you $10 million either.)

So despite all the good things your product may do and may say about you, your corporate image may ultimately have to stand on its own two feet.

What are the most frequent mistakes organizations make in positioning themselves?

1. **Reaching too far** From some companies' communications, you'd conclude they're just miserable with their current positions. But what's wrong with second place? Pepsi, Avis, Ford, *Newsweek*, J. C. Penney, Firestone, Zenith, and Chase Manhattan are all considered strong alternatives to the leader.
2. **Trying to be all things to all people** The result is terminal blandness of message.
3. **Choosing the wrong name** The United Shoe Machinery Company disappears into the absolute anonymity of USM Corporation. International Silver Company tarnishes itself into Insilco.
4. **Trying for a free ride** The makers of Alka-Seltzer develop a new product to compete with two cold remedies, Dristan and Contac. They dub it Alka-Seltzer Plus. But instead of eating into the Dristan and Contac market, the new product wheels around and eats into the Alka-Seltzer market. (One position per product name is the rule.)

a single word—pressure. By the early 1970s pressure began to build for a re-shaping of traditional advertising approaches. For a variety of reasons, companies had no choice but to strengthen their role in institutional advertising.

The sudden jolt brought about by the Arab oil embargo of the early 1970s changed the rules for a number of advertisers. Oil companies, in particular, no longer had to worry about selling their products, but rather about staying in business. In addition, the more sophisticated, college-educated public of the 1970s intuitively distrusted advertising. One study found that even among business people, 42 percent believed "the public's faith in advertising is at an all-time low." Moreover, many thought that business—and especially big business—had shifted its role in the public psyche from hero to villain.[2] Advertising's most ferocious critics were in the consumer and regulatory areas. Consumer advocates and regulators began to zero in on large corporations and the advertisements they ran. Soon, large companies became once again "everyone's favorite candidate for slaughter."[3]

Counteradvertising

With attacks reminiscent of the earlier muckrakers, consumer advocates of the 1970s went after big business advertising with a vengeance. The weapon they used to attack corporate advertisers was the same tool corporate advertisers used—advertising. Public interest groups sprang up on both coasts to create their own ads in answer to the claims of large corporate advertisers (Figure 12–1). One such concern, Public Media Center (PMC) of San Francisco, adopted this as its creed:

> To represent the unrepresented—in the task of providing media access to those who have important, often vital, information or concerns to share with the public, but who have been denied access to the communications media in this country because of a lack of funds, a lack of professional skills, or because their message was deemed too controversial.[4]

Not only did groups like PMC have the privately donated funds and skills necessary to create professional advertising, but they targeted most efforts at questioning the claims of established advertisers. For example, a typical consumerist-sponsored ad from PMC was a radio spot protesting nuclear power plants. In the ad an announcer for nuclear plants explained that nuclear technology, like all technology, was a great advancement. The ad finished with the tape speeding up and racing out of control.

Radio and television stations and newspapers were not obligated to accept such public service advertising, but a few publications and stations did, particularly those on public broadcasting channels. When such counteradvertising was accepted, it ran free of charge, falling within the Federal Communications Commission Fairness Doctrine that allows equal broadcast time for opposing viewpoints on controversial issues.

Corrective Advertising

Increased federal pressure was another major reason for the spread of institutional advertising in the 1970s. The Federal Trade Commission (FTC), for years one of the meeker government agencies, suddenly sprouted teeth in 1970, when it waged a vigorous campaign to deter advertisers from making claims they could not back up with material facts.[5] The cutting edge of the FTC offensive was a corrective advertising campaign, in which advertisers had to correct any advertising claims found to be false and misleading.

One example was Ocean Spray Cranberry Juice Company, which claimed that its product contained "more food energy" than other drinks. Food energy, according to the FTC, meant nothing more than calories. The commission ordered Ocean Spray to run ads stating clearly that previous claims of having more food energy simply meant that the product contained more calories.

Although the FTC succeeded in the Ocean Spray case, it was less successful in an attempt to force ITT Continental Baking to run corrective treatment for its Wonder bread ads. The commission claimed that Wonder bread wasn't any different from other breads even though it boasted it "could build strong bodies 12 ways." The commission claimed that by "implying Wonder Bread is unique," the company's advertising was misleading. ITT appealed the FTC ruling, and a judge ruled, "The record fails, by a wide margin, to show that asserted false aspects of this advertising are presently contributing to Wonder bread sales or that such aspects have ever had any impact on sales."[6]

In addition to attempts at corrective advertising, government regulators also tried to counter certain advertisements to which they objected. In 1967, for example, the government ordered TV and radio stations to make free time available for messages that said cigarette smoking was dangerous to health. Eventually, cigarette manufacturers removed their ads from the airwaves. Interestingly, in the first year that cigarette advertisements disappeared from TV and radio, cigarette sales rose to record levels.

Another government maneuver to regulate advertising claims was the FTC's Substantiation Program, which attempted to make advertisers document claims they made on price, safety, performance, and effectiveness. Although most advertisers strongly objected to the harsh FTC scrutiny, by the mid-1970s most had toned down their product claims that they couldn't fully defend. In sum, the rules and the substance of advertising changed dramatically in just a few years.

EMERGENCE OF IMAGE ADVERTISING

In the face of such hostile pressure from its critics, advertising in the 1970s took a new turn. Advertisers sought to broaden the use of nonproduct ads to create more responsible images for their firms. Instead of products, they advertised programs, many of which were in the public interest. They talked about

This oil executive will go to bed hungry tonight.

Diana Church

HIS COMPANY earned almost two billion dollars in profits* last year, but that's not enough for him. Because he knows the world is running out of fossil fuels, and unless he can move in and monopolize a new power source, in the same way he's monopolized oil, he's going to be out of a job before very long.

That's why he says his company's astronomical profits aren't excessive—because he needs those profits to maintain his power. That's why he's asking for huge new handouts and tax incentives from the taxpayers—because he wants the government to pay the bills, and his company to reap the benefits.

If he doesn't get what he wants, he may not be able to go on collecting his $300,000 a year salary. He may not be able to go on manipulating the world energy market to the benefit of his stockholders and to the detriment of everyone else. He may be forced to give way to a system where the public controls the public resources for the public good.

If you think America's energy supply is too important to be left to a few huge multinational conglomerates, write your elected representatives and tell them that. The oil industry is making its voice heard in Washington. Isn't it time the shivering majority was heard from?

* After-tax oil profits—1973 (millions of dollars)	First nine months of 1973	Increase over 1972
Exxon	1,656	59.4%
Mobil	571	38.3%
Texaco	839	34.9%
Gulf	570	60.1%
Standard Calif.	560	39.7%
Standard Indiana	390	32.2%
Shell	253	40.6%
Continental	153	23.4%
Atlantic-Richfield	178	36.9%
Total all nine	5,170	45.2%
All oil companies	52,500	30.3%

Prepared by Public Interest Communications

ENERGY SHOULD BE EVERYBODY'S BUSINESS

FIGURE 12–1   These two ads, both critical of the nation's oil companies, were prepared by Public Interest Communications in the early 1970s and ran free of charge in several newspapers. (Courtesy of Public Interest Communications)

The oil companies have us over a barrel

THE NATION'S OIL COMPANIES control the nation's energy supply. And when they want something, they get it. All they have to do is claim that it's not profitable enough for them to produce the energy we need, and the government rushes to make all the concessions the industry wants. The government doesn't even have its own figures on the nation's oil supply—they get all their figures directly from the industry, and make no attempt to have them independently verified.

So if the oil industry wants higher prices, relaxed environmental requirements, the

Alaska pipeline, offshore drilling, more tax handouts, and less competition from independent dealers, they simply allow a shortage to occur, and hold our energy supply for ransom.

We think it's time energy policy was based on public need, not corporate greed.

Don't be left out in the cold—write your congressman and insist on public control of the public's resources.

After-tax oil profits—1973
(millions of dollars)

	First nine months of 1973	Increase over 1972
Exxon	1,656	59.4%
Mobil	571	38.3%
Texaco	839	34.9%
Gulf	570	60.1%
Standard Calif.	560	39.7%
Standard Indiana	390	32.2%
Shell	253	40.6%
Continental	153	23.4%
Atlantic-Richfield	178	36.9%
Total all nine	5,170	45.2%
All oil companies	52,500	30.3%

Prepared by Public Interest Communications

ENERGY SHOULD BE EVERYBODY'S BUSINESS

FIGURE 12–1 *continued*

YOU MAKE THE CALL

Messing with Mr. Rogers

By the mid-1980s Burger King had become one of the most aggressive national advertisers. The company was particularly aggressive when it came to poking fun at arch rival, McDonald's. In 1985 Burger King sought to distance itself from its rival by emphasizing that it flame-broiled its hamburgers, whereas McDonald's fried its meat.

To illustrate the difference in the two burgers, in one commercial Burger King decided to parody Fred Rogers, star of the popular children's show "Mr. Rogers' Neighborhood," which appeared nationally each day on the Public Broadcasting System.

The $150,000 commercial—with an imitator named Mr. Rodney teaching his audience to say the word *McFrying*—ran nationwide for three days before a distressed call came in to Burger King headquarters. The caller was none other than Mr. Rogers himself. And the silver-haired, soft-spoken neighborhood landlord was madder than a dog. Mr. Rogers objected fiercely to the commercial. "To have someone who looks like me doing a commercial is very confusing for children," said the mild-mannered Rogers. He appealed to Burger King's marketing vice president to pull the popular 30-second spot.

QUESTION

If you were Burger King's marketing vice president, would you kill the commercial?

---

social responsibility, equal employment hiring, and minority assistance. Figure 12–2 is a good example of image advertising by Gulf in early 1972.

This shift from institutional advertising to image advertising was a subtle one. As one ad agency executive put it, "It was a shift from what the company is doing to why it is doing these good things for the public."[7] Advertising headlines of the period underscored the social responsibility theme.

At U.S. Steel, Community Life Is Our Life-Style

At Chase, We Helped the Black Magazine That's Helping Black Businessmen

At Texaco, We Don't Talk About Opportunities. We Create Them.

For a while, image advertising ruled the day. But almost as quickly as they had appeared, the image ads began to run into problems.

Problems with the Image

By the mid-1970s people began to distrust image advertising. As one student of the field put it, "Enchantment with image ads lessened because of their attempts to try to 'con' audiences, and because too many ignored the rules of sound communication by trying to impose the advertisers' message on the public."[8]

Then, too, issues involved in image advertising were more complex than those involved with selling products. Images by nature are amorphous, whereas products are tangible. People believed the merits of a particular toothpaste or bar of soap because they could taste or feel them, but they were less likely to take on faith the corporate claim of brotherhood, team play, or social responsibility simply by being told that the advertiser practiced it.

Finally, image advertising was suspect even within many of the corporations sponsoring it. In many cases top management, perhaps because of its lack of understanding about the objectives behind image advertising, apparently didn't trust its own ads.[9] And feedback measurements on image ads were difficult to conceive and implement. Management, which may have grudgingly accepted image advertising on faith, seemed to quickly tire of the idea.

ISSUES ADVERTISING IN THE 1980s

The logical extension of image advertising was the birth of issue, or advocacy, advertising in the mid-1970s and its blossoming in the 1980s. Issues advertising, unlike its predecessor, didn't aim to be all things to all people. Its objective was to convey the sponsor's viewpoint on matters of some controversy. Ads were informational, factual, and persuasive. Many tried to be hard-hitting and let the public know exactly where the firm stood on certain issues.

The growth of issues advertising in the 1980s was attributable to several factors.

■ Many business executives believed that journalists were, in the words of business professor S. Prakash Sethi, "economic illiterates," who limited the extent to which business would be given a fair hearing in the media.

■ Corporate leaders became more aggressive in responding to their critics, recognizing that past silence generally had been counterproductive.

■ A Supreme Court decision in 1978 (see Bellotti case in chapter 22) held that corporate speech was entitled to First Amendment protection, thereby eliminating many earlier restrictions against such speech. As Chase Manhattan Chairman Bill Butcher put it, "A company not only has rights and privileges like an individual person, but also responsibilities and duties. Any person who claims his rights but shuns his responsibilities fails to contribute to the betterment of mankind and, therefore, has no claim on the respect of mankind. I believe the same holds true for corporations."[10]

If you've made up your mind that the guys who run oil companies are bad guys, this isn't your ad.

But if you like to keep an open mind, keep reading. And when you're through, we'd like you to believe one thing: that Gulf is every bit as concerned about preserving and restoring the environment as you are.

One way we can get you to believe this is to tell you what we're doing. So here's what we're doing:

First, we've spent a lot of money fighting pollution for many years—$45 million in 1971 alone, and a projected $196 million during the next five years. And it's bought us some very useful equipment and processes.

It's bought us (and our neighbors) smokeless flare tips at plants and refineries—to insure 100% combustion of hydrocarbons when gases are vented for safety measures.

Closed circuit TV monitoring of flares for combustion

The trouble with being a big, successful oil company is that nobody believes a word you say.

FIGURE 12–2   This Gulf ad, which appeared in *Black Enterprise* magazine in 1972, is a typical image ad. (Courtesy of Gulf Oil Corporation)

control. Roofs that float on liquid storage tanks to prevent vapor formation and escape. Gulfining—a process that removes sulfur from home heating oil. And hydrodesulfurization—to produce fuel that reduces sulfur dioxide emissions at industrial and power generating plants.

We're also making progress in abating automotive exhaust emissions. With low-lead gasoline. And a smoke-suppressant additive that helps to minimize emissions from diesel-powered vehicles.

Before you can correct pollution, you have to trace it. So we built three mobile detector vans to use at Gulf plants: one pinpoints emissions into the air; another pinpoints emissions into the water; and the third determines on the spot the best way to treat effluents.

We transport vast amounts of petroleum by transoceanic tankers. So we use special loading devices that keep accidental spills on board or in dock—and out of the water. And we have a major research program on clean-up technology.

We're concerned with wildlife, too. That's one reason we donated the land for the Tinicum Wildlife Preserve in Pennsylvania. It's a major stopping place for migratory birds that travel the Atlantic Flyway. And we've assisted several environmentalists in getting an interstate highway reconstructed so that the natural state of the land can be preserved.

One of the problems with preserving natural resources is that we're simultaneously fighting a national energy shortage. So we're looking for new, ecologically sound fuel sources from coal, tar sands and shale. And we've entered the nuclear energy field. Our choice of nuclear power systems is a High Temperature Gas-cooled Reactor (HTGR) that uses less uranium and discharges only about ⅔ as much waste heat as other nuclear systems now in commercial operation.

We may some day face a water shortage. So we've developed a way to purify brackish water and are working on ways to desalt sea water economically.

This is some of the work Gulf is doing. We know we have a lot more to do. But we're determined to do it. And we'd like you to believe that.

An Equal Opportunity Employer
Gulf Oil Corporation

FIGURE 12–2 *continued*

YOU MAKE
THE CALL

The Unwanted "Extra" in Corona Beer

Midway through 1987 the importer of Corona Extra, the most successful foreign beer in America, had a problem—a real problem. In a several-week period during the summer, Corona was the victim of an urban myth, apparently started by a jealous competitor, that the beer's unique flavor was the result of its being contaminated with urine at the brewery in Mexico City.

Barton Beers, which imports Corona to the United States, kept getting calls from people who had heard the rumor. The number of calls reached the point that Barton went to court in July, suing Luce and Son, which imports Corona's main competitor Heineken, on the grounds that Luce representatives were spreading the rumor. In an out-of-court settlement Luce and Son made a public statement that Corona was "free of any contamination."

Nonetheless, the rumor persisted. And U.S. sales, which had grown 170% over the previous year, dropped as much as 80% in some areas. In Orange County, California, the Corona representative was besieged about the rumor by 35 separate retailers. So the question that faced Barton Beers executives in late summer 1987 was "To advertise or not to advertise?"

QUESTIONS

1. If you were Corona's public relations director, would you advertise?
2. Why or why not?
3. If you did advertise, what would you say?

- The news media, stunned by a proliferation of corporate advertisements criticizing its treatment of business (Figure 12–3), began to acquiesce to corporate requests for equal time.
- The FTC, dubbed the "national nanny" in its earlier salad days, narrowed its approach to deceptive advertising during the Reagan years. Instead of vigorously pursuing national advertisers, the FTC generally relaxed its substantiation program. Advertisers were thus less concerned about their overall image and more interested in publicly pursuing the issues that affected them most.[11]

Networks began allowing a trifle more advocacy and controversial corporate comment than had previously been the case. ABC-TV, for one, allowed Kaiser/Aluminum & Chemical Corporation to present an unedited rebuttal to an earlier ABC report on unsafe aluminum housing wire. ABC also began to accept issue commercials on its late-night programming. Not to be outdone, CBS devoted an entire 1981 edition of "60 Minutes" to a critical look at itself, *as advertised in* THE WALL STREET JOURNAL.

We're not giving in.
We're going on.

For the past several months there's been a lot of talk that we'd soon be out of business. There's no denying that we've had our share of troubles. But we're not ready to give in.

We know it'll be tough. But we have the support of some very dedicated people. Like our suppliers. Our dealers. Our customers. And especially our employees. They've made a lot of personal sacrifices. Because they're determined to help turn this company around.

So are we.

We've re-organized our entire operation. From top. To bottom. We're putting all our resources behind our proven strengths: Trucks and farm equipment. Because both of these are winners.

Take a look at the facts.

Fact. During the first six months of this year, we outsold everyone in medium and heavy trucks. And that's no fluke. For the past 36 months we've outsold everyone in the industry. More people stood by International trucks than any other.

Fact. Our farm equipment continues to be the best in the world. Just look at our 50 Series tractors. Our Axial Flow combines. Our Early Riser planters. They are the most innovative, most advanced machines available. That's why in the last seven months alone...even in this tough economy...over 33,000 farmers have invested in International farm equipment. And we're committed to continue making the best equipment in the field. Today. And tomorrow.

Because we're getting ready for tomorrow.

We have nearly 700 million dollars invested in continuing product development for both trucks and farm equipment. That's so we can keep making the best machines you can buy. And we're backing that up with over half a billion dollars in readily available parts.

Today, we're trimmer and tougher than ever before. And we're building the best trucks and farm equipment in the world. And we plan to keep building them tomorrow.

Because we're not giving in. We're going on.

International Harvester

FIGURE 12–3   In the summer of 1982, the huge International Harvester Company was widely rumored in the media to be on the verge of bankruptcy. To counter such damaging talk, the company hammered back with this full-page ad in the *Wall Street Journal*. By 1986 the company had changed its name to Navistar. (Courtesy of Navistar, formerly International Harvester)

providing opportunity to various observers, including corporate media critics, to comment on the program's practices in covering news stories. And in 1985 the Public Broadcasting System (PBS) aired a Vietnam retrospective program, produced by the conservative Accuracy in Media group and designed to rebut an earlier PBS broadcast.

By 1980, 90 percent of America's independent television stations were accepting advocacy or opinion commercials, compared to about 50 percent five

SHE'S GOT HER MOTHER'S EYES, HER FATHER'S NOSE AND HER UNCLE'S DEFICIT.

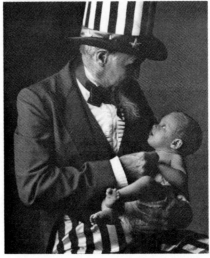

It's quite a legacy her uncle has handed her. (Her favorite uncle, at that.) Annual federal deficits approaching $200 billion. A current national debt of $1.6 trillion. Potentially, $13 trillion by the year 2000.

When the numbers get this big, they tend to get meaningless. Until you look at it this way. If federal deficits continue at their current rate, it's as if every baby born in 1985 will have a $50,000 debt strapped to its back.

The great debate over deficits, of course, no longer centers on whether or not they should be reduced, but how.

One side favors raising taxes. But whose? 90% of all personal taxable income already comes from tax brackets of $35,000 and below. Does anyone seriously suggest increasing the tax burden of lower and middle income families?

Well then, the argument follows, tax the rich. But, if the federal government took every penny of every dollar over the $75,000 tax bracket that isn't already taxed—not

a surcharge, mind you, but took it all—it would only collect enough to run the country for a week. Besides, there's no guarantee that Congress would spend less money if we all gave them more.

The alternative seems clear. Cut spending. But, again, the question is how.

We're W.R. Grace & Co. While our business interests in chemicals, natural resources and consumer

services are worldwide, our primary interest is in the future of America's economy. That's where any corporation's best interest lies.

To that end, our chairman headed a presidential commission that identified ways to end abuses in federal spending. It found 2,478 ways. Specific ways.

The President has seen the report. So has Congress. We think you should know what they

know. There's a booklet that summarizes it all. For your free copy, write to this address: USA DEBT, Dept. U, P.O. Box 3190, Ogden, Utah 84409.

Unfortunately, almost 75% of the commission's recommendations won't be implemented unless Congress acts on them. And, sometimes, the words "Congressional action" are mutually exclusive. That's why we all have to take action first.

Read the booklet. If it gets you angry, it's up to you to get things changed. Write to Congress. If you don't think that'll do it, run for Congress.

Our children and grandchildren don't deserve to pay for our mistakes. We should be passing on to them a healthy economy and a high standard of living. That should be their inheritance. That should be their birthright.

GRACE
One step ahead
of a changing world.

W.R. Grace & Co., 1114 Avenue of the Americas, New York, N.Y. 10036

FIGURE 12–4 W. R. Grace & Co., inspired by its fiery chairman Peter Grace, launched an issues advertising campaign to highlight the perilous nature of a steadily escalating federal deficit. Grace complemented its print ads with two 60-second commercials, one of which was banned in 1986 by the three major networks because it was seen as "too controversial." The other ad, curiously, was accepted by two of the three networks. (Courtesy of W. R. Grace & Co.)

years earlier. By 1984 total spending by the 10 leading U.S. corporate advertisers for what could be classified as public relations advertising had surpassed $300 million.[12] And the issue ads of the 1980s were more pointed than at any previous time. Figure 12–4, for example, shows an ad from W. R. Grace & Co., designed to warn readers of the dangers of a burgeoning federal budget deficit.

Issues Advertising in the Oil Industry

By far the leading proponent of issues advertising was the oil industry, barraged by critics who claimed that it profited from the nation's energy miseries. As one advertising executive put it, the realization of worldwide energy shortages made it nonsensical "to promote traffic into Arco stations when there wouldn't be enough gas to go around."[13]

Initially, the oil companies reacted to the energy crisis by sponsoring factual ads explaining the origins of the problem and exhorting the public to conserve energy. But these ads failed miserably. As Texaco's advertising general manager put it,

> We had not done as good a job as we should have in bringing our story to the people and their representatives. We sincerely believe the facts are on our side, but we failed to bring those facts home to the public. We cannot afford to fail again.[14]

The direction the industry chose to prevent failure was that of hard-line issues advertising. For example, in late 1974, when legislators challenged oil firms on the truth of their supply shortage, Texaco responded with full-page ads claiming: "We're Not Holding Back Anything."

Of all the large companies, none was more demonstrative and vocal in issues advertising than Mobil Oil. Each Thursday Mobil bought space opposite newspaper editorial pages across the country to holler, plead, and proselytize. And Mobil didn't mince words. "Don't read these ads if you've made up your mind about oil profits," began a typical ad. Another urged readers to "fight the two-times-two-equals-five logicians who think the same outfit that brings you the U.S. mail can find oil three miles under the ocean bottom." Strong words. Tough talk. Admonition bound to evoke criticism.

> While the big guns of Mobil's ads on the op-ed page thundered their message to the groggy readers of the *New York Times,* a team of fast-talking Mobil flacks were busying themselves with the public interest consumer groups and environmental groups.[15]

The Mobil ads that created such controversy (illustrated in Figures 12–5 through 12–7) were largely the idea of Mobil's public affairs director Herbert Schmertz, a former labor lawyer and assistant to Robert Kennedy. Mobil's public relations staff conceived of and wrote the ads; an advertising agency executed them. Schmertz attempted to place Mobil's issues ads on television networks, but they initially rebuffed him, saying that such advertising would

If we tell you oil companies don't make enough profit, you'll have a fit.
Oil companies don't make enough profit.
Sorry.

It has been more than five years since we first ran an advertisement under this headline. Back, even, before our profits were called "obscene."

Today, the oil industry is being charged with things like "ripoffs" and "profiteering." And the reason for these accusations hasn't changed much since 1972: continued misunderstanding about just how profitable the industry *really* is.

In the years since the oil embargo brought on that "obscene profits" nonsense, for example, Mobil's annual *revenue* has increased steadily. But our revenue, like your salary, is shared with federal, state, and local governments. It also pays the bills, buys crude oil, and pays royalties.

What's left after all the bills and taxes are paid is net income, or *profit,* which last year amounted to just 3.8 cents for every dollar Mobil Oil took in. Out of this profit, dividends are paid to shareholders. What's left provides some of the money to look for new supplies of oil and gas. In fact, looking for oil and gas is so expensive, we have to borrow money to help finance the search.

Mobil Oil's profit per dollar of revenue of 3.8 cents is substantially lower than the 4.6-cent average return on revenue for all U.S. industry. Measured by the same yardstick, the oil industry as a whole last year was just a little better than average, with a 5.0 percent return on revenue. But this still can't hold a candle to the 8.5 percent return for the pharmaceutical industry, 6.4 percent for broadcasting and motion pictures, or 6.1 percent for soaps and cosmetics, to name just three other industries.

Another measure of corporate profitability is return on shareholders' equity—net income expressed as a percentage of the company's net worth. Last year, that number for Mobil Oil was 13.2 percent, the oil industry was at 13.0 percent, and all U.S. industries were at 13.3 percent.

These results put oil about halfway down a list headed by the broadcasting and motion picture industry, whose return on shareholders' equity for 1976 was a whopping 21.0 percent. Others near the top were soaps and cosmetics, 16.3 percent; and publishing and printing, 14.7 percent. Motor vehicles were slightly better than oil at 13.8 percent. Food was below oil at 12.8 percent and office equipment was at 11.5 percent. So, many industries did better than we did and others did worse.

And last year wasn't an unusual one, either for us or other industries. With few exceptions, oil industry profits have traditionally been near the median for U.S. industry as a whole.

In the final analysis, these comparisons provide ample proof that the myth of oil company "greed" is just that—a myth. If more is needed, however, it can be found in a recent financial analysis of 30 petroleum companies. It showed that, in the years since the embargo, the companies' profits increased by $6.7 billion, while their investments increased $14.6 billion. In other words, they *spent* more money than they *earned* in profits, borrowing against the expectation of future earnings.

This fact probably prompted a recent draft study made for the Federal Energy Administration to say: **"Return on oil company stockholder equity is not excessive compared with other manufacturing industries.... Oil companies have consistently been making capital expenditures in excess of available internally generated funds.... It appears that a choice may have to be made between allowing higher profits or probably seeing lower capital expenditures for privately financed energy development efforts."**

And that's why we say we don't make enough profit.

Mobil

©1977 Mobil Corporation

FIGURE 12–5 In 1977, when Senator Henry Jackson labeled oil company profits "obscene" at a congressional hearing, Mobil immediately challenged the assertion. (Copyright © 1977 Mobil Oil Corporation)

"There is a better way"

As responsible businessmen committed to South Africa and the welfare of all its people, we are deeply concerned about the current situation.

We believe that the reform process should be accelerated by:

● Abolishing statutory race discrimination wherever it exists;

● Negotiating with acknowledged black leaders about power sharing;

● Granting full South African citizenship to all our peoples;

● Restoring and entrenching the rule of law.

We reject violence as a means of achieving change and we support the politics of negotiation.

We believe that there is a better way for South Africa and we support equal opportunity, respect for the individual, freedom of enterprise and freedom of movement.

We believe in the development of the South African economy for the benefit of all of its people and we are, therefore, committed to pursue a role of corporate social responsibility and to play our part in transforming the structures and systems of the country toward fair participation for all.

The advertisement reprinted above ran in leading newspapers in South Africa. It was signed by more than 90 major companies operating there, including the affiliates of several U.S. corporations. We're proud that Mobil Oil Southern Africa (Pty) Limited was one of the signers, just as we're proud that here in the U.S., in 1977, Mobil Oil Corporation was an original signatory of the Sullivan Principles.

The fact is that Mobil and its affiliates in South Africa have opposed apartheid in both word and deed for a decade or more.

Mobil workplaces and company facilities in South Africa are desegregated. All employees are treated equally. All employees doing equal and comparable work receive equal pay.

These are among the conditions embraced by all companies who sign the Sullivan Principles. They are also pledged to provide training and opportunity for advancement, and here, too, the Mobil companies in South Africa have a positive story to tell. Hundreds of our employees who are black, colored, or Asian (South African government terminology, not ours) have moved into semi-skilled, skilled, and supervisory jobs. Some supervise whites. Some have entered management. Working conditions for black employees have improved in an ongoing process of long duration,

and we hope it will be allowed to continue.

The 12 original signers of the Sullivan Principles have now grown to 152 American companies. Together, they and their affiliates have spent more than $130 million since 1978 on health, education, community development, training, and housing for blacks and other nonwhites in South Africa.

Those who would pressure American companies to withdraw from South Africa are doing a disservice to the objective they share with both the American and South African business communities—an end to apartheid, as peacefully and as quickly as possible. Their actions are unproductive and unfairly punitive.

● The business community in South Africa—including the affiliates of American corporations—is a most effective instrument for social and economic change. Just reread the ad we've reprinted if you have any doubts on that score. Forcing American companies to withdraw would end their constructive role.

● Disinvestment would punish the very people we are all trying to help and render meaningless the gains they have already made. Boycotting the stock of companies with interests in South Africa is an attempt to punish the companies working for change.

Mobil®

© 1985 Mobil Corporation

FIGURE 12–6 Well into its second decade of op-ed advertising, Mobil was still going strong in 1985. Although some criticized the company for "preaching to the choir," Mobil pushed on. Why? Well, as Mobil itself put it, "When our messages add to the spectrum of facts and opinion available to the public, even if the decisions are contrary to our preferences, then the effort and cost are worthwhile." (Copyright © 1985 Mobil Oil Corporation)

FIGURE 12–7 Occasionally, in the midst of "talking turkey" on public issues, Mobil took a deep breath and relaxed its offensive. (Copyright © 1980 Mobil Oil Corporation)

precipitate "demands for equal time."[16] Schmertz then turned the rejection by the networks into a public relations victory by offering to buy equal time for his adversaries. The networks refused the offer.

As previously noted, the impact of Mobil's advocacy advertising campaign was difficult to measure. A 1976 Louis Harris survey revealed that Mobil was regarded somewhat more favorably than some other oil companies. Of the people who were familiar with Mobil, 69 percent regarded it as a "progressive, forward-thinking company" compared with an average of 66 percent for all the oil companies in the survey. On the question of "helping to improve the quality of life," 60 percent thought well of Mobil, compared with an average of only 53 percent for all the companies. No company came out well on the question of "keeping profits at reasonable levels"; only 34 percent agreed that Mobil did so.[17]

Indeed, Mobil's management made no claim that the company had moved public opinion on specific issues. However, few argued that the program was not without value. Indeed, Mobil has continued its advertising activism even after Schmertz's retirement. As one public relations agency executive put it, "The days of sweetness and light in image advertising are over. Mobil's ads are vigorous and show that the company has conviction."[18]

PURPOSES OF PUBLIC RELATIONS ADVERTISING

Traditional public relations, or nonproduct, advertising—as opposed to image or issue positioning—is still very much in practice for specific purposes. Such advertising can be appropriate for a number of mutually supportive activities.

1. **Mergers and diversifications** When a company merges with another, the public needs to be told about the new business lines and divisions. Advertising provides a quick and effective way to convey this message.
2. **Personnel changes** A firm's greatest asset is usually its managers, its salespeople, and its employees. Presenting staff members in advertising not only impresses a reader with the firm's pride in its workers, but also helps build confidence among employees themselves.
3. **Organizational resources** A firm's investment in research and development implies that the organization is concerned about meeting the future intelligently, an asset that should be advertised. The scope of a company's services also says something positive about the organization.
4. **Manufacturing and service capabilities** The ability to deliver quality goods on time is something customers cherish. A firm that can deliver should advertise this capability. Likewise, a firm with a qualified and attentive servicing capability should let clients and potential clients know about it.
5. **Growth history** A growing firm, one that has developed steadily over time and has taken advantage of its environment, is the kind of company with which people want to deal. It is also the kind of firm for which people will want to work. Growth history, therefore, is a worthwhile subject for nonproduct advertising.
6. **Financial strength and stability** A picture of economic strength and stability is one that all companies like to project. Advertisements that highlight the company's financial position earn confidence, customers, and corporate stockholders.

"Once people called us The Proud Bird. Lately they've been calling us other names."

"Continental is no stranger to success. As 'The Proud Bird,' passengers were calling weeks in advance to be sure of getting a seat with us. But recently, while we combined the operations of four airlines, we grew so fast that we made mistakes. Misplaced baggage. Delays. Reservation errors. You were frustrated and angry. And a lot of hard-working people at Continental were pretty embarrassed.

"It's led us to an intensified commitment to quality. And it's beginning to pay off: Latest reports show Continental's back as one of the top two airlines in on-time arrivals. But we're out to be 'America's Best.' To get there, we're investing more than $1.25 billion this year alone — to upgrade airport facilities and aircraft, and to expand our fleet.

"We're continually evaluating and adjusting our flight schedules for better connections and on-time performance. Working to decrease lost baggage — an area where we've already improved 100% in the last six months. Even adding special trouble-shooters at major airports who can respond instantly if problems occur. But that's just the start.

"We think we'll be the talk of the airline industry. And believe me, it won't sound anything like what you've been hearing lately."

Frank Lorenzo, Chairman, Continental Airlines

 CONTINENTAL

© 1987 Continental Airlines, Inc.

FIGURE 12–8   In 1987, with Continental Airlines criticized in the wake of rapid mergers and deteriorating service, the company and its gutsy chairman, Frank Lorenzo, decided to go public with this equally gutsy public relations ad. (Courtesy of Continental Airlines)

7. **Company customers** Customers can serve as a marketing tool, too. Well-known personalities who use a certain product may be enough to win additional customers. This strategy may be especially viable in advertising for higher-priced products, such as expensive automobiles or sports equipment.

8. **Organization name change** Occasionally, firms change their names (Jersey Standard to Exxon, American Metal Climax to AMAX, First National City Corporation to Citicorp). To stick in people's minds, a name change must be well promoted and well advertised. Only through constant repetition will people become familiar with the new identity.

9. **Trademark protection** Companies such as Xerox and Coca-Cola, whose products are household names, are legitimately concerned about the improper generic use of their trademarks in the public domain. Such companies run periodic ads to remind people of the proper status of their marks. In one such ad, a perplexed secretary reminds the boss, "If you had ordered 40 photocopies instead of 40 Xeroxes, we wouldn't have been stuck with all these machines!"

10. **Corporate emergencies** Occasionally, an emergency situation erupts—a labor strike, plant disaster, or service interruption. One quick way to explain the firm's position and procedures without fear of distortion or misinterpretation by editors or reporters is to buy advertising space. This tactic permits a full explanation of the reasons behind the problem and the steps the company plans to take to resolve the dilemma (Figure 12–8).

PUBLIC RELATIONS ADVERTISING IN THE 1990s

The end of the Reagan era, coupled with a rash of ethical transgressions among institutions, may signal a reemergence of public relations advertising in the 1990s. Pressure on nonprofit organizations to prove why they, rather than others, deserve contributions will intensify. Hospitals—faced with declining patient enrollments, increased competition, and rising costs—will have to position themselves in a manner unique enough to stay in business. In business, regulatory pressures, consumer demands, and class action suits will continue to be the order of the day. A return to public relations advertising will be one way for organizations to take their case directly and immediately to the public.

For such advertising to work in the overcommunicated, skeptical, and sophisticated society of the 1990s, institutions must keep in mind seven cardinal rules of public relations advertising.

1. **Ads must strengthen the bottom line.** The institution must keep in mind its own best long-term interest in its advertising. An organization pays for an ad for selfish reasons. For example, when Dresser Industries warned that "American jobs will be lost if Middle East-dependent firms, like Dresser, are subject to more boycott legislation," the bottom-line impact on Dresser and the country was clear.

2. **Ads must be clear**. One purpose of public relations advertising is to promote understanding. If message and motives are cloudy, people simply won't understand, no matter how well conceived the ad is.

3. **Ads must be supported by top management**. The more controversial a public relations ad, the better it is. An ad that is watered down is one that is doomed to failure. Top management must be prepared to take the heat and support the advertising. For example, when New York builder Donald Trump took out ads in 1988 to talk about protectionism, they began, "Japan is taking advantage of us." Top management—that is, Trump himself—was fully supportive.

4. **Ads must persuade**. Again, this is the basis of advertising. Ads shouldn't just inform; they must be persuasive. When public interest groups opposed Judge Robert Bork's nomination to the Supreme Court in 1987, they initiated a public relations advertising campaign that said in part, "We're one vote away from losing our most fundamental rights . . . choosing between sterilization and job loss . . . declaring illegal the use of birth control . . . not being protected from sexual harassment." In other words, they used fear to persuade, and Bork's nomination was defeated.

5. **Ads must sell the persuaded**. All advertising, especially the public relations variety, must appeal to what the public wants—not what the organization wants. This is a subtle distinction that is often lost on public relations advertisers (Figure 12–9).

6. **Ads must be honest**. Any advertiser is suspect. All ads begin with a bias. If the organization is to be believed, the ad itself must be scrupulously straightforward and honest. Such was not the case when the head of the United Transportation Union in 1987 ostensibly paid for an ad in the *New York Times* appealing for support to fight a ban on smoking in commuter trains. Several days later, it was revealed that the ad was secretly paid for by the Philip Morris Tobacco Company.

7. **A sense of humor helps**. Organizations, particularly big ones, can't take themselves too seriously, especially in public relations advertising. Humor disarms a skeptical populace, and a light touch can help to influence readers toward a particular viewpoint.

EFFECTIVENESS OF PUBLIC RELATIONS ADVERTISING

The effectiveness of public relations advertising, particularly with legislators and other opinion leaders, remains an open question. Critics charge that many image and issues ads are examples of organizations "talking to themselves." Indeed, most issues advertisers consider their competitors as important targets for such advertising.

The likelihood of continued nonproduct advertising presents important new challenges for public relations professionals, used to dealing with adversarial publics. As advertising moves further into the realm of issues and posi-

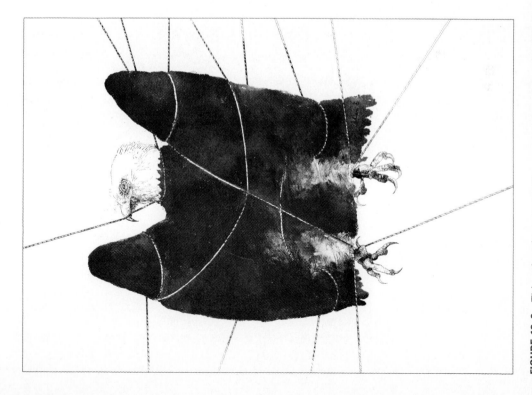

FIGURE 12–9 This ad makes compelling arguments about the anachronistic laws that govern commercial banks in the United States. But are these arguments personal enough to persuade consumers to take action? (Courtesy of Chase Manhattan Bank)

BETWEEN THE LINES

Issues Advertising to the Rescue

Although many companies in the 1980s began using issues advertising to go on the offensive against critics, issue ads were useful as a quick defense, too. Consider the following chain of events involving Citibank, one of the world's most powerful institutions.

On December 21, 1981, after Soviet-style authoritarianism had snuffed out a democratic movement in Poland, the *Wall Street Journal* quoted a high-ranking Citibank executive as saying, "Who knows which political system works? The only test we care about is, 'Can they pay their bills?' " On December 22 the *Journal* and other newspapers around the nation began receiving scathing letters to the editor, denouncing the Citibank position. On December 23 the president of the United States, in a nationally televised address, urged Americans to place a candle in their windows in solidarity with the Polish people.

Three days later, on December 26, a full-page ad appeared in the *New York Times* that was headlined "Peace and Freedom on Earth," picturing a lighted candle and quoting the president's call for all Americans to show support for their brave Polish brethren (Figure A).

The ad's sponsor?

Yup.

FIGURE A (Courtesy of Citibank)

In fact, we've made it a tradition. The reason is simple: we've got the best on our side.

In health, education and municipalities, Clark Burrus, Craig Bouchard and their people have made us the #1 bank for the hospital industry. The #1 U.S. Government bank in the Midwest. The #1 bank for Illinois municipalities. The leader in innovative college and university finance. By far.

In communications finance, no one can touch us. Led by Jackie Hurlbutt, we offer more expertise in cable, broadcasting, newspapers and telecommunications than anyone. Anywhere. That's a commitment backed by nearly $2 billion in loans outstanding.

In real estate finance, we're a lead bank to the country's leading real estate and mortgage companies. With Dan Lupiani and his experienced team, our clients get a combination of market knowledge and financial expertise that's hard to beat.

For more than a dozen specialized industries, First Chicago has the players, the speed, the depth, the drive.

All we need is you.

SPECTACULAR PERFORMANCE IS NOTHING NEW TO CHICAGO.

Performance has always been a Chicago tradition.

FIRST CHICAGO

FIGURE 12–10 First Chicago's advertising campaign combined the best of marketing promotion and public relations techniques in an ad series that at once appealed to societal values and civic pride in addition to highlighting the institution's premier standing in certain markets. (Courtesy of First Chicago)

tions, public relations professionals will be called on to play a greater role. To be sure, as organizations are called on to explain themselves more on such issues as credit, guarantees, social responsibility, minority hiring, and product claims, public relations practitioners will be asked to pick up an increasing share of the decision-making and creative burden.

In so doing, practitioners must be sensitive to using the channel of advocacy advertising in a thoughtful way. As Professor S. Prakash Sethi puts it,

> Increased access to the marketplace carries with it the obligation to use such access in a responsible manner. Business has most to lose from public misinformation and, therefore, should take every possible step to improve the quality of public information and debate. This would lead to better public understanding of complex issues affecting business and society and would improve the process of public policy formulation.[19]

Clearly, the real advertising giants in the 1990s and beyond may not be those companies that triumph in the marketplace of products, but rather those that are effective in the marketplace of ideas (Figure 12–10).

NOTES

1. Mead & Bender Communications, *Advertising in the National Interest*, Boston, MA: Mead & Bender Communications, January 1979.
2. Steven A. Greyser and Bonnie B. Reece, "Businessmen Look Hard at Advertising," *Harvard Business Review* (May-June 1971): 18.
3. "Problems of the Credibility of Big Business," *National Observer*, 26 January 1975, 14.
4. Public Media Center Annual Report, 1974/1975. (Available from the Public Media Center, 2751 Hyde St., San Francisco, CA 94109.)
5. Staff report to the Federal Trade Commission on the Ad Substantiation Program, prepared by Hon. Frank E. Moss, 31 July 1972. (Available from the U.S. Government Printing Office, Washington, DC, order no. 80–9410, 1972.)
6. "ITT Continental Baking Unit Is Backed by Examiner on Wonder Bread Ads," *Wall Street Journal*, 29 December 1972, 4.
7. Audrey Allen, "Corporate Advertising: Its New Look," *Public Relations Journal* (November 1971): 6
8. Philip Lesly, "Business Faces a Change of Voice," *Public Relations Journal* (November 1971): 15.
9. W. H. Depperman, "PR Advertising Is a Misunderstood Tool," *Advertising & Sales Promotion* (April 1966).
10. Willard C. Butcher, "Total Corporate Responsibility in the 80s," address at the University of North Carolina, Charlotte, NC, 16 October 1981.
11. Christine Dugas, "Deceptive Ads: The FTC's Laissez-Faire Approach Is Backfiring," *Business Week*, 2 December 1985, p. 136.
12. Josephine Curran, "Corporate Advertising Expenditures," *Public Relations Journal* (December 1985): 28.

13. Audrey Allen, "Corporate Advertising: Its New Look," 6.
14. "Oil's New Sell," *Time*, 11 November 1974, 30.
15. Alexander Cockburn and James Ridgeway, "How Big Oil Pushes Its Message," *Village Voice*, 6 October 1975, 17.
16. Michael Gerrard, "This Man Was Made Possible by a Grant from Mobil Oil," *Esquire* (January 1977): 142.
17. Irwin Ross, "Public Relations Isn't Kid Glove Stuff at Mobil," *Fortune* (September 1976): 202.
18. "Hammond Backs 'Message' Advertising," *Jack O'Dwyer's Newsletter*, 29 October 1975, 3.
19. S. Prakash Sethi, "Battling Antibusiness Bias: Is There a Chance of Overkill?" *Public Relations Journal* (November 1981): 64.

SUGGESTED READINGS

Curran, Josephine. "Corporate Advertising Expenditures." *Public Relations Journal* (December 1985): 28–40.

Dardenne, Peg. "The Cost of Corporate Advertising." *Public Relations Journal* (November 1981): 30–35, 38–42.

Denbow, Carl J., and Hugh M. Culbertson. "Linkage Beliefs and Diagnosing an Image." *Public Relations Review* (Spring 1985): 29–37. The authors diagnose the public image of an osteopathic medical clinic to develop a rational public relations program.

Dugas, Christine. "Deceptive Ads: The FTC's Laissez-Faire Approach Is Backfiring." *Business Week*, 2 December 1985, 136–140.

Garbett, Thomas F. "Corporate Advertising: The What, the Why, and the How." New York: McGraw-Hill, 1981.

Haller, Robert T. *Creative Power! Grow Faster with New Proactive Tactics in Advertising and Public Relations.* New York: Leister & Sons, 1987.

Newsom, Douglas A. "Conflict: Who Gets Media Attention—And Why?" *Public Relations Review* (Fall 1983): 35–39.

Sachs, William S. "Corporate Advertising: Ends, Means, Problems." *Public Relations Journal* (November 1981): 14–17.

Sethi, S. Prakash. "Battling Antibusiness Bias: Is There a Chance of Overkill?" *Public Relations Journal* (November 1981): 22–24, 64.

———. *Handbook of Advocacy Advertising: Concepts, Strategies, and Applications.* Cambridge, MA: Ballinger, 1987.

Welty, Ward. "Is Issue Advertising Working?" *Public Relations Journal* (November 1981): 29.

"When You Are Considering Corporate Advertising." *Public Relations Journal* (November 1981): 21. Guidelines are given for approaching the task of running an advertising program.

The Bank That Cried "Wolf!"

In the fall of 1975, Chase Manhattan Bank told the world, through a series of advertisements in major national media, that it was very worried. The object of Chase's concern was an impending shortage of capital, which the bank thought threatened the nation. Chase said in its ads that the United States was "underinvesting $400 million each day," and that if that trend continued, there would be a shortfall of $1.5 trillion in 10 years. Translated into common terms, that shortfall would mean a decline in growth and prosperity in the United States. To underscore its concern, Chase announced that it had decided to cry "Wolf!" and said it would debate the capital formation argument anywhere and any time (Figure A, p. 324).

One person who wanted to take the bank up on its offer was a 28-year-old data processing executive in Helena, Arkansas, Robert Sitarzewski. Seeing the Chase ads in a national magazine in September, Sitarzewski wrote Chase's chairman, David Rockefeller, saying, "You don't know what you're talking about." Sitarzewski then challenged the New York banker to a public debate.

After several weeks Mr. Sitarzewski received a response from Chase's corporate communications director advising him that although Mr. Rockefeller would not be able to debate, the bank's chief domestic economist would accept the challenge. And so the Great Debate was planned.

In the spring of 1976, Chase sent Richard Everett, vice president and head of Chase's domestic economic policy unit, to Helena, via the bank's private jet. Everett was accompanied by several bank employees. The event attracted print and electronic media representatives from across the country. Network television covered. Wire services were represented. The *Washington Post* sent its reporter. So did the *New York Times*. As the wife of Helena's mayor put it, "This is the first time since the Civil War we've had this many Yankees in town."

During the debate, which took place in a local community college auditorium, Sitarzewski told the audience of about 600 that the free functioning of the market would allocate the nation's resources adequately. He said the bank's proposals to stimulate capital investment would "destroy the American capitalistic system." Everett parried that the federal government would have to provide more tax incentives for industry, encourage personal savings, and attract foreign investments "or the economy would suffer major setbacks."

And who won the Great Debate? Most of the hundreds of follow-up media accounts called the contest a draw. The Associated Press, however, quoted one member of the audience as saying, "Sitarzewski clearly won because he made the bank come to Helena, Arkansas."

QUESTIONS

1. Do you think the bank handled the challenge correctly?
2. How would you have modified Chase's response?
3. Do you agree with the audience member that Sitarzewski won the debate?
4. What do you think Chase got out of the debate?
5. From a public relations standpoint, was Chase correct in participating?

"Wolf!"

The Chase is crying "Wolf!" Again. And we mean it. Again.

America is faced with a shortage of capital. Capital vital to the healthy growth this nation must have if it is to maintain and improve the living standards of all Americans.

In 1952, we published a study warning against government disincentives to the continuing search for natural gas. We raised more caution flags in 1956, 1957, and 1961 about industry's ability to continue to deliver low-cost petroleum energy.

We were accused of crying "Wolf!" at that time. And indeed we were. But it was no pretense.

Our warnings were based on hard facts which became even harder with every disappearing drop of cheap imported oil.

Today we face an equally hard set of facts regarding the level of capital formation and mounting capital needs:

Fact 1: The next ten years will require twice as much capital as the past ten.

Fact 2: It will take a tremendous effort of husbanding sources and resources — far more than it took to win World War II or to put a man on the moon.

Fact 3: We will be lucky if there is as much as $2.6 trillion for building and rebuilding our industrial capacity.

Fact 4: Set against the needs of $4.1 trillion, there'll be a shortfall of $1.5 trillion.

Which means we will be under-investing $400 million a day every day for the next ten years.

The highest priority of our economy right now should lie in the nurture and stimulation of capital formation. Because everything the American people need and want grows out of that.

How do we deal with the problem? Chase proposes a six-part action program:

• Provide sufficient inducements for an ever-growing base of personal savings.

• Establish more realistic guidelines for depreciation allowances.

• Give preferential tax treatment for retained corporate earnings used for investment purposes.

• Ameliorate our relatively harsh treatment of capital gains compared with that of most other countries.

• Stabilize our monetary and fiscal policies to prevent violent swings in the economy.

• Eliminate unnecessary controls. And do away with outmoded government regulations and agencies that restrict our free market economy.

Capital formation must be government's business, businesses' business, labor's business, banking's business — everybody's business.

Your business.

CHASE

FIGURE A   (Courtesy of Chase Manhattan Bank)

13

Publicity Techniques

N o matter whether you work for the largest manufacturing company, the poorest politician, or the tiniest nonprofit organization, chances are good that if you are engaged in public relations work, attracting positive publicity will be among your primary responsibilities. Securing publicity is perhaps the most well-known aspect of public relations work. Certainly, it is the function most associated with public relations. In fact, in most people's minds, publicity *is* public relations.

Publicity, through news releases and other methods, is designed to broaden knowledge and positive recognition of an organization, its personnel, and its activities. Publicity is most often gained by dealing directly with the media, either initiating the communication or reacting to inquiries. Publicity differs dramatically from advertising, despite the fact that most people confuse the two.

Advertising possesses the following characteristics:

1. You pay for it.
2. You control what is said.
3. You control how it is said.
4. You control to whom it is said.
5. To a degree, you control where it is put in a publication or on the air.
6. You control the frequency of its use.

Publicity, on the other hand, offers no such controls. Typically, publicity is subject to review by news editors, who may decide to use all of a story, some of it, or none of it. When it will run, who will see it, how often it will be used—all such factors are subject, to a large degree, to the whims of a news editor. However, even though publicity is by no means a sure thing, it does offer two overriding benefits that enhance its appeal, even beyond that of advertising.

- First, although not free, it costs only the time and effort expended by public relations personnel and management in attempting to place it in the media (Figure 13–1). Therefore, relatively speaking, its cost is minimal, especially when compared with the costs of advertising and assessed against potential returns.
- Second and most important, publicity, which appears in news rather than in advertising columns, carries the implicit endorsement of the publication in which it appears. In other words, publicity is perceived as objective news rather than self-serving promotion, which translates into the most sought-after of commodities for an organization—credibility. And this is the true value of publicity over advertising.

SECURING PUBLICITY

Gaining access to the media is a common problem among organizations wishing to attract positive publicity. People often complain that the media are more interested in bad news than in anything positive. To a degree, this complaint is valid. Although no two reporters or editors can agree on what constitutes news, more often than not, news is the sensational, the unusual, or the unexpected. And oftentimes for an organization, this equals bad news. Indeed, in recent years large multinationals like Mobil Oil and Kaiser Aluminum have taken the unprecedented step of purchasing media air time to tell their side of a story.

Obviously, most organizations lack the resources to do this. But clearly, every organization yearns to earn positive mentions in the media. And this objective is indeed attainable. Overall, what's required is a basic, common sense knowledge of the media people with whom you're dealing and a sense of courtesy, responsiveness, and respect in dealing with them. It bears repeating: journalists—or at least most of them—are people, too. Treat them that way, and the goal of penetrating the print or broadcast barriers lies within reach. The next several pages offer specific suggestions for developing a positive relationship with the media.

Variety of Forms

Occasionally, events trigger an immediate need to disseminate company news. A sudden change in management, a fire or explosion at a plant, a labor strike or settlement—all engender the need for news publicity. In a more controlled sense news publicity is used to announce plant openings, executive speeches, groundbreakings, charitable donations, major appointments, and product changes.

- **Feature** Less news-oriented material provides the media with features: personality profiles on management and company personnel, helpful hints from company experts, case studies of ongoing and successful company programs,

FIGURE 13–1 Media relations has become so important for many large companies that they now advertise names and locations of their press relations staffs so that journalists know where to obtain information about the firm. (Courtesy of Con Edison, the Tobacco Institute, Exxon Corporation, and Texaco)

FIGURE 13–2 The more interesting the photo, the better chance it has of being used in the media. Once a photo appears in print, the reader often presumes that the publication (not the sponsoring agency) took the picture and therefore considers it news. These Kodak photos, which portray the company's exhibition at Florida's Epcot Center, are examples of excellent publicity photos. (Photos courtesy of Eastman Kodak)

innovative ways of opening up production bottlenecks, or unusual applications of new products. Practitioners also often help freelance writers in this task.

■ **Financial** Generally, this material concerns earnings releases, dividend announcements, and other financial affairs. The Securities and Exchange Commission requires that all publicly held companies announce important financial information promptly through the media and news wires.

■ **Product** Publicizing new or improved products has enormous potential to aid bottom-line profits. However, such publicity should be used judiciously so that the media do not feel that the organization is going overboard in attempting to boost sales.

■ **Picture** The old maxim "A picture is worth a thousand words" is particularly true in public relations. Good photos can frequently tell a story about a new product or company announcement without the necessity of a lengthy news release. If an accompanying photo caption of three or four lines is pointed and provocative, the photo has an even greater chance of being used (Figure 13–2).

AVENUES OF PUBLICITY

Many vehicles can be used for publicity purposes—from skywriting to pennysavers to the bullhorn at a political rally. The four most important avenues for publicity remain newspapers, magazines, radio, and television.

Newspapers

Even though television has become a major news disseminator, newspapers continue to hold their own as a news source. A survey by Audits & Surveys showed that television and newspapers were on a par in terms of cumulative daily exposure. Any day of the week, in fact, almost 70 percent of the adult population watches some television news and reads at least one newspaper.[1]

Newspapers provide more diversity and depth of coverage than television or radio. It may be for this reason that approximately 63 million copies of daily newspapers are sold each day. Newspapers range from giant dailies with circulations approaching two million to small weekly papers, written, edited, and produced by a single individual. There are approximately 1,730 daily newspapers in the United States, 78 percent of which are afternoon papers (Tables 13–1 and 13–2).

In recent years, as operating costs have skyrocketed and many Americans have left central cities for the suburbs, some urban papers have folded. In such cities traditional competition between the morning and evening newspapers has diminished. Frequently, both newspapers are printed at the same plant with the two editorial and advertising staffs sharing the same facility. Over the decade ending in 1982, 50 pairs of U.S. newspapers merged their staffs. Occasionally, the same publishing firm owns both papers. The huge Rochester-

TABLE 13–1 This table lists the 20 largest daily newspapers (according to 1987 daily circulation) in the United States. By September 30, 1987, the nation's largest daily circulation newspaper remained the *Wall Street Journal*, with slightly under two million readers daily. *USA Today*, published by Gannett Company, showed a strong circulation gain. (Courtesy of American Newspaper Publishers Association)

Newspaper	Circulation
Wall Street Journal	1,961,846
USA Today	1,324,223
New York Daily News	1,285,869
Los Angeles Times	1,113,459
New York Times	1,022,899
Chicago Tribune	765,371
Washington Post	761,142
New York Post	690,915
Detroit News	686,787
Detroit Free Press	649,312
Newsday	641,363
Chicago Sun-Times	604,862
San Francisco Chronicle	568,088
Philadelphia Inquirer	508,496
Boston Globe	502,521
Newark Star-Ledger	467,549
Cleveland Plain Dealer	447,033
Baltimore Sun	407,439
Houston Chronicle	406,776
Miami Herald	398,612

SOURCE: Audit Bureau of Circulations, New York, 30 September 1987.

based Gannett chain, for example, owns 97 daily newspapers reaching 6 million readers as well as 8 TV stations and 15 radio stations.

In 1982 Gannett launched its most ambitious project to date with the publication of *USA Today,* a truly national newspaper, transmitted from Rosslyn, Maryland, to major American cities via satellite. The paper costs Gannett upwards of $50 million per year. The full-color newspaper lists daily news from all 50 states, offers national weather, sports, and business and downplays international news. Gannett's hope is that *USA Today* will shortly become "America's hometown newspaper." Critics charge that *USA Today*'s abbreviated articles are fast-food journalism and derisively label the publication "McPaper." Nevertheless, early results are encouraging as *USA Today* circulation and advertising revenues exceed projections. By mid-1988 its circulation had reached 1.5 million, second only to the *Wall Street Journal.*

Despite the loss of journalistic competition in many cities, the newspaper is still a primary target for media relations activities. To practitioners and their managements, penetrating the daily with positive publicity is a critical challenge. To many corporate managements, favorable publicity in the *New York Times* is a special achievement. To politicians a complimentary story in the *Washington Post* is equally cherished. In other communities a positive piece in the local daily is just as rewarding.

TABLE 13-2 This table lists the 20 largest newspaper companies (again, according to 1987 daily circulation) in the United States. The 89 dailies put out by Gannett reached more than six million readers every day. (Courtesy of American Newspaper Publishers Association)

Company	Daily Circulation*	Number of Dailies	Sunday Circulation*
Gannett Company	6,029,745	89	5,673,718
Knight-Ridder	3,840,387	31	4,643,057
Newhouse Newspapers	3,018,247	26	3,775,683
Tribune Co.	2,706,970	9	3,552,635
Times Mirror Co.	2,566,586	8	3,081,478
Dow Jones & Company	2,536,377	24	418,297
New York Times Co.	1,821,089	27	2,370,587
Thomson Newspapers [USA]	1,725,977	102	1,303,244
Scripps Howard	1,598,375	22	1,708,427
Hearst Newspapers	1,441,031	15	2,509,392
Media News Group	1,394,620	27	1,556,817
Cox Enterprises	1,274,973	20	1,569,465
News America Publishing	1,193,595	3	489,792
Ingersoll Newspapers	1,077,369	37	922,756
Capitol Cities/ABC	944,832	9	908,387
Freedom Newspapers	926,261	29	934,509
Chronicle Publishing Co.	894,033	8	772,110
Central Newspapers	817,179	7	940,048
Washington Post Co.	815,947	2	1,156,415
Donrey Media Group	753,856	55	746,510

SOURCE: Morton Research; Lynch, Jones & Ryan; Audit Bureau of Circulations.

*Average for six months prior to 30 September 1987.

One newspaper that is a frequent target for public relations professionals, particularly those who work for publicly held firms, is the *Wall Street Journal.* The *Journal,* commonly called the business bible, prints several daily editions for different geographic regions. Although its circulation is nearly two million, more than four million people a day read the paper because of high pass-along readership. The paper is put together by 200 reporters and 120 editors and bureau chiefs worldwide. The average annual income of a *Journal* subscriber is close to $62,200. More than one-half of its readers are employed in professional or managerial occupations; 262,000 are company presidents. Thus, the *Wall Street Journal* is a prime target for public relations publicity initiatives, including all four U.S. editions and the Asian and European editions as well.

Not to be overlooked in media relations are the suburban newspapers, the small-city dailies, and the nearly 7,500 weekly newspapers. All are targets for news releases and story ideas. When an organization has a branch or plant in an area, these local media contacts can be of critical importance, particularly for consumer product publicity.

Andrew S. Edson

Andrew S. Edson is senior vice president and general manager of the New York office of Padilla, Speer, Beardsley, Inc., a leading Minneapolis-based public relations agency. Edson's extensive background in public relations includes periods as an account executive for Harshe-Rotman & Druck and for Ruder & Finn. He was also assistant director of corporate public relations for the Anaconda Company and public affairs man-

ager for Citicorp. Edson has taught public relations at Pratt Institute and New York University and lectures frequently on public relations subjects.

How would you define public relations?
Advertising is what you pay for. Public relations is what you pray for.

How does one deal effectively with the media?
You must know the media you plan to deal with. Read the pertinent publications, listen to or watch the actual program. In short, do your homework beforehand. This will show when you write that first pitch letter or make the introductory call. Honesty also counts. Don't hide under a hundred platitudes once you've established a contact. If you cannot effectively answer a question or aid a journalist, be truthful and let that person know. It'll pay off in the long run.

How important are contacts in media relations?
Very. If you develop a good working relationship with members of the fourth estate, you, too, can engage in a game of "give and go." It's not imprudent to ask a favor or question a journalist. Basically, it's a two-way street. The newsperson wants your help when he or she needs it. Conversely, there will come a day when you will need a favor in return. Good media contacts are invaluable in practicing public relations.

What is the proper relationship between a journalist and a public relations practitioner?
Some say at "arm's distance," while others make it a habit of getting to know a journal-

ist on an almost personal and social basis. There really isn't any concrete formula for setting the tone of a practitioner/journalist relationship. Common sense and an adherence to a professional code of ethics, such as that of the Public Relations Society of America, more than anything else, constitute what is proper and improper.

What steps do you follow in publicizing a client?
I first try to put together a publicity plan that will help the client achieve his objectives through proven strategies and action programs. Sure, everyone would love to be in the *New York Times* or *Wall Street Journal* or on ABC's "Good Morning America" program, but it doesn't always happen. While your client may push for his or her appearance in a national book, the company and its products may be more appropriate for a series of bylined articles in trade publications (not at all unlike hitting a few singles in baseball) before pitching a major book or program. Those singles will help you get a home run and build a better case for pitching your client before other target media. Keep in mind the reprint potential of trade articles as calling tools for your sales force, for direct mail to shareholders, as information vehicles to financial analysts, and for simplifying a technical subject to a business journalist. Your success or failure, however, shouldn't be measured on the sheer volume of clippings or articles. Always remember what management's objectives were from the outset and go from there.

Is it wise to phone a busy journalist to assess his or her interest in a story?
That depends on how well you know the person, whether he or she is on a breaking deadline, and how comfortable you feel in "cold pitching" a story. If you're aware that the afternoon is the worst possible time to call someone at the *Wall Street Journal,* for example, unless you've a fast-breaking news story, engage in conversation in the A.M. It's certainly faster to discern interest in an idea by telephone than it is by mail.

Are clients understanding when they don't attract publicity?
Some are. Some aren't. If you make the client aware from the outset of the success/ failure ratio and don't make any unnecessary promises, then you won't get harmed. All too often, public relations practitioners get overzealous and almost guarantee that certain things will happen when they may not. Unlike advertising, we don't control what gets into print, or heard on the airwaves, or seen on the tube.

What special tips can you offer in dealing with the media?
Be honest, forthright, and cooperate with the media person in a professional manner. Don't forget to send a proper thank you note when the occasion calls for it. Think of your relationship as continuing, not a one-shot deal. Stay in touch, even if you have nothing in particular to sell.

Successful Placement   How does a practitioner place a story in a newspaper? After getting the release written, the following hints may help achieve placement.

1. **Know deadlines.** Time governs every newspaper. The *New York Times* has different deadlines for different sections of the paper, with its business section essentially closing down between 6:00 and 7:00 P.M. News events should be scheduled, whenever possible, to accommodate deadlines. An old and despised practice (at least by journalists) is to announce bad news right around deadline time on Friday afternoon, the premise being that newspaper journalists won't have time to follow up on the story and that few people will read Saturday's paper anyway. Although this technique may work on occasion, it leaves reporters and editors hostile.

2. **Generally write, don't call.** Reporters are barraged with deadlines. They are busiest right around deadline time, late afternoon for morning newspapers and morning for afternoon papers. Thus, it's preferable to mail or send news releases by messenger rather than trying to explain them over the telephone. Also, follow-up calls to reporters to "make sure you got our release" should be avoided. If reporters are unclear on a certain point, they'll call to check.

3. **Direct the release to a specific person or editor.** Newspapers are divided into departments—business, sports, style, entertainment, and the like. The release directed to a specific person or editor has a greater chance of being read than one addressed simply to "editor." In smaller papers, for example, one person may handle all financial news. At larger papers the financial news section may have different editors for banking, chemicals, oil, electronics, and many other specialties. Public relations people should know who covers their beat and target releases accordingly.

    Public relations professionals should also know the differences in the functions of newspaper personnel. For example, the publisher is the person responsible for overall newspaper policy. The editorial editor is generally responsible for editorial page content, including the opinion-editorial (op-ed) section. The managing editor is responsible for overall news content. These three should rarely, if ever, be called to secure publicity. That leaves the various section editors and reporters as key contacts for public relations practitioners.

4. **Make personal contact.** Knowing a reporter may not result in an immediate story, but it can pay residual dividends. Those who know the local weekly editor or the daily city editor have an advantage over colleagues who don't. Also, when a reporter uses your story idea, follow up with a note of commendation—particularly on the story's accuracy.

5. **Don't badger.** Newspapers are generally fiercely independent about the copy they use. Even a major advertiser will usually fail to get a piece of puffery published. Badgering an editor about a certain story is bad form. So is complaining excessively about the treatment given a certain story. Worst

of all, it achieves little to act outraged when a newspaper chooses not to run a story. Editors are human beings, too. For every release they use, dozens get discarded. If a public relations person protests too much, editors will remember.

6. **Use exclusives sparingly.** Sometimes public relations people promise exclusive stories to particular newspapers. The exclusive promises one newspaper a scoop over its competitors. For example, practitioners frequently arrange to have a visiting executive interviewed by only one local newspaper. Although the chances of securing a story are heightened by the promise of an exclusive, there is a risk of alienating the other papers. Thus, the exclusive should be used sparingly.

7. **When you call, do your own calling.** Reporters and editors generally don't have assistants. Most do not like to be kept waiting by a secretary calling for the boss. Public relations professionals should make their own initial and follow-up calls. Letting a secretary handle a journalist can alienate a good news contact. And above all, be pleasant and courteous.

Magazines

Magazine publishing experienced a renaissance in the 1980s. Even though some of the nation's most prominent magazines have closed down—*Look* and *Collier's,* for example—many others, particularly specialized publications, have sprung up in their place: from gossip-oriented magazines such as *People* and *Us* to publications a little further afield, such as *Wet,* "the magazine of gourmet bathing"; *Chocolate News,* a bimonthly featuring every imaginable form of chocolate; and the *Razor's Edge,* which caters to women sporting shaved heads.

Today, approximately 11,000 magazines are published in the United States. They can generally be classified into general interest, news, quality, business-oriented, trade, men's/women's interests, and special interest.

- **General interest** These magazines are aimed at the entire population and are designed to appeal to all groups. The two largest are *Reader's Digest* and *TV Guide.* Although differing in format and treatment, they both appeal to millions of readers.
- **News** These weeklies summarize news events, provide background, and add depth to evolving stories. *Time, Newsweek,* and *U.S. News and World Report* dominate this group. *Time,* the first news magazine, made its debut in 1923 and now has a circulation in excess of four million.
- **Quality** These publications are targeted to a more selective readership. *Smithsonian, National Geographic, Harper's, Saturday Review,* and *The New Yorker* are examples. Often these magazines offer more scholarly writing than news magazines do. Some, such as *The Nation* and *The New Republic,* have more limited circulations but command national respect as journals of political insight.

■ **Business-oriented** *Forbes, Business Week, Money, Dun's, Working Woman, Fortune,* and *Barron's* are among the fastest-growing of all periodicals. All influence the attitudes of the nation's business leadership and are the objects of considerable public relations activity. One area of rapid growth is that of regional business journals. Indeed, the Association of Area Business Publications, organized in late 1978 with 14 members, soon had 50 publishers with a combined circulation in 60 tabloids and magazines of more than 900,000. And there were perhaps another 30 to 40 similar publications across the nation ready to join the group. As the association's executive director explained the boom, "It's very simple. There's a tremendous hunger for local and regional business news. The national business publications can't possibly begin to touch it. And the local dailies, for the most part, do a very poor job."[2]

■ **Trade** Magazines such as *Advertising Age, Supermarket Age, Iron Age, Convenience Store News, Metalworking News,* and many others are trade-oriented and are important publicity targets for practitioners serving in specific fields. Most of these are avidly read in the industry.

■ **Men's/women's interest** These magazines cater specifically to either the men's or women's market. For example, *Playboy* and *Penthouse* are clearly designed for men, whereas *Cosmopolitan, Vogue, Glamour,* and *Playgirl* are aimed at women. Teenage girls have *Seventeen, Teen, Model,* and *Sassy,* which sports headlines like "Losing Your Virginity—Read This Before You Decide." One recent trend in these magazines has been toward body toning. A clutch of new titles—*Shape, Fit, Pretty Body,* and *Slimmer*—have taken their place next to the more traditional *Better Homes and Gardens, Ladies' Home Journal, Ms.,* and *Mademoiselle.* All, once again, are excellent outlets for potential public relations placements.

■ **Special interest** These periodicals target virtually every special interest group: black life-style—*Ebony* and *Jet;* science—*Popular Mechanics* and *Scientific American;* farming—*Farm Journal;* journalism—*The Quill* and *Editor & Publisher;* sports—*Sports Illustrated, Sport,* and *Runner;* success—*Vanity Fair, GQ,* and *Manhattan, inc.;* aviation—*Flying, Air Cargo,* and *Aviation Week;* and on and on. And this doesn't include magazines for airline passengers, homosexuals, classic car owners, apartment dwellers, divorced persons, and marijuana smokers. Even *Wet* has 45,000 regular readers.

Successful Placement How does one take advantage of the magazine boom? Magazine placement differs from newspaper placement in a number of ways. For one thing, magazines have longer lead times than newspapers: stories take longer to get printed, so articles must be less time-oriented than daily press material and must be written more in a feature style. They must also be scheduled further in advance. Here are five general suggestions for attempting to place publicity in magazines.

Blimp Wars

Perhaps the most unusual publicity vehicle in the 1980s was the airship made famous by the Goodyear Tire & Rubber Company. Goodyear was so protective of its blimp as a publicity vehicle that when the Fuji Photo Film Company in 1986 began using its own blimp in television ads and as a flying billboard, Goodyear sued Fuji. The company charged that too many blimps would spoil its franchise, which had been trademarked for many years in promoting tires. Goodyear sought to stop anyone else from using the blimp as a unifying theme in promotions.

With companies such as McDonald's, Resorts International, and Citibank also starting to use airships as publicity vehicles, blimp wars have only just begun.

(Courtesy of Fuji Photo Film USA, Inc.)

(Courtesy of Goodyear Tire & Rubber Co.)

1. **Choose target publications carefully**. Know what the magazine uses. Read and study back issues for at least six months to determine whether your subject fits.
2. **Innovate**. Magazines like creative ideas and shun run-of-the-mill material. Suggest new approaches and break new ground. Retreaded news releases seldom have a chance.
3. **Take care with the cover letter**. A short cover letter can help sell a story idea. The letter should state simply why it's in the magazine's best interest to publish the suggested story. The letter should be just thorough enough to interest the editor and make the sale without supplying the finished article.
4. **Use exclusives**. With public relations material, many magazines insist on exclusives. For example, *Time* may not accept a feature idea or a bylined guest column from an executive if *Newsweek* has already run such an article from the same executive. As a matter of courtesy and prudence, practitioners should seek only one placement per story idea in a particular magazine category. If the idea is rejected by the first choice, the practitioner should then approach the next choice.
5. **Use freelancers**. Magazines frequently buy articles from freelance writers. Some freelancers know magazine editors well enough to have a feel for what the editors like. A practitioner should stay in contact with freelancers, who are willing recipients of story ideas that can then be marketed by the writers to magazine editors.

Radio and Television

For more than two decades, radio was the nation's dominant electronic news source. Then came television, and radio slipped into a subordinate position. Although the golden years of radio may have passed, the medium is still important as a news source. Here are the facts.

1. During the average week the radio is heard by adults in close to 95 percent of the homes in the United States.
2. The number of radios in cars rose from under 50 million in 1962 to 122 million by 1985.
3. On a typical day the average college or high school student spends about three hours with a radio.

As TV has taken on the entertainment characteristics of radio, radio has moved more strongly into news dissemination. At least one all-news radio station is available in major cities, broadcasting a constant stream of news around the clock. Several radio networks—including ABC, NBC, CBS, and Mutual—compete to service the approximately 6,000 stations in the United States. Radio journalists are often receptive to the story ideas of public relations people.

Television also offers a variety of opportunities, particularly on the local level, for groups to tell their stories through film, videotape, and on-the-air

Publicity is just one weapon in the arsenal of public relations communicators. The variety of promotional vehicles available to public relations professionals is limited only by the imagination of the practitioner.

- Employee magazines, such as Chase Manhattan's *Chase Directions,* can be enormously helpful in conveying management messages in a palatable, colorful way that employees understand and appreciate.

- Comic books, such as *Meet the Bank* of the American Bankers Association, can be a friendly way to introduce children to products and services they will grow up with.

- A bit more revolutionary is the Anaglifics[R] system, which uses 3-D technology to bring products and services to larger-than-life dimensions in magazine advertisement inserts, direct mail pieces, and retail displays.

The next several pages illustrate the diversity of colorful promotional vehicles available to public relations practitioners.

Publications of all varieties are outstanding ways to target organizational themes to particular constituents.

- The Noranda Group, a Canadian manufacturer dealing in natural resources, used every page of its *Panorama* magazine to combine headlines, copy, design, and color to grab employee attention about matters of considerable corporate concern.
- Hamilton College combined an attractive recruiting brochure with a 17-minute videotape in which the same students talked about life at Hamilton, both inside and outside the classroom.
- Chase Manhattan's Individual Banking Group used its publication to pass along "marketing ideas that worked" to fellow employees engaged in retail banking around the globe.

Much less traditional than using publications to convey messages are the promotional vehicles illustrated on the pages that follow. These run the gamut.

- When concerned American Indian parents in Minneapolis wanted to change people's minds about using Indians as mascots, they came up with a blunt but effective poster that not only received national attention but also caused local athletic teams to change their nicknames.
- When the Potato Board in Denver wanted to promote good old spuds as "America's favorite diet food," it portrayed its product as a lovable staple through a general information package of cookbooks, posters, and colorful ads.
- When Chicago-based Levy Restaurants was selected to create, own, and operate two new outlets at Walt Disney World, Levy worked with Tassani Public Relations, Inc., to supply the press with oversized Mickey Mouse gloves to handle the "hot" news announcement.
- Thompson Printing Company of New Jersey hand-printed promotional reminders on its complimentary stationery.
- Jesse Jackson's National Rainbow Coalition used an appropriately colorful button to promote the candidate in 1988.
- Coffey Communications devised and marketed special senior citizens publications, called *Senior Edition,* for hospitals everywhere.

The free trade deal that has been negotiated between Canada and the United States will be very good for Noranda employees and shareholders.

About a quarter of Canada's national income and more than 2 million of our jobs depend on this trade, which is under increasing threat from U.S. protectionism. Lumber, potash and copper strip are three recent examples of our products that have faced restrictions on entry to the U.S. market, and the list threatens to grow larger.

Under the terms of the agreement, barriers to trade in goods and services will be eliminated over a period ranging up to 10 years, and a more effective means of resolving trade disputes will be put in place. At the same time, our cultural industries will continue to be protected and our social programs will not be affected.

By providing more secure access to the U.S. market, the free trade deal will improve the position of Noranda's existing operations as well will make Canada an increasingly attractive place in which to invest and expand. Virtually every independent study has concluded that it will significantly improve the living standards and quality of life for Canadians in every region of the country.

Past efforts to negotiate free trade with the U.S. have faced strong opposition from the business community because it was afraid it couldn't compete, but now we have grown up. We have confidence in our ability to prosper and grow under free trade. The deal is supported strongly by both big and small business as well as the consumer movement.

Critics of the deal, while conceding that our living standards may improve, seem to base their opposition on the fear that we may lose our sovereignty and identity. This seems to represent a peculiar view of what it means to be a Canadian. Our identity is not so fragile and our values are not so shallow that they are somehow going to be destroyed by improved access to the U.S. markets.

Over the next few months, free trade will be the subject of fierce debate in this country. The deal is not perfect, but it represents a real improvement over what is now in place. Hopefully, the debate will be based on fact and informed opinion rather than partisan politics and ideology.

Alfred Powis
Chairman and Chief Executive Officer
Noranda Inc.

WHAT IT MEANS TO NORANDA

Noranda Inc. had sales of approximately $6.2 billion in 1986.

This money is from selling the resources we harvest, mine or manufacture. In fact, Noranda Inc. is listed by *Fortune* magazine as number 214 in their annual top international 500 companies (ranked by sales and excluding U.S. companies). The company's customers are in 65 countries around the world. The Noranda Group is an example of how rich Canada is in resources and how important its world trading partners are.

1987 has been the year of free trade. Much has been heard both for and against the free trade agreement. Where does Noranda stand?

Noranda supports the free trade agreement that was signed on October 3, 1987.

In the terms of this agreement, the two countries, Canada and the United States, would have free trade by the turn of the century. And both countries benefit.

Although Noranda sells many different kinds of products to many countries around the world, Noranda's biggest customer for its goods is the United States.

In the recent past, protectionism has been evident in the two countries. (Protectionism is when one country uses or encourages restrictions on imports because of relatively inefficient domestic producers who cannot compete successfully with foreign producers.) This protectionism against some of the products Noranda sells, has been harmful to the company's financial health. Although Noranda Inc. is showing a profit, the long-term effect of countervailing duties already imposed by the United States have not yet fully been felt.

The free trade agreement will provide a mechanism to resolve disputes arising from these protectionist measures now in effect.

The majority of businesses within Noranda are competitive with similar industries in other countries. And while there are businesses in the Noranda Group that will have to increase their competitive edge in the world marketplace, the company is able and ready to meet foreign competition.

Close to 80% of Canada's exports flow to the United States. About a quarter of the country's national income and over two million jobs are dependent upon this trade. External Affairs Canada has put out a booklet, called "Overview," which discusses some of the major points in the agreement:

"The Agreement will provide a regime which will ensure that 'Canadians and Americans alike can plan, invest, grow and compete more effectively with one another and in the global market.' The wide scope of the Agreement is indicated from the outset in the agreed objectives. The Agreement will:

-- eliminate barriers to trade in goods and services between the two countries;

-- facilitate conditions of fair competition within the free-trade area;

-- significantly expand liberalization of conditions for cross-border investment;

-- establish effective procedures for the joint administration of the Agreement and the resolution of disputes;

-- and lay the foundation for further bilateral and multilateral cooperations to expand and enhance the benefits of the Agreement."

There have been many arguments against free trade, and one which is most hotly debated is the issue of sovereignty. Allan Gotlieb, Canadian Ambassador to the United States, in a recent *Globe and Mail* article, stated: ". . .we should not

How To Make The Right Moves

Most guests at the suburban Chicago hotel were either buying a last drink at the bar or going to bed. But the rooms rented by Chase employees buzzed with activity as reports were typed on portable computers, and tasks were planned for the next day.

Months later, Chase Home Mortgage Corporation (CHMC) would complete its acquisition of Lyons Mortgage Company's $2.5 billion servicing portfolio and 11-office branch network.

For the Individual Bank overall, acquisitions are an important part of the growth strategy (see page 5). In the last 12 months, CHMC alone acquired two companies and four major servicing portfolios. The Lyons purchase boosted CHMC into the ranks of the top U.S. mortgage banks and gave Chase a solid foothold in the Midwest.

No acquisition is easy, and Lyons was no exception. But it helped to have a team of CHMC business specialists and Chase corporate staff ready to go the moment Lyons became available. Here's the approach they took:

CHASE HOME MORTGAGE CORPORATION

1. FORGE A PLAN OF ATTACK

Four years ago, Steve O'Brien of Chase Corporate Development and Carol Yorke of Chase Management Science began to work with CHMC on an acquisition strategy. They first defined criteria: location, servicing volume and origination capability. Next, working with Corporate Controller, they built a business model to help evaluate an acquisition candidate and estimate a competitive purchase price.

2. MOBILIZE THE TEAM

Last April, CHMC learned that an Illinois-based savings and loan company wanted to sell its mortgage business. A team headed by Fred Koons, CHMC president, Mr. O'Brien and Geoff Dreyer, then CHMC's Corporate Development manager, flew to Chicago to tour Lyons's home office and visit the servicing plant.

"Buying a business is tough," says Mr. O'Brien. "You have to learn about it quickly." Part of the team stayed in Illinois to come up with an offer, and the rest went back to New York to analyze what Lyons's business would do for CHMC. The verdict: It looked like a good fit.

CHMC's bid, submitted in late April, beat the offers of several other suitors.

Two weeks later, 40 people from CHMC and such Chase staff units as Corporate Controller, Human Resources and Legal descended on Lyons's offices to begin the due diligence process—a week-long, in-depth examination of the business—to make sure CHMC was getting what it expected. Since its bid had been made subject to due diligence, CHMC could still withdraw.

3. KNOW THE BUSINESS INSIDE OUT

Mike Hart, National Standards and Procedures manager, was responsible for training the Lyons branch staff in CHMC operating procedures. He also oversaw the installation of computer equipment and the sorting out of local

4. HAMMER OUT THE ISSUES

Underwriters directed by CHMC Chief Credit Officer Barbara Sanders pored over mortgage documents. CHMC Chief Operating Officer Rich Mirro and his staff examined servicing procedures, and Jim Panepinto's National Production team toured the branches and met with Lyons's employees.

"We looked at people's skills and verified the servicing information," says Mr. Mirro. "I wanted to know more about their business than they did."

After spending 12-hour days at Lyons, team members listed their concerns and any open issues in a 60-page on-site summary.

The Chase negotiating team intensively reviewed the information gathered during due diligence. Strategy sessions during the six-week negotiations "helped us know when to compromise and when to hold the line," Mr. Mirro says.

After the agreement was signed in early August, about a half-dozen CHMC people set up temporary residence in Lyons's Rolling Meadows headquarters to ensure a smooth transition.

5. MAKE IT CHASE

legal requirements.

A different task confronted Jim Tireman, at the time National Loan Documentation manager. He supervised the transfer of Lyons's portfolio to CHMC's new regional servicing center, which he now heads, in Tampa. (The Tampa production facility was acquired only five months earlier.) Like most CHMC employees on the team, Mr.

Tireman juggled his regular duties with this assignment.

"I'll spend three da. a each week in Rolling Meadows and two at our New Jersey headquarters in Montvale," he says. "And the systems manager in Tampa called me every day to let me know how they were doing."

In the end, dozens of CHMC and other Chase people had a role

in bringing Lyons into CHMC's fold —and kept CHMC running at the same time.

"This is a story of vitality and teamwork, of how we responded to opportunities in the marketplace," Mr. Koons says. "We moved quickly to coordinate expertise that crossed traditional borders in the corporation."

Doug Milrod

The team of specialists involved in the Lyons acquisition included (left to right): Geoff Dreyer, formerly CHMC Corporate Development; Rita Blaziar, CHMC Credit; Carol Yorke, Chase Management Science; Mike Hart, CHMC National Standards and Procedures; and Steve O'Brien, Chase Corporate Development.

Bottom-Line Sense

At the CHMC-Lyons Mortgage deal shows, purchasing a business or a portfolio takes intensive effort. At the same time, it can add significant long-term value to the Individual Bank's bottom line.

"Acquisitions let us move quickly into strategically important businesses," says Ken Jablon, Individual Bank Strategic Planning manager. "For example, when we wanted to offer discount brokerage services, we bought Rose & Company instead of starting our own firm." (Chase purchased the Chicago-based brokerage in 1983.)

Another important benefit is added production capability. The purchase of Tampa-based Freedom Home Mortgage last year gave CHMC additional servicing capacity in a low-cost area. That extra capacity was put to good use when CHMC bought the Lyons portfolio, enabling it to service those loans inexpensively.

Acquisitions can also help businesses increase market share. After buying nearly 200,000 revolving credit accounts from Atlantic Financial Federal last year, Direct Response became the second-largest lender of unsecured revolving credit in the U.S.

"For an organization to keep growing as fast as the Individual Bank has—nearly 25 percent, on average, in each of the last three years—it has to keep an eye open for acquisition candidates," Mr. Jablon says.

Both eyes open, in fact.

MONTREAL BANK NET INCOME
($ millions)

1986   1987   1988
Business Plan

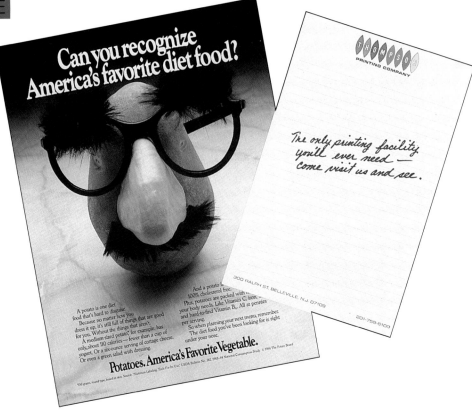

This News Is So Hot,
It Needs To Be Handled
With Special Gloves...

Posters, ads, oversized gloves, messages on stationery, colorful buttons, and special publications for special publics—all are promotional vehicles available to public relations communicators.

More promotional ideas from the minds of imaginative public relations professionals include:

- CPC/Best Foods produced a Mazola Corn Oil cookbook for the Olympics, with the help of New York's Howard Marlboro Group.
- Belmont Park in Nassau County, New York, created a lively and classy direct mail offering to solicit group-rate clients.
- An internal/external publication for Pizza Hut employees and franchisees as well as for key news and trade media let all constituencies know the company's key strategies for growth in the 1990s.
- A provocative press kit for the Toys for Adults Show[R], which toured the United States in 1987, was the vehicle selected to introduce the $100 million of merchandise on hand—from state-of-the-art electronics to cars, boats, furs, Jacuzzis, and much, much more.
- The ultimate promotional vehicle—human beings—was the device used by Days Inns of America, which assembled 300 corporate employees in the shape of the Days Inns sunburst logo to celebrate National Tourism Awareness Day in 1988.

Belmont Park

The Group Experience

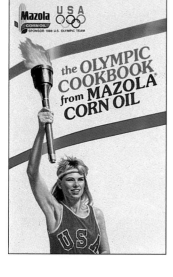

DAYS INNS OF AMERICA

Michael Pugh/Atlanta

When the Vote America Foundation wanted to get out the vote, it relied on a series of promotional vehicles, including print ads with celebrities such as Bill Cosby, comedian Yakov Smirnoff, and major league baseball commissioner Peter Ueberroth. But its most memorable promotion was the gripping spot shown here that ran as a television commercial.

One of the most unique promotional vehicles in the age of the 1990s is the technique of video architecture, offered by Jara Associates, a New York City video design and engineering company that invented, wrote, and produced 3-dimensional promotional excitement for clients. Jara produced everything from multimonitor videos to space-age trade show exhibits, including this striking display for Xerox.

The promotional vehicles illustrated in this special feature are just the tip of the innovative iceberg of creative communications vehicles available to public relations practitioners. In the years ahead, as the clutter of communications in society becomes even greater, the necessity of distinguishing messages in innovative and imaginative ways will be a significant challenge for the practice of public relations.

Myopic Meg and the Great Flack Flap

Nobody ever said newspaper editors were the most rational of beings. Take Meg Greenfield, the respected editorial page editor of the *Washington Post*. Because Greenfield's domain is widely read by the movers and shakers of America, it is a frequent target of public relations-authored, op-ed articles. So frequent, in fact, that midway through 1982 Greenfield blew her journalistic cork.

In a blistering memo to her fellow editors, Greenfield lashed out at public relations counselors as "wolves," "slaves," and "that damned crowd." "I, myself, have told some slave or other from H&K [public relations firm] that we don't traffic with press agents, that if her client, a college president, had business to transact with us, then the college president should call," Greenfield huffed in her confidential memo.

Obviously unaware, or perhaps unconcerned, that politicians and business executives also regularly have their bylined editorials ghost-written by public relations people, Greenfield said she would still entertain these articles as long as public relations agencies weren't involved.

It wasn't long, of course, before the memo leaked and the counterattack began. *Advertising Age* made Greenfield's memo a cause célèbre. Soon the editorial section of the *Post* was flooded with both critical letters and—ironically for Greenfield, who wanted to be rid of such things—invitations to lunch from public relations people wanting to explain their views. One public relations counselor caustically pointed out that Greenfield didn't write her memo until the *Post*'s major competitor, the *Washington Star*, had gone out of business.

In any event the "great flack flap," as one magazine labeled it, seemed to end in a stand-off, with most *Post* editors continuing to accept material from public relations consultants as usual and Greenfield, as she put it, not getting "this stuff anymore."*

*Carl Cannon, "The Great Flack Flap," *Washington Journalism Review* (September 1982): 35.

interviews. There are about 1,150 television stations in the United States. Each week night about 44 million Americans get their news from one of the three major television network shows. In the 1980s TV news has experienced a resurgence, with networks launching late night and early morning news shows.

Additionally, the networks, local stations, and public broadcasting all feature interview programs to complement nightly news shows. Also, with cable television introducing a host of business and economics-oriented programs, the networks, too, have begun to increase their quantity of business and economic news. Unfortunately, many Americans think that by watching TV, they are getting all the news. TV news personnel are the first to admit that their coverage is, of necessity, capsulized and condensed. The typical 30-minute show provides less than 20 minutes of news coverage. In terms of words, a TV news show would fill only about one-half page of the average daily newspaper. When Edward R. Murrow was reminded of this fact by a listener, he changed his opening from "This is the news" to "This is *some* of the news." People who rely solely on television for their news are missing much of what's happening in the world, the nation, and their own community.

Film and videotape are the special appeals of television and are used liberally to heighten the impact of stories. Practitioners should be aware that occasionally an important story that lacks film may be limited in its air time, whereas a less important one with film may receive greater play. This, of course, helps influence people's judgments about the relative importance of specific news. Indeed, broadcasters are often faulted by their critics for using faulty judgment in visually biasing viewers with only one side of a story.

Nevertheless, TV's growth is indisputable. In the 1980s cable television also grew dramatically. By 1985 nearly half of all U.S. households subscribed to cable TV. As a result, the three networks' share of prime-time ratings declined by about 11 percent from 1979 to the early 1980s. Perhaps the most stunning attempt at news on cable has been entrepreneur Ted Turner's Cable News Network (CNN), a 24-hour-a-day video news service, which reaches 80 percent of the cable population and has tried admirably to match the networks in world news coverage. In addition, companies like Warner-Amex have promised further use of two-way systems to link viewers with the programs they watch. The pioneer of such systems, the QUBE limited two-way system in Columbus, Ohio, proved successful, and Warner-Amex, for one, planned to spend $150 million over three years to expand its two-way capacity. In the 1990s half the television sets in America will be hooked up to cable, which will become a $200-billion-a-year industry. The possibility for publicity placement on cable television is enormous.

Beyond cable, private television networks have also begun to pop up. The nation's first private business network, launched by the U.S. Chamber of Commerce in 1982, was called BIZNET. It transmitted programs from the Chamber's Washington, DC, headquarters via communications satellite to subscribers around the country. One BIZNET wrinkle was the opportunity for interaction between audience members (generally business groups) and speakers (generally government officials) through audio hookups. BIZNET was followed by a number of other so-called narrowcasting efforts, especially by business groups interested in seizing equal time with target audiences.

Successful Placement   The public relations professional can approach radio and television similarly for publicity placement, using these guidelines:

1. **Generally call, don't write.** Radio and television are more telephone-oriented than newspapers are. To begin each day, radio news directors and television assignment editors plot their staff assignments. A phone call to

these people—and generally not to reporters or correspondents themselves—during their early scheduling periods may evoke some interest.
However, most news directors appreciate advance warning, so an early letter about an upcoming event may be a good idea.

2. **Keep the story simple**. Radio and TV don't have the editorial space that
newspapers and magazines offer. Rarely does a radio story last one minute—the equivalent of perhaps a page and a half of triple-spaced copy. Television stories may be a bit longer, but not much. Therefore, the more succinct a story is, the better.

3. **Know deadlines**. Deadlines in radio and TV may be even stricter than in
newspaper work. Unless a TV story can be filmed or taped in time to return
for the six o'clock news (ideally, mid-morning), it will be useless. Radio
offers greater flexibility since interviews can be taped on-the-scene or on
the telephone and aired immediately. Frequently, short interview snatches
or "actualities" from longer interviews are aired. In any event it's a good
idea to schedule radio and TV publicity early enough in the day to avoid
running up against competition from unexpected breaking news.

4. **For TV be visual**. TV assignment editors are rarely interested in nonvisual
stories. Talking heads (shots of people moving their mouths and nothing
else) are anathema to TV producers. On the other hand, stories that offer
dramatic, interesting visuals may have a good chance of being used (Figure
13–3).

5. **Get to know the talent coordinator/producer**. In placing clients on radio
and television talk shows, it helps to know the people who book the talent.
Talk shows are excellent vehicles through which to discuss products, books,
or ideas. Earning the trust of the talent coordinator or producer will help
ensure that invitations continue to appear.

Wire Services

Two news-gathering organizations form the backbone of the nation's news system, supplying up-to-the-minute dispatches from around the world to both the
print and electronic media. The Associated Press (AP) and United Press International (UPI) wire services compete to deliver the most accurate news first.
Both services write in a simple, understandable style. The AP serves more than
8,000 clients—newspapers, magazines, TV, and radio stations—and UPI serves
nearly 5,000. Each has bureaus in more than 100 countries, and both believe
it is their role to be there when the news happens. Regrettably, in 1986 UPI
suffered financial problems that left its future in doubt. The death of UPI would
be a most unfortunate blow to journalism and public relations.

Staging as intense a rivalry on the financial side are two business wires—
Dow Jones and Reuters. These wires specialize in business-oriented news.
(Reuters also provides a general news service outside the United States.) When
a company releases news that may influence the decision of an investor to
hold, sell, or buy the company's stock, it is required to release the information

FIGURE 13–3 Television is always looking for a visual angle. And that's just what Guinness World of Records and its public relations counselor, Dorf & Stanton, came up with in the spring of 1988 to publicize the opening of the renovated Guinness World of Records in New York City. Specifically, they had Bruce Block, holder of the record for cigar box balancing, demonstrate his talent. And the cameras rolled to the tune of 15,470,000 viewers reached through television coverage. (Courtesy of Guinness World of Records/Dorf & Stanton Communications)

promptly to the broadest group of investors. In such an instance, Dow Jones, Reuters, and the local press are notified simultaneously. Dow Jones and Reuters news wires, like those of AP and UPI, are found in newspaper offices, brokerage firms, banks, investment houses, and many corporate offices throughout the country.

Additionally, commercial wire services, such as PR News Wire and Business Wire, distribute public relations material to news outlets nationwide. Unlike AP and UPI, these commercial wires charge organizations a fee for running news release stories verbatim on their wires. Such commercial wires serve as an effective backup, ensuring that announcements at least reach news outlets.

One commercial publicity experiment that failed miserably was the scheme launched by the *Los Angeles Times* in 1988 to accept news releases as paid advertising. The *Times* proposed to run each week a section called "Corporate News," to announce the "latest breakthroughs, favorable earnings reports, executive promotions, stock offerings . . . whatever you want them to know, when you want it known." Although the *Times* offered the space at a reduced rate, U.S. public relations people refused to adopt the practice common in some other countries of buying space for publicity/advertising. Quickly, the *Times* postponed its innovation.

One phenomenon that is growing is teleconferencing as a means of disseminating organizational news. Teleconferencing combines television with phone hookups so that participants can be seen and questions asked from remote locations. In one such teleconference General Mills Corporation announced the results of a survey of working families through an elaborate 18-city, satellite TV hookup. With General Mills executives presiding at a news conference in New York, reporters from around the country called in to pose questions about the survey. A similar hookup was used in late 1982 when Johnson & Johnson reintroduced extra-strength Tylenol after its first removal from the market (see the case study at the end of this chapter). The Tylenol teleconference received front page publicity across the nation.

Feature syndicates, such as North American Newspaper Alliance and King Features, are another source of editorial material for newspapers and magazines. They provide subscribing newspapers with a broad spectrum of material ranging from business commentaries to comic strips to gossip columns. Some of their writers—such as Art Buchwald, Jack Anderson, and Jane Bryant Quinn—have built national reputations. Many such columnists depend heavily on source material provided by public relations personnel.

MEDIA DIRECTORIES

Another publicity support is the media directory, which describes in detail the various media.

1. *Ayer's Directory of Publications* lists about 20,000 publications, including daily and weekly newspapers as well as general circulation, trade, and special

interest magazines. *Ayer's* also includes the names, addresses, and phone numbers of publication editors.

2. *Bacon's Publicity Checker* provides data on almost 5,000 U.S. and Canadian trade and business publications, organized in some 100 categories—from accounting and advertising to woolens and yachting. *Bacon's* includes editors, addresses, and phone numbers.

3. *Broadcasting Yearbook* contains information on radio and TV stations in the United States, Canada, and Latin America. It also lists key personnel, addresses, and telephones.

4. *Editor & Publisher Yearbook* lists newspapers across the United States (daily, weekly, national, black, college and university, foreign language) and their personnel.

5. *Working Press of the Nation* is a five-volume effort. It lists locations and editorial staff for the following media: newspapers, magazines, radio, television, feature writers, syndicates, and house magazines.

6. Specialized directories—from *Hudson's Washington News Media Directory* and *Congressional Staff Guide* to the *Anglo-Jewish Media List*—and various state media directories, published by state press or broadcasters' associations, are also excellent resources for publicity purposes. Appendix C offers a comprehensive list of leading media directories, compiled from *O'Dwyer's PR Services Report*.

MEASUREMENT ASSISTANCE

After an organization has distributed its press materials, it needs an effective way to measure the results of its publicity. A variety of outside services can help.

Press Clipping Bureaus

Some agencies will monitor company mentions in the press. These press clipping bureaus can supply newspaper and magazine clippings on any subject and about any company. The two largest, Burrelle's and Luce, each receive hundreds of newspapers and magazines daily. Both services dispatch nearly 50,000 clippings to their clients each day. Burrelle's, for example, employs about 800 people and subscribes to about 1,800 daily newspapers, 9,000 weeklies, 6,000 consumer and trade magazines, and various other publications.

These bureaus may also be hired in certain regions to monitor local news or for certain projects that require special scrutiny. Most charge monthly fees plus about $.70 per clipping. For a practitioner who must keep management informed of press reports on the firm, the expense is generally worthwhile.

Broadcast Transcription Services

Press clipping bureaus are generally not equipped to monitor radio and television stations for client mentions. Consequently, specialized transcription services have arisen to monitor broadcast stories. A handful of such broadcast transcription services exist in the country, the largest being Radio-TV Reports, with offices in several cities. This firm monitors all major radio and TV stations around the clock, checking for messages concerning client companies. After a client orders a particular segment of a broadcast program, Radio-TV Reports either prepares a typed transcript or secures an audiotape. Costs for transcripts are relatively high, with a one-page news item costing upwards of $25.

Broadcast transcription entered the computer age in 1983 when a firm called Mediascan supplied clients with daily verbatim transcripts of network news programming, transmitted by computer to word processors.

Content Analysis Services

A more sophisticated analysis of results in the media is supplied by firms that evaluate the content of media mentions concerning clients. Firms such as Ketchum Public Relations and PR Data use computer analysis to discern positive and negative mentions about organizations. Although this measurement technique is rough and somewhat subjective, it nevertheless enables an organization to get a clearer idea about how it is being portrayed in the media. However, such press clipping computer analysis stops short of being a true test of audience attitudes.

HANDLING INTERVIEWS

Public relations people coordinate interviews for both print and broadcast media. Most executives are neither familiar with nor comfortable in such interview situations. For one thing, reporters ask a lot of searching questions, some of which may seem impertinent. Executives aren't used to being put on the spot. Instinctively, they may resent it. So the counseling of executives for interviews has become an important and strategic task of the in-house practitioner as well as a lucrative profession for media consultants.

Print Interviews

The following 10 do's and don'ts are important in newspaper, magazine, or other print interviews.

1. **Do your homework in advance.** An interviewee must be thoroughly briefed—either verbally or in writing—before the interview. Know what the interviewer writes, for whom she writes, and what her opinions are. Also determine what the audience wants to know.
2. **Relax.** Remember that the interviewer is a person, too, just trying to do a good job. Building rapport will help the interview.
3. **Speak in personal terms.** People distrust large organizations. References to "the company" and "we believe" sound ominous. Use "I" instead. Speak as an individual, as a member of the public, rather than as a mouthpiece for an impersonal bureaucracy.

Sputtering Spungen Meets the Press

Cable Electronics was one of the hottest high-technology firms in the country. So hot, in fact, that *Forbes* magazine asked to interview its chairman, Charles Spungen, about the company's remarkable growth. An engineer by background, Spungen had little experience with the press. Nevertheless, he passed up the opportunity for a preinterview briefing from his public relations director, choosing to get a haircut instead. Immediately after the haircut, he greeted *Forbes* reporter James White at the door of his office, and the interview commenced.

White: Your growth has been phenomenal. To what do you attribute the rapid rise in your profits?

Spungen: We've been on the ball, Jimmy. And we're damn good at what we do. Our products are better. Our people work harder. And we produce. Simple as that.

White: What do you think your competitors have been doing wrong?

Spungen: In the case of Telcom, they've been playing catch-up ball for four years. They just can't seem to get on track. Suncom is another story. Their management is weak.

White: What about Apex?

Spungen: Apex couldn't come in third in a three-man race! But gloriosky! Don't quote me on that one.

White: What, briefly and specifically, are some of the new products you're working on?

Spungen: We're looking at a new micro-processing line. I can't say much about it now, but we think it will be revolutionary.

---

4. **Welcome the naive question.** If the question sounds simple, it should be answered anyway. It may be helpful to those who don't possess much knowledge of the organization or industry.

5. **Answer questions briefly and directly.** Avoid rambling. Be brief, concise, and to the point. An interviewee shouldn't get into subject areas about which he knows nothing. This situation can be dangerous and counterproductive when words are transcribed in print.

6. **Don't bluff.** If a reporter asks a question that you can't answer, admit it. If there are others in the organization more knowledgeable about a particular issue, the interviewee or the practitioner should point that out and get the answer.

7. **State facts and back up generalities.** Facts and examples always bolster an interview. An interviewee should come armed with specific data

White: Didn't I read something about that in the trade press several months ago?

Spungen: I wasn't aware of it if you did.

White: I learned that yesterday you were served with a suit from a group of minority and women employees. Can you tell me a bit more about this suit and what it might mean for your company's future profit outlook?

Spungen: Well, we were notified about that in a confidential correspondence from the court. I absolutely cannot talk about that issue, either to confirm or deny the existence of any such suit.

White: But wouldn't such a suit be potentially damaging to the company?

Spungen: Look, we get sued all the time by various people. To highlight a suit by a few disgruntled employees would be playing into their hands. I certainly wouldn't want to get involved in publicizing these people. So let's drop the subject, O.K.?

QUESTIONS

1. If you were Spungen's public relations director, what would you have included in your briefing (had you had it) prior to the interview?
2. Do you think Spungen's answers were responsive?
3. How would you rate his response to the question about competition?
4. What do you think White might do with the off-the-record information Spungen gave him?
5. Do you think Spungen was right in standing his ground when White raised the minority suit issue? How might he have better handled the question?

that support general statements. Again, the practitioner should furnish all the specifics.

8. **If the reporter is promised further information, get it to her quickly.** Remember, reporters work under time pressures and need information quickly to meet deadlines. Anything promised in an interview should be granted soon. Conveniently forgetting to answer a request may return to haunt the organization when the interview is printed.
9. **There is no such thing as off the record.** A person who doesn't want to see something in print shouldn't say it. It's that simple. Reporters may get confused as to what was off the record during the interview. And although most journalists will honor an off-the-record statement, some may not. Usually, it's not worth taking the risk. Occasionally, reporters will agree not to attribute a statement to the interviewee but to use it as background.

Mostly, though, interviewees should be willing to have whatever they say in the interview appear in print.

10. **Tell the truth**. Telling the truth is the cardinal rule. Journalists are generally perceptive; they can detect a fraud. So don't be evasive, don't cover up, and, most of all, don't lie. Be positive, but be truthful. Occasionally, an interviewee must decline to answer specific questions but should candidly explain why. This approach always wins in the long run.*

After the interview the practitioner might call the reporter to determine her assessment of the interview. Generally, reporters will say frankly how the interview (and the interviewee) turned out. The practitioner should try to improve the interviewee in future interview situations.

Broadcast Interviews

As the broadcast media, particularly television, have become more potent channels of news to the public, executives are being called on to appear on news and interview shows to air their viewpoints. For the uninitiated and the unprepared, a TV interview can be a harrowing experience.

To be effective on TV takes practice. Executives and public relations people must accept guidance on acting appropriately before the camera. In recent years elaborate programs have been constructed by counseling firms to teach executives how to act on TV. The following 11 do's and don'ts may help.

1. **Do prepare**. Preparation is the key to successful broadcast appearances. Executives should know the main points they wish to make before the interview begins. They should know the audience. They should know who the reporter is and something about the reporter's beliefs. They should also rehearse answering tough hypothetical questions before entering the studio.

2. **Do be yourself**. Interviewees should appear relaxed. Smiles are appropriate. Nonverbal signs of tension (clenched fists, gripping the arms of a chair, or tightly holding one hand with the other) should be avoided. Gesturing with palms open, on the other hand, suggests relaxation and an eagerness to discuss issues. Giggling, smoking, or chewing gum should be avoided during the interview. Proper posture is also important.

3. **Do be open and honest**. Television magnifies everything, especially phoniness. If facts are twisted, it will show. On TV a half-truth becomes a half-lie. Credibility should be established early.

4. **Do be brief**. TV and radio have no time for beating around the bush. Main points must be summarized at the beginning of sentences. English must be understandable; neither the reporter nor the public can be expected to be familiar with technical jargon.

---

*For additional practical pointers, see William J. Ardrey III, "The Editorial Interview: How to Get the Most Out of It," *Public Relations Journal* 23 (January 1973): 19–22 and Richard W. Soell, "When Management Meets the Press," *Public Relations Journal* (January 1971): 21–22.

5. **Do play it straight; be careful with humor.** An interviewee can't be giddy, vacuous, or irreverent. Attempts to be a comic may be interpreted as being foolish. However, the natural and relaxed use of appropriate humor may be a big plus for getting a point across. If humor does not come naturally, interviewees should play it straight. That way, they won't look stupid.

6. **Do dress for the occasion.** Bold patterns, checks, or pinstripes should be avoided; so should jewelry that shines or glitters. Skirts should fall easily below a woman's knees. Men's socks should be high enough to prevent a gap between socks and pants. Colors on shirts, socks, suits, and accessories should generally be muted.

7. **Don't assume the interviewer is out to get you.** Arguments or hostilities come through clearly on TV. In a discussion on a controversial subject with a professional interviewer, the guest usually comes out looking like the bad guy. All questions, even naive ones, should be treated with respect and deference. If an interviewee becomes defensive, it will show.

8. **Don't think everything you say will be aired.** TV is a quick and imperfect medium. When Equitable Life Assurance fired several hundred managers, a reporter spent hours chatting with top Equitable executives. That evening 30 seconds' worth of interviews was aired. In other words, to make a point on TV, one needs to be brief and direct in responses.

9. **Don't let the interviewer dominate.** Interviewees can control the interview by varying the length and content of their responses. If a question requires a complicated answer, the interviewee should clarify that before getting trapped in an incomplete and misleading response. If interviewees make mistakes, they should correct them and go on. If they don't understand a question, they should ask for clarification.

10. **Don't say, "No comment."** "No comment" sounds evasive (Figure 13–4). If interviewees can't answer certain questions, they should clearly explain why. Begging off for competitive or proprietary reasons is perfectly allowable as long as some explanation is offered.

11. **Do stop.** One regularly practiced broadcast technique is to leave cameras running and mikes on even after an interviewee has responded to a question. Often the most revealing, misleading, and damaging statements are made by interviewees embarrassed by the silence. They should not fall for the bait; silence can always be edited out later. The interviewer knows that, and the interviewee should, too, before getting trapped.

These are just a few hints about dealing with what often turns out to be a difficult situation for the uninitiated. In general, the best advice for an interviewee is to be natural, straight, and prepared.*

---

*For additional practical pointers, see Elliot Frankel, "Learning to Conquer 'Mike' Fright," *Washington Journalism Review* (July/August 1982): 29–33; Paul Lockwood, "Speak into the Mike, Please!" *Enterprise* (November 1977): 12, 13; and Dick Martin, *The Executive's Guide to Handling a Press Interview* (New York: Pilot Books, 1977), 12–13.

FIGURE 13–4 Typical of an enlightened media relations attitude is this ad by Adolph Coors Co., a firm that once had been criticized in the media as espousing a particularly silent posture. (Courtesy of Adolph Coors Co.)

Press Conferences

Press conferences, the convening of the media for a specific purpose, are generally not a good idea. Unless an organization has real news to communicate, press conferences can flop. Reporters don't have the time for meetings offering little news. Therefore, before attempting a conference, ask this question: Can this information be disseminated just as easily in a news release? If the answer is yes, the conference should be scratched.

Eventually, though, every organization must face the media in a conference—in connection with an annual meeting or a major announcement or a presentation to securities analysts. The same rules and guidelines hold true for dealing with the press in conference as in a one-on-one interview. Be honest, candid, forthright, and fair. Follow these additional guidelines in a press conference.

1. **Don't play favorites; invite representatives from all major news outlets.** Normally, it makes sense to alert wire services, which in turn may have the resources to advise their print and broadcast subscribers. For example, both the AP and UPI carry daily listings, called day books, of news events in major cities.

2. **Notify the media by mail well in advance of the conference and follow up by phone.** Ordinarily, the memo announcing the event should be straightforward and to the point, listing the subject, date, time, and place as well as the speaker and the public relations contact's name, title, and phone number. If possible, the memo should reach the editor's desk at least 7 to 10 days before the event. Also, the day before the event, a follow-up phone call reminder is wise.

3. **Schedule the conference early in the day.** Again, the earlier in the business day, the better, particularly for TV consumption.

4. **Hold the conference in a meeting room, not someone's office.** Office auditoriums and hotel meeting rooms are good places for news conferences. Chairs should be provided for all reporters, and space should be allowed for TV crews to set up cameras. The speaker at the conference should preside from either a table or a lectern so that microphones and tape recorders can be placed nearby.

5. **The time allotted for the conference should be stated in advance.** Reporters should be told at the beginning of the conference how much time they will have. Then no one can complain later.

6. **Keep the speaker away from the reporters before the conference.** Mingling prior to the conference will only give someone an edge. Keep all reporters on equal footing in their contact with the speaker.

7. **Prepare materials to complement the speaker's presentation.** The news conference is an apt place for a press kit, which should include all the pertinent information about the speaker, the subject, and the organization.

8. **Let the reporters know the end has come.** Just before the stated time has elapsed, the practitioner should announce to the reporters that the next question will be the last one. After the final question the speaker should thank the reporters for coming and should take no more questions. After the conference some reporters (particularly broadcast journalists) may want to ask follow-up questions on an individual basis. Do so only if all reporters have an opportunity to share in the one-on-one format.

Remember, the purpose of a news conference is to enable reporters to ask questions. Questions should be handled as they would be with a single reporter. Every reporter should have a chance to speak up, and no reporter should be allowed to dominate. Often, it is up to the practitioner to be sure that the conference goes according to schedule and format.*

*For additional practical information, see Sam Justice, "Dealing with the Financial Press," monograph, *Corporate Shareholder Press,* September 1978; and Dick Martin, *Handling a Press Interview,* 12–13.

YOU MAKE THE CALL

The Agitated Administrator

Chee Chee Gomez of the Eyewitness News team is at Elmsford Psychiatric Center to film an interview with hospital administrator Neal Shapiro. Earlier in the day an Elmsford patient had escaped and molested a woman in a city park before being captured.

Shapiro—his tie undone and his lip curled—agrees to take a few minutes for the interrogation.

Gomez: Mr. Shapiro, how could a patient with such a long history of mental illness be allowed to roam free on the grounds of the hospital and then escape undetected?

Shapiro: In the first place, our patients are generally supervised as they perform their regular chores during the day. We have about 40 very able guards. Each one has either been a regular police officer or a corrections officer and is also trained in working with mental patients. We have had a few isolated incidents in the past several years, but nothing that I would call major. Our guards, as I said, go through a thorough training period before being assigned here. Generally, they supervise very well, and we haven't had much trouble. This case was a fluke. The man simply slipped away. I mean, what would you have us do? Chain him to his bed? This guy had a real history of severe problems. He should never have gotten away. Somebody just blew it.

But let me add that there was no way we could envision that he would ever do such a thing. For one thing, over the past several months he has been an excellent patient. He has taken his treatment, reacted well to supervision, and generally caused no problems. In this particular case, he probably just slipped away for a second, and something snapped.

There is no way, it seems to me, that you can fault the institution on such an isolated incident. I simply do not feel that undue criticism of the institution or our supervisory staff in this case is warranted. Now, that's all I care to say.

QUESTIONS

1. What do you think of Shapiro's response?
2. If you wanted to portray Shapiro and his institution as the villain in this case, how would you edit his answer on film?
3. If you wanted to portray Shapiro and his institution as blameless, how would you edit the film?
4. If you were Shapiro's public relations adviser, how would you have suggested he answer questions?

Press Junkets

A junket is a kind of press conference on wheels. It is usually billed as an information visit by journalists to a particular site, paid for by a sponsoring organization. The purpose of the trip—for example, film critics to Hollywood to screen a new film or travel writers to a far-away island to sample its hospitality—is to secure positive publicity. In 1986, in the largest press junket ever, Walt Disney World flew 10,000 journalists to Florida to celebrate its fifteenth anniversary.

Some news organizations flat-out reject junkets. *Harper's Magazine*, for instance, has a policy "not to solicit or accept contributions or subsidies from interested parties on matters on which the magazine plans to write." Others are less doctrinaire. Indeed, less prosperous publications find junkets a good way to report on out-of-the-way places and events that they couldn't afford to cover otherwise. As the *New Republic*'s editor put it, "If you have honest people going, they will not be persuaded by the purchase of an airplane ticket for them."

Nonetheless, journalistic junkets should be arranged with extreme care. Occasionally, in fact, a sponsoring organization has been sandbagged by a cynical journalist who accepted the firm's generosity only to write sarcastically of the excesses viewed or received. The bottom line on junkets is for public relations professionals to approach them with extreme caution.

PROFESSIONALISM: THE KEY

As is true with any other specialty in public relations work, the key to securing publicity is professionalism. Because management relies on the practitioners for expertise in handling the media effectively, practitioners must not only know their own organization and management, but must also be conversant in and respectful of the role and practice of journalists. In chapter 14 the proper relationship between journalists and public relations people is further examined.

Publicists, who charge clients for getting their names in print or on the air, are the latest innovation in the relationship between journalists and public relations people. One Mill Valley, California, practitioner received extensive publicity when he announced his publicity price list in 1987—$24,075 for a placement on "20/20," $21,560 for a placement on "NBC Nightly News," $21,400 for a placement in the *Wall Street Journal*, and $21,135 for a placement in *People* magazine. Such schemes, however, are in the minority. Indeed, the best public relations/media relationship—probably the only successful one over the long term—is based on mutual understanding, trust, and respect.

NOTES

1. Leo Bogart, "The Public's Use and Perception of Newspapers," *Public Opinion Quarterly* 48 (Winter 1984): 709.
2. Bill Hogan, "The Boom in Regional Business Journals," *Washington Journalism Review* (July/August 1982): 35.

SUGGESTED READINGS

American Society of Journalists & Authors Directory (1501 Broadway, New York, NY 10036). Freelance writers.

Ayer Public Relations/Publicity Stylebook. Fort Washington, PA: IMS Press (426 Pennsylvania Ave.).

Barhydt, James D. *The Complete Book of Product Publicity.* New York: AMACOM (135 W. 50th St.), 1987.

Bennett, Michael J. "The 'Imperial' Press Corps." *Public Relations Journal* (June 1982): 10–13.

Caruba, Alan. "Satellite TV: New Way to Educate Physicians." *Public Relations Journal* (October 1981): 20.

Danzig, Fred, and Ted Klein. *Publicity: How to Make the Media Work for You.* New York: Scribner, 1985.

Hattal, Alvin M., and Daniel P. Hattal. "Videoconferencing." *Public Relations Journal* (September 1984): 21–26.

Hospitals and the News Media: Guide to Media Relations. Chicago, IL: AHA (P.O. Box 99376), 1985.

International Directory of Special Events & Festivals. Chicago, IL: Special Events Reports (213 W. Institute Place).

Jefkins, F. *Planned Press & Public Relations.* Glasgow, Scotland: Blackie, 1986.

Johnson, Daniel. "Try This Approach for Breaking News." *Public Relations Journal* (September 1981): 28–29.

Kowal, John Paul. "Understanding the Media: If a Newspaper Hums, Hum Back." *Public Relations Quarterly* (Summer 1981): 11.

Ledingham, John A. "Interviewing and Role Playing to Prepare for the Media." *Public Relations Quarterly* (Fall 1984): 28–31.

Mullen, Richard. "Formula for Quiet Sponsorship." *Public Relations Journal* (September 1984): 18–20.

National Research Bureau. *Working Press of the Nation.* (Available from the author, 242 N. 3rd Street, Burlington, IA 52601.) Each of multiple volumes covers a different medium—newspapers, magazines, radio-TV, feature writers, syndicates, and house organs.

Network Futures (Television Index, 40–29 27th St., Long Island City, New York 11101). Monthly.

Nickels, W. *Marketing Communication & Promotion.* New York: John Wiley & Sons, 1984.

O'Dwyer, Jack, ed. *O'Dwyer's Directory of Corporation Communications.* New York: J. R. O'Dwyer, 1985. Guide provides a full listing of the public relations departments of nearly 3,000 companies and shows how the largest companies define public relations and staff and budget for it.

———. *O'Dwyer's Directory of PR Firms.* New York: J. R. O'Dwyer, 1985. This directory has listings of 1,200 public relations firms. In addition to information on executives, accounts, type of agency, and branch office locations, the guide offers a geographical index to firms and cross-indexes more than 8,000 clients.

PR Aids' Party Line. (Available from 221 Park Ave., S, New York, NY 10003.) This information service weekly, published on Monday, lists editorial placement opportunities in all media, including network and local radio and TV.

Professional Guide to Public Relations Services. 2d ed. Englewood Cliffs, NJ: Prentice-Hall, 1980. Guide describes and evaluates more than 1,000 services, including clipping bureaus, mailing house media guides, translators, prop houses, film and record producers and distributors, and mat suppliers.

Public Relations Aids, Inc. (221 Park Ave., S, New York, NY 10003). Computerized media system lets a client select local broadcast media by market, type of programming, power of radio stations, network for TV, department (news, program, women's interest, public service, etc.).

Publicity Handbook. Minneapolis, MN: Brum & Anderson (425 Lumber Exchange Bldg.), 1984.

Rein, Irving, Philip Kotler, and **Martin Stoller.** *High Visibility.* New York: Dodd Mead & Company, 1987.

Rowan, Ford. *Broadcast Fairness: Doctrine, Practice, Prospects.* White Plains, NY: Longman, 1984.

Ruffner, R. *Handbook of Publicity and PR for the Nonprofit Organization.* Englewood Cliffs, NJ: Prentice-Hall, 1985.

Schmertz, Herb. *Good-Bye to the Low Profile: The Art of Creative Confrontation.* Boston, MA: Little, Brown & Co., 1986.

Spitzer, Carlton E. "Fear of the Media." *Public Relations Journal* (November 1981): 58–63. Business fears the media and usually acts accordingly. It is time for both adversaries to clean up their houses and develop a more productive relationship.

Syndicated Columnists. New York: Richard Weiner, 1979. This book gives information on how to locate major columnists in 24 subject categories as well as offering a description of the major syndicates and columnists.

Turow, Joseph, and **Ceritta Park.** "TV Publicity Outlets: Preliminary Investigation." *Public Relations Review* (Fall 1981): 15–24.

Weiner, Richard. *Professional's Guide to Publicity.* New York: Richard Weiner, 1976.

———, ed. *News Bureaus in the U.S.* New York: Richard Weiner, 1981. This media guidebook lists information on 500 bureaus maintained by newspapers, magazines, business publications, and wire services in 23 major cities.

What to Do When the Media Contact You (New York State Bar Association, Dept. of Communications & Public Affairs, One Elk Street, Albany, NY 12207).

Young, Lewis H. "The Media's View of Corporate Communications in the '80s." *Public Relations Quarterly* (Spring 1982): 9–11.

Dashing Dan Gets Bushwhacked

It was the first great debate of 1988, or at least nine minutes of great TV. What happened on the "CBS Evening News" on January 26, 1988, will probably have implications for years to come for presidential campaigns, media coverage, and preparation prior to publicity.

A feisty Vice President George Bush, appearing live from the White House, attacked CBS anchorman Dan Rather for impugning his character during Bush's run for the Republican nomination. Bush also accused Rather and CBS of misrepresenting themselves in obtaining the interview. He said that CBS had promised his appearance would be for a political profile, not a rehash of the arms-for-hostages issues that had set off the Iran-contra affair and had clouded Bush's candidacy.

At one point during the interview, Bush seemed to stun Rather by referring to the anchorman's much-noted walkout from the set of the "CBS Evening News" a few months earlier, when a broadcast tennis match ran too long. Rather's walkout had caused CBS to transmit a blank signal for nearly seven minutes, and the anchorman was roundly criticized by others in the profession, including his predecessor, Walter Cronkite.

"I want to talk about why I want to be president," Mr. Bush said in the interview. "It's not fair to judge my whole career by a rehash on Iran. How would you like it if I judged *your* career by those seven minutes when you walked off the set in New York?" When Rather did not immediately answer, Bush asked again, "How would you like that?"

Bush was initially angered when his interview was preceded by a taped report that suggested that he had played a greater role in the Iran-contra affair than had been previously acknowledged. After the airing of the report, Bush threatened to cancel the interview. But he didn't. Instead, Bush went on and immediately got feisty. "You've impugned my integrity by suggesting here that I didn't tell the truth. I'm asking for fair play," the vice president said.

What followed was nine minutes of shouting and cross-talk, broadcast mayhem, and great theater all at the same time. CBS news was understandably stunned by the vice president's combativeness. After the broadcast it issued a statement saying that it had negotiated for the interview for three weeks and had told Bush campaign aides "that the interview would be 'issue-oriented and tough.'"

Bush, after the interview, was unrelenting. "I'm very upset about it," he told CBS staff members afterwards. "Tell your goddamned network that if they want to talk to me again to raise their hands at a press conference. No more Mr. Insider stuff after that!"

The winner around the country—10 million households watched the mugging—was not even close. CBS switchboards were flooded with phone calls, overwhelmingly critical of Rather and supportive of Bush. So spirited was the backlash against Rather's badgering of Bush that CBS affiliates debated whether to formally protest the anchorman's performance. Bush, who up to that point in the campaign had been derisively called a wimp by his opponents, was clearly reinvigorated.

But there was more than met the eye. The confrontation that appeared on the screen to millions of viewers at home was just a part of the story. It had all begun about a month before the interview. When the vice president saw the CBS letter inviting him to participate with the anchorman, he wrote on his copy, "I feel confident with Rather. Make sure this guy gets reply soon." Immediately, the Bush people began negotiating with CBS over the ground rules. For one thing the Bush people insisted that the interview be live or not at all. Early on, they suspected that the interview would be highly confrontational, and they didn't want CBS to be able to edit anything.

CBS, for its part, was uncomfortable. Live interviews, particularly on nightly news shows, are unpredictable. Whereas a taped interview allows for network editing and shaping, a live interview gives the subject a chance to manipulate the conversation. He can filibuster, evade a probing question, and generally be too elusive to pin down. Nonetheless, CBS finally agreed to do the interview live, and Rather's associates warned Bush's staff that the anchorman's questions were going to be "tough and pointed."

On the weekend before the broadcast, CBS began airing promotions for the Bush-Rather interview and calling political writers to let them know CBS would be airing the "first interview on Iran-contra that Bush has done with any network." The day of the interview, Rather had three one-hour rehearsals with the people involved in the broadcast. He was coached as if he were a candidate preparing for a debate or a boxer preparing for a fight, rather than a journalist going into an interview.

The Bush camp reportedly knew full well that they were heading into an ambush, and they prepared the vice president accordingly. Before the interview one of Bush's advisers predicted that "the vice president would be prepared to answer the questions and may indeed have something of his own he wants to go into." That "something of his own" was apparently the reference to Rather's walking off the set. If so, then the vice president was well prepared for the Iran-contra segment. And his initial barrage, which left Rather stunned and reeling, might well have been rehearsed in advance.

Whatever. What is indisputable is that the bout with Rather turned the tide for George Bush's campaign. The publicity submerged once and for all the wimp image, and George Bush walked away with his party's presidential nomination.*

QUESTIONS

1. Had you been George Bush's public relations counselor, how would you have prepared him for the Rather debate?
2. Had you been Dan Rather's public relations counselor, how would you have prepared him for the Bush debate?
3. From your knowledge of this case, which one of the combatants do you think was perceived as the bully. Why?
4. Do you think George Bush planned the whole thing? Why or why not?

---

*For additional information on this case, see Peter J. Boyer, "Rather's Questioning of Bush Sets Off Shouting on Live Broadcast," *New York Times*, 26 January 1988, A1, 9; David Colton and Matt Roush, "On-Air Bash: Who Got Mugged?" *USA Today*, 26 January 1988, 1–2A; E. J. Dionne, Jr., "Bush Camp Feels Galvanized After Showdown with Rather," *New York Times*, 27 January 1988, A1, 9; Ned Schurman, "Bush vs. Rather: A Tonic for TV News," *New York Times*, 27 January 1988, A27; Gerald F. Seib and Monica Langley, "Bush Wins a Clear Victory in TV-Interview Spat but Doesn't Dispel His Iran-Contra Problems . . ." *Wall Street Journal*, 27 January 1988, 52; Richard Stengel, "Bushwhacked!" *Time*, 8 February 1988, 16–20.

PART THREE
The Publics

Media

T he media comprise the public that is most associated with public relations work. As noted, most people believe that the term *public relations* is synonymous with *publicity*. It isn't. But few people are able to distinguish between securing favorable publicity for an organization and winning positive public relations.

Without question publicity, as discussed in chapter 13, is a critical activity for most public relations professionals. The focus of this chapter, however, is the broader area of media relations. A good working relationship with the media is imperative for any successful communications program. Dealing with the media has traditionally been a primary responsibility for public relations practitioners. Media relations, in fact, has developed into a career specialty for many in the field.

Ours is a mass-media society, where learning and knowledge come through newspapers, television, radio, magazines, books, and films. To the traditional means of transmitting information (the classroom, pulpit, lecture hall, and face-to-face encounters) have been added such devices as satellite communication networks, computerized printing technology, and even two-way cable television.

In our society the media play a major role in shaping opinions, values, and knowledge. Indeed, if an item isn't in the news, it may as well never have happened. If it makes page one, it not only happened, but is also important. If it makes page 40, it may have happened but isn't terribly important. Or so we think.

The mass media also influence today's issues. When they zero in on a particular individual or institution, the results can be devastating. Recent U.S. history is studded with examples of people and agencies whose power and influence have been cut short as a result of their attracting extensive, critical media attention. Presidential appointments in recent years have been particularly vulnerable.

■ President Reagan's Supreme Court nominations in 1987 were treated especially harshly by the media. First Judge Robert Bork and then Judge Douglas Ginsburg were attacked by an unrelenting press corps, and both nominations were withdrawn. Bork, unquestionably one of the brightest jurists to come before the Senate for confirmation, was portrayed as being anti-woman, antiblack, and anti-just-about-everything-else. Ginsburg, a Yale law professor, was pummeled when he admitted smoking marijuana in his youth.

■ Later in the Reagan administration, the president's trusted aide, Edwin Meese, nearly failed in his bid to become U.S. attorney general when the media dug up questionable loans with which he was involved. Then when Meese got the job, the media continued to hound him. Things got so bad that in 1988, Meese canned his Justice Department press secretary for not representing him forcefully enough with the media. And several months later Meese himself resigned.

■ Nor was President Carter's administration immune from media attack. After newspaper reports revealed questionable personal financial dealings by Bert Lance prior to his being selected by President Carter as the nation's director of the Office of Management and the Budget, the Georgia banker went before the Congress and a national television audience to deny the various allegations. Shortly after his testimony, he resigned from the administration.

■ President Carter's chief drug advisor, Dr. Peter Bourne, also resigned after newspaper stories revealed first that Bourne had written a false prescription for an employee and later that he had occasionally smoked marijuana.

■ During President Ford's administration, Secretary of Agriculture Earl Butz resigned when a magazine revealed a tasteless joke that Butz had recounted in confidence to a reporter aboard an airplane.

The vigilance of the media in exposing fraud, deception, and questionable practices in society is traditional (Figure 14–1). During the late 1940s, in one of the most celebrated and tragic examples, columnists Drew Pearson and Walter Winchell attacked the nation's first secretary of defense, James Forrestal. These attacks contributed to Forrestal's eventual physical and mental breakdown and ultimate resignation. He was hospitalized after leaving office, and in 1949 he jumped to his death from the 16th floor of Bethesda Naval Hospital.[1]

The media's crowning achievement was their exposure of the Watergate break-in, which eventually led to the resignation of President Nixon. The success of the *Washington Post* in getting to the bottom of Watergate triggered an immediate reaction throughout journalism to focus on abuses of power in all areas of society. Regrettably, this focus on abuse itself led to abuses by some journalists. Even Carl Bernstein, one-half of the *Post* Woodward-Bernstein Watergate reporting team, concluded, "Post-Watergate has been marked by the elevation of gossip and celebrity journalism."[2]

Nowhere has investigative reporting taken off so dramatically as on the tube. By the early 1980s investigative reporting had gained a solid foothold in

Ships that didn't pass in the night

Remember a few years back when the big news turned out to be no news? We saw stories about mysterious ships alleged to be lurking offshore awaiting an increase in oil prices—phantom tankers that no one, not even the Coast Guard, could ever find.

Maybe the media's enlightenment over these specious articles did some good—because nowadays we encounter far fewer energy stories based on phantom facts. Energy reporting has been gaining stature—more depth, more expertise, more sophistication—and one result is a public that's much better informed on energy issues. And we're a lot less upset by what we read about our business.

We've tried to keep up our own record of being forthright and forthcoming when a story involved Mobil—or, for that matter, any energy subject on which our information and insights are sought. We try to tell it like it is. Factually.

And let the ships fall where they may.

Mobil

FIGURE 14–1 The oil companies have had their share of problems with investigative reporting. However, as this Mobil ad demonstrates, when the oil giants believe the media have learned from past mistakes, they occasionally duly acknowledge. (Courtesy of Mobil Oil Corporation)

INTERVIEW

Myron Kandel

Myron Kandel is one of the country's best-known financial writers and broadcasters. After serving as financial editor of three major newspapers, he switched to television in 1980 and helped start Cable News Network, the 24-hour, all-news television network. He continues to serve as CNN's financial editor and on-air economics commentator. Kandel lectures frequently and has taught journalism at Colum-

bia University Graduate School of Journalism and City College of New York. He is the author of *How to Cash In on the Coming Stock Market Boom,* published in 1982.

What's the quality of business news on television?

Business news, once the wasteland of television news coverage, has made great strides over a relatively short period of time. It was as recently as June 1980 that Cable News Network began broadcasting the first nightly half-hour business news program in the history of network television. Now, many other news organizations—on cable and public television, in syndication, and to a lesser extent on the broadcast networks—are offering a wide assortment of business news programming. Up to now, however, local television stations have not devoted any real resources or time to such coverage.

What do journalists think of public relations people?

It once was the conventional wisdom that journalists and public relations people were adversaries. I like to think of them, instead, as fellow communicators with different agendas. As long as each understands the other's goals, the relationship can be productive both ways. Some news people—a declining percentage, I think—still dismiss PR people as mere flacks, trying to foist untrue, misleading, or inappropriate facts or stories on the media. Although there may be some of those types still around, that's an antiquated image.

As PR people get more and more professional, that image will continue to diminish.

What kind of public relations person do you appreciate?

The PR person I like best is the one who knows what my news organization does, understands our needs, and is responsive to them. Conversely, those I like least don't know enough, or don't care enough, to relate to us specifically. This doesn't mean that a good PR person must necessarily grant our every request. But, first, he or she should know what we do, what kind of programming we're presenting, and who the relevant contacts are. They should understand our time constraints and deadlines and should get back to us accordingly, even if they can't provide a definitive answer. It's always a pleasure to find a PR person who anticipates a need and offers a way to meet it.

A spokesperson who is knowledgeable about his or her organization and has the necessary access to the top to get queries answered impresses me the most. The least impressive are those who obviously don't have the confidence of management to speak for the organization. I'm surprised at how often supposedly professional people are in that situation.

What problems have you encountered with public relations people?

I can't remember an occasion where a PR person lied to me deliberately, but there have been instances where they passed on incorrect information because they themselves were misinformed or were kept in the dark. That kind of situation undermines their credibility and sours any relationship that previously existed. Credibility and integrity are two attributes that any professional PR person must safeguard jealously.

Are most reporters hostile to organizations?

They often give that impression because they must be probing in their questioning and unwilling to accept statements they're given at face value. Rather than hostile or antiestablishment, they are nonestablishment, and that approach may seem hostile. Some news people do have biases that creep into their reports. As an editor, it's my responsibility to see that this does not happen. If a persistent pattern exists, I would welcome being informed about it. The principal goal of any news organization is to present the news fairly and objectively.

What is the status of the relationship between journalists and public relations people?

I like to refer to the state of the journalist-public relations relationship as an uneasy alliance, meaning that although they work together, each side may on occasion have a different objective. Nearly all the time, but not always, they share the goal of truth. They always share a desire for accuracy. The trend in recent years has been toward greater professionalism on both sides, and that means more respect and cooperation.

television news. But this, too, was not without significant problems. Said Dan Rather about the investigative program that helped land him the top anchor position at CBS news, "On '60 Minutes' we make mistakes so often, violating the basics of accuracy, clarity, or fairness, that sometimes it shatters me. If with our budget and our staff and time, we make so many mistakes in exposé material, what's it like under less luxurious circumstances?"[3]

Rather's words were prophetic. Several years after he uttered them, the vaunted CBS news team was embarrassed by several court cases, one brought by former General William Westmoreland, accusing the network of malice in its coverage of the news. Although CBS managed to win its bouts in court, its luster as an unbiased investigator was severely tarnished.

Whether a positive or negative development—or, as is more likely the case, a combination of the two—the emergence of investigative reporting has placed added pressure on public relations practitioners, who, as the primary voice of management, seek honest, fair, and accurate treatment of their organizations in the media.

WHAT RESEARCH TELLS US ABOUT THE MEDIA

The relationship between journalists and public relations people has never been an easy one. The former often accuse the latter of withholding information. The latter often accuse the former of liberal, one-sided reporting. Recent research corroborates an uneasy relationship between those who interview and those who are being interviewed. In one 1987 telephone survey of 100 top-level executives, 59 percent of those polled claimed that they "invariably get misquoted" by the press. "Journalistic ignorance" was cited by 39 percent, with 25 percent saying that journalists were guilty of an "overemphasis on the negative." Another 22 percent cited "sensationalist tendencies," and 12 percent cited clear-cut "bias" among members of the press.[4]

As to a liberal bias among journalists, a 1986 study of so-called elite journalists working for major news organs in Washington and New York found evidence to support such a view. The authors concluded that evidence "does not imply a conspiracy to exclude conservative voices, but merely reflects the human tendency to turn more often to those you trust, and to trust most those who think most like you do." They suggest that when it comes time to find expert commentary on policy issues, it is the liberal left that most often provides that commentary. As proof, they cited investigations of articles on welfare reform, consumer protection, nuclear energy, and other issues for which liberal sources were quoted significantly more than conservative ones.[5]

According to other research, public relations practitioners deny the accusation that they withhold information. In the mid-1970s one national survey revealed that most practitioners disagreed with the statement that they "try to deceive journalists by attaching too much importance to unimportant events." In contrast, almost all journalists agreed with this statement.[6]

Turning the Cameras on "Open Mike"

No investigative journalist has gained as fearsome a reputation for catching subjects off guard as television reporter Mike Wallace of CBS-TV's "60 Minutes." Indeed public relations professionals live in dread of the day that Mike Wallace appears at their door. That's why in January 1982 many public relations practitioners may have felt a bit more chipper than usual when they read that Mike Wallace had been caught at his own game.

The story started when Wallace took his "60 Minutes" crew to the San Diego Federal Savings and Loan Company to interview a vice president on the plight of low-income Californians—most of them either black or Hispanic with minimal reading skills—who faced foreclosures after signing contracts for expensive air conditioners without realizing that their houses served as collateral. As a precondition of the interview, San Diego Federal insisted on filming the proceedings for its own use.

During a break in the filming, with the CBS camera off but the San Diego Federal camera still rolling, Wallace commented on the complex lien-sale bank contracts. "You bet your ***** they are hard to read," he said, "if you're reading them over the watermelon or over the tacos!" Thereupon, according to observers, Mike began to laugh uproariously—but not for long.

A few weeks later Wallace learned that the San Diego Federal crew had videotaped his off-hand remark, and he and CBS tried desperately to retrieve the offensive tape from the bank. They failed, and the story received nationwide coverage. Later, Wallace called the retrieval idea a "lame one," and he and CBS apologized for the racially disparaging remark.

Ironically, during a prior "60 Minutes" show about the behind-the-scenes workings of the broadcast, Wallace was asked how he would feel if a hidden camera one day captured some embarrassing material about him. "I wouldn't like it," he replied. Boy, was he right!

Other, more recent studies show that neither journalists nor public relations people hold the strong negative views that may once have been common. According to several studies since 1977, there seems to be a fairly high level of mutual respect within the two camps: journalists tend to think that most public relations people do a good job and vice versa.

As for the general public, one 1985 study revealed that the public has a high level of confidence in the media.[7] This confidence is affected from time to time by controversial events, such as the Bush-Rather debate discussed in chapter 13. After his bout with Bush, Rather's favorability rating fell a monumental 18 points. His fall coincided with a general weakening of support for news organizations in the late 1980s, particularly network news. Early in 1988 only 44 percent of the public believed that "news organizations get the facts straight," an 11 point drop in 2½ years.[8] Despite the decline, twice as many people still "trusted" Rather more than Bush to tell the truth.

OBJECTIVITY IN THE MEDIA

Total objectivity in reporting is unattainable: it would require complete neutrality and near-total detachment in reporting a story. Most people start with biases and preconceived notions about almost any subject. Reporting, then, is subjective. Nevertheless, scholars of journalism believe that reporters and editors should strive for maximum objectivity.

After the turn of the century, when muckrakers exposed the questionable practices of the public-be-damned capitalistic entrepreneurs, American journalism was dominated by reporters seeking to learn the answers to six key questions: who, what, where, when, why, and how. After World War I, reporters became more interpretive. Led by the examples of the *New York Herald Tribune* newspaper and *The New Yorker* magazine, reporters embellished stories by going beyond the official viewpoint, interviewing not only participants in a news event but also spectators.

After World War II, another reporting refinement began to develop: advocacy journalism. Advocacy journalists tended to take sides and support causes in reporting. By the 1960s, journalists—both reporters and columnists—enlarged the advocacy concept to become more investigative. They sought more depth and meaning in their reporting. Occasionally, they didn't investigate thoroughly enough. For example, reports that vice presidential candidate Senator Tom Eagleton had been arrested for drunken driving helped remove him from the 1972 ticket. After the candidate had been discredited, columnist Jack Anderson admitted that the story he had initiated was based on questionable information. In another example, this one in the early 1970s, when an uprising at New York State's Attica prison took the lives of several people, journalists didn't question the claim of corrections officials that prisoners had slashed the throats of the hostages. Autopsies revealed that no throats had been slashed and that official versions of what happened were false and misleading.

By the 1970s, yet another form of journalism had begun to develop, the so-called new journalism. In approaching a story, new journalists secured all the facts that conventional reporters got but kept going, saturating the story with dialogue, facial expressions, details of the setting, gestures, habits, manners, and behavioral patterns, in the hope of painting scenic pictures for readers. This style frequently took liberties in order to juxtapose time sequences and protect actual identities. However, it was slow to catch on and seemed restricted to pace-setting publications (*New York Magazine, Rolling Stone, Esquire*) as well as campus newspapers. Although it had less application to general newspaper reporting, some of the leading practitioners of new journal-

Confessions of a Media Maven

Dealing with the media for fun and profit, even for an experienced public relations hand, is a constant learning experience. Often, such learning is achieved the hard way.

By the spring of 1984, many of the nation's largest banks were a bit jittery about negative publicity about their loans to lesser developed countries. One of the most vociferous bank bashers was Patrick J. Buchanan, a syndicated columnist who later became President Reagan's communications director.

After one particularly venomous syndicated attack on the banks, a certain bank public affairs director wrote directly to Buchanan's editor asking whether he couldn't "muzzle at least for a little while" his wild-eyed columnist. The letter's language, in retrospect, was perhaps a bit harsh.

Some weeks later, in a six-column article that ran throughout the nation, Mr. Buchanan wrote in part:

> Another sign that the banks are awaking to the reality of the nightmare is a screed that lately arrived at this writer's syndicate from one Fraser P. Seitel, vice president of Chase Manhattan.
>
> Terming this writer's comments "wrong," "stupid," "inflammatory," and "the nonsensical ravings of a lunatic," Seitel nevertheless suggested that the syndicate "tone down" future writings "at least 'til the frenetic financial markets get over the current hysteria."*

The columnist went on to describe the fallacy in bankers' arguments and ended by suggesting that banks begin immediately to cut unnecessary frills—such as directors of public affairs.

Moral: Never get into a shouting match with somebody who buys ink by the barrel.

Secondary moral: Just because you write a textbook doesn't mean you know everything!

---

*Patrick J. Buchanan, "The Banks Must Face Up to Losses on Third World Loans," *New York Post,* 12 July 1984, 35.

---

ism—Jimmy Breslin, Gay Talese, and Pete Hamill, for example—started by using the form in newspaper writing.[9]

In the early 1980s new journalism was clobbered by two particularly embarrassing incidents. In one, *New York Daily News* columnist Michael Daly was found to have fabricated a column purporting to be an interview with a woman whose son had been murdered in Ireland. Daly was promptly fired. The other incident was an even more celebrated and more embarrassing case.

THE JOURNALIST'S Creed

I believe IN THE PROFESSION OF JOURNALISM.

I BELIEVE THAT THE PUBLIC JOURNAL IS A PUBLIC TRUST; THAT ALL CONNECTED WITH IT ARE, TO THE FULL MEASURE OF THEIR RESPONSIBILITY, TRUSTEES FOR THE PUBLIC; THAT ACCEPTANCE OF A LESSER SERVICE THAN THE PUBLIC SERVICE IS BETRAYAL OF THIS TRUST.

I BELIEVE THAT CLEAR THINKING AND CLEAR STATEMENT, AC-CURACY, AND FAIRNESS ARE FUNDAMENTAL TO GOOD JOUR-NALISM.

I BELIEVE THAT A JOURNALIST SHOULD WRITE ONLY WHAT HE HOLDS IN HIS HEART TO BE TRUE.

I BELIEVE THAT SUPPRESSION OF THE NEWS, FOR ANY CONSIDER-ATION OTHER THAN THE WELFARE OF SOCIETY, IS INDEFENSIBLE.

I BELIEVE THAT NO ONE SHOULD WRITE AS A JOURNALIST WHAT HE WOULD NOT SAY AS A GENTLEMAN; THAT BRIBERY BY ONE'S OWN POCKETBOOK IS AS MUCH TO BE AVOIDED AS BRIBERY BY THE POCKETBOOK OF ANOTHER; THAT INDIVIDUAL RESPONSIBIL-ITY MAY NOT BE ESCAPED BY PLEADING ANOTHER'S INSTRUC-TIONS OR ANOTHER'S DIVIDENDS.

I BELIEVE THAT ADVERTISING, NEWS AND EDITORIAL COLUMNS SHOULD ALIKE SERVE THE BEST INTERESTS OF READERS; THAT A SINGLE STANDARD OF HELPFUL TRUTH AND CLEANNESS SHOULD PREVAIL FOR ALL; THAT THE SUPREME TEST OF GOOD JOURNAL-ISM IS THE MEASURE OF ITS PUBLIC SERVICE.

I BELIEVE THAT THE JOURNALISM WHICH SUCCEEDS BEST—AND BEST DESERVES SUCCESS—FEARS GOD AND HONORS MAN; IS STOUTLY INDEPENDENT, UNMOVED BY PRIDE OF OPINION OR GREED OF POWER, CONSTRUCTIVE, TOLERANT BUT NEVER CARE-LESS, SELF-CONTROLLED, PATIENT, ALWAYS RESPECTFUL OF ITS READERS BUT ALWAYS UNAFRAID, IS QUICKLY INDIGNANT AT IN-JUSTICE; IS UNSWAYED BY THE APPEAL OF PRIVILEGE OR THE CLAMOR OF THE MOB; SEEKS TO GIVE EVERY MAN A CHANCE, AND, AS FAR AS LAW AND HONEST WAGE AND RECOGNITION OF HUMAN BROTHERHOOD CAN MAKE IT SO, AN EQUAL CHANCE; IS PROFOUNDLY PATRIOTIC WHILE SINCERELY PROMOTING IN-TERNATIONAL GOOD WILL AND CEMENTING WORLD-COMRADE-SHIP; IS A JOURNALISM OF HUMANITY, OF AND FOR TODAY'S WORLD.

Walter Williams

DEAN SCHOOL OF JOURNALISM, UNIVERSITY OF MISSOURI, 1908-1935

FIGURE 14–2 "The Journalist's Creed" was coined after World War I by Dr. Walter Williams, dean of the School of Journalism at the University of Missouri. (Courtesy of the University of Missouri School of Journalism)

Washington Post reporter Janet Cooke was awarded journalism's highest honor, the Pulitzer Prize, for a front-page story about an eight-year-old heroin addict. As was later revealed, Cooke's searing story lacked only one ingredient—truth. It was, in fact, all a lie, created in the fertile imagination of the reporter and slipped by red-faced *Washington Post* editors. Cooke was summarily stripped of her Pulitzer and fired from the *Post,* but the damage was done. By the late 1980s then, although journalists still frequently interpreted what they observed (the so-called trust-me journalism), they also exhibited a renewed sense of the importance of reporting the true facts.

One innovation in the 1980s was the emergence of media watchdog organizations, most financed by conservative foundations and large companies. Typical was the Media Institute, headquartered in Washington, DC, which kept track of media treatment of issues—from the handling of the oil crisis in the mid-1970s to the TV portrayal of business executives in prime time situation comedies as "con men, crooks, and clowns." Indeed, many Americans thought the typical businessperson was J.R., the dastardly central character on the TV show "Dallas," rather than the people featured on the pages of *Fortune* magazine.

In general, though, the who, what, why, where, when, and how approach to reporting still dominates American journalism. Reporters are interested in learning the truth about an issue. However, finding out often requires a high degree of subjective judgment. Thus, if an organization expects fair and positive treatment in print or on the air, its statements must always hold up when subjected by the media to a test of truth. Figure 14–2 details a journalist's creed.

MEDIA'S VIEW OF OFFICIALDOM

By virtue of their role, the media view officials, particularly business and government spokespersons, with a degree of skepticism. Reporters shouldn't be expected to accept on faith the party line. By the same token, once a business or government official effectively substantiates the official view and demonstrates its merit, the media should be willing to report this accurately without editorial distortion.

Stated another way, the media-business/government relationship should be one of healthy adversaries rather than bitter enemies. Unfortunately, this is occasionally not the case. Journalist Edith Efron has said, referring to the relationship between business and the media, "The antagonism to capitalism on the nation's airwaves, the deeply entrenched prejudice in favor of state control over the productive machinery of a nation, is not a subjective assessment. It is a hard cultural fact."[10] Indeed, some journalists tend to look at government, business, and all forms of authority as the enemy.

Fortunately, such journalists are in the minority. Most want to get the facts from all sides. And they acknowledge and respect the public relations practitioner's role in the process. If they are dealt with fairly, they will recip-

YOU MAKE THE CALL

All the News That's Fit to Print

A frequent media complaint about organizational executives is that they don't understand, appreciate, or recognize what constitutes news. But what is news? The answer to that question is by no means cut and dried, as the following real-life example illustrates.

Midway through 1985 the *Bakersfield Californian* newspaper received a call over the police scanner reporting a drowning at a nearby lake. Arriving at the scene, the *Californian* photographer encountered divers searching for a five-year-old child.

After about 15 minutes the boy's body was discovered and brought to a grass embankment, where the distraught family gathered around it. Although sheriff's deputies prevented a local television crew from filming the tragedy, the *Californian* photographer ducked under a sheriff's outstretched arms and shot eight frames with a 24mm lens and motor drive. He then raced back to town to print the pictures.

On seeing the prints, the *Californian* metropolitan editor called his managing editor at home to ask whether the paper could print one of the pictures, even though the paper's policy generally prohibited publishing pictures of dead bodies. The editors decided that the picture was too powerful *not* to run. There had been other drownings in the same location that summer, and the editors thought the picture would remind parents to be more careful.

The next day a picture ran in the *Californian,* showing the child's father kneeling over his son's body. The boy's face was clearly visible. Directly above, a rescue worker tried to comfort members of the boy's grieving family. Several small children looked on in the background.

And there you have it—News, as defined by the *Bakersfield Californian.* But was this truly a community service, or was it, more correctly, a gross invasion of privacy?

QUESTION

What do you think?

rocate in kind. However, some executives fail to understand the essential difference between the media and their own organizations. As described by former journalist and presidential press secretary Ron Nessen, "The reporter wants to get all the information he can and interpret it as he sees fit, while the people in organizations he covers want things to be presented in the best light."[11] Because of this difference, some executives consider journalists to be feared adversaries, and they fear and distrust the media.

Thoughtful journalists, of course, abhor the enemy tag. They implore officials in business and government to continue to talk to the media, to explain complex issues so that the public can better understand them. According to Lewis H. Young, former editor-in-chief of *Business Week* magazine, "The chief executive officer has to learn to be comfortable with the press. And the only way to be comfortable with the press is to get to meet media people, to talk to them, to go out for lunch with them, go out to dinner with them, and get used to the kinds of things that they're going to ask about, what they're interested in."[12] Based on the deep-seated distrust that some business and government people reserve for the media, Young's wish is no easy task.

OFFICIALDOM'S VIEW OF THE MEDIA

In the 1980s the pervasive fear and distrust of the news media among executives, particularly among those in business, seemed to diminish. To be sure, there were still those who charged that the media were liberally biased.

- Senator Jesse Helms formed a Fairness in Media group and attempted to take over CBS. The attempt failed.
- President Reagan's science adviser, George Keyworth, charged that the national press was drawn predominantly from a narrow fringe element on the far left and was "intent on trying to tear down America."[13]
- President Reagan himself, in an unusual slip of the lip after posing for White House photographers, muttered an ever-so-audible "Sons of bitches," when besieged by reporters to respond to the 1986 overthrow of Philippine President Ferdinand Marcos.

Nonetheless, as the 1980s wore on and the 1990s beckoned, the trust between people in power and people who report the activities of the powerful increased a bit. In one 1981 study some 71 percent of executives considered themselves "usually accessible to the media." However, 73 percent of those polled believed that "fewer than half the reporters understand the subject they are writing about."[14] In another study of top communications officers in 1,300 large corporations, the broad majority said that senior executives were actively participating in news interviews and that, in general, corporate spokespersons were treated fairly in most interviews.[15]

One of the best at handling the media was Federal Reserve Board chairman Alan Greenspan, whose secretary instinctively asked reporters, "Are you on deadline?" Greenspan's concern for the media made him one of the most sought-after and favorably reviewed spokespersons on economic issues.

Most media studies later in the decade were inconclusive. A 1985 study by the American Society of Newspaper Editors concluded that 75 percent of adults in the country "have some problem with media credibility." However, a year later a study commissioned for Times Mirror Co., the publisher of the *Los Angeles Times,* found "there is no credibility crisis for the nation's news media." Among the findings from the 5,000 interviews were that 79 percent believed the media care about the quality of their work; 72 percent rated them "highly professional"; and 55 percent said the media are accurate.[16]

Nonetheless, some observers aren't convinced that the public is wholly trusting of the media. In commenting on his own paper's poll of the public, *Los Angeles Times* political analyst William Schneider said, "This poll does not prove or disprove the charge that the media is [sic] politically biased, but it does show that if there is any bias, it hasn't crept into the news coverage to the extent that the public feels aggrieved by it. The potential for bias is there, but so far, readers seem to feel only a healthy skepticism toward the media, not widespread disgruntlement."[17]

With the media and the public—particularly government and business officials—still not on the same philosophical wavelength, the challenge for public relations professionals to foster a closer working relationship between their organizations and the media continues to be a major one.

ROLE OF PUBLIC RELATIONS

How can public relations practitioners correct what may well be a distrustful, fearful relationship between organizations and the media? First, they can pinpoint the reasons for past grievances. Perhaps a firm has traditionally refused to talk to reporters, played favorites among media people, or gone over a reporter's head to complain to an editor. The first job of a public relations person is to reverse any of these red-flag practices that may exist. Second, an organization can establish a formal media relations policy (Figure 14–3), perhaps including these elements:

1. Appointing one person as the official spokesperson for the organization, ordinarily the public relations director.
2. Implementing an open news policy, informing news outlets of bad news as well as good news. Although many organizations find the reporting of bad news a bit hard to stomach, in the long run it's better for an organization to volunteer and thus control the announcement of bad news, rather than let an investigative journalist discover the story and exaggerate its significance.
3. Establishing a news-gathering apparatus within the organization to better keep journalists informed of current developments.
4. Rebuilding contacts with the media. Frequently, getting to know journalists can help attain this objective. Some may disagree with the practice, but according to Dow Jones News Service editor Robert L. Rettig, "It is a good idea for practitioners to take press members to lunch to get to know them and their points of view."[18] Such sessions should be low-key, friendly visits, perhaps to introduce story ideas, perhaps not. Such personal contact may pay off in the future.

A good public relations person can be a great help to a journalist. Generally, practitioners are the first people reporters call inside an organization. Frequently, the reporter's questions can be handled directly or channeled to a

Organization and Policy Guide

Unit with Primary Responsibility for Review Corporate Communications

It is frequently in Chase's best interest to take advantage of interest from the media to further the reputation and services of the bank. In dealing with the media, Chase officers must be careful to protect the best interests of the bank, particularly with regard to the area of customer confidence.

The following policies will serve as a guideline for media relationships. Specific questions regarding the media relationships should be addressed to the Public Relations Division.

Inquiries from the Media

Most journalists call the Public Relations Division when they need information about the bank or wish to arrange an interview with a bank officer. Many times, Public relations officers are able to handle inquiries directly. Occasionally, however, more complex questions require input from appropriate bank officers. In these cases, inasmuch as journalists are often under deadline pressures, it is important that bank officers cooperate as fully and respond as promptly as possible. Such cooperation enhances Chase's reputation for integrity with the news media.

Less frequently, reporter inquiries will go directly to line officers. In this case, either one of two responses may be appropriate:

1. If a journalist seeks simple, factual information such as Chase's current rate on a particular savings instrument or the factual details of a new bank service, officers may provide it directly.

2. If a reporter seeks Chase policy or official opinion on such subjects as trends in interest rates, legislation, etc., responses should be reviewed with the Public Relations Division. If an officer is unfamiliar with a particular policy or requires clarification of it, he or she should always check first with the Public Relations Division before committing the bank in print.

In talking with a reporter, it is normally assumed that whatever a bank officer says may be quoted and attributed directly to him or her by name as a spokesperson for the bank. An officer not wishing to be quoted must specify that desire to the journalist.

Most reporters with whom the bank deals will respect an officer's wishes to maintain anonymity. Most journalists recognize that it is as important for them to honor the wishes of their sources at the bank as it is for the bank to disseminate its comments and information to the public through the news media. Chase's policy toward the media should be one of mutual trust, understanding and benefit.

Interviews With the Media

In order to monitor the bank's relationships with journalists, all requests for interviews with bank officers by journalists must be routed through the Public Relations Division.

As a rule, public relations officers check the credentials of the journalist and determine the specific areas of inquiry to be examined. The public relations officer will then decide whether the interview is appropriate for the bank. When the decision is affirmative, the public relations officer will discuss subject matter with the recommended interviewee and together they will decide on a course of action and Chase objectives for the interview.

A member of the public relations staff is normally present during any face-to-face interview with an officer of the bank. The purpose of the public relations staffer's attendance is to provide assistance in handling the interview situation as well as to aid the reporter with follow-up material.

When a reporter calls an officer directly to request an interview, the officer should check with the Public Relations Division before making a commitment.

Authorized Spokespersons

Vice presidents and above are normally authorized to speak for the bank on matters in their own area of responsibility.

Normally, officers below the level of vice president are not authorized to speak for attribution on behalf of the bank except where they are specialists in a particular field, such as technical directors, economists, etc.

Exceptions may be made in special situations and in concert with the Public Relations Division.

Written Material for the Media

Chase articles bylined by officers may either be written by the officer approached or by a member of the public relations staff. If an officer decided to author his or her own article, the public relations division must be consulted for editing, photographic support and policy proofing.

Occasionally, customers or suppliers may wish to include Chase in an article or advertisement they are preparing. This material too must be routed through the Public Relations Division for review.

FIGURE 14-3 This press relations policy of Chase Manhattan Bank is typical of that found in many large organizations. Relationships with the media are generally encouraged, with the public relations division taking overall responsibility for all of the bank's relationships with journalists. (Courtesy of Chase Manhattan Bank)

BETWEEN THE LINES

"Please Don't Quote Me"

All the trust and credibility and guidance in the world can't correct the damage done when a person realizes, too late, that anything said is fair game for a reporter. The final two paragraphs of a *Wall Street Journal* profile of hard-nosed Chicago banker A. Robert Abboud bear out that truth.

> In Houston, there is a chance that Mr. Abboud actually will become the man who saved the bank. But in his hometown, he will probably always be the man who was fired. A Chicago executive, having offered one positive remark after another about Mr. Abboud, concludes a long interview with an odd request, "Please don't quote me."
>
> The executive, Robert P. Gwinn, chairman of Encyclopaedia Britannica, was a First Chicago director when Mr. Abboud was fired. Publicly praising Mr. Abboud, Mr. Gwinn says, might anger inner-circle Chicagoans. "To the group I travel with now," Mr. Gwinn explains, "Bob is sort of on their *S* list."*

*Jeff Bailey, "Still Bitter at Firings, Abboud Hopes Bailout Will Help His Image," *Wall Street Journal,* 7 March 1988, 1.

---

more knowledgeable source within the organization. Often, the intermediation of a practitioner can help journalists reach company sources. In addition, public relations professionals can arrange interviews between journalists and executives. Frequently, practitioners sit in on such interviews to assist interviewees and reporters. The role of the practitioner in these situations should not be to obstruct the interview but to facilitate it.

At the heart of the journalist-practitioner relationship is credibility and trust. True, the two professions march to the beat of different drummers, but they should respect each other's views and responsibilities. Only through mutual respect can adversarial relationships be avoided. Lasting respect can neither be bribed nor bullied. It must be earned through the consistent practice of fair, open, and honest dealings and, again, through the highest degree of professionalism.

1. Walter Mills, *The Forrestal Diaries* (New York: Viking Press, 1951) and Jack Anderson with James Boyd, *Confessions of a Muckraker* (New York: Random House, 1979).

2. Cited in "Reporter Attacks Press," *Editor & Publisher*, 4 November 1978, 38.

3. "Investigative Reporting: Handle with Care," *RTNDA Communicator* (Washington, DC: Radio Television News Directors Association, March 1982): 5.

4. Judith A. Mapes, "Top Management and the Press—The Uneasy Relationship Revisited," *Corporate Issues Monitor*, Egon Zehnder International, vol. 11, no. 1 (1987): 2.

5. S. Robert Lichter, Stanley Rothman, and Linda S. Lichter, *The Media Elite: America's New Powerbrokers* (Bethesda, MD: Adler & Adler, 1986).

6. John V. Pavlik, *Public Relations: What Research Tells Us* (Newbury Park, CA: Sage Publications, 1987): 59.

7. Ibid.

8. Bush-Rather Debate Adds to Eroding Public Attitudes Toward News Media," *PR Reporter Purview* (9 May 1988): 1.

9. Tom Wolfe, *The New Journalism* (New York: Harper & Row, 1973).

10. Chester Burger, "How to Meet the Press," *Harvard Business Review* (July–August 1975): 62.

11. "Sound Advice About Media Relations," *Public Relations News* 33, no. 47 (21 November 1977): 1.

12. Lewis H. Young, "The Media's View of Corporate Communications in the '80s," *Public Relations Quarterly* (Fall 1981): 10.

13. Albert R. Hunt, "Media Bias Is in Eye of the Beholder," *Wall Street Journal*, 23 July 1985, 32.

14. Roger Ricklefs, "Business Relations with the Press: Three Versions of the Way It Is," *Wall Street Journal*, 6 July 1981, 15.

15. "Antagonism: Myth or Reality?" *Public Relations Journal* (November 1981): 62.

16. Jack Kelley, "An Absence of Malice," *USA Today*, 16 January 1986, 6A.

17. "News Study Shows Public Is Both Confident and Skeptical of the News Media," *PR Reporter*, 11 November 1985, 4.

18. "Must PR and the Press Be Adversaries?" *Corporate Shareholder*, 24 January 1979, 3.

NOTES

SUGGESTED READINGS

Bacon's Media Alerts. Chicago, IL: Bacon Publishing Co. (332 S. Michigan). Bimonthly.

Boot, William. "Capital Letter: The New Tattlers." *Columbia Journalism Review* (January/February 1988): 14–18. New York: Columbia University. This article discusses distinguishing between news and gossip.

Danzig, Fred, and **Ted Klein.** *Publicity: How to Make the Media Work for You*. New York: Scribner, 1985.

"Funding the News: Nonprofits and the Media Elite." *Organization Trends*. Washington, DC: Capital Research Center (1612 K Street, NW, Suite 605), December 1987.

Gold, Vic. "Time to Rethink Public Relations Role?" *Media Institute Forum* (November/December 1984): 1–4.

Hunt, Albert R. "Media Bias Is in Eye of the Beholder," *Wall Street Journal*, 23 July 1985, 32.

Media News Keys (40–29 27th St., Long Island City, NY 11101). Weekly.

Newsletter on Newsletters (P.O. Box 311, Rhinebeck, NY 12572). Weekly.

"The People and the Press." New York: Times Mirror Co., January 1986. An investigation of public attitudes toward the news media was conducted by the Gallup organization.

Rowan, Ford. *Broadcast Fairness: Doctrine, Practice, Prospects*. White Plains, NY: Longman, 1984.

Schramm, Wilbur. *Men, Messages, and Media: A Look at Human Communication*. New York: Harper & Row, 1973. This analysis of the communications process and its effects on mass communication in society contains an insightful look at the "War of the Worlds" broadcast and the Kennedy/Nixon debates.

Shapiro, Andren. *Media Access*. Boston: Little Brown & Co., 1976. This offers a legal guide.

Ungurait, Donald F., Thomas W. Bohn, and **Ray Eldon Hiebert.** *Media Now*. White Plains, NY: Longman, 1986.

The Media Relations Ruckus at Goliath Industries

Compared to that of most organizations, the media relations policy at Detroit's huge Goliath Industries was exemplary. The company, the nation's largest manufacturer, was generally forthright in its public statements and frequently led industry on such issues as corporate disclosure and South African business policy.

Goliath was such a business leader, in fact, that most observers were puzzled one May 18, when C. A. Wheat, Goliath's vice-chairman and likely successor to the firm's president, unexpectedly resigned. In response to Wheat's departure, Goliath Industries issued a terse news release indicating that Wheat was leaving "to pursue personal business opportunities." Goliath refused to amplify the brief announcement, despite constant prodding by the media. The company cited as its primary reason for secrecy the concept of privacy with respect to personnel records.

The announcement that Wheat was leaving the $325,000-a-year job started rumor mills humming, not only in Detroit but throughout the nation. The media, predictably, refused to drop the story. Eventually, one enterprising reporter turned up the fact that Wheat had been asked to leave by Goliath's president, as a result of an internal audit that reportedly revealed conflicts in Wheat's handling of a customer with whom Wheat shared business interests.

After this revelation the Goliath story became fair game for business journalists everywhere. The firm quickly acknowledged the existence of the internal audit but refused to discuss its content, claiming that such a confidential matter was exempt from its internal disclosure code. Details of the report were subsequently made public by the *Detroit Free Press*. Indeed, even Wheat acknowledged the accuracy of the transactions described, maintaining that there was nothing improper about them.

In the months that followed *l' Affaire Wheat,* as the Detroit newspapers called it, it was revealed that the Federal Bureau of Investigation had launched a probe of the matter, and a federal grand jury had also been impaneled to investigate. Eventually, Wheat was cleared of all possible violations of law. Nevertheless, the positive public image of Goliath Industries had suffered a tremendous blow. *Forbes* magazine labeled it "the industry's biggest public relations blunder in years." One source close to Goliath's board of directors summed it up by saying, "It could not have been handled any worse."

QUESTIONS

1. Had you been Goliath's public relations director, what strategy would you have recommended on May 18?
2. What would you have suggested the firm do after the revelation of the internal audit?
3. How would you suggest that Goliath management handle the Wheat affair at the company's next annual meeting? Should they bring it up at all? What should they say?

15

Employees

The first step in promoting positive external public relations is achieving good internal public relations. If management speaks out of one side of its mouth to its external constituencies and out of the other to its internal groups, it will lose credibility. And employees must be solidly on management's side; without their support a company is unlikely to communicate convincingly with the outside world. In effect, every employee is a public relations spokesperson for the organization. Consequently, practitioners are finding more and more that "sound public relations begins at home"[1] (Figure 15–1).

Internal communications has become a hot ticket in public relations. Management traditionally tended to view employees as a mass, rather than as individuals with unique interests, needs, and wants.[2] Now, good management realizes that a satisfied and enthusiastic employee is an extremely effective and credible public relations advertisement.

Study after study confirms that an employee's preferred source of internal communication is face-to-face contact with an immediate supervisor. Speaking directly with the boss beats all other types of internal communication, hands down. One 1988 poll by Louis Harris and Associates of more than 1,000 office workers indicated that most of them wanted managers who let them help make decisions, encouraged free exchange of information, and were honest and ethical. Nearly two-thirds of those polled favored a more participatory management style at all levels of decision making.

In line with this thinking, such management texts as *In Search of Excellence* and *Reinventing the Corporation* have exhorted management to "wander around, share their 'vision' with the troops and keep the workers informed." Nonetheless, based on a 1986 survey of 48,000 employees by Opinion Research Corporation, "Downward communication, measured by employees' ratings of their companies on letting them know what is going on, is rated favorably by fewer than half of employees in all groups."[3] So although most agree that candid communications between management and employees is critical, much more needs to be done to get through to the employee public.

Pardon our pride.

For generations GE and RCA have touched the lives of millions of people. We have embodied the creative spirit of America. Its technological greatness, scientific advances, dynamism and movement.

We have entertained America and defended it. Illuminated its homes and made its airwaves dance.

Above all, we have been a pulse of progress and free enterprise.

The planned merger of our two great companies is an event that makes us very proud. And equally optimistic.

We will be a company whose strengths will have profound and beneficial effects. A company that will compete with anyone. Anywhere. In every market we serve.

We are proud of the people who over the years have built our two companies into great organizations achieving modern-day miracles. And of the people who've worked so diligently to keep our companies great — through periods of economic difficulties and technological change.

We are two companies with proud pasts. We will become one company with an important future. For the people of this country and countless millions of others around the world.

All will benefit from our products, our services, and our capabilities.

That makes us especially proud. And very enthusiastic.

FIGURE 15–1 Late in 1985 the merger of two huge companies, General Electric and RCA, was heralded by this full-page ad that appeared in the nation's leading newspapers. The ad was designed as much to reinforce employee morale as to win public support. (Courtesy of General Electric Co.)

The employee public itself is composed of numerous subpublics: hourly workers, salaried workers, supervisory staff, union members, official staff, craftsmen, and white-collar workers. With such a diverse mix of subpublics, mass communications aimed at no group in particular may not succeed. Internal communications, like external messages, must be targeted to reach specific subgroups. And communications must be continuous to consistently reinforce management's interest in its employees.

In recent years several trends have affected employee communications.[4]

- **Externalization of communications** With a greater emphasis on relations with the media, government officials, opinion leaders, and external constituencies of all stripes, the need has intensified for employee communication not only to be in sync with the external program, but also to play a larger role in the overall corporate communications function.
- **Targeting of the organization** As interest groups swipe at corporations, in particular, employees become much more important to their firms as voters, advocates, and concerned citizens in the political process.
- **Changing nature of the internal audience** Employees no longer accept organizational pronouncements at face value. The staff today is generally younger, better educated, increasingly female, ambitious, and career-oriented at all levels. Today's more hard-nosed employee demands candor in communication.
- **Businesslike approach to employee communications** Larger budgets and staffs in internal communications functions have allowed a greater emphasis on research-oriented services, such as climate studies, effectiveness audits, economic education programs, and the like.
- **Nonprint emphasis** Face-to-face communication has been emphasized, whereas more impersonal, print-oriented communication has diminished in relative importance. More emphasis has been placed on small group meetings, visibility of top executives, and use of audiovisual—particularly video—communications.

One goal of all employee communications must be credibility. The task for management is to convince employees that it not only wants to communicate with them, but also wishes to do so in a truthful, frank, and direct manner.

CREDIBILITY: THE KEY

The employee public is a savvy one. Employees can't be conned, because they live with the organization every day. They generally know what's going on and whether management is being honest with them. That's why management must be truthful. One employee communications manager summarized the problem succinctly:

Robert S. Cole

Robert S. Cole is vice president and director of communications for the New York State Bankers Association. He has also served as manager of Bank of America's public relations activities in the Eastern United States and Canada, director of development for the Deafness Research Foundation, and assistant director of public relations at Queens College. A former reporter for the *New York Daily News,* he teaches public relations at St. John's University and is the author of *The Practical Handbook of Public Relations.*

What are the fundamental principles in dealing with employees?

Management must be honest with employees, maintain a two-way flow of communications, and be willing to share bad, as well as good, news. Most of all, management has to demonstrate through verbal, print, and electronic communications that it genuinely cares about getting information to and from its staff.

How can employee communications influence morale?

Very simply, informed workers are better workers; hence, happier and more productive men and women. If managed well, an internal communications program can convince employees that they'll be told what they need to know to maximize their value to the organization and that they are welcome to contribute ideas, opinions, and criticisms to the deliberation process.

Should certain information (e.g., layoffs, losses, lawsuits, etc.) be kept from employees?

Never and yes. Never on layoffs, losses, lawsuits, or the like because these are important stories that must be shared with employees, who have a right and a need to know about them. Moreover, these stories will be covered in the media and through the grapevine anyway. If employees, on learning of such incidents, don't believe they'll get the real facts through internal communications, the company has a credibility problem—probably a morale problem, too. Yes, however, on the small number of details that violate employee or customer confidentiality. But employees should then be told why they can't have all the facts.

What are the most effective ways to communicate to employees?
It's hard to generalize. Some people prefer to get their information in print; others remember it better if they are told verbally by their boss—or their boss's boss. With apologies for the mom-and-apple-pie message, I believe honesty, timeliness, thoroughness, and a willingness to receive as well as dispense information have to be a part of the process, regardless of how the message is conveyed.

Is the employee house organ an outmoded concept?
I hope not; some of the nicer people I know are house organ editors. More important, people are used to (and receptive to) receiving information in printed form at regular intervals. Additionally, the permanence of words on paper provides a valuable historic perspective. I think, however, that the con-

cept of a house organ serving as the beginning and the end of employee communications is outdated. There are too many other written, electronic, and verbal vehicles at our disposal for communicators to think they can call it a day after putting a house organ issue to bed.

What are the characteristics that distinguish good employee communicators from mediocre ones?
The ability to (1) educate in an entertaining manner, (2) show how jobs and processes fit into the overall operation, (3) explain how what happens outside the organization can affect the bottom line, and (4) find interesting, work-related ways to get the clerical staff (as opposed to officers only) into company publications. Creativity, flexibility, and empathy help a lot, too. Finally, smart employee communicators recognize that employees and their families are potential good-will ambassadors. They act accordingly.

How important is top management involvement in employee communications?
Very. Top management must recognize (via budget and staff allocations) the importance of employee communications. They must also participate in the process as spokespeople and listeners, and they must encourage middle management to do the same.

About the only authority you hold today as a manager is the authority of your passion for the truth and your integrity. The sticks are pretty much gone. The carrots are not what they used to be. Loyalty to the organization per se is pretty much gone. Your best hope is your credibility with your people.[5]

Surveys show that employees desperately want to know top management's views on a host of internal matters. For example, employees want to find out in what direction an organization is headed, why it has chosen to go that way, and what their personal role in the new direction will be. Even though employees understand that policy decisions rest with management, they nevertheless desire and appreciate the opportunity to contribute to policy formulation.[6]

In dealing with organized labor, in particular, communications candor is extremely important for management. The role of the union in the organization must be clearly understood by public relations professionals, whose job is to enhance communications between management and union members. In times of economic stress, such as those that have afflicted certain sectors from time to time in the 1970s and 1980s, it is imperative that a sense of teamwork be established between union members—indeed, all employees—and management. For example, in the early 1980s when U.S. auto manufacturers suffered dislocations because of declining sales, increased foreign competition, and retooling for more fuel-efficient cars, management and labor had to work more closely together in the major auto companies. Chrysler advertised the benefits of American labor. General Motors announced that hourly workers as well as top executives and members of the board of directors would take pay cuts until the company reemerged. In both cases the esprit de corps was briefly interrupted by subsequent developments, but the spirit of the times demanded that management and labor work together to solve the common problems of their organizations.

In any organization employees must feel that they are appreciated. They want to be treated as important parts of an organization; they should not be taken for granted, nor should they be shielded from the truth. Thus, the most important ingredient of any internal communications program must be its credibility.

EMPLOYEE COMMUNICATIONS OBJECTIVES

The overriding objective in any employee relations or employee communications campaign is to stimulate increased productivity among the staff so that the organization does better. That means communicating first and foremost what management wants employees to know and second—and almost as important—what employees want to know. The first step in any employee communications program is to set objectives. Here are several offered by Rockwell International, a conglomerate with offices around the world.

1. To keep all communications understandable and to avoid ambiguity or lack of clarity
2. To communicate regularly, not just in crisis situations
3. To provide completely reliable information and to present all the facts needed to arrive at a reasonable judgment
4. To disseminate information—particularly about changes—in advance of, not after, the fact
5. To communicate on the basis of what employees want to know about their company and their jobs and to provide information helpful to employees in understanding and performing their job responsibilities
6. To recognize the accomplishments and contributions of employees
7. To clarify the reasons for policies and procedures and to build an understanding of the economic facts of business life required for a successful operation
8. To stimulate awareness on the part of employees that the company has a sincere interest in their security and well-being
9. To help develop a sense of employee pride in association with a progressive company
10. To encourage employee participation in the company's support of worthwhile community projects and civic affairs
11. To encourage employees to express attitudes and opinions and to provide for a free flow of information both upward and downward
12. To present a continuing overview of company products and operations so that employees are knowledgeable about their company

Growing out of these general objectives must be a predetermined list of tactical objectives for employee communications. Although management concerns vary with changing situations, the following tactical objectives are commonly addressed in employee communications.

1. Achievement of production quotas to meet delivery promises on schedule
2. Achievement of quality standards and reduction of defects to meet customer demands
3. Achievement of cost-reduction goals
4. Achievement of productivity improvements from new equipment and procedures and from changes in facilities, machines, and methods
5. Introduction of new practices, changes in work standards, restructuring of jobs, and changes in classifications and pay rates
6. Resolution of employee dissatisfaction, strike threats, and strikes through sound understanding of the issues

EMPLOYEE COMMUNICATIONS METHODS

Once objectives are set, a variety of techniques may be adopted to reach the staff. The initial tool is research. Before any communications program can be implemented, communicators must have a good sense of staff attitudes. Perhaps the most beneficial form of research to lay the groundwork for effective employee communications is the internal communications audit. This consists essentially of old-fashioned personal, in-depth interviews to determine staff attitudes about their jobs, the organization, and its management, coupled with an analysis of existing communications techniques. The findings of such audits are often startling, always informative, and never easily ignored.[7]

Once internal communications research is complete, the public relations practitioner has a clearer idea of the kinds of communications vehicles that make sense for the organization. Several of the more popular vehicles are discussed here.

Employee Publications

Many years ago the company-sponsored newspaper was considered a good way to prevent barriers between management and employees. Although the format and content of the employee newspaper (or increasingly, news magazine) has changed over time, the broad concept of informing the staff through one major corporate publication has stood the test of time. Before creating such a newspaper, however, an organization must answer several basic questions.

1. Whom will this paper attempt to reach?
2. What kinds of articles will be featured?
3. How should each issue be budgeted?
4. What format will the paper take?
5. What should the paper accomplish with respect to the target readers?
6. How frequently should it be published?
7. Who in the organization should produce the publication—the public relations or personnel department?

The answers to these questions depend on which organization is doing the asking. Internal communications needs differ from one organization to the next.

In general, publications should clearly interpret management's policies to the staff and, whenever possible, serve as a two-way communications vehicle, expressing staff concerns as well. Traditionally, employee publications purposely overlooked news about controversial company-related issues. Instead, they included a plethora of items about management's benevolence and employees at work and play. In recent years a hint of controversy has slowly crept into some employee publications. Nonetheless, the single most important subject to employees is job information that affects them, the organization, and their jobs (Figure 15–2).

Employee newsletters should appear regularly, on time, and with a consistent format. Employees should expect them and look forward to them. In recent years organizations have sacrificed elaborate graphics for more immediate information dissemination. Specifically, large companies with far-flung

THE BAGEL BUGLE

SPECIAL
Lender/Kraft
WEDDING EDITION

Published by Lender's Bagel Bakery, Inc.

WEDDING OF THE CENTURY

INNISBROOK, Florida — Lender's Bagels and Kraft Inc. tied the knot in a spectacular wedding celebration held here on Saturday, September 15.

The joining of the two dynamic food companies was symbolized in a colorful ceremony which included eight-foot-high replicas of Kraft and Lender's products marching down the aisle.

"This is the proudest moment of our lives," said Murray and Marvin Lender as they escorted Len, the groom.

The bride, Phyl, was given away by the president of Kraft's Retail Food Group, Keith Ridgway. Len and Phyl had been dating for 20 years.

The weekend was filled with much eating, drinking and merriment as a crowd of more than 250 people including brokers, wives and associates enjoyed the luxurious accommodations at Innisbrook, the world-famous resort hotel in Tampa.

Most guests gained at least five pounds.

FIGURE 15–2 One of the most unusual employee publications in recent years was this issue of the *Bagel Bugle,* published by Lender's Bagel Bakery of West Haven, Connecticut. Lender's commemorated its merger with Kraft, maker of Philadelphia cream cheese, with this special "wedding" edition. (Courtesy of Lender's Bagel Bakery)

networks have begun to transmit employee newsletters electronically over proprietary data networks. In more traditional setups the mix of employee-related and organization-oriented features that appeal to employees may include the following:[8]

- **Staff photographs** People love to see themselves in the papers.
- **On-the-job stories** People appreciate reading about their neighbor's job.
- **How-to-do-it case studies** Co-workers' success stories are always interesting, especially if the reader can benefit from the experience. Case studies also aid morale.
- **Candid camera** It's fun to see other people caught in the act of being themselves.
- **Policy-philosophy articles** People crave the background of company policies and philosophies.
- **Educational quizzes** People like to learn about the organization, especially if the learning process is in an interesting format, such as a quiz.
- **Retiree articles** Retirees are among the most devoted publics of employee publications. Writing about them helps bolster this relationship.
- **Departmental features** Written in a lively fashion, features about the activities and successes of different departments can be beneficial for organizational understanding.
- **The "you" approach** The key to writing *for* people is writing *about* people. A good internal newspaper brings the reader directly into the story. This approach enhances knowledge and appreciation of an organization, while instilling pride in the individual.

The best employee publications are those that speak candidly to the staff about the organization. Among the best was *ARCO Spark,* the internal publication of the Atlantic Richfield Company in the mid-1980s. *ARCO Spark* included a "Letters to the Editor" column that printed some missives critical of the company, its management, and even *ARCO Spark* itself. Another segment of the paper was an "Employee Opinion Section," which featured anonymous staff questions and answers. For example, "I would like to know why the chairman rates an annual salary of $625,000 and the president rates $440,600?" Such frankness made *ARCO Spark* unique among employee publications.

Another trailblazing employee publication is the phone company's *AT&T Journal.* So bold is this publication that in 1988, when AT&T's amiable chairman James Olson died unexpectedly, *AT&T Journal* dedicated the next edition to the late chairman and included an article counseling managers on "how to help themselves and others deal with grief" (Figure 15–3).

Employee publications have historically served as principal organizational entry points for public relations beginners. The total U.S. circulation of employee publications has been estimated at more than 200 million—well in excess of total U.S. daily newspaper circulation. Therefore, job availabilities are more plentiful in the employee publications area than in most other public

When something terrible happens

Mourning is a process. When people go through it in the workplace, managers need to understand how to help themselves and others deal with grief.

by Don Vandegrift

The man was struggling with the reality of the untimely death of Jim Olson. "To be honest with you, I don't like going through the process right now of assessing the loss of this man to this company. It's just too difficult to move from the feeling level to the intellectual level so soon.

"My sense of personal loss is much too acute. I haven't allowed myself to think about the full meaning of his death since I got the news."

The employee was in one of the stages of mourning—what the experts call denial. If this sense of loss follows the usual pattern, he will move from denial to anger, guilt, anxiety, disorganization, despair, and powerlessness—not necessarily in that order and not necessarily including every one of these emotions.

The time it will take him to work through the process is personal. It varies with each individual. And mourning is a process—a necessary process not understood by most. This is particularly true of death in the workplace, a topic sadly current in this corporation. It includes not only the loss of a leader but also the death of a colleague—the person who sits at the desk next to you —a member of your staff, or your boss.

As with all processes, mourning can be managed. That may sound cold, but it *must* be managed, or the results of not facing the loss can be disastrous to morale, production, teamwork—

nearly everything that makes an organization effective.

So every supervisor needs to learn how to deal with the individual emotions of his or her staff following a death in the group or in the larger organization. At the same time, the supervisor has to handle his or her own emotions.

Where do you go to get guidance on this subject?

It's not easy. There are countless books and articles on living through the deaths of spouses, parents, children, and friends, and other books on dealing with sudden losses, such as those resulting from accidents and suicides. But it's hard to find books or articles on death in the workplace.

for example, from selfish reactions to a death: "What does it mean to me? to the business?"

Discussion also helps to actualize the loss of a fellow worker. There is a

The results of not facing a loss can be disastrous to morale, production, teamwork—nearly everything that makes an organization effective.

certain unreality to death, and a frank talk about the details of a person's death and the circumstances surrounding it can bring some people out of the initial shock and numbness resulting from a tragedy to the realization that someone who was part of your day-to-day life is not coming back.

Facing reality in this fashion can

What's left is to extrapolate what is common to all personal loss and grieving into the work situation. And one message above all comes through clearly in material on the subject: we must accept the fact that grief and mourning are normal, and supervisors should be prepared to provide a channel for everyone involved to mourn in their own way and their own time.

This is particularly difficult in the business world, where emotion of the depth that grief produces has not been traditionally acceptable and might even be thought to be frivolous in some quarters. So, in effect, the supervisor must almost give permission to grieve.

Experts agree that conscious grieving over a loss is necessary if people expect to get on with business. One way the supervisor can facilitate the process is to call a special meeting to talk about the deceased or to make such a talk part of a regular staff meeting. Unlike regular business discussions, which help staffs examine complex issues or reach consensus, this type of discussion will allow people to examine their own feelings about the deceased.

Discovering that there are no good or bad feelings—only feelings— may help wipe away guilt stemming,

help a corporate team deal with the practical aspects of the job ahead without the person who died. The process forces introspection and turns energies back toward life. Far from seeming insensitive to the loss suffered by the members of the work group, the entire process can be helpful to them. Death is a crisis—another form of change.

But a warning is necessary here: don't rush the grieving process. Allow for individual differences and continue to provide support, with an understanding that grief and mourning are normal.

Another way of helping people reach restoration and recovery—what counselors on grief call reorganized behavior—is public acknowledgment of the company. This acknowledgment could range from the personal remembrances of individuals in a group to full-scale memorials, possibly involving the entire company.

All of this applies equally in the case of people who had only a superficial relationship with the one who died. The determining factor is not necessarily the closeness or the social significance of the relationship, but the importance that the griever assigns to the lost person. For example, the death of a leader who symbolized important values can be seen as a personal loss by a great many people, and the mourning period should be handled in a fashion similar to those already mentioned.

It is important to demonstrate that the company is interested in people. These efforts to guide people through grief reinforce the company's interest in people by revealing the humaneness of an honest display of emotion.

In general, being an understanding, sensitive human being seems to be the key to managing through mourning. When those whom you supervise—and you—can recall the deceased person and the circumstances of the death without pain, you know you've done your job. ■

Much of this article is based on discussions with Alan Youngblood, of the health affairs organization; Joan Tracey, New York/New Jersey regional manager of the employee assistance program (EAP) and her staff of consultants; and AT&T psychologist Dr. Joel Moses. The EAP coordinator in your region is a good source for guidance on managing the mourning process. Books of interest include the following:

On Death and Dying, by Dr. Elisabeth Kübler-Ross.

Death, Grief, and Mourning, by John S. Stephenson.

The Courage to Grieve, by Judy Tatelbaum.

Grief Counseling and Grief Therapy, by J. William Worden, Ph.D.

For more information

FIGURE 15-3 One of the gutsiest of the new employee publications, *AT&T Journal,* ran this article to help employees cope with their grief over the sudden death of AT&T chairman James Olson in May 1988. (Reprinted by permission of AT&T)

YOU MAKE THE CALL

The Quackenbush Beacon

Quackenbush Manufacturing has 15 plants in 10 states. It is a diversified manufacturer with 30,000 employees and one internal newspaper, the *Quackenbush Beacon*, to reach them. Editor Sammy Shram prides himself on distributing the *Beacon* without fail every other Wednesday. Since the *Beacon* is the only communications vehicle that unites the entire Quackenbush staff, Shram is responsible for informing employees about company developments and management policy.

At 1:30 P.M. on the Monday before publication, Shram and his public relations colleagues are advised that the Eau Claire plant has blown up. Early reports indicate that 5 to 10 Quackenbush employees may have been killed. Many others are injured. The fire and subsequent explosion were caused, according to rumors, by a disgruntled ex-Quackenbush employee. Only the quick thinking of plant manager Carlos Sledge, who sounded the alarm early, averted a more serious disaster.

Because the *Beacon* will be published in two days, Shram must decide quickly how to treat the Eau Claire disaster. His absolute deadline for copy is in one hour.

QUESTIONS

1. Should Shram run the story in his next edition? Why or why not?
2. If he does, how should he treat it? If he doesn't, should he report it in the edition after next?
3. If you were a reporter for the *Eau Claire Daily Blat* and had only the information recorded in this case study, how might your report differ from that of the *Quackenbush Beacon*?

---

relations positions. Indeed, one organization devoted originally to internal communications, the International Association of Business Communicators (IABC), has, in a relatively short time, come to rival the much older Public Relations Society of America. With more than 120 chapters throughout the United States, Canada, and the United Kingdom and affiliates in 15 countries, the IABC helps set journalistic standards for communicators.[9]

Management Publications

Managerial employees must know what's going on in the organization, also. The company needs their support. Continual, reliable communication is one way to ensure it. Many firms publish frequent bulletins for management with updates on personnel changes, office relocations, new telephone numbers, and revised company policies. Occasionally, special bulletins concerning new product developments, breaking company news, or other matters of urgent interest are circulated.

More formal publications, such as management magazines, are often more technical and more confidential than related employee newspapers. For example, a firm may release its corporate mission to all employees through the employee newspaper but may reveal its business profitability objectives only in the management magazine. This element of confidentiality is always a sensitive one. Employees occasionally object that internal publications don't reveal enough pertinent details about corporate decisions and policy. One common complaint is that outside newspaper reporters "know more than we do about our own firm's activities." Although limitations may be necessary for certain issues, those who run the organization must try to be as candid as possible, with fellow managers in particular.

Because of the very personal, vested interest of a manager in an organization, management publications are generally among the best read of any internal communication. They shouldn't be underestimated as a way to build confidence, enhance credibility, and promote a team spirit.

Employee Annual Reports

It often makes sense to print a separate annual report just for employees. Frequently, the lure of this report—published in addition to the regular corporate shareholder annual report—is that it is written for, about, and by the employees.

Most employees do care about how their organization functions and what its management is thinking. The annual report to the staff is a good place to discuss such issues informally, yet candidly. The report can be both factual, explaining the performance of the organization during the year, and informational, reviewing organizational changes and significant milestones during the year. It can also be motivational in its implicit appeal to team spirit and pride.

Staff reports observe few hard-and-fast rules about concept and format. In the report shown in Figure 15–4, the main focus is on what it all means to the employee. Staff annuals can be as complex as the shareholder annual report itself or as simple as a brief outline of the highlights of the year for the company. Typical features in the employee annual report include the following:

1. **Chief executive's letter** A special report to the staff reviewing the performance and highlights of the year and thanking employees for their help.
2. **Use-of-funds statement** Often a graphic chart describing how the organization used each dollar it took in.
3. **Financial condition** Frequently a chart describing the assets and liabilities of the corporation and the stockholders' equity.

FIGURE 15–4 The Jim Walter Corporation is one company that regularly distributes a special annual report to employees—in good and bad times. Even when the company has a subpar year, management commends employees for their contributions, recognizing an important tenet of employee communication, that winning the approval of the staff is the first step to winning the approval of external publics. (Courtesy of Jim Walter Corporation)

4. **Description of the company** Simple, graphic explanation of what the organization is and where its facilities are located.
5. **Social responsibility highlights** Discussion of the organization's role in aiding society through monetary assistance and employee participation during the year.
6. **Staff financial highlights** General description, usually in chart form, of salaries, benefits, and other staff-related expense items.
7. **Organizational policy** Discussion of current issues about which management feels strongly and for which it seeks employee support.
8. **Emphasis on people** One general theme throughout the report should be the importance of the people who make up the organization. This theme may take the form of in-depth profiles of people on the job, comments from people about their jobs, and/or pictorial essays on people at work.

Employees appreciate recognition. The special annual report is a measure of recognition that does not go unnoticed—or unread—by a firm's workers.

Bulletin Boards

Bulletin boards are making a comeback—in corporations, hospitals, and other organizations. For years they were considered second-string information channels, generally relegated to the display of federally required information and policy data for such activities as fire drills and emergency procedures. Most employees rarely consulted them. But the bulletin board has experienced a renaissance and is now being used to improve productivity, cut waste, and reduce accidents on the job. Best of all, employees are taking notice.

How come? For one thing, yesterday's bulletin board has become today's news center. It has been repackaged into a more lively, visual, and graphically arresting medium. Using enlarged news pictures and texts, motivational messages, and other company announcements—all illustrated with a flair—the bulletin board has become a primary source of employee communications (Figure 15–5). Hospitals in particular have found that a strategically situated bulletin board outside a cafeteria is a good way to promote employee understanding and cooperation.

One key to stimulating readership is to keep boards current. One person in the public relations unit should be assigned to this weekly task.

Internal Television

Just as increasing numbers today are receiving their external news from television, so, too, is television—more specifically, videotape—becoming an internal medium of preference for many organizations. Faced with the fact that upwards of 80 percent of the public gets much of its news from television, major companies have headed to the tube to compete for their employees' attention. One TV consultant estimated that 7,500 corporations spent almost

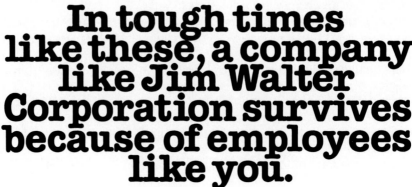

In tough times like these, a company like Jim Walter Corporation survives because of employees like you.

Thanks for your hard work and perseverance in 1981. Let's make 1982 a better year for all of us.

FIGURE 15–5 Sometimes the most effective and well-read bulletin board announcements carry simple messages like this. (Courtesy of Jim Walter Corporation)

$3 billion on some form of video production in 1983, compared with 5,000 companies spending $1.5 billion in 1980.[10]

Internal television can be demonstrably effective. A 10-minute videotape of an executive announcing a new corporate policy imparts hundreds of times more information than an audiotape of that same message, which, in turn, contains hundreds of times more information than a printed text of the same message.[11]

But internal television is not without serious dangers. For one thing, unless in-house television is of comparable broadcast quality to commercial TV, employees may be turned off. The following problems typical of in-house television may scuttle any attempt to reach employees.

1. **Too much talk**   In-house TV attempts are notorious for talking heads—narrators spending interminable minutes narrating without any action on the screen.
2. **Poor scripts**   Script-writing ability is a special skill, difficult to find in the typical organization.
3. **Limited equipment and staff**   Good quality television demands keeping abreast of technological breakthroughs. Even the wealthiest organizations may find it difficult and too expensive to try to keep up with the pace of television technology.
4. **Lack of creativity**   Creativity in television encompasses a number of aspects, including writing, photography, editing, and production. All require special technical expertise that many firms are unlikely to have.
5. **Failure to communicate**   If extensive time and effort are put into the technical production of a TV show, the content may be overlooked. Consequently, the people in the target audience may never get the desired message.
6. **Poor acting**   Public relations professionals, despite what their critics say, are generally not actors. In-house casting may not suffice.
7. **Poor voices**   In television the voice should fit the subject, script, and audience. This requirement isn't easy to meet when drawing from existing corporate talent.
8. **Poor music**   Proper music selection requires skill as well as access to good music libraries.
9. **Poor direction**   A good director is second in importance only to a good script.
10. **Poor production quality**   The sophisticated viewer (the typical employee) is aware of camera moves, lighting, picture framing, editing, sound quality, sound mixing, color, graphics, and art. If these elements are inferior, the viewer won't be convinced.
11. **Program length**   Most corporate video directors tend to make programs too long. Any program over 12 minutes may lose audience attention.[12]

In addition to insufficient competence and resources, in-house video can be plagued by poor public relations planning. The key to effective in-house TV is first to examine internal needs, then to plan thoughtfully before using the medium, and finally to reach target publics through the most sophisticated and high-quality programming available. If the organization cannot afford high-quality video, it simply should not get involved.

Face-to-Face Meetings

For good staff-management relations many organizations have concluded that there is no substitute for face-to-face meetings. Some firms formalize the meeting process by mixing management and staff in a variety of formats, from gripe sessions to marketing/planning meetings. In many organizations the concept of skipped-level meetings is a popular and productive form of communication, in which top-level managers meet periodically with employees at levels several notches below them in the organizational hierarchy. Such sessions introduce people who rarely get the opportunity to communicate with each other and often result in productive new ideas and associations that ultimately benefit the firm.

Just as with any other form of communication, the value of meetings lies in their regularity and substance. Meetings held only occasionally are not as productive as meetings scheduled periodically to realize target communication objectives. One such successful program was the quarterly, two-way, two-hour management open forum of Cedars-Sinai Medical Center in Los Angeles, a 1,000 bed, 5,000 employee urban facility. This program was designed as an off-the-cuff question-and-answer session for middle managers. In each get-together about 15 percent of the hospital's more than 500 managers—department heads were excluded—were encouraged to ask questions of top hospital staff members. Questions were rarely mild, but answers generally told managers why the hospital chose to take certain actions. The meetings, according to the internal communications manager who ran them, were not only effective but also inexpensive to boot.[13]

Other Methods

A variety of other methods are available for employee communications.

- **Open houses**   An open house gives relatives, friends, and neighbors an opportunity to see the workplace firsthand. Often, industrial firms hold family nights at plant locations. These events must be carefully planned and thoroughly organized; committees should be assigned to coordinate such areas as invitations, souvenirs, exhibits, and refreshments.
- **Management media summaries**   To help management stay aware of what the media are saying about the organization, regular media summaries can be compiled and distributed. For example, the 3M Company delivers its "News Scanner" service to top management by 10:00 A.M. daily. The United Technologies Company, in addition to distributing a "Morning News Sum-

The Bilgewater Breakthrough

For 20 years the *Bilgewater Bugle* has served the faculty of Bilgewater College. The *Bugle* reports regular employee newspaper fare, including research grants, personnel changes, and employee features. Bilgewater's public information office has not surveyed faculty opinions about the *Bugle* for some time, but director Chico Chesterton feels it's time for a change. "Television," according to Chesterton, "is the name of the game these days. What we really need is a video house organ to complement the *Bugle*, for faculty and students."

In setting out to convince the college president, Chesterton posits the following:

1. Since students spend more time watching television than they do reading, TV is an excellent way to inform them about the school's policies and programs.
2. TV monitors can be situated throughout student and faculty lounges so that in-house television can be continuously broadcast during the lunch hour. In this way, normal class time need not be disturbed.
3. Students and faculty might be quite willing to watch the lunchtime TV shows as they relax before or after they have eaten or after their normal shopping and browsing time at the numerous stores in the area.
4. People will like seeing their fellow students and teachers in the roles of television personalities.
5. Students will appreciate having a choice between the daily feature films shown in the student union and the in-house TV shows shown in the lounge.
6. The constant broadcast of in-house television may help motivate those who normally sleep in the lounge during their lunch period.
7. By seeing faculty and administration in interviews on the screen at lunchtime, students and teachers will feel closer to and more a part of the college team.

QUESTION

What do you think of Chico's reasoning?

mary," also posts "Noon News Briefs" in its executive dining room. At Mobil an elaborate system of newswires, videotape recorders, and press clipping monitors keeps corporate management aware of virtually any item concerning the energy industry or the company.

■ **Employee activities** Many organizations sponsor special after-hours employee activities (subsidized sports, picnics, cultural affairs) to promote em-

Here's how you can speak up.

Of all the people who will become involved in the Chemical Facts of Life program, none are more important than the 62,000 Monsanto employes and their families.

Starting with our Chairman and President, Monsanto executives already are speaking to nationally prominent groups about the Chemical Facts of Life.

This "Speak Out" portion of the program will be expanded until we have a huge cadre of Monsanto employes giving speeches at every level ranging from civic clubs in the smallest plant community, to major conventions and meetings of national groups.

The task of informing local, state and national lawmakers and regulators will receive special emphasis through intensified activities in our Washington office and a companywide "Grass Roots" program designed to reach legislators on a one-to-one basis.

But most important of all is your role. The role of the employe. We want you to participate in the program. We suggest you take the following steps.

1. Learn the chemical facts.

Over the next several months, we'll provide you with a continuing flow of information through plant newspapers, Chemical Fact Bulletins and in other ways.

(The Chemical Facts of Life booklet itself contains a wealth of material to support intelligent conversation about chemicals and their usage.)

2. Speak out when the opportunity arises.

Several times a day, each of us has an opportunity to speak out on behalf of our industry, our company and our products. To neighbors, relatives, friends, business associates, customers, suppliers.

And even to store clerks, bank tellers, taxi drivers. To anyone we may come in contact with.

3. Send us your comments.

This is not a one-way program. We want your comments, suggestions and advice.

Do you have any thoughts about other ways to tell our message to the country and the world?

Would you like extra materials to distribute among your non-Monsanto associates?

Would you like to participate in a speaker's bureau? Does your civic club or church group need a speaker?

The "Chemical Facts of Life" committee would like to hear from you.

If you would like to get involved in any way, or if you have any comments, please drop a note to Chemical Facts of Life, Dept. A3NB, Monsanto, 800 N. Lindbergh Blvd., St. Louis, Missouri 63166.

© Monsanto Company 1977

FIGURE 15–6   This excerpt from a Monsanto Company employee booklet shows the importance of internal communication to achieve an external purpose. Monsanto sought the aid of its 62,000 employees around the world in speaking out about the role of chemicals in society. (Courtesy of Monsanto Co.)

ployee morale. Workers appreciate these activities; however, organizations should be careful not to appear paternalistic in these kinds of sponsorships.

- **Telephone hotlines**   Some companies have introduced two-way telephone hotlines, which allow employees to pose job-related questions to public relations or personnel representatives. Calls are designed to convey concern for employee problems and are kept confidential.
- **Management-employee task forces**   An offshoot of face-to-face meetings is the formation of task forces composed of managers and subordinates throughout the organization. These task forces, charged with such responsibilities as keeping the premises clean, organizing emergency plans, and keeping the company ethical, also have an ancillary objective—to enhance employee communications (Figure 15–6).

Beyond these devices more exotic activities exist in great number. In 1987, when it was faced with a government investigation about insider trading, securities firm Drexel Burnham Lambert created a four-minute music video for internal distribution to perk up morale. It featured employees lip-synching to a Billy Ocean hit single, slightly altered to fit their needs. Another beleaguered securities company, E. F. Hutton, created "The Hutton Neighborhood Coloring Book" to motivate the firm's employees as the company tried to recover from its conviction on federal mail and wire fraud charges. However, a year later, when Hutton's former chairman became the subject of scandalous articles in the press, the Hutton coloring book became a laughingstock.

Much more likely to pay off in employee communications is "management by walking around," or just plain MBWA. MBWA is a tried and true technique that consists of chance encounters at the water cooler, in the cafeteria or corridor, and even in the restrooms. Indeed, one of the most effective ways to communicate with employees is simply to ask, "How are things going?"

DEALING WITH THE GRAPEVINE

In many organizations the company grapevine is one of the most powerful means of communications. But the rumor mill can be devastating. As one employee publication described the grapevine:

> It's faster than a public address announcement and more powerful than a general instruction. It's able to leap from L.A. to San Francisco in a single bound. And its credibility is almost beyond Walter Cronkite.

Rumors, once they pick up steam, are difficult to stop. Consequently, an organization must work to correct rumors as soon as possible, because employees tend to distort future events to conform to a rumor.

Identifying the source of a rumor is often difficult, if not impossible. And it's usually not worth the time. However, dispelling the rumor quickly and frankly is another story. Often a bad news rumor—about layoffs, closings, and so on—can be most effectively dealt with through forthright communication. Generally, an organization makes a difficult decision after a thorough review of many alternatives. The final decision is often a compromise, reflecting the needs of the firm and its various publics, including, importantly, the work force. However, in presenting a final decision to employees, management often overlooks the value of explaining how it reached its decision. By comparing alternative solutions so that employees can more clearly understand the rationale behind management decisions, an organization may make bad news more palatable.[14]

As demonic as the grapevine can become, it shouldn't necessarily be treated as the enemy in effective communications with employees. A company grapevine can be as much a communications vehicle as internal publications or employee meetings. It may even be more valuable because it is believed, and everyone seems to tap into it. One company, in fact—Sun Company of Radnor, Pennsylvania—regularly reported about the corporate grapevine in its internal publication, *Sun News*. In one article the newspaper discussed certain

Sun middle managers "who would rather die than say yes or no or anything."[15]

Again, the best defense against damaging rumors is a strong and candid communications system. Historically, the function of internal communications has bounced like a Ping-Pong ball between the provinces of public relations and personnel. However, where the function resides is much less important than the role it plays. If employee communicators are competent and if management stands wholeheartedly in support of their efforts, the culture of an organization will likely be a positive and productive ingredient in the firm's performance.

NOTES

1. Charles S. Steinberg, "Where Good PR Begins," *Public Relations Journal* (September 1976): 30–31.
2. Richard W. Darrow, "Employee Communications—Neglected Need," *New York Times,* 28 December 1975, F10.
3. Walter Kiechel III, "No Word from on High," *Fortune,* 6 January 1986, 125.
4. Roy G. Foltz, "Learning to Speak with One Voice," *Public Relations Journal* (July 1982): 30–31.
5. Roger M. D'Aprix, "The Human Corporation," speech delivered to the Southeast District Conference of the Public Relations Society of America, 8 February 1978.
6. Roy G. Foltz, "Credibility: Its Erosion," *The Personnel Administrator* (September 1976): 16.
7. Ronald Goodman and Richard S. Ruch, "The Role of Research in Internal Communication," *Public Relations Journal* (July 1982): 19.
8. Interview with Robert S. Cole, East Coast public relations manager, Bank of America, 5 September 1978.
9. For further information about the International Association of Business Communicators, write IABC, 807 Market Street, Suite 940, San Francisco, CA 94102.
10. Dennis Blank, "What's on TV Today? It Could Be the Boss," *USA Today,* 1 November 1984, 6b.
11. Douglas P. Brush, "Internal Communications and the New Technology," *Public Relations Journal* (February 1981): 10–11.
12. Jack Moss, "20 Things Wrong with In-Plant AV," *Photo Methods for Industry* (October 1973): 46.
13. Andrea Platt Hecht, "How to Bring Middle Management into the Communication Process," *Public Relations Journal* (October 1981): 16.
14. "Communicating Bad News," *Kwasha Lipton Newsletter* 15, no. 3 (July 1982): 1.
15. Eric Larson, "Corporate Grapevine Produces Ripe Fruit for Robert Finucane," *Wall Street Journal,* 18 March 1981, 1.

Anderson, Walter. *Handbook of Business Communications.* (Available from Box 243, Lenox Hill Station, New York, NY 10021.)

Blewett, Steve. "On Being a Pro: A House Organ Editor Speaks." *Public Relations Quarterly* (Summer 1981): 9–10.

Burger, Chester. "How Management Views Public Relations." *Public Relations Quarterly* (Winter 1983): 27–30.

Corbett, William. "The Bottom Line in Internal Communications: The Human Factor." *Tips & Tactics* (supplement of *PR Reporter*). 30 May 1988. The writer stresses how important informed, motivated staffers are to their firms. He goes on to detail various channels of company communications.

Employee Annual Report and Update. Chicago, IL: Ragan Communications (407 S. Dearborn), 1986.

Erb, Lyle L. "There's a Moral Here Somewhere." *Public Relations Quarterly* (Winter 1981–1982): 23–24.

Gitter, A. George. "Public Relations Roles: Press Agent or Counselor?" *Public Relations Review* (Fall 1981): 35–41.

How to Prepare and Write Your Employee Handbook. New York: AMACOM (135 W. 50th St.), 1984.

Kiechel, Walter III. "No Word from on High." *Fortune,* 6 January 1986, 125–126.

Nowlan, Stephen E., and Diana R. Shayon. "Reviewing Your Relationship with Executive Management." *Public Relations Quarterly* (Winter 1984): 5–11.

Seiler, Roger, and Michael J. Enzer. "How to Select and Use Motivational Films." *Public Relations Journal* (July 1981): 26.

SUGGESTED
READINGS

Much Ado About Mary

Internal gossip and rumors can be devastating to any organization. But rarely in the history of corporate America have internal rumors proved as destructive as the ones that led to the resignation of a promising young woman executive from the Bendix Corporation in the fall of 1980.

The saga went like this. Mary Cunningham, her degree from Harvard Business School freshly in hand, joined Bendix in June 1979 as executive assistant to the company's chairman, William M. Agee. Prior to entering Harvard, Cunningham had served as a junior officer of Chase Manhattan Bank for three years. Agee was known as something of a corporate maverick. Only in his early 40s—young for a major company CEO— Agee rose swiftly to the top by shaking things up at Bendix through acquisitions, personnel changes, and assorted bold business strokes.

A year after she joined Bendix, Mary Cunningham was promoted to vice president for corporate and public affairs. Although she had no experience in the communications field and the move was roundly criticized by public relations professionals, Agee stuck by the decision.

Inside the company, gossip about the "special relationship" between Cunningham and Agee began to circulate after her promotion. Insiders pointed to a number of public signs that the relationship might be more than strictly business.

- A television camera focused on former President Gerald Ford at the 1980 Republican National Convention in Detroit happened to find Agee and Cunningham sitting next to him.

- Some Bendix people suggested that Agee was less accessible than he had once been, and Cunningham's growing influence with him did not help to allay suspicions.

- In August 1980 Agee and his wife of 23 years got a divorce so quickly that it surprised even top officials at Bendix.

In light of the fact that Cunningham, a single woman, and Agee, a newly divorced man, were so close, it wasn't long before the Agee-Cunningham relationship became the major topic of conversation in the corridors of Bendix.

In September 1980 Agee suddenly fired his chief operating officer, and in the wake of that firing the executive vice president for strategic planning also resigned. Almost immediately, Agee appointed Cunningham as new Bendix vice president for strategic planning—just 15 months after she had graduated from Harvard Business School. Said Chairman Agee about his new strategic planning director, "She has been my right and left arm ever since she came into the company. She is the most vital and important person within the company and has played an important part in conceptualizing the strategy."

Agee also appeared before the executive committee of the Bendix board to personally refute the rumors about a romantic involvement between himself and Cunningham.

Cunningham also appeared at the meeting and offered to resign. But she argued that doing so would appear to corroborate the rumors and set the terrible precedent that, as *Fortune* magazine put it, "rumors can dictate policy." The board did not push for her resignation. Fortunately for all concerned, the media in general had not yet noticed the rumored Agee-Cunningham relationship.

But then the Bendix chairman went a tad too far. At a meeting in late September before more than 600 Bendix employees, Agee acknowledged the rumors about Cunningham and himself. He staunchly defended his strategic planning director on the basis of her qualifications, and he vigorously denied that her advancement had anything to do with "a personal relationship that we have." Agee apparently believed that a public discussion of the matter would once and for all clear the air. He was wrong.

His comments to the employees set off an avalanche of press coverage, and Mary Cunningham literally became a household word across America. As *Fortune* put it, "Top corporate executives in the U.S. have been accused of almost everything imaginable except having romances with one another." Predictably, in late October 1980 Mary Cunningham resigned from Bendix. As for Agee, he said he had learned some valuable lessons from the Cunningham flap, the most salient of which was the old Henry Ford II saying, "Never complain, never explain." Agee added that he did not believe there would be any long-term negative impact on Bendix.

Nonetheless, two years later, when Bendix attempted to acquire the huge Martin Marietta Corporation, the Bendix chairman was again publicly criticized for taking his wife of just a few weeks—the former Mary Cunningham—along with him to Bendix-Martin merger discussions. Summarized one Bendix operating executive in reference to the company's battering from the swirl of rumors surrounding Agee and Cunningham, "It's not like dealing with spark plugs."*

QUESTIONS

1. Was it wise for Agee to confront the executive committee of the Bendix board on the Cunningham rumors?
2. Was it wise for him to discuss the Cunningham relationship at the meeting of employees?
3. If Agee had said nothing about the Cunningham situation at the employees' meeting, what might have been the result?
4. Based on this case, do you think going public to nip a budding rumor is always the best policy?
5. Had you been Agee's public relations counselor in the midst of the Cunningham controversy, what public stance would you have recommended the company adopt?

---

*This case was excerpted largely from Peter W. Bernstein, "Upheaval at Bendix," *Fortune*, 3 November 1980, 48–56.

16

Government

The growth of public relations work, both with and in the government, has been explosive over the past decade. The burgeoning of the federal government itself is a relatively recent phenomenon. Since 1970 some 20 new federal regulatory agencies have sprung up, from the Environmental Protection Agency to the Consumer Product Safety Commission to the Department of Energy to the Occupational Safety and Health Administration. Moreover, according to the General Accounting Office, some 116 government agencies and programs now regulate business. In the 1950s and 1960s the business community was primarily interested in keeping government at arm's length, but today, as one corporate official put it, "The chief executive is seeing increasingly that more and more of the day-to-day decisions are made, not in his boardroom, but in Washington."[1]

In the 1990s chief executive officer trips to Washington will reach a new high as issues such as trade and budget deficits, high interest rates, tax changes, and a variety of others affect many companies that in the past believed government decision makers didn't matter to them. Accordingly, organizations are upgrading and expanding their own government relations functions.

As for the government itself, its public relations function has also been expanded and enhanced. Although President Nixon preferred advertising professionals as his closest advisors, in the Reagan administration numerous public relations professionals hold key slots.

Ironically, the public relations function has traditionally been something of a stepchild in the government. In 1913 Congress enacted the Gillett amendment, which almost barred the practice of public relations in government. The amendment stemmed from efforts by President Theodore Roosevelt to win public support for his programs through the use of a network of publicity experts. Congress, worried about the potential of this unlimited presidential persuasive power, passed an amendment stating: "Appropriated funds may not be used to pay a publicity expert unless specifically appropriated for that purpose."

Several years later, still leery of the president's power to influence legislation through communication, Congress passed the gag law, which prohibited "using any part of an appropriation for services, messages, or publications designed to influence any member of Congress in his attitude toward legislation or appropriations." Even today, no government worker may be employed in the practice of public relations. However, the government is flooded with public affairs experts, information officers, press secretaries, and communications specialists.

PUBLIC RELATIONS IN GOVERNMENT

Unfortunately, when people think about public relations in government, they tend to envision a blonde bombshell bursting onto the Capitol scene, a piggish congressman stuffing cash in his pockets as a secret videotape camera records the scene, or some senator or another checking into a hospital for treatment of some kind of antisocial behavior. Such predilections are indeed unfortunate and unfair.

Most practitioners in government communicate the activities of the various agencies, commissions, and bureaus to the public. As consumer activist Ralph Nader has said, "In this nation, where the ultimate power is said to rest with the people, it is clear that a free and prompt flow of information from government to the people is essential."

It wasn't always as essential to form informational links between government officials and the public. In 1888, when there were 39 states in the Union and 330 members in the House of Representatives, the entire official Washington press corps consisted of 127 reporters. Today there are close to 4,000 full-time journalists covering the capital.

In 1980 the U.S. Office of Personnel Management said there were 3,033 specialists in public information in the government, 2,272 in writing and editing, 1,722 in technical writing and editing, 1,659 in visual information, 1,090 in foreign information, 2,199 in editorial assistance, and 182 in foreign language broadcasting. That would mean that government at the start of the decade employed 12,157 people who could generally be characterized as practicing public relations.[2]

During the early Reagan years, spending commitments for public relations in 13 cabinet departments and 18 independent agencies fell slightly. But by 1985, with the government communications machine humming at full tilt, cabinet departments and agencies, exclusive of the United States Information Agency itself, spent close to $340 million. The big spenders were Health and Human Services with $56 million, the Energy Department with $47 million, and the Defense Department with $46 million.[3]

The volume of information initiated in Washington is so great that it is almost impossible for newspapers to cover the capital without the assistance of public relations professionals. In the words of columnist James J. Kilpatrick, "Those of us who try to cover Washington, however feebly, are utterly dependent upon the information officers. . . . What counts is the integrity of the information men."

United States Information Agency

Most far-reaching of the federal government's public relations arms is the United States Information Agency (USIA), which for a brief time was called the International Communications Agency. USIA employs nearly 9,000 people and functions in 129 countries around the world. Its budget in 1988 was $820 million. Although that might seem rather hefty as public relations budgets go, USIA officials claim that the USSR has 77,000 people and a budget of about $3 billion to perform this same function.

USIA's primary mission is "to support the national interest by conveying an understanding abroad of what the United States stands for as a nation and as a people; to explain the nation's policies and to present a true picture of the society, institutions, and culture in which those policies evolve."[4] Under the direction of such well-known media personalities as Edward R. Murrow, Carl Rowan, and Frank Shakespeare, the agency prospered. However, under the Reagan administration's director, Charles Z. Wick, USIA became an unsurpassed force in communicating America's message. One of Wick's innovations was WORLDNET, a 30-country satellite television network, dubbed the "jewel in the crown" of USIA communications techniques. Other USIA vehicles include the following:

1. **Radio** Voice of America has 111 transmitters, broadcasts in 42 languages, and reaches 120 million people in an average week. In addition to Voice of America, the USIA in 1985 began Radio Marti, in honor of José Marti, father of Cuban independence. Radio Marti's purpose is to broadcast to Cuba in Spanish and "tell the truth to the Cuban people."
2. **Film and television** USIA annually produces and acquires an extensive number of films and video cassettes for distribution in 125 countries.
3. **Media** About 25,000 words a day are radio-teletyped to 214 overseas posts for placement in the media.
4. **Publications** Overseas regional service centers publish 16 magazines in 18 languages and distribute pamphlets, leaflets, and posters to more than 100 countries.
5. **Exhibitions** USIA designs and manages about 35 major exhibits each year throughout the world, including Eastern European countries and the Soviet Union.
6. **Libraries and books** USIA maintains or supports libraries in over 200 information centers and binational centers in more than 90 countries and assists publishers in distributing books overseas.
7. **Education** USIA is also active overseas in sponsoring educational programs through 111 binational centers where English is taught and in 11 language centers. Classes draw about 350,000 students annually.

Robert K. Gray

Robert Keith Gray is chairman of Hill and Knowlton USA and vice chairman of Hill and Knowlton. He was honorary chairman of the 1985 Presidential Inaugural Committee and co-chairman of the 1981 Reagan-Bush campaign. He is former vice chairman and head of Washington operations for Hill and Knowlton. Prior to joining Hill and Knowlton in 1961, Gray served the Eisenhower administration in various capacities, including appointment secretary to the president and cabinet secretary. He is the author of *Eighteen Acres Under Glass,* an account of his years at the White House.

What makes a good lobbyist?
There is no magic concoction from which a lobbyist is brewed. Likewise, there is no one trait or skill that separates the effective lobbyist from the ineffective one. A knowledge of the legislative process certainly is essential. The rules under which the House and Senate operate govern the lobbyist's course of action. Plainly and simply, know Capitol Hill; its faces, which are many and always changing; its pace, which can be hectic; and its rules.

A member of Congress survives by keeping one eye on a given issue and the other on the clock, so you have to know the limitations of a member's time. Prepare your client's case carefully, target your member; then, when you have been granted an audience, state your case intelligently and crisply. A tip: If it takes less than the time allotted, you will improve your chances for a quick appointment the next time you ask for one.

In lobbying, are ''contacts'' everything?
No! A good case is far more important than a good contact. A friend in the right place, a press aide who was particularly cordial at a dinner party, your high school sweetheart who vowed to marry a member of Congress and did—contacts like these can and often do serve the lobbyist well. But they do not make the lobbyist; it is the other way around. A good lobbyist develops contacts and learns to

keep them. The secret is maintaining a productive relationship with a given contact year in and year out. Public relations, lobbying, politics—all are give-and-take professions. The best lobbyists operate under the "What can I do to help you?" maxim.

What is the most common mistake lobbyists make?
Operating with less than full facts. Know your issue, know it well! There is nothing more basic to the lobbyist than preparation. On the other hand, the member should be informed and intrigued by your proposal, not overwhelmed by it. Inexperienced lobbyists sometimes press too hard. They oversell their cases, insist on presenting more information than anyone has time to read or wants to hear.

How important are lobbyists in influencing legislation?
Today's legislator, given the preponderance of issues and the limits of time, is overworked and often underinformed. The complexities of our society spread the member and his or her staff so thin that they can only hope to know the general line on a plethora of issues.

In this arena the lobbyist offers the legislator refined information about how a certain issue will affect employment, products, prices, etc. The lobbyist thus provides practical application to legislative theory.

The modern legislator understandably is very responsive to those who bring clear understanding to issues. The lobbyist fills an information void with solid facts and persuasive arguments.

How does a small organization get involved in influencing the legislative process?
A small organization—for that matter a single individual—can be an effective lobbyist. The private citizen has an opportunity to contact members of Congress every time the postman goes past his door or every time he passes his telephone. When a constituent has kept his lines current with a member of Congress, has been helpful to him in his campaigns, and is known to the member as a constituent of knowledge and reputation in the district, then his communication may have more impact on the member's vote than all the high-priced lobbyists in Washington.

How do you answer the critics who say special interest groups are a pox on good government?
The term *special interest* has taken on a pejorative connotation, as if it were somehow Cain to the public interest's Abel. The special interest groups serve the public interest, for they are the means by which those citizens most affected by particular legislation or legislative considerations in a particular area can most effectively present their views. The legislative system is an adversarial process. Special interest groups are no pox on government but are acting on their First Amendment right to air their views before a forum of elected officials, and they are doing so in an ever more organized way.

Government Bureaus

Nowhere has government public relations activity become more aggressive than in federal departments and regulatory agencies (Figure 16–1). Many agencies, in fact, have found that the quickest way to gain recognition is to increase public relations aggressiveness.

The Federal Trade Commission (FTC), which columnist Jack Anderson once called a "sepulcher of official secrets," opened up in the late 1970s to become one of the most active of government communicators. As a former FTC director of public information described the agency's attitude, "The basic premise underlying the commission's public information program is the public's inherent right to know what the FTC is doing."[5] When the FTC found a company's products wanting in standards of safety or quality, it often announced its complaint through a press conference. Although corporate critics branded this process "trial by press release," it helped transform the agency from a meek, mild-mannered bureau into an office with real teeth.

Other government departments have also stepped up public relations efforts. The Department of Defense has a public affairs budget of $31 million and a staff of more than 1,000 people. The Air Force alone has a worldwide public affairs staff of 200. Its internal audience consists of 600,000 people in uniform, plus their families. In 1986 the Air Force answered about 35,000 letters from school children inquiring about this military branch.[6] The Department of Health and Human Services has a public affairs staff of 550 people. The departments of Agriculture and Treasury also have substantial communications staffs. Even the Central Intelligence Agency has a 20-person group of public affairs experts.

The most proficient government agencies in public relations must nonetheless work constantly at improving relationships with taxpayers. As the case study at the end of this chapter illustrates with the *Challenger* disaster of the National Aeronautics and Space Administration in 1986, a government agency's credibility takes years to build up but just a few tragic seconds to lose.

The President

Despite early congressional efforts to limit the persuasive power of the nation's chief executive, the president today wields unprecedented public relations clout. Almost anything the president does or says makes news. The broadcast networks, daily newspapers, and national magazines follow his every move. His press secretary provides the White House press corps (a group of national reporters assigned to cover the president) with a constant flow of announcements supplemented by daily press briefings. Unlike many organizational press releases that seldom make it into print, many White House releases achieve national exposure.

Although most journalists resent administration attempts at news management (some call it news manipulation), most succumb to it. As one publi-

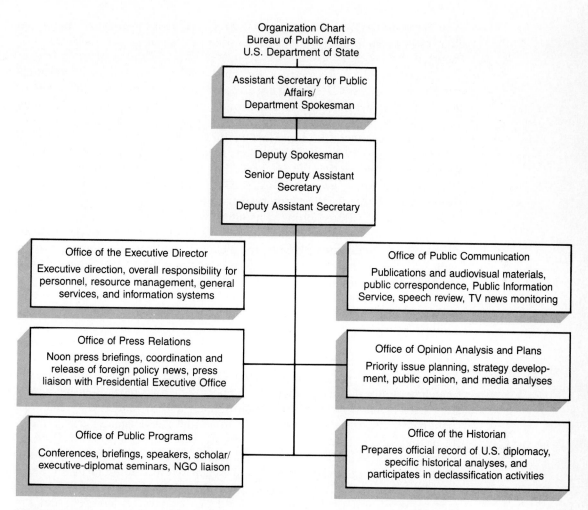

**Organization Chart
Bureau of Public Affairs
U.S. Department of State**

Assistant Secretary for Public Affairs/
Department Spokesman

Deputy Spokesman

Senior Deputy Assistant Secretary

Deputy Assistant Secretary

Office of the Executive Director
Executive direction, overall responsibility for personnel, resource management, general services, and information systems

Office of Public Communication
Publications and audiovisual materials, public correspondence, Public Information Service, speech review, TV news monitoring

Office of Press Relations
Noon press briefings, coordination and release of foreign policy news, press liaison with Presidential Executive Office

Office of Opinion Analysis and Plans
Priority issue planning, strategy development, public opinion, and media analyses

Office of Public Programs
Conferences, briefings, speakers, scholar/executive-diplomat seminars, NGO liaison

Office of the Historian
Prepares official record of U.S. diplomacy, specific historical analyses, and participates in declassification activities

FIGURE 16–1 The Bureau of Public Affairs in the U.S. Department of State is typical of the public information mechanism in a federal department. The assistant secretary for public affairs in the State Department and in most other federal agencies reports directly to the secretary. (Courtesy of United States Department of State)

cation put it, "The ways a President can influence the news are endless. For example, announcements of favorable developments are made from the White House, while gloomy tidings are usually reported by individual agencies."[7]

Typical of such news management was President Jimmy Carter's administration in the late 1970s. When his image as a forceful leader began to wane in late 1978, he brought in media specialist Gerald Rafshoon to help improve it. Thereafter, the president began announcing federal grants in local communities, holding town meetings around the country, and even taking adventurous vacations, such as a raft trip down the Idaho rapids. Some believed that even the historic Camp David summit, which brought together the traditional enemies of Israel and Egypt, was (at least below the surface) a Rafshoon production.

Ronald Reagan was perhaps the most masterful presidential communicator in recent history. Reagan gained experience in the movies and on television, and even his most ardent critics agreed that he possessed a compelling stage presence. So formidable were the persuasive powers of "the great communicator" that when CBS broadcast a critical 1982 documentary against Reagan's budget cuts, White House reporters objected strenuously to the president and his aides for singling the broadcast out for criticism. "How can you say that it [White House criticism] is not going to have a chilling effect on our profession?" moaned a Washington correspondent.[8] In the face of such media anxiety, the White House dropped its offensive.

Later, in the spring of 1983, when Reagan's interior secretary James Watt forbade the popular music group, the Beach Boys, from performing on the Capitol Mall on the Fourth of July, the president's communication savvy again saved the day. He immediately presented Watt with a plaster foot to symbolize where he had "shot himself." The Reagan gesture once again reversed an embarrassing situation and resulted in even more goodwill for the "great communicator."

Reagan's greatest public relations test came in the last years of his presidency, when his administration tried to defend its Iran initiative, including the shipment of arms to Iran in exchange for American hostages and the later funneling of illegal arms payments to support the contra rebel offensive in Nicaragua. To defend this program, Reagan's aides in 1987 launched an elaborate "spin patrol" to alter the direction, or spin, of news coverage, especially analyses of the president's actions, so that the Reagan view of events won out on the networks and in the major newspapers. In one graphic description of this effort, former Reagan chief of staff Don Regan wrote, "Some of us are like a shovel brigade that follows a parade down Main Street, cleaning up."[9] Despite such setbacks, Ronald Reagan, who held fewer news conferences than any president since Richard Nixon, was largely credited with possessing more potent communications skills than any other chief executive in the nation's history.

The President's Press Secretary

Some have called the job of presidential press secretary the second most difficult position in any administration. The press secretary is the chief public relations spokesperson for the administration. Like practitioners in private industry, the press secretary must communicate the policies and practices of the management (the president) to the public. Often it is an impossible job.

In 1974 Gerald terHorst, President Ford's press secretary, quit after disagreeing with the pardon of former President Richard Nixon. Said terHorst, "A spokesman should feel in his heart and mind that the chief's decision is the right one so that he can speak with a persuasiveness that stems from conviction."[10] A contrasting view of the press secretary's role was expressed by terHorst's replacement in the job, former NBC reporter Ron Nessen. Said Nessen, "A press secretary does not always have to agree with the President. His first loyalty is to the public, and he should not knowingly lie or mislead the press."[11] Still a third view of the proper role of the press secretary was offered by a former public relations professional and Nixon speech writer who became a *New York Times* political columnist, William Safire.

> A good press secretary speaks up for the press to the President and speaks out for the President to the press. He makes his home in the pitted no-man's-land of an adversary relationship and is primarily an advocate, interpreter, and amplifier. He must be more the President's man than the press's. But he can be his own man as well.[12]

In recent years the position of press secretary to the president has taken on increased responsibility and has attained a higher public profile. Jimmy Carter's press secretary, Jody Powell, for example, was among Carter's closest confidants and frequently advised the president on policy matters. Powell's successor as press secretary, James Brady, was seriously wounded in 1981 by a bullet aimed at President Reagan as they both departed from a Washington hotel. Although Brady was permanently paralyzed, he retained his title as presidential press secretary and returned for limited work at the White House.

Brady was then replaced by Larry Speakes, a former Hill and Knowlton executive, who was universally hailed by the media for his professionalism. During Reagan's second term Speakes apparently was purposely kept in the dark by Reagan's military advisors planning an invasion of the island of Grenada. An upset Speakes later apologized to reporters for misleading them on the Grenada invasion.

Later in the Reagan term, Speakes was included early and forthrightly in several pending crises. When informed early, the deputy press secretary was more than up to the task. In one instance midway through Reagan's second term, when Ferdinand Marcos was rumored to be seeking asylum in the United States as his power base in the Philippines tottered, Speakes told inquiring journalists, "I'm in a situation right now where we just prefer to remain silent. There are things we know that we're not talking about right now for obvious reasons."

Unfortunately for Speakes, when he resigned in 1988 and published a controversial book about his White House experience, passages involving fabricated presidential quotes (see chapter 5) made him an easy target for retrospective criticism. Speakes was replaced by a low-key, trusted, and respected lifetime public relations practitioner, Marlin Fitzwater. Fitzwater distinguished himself in the last two years of the Reagan presidency as a straight-shooting, always-available public relations professional.

Over the years the number of reporters hounding the presidential press secretary—dubbed by some an imperial press corps—has grown from fewer than 300 reporters during President Kennedy's term to around 3,000 today.

Salaries of $40,000 to $50,000, relatively rare in most newspaper offices in prior years, are today commonplace in Washington bureaus. And TV network White House correspondents command six-figure incomes, with each major network assigning two or three correspondents to cover the White House simultaneously. Dealing with such a host of characters is no easy task. Perhaps Lyndon Johnson, the first chief executive to be labeled an imperial president by the Washington press corps, said it best when asked by a TV reporter what force or influence he thought had done the most to shape the nature of Washington policy. "You bastards," Johnson snapped.[13]

DEALING WITH GOVERNMENT

The business community, foundations, and philanthropic and quasi-public organizations have a common problem—dealing with government, particularly the mammoth federal bureaucracy. Because government has become so pervasive in organizational and individual life, the number of corporations and trade associations with government relations units has grown steadily in recent years.

Government relations people are primarily concerned with weighing the impact of impending legislation on the company, industry group, or client organization. Generally, a head office government relations staff complements staff members who represent the organization in Washington and state capitals. These representatives have several objectives.

1. To improve communications with government personnel and agencies
2. To monitor legislators and regulatory agencies in areas affecting constituent operations
3. To encourage constituent participation at all levels of government
4. To influence legislation affecting the economy of the constituent's area as well as its operations
5. To advance awareness and understanding among lawmakers of the activities and operations of constituent organizations

Carrying out these objectives requires knowing your way around the federal government and acquiring connections. A full-time Washington representative is often employed for these tasks.

To the uninitiated, Washington (or almost any state capital) can seem an incomprehensible maze. Consequently, organizations with an interest in government relations usually employ a professional representative, who may or may not be a registered lobbyist, whose responsibility, among other things, is to influence legislation. Lobbyists are required to comply with the federal Lobbying Act of 1947, which imposes certain reporting requirements on individuals or organizations that spend a significant portion of time or money attempting to influence members of Congress on legislation. Some have described this act as "vague, essentially unenforceable, and in need of revision."[14] The Su-

A Close Call for the Great Communicator

Every iota of Ronald Reagan's communications skill was tested in the spring of 1985, when the president agreed to visit a West German cemetery that turned out to be a burial place for former Nazi SS troops. Jewish and veterans groups implored the president to boycott the cemetery. Indeed, Reagan's advisors were apparently split on whether he should go through with the visit. But in the end, potential embarrassment of West German government officials made the trip to the cemetery at Bitburg an imperative stop.

Right up until the visit, the Washington press corps wrote of little else. Bitburg dominated the daily headlines and evening news broadcasts. And Reagan was the villain. On the day of the fateful visit, ABC and NBC covered it live, and CBS dispatched its anchor, Dan Rather, to London to interview news correspondents who covered World War II.

The president, like a Christian thrown to the lions, was painted inescapably into a corner. And the world waited to see whether the "great communicator" could once again wriggle out of his predicament. He did.

Reagan's trip to the Bitburg cemetery was brisk and uneventful. He immediately left the cemetery to visit a nearby concentration camp at Bergen-Belsen. Referring to the 5,000 victims of the Nazi holocaust buried at the Bergen-Belsen site, Reagan said, "Here they lie—never to hope, never to pray, never to love, never to heal, never to laugh, never to cry." So moving and memorable was Reagan's stirring speech at the former Nazi death camp that days later most Americans remembered little else—including the controversy that had preceded the West German trip.

Chalk up another one for the great communicator.

preme Court did rewrite the law in 1953 and greatly narrowed the act's application in order to find it constitutional.

In point of fact, one need not register as a lobbyist in order to speak to a senator, congressional representative, or staff member about legislation. But a good lobbyist can earn the respect and trust of a legislator. Because of the need to analyze legislative proposals and deal with members of Congress, many lobbyists are lawyers with a heavy Washington background. Lobbying ranks are filled with former administration officials and congressional members, who often turn immediately to lobbying when they move out of office.

Although lobbyists, at times, have been labeled everything from influence peddlers to fixers, such epithets are generally inaccurate and unfair. Today's lobbyist is more likely to be "a technician, competent and well-informed in his

YOU MAKE THE CALL

Defusing the Dioxin Controversy

In early 1987 the nation's paper manufacturers faced an impending disaster. Dioxin, the cancer-causing chemical, was believed to be bubbling up in the bleaching process of paper mills, contaminating discharges and pulp in tiny quantities. It seemed unavoidable that the substance would turn up in every-day products. As one official at the American Paper Institute (API) warned colleagues, "The industry could be responding to claims of skin rashes, upset stomachs, aches and pains, animal ills, bad tasting water, etc., all blamed on our products or processes."

So, rather than waiting for the dioxin shoe to drop, the industry took immediate action. Fueled by a $300,000 industry war chest, the paper industry set out to manage public and official views of the controversy.

- It independently tested its products.
- It worked hand in hand with the Environmental Protection Agency, surveying the pollution of paper mills around the country.
- It hired outside experts, who challenged the EPA's view of dioxin risks.
- It trained industry spokespersons to take to the airwaves for interviews about dioxin.
- It launched a consumer survey to assess the public's knowledge of the product.
- It met with journalists of influential media to discuss dioxin.

The industry's objective, according to an API executive, was "that accurate information get out." And the industry agreed to have a quick response plan and team in place for the day when the dioxin issue would become public news.

One way the industry succeeded in getting the news out objectively was to encourage the EPA itself to discuss dioxin with the media in a balanced,

---

field . . . performing a vital function in furnishing Congress with facts and information."[15] Indeed, the lobbyist's function is rooted in the First Amendment right of all citizens to petition government.

What Do Lobbyists Do?

Lobbyists inform and persuade. Their contacts are important, but they must also have the right information available for the right legislator. The time to plant ideas with legislators is well before a bill is drawn up, and skillful lobbyists recognize that timing is critical in influencing legislation. The specific

nonhysterical manner. API representatives met regularly with the EPA to discuss the hazards of dioxin and the way the industry was containing them. According to industry memoranda, the paper manufacturers sought to "avoid confrontations with government agencies which might trigger concerns about health risks or raise the visibility of the issue generally."

In September, when the EPA finally held a news conference disclosing dioxin in the pulp and discharges of paper mills, the effect on the public was muted. The EPA's announcement was reasoned and reasonable, helping avert public alarm. Basically, the EPA acknowledged that it and the industry had the potential dangers of dioxin well in hand. Environmentalists, who later criticized the public relations offensive of the paper industry, could only shake their heads at having been caught so off guard.*

QUESTIONS

1. What do you think was key to the paper industry's public relations strategy?
2. Why did the industry enlist the support of the Environmental Protection Agency?
3. Would you have attempted to enlist the support of environmentalists early on to avoid later criticism?
4. What strategy should the industry adopt for the future in terms of this dioxin issue?

---

*Michael Weiskopf, "Paper Industry Campaign Defused Reaction to Dioxin Contamination," *Washington Post*, 25 October 1987.

---

activities performed by individual lobbyists vary with the nature of the industry or group represented. Most take part in these activities:

1. **Fact-finding** The government is an incredible storehouse of facts, statistics, economic data, opinions, and decisions, which generally are available for the asking.
2. **Interpretation of government actions** A key function of the lobbyist is to interpret for management the significance of government events and the potential implications of pending legislation. Often, a lobbyist predicts what can be expected to happen legislatively and recommends actions to deal with the expected outcome.

3. **Interpretation of company actions** Through almost daily contact with congressional members and staff assistants, a lobbyist conveys how a specific group feels about legislation. The lobbyist must be completely versed in the business of the client and the attitude of the organization toward governmental actions.

4. **Advocacy of a position** Beyond the presentation of facts, a lobbyist also advocates positions on behalf of clients, both pro and con. Often, hitting a congressional representative early with a stand on pending legislation can mean getting a fair hearing for the client's position. Indeed, few congressional representatives have the time to study—or even read—every piece of legislation on which they are asked to vote. Therefore, they depend on lobbyists for information, especially for information on how proposed legislation may affect constituents.

5. **Publicity springboard** More news comes out of Washington than any other city in the world. It's the base for thousands of press, TV, radio, and magazine correspondents. This multiplicity of media makes it the ideal springboard for launching organizational publicity. The same holds true to a lesser degree in state capitals.

6. **Support of company sales** The government is one of the nation's largest purchasers of products. Lobbyists often serve as conduits through which sales are made. A lobbyist who is friendly with government personnel can serve as a valuable link for leads to company business.

For all of this, lobbying today has become big business. In 1986 lobbying costs hit $61 million, 25 percent more than the year before, and the number of registered Washington lobbyists increased from 6,000 to more than 8,000. The three largest lobbying budgets reported were those of the Citizens for Sensible Control of Acid Rain ($3 million), the National Committee to Preserve Social Security and Medicare ($3 million), and Common Cause ($2 million). Other groups that spent in excess of $1 million included the National Association of Letter Carriers, American Council of Life Insurance, and the environmental group the Sierra Club.

Grass Roots Lobbying

Particularly effective recently has been the use of indirect, or grass roots, lobbying (as opposed to conventional lobbying by paid agents). The main thrust of such lobbying is to mobilize local constituents of congressional members, together with the general public, to write, telephone, telegraph, or buttonhole members of Congress on legislation.

Grass roots lobbying is a tactic that has been used most effectively by everyone from so-called consumer advocates, such as the Ralph Nader organization and Common Cause, to President Ronald Reagan. In the early 1980s a resurgence of citizens' activism, not seen since the 1960s, began to appear.

Coalitions formed on both national and local levels on issues from arms to economics. Locally, tenants' organizations, neighborhood associations, and various other local groups won significant concessions from government and corporate bodies. Nationally, the nuclear freeze campaign, for one, made its way onto many 1982 state election ballots and received widespread support.

The success of such grass roots campaigns was not lost on big business. Business learned that grass roots lobbying—applying pressure from the 50 states and the 435 congressional constituencies, from corporate headquarters to plant communities—was at the heart of moving the powers in Washington. In one of the most successful grass roots campaigns in history, the upstart money market fund industry in 1981 soundly trounced the more entrenched banking establishment by organizing a massive grass roots letter-writing campaign. Constituents from all over the country wrote their congressional representatives and state legislators, telling them to keep their hands off the money funds. One outgrowth was that threatened legislation to limit the funds never was instituted.

Such indirect lobbying may seek to (1) persuade community leaders to meet directly with their congressional representative; (2) mobilize telephone calls and individualized letters to congressional members; (3) instigate mass mailings of postcards or coupons from advertisements; or (4) exhort shareholders, members, employees, and customers to pressure Congress.[16]

Whatever the objectives, grass roots lobbying and lobbying in general are very much in vogue. Rare is the group not represented in Washington. The popcorn industry has its Popcorn Institute. The automatic telephone dialing service industry has a lobbyist. So does the International Llama Association. Prohunters have Safari Club International, and antihunters have the Fund for Animals. All believe their efforts are worthwhile.

Lobbyists are a gritty breed. Even the underdog is positive that somewhere in the vast network of official Washington there is a friendly ear, no matter how out of favor the cause may currently be. The lobbyist's task: to find it, cherish it, nurture it, and finally ask it a favor.[17]

POLITICAL ACTION COMMITTEES

A fast-growing and perfectly legal mechanism for unified support of political candidates by members of incorporated bodies is the political action committee (PAC). Between 1974 and 1980 the number of federally registered PACs nearly quadrupled, with the largest increase coming from corporations (Figure 16–2). Today, one-half of the 2,300 PACs in the United States are sponsored by corporations. The Federal Election Commission, which gathers and reports figures from all PACs, recorded PAC receipts from January 1979 to August 1980 as $113 million, the majority of which went to support political candidates.

For many years the law prohibited corporations from making direct political contributions. In recent years, however, the Federal Election Campaign

What is ChasePAC?
   ChasePAC is a registered Political Action Committee—that is, an organization empowered to solicit donations from Chase personnel and to contribute these funds to political candidates on the federal, state and local levels. ChasePAC's affairs are conducted in accordance with federal and New York State laws. ChasePAC is registered with the Federal Election Commission in Washington and with the State Board of Elections in Albany.

What statutory authorization is there for establishment of corporate PACs?
   Establishment of corporate PACs has been authorized by the Federal Election Campaign Act and by the New York State Election Law. In fact, operation of a PAC is the only legally sanctioned way in which a bank or corporation may involve itself in fund-raising in connection with any campaign for federal public office. As you know, Chase is prohibited by law from contributing corporate funds to candidates or political committees in connection with any election for federal public office.

How many similar Political Action Committees are in existence?
   Since enactment of the Federal Election Campaign Act, the corporate PAC movement has mushroomed. Today there are more than 1,000 such committees in existence, including over 100 PACs in the banking industry nationwide and in about a half dozen major banks headquartered in New York City.

What is the purpose of ChasePAC?
   The purpose of ChasePAC is to provide a convenient way for Chase personnel to pool their personal funds in order to extend tangible support on both the federal and state levels to political candidates whose views on important issues are consistent with Chase positions.

How much would any candidate receive from the fund?
   It is anticipated that a typical contribution would range between $200 and $400. This level of giving appears to be consistent with the pattern of other corporate Political Action Committees.

CHASE believes that sound government can only be achieved through the full participation of its citizens. As a result, The Chase Manhattan Corporation has established a Political Action Committee (ChasePAC) to give its staff members a means to contribute as a group to responsible men and women who seek public office.

   To find out more about ChasePAC and how you can participate in its activities, we invite you to read this Fact Book which has been prepared to explain how ChasePAC works and to answer questions you may have about the organization.

   You will also find an enrollment card printed in this booklet. Please use this card at the time you decide to join your fellow Chase staff members in contributing to this political action fund.

   If after reading this brochure you have any further questions, you may contact Herbert W. Abrams, Treasurer of ChasePAC, 552-3733.

FIGURE 16–2   This question-and-answer sheet, mailed to each potential member of the Chase Manhattan Bank Political Action Committee, offers the kind of simple explanations that are typical of most corporate PACs. (Courtesy of Chase Manhattan Bank)

Act of 1971 with subsequent amendments has generally allowed incorporated bodies to "solicit funds, maintain them in a segregated fund, pay all expenses of the fund, and disperse the funds at the discretion of the organization's management."[18]

   Although some politicians publicly voice concern about the clout of PACs in influencing elections, the facts thus far indicate that such fears are premature. Most corporate and union PACs have lacked the large sums to dominate elections. However, PAC numbers are growing—from 89 in 1974 to 1,700 in 1986. Contributions by PACs to individual candidates averaged $500 for Congress and $1,000 for the Senate in 1983–84. Donations go mainly to incumbents and they're split fairly evenly—in 1984, business contributed about $21 million to Democrats and about $24 million to Republicans.

   To be sure, the role of PACs in the electoral process is bound to increase in the 1990s.

DEALING WITH CONGRESS

The name of the game in government relations is influencing legislation. And the key to such influence is good information. Legislators work on information. Hence, it is the timely presentation of accurate information that counts. A key vote may be affected by other considerations from time to time, but usually members of Congress are most sensitive to what will affect the voting in their area.

Testify

One way to reach Congress, of course, is by giving testimony in connection with legislation, a special investigation, or a nonlegislative study designed to examine a particular issue. Cleverly staged hearings on shocking topics are quite the rage in Washington today. By feeding the media's appetite for dramatic news, oversight hearings provide members of Congress with valuable publicity that sidesteps the frustrating and often thankless legislative process. One senator's agenda for a legislative session included hearings on child abuse, rape, spouse beating, alcoholism, and drugs—just for starters.

Congressional witnesses must do their homework. They must write out their testimony and know it well enough to explain it confidently and articulately. They should also prepare for sharp interrogation by members of Congress. Even if testifying on legislation with general backing, there are always at least two points of view that invariably emerge in every hearing: Republicans versus Democrats, conservatives versus liberals, business versus labor, one-worlders versus protectionists—the gamut of ideological, philosophical, ethnic, and religious viewpoints.

Write

Another effective means of getting through to a busy legislator is by writing. Members of Congress and state government receive scores of letters. Part of their job is to read them.

A letter should be brief and to the point. It should identify the subject clearly, giving the bill number if that is what is at issue. The best time to write is when a bill is in committee; legislators are more responsive when a bill is being discussed in the committee forum.

Letters should also be original. Often lobbying groups direct thousands of form letters to government officials. Typically, these form appeals are tossed. So it's much better to tailor each letter, keeping in mind that the purpose is to convince, not intimidate.

Finally, it's important to learn the names of the people behind the official. More than 14,000 staff members work on Capitol Hill in Washington, supporting members of Congress. Often a letter directed to one of these staff associates, who may wield significant influence, may be more valuable than a letter to the actual legislator.

The "Be" List of Getting Through to Legislators

Pat Choate, a veteran government relations professional of TRW, offers the following "be" list for anyone wishing to get through to legislators.

- **Be independent.** Policymakers value an independent view.
- **Be informed.** Government thrives on information. Timely facts, a deep knowledge of the subject, and specific examples are invaluable.
- **Be bipartisan.** Matters are more likely to be addressed on merit if approached in a bipartisan manner. Although it is necessary to be sensitive to political nuances, politics is best left to the politicians.
- **Be published.** Clear and cogent thinking, in articles and op-ed pieces, is noticed in Washington and at the state house.
- **Be broad-minded.** Don't peddle petty self-interest. Address the broader interests, and your counsel will be sought.
- **Be persistent.** A long-term, persistent commitment of time is mandatory in dealing with legislators.
- **Be practical.** Politicians value practical recommendations they can defend to their constituents.
- **Be honest.** Politicians and the press are skilled at spotting phonies. Honesty is the best policy. It works.*

*Cindy Skrzycki, "Possible Leaders Abound in Business Community," *Washington Post,* 24 January 1988.

Visiting the Capitol

Perhaps the most effective way of reaching legislators is to visit them. First, arrange to meet your representative or senator early in a congressional session, not to press for consideration of particular legislation, but rather to introduce yourself. If there is particular legislation in which you are interested, also see your legislator early in the process. You must track the subcommittee calendars closely; decisions in subcommittees are critical and their impact grossly underestimated.

When you get inside the door, realize that your representative's time is short. Usually, you've got 15 minutes to make your case. What the representative wants to know is this:

1. What's the problem?
2. What does it mean to my state or district in terms of the economy, jobs, or general welfare?
3. How can I help?

Tell your representative of your concern as simply and succinctly as possible.

After the visit follow up with a short letter to the legislator or legislative aide and keep track of legislative developments. An occasional reminder nudge may be helpful. But too much pressure will be counterproductive. Just as in dealing with the media, the best relationships between you and your legislator or all-important aides are developed over time and are based on mutual trust.[19]

DEALING WITH LOCAL GOVERNMENT

In 1980 Ronald Reagan rode to power on a platform of New Federalism, calling for a shift of political debate and public policy decisions to state and local levels. Thus, it became more important for public relations people to deal with local, state, and regional governments.

Dealing with such local entities, of course, differs considerably from dealing with the federal government. For example, opinion leaders in communities (those constituents with whom an organization might want to affiliate to influence public policy decisions) might include such sectors as local labor unions, teachers, civil service workers, and the like. Building consensus among such diverse constituents is pure grass roots public relations.

The very nature of state and local issues makes it impossible to give one, all-encompassing blueprint for successful government relations strategies. Public relations advertising may be appropriate in some cases. Area philanthropic contributions may be called for. And certainly, closer contact with local legislators to impress them with the investment, facilities, and jobs created by the organization will become increasingly important. Through the 1990s increased government relations attention will be directed at effectively reaching the relatively new audiences of state, local, and regional lawmakers.

NOTES

1. Vasil Pappas, "More Firms Upgraded Government-Related Jobs Because of Sharp Growth in Federal Regulations," *Wall Street Journal*, 11 January 1980, 1.
2. Harry F. Rosenthal, "U.S. Devotes Millions to PR Experts," *Washington Post*, 30 May 1983, A13.
3. Nathaniel C. Nash, "Outlays for Public Relations," *New York Times*, 24 March 1986, D2.
4. *Forty-Fifth Report to the Congress.* Washington, DC: United States Information Agency, 30 June 1977.
5. David H. Buswell, "Trial by Press Release?" *NAM Reports*, 17 January 1972, 9–11.
6. "How the U.S. Air Force Communicates," *IABC Communication World*, May 1987: 14.
7. "Managing the News, White House Style," *U.S. News & World Report*, 4 September 1978, 17.
8. "White House Fights Back," *Washington Journalism Review* (June 1982): 38.
9. Kenneth T. Walsh and Dennis Mullin, " 'Spin Patrol' on the March," *U.S. News & World Report*, 1 December 1986: 17.
10. Robert U. Brown, "Role of Press Secretary," *Editor & Publisher*, 19 October 1974, 40.
11. I. William Hill, "Nessen Lists Ways He Has Improved Press Relations," *Editor & Publisher*, 10 April 1975, 40.
12. William Safire, "One of Our Own," *New York Times*, 19 September 1974, 43.
13. Michael J. Bennett, "The 'Imperial' Press Corps," *Public Relations Journal* (June 1982): 13.
14. Frederick J. Krebs, assistant general counsel of the Chamber of Commerce of the United States, in testimony before the Senate Government Affairs Committee, 14 February 1978.
15. Jules Witcover, "The Lobbyist's Act," *Washington Post*, 16 March 1975, 26.
16. Charles Mohr, "Business Using Grass-Roots Lobby," *New York Times*, 17 April 1978, A1.
17. Gordon Chaplin, "Lobbying the Underdog," *Washington Post Magazine*, 28 May 1978, 18.
18. William L. Dupuy, "The Political Action Committee and the Public Relations Practitioner," *Public Relations Quarterly* (Spring 1981): 14.
19. E. Bruce Peters, "You Can Be Wise in the Ways of Washington," *Enterprise* (December 1981/January 1982): 8–9.

SUGGESTED READINGS

Bernays, Edward L. "The PR Proficiency of the Reagan Administration." *Public Relations Quarterly* (Spring 1981): 20.

Brown, David H. "Government Public Affairs—Its Own Worst Enemy." *Public Relations Quarterly* (Spring 1981): 4–5.

Dupuy, William L. "The Political Action Committee and the Public Relations Practitioner." *Public Relations Quarterly* (Spring 1981): 14–16.

Gilbert, William H. *Public Relations in Local Government.* Washington, DC: International City Management Association (1140 Connecticut Ave., NW), 1975.

Goldstein, Stephanie. "Hi, I'm from Government, and I Want to Help You." *Public Relations Journal* (October 1981): 22–24.

Government/Press Connection: Press Officers and Their Offices. Washington, DC: Brookings Institution, 1984. Free.

Hess, Stephen. *The Government/Press Connection.* Washington, DC: Brookings Institution, 1984.

Hesse, Michael B. "Strategies of the Political Communication Process." *Public Relations Review* (Spring 1981): 32–47.

How to Find Business Intelligence in Washington. Washington, DC: Washington Researchers Publishing Co., 1988.

Hudson, Howard Penn. "Working with Federal Government." *Public Relations Quarterly* (Spring 1981): 6–13. Relations with the federal government are less hostile today than in previous years. There is more acceptance that one can work within the framework of the government.

Hudson, Howard Penn, and **Mary Elizabeth Hudson,** eds. *Hudson's Washington News Media Contact Directory.* (Available from 2626 Pennsylvania Ave., NW, Washington, DC 20037.) This directory lists the Washington correspondents for major newspapers (by state or origin), news bureaus, foreign newspapers and news services, radio and TV networks (both domestic and foreign), magazines, specialized newsletters and periodicals, freelance writers, and photographic services.

Lobsenz, Amelia. "Representing a Foreign Government." *Public Relations Journal* (August 1984): 21–24.

Manthorne, Joseph P. *Public Relations Tips in Small Business, the Arts, Education and Service Organizations.* Natick, MA: Manthorne Co. (48 Charles Street), 1987.

Miller, William H. "Business Gets Its Lobbying Act Together." *Industry Week,* 5 December 1977, 66–76.

Napolitan, Joseph. "100 Things I Have Learned in 30 Years as a Political Consultant." (Available from Public Affairs Analysts, 342 Madison Ave., New York, NY 10173.) Paper for the 19th annual conference of the International Association of Political Consultants, November 1986.

National Directory of State Agencies 1987 (5161 River Rd., Bethesda, MD 20816).

Reaburn, Gordon C. "How to Get Congress' Attention." *Public Relations Journal* (May 1981): 42.

Robinson, Gilbert A. "The New Look at CIA." *Public Relations Journal* (December 1981): 12–15.

Rogozinski, Jan. "The New Federalism and Public Relations." *Public Relations Journal* (March 1982): 12–14, 16. The shift of public policy decisions to the state and local levels will give new importance to local attitudes and will create new challenges for public relations.

Social Science Writer (10606 Mantz Rd., Silver Spring, MD 20903). Monthly.

Spitzer, Carlton E. "Should Government Audit Corporate Social Responsibility?" *Public Relations Review* (Summer 1981): 13–28.

Timberg, Robert. "The Hill Handlers." *Washington Journalism Review* (June 1985): 39–43.

Trent, Judith, and **Robert Friedenberg.** *Political Campaign Communication: Principles and Practices.* New York: Praeger, 1984.

NASA's *Challenger* Disaster

The National Aeronautics and Space Administration (NASA) had one of the largest public affairs budgets in government—almost $20 million. That included not only $5 million for public information but also $3.5 million for public services, such as handling more than two million visitors annually at nine space centers. Traditionally, NASA was regarded as one of the smartest, most buttoned-up public information efforts in government.

NASA's spotless information reputation lasted until January 28, 1986, when, in just 73 seconds, the agency—and the nation—suffered an unprecedented tragedy: the space shuttle *Challenger* exploded before a national television audience. Its crew of seven—which included America's first citizen-astronaut, New Hampshire high school teacher Christa McAuliffe—was killed.

Not only was the *Challenger* explosion a national tragedy, but NASA's public relations handling of the aftermath was also viewed as a disaster in its own right. For one thing, when TV screens clearly showed a fireball less than two minutes into the launch, NASA's mission control commentator coolly spoke of a "major malfunction" and "apparent explosion." In addition, although NASA's public relations emergency plan emphasized the importance of issuing a public statement within 20 minutes of an accident, noting that "rumors and speculation creating further problems will result if release is delayed," the agency waited almost five full hours to hold a news conference to explain what had happened. Even then, NASA's shuttle chief, who presided at the news conference, offered little in the way of new information to the hundreds of reporters who attended. What made the information vacuum even worse was the fact that millions of school children around the nation, intrigued by the presence in space of the first teacher-astronaut, were tuned in to the shuttle's flight.

In the days immediately following the disaster, NASA impounded all documents pertaining to the launch. Even the weather report and temperature readings in the hours before lift-off became classified information. The unwillingness of the space agency to release substantive information on the explosion forced reporters to rely on unofficial, unnamed sources. Some sources speculated that sabotage was involved. Others, who had been covering the space agency for some 20 years, speculated that a flame from the solid-fuel booster rocket was the likely trigger of the explosion. As a subsequent presidential commission revealed, this theory wasn't far from wrong.

NASA officials stuck to their position that no information would be released until the facts were known. As one NASA employee put it, their first reaction was to draw the wagons in a circle to fight off attacks on the shuttle program and the agency's operations. Predictably, the media objected violently to NASA's withholding of information, claiming that NASA had turned a significant loss of human life and technology into a public relations fiasco that would undermine the agency's credibility and prestige for years to come.

How prophetic that claim was! The next 2½ years for NASA were nightmarish. NASA's public relations performance in the *Challenger* disaster was picked apart from numerous perspectives. The media bridled at NASA's directive that ships returning *Chal-*

lenger debris wait offshore until dark so that video crews and photographers could not shoot them without special equipment. The media were also incensed when NASA sent empty ambulances to a nearby Air Force base hospital as a diversion when astronaut remains were returned.

Nor was the manufacturer of the solid-fuel rocket, Morton Thiokol, spared the media's wrath. Morton Thiokol scarcely mentioned its role in the tragedy in its 1986 annual report, and the media took note. Specifically cited in media reviews was Thiokol's failure to mention that its rockets were blamed for the accident or that the presidential commission investigating the tragedy concluded that Thiokol managers had overruled lower-ranking engineers who argued against the launching. Little wonder that it was front page news in June 1988 when Thiokol announced that it would not bid to build the next generation of rocket motors for U.S. manned space shuttles.

All in all, the *Challenger* disaster was as much a public relations tragedy as it was a human one. The public relations mishandling by those associated with the *Challenger* clearly resulted in long-term damage to America's space program.*

QUESTIONS

1. How soon after the *Challenger* disaster should NASA have held its news conference?
2. Assuming few of the facts were known at the time, what key messages should NASA officials have tried to convey at the news conference?
3. How would you assess NASA's policy of impounding all documents in the days following the disaster and not reporting information until all the facts were known?
4. Would the agency have been justified in stating probable causes of the disaster?

---

*For further information on the *Challenger* disaster, see: William J. Broad, "Thiokol Is Ending Booster Output on Space Shuttle," *New York Times*, 7 June 1988, 1; Matt Moffett and Laurie McGinley, "NASA, Once a Master of Publicity, Fumbles in Handling Shuttle Crisis," *Wall Street Journal*, 14 February 1986, 23; John Noble Wilford, "*Challenger*, Disclosure and an 8th Casualty for NASA," *New York Times*, 14 February 1986, B5; and "The Space Shuttle Tragedy," *Public Relations News*, 10 February 1986, 1.

17

The Community

President Calvin Coolidge once said, "The business of America is business." Today, some argue, "The business of business is America." In the early 1960s any business executive worth his salt would have stated immediately that a company's job is to make money for its owners—period. Indeed, Nobel Prize–winning economist Milton Friedman argued just that—that the corporation's responsibility is to produce profits and that the cost of corporate social goals amounts to a hidden tax on workers, customers, and shareholders.

Professor Friedman is in the minority. More and more, companies and other organizations acknowledge their responsibilities to the community: helping to maintain clean air and water, providing jobs for minorities, and, in general, enhancing everyone's quality of life. This concept of social responsibility has become widely accepted among enlightened organizations. For example, most companies today donate a percentage of their profits to nonprofit organizations—schools, hospitals, social welfare institutions, and the like. Employee volunteer programs, to assist local charitable groups, are also commonplace. In the 1990s social responsibility is no longer the exception but the rule among organizations.

This enlightened self-interest among executives has taken time to develop. The social and political upheavals of the 1960s forced organizations to confront the real or perceived injustices inflicted on certain social groups. The 1970s brought a partial resolution of those problems as government and the courts moved together to compensate for past inequities, outlaw current abuses, and prevent future injustice.

The 1970s also saw a more conciliatory response from business toward societal concerns. Indeed, business bore a major share of carrying out social programs because it was the principal repository of the nation's economic resources.[1]

In the 1980s the conflict between organizations and society became one of setting priorities—of deciding which community group deserved to be the beneficiary of corporate involvement. Most corporations today accept their role as an agent for social change. As the former Federated Department Stores president Howard Goldfeder put it:

> We continue to be mindful of the fact that we are citizens of the communities we serve, that we're neighbors, voters, taxpayers, that our children attend the same schools, drink the same water, drive the same streets and highways as our customers.[2]

Basically, every organization wants to foster positive reactions in the community and avoid negative responses. To achieve community acceptance and approval, most organizations, regardless of size, find the role of community relations a critical one. What positive community relations boils down to is convincing neighbors that the organization is a good citizen, cares about its community, and offers a good product or service at a fair price.

COMMUNITY COMPONENTS AND EXPECTATIONS

The community of an organization can vary widely, depending on the size and the nature of the business. The mom-and-pop grocery store may have a community of only a few city blocks; the community of a Buick assembly plant may be the city where the plant is located; and the community of a multinational corporation may embrace much of the world.

Who are the principal members of a firm's community? At the local level there are several discrete types of community members.

- **Community leaders** These are the shapers of opinion in the community: public officials, major employers, old-guard families, vocal advocates, and, occasionally, informal thought leaders. They can generally be reached through regular contact with influential local groups, face-to-face meetings, and special mailings.
- **Local press** It is important to get to know the local news media for effective community relations. However, attempting to coerce the media by purchasing or canceling advertising should not be contemplated. More practical is getting to know local journalists in an informal, low-pressure way.
- **Civic groups** There are many ways to reach local civic groups: regularly donating to local charities, using radio programs, forming a speakers' bureau to meet local organizations, filling emergency needs, or providing free movies for use by nonprofit groups.
- **Students, faculty, school officials** Educating young people and informing their mentors about the benefits of the firm is time well spent. Eventually, students will become customers and employees.
- **Municipal employees and local officials** Organizations should encourage employees to take active roles in city council, the police or fire commission, civil defense, and other municipal agencies. Concerned citizenship on the individual level translates directly into corporate community concern.

- **Local merchants, industrialists** A brief congratulatory letter to a business person recently honored or promoted is always welcomed. So, too, are visits to new merchants, industry officials, and new residents to acquaint them with the local community.
- **Women, homemakers** Increasingly, women are becoming as important a public as any in a community. Their rise in the labor force gives them greater knowledge and resources for family decisions. At the same time, the role of women in the work force has caused employers to reach out with childcare, pregnancy leaves, flexible hours, and so on. Retailers and service providers pay maximum attention to what women want, since they are responsible for a steadily expanding percentage of buying decisions.

Again, key constituencies vary from community to community, but everyone today seems organized. So much so, in fact, that when Phil Donahue devoted his 1988 network talk show to the problems of a New York City homeless woman named Joyce Brown, the woman arrived on the set with a vocal cadre of fellow homeless citizens. Every organization must learn which publics in its community are organized and capable of influencing others. Knowing which civic group is more influential with the alderman and which alderman is more influential with the mayor, for example, may be of crucial importance to the management of a local organization. Identifying and being able to tap influence networks is a valuable skill of the community relations specialist.

What the Community Expects

Communities expect from resident organizations such tangible commodities as wages, employment, and taxes. But communities have come to expect intangible contributions, too.

- **Appearance** The community hopes that the firm will contribute positively to life in the area. It expects facilities to be attractive, with care spent on the grounds and the plant (Figure 17–1). Increasingly, community neighbors object to plants that belch smoke and pollute water and air. Occasionally, neighbors organize to oppose the entering of factories, coal mines, oil wells, drug treatment centers, and other facilities suspected of being harmful to the community environment. Government, too, is acting more vigorously to punish offenders and to make sure that organizations comply with zoning, environmental, and safety regulations.
- **Participation** As a citizen of the community, an organization is expected to participate responsibly in community affairs, such as civic functions, park and recreational activities, education, welfare, and support of religious institutions. Organizations generally cannot shirk such participation by blaming headquarters' policy.

IF EVERYBODY LOVES NEW YORK SO MUCH, WHY IS IT SO DIRTY?

With all the hoopla about "I Love New York," everybody seems to have overlooked something—the garbage problem.

Maybe love is blind. Because New York does have a major litter problem. On Broadway. In front of our movie theaters. Our best restaurants. Your neighborhood. And unless we all do something about it fast, it'll reach awesome proportions.

So let's not put up with it anymore. When you see a piece of litter, it won't hurt to pick it up. If there's a pile of loose garbage in front of a restaurant, don't eat there. If your neighborhood store has a mess out front, tell them. It'll do you some good and it'll do the store some good. Who knows—New York may wind up not only a great place to visit, but an even greater place to live. For more information on how to clean up your city, call We Care About New York, Inc. at 619-3100.

NEW YORK LET'S CLEAN UP NEW YORK.

 **THE CHASE IS ON**

We Care About New York, Inc. and the City of New York

- **Stability** A business that fluctuates sharply in volume of business, number of employees, and taxes paid can adversely affect the community through its impact on municipal services, school loads, public facilities, and tax revenues. Communities prefer stable organizations that will grow with the area. Conversely, they want to keep out short-term operations that could create temporary boom conditions and leave ghost towns in their wake.

- **Pride** Any organization that can help put the community on the map simply by being there is usually a valuable addition. Communities want firms that are proud to be residents. For instance, to most Americans Battle Creek, Michigan, means cereal; Hershey, Pennsylvania, means chocolate; and Armonk, New York, means IBM. Organizations that help make the town usually become symbols of pride.

What the Organization Expects

Organizations expect to be provided with adequate municipal services, fair taxation, good living conditions for employees, a good labor supply, and a reasonable degree of support for the business and its products. When some of these requirements are missing, organizations may pick up and move to communities where such benefits are more readily available.

New York City, for example, experienced a substantial exodus of corporations during the 1970s, when firms fled to neighboring Connecticut and New Jersey as well as to the Sun Belt states of the Southeast and Southwest. These became commercial centers because of tax moratoriums, lower labor costs, and business incentives. New York state and city legislators responded to the challenge by working more closely with business residents in such areas as corporate taxation. By the 1980s not only had the corporate flight to the Sun Belt been arrested, but some firms decided that they agreed with the "I Love New York" ad campaign and returned to the state.

The issue for most urban areas, faced with steadily eroding tax bases, is to find a formula that meets the concerns of business corporations while accommodating the needs of other members of the community.

COMMUNITY RELATIONS OBJECTIVES

Research into community relations indicates that winning community support for an organization is no easy task. One 1977 study suggested that the goal of compatibility between organization and community "is quite unrealistic in many situations." Researchers found that conflict often exists between a community and an agency or corporation that is controlled elsewhere.[3] Additional community relations research has shown that a high level of public commu-

FIGURE 17–1 Every community wants its corporate citizens to care about its appearance. In this case, Chase Manhattan Bank let its customers know that it, too, cared about cleaning up its headquarters' city. (Courtesy of Chase Manhattan Bank)

Mary Stewart Hall

Dr. Mary Stewart Hall is vice president of corporate contributions at Weyerhaeuser Company, a large, diversified forest products and paper firm. She directs all aspects of corporate philanthropy, volunteerism, and employee campaigns. She is also a trustee of the Weyerhaeuser Company Foundation, and she lectures and writes extensively. Her latest book, *Getting Funded: The Complete Guide to Proposal Writing,* was published in 1988.

What should be the proper relationship between an organization and the community?
The proper relationship is an understanding of and commitment to enlightened and interdependent self-interest. Business cannot survive without healthy communities, and communities draw sustenance from profitable businesses.

What constitutes an organization's social responsibility?
In years past, firms were judged to be responsible if they produced a safe and good product at a reasonable price, made an appropriate return for stockholders or owners, and treated employees and suppliers fairly. We then entered a period when some level of corporate philanthropy and community investment was added to these expectations. We are now in an era when, because of the interdependence of business and communities, social leadership is a necessary component of corporate responsibility. This means assuming proactive involvement in everything from guaranteeing affirmative equal opportunity to assuring that we remain compet-

nication does not always lead to increased support for a newly introduced community relations program.

Such studies indicate something of the difficulty in achieving rapport with community neighbors. One device that is helpful is a written community relations policy. A community relations policy must clearly define the philosophy of management as it views its obligation to the community. Employees, in

itive through sound educational systems to finding ways to cope with significant environmental concerns.

How socially responsible are most organizations today?

Most businesses want to be socially responsible, but only a relative few have moved into the arena of social leadership. We will see this change as more and more firms realize they cannot rely on others to solve challenges whose solutions are essential to the future survival of both communities and corporations.

Why should a company give part of its profits to charity?

A strong case for corporate philanthropy can be made by focusing on the intersection of community needs and a firm's self-interest. Rather than being charity, philanthropy then becomes a form of investment. Some businesses may want to concentrate on improving communities in which they are located. This lowers future costs because it makes it possible to recruit employees without paying premium salaries. Another example is strengthening educational organizations to prepare future employees or to provide the basic technical and scientific knowledge necessary for product development. Each business needs to identify the opportunities that are most important to them and then concentrate on those where they can make a difference.

How ethical are most organizations today?

Most firms are very ethical, but some are not as ethical as they might be because their concept of ethics is limited. A truly ethical firm has carefully identified how its behavior impacts each stakeholder, including the community. It understands the necessity of going beyond just a written code of values and behaviors. Ethical behavior requires the ability to make ethical judgments in every decision.

Do big companies really listen to the ''little man'' today?

In my experience most firms really do want to listen to everyone. But practically, this is hardest for big firms because they have all of the same problems and constraints of any large bureaucracy. I have always been a bit surprised that it took some businesses as long as it did to realize that if they really want to listen, it has to start with the very first employees with whom people come into contact—the sales force, the telephone operators, the receptionists, the people who open and sort the mail, and so forth. Firms that are really dedicated to service for everyone now understand the need to pay attention to these fundamentals.

particular, must understand and exemplify their firm's community relations policy; to many in the community, the workers *are* the company.

Equally important, a clear set of community relations objectives must be enumerated so that employees have a clear idea of the organization's goals in promoting favorable public opinion within the community. Typical objectives might include the following:

1. To tell the community about the operations of the firm: its products, number of employees, size of payroll, tax payments, employee benefits, growth, and support of community projects
2. To correct misunderstanding, reply to criticism, and remove any disaffection that may exist among community neighbors
3. To gain the favorable opinion of the community, particularly during strikes and periods of labor unrest, by stating the company's position on issues involved
4. To inform employees and their families about company activities and developments so that they can tell their friends and neighbors about the company and favorably influence opinions of the organization
5. To inform people in local government about the firm's contributions to community welfare and to obtain support for legislation that will favorably affect the business climate in the community
6. To find out what residents think about the company, why they like or dislike the organization's policies and practices and how much they know of company policy, operations, and problems
7. To establish a personal relationship between management and community leaders by inviting leaders to visit the plant and offices, meet management, and see employees at work
8. To support health programs through contributions of both funds and employee services to local campaigns
9. To contribute to culture by providing funds for art exhibits, concerts, and drama festivals and by promoting attendance at such affairs (Figure 17–2)
10. To aid youth and adult education by cooperating with administrators and teachers in providing student vocational guidance, plant tours, speakers, films, and teaching aids and by giving financial support to higher education
11. To encourage sports and recreational activities by providing athletic fields, swimming pools, golf courses, and/or tennis courts for use by community residents and by sponsoring teams and sports events
12. To promote better local and county government by encouraging employees to run for public office or volunteer to serve on administrative boards; lending company executives to community agencies or to local government to give specialized advice and assistance on municipal problems; and making company facilities and equipment available to the community in times of emergency
13. To assist the economy of the community by purchasing operating supplies and equipment from local merchants and manufacturers whenever possible
14. To operate a profitable business to provide jobs and to pay competitive wages that increase the community's purchasing power and strengthen its economy
15. To cooperate with other local businesses in advancing economic and social welfare through joint community relations programs, financed and directed by the participating organizations

FIGURE 17–2   Typical of programs to win community support, Chase Manhattan Bank annually awards $600,000 to hundreds of small nonprofit organizations—from block associations to volunteer ambulance groups to neighborhood theatrical companies— through its New York City metropolitan area neighborhood grants program. (Courtesy of Chase Manhattan Bank)

All these community relations objectives not only make sense in terms of social responsibility, but also promote good business. Many organizations, from hospitals to department stores to corporate multinationals, have learned that an effective community relations program can translate into ample benefits in recruitment, tax treatment, and public support for the organization and its beliefs.

Emergence of Public Affairs

In recent years community relations has evolved into the more all-encompassing activity of public affairs. Although a precise definition of *public affairs* is elusive, this Conference Board definition is a good one.

A significant and substantial concern and involvement by individuals, business, labor, foundations, private institutions, and government with the social, economic, and political forces that singly or through interaction shape the environment within which the free enterprise system exists.

The emergence and expansion of public affairs activities is a response to public demands that organizations act responsibly in employee hiring and promotion, product safety and pricing, advertising, merchandising, and labeling.

Distinctions between public relations and public affairs are often blurry, and in some organizations the functions may overlap. Certain differences, however, are clear. The public affairs function usually operates through either the political or the social service process; practitioners tend to be knowledgeable about liberal arts or political science. In contrast, public relations usually operates through the communications process, with practitioners oriented toward journalism. As public relations counselor John W. Hill once said, "The difference between the two functions is marked by an exceedingly fine line. Actually, the two activities are brothers under the skin."

Even though no clear-cut distinction between the two functions has yet been established, the team concept of many large organizations helps guard against duplication of efforts. In smaller operations these two functions are often combined.

SERVING SPECIAL PUBLICS

One aspect of public affairs that has emerged with increasing importance in recent years has been that of serving so-called special publics, most particularly women, blacks, and Hispanics. A detailed analysis of these special publics goes beyond the scope of this text, but some understanding is important.

Women

Although women have always been a prime target for advertisers (especially for products related to the roles of homemaker and mother), it was not until the women's liberation movement of the 1960s and 1970s that women became a primary group for public relations. By the 1980s women had, indeed, come a long way. Today, women constitute an important source of discretionary income. Close to 70 percent of all American women between the ages of 18 and 64 work outside their homes. And that number is increasing. Three-quarters of all working women are employed full-time (30 or more hours per week). More than two-thirds of women with school-aged children also work.

Women's increased consciousness of sexual bias against them has greatly affected the public relations field. Women have demanded proper pay, opportunities for promotion, and equal rights in the workplace. Practitioners must be sensitive to the special problems in reaching women and must avoid sexist language in internal messages. Indeed, in public relations, banking, and many other fields, the work force is being increasingly dominated by women.

Making Amends at the Bank of Boston

Right up until February 1985, the Bank of Boston—New England's largest financial institution, with more than $20 billion in assets—had always managed to steer clear of negative publicity. The Bank of Boston's image in the community was austere, aloof, and generally above the fray.

In February 1985, though, the Bank of Boston was thrust into the news when it pleaded guilty to federal charges that it had failed to report to the Internal Revenue Service $1.2 billion in large cash transactions with other banks. Federal law requires banks to report such transactions to help federal investigators follow a paper trail to organized crime enterprises.

In the wake of the scandal, the bank characterized the problem as a "systems error," a statement quickly dismissed by Treasury Department officials. At his first press conference in 36 years with the bank, the Bank of Boston's disdainful chairman William Brown denied that federal investigators had linked the bank to organized crime—just as reports surfaced that New England's largest Mafia family enjoyed privileged client status at one of the bank's local branches.

In the midst of the resultant money-laundering probe, Brown fired off a letter to shareholders complaining of "inaccuracies and misunderstandings" in media coverage of the bank's problems but failed to mention that the bank was involved in an organized crime investigation. Brown also refused virtually all interviews to discuss the bank's problems. The bank's attitude in handling the crisis compelled one rival banker to suggest, "They just project an elitist, uncaring attitude." And for five months the Bank of Boston did little to alter this negative perception.

But then in June the bank launched an aggressive community relations campaign to win back public support. To address the problem of child kidnapping, the bank hired Boston Celtics basketball player M. L. Carr and initiated a free fingerprinting program for New England children (Figure A, p. 442). Carr, one of the most endearing athletes in New England, toured the state on behalf of the bank, to meet with children. Again using Carr as chief spokesman, the Bank of Boston initiated a Shoot Straight Basketball Clinic and M. L. Challenge: Stand Tall Against Drugs Program to educate local athletes about the dangers of drug abuse.

When the New England Patriots football team began winning at an amazing clip, Bank of Boston took out full-page ads hailing the Patriots' well-liked coach, Raymond Berry. The Patriots later made the 1986 Super Bowl, and the Bank of Boston ad generated hundreds of commendation letters.

M.L.Carr will be there to give your kid a hand.

Now, when you pick up a Kid Print™ home fingerprinting kit at Bank of Boston, you can receive M.L.Carr's autographed handprint and photo… from M.L. Carr himself, while he's at the bank.

Fingerprinting is still the most positive form of identification your child can have. And with Kid Print,™ it's safe, clean and easy to use. You get step-by-step instructions on how to fingerprint your children in the privacy of your own home. There's even a place for an up-to-date physical record of each child. You do it all at home, and you keep it at home. And we hope you never have to use it. But should anything happen, those prints could be as precious as life itself.

While supplies last, come in and ask for your Kid Print™ kit…and let M.L. Carr give your kids a hand. Remember, protecting your child begins at home.

Where: When:

BANK OF BOSTON

© 1985 The First National Bank of Boston

Finally, almost one year to the day that the cash transaction scandal had rocked the bank, the giant financial institution invited reporters to examine an elaborate new training program for employees, to warn them of the dangers of violating federal currency laws. The new program generated positive, region-wide publicity for the bank.

By March 1986 the Bank of Boston, predicted by some to have "an image problem likely to shadow it for years," enjoyed both a steadily escalating stock price and a reputation that appeared to be on the rise.*

QUESTIONS

1. How would you assess the Bank of Boston's immediate handling of the currency transaction problem?
2. Would you have delayed for several months before launching the community relations program?
3. Why do you think the Bank of Boston chose sports stars like M. L. Carr and Raymond Berry as the focus of its programs?
4. How visible do you think the Bank of Boston's chairman should have been in the community relations program?
5. Do you think the Bank of Boston will, as predicted, have "an image problem likely to shadow it for years"?

FIGURE A (Courtesy of Bank of Boston)

---

*For further information on the Bank of Boston situation, see Alex Beam, "Bank of Boston: A Public Relations Nightmare," *Business Week,* 4 March 1985, 38; Michael Isikoff, "Bank of Boston in Spotlight," *Washington Post,* 3 March 1985, F1, 4; Francine Kiefer, "Bank of Boston, Its Image Needs Laundering," *Christian Science Monitor,* 4 March 1985, 25–26; and David Wessel and Bob Davis, "Bank of Boston Faces Image Problem Likely to Linger for Years," *Wall Street Journal,* 7 March 1985, 1, 29.

Women are also critical in the areas of consumer relations and product publicity. They still do about 90 percent of family food shopping and are more and more responsible for the purchase of expensive items, such as automobiles and furniture. Working women have proven less brand-loyal and less easily persuaded than their nonworking counterparts. Although women have become more assimilated into the general work force, they still remain a special public that must be considered by public relations practitioners.

Blacks

Blacks, too, have become increasingly important in American society. Today, 25 of the nation's largest cities—including Chicago, Detroit, and Los Angeles—have a majority population of blacks, Hispanics, and Asians. Blacks represent almost 12 percent of the U.S. population and earned a total income of $172 billion in 1984. The number of black families with incomes in excess of $15,000 is seven times as great as it was in 1970. Indeed, as the 1984 *Black Book* summarized:

> A new breed of black American has emerged who is impacting upon decisions and implementing policies at every level of American life. They are more willing to contribute economically to our future in America, more apt to reject the status quo, more assertive and aggressive, ready to seize every opportunity available, and willing to create opportunities where none exist.[4]

Despite their continuing evolution in the white-dominated workplace, blacks can still be reached effectively through special media. Black-oriented magazines—such as *Ebony, Jet, Black Enterprise,* and *Essence*—are natural vehicles. So, too, are the black-oriented dailies of major cities, such as the *Amsterdam News* in New York City and the *Daily Defender* in Chicago. Such newspapers are controlled, for the most part, by active owners whose personal viewpoints dominate editorial policy. Black-oriented news media should definitely be included in the normal media relations functions of an organization. Already, there is a Black Public Relations Society, begun in 1982, with chapters in Chicago, Los Angeles, New York City, Philadelphia, and Washington, DC, and a 100-person membership.

Indeed, blacks today are a potent force in the marketplace. When the Adolph Coors Company became embroiled in lawsuits charging discrimination in hiring and was widely criticized for controversial remarks made by its chairman, the Colorado beer brewer was the object of a nationwide boycott by black and Hispanic groups in 1983. So determined was Coors to clean up its image that it bought boxing equipment for Hispanic youths in Denver, reproduced paintings of historical black figures, and hosted a reception for black Nobel Prize winners. Coors also initiated a wide-scale push to conduct business with minority law firms, banks, advertising agencies, and public relations firms. As a result, Coors beer gained popularity with blacks. And like Coors, other consumer product companies have increasingly beamed communications messages toward winning the support of black Americans (Figure 17–3).

For 52 years we at General Foods researched how kids react to color— the color of food, of packages, etc. Along the way, we made a more valuable discovery:

Kids are color blind

Racial prejudice is not genetically inborn.
It's taught. Once taught, it's almost impossible
to unteach. Corporately, General Foods has been fighting
the unfair social effects of racial prejudice for years:
with contributions to many national civil rights organizations.
And we practice equal opportunity employment. But prejudice
will die only as soon as we stop teaching it in the home,
and perpetuating it outside the home. For our
children always sense what we really mean
—so behind the slightest slur looms the
shadow of a most subtle,
a most insidious "contemporary"
slavery.

**GENERAL
FOODS**

FIGURE 17–3   As minorities have increased their clout as American consumers, large companies have turned to minority media for targeted promotion. Often this is accomplished through the services of minority-owned advertising and public relations agencies. (Courtesy of Uniworld Group and General Foods Corporation)

Hispanics

Hispanics, like blacks, make up a growing portion of the labor and buying markets in major American cities. There are 20 million Hispanics in the United States; their median family income is more than $16,000, as compared to $13,000 for U.S. blacks. More than 70 percent of all U.S. Hispanics reside in California, Texas, New York, and Florida. Radio stations and newspapers communicating in Spanish in these market areas, such as New York City's *El Diario* and *La Prensa*, are prominent voices in reaching Hispanics.

The diverse Hispanic market is composed of Mexicans, Cubans, Puerto Ricans, and persons from virtually every other Spanish-speaking country in the world. Since 75 percent of them communicate primarily in Spanish, smart organizations can readily identify and target this public—and increase their retail sales—simply by communicating in Spanish. One public relations agency, Fleishman-Hillard, has devoted an entire division to serving Hispanic needs.

Other ethnic groups—particularly Asians—have also increased their role in the American marketplace. And as blacks, Hispanics, and other minorities continue to play a more prominent role in American affairs, the field of public relations can be expected to increase its commitment to these special publics.

NONPROFIT PUBLIC RELATIONS

Many public relations professionals make their living in the nonprofit realm, working for hospitals, schools, civic organizations, social welfare agencies, and the like. Nonprofit organizations are in business to serve the community around them, and the practice of public relations is integral to the viability of such organizations.

Public relations practitioners at nonprofits engage in the same activities that their for-profit brethren do. They write speeches, deal with the press, communicate with employees, and counsel management. But one activity that nonprofit practitioners engage in that corporate practitioners do not is fund-raising. Nonprofit organizations depend on contributions to sustain them. And lately, such sustenance has been getting harder and harder to come by. A study by the Council for Financial Aid to Education found that in 1986 gifts to education and other causes by leading corporate donors declined for the first time in 16 years. Another study by the Conference Board showed a 2.5 percent decline in charitable giving among leading corporate donors, with half of the major contributors—those donating more than $10 million annually—cutting back up to 78 percent.[5] With the wave of mergers and takeovers that have upset the U.S. corporate balance, coupled with government cutbacks, the fundraising activities of nonprofits have become that much more important.

A knowledge of fund-raising techniques is especially important to beginning practitioners who, once hired in the public relations office of a college, hospital, charitable organization, or other nonprofit, are soon confronted with questions about how public relations can help raise money for the organization. Here are a dozen tried-and-true rules to follow in writing fund-raising letters.

1. Don't be afraid to ask for more money.
2. Develop a conversational writing style.
3. Establish a deadline.
4. Use compelling pictures.
5. Be an optimist, not necessarily a realist.
6. Know your audience before you write your letter.
7. Don't shout in a letter—avoid all-caps—but do underline for emphasis.
8. Advertise your postage—use a slogan on your postal indicia.
9. Get to the point—chop the warm-up.
10. Remember that women give the majority of gifts. Write to them.
11. Remember that men give larger gifts. Write to them, too.
12. Consider using a P.S. to take one final shot at the potential donor (Figure 17–4).

HEALTH AND HOSPITALS

Perhaps no industry in the nonprofit world has been more affected by the growth of public affairs in general and community relations in particular than the health and hospital field. The health and hospital industry is among the nation's largest employers: it is a nearly $400 billion enterprise consisting of about 7,000 institutions that serve hundreds of millions of people annually.

Hospitals today are in a state of unprecedented flux.

- Doctors are moving out on their own, creating competition for hospitals.
- New survival organizations with not-for-profit holding companies and profit-center units are proliferating.
- Huge chains, such as the Hospital Corporation of America and Humana, are causing great concern among hospital boards and administrators regarding takeovers, mergers, and competition.
- A highly competitive environment exists among once-coexisting hospitals.
- There has been an enormous decline in the number of beds filled and an increase in home health care.
- Emergency-care centers—so-called doc-in-the-box facilities—have sprung up to compete head-to-head with hospital emergency rooms.
- Costs for hospital services have skyrocketed, and hospitals have become centers of scientific progress.

One outgrowth of this dynamic environment has been an increasing concern among doctors, administrators, and trustees about positioning the hospital through public relations efforts.

A reality for hospital public relations practitioners today is the need to market the health services that people require rather than creating an artificial

COVENANT HOUSE

460 WEST 41 STREET, NEW YORK, N.Y. 10036
(212) 613-0300

Friday, 10:40 PM

Dear Friend,

A lady should never get this dirty, she said.

She stood there with a quiet, proud dignity. She was incomparably dirty -- her face and hands smeared, her clothes torn and soiled. The lady was 11.

My brothers are hungry, she said. The two little boys she hugged protectively were 8 and 9. They were three of the most beautiful children I'd ever seen.

Our parents beat us a lot, she said. We had to leave. The boys nodded mutely. We had to leave, one of them echoed. The children did not cry. I struggled to manage part of a smile. It didn't come off very well. The littlest kid looked back at me, with a quick, dubious grin. I gave him a surreptitious hug. I was all choked up.

I would like to take a shower, the lady said.

Eighteen years ago, I did not know that there were thousands of runaway, abused and abandoned children like these in this country.

I learned the hard way.

One night, in the winter of 1969, six teenage runaways knocked on the door of my apartment where I was living to serve the poor of New York's Lower East Side. Their junkie pimp had burned them out of the abandoned tenement they called "home." They asked if they could sleep on my floor. I took them in. I didn't have the guts not to.

Word of mouth traveled fast. (It does among street kids). The next day four more came. And kids have been coming ever since. It was these kids -- with no place else to go -- homeless, hungry, lacking skills, jobs, resources -- that compelled me to start Covenant House over eighteen years ago. Today our crisis centers help tens of thousands of kids from all over the country -- and save them from a life of degradation and horror on the streets.

Kids like the eleven-year-old lady and her very brave little brothers. They were easy to help: to place in a foster home where beautiful kids are wanted and loved, and made more beautiful precisely because they are wanted and loved.

But sadly, not all of the more than 20,000 kids who will come to Covenant House this year will be that lucky. These kids have very few options. Many of them will have fallen victim to the predators of the sex-for-sale and pornography "industry."

One of them put it to me very simply, and very directly:

"Bruce, I've got two choices: I can go with a john (a customer) and do what he wants, or I can rip somebody off and go to jail. I'm afraid to go to jail, Bruce. I can't get a job ... I've got no skills. I've got no place to live."

This child is 16. I do not know what I would have done if I were 16 and faced with that impossible choice.

They are good kids. You shouldn't think they're not good kids. Most of them are simply trying to survive. When you are on the street, and you are cold and hungry and scared and you have nothing to sell except yourself, you sell yourself.

There was a time when I was forced to turn these kids away simply because there was no room. I can't do that anymore. I know only too well what the street holds in store for a kid all alone. That is why we run Covenant House, and that is why we keep it open 24 hours a day, seven days a week -- to give these kids an alternative, an option that leads to life and not death.

These kids come to us in need, from every kind of family background. Boys and girls. White, Black and Hispanic. Children -- sometimes with children of their own. Innocent and streetwise. They are your kids and mine. Their number is increasing at a frightening rate.

We are here for them because of you. Almost all of the money that we need to help these kids comes from people like you.

A lady should never get that dirty. And a good kid should not be allowed to fall victim to the terror of street life. As more good kids come to us, we need more help. We need yours. Won't you send whatever contribution you can in the enclosed envelope today?

Thanks for my (no, our) kids.

Peace,

Father Bruce Ritter

P.S. I'm enclosing a brochure that will tell you a little bit more about the thousands of kids who come to us each year. I hope you will read it, and give our kids whatever help you can. Thanks!

FIGURE 17-4 Covenant House, a New York City nonprofit organization that houses runaway children, is famous for its poignant and pointed fund-raising letters. (Courtesy of Covenant House)

Candlelight, Chateaubriand, and the 10 O'clock Blood Pressure Reading

Falling occupancy rates and increased competition in the health care industry have prompted some hospitals to compete for patients who don't mind paying more for a nice place to recover.

- At Doctors Hospital of Jefferson in suburban New Orleans, patients can soak in hot tubs, get their hair or nails done in their rooms, and use free secretarial service around the clock.
- At Mount Sinai Medical Center in Minneapolis, patients are served appetizers of herring and pickled vegetables, then move on to Chateaubriand, and view movies on large-screen television sets.
- At Baylor University Medical Center in Texas, luxury suites come equipped with a desk, color television set, refrigerator, coffee maker, and fold-out couch for overnight guests.

Such comfort has its price. At Mount Sinai Hospital in Miami, a suite costs $560 a day, compared with $290 for a private room and $250 for a semiprivate room. At New York City's Presbyterian Hospital, suite patients pay as much as $350 more than those in semiprivate rooms.

Such fancy treatment for a privileged few has caused health care critics to complain that the money could be better spent on improving care for the poor or remodeling rooms used by a wider range of patients. Nonetheless, argue hospital trustees, in an age when hospitals are under increasing competitive pressure, creating a unique appeal for a hospital has become the name of the game.

demand. Community needs must be considered along with institutional needs to determine what hospital services will be offered, who will be served, and what effect this will have on pricing, referral, and access to health care.

Marketing also means educating hospital publics through such vehicles as open houses that demonstrate and explain services, sponsorship of health and medical events and seminars, and distribution of health-related information through newspaper columns, radio spot announcements, television interviews, and telephone hotlines. Indeed, the increase of medical-care costs has enhanced the importance of health education as a primary source of hospital-community interaction.

Community relations is a key aspect of hospital public relations. Practitioners must keep neighborhoods informed about such controversial programs as alcohol and drug treatment and must involve area residents as much as possible in hospital affairs. One critical function of hospital public relations practitioners is to seek out human interest stories for the media to demonstrate the hospital's concern for its community.

Competing with hospitals and also depending largely on public relations to communicate its role is the health maintenance organization (HMO), an association of physicians that emphasizes early detection of potential health concerns. Some predict that HMO enrollment will grow to more than 20 million people by 1990. The public relations challenge of HMOs includes persuading the public that regular health maintenance can detect and help prevent illness and that the HMO approach warrants their participation.

With hospital costs continuing to rise, medical practice is being placed under increased scrutiny, and corporations are taking over an increasing number of hospitals and health care facilities. The importance of hospital public relations promises to increase in the future, and health care public relations will be a growing repository for public relations professionals.

SOCIAL ACTIVISM HANGS ON

The activist movement, which began on college campuses in the late 1960s during the Vietnam War, has today evolved into a tamer movement, one that pressures corporations to deal responsibly with societal issues. Here's a sampling of activist groups that regularly tweak the American establishment.

- **Project on Corporate Responsibility** Formed in the late 1960s, the project's early efforts were directed primarily at General Motors. The project got credit for shaking up the automaker into appointing the first black to its board of directors, naming an air pollution expert as the firm's first vice president of environmental activities, and depositing $5 million in minority-owned banks.
- **Nader's Raiders** The several organizations spearheaded by consumer crusader Ralph Nader publish reports on abuses in a wide range of areas: air pollution, banking, birth control pills, nursing homes, government regulatory agencies, corporate democracy, and so on.
- **Council on Economic Priorities** The council provides information to investors wishing to base investment decisions on the social policy of corporations as well as on their financial performance.
- **National Affiliation of Concerned Business Students** This group, formed in the mid-1970s, is primarily concerned with social activism among business school students. It has backed such reform proposals as guaranteed annual income for all Americans, negative income tax, consumerism, and the application of private management techniques to the public sector.
- **National Council of Churches** Composed of more than 30 Christian denominations, this group lobbied aggressively in the 1970s and 1980s against corporate and university support of the apartheid policies of the South African government.

In addition to these larger, more organized groups, corporate shareholders concerned about a wide variety of miscellaneous issues regularly let organizations know how they feel. The emergence of so many social activists has caused the term *social responsibility* to become a permanent part of the corporate lexicon.

Once social activism drove organizations to become more responsible to their communities, but this is no longer the case today. Organizations need little prodding to give back something to the communities in which they reside. Community relations is practical today primarily because it makes good business sense. As former Chase Manhattan Bank chairman David Rockefeller put it:

> The business sector is undertaking increasingly to make genuine headway against major urban problems. More must be done, certainly. More to emphasize coordinated programs than isolated projects; more to strengthen the educational system to overcome the difficulties of upgrading performance; more to promote cooperative efforts among business, government, and the minority communities. But the heartening signs of progress to date suggest a willingness on the part of this vital triad to cooperate, fully recognizing that in striving for solutions they are living up not only to the best of American ideal, but also to the wisest of American self-interest.[6]

1. S. Prakash Sethi, "Business and Social Challenge," *Public Relations Journal* (September 1981): 31.
2. *How to Survive Happily in the Community and with the Press and the Government*, brochure, Federated Department Stores, 7 West 7th Street, Cincinnati, OH 45202, February 1981.
3. John V. Pavlik, *Public Relations: What Research Tells Us* (Newbury Park, CA: Sage Publications, 1987), 109.
4. "As Minorities Grow in Number and Influence, They Will Become Vital Publics," *PR Reporter* 28, no. 6, 11 February 1985, 1.
5. Fraser P. Seitel, "Corporate Philanthropy: Surviving in Hard Times?" *Leaders* (July 1987): 82.
6. David Rockefeller, "Corporate Responsibility: A Call for Joint Business Investment in Society," *Black Enterprise* (March 1972): 85.

NOTES

SUGGESTED READINGS

Basic Guide to Hospital Public Relations. Chicago: AHA (P.O. Box 99376).

Blake, Rich. "Reaching the Ninth Largest Market." *Public Relations Journal* (June 1985): 30–31. This article discusses the need for companies to more actively market to minorities.

Bonus, T. *Improving Internal Communications* (college). Washington, DC: Case (11 DuPont Circle).

Brown, Peter C. *The Complete Guide to Money Making Ventures for Nonprofit Organizations.* Washington, DC: Taft Group (5130 MacArthur Blvd., NW), 1987.

Community Relations Report (P.O. Box X, Bartlesville, OK 74005).

Cooper, Michael. "Crisis Public Relations." *Public Relations Journal* (November 1981): 52–57.

Corporate Giving Watch. Washington, DC: Taft Group (5130 MacArthur Blvd., NW).

Curtis, Lynn A. "The Power of Neighborhood Self-Help Programs." *Public Relations Review* (Spring 1982): 6–14.

Dannelley, Paul. *Fund Raising & Public Relations: A Critical Guide to Literature and Resources.* Norman: University of Oklahoma Press, 1986.

Effective Public Relations for Colleges. Washington, DC: Case (11 DuPont Circle).

Escobar, Frank. "Public Relations and the Minority Community." *Public Relations Journal* (July 1981): 27–28. Public relations programs have not kept pace with organizations' attempts to resolve their problems with minority communities.

Finn, David. *The Corporate Oligarchy.* New York: Simon & Schuster, 1969.

Grunig, James A., and **Daniel A. Ipes.** "The Anatomy of a Campaign Against Drunk Driving." *Public Relations Review* (Summer 1983): 37–52. This article explains how a campaign against drunk driving developed and how the campaign was supplemented by enforcement, engineering, and interpersonal support.

Harrison, Bruce. "Environmental Activism's Resurgence." *Public Relations Journal* (June 1982): 34–36. Despite a national commitment to environmental health, activists are stepping up their activities, including fund-raising and grass roots campaigns.

Hicks, Nancy J., and **David T. McKee.** "Integrated Strategies: A Successful Approach to Hospital Public Relations." *Public Relations Journal* (October 1981): 14–16.

Making Community Relations Pay Off. Washington, DC: Public Affairs Counsel, 1987.

Reich, Charles A. *The Greening of America.* New York: Random House, 1970.

Sethi, S. Prakash. "Business and Social Challenge." *Public Relations Journal* (September 1981): 30–31, 34. According to the author, business cannot participate effectively in the political process until it articulates who and what it is socially and what role its products and services play culturally.

Sutula, Dolores A. "Community Education as a Communications Tool." *Public Relations Journal* (February 1981): 27–28. This article gives an example of how one hospital tackled major community relations problems.

Three Mile Island

Prior to March 28, 1979, most of the nation's electric utilities had little use for public relations and preferred a low-key business style, out of the public spotlight and off the front page. Occasionally, a utility official would come forward to defend the industry, particularly the cause of nuclear power, in the face of adversary criticism. For example, in 1978, when a magazine in Harrisburg, Pennsylvania, wrote about a fictional disaster at a nearby nuclear power plant, chief executive officer Walter Creitz of the Metropolitan Edison Company, which operated the plant, publicly complained about the "blatantly distorted" writing. Later, when the York *Daily Record* ran a four-page series calling attention to "grave safety defects" at a plant, Creitz again spoke up, calling the series tantamount "to someone yelling fire in a crowded theater."

How ironic! On March 28, 1979, Creitz, Metropolitan Edison, and the Three Mile Island plant plunged into the scariest nuclear nightmare in the nation's history. Overnight, Three Mile Island and nuclear power became the most prominent issues in the country, with newspapers, magazines, and network broadcast media all focused on the events in southeastern Pennsylvania.

What happened was that an accident in the reactor's core caused the danger of a meltdown, which ultimately could have led to lethally radioactive gases escaping into the atmosphere. Initially, Metropolitan Edison spokespersons explained that a pump had broken down in the reactor and that this

malfunction was regarded by engineers as a normal aberration, no cause for panic. This reassurance sounded suspiciously akin to the script of *The China Syndrome*, a then-current Jane Fonda–Jack Lemmon movie about a nuclear accident.

Later, Metropolitan Edison spokespersons announced that a small amount of radioactive water had leaked onto the floor of the reactor's containment building. They said that they had declared an emergency and had notified proper state and local authorities. State police thereupon blocked off the bridges leading to the 600-acre island. The company then issued a statement:

> There have been no recordings of any significant levels of radiation and none are expected outside the plant.
> The reactor is being cooled according to the design by the reactor cooling system and should be cooled by the end of the day. There is no danger of a meltdown. There were no injuries either to plant workers or to the public.

Shortly after the company released this statement, Pennsylvania officials flew over the plant in a helicopter and detected a small release of radiation into the environment. How much radioactivity had leaked? When reporters persisted, Creitz said, "I'll be honest about it: I don't know."

By March 30 Harrisburg was inundated with 300 reporters from around the world. In the days to follow, Pennsylvania officials, as well as representatives of the National Nuclear Regulatory Commission, were calling the Three Mile Island plant failure "one of the most serious nuclear accidents to occur in the United States." And the industry became a national scapegoat. Nevertheless, Metropolitan Edison spokespersons still contended, "We didn't injure anybody. We didn't overexpose anybody. We didn't kill a single soul. The release of radioactivity off-site was minimal." Interestingly, when Senator Edward Kennedy requested Creitz to testify to the health subcommittee a few days after the accident, Creitz declined and sent a subordinate in his place.

The events at Three Mile Island did not reflect well on public relations practitioners. For example, the governor of Pennsylvania said that "the lack of credible information" was of major public concern.* Journalists on the scene agreed: "Sources and public-information people were hard to reach. When reached, they gave out conflicting stories. And it turned out they were all guessing."** Largely because of the events at Three Mile Island, the future of nuclear power in America appeared unclear. What *was* clear, however, was that the nuclear power industry had seriously damaged its credibility largely because of the confusion over Three Mile Island.

Perhaps the only bright spot in the otherwise dim immediate future of the industry was the boon Three Mile Island provided to public relations. A year after the accident, Metropolitan Edison officials invited reporters on a tour of the renovated Three Mile Island facility in anticipation of hearings on the possible restarting of the unit. In addition, the nuclear power industry itself launched "truth squads" to tour the country, frequently shadowing antinuclear celebrities like Jane Fonda and her husband, Tom Hayden, to debate on radio and television the virtues of nuclear power. Because of Three Mile Island, the industry did, indeed, come out of the closet. "Just because we're no longer thought of as the community good guys," said one utility communications director, "doesn't mean we're going to roll over and play dead." Said another, "It's either fight or give up the ship."

QUESTIONS

1. What mistakes did Metropolitan Edison make in its public relations approach at Three Mile Island?
2. Should the company have been better prepared for a potential accident at its plant?
3. Had you been Metropolitan Edison's public relations director, what role would you have suggested for Creitz? for yourself?
4. How would you suggest the industry set about picking up the pieces of its damaged credibility?

---

*Albert B. Crenshaw, "Thornburgh Faults Information Quality after A-Plant Incident," *Washington Post*, 22 August 1979, A9.

**Peter M. Sandman and Mary Paden, "At Three Mile Island," *Columbia Journalism Review* (July/August 1979): 47.

Consumers

18

American consumers today—more than at any other time in our history—are well aware of their rights. Consumers simply will not tolerate defective merchandise, misleading advertising, packaging and labeling abuses, quality and safety failures, inadequate service and repair, diffident corporate complaint-handlers, incomprehensible or inadequate guarantees and warranties, or slow settlements when products don't live up to advance claims.

In other words, doing business today means dealing with consumerism, and the movement is exerting increasing clout in the marketplace. Conditions that enabled Ralph Nader's Public Citizens to collect more than $1 million annually from consumers throughout the nation testify to the public's acceptance and support of the movement. Surveys corroborate that consumers believe in it. A typical research study found that most people supported the following consumerist efforts:[1]

1. Formation of a federal agency for consumer advocacy
2. Adoption of a periodic convention for government, business, and consumer representatives to construct long-term consumer policies
3. Establishment of consumer complaint bureaus in local communities
4. Creation of independent test centers to evaluate the safety of potentially dangerous products, to be run by either government agencies or private consumerist groups
5. Adoption of consumer affairs as a compulsory subject in high schools
6. Requirement of large companies to employ senior officers responsible for consumer affairs
7. Encouragement of large corporations to include on their boards of directors several public or consumer representatives

As the findings of this study suggest, many Americans believe that consumers need assistance in ensuring that products and services meet the highest standards of safety and quality.

GROWTH OF THE CONSUMER MOVEMENT

Although consumerism is considered to be a relatively recent concept, legislation to protect consumers first emerged in the United States in 1872, when Congress enacted the Criminal Fraud Statute to protect consumers against corporate abuses. In 1887 Congress established the Interstate Commerce Commission to curb freewheeling railroad tycoons.

However, the first real consumer movement came right after the turn of the century when journalistic muckrakers encouraged legislation to protect the consumer. Upton Sinclair's novel *The Jungle* revealed scandalous conditions in the meat-packing industry and helped establish federal meat inspection standards as Congress passed the Food and Drug Act and the Trade Commission Act. In the second wave of the movement, 1927 to 1938, consumers were safeguarded from the abuses of manufacturers, advertisers, and retailers of well-known brands of commercial products. During this time Congress passed the Food, Drug, and Cosmetic Act.

By the early 1960s the movement had become stronger and more unified. President John F. Kennedy, in fact, proposed that consumers have their own Bill of Rights, containing four basic principles.

1. **The right to safety**—to be protected against the marketing of goods hazardous to health or life
2. **The right to be informed**—to be protected against fraudulent, deceitful, or grossly misleading information, advertising, labeling, or other practices and to be given the facts needed to make an informed choice
3. **The right to choose**—to be assured access, whenever possible, to a variety of products and services at competitive prices
4. **The right to be heard**—To be assured that consumer interests will receive full and sympathetic consideration in the formulation of government policy

In 1962 the first National Consumer Advisory Panel was established to "bring to the president's attention matters relating to the consumer." Two years later President Lyndon Johnson appointed the first special assistant to the president for consumer affairs. In 1971 President Richard Nixon expanded the concept still further with the creation of the Office of Consumer Affairs, which was given broad responsibility to analyze and coordinate all federal activities in the field of consumer protection.

Federal Consumer Agencies

Today a massive government bureaucracy attempts to protect the consumer against abuse; upwards of 900 different programs, administered by more than 400 federal entities. Key agencies include the Justice Department, Federal Trade Commission, Food and Drug Administration, Consumer Product Safety Commission, and Office of Consumer Affairs.

■ **Justice Department** The Justice Department has had a consumer affairs section in the antitrust division since 1970. Its responsibilities include the enforcement of such consumer protection measures as the Truth in Lending Act and the Product Safety Act.

- **Federal Trade Commission** The FTC, perhaps more than any other agency, has vigorously enforced consumer protection. Its national advertising division covers television and radio advertising, with special emphasis on foods, drugs, and cosmetics. Its general litigation division covers areas not included by national advertising, such as magazine subscription agencies, door-to-door sales, and income tax services. Its consumer credit and special programs division deals with such areas as fair credit reporting and truth in packaging.
- **Food and Drug Administration** The FDA is responsible for protecting consumers from hazardous items: foods, drugs, cosmetics, therapeutic and radiological devices, food additives, and serums and vaccines.
- **Consumer Product Safety Commission** This bureau is responsible for overseeing product safety and standards.
- **Office of Consumer Affairs** This agency, the central point for consumer activities in the government, publishes literature to inform the public of recent developments in consumer affairs.

By the 1980s the public had become increasingly disenchanted with non-stop government growth. With the cost of government regulation estimated at more than $100 billion per year, presidents Carter and Reagan both espoused a platform of reducing the size of government bureaucracy.[2] Under Carter several industries, most notably the airlines, were deregulated. Ironically, with the regulatory gloves off, several airlines couldn't compete and went bankrupt. Under President Reagan, the FTC, in particular, toned down its investigative offensive into the affairs of business. Although some applauded this removal of government intervention in the market process, others objected that unregulated companies would run roughshod over the American consumer.

Regardless of whether more or less government protection is needed, corporations in the 1990s will continue to have to deal with those who regulate them. Companies from banks to public utilities to consumer product firms must communicate directly and frequently with the regulators in Washington. Often the best policy is to keep regulators advised of corporate developments and to work at winning their understanding, if not their support.

Consumer Activists

The consumerist movement has attracted a host of activists in recent years. Private testing organizations, which evaluate products and inform consumers about potential dangers, have proliferated. Perhaps the best known, Consumers Union, was formed in 1936 to test products across a wide spectrum of industries. It publishes the results in a monthly magazine, *Consumer Reports*, which reaches about 3.5 million readers. Often an evaluation in *Consumer Reports*, either pro or con, greatly affects how customers view particular products (see this chapter's case study). Consumers Union also produces books, a travel

Stephen Brobeck

Stephen Brobeck has served as executive director of the Consumer Federation of America (CFA) since 1980. A federation of 220 groups with more than 30 million members, CFA is the nation's largest consumer advocacy organization. Brobeck frequently testifies before congressional committees and is often interviewed by the national news media. He has co-authored two books, *The Bank Book* and *The Product Safety Book*.

Are consumers today more enlightened?
It's unclear whether consumers are smarter shoppers than they were 20 years ago. There is no question, however, that they're more aware of their interests as consumers and of the obligations of sellers.

Are companies today more enlightened?
Most companies not only are aware that consumers expect more from them but also have taken steps—ranging from improved product quality to effective complaint resolution—to meet these higher expectations.

newsletter, a column for 450 newspapers, and monthly features for network television. It has an annual budget of $70 million.

Consumers have also begun taking a more active role in their own affairs. The Consumer Federation of America was formed in 1967 to unify lobbying efforts for proconsumer legislation. Today, the federation consists of 200 national, state, and local consumer groups, labor unions, electric cooperatives, and other organizations with consumer interests.

Although companies often find activists' criticism annoying, the emergence of the consumer watchdog movement has generally been a positive development for consumers. Ralph Nader and others have forced organizations to consider, even more than usual, the downside of the products and services they offer. Smart companies have come to take seriously the pronouncements of consumer activists.

What is the general state of consumer relations in America?

Although consumer relations can vary widely from company to company and even from industry to industry, it is far more advanced than 20 years ago. Just one indication is that the Society of Consumer Affairs Professionals in Business, founded only in 1973, has 1,500 members.

How important today is the consumer movement?

Over the past decade the consumer movement has had successes and disappointments. But organizations such as Consumers Union, Center for Science in the Public Interest, CFA, and state public utility advocates are far stronger institutionally than they've ever been. And they continue to enjoy strong public support.

What are the responsibilities of an organization to the consumers of its products?

Most importantly, to provide good value in products—quality that is never less than satisfactory at a reasonable price. In addition, sellers must supply accurate, useful prepur-chase information and respond adequately to postpurchase requests for information or redress.

What's the worst situation you've ever run into as a consumer advocate?

While working with a self-help complaint resolution group in the 1970s, I encountered several dozen sellers who stole from their customers. Typically, these were home repair contractors, appliance repairmen, or mail order firms that received payments from customers yet supplied no product value, sometimes no product at all.

How should a company react to criticism of its products by consumers, advocates, or the media?

If the criticism is totally baseless, correct it with an objective, documented response. However, if the complaint is valid, acknowledge the problem and explain how it will be corrected. Research shows that resolving an individual complaint, or generic problem, can build company credibility and customer satisfaction.

Business Gets the Message

Obviously, few organizations can afford to shirk their responsibilities to consumers. Consumer relations divisions have sprung up, either as separate entities or as part of public relations departments. The title of vice president for consumer relations is showing up with more frequency on corporate organization charts.

In many companies consumer relations began strictly as a way to handle complaints, an area to which all unanswerable complaints were sent. Such units have frequently provided an alert to management. In recent years some companies have broadened the consumer relations function to encompass such activities as developing guidelines to evaluate services and products for management, developing consumer programs that meet consumer needs and in-

January 21, 1985

Mr. David Kemp
176 West 87th Street
New York, NY 10024

Dear Mr. Kemp:

Clearly we screwed up. Please accept our apologies.

Attached is a check for $168.00, which represents a full
refund.

Again, please accept our apologies.

Sincerely,

Kingsley G. Morse,
President

KGM:nj
Encl.

FIGURE 18–1 Here's a refreshingly straightforward response, from the chief executive officer no less, that is guaranteed to restore consumer confidence in Command Airways. (Courtesy of Command Airways)

crease sales, developing field-training programs, evaluating service approaches, and evaluating company effectiveness in demonstrating concern for customers.

Typical of such increased concern was the response of the Swingline company to consumer complaint letters about its Tot stapler; the company not only reconstituted the small stapler but also sent a new model free of charge to people who complained. The airlines, often criticized for poor service and deteriorating quality, also responded quickly to consumer complaints. In 1987, when Delta Air Lines was the subject of newspaper headlines about its safety failures, the company's president wrote each employee and every Delta Frequent Flyer participant, explaining how "puzzling and frustrating" the headlines were, as well as the events that had triggered them. He assured these important publics that "the safety and professionalism of our operation is something we take very seriously and never joke about."

In adopting a more active consumerist philosophy, many firms have found that consumer relations need not take a defensive posture. Instead, positive customer relations can be an effective marketing tool to enhance an organization's reputation as a concerned supplier of products that satisfy consumer desires (Figure 18–1).

Accordingly, the consumer affairs function has grown in stature. Today, there is a Society of Consumer Affairs Professionals in Business (SOCAP). In a poll of its members, SOCAP found that 80 percent regularly reported consumer trends to management, 70 percent developed consumer education materials on a regular basis, half met occasionally with consumer representatives, and nearly half consulted with government agencies on a periodic basis.

CONSUMERIST PHILOSOPHY

Most companies begin with the premise that customers, if they are to remain customers, deserve to be treated fairly and honestly. Historically, the companies that initiated their own activist consumer affairs units have been those to escape the wrath of outside activists. The Grand Union Company, second oldest food chain in the nation, is a good example. Grand Union's consumer affairs department began in 1970 to recommend policies and procedures to the company, monitor performance, and effect changes in the best interests of consumers. Stealing a page from JFK, Grand Union drew up its own Consumer Bill of Rights, which is illustrative of a forward-thinking, consumer-oriented company.[3]

1. **We believe that the consumer has a right to know.** Grand Union was among the first to introduce unit pricing, listing price-per-measure information on its packages. More than 5,000 Grand Union items were unit-priced, and the company explained how to use the new system in large window posters and placards in its stores.
2. **We believe that the consumer has the right to choose.** Grand Union made it policy to always give customers a choice between nationally advertised brands and its own brand.
3. **We believe that the consumer has the right to expect to find advertised specials in the store, in adequate quantity and variety.** Grand Union was among the first to offer rain checks, entitling customers to purchase out-of-stock specials at the same price even after the sale had concluded.

4. **We believe in the consumer's right to protection from unsafe products.** Grand Union was among the first to voluntarily switch to a system of open dating, allowing customers to determine the freshness of perishable and semiperishable products. The company also maintained its own test laboratory and sponsored in-store cleanliness programs.

5. **We believe in the consumer's right to be heard.** In addition to its complaint bureau, Grand Union provided customers with addressed, postage-paid letter forms, pens, and writing desks in its stores. The company promised that each letter received would be acted on and replied to promptly.

6. **We believe that the consumer has a right to be completely satisfied in any dealings with the company.** Grand Union advertising stressed nutritional education as well as straight product messages. Early in the fuel crisis of the mid-1970s, Grand Union converted its company fleet of almost 200 trucks in the New York City metropolitan area from gasoline to diesel power, thus reducing pollution. The company also stopped burning its trash and instead had it carted away or recycled. Even though the Grand Union Bill of Rights was among the first, the enlightened consumer relations policy it reflected was emulated by many other organizations in subsequent years (Figure 18–2).

Consumerist Objectives

Building sales is the primary consumer relations objective. A satisfied customer may return; an unhappy customer may not. Here are some typical goals.

- **Keeping old customers** Most sales are made to established customers. Consumer relations efforts should be expended to keep these customers happy. Pains should be taken to be responsive to customer complaints and reactions. For example, when devastating hurricanes rocked the Houston, Texas, area in 1984, the Houston-based Exxon Company wrote all its cardholders in the area, offering heartfelt sympathy and special credit card payment terms.

- **Attracting new customers** Every business must work constantly to develop new customers. In many industries the prices and quality of competing products are similar. Customers may base decisions among brands on how they have been treated.

- **Marketing new items or services** Customer relations techniques can influence the sale of new products. Thousands of new products flood the market each year, and the vast array of information about these products can confuse the consumer. In 1980 General Electric research revealed that consumers want personalized service and more information on new products but generally lack the time to investigate a product fully before buying. Consequently, General Electric established the GE Answer Center, a national toll-free, 24-hour service that informed consumers about new GE products

A Customer's Bill Of Rights

1. A customer has the right to courteous, considerate treatment at all times by all members of the seller organization.

2. A customer has the right to receive accurate information about features, applications, prices and availability of products or services which are offered for sale.

3. A customer has the right to have his or her expectations met that quality, price and delivery of the product or service will be as represented prior to having made the purchase.

4. A customer has the right to be served by skilled, knowledgeable personnel dedicated to representing his or her best interests with other departments in the seller organization.

5. A customer has the right to be promptly and fully informed when the seller's commitment cannot be met as originally stated.

6. A customer has the right to complain—and to receive prompt, fair handling and resolution of the complaint on its merits.

7. A customer has the right to expect extra effort by the seller's personnel in genuine emergencies, regardless of their cause.

8. A customer has the right to expect honesty and integrity at all levels in the seller organization, and assurance that all legal requirements have been met and rights observed.

9. A customer has the right to expect teamwork from the seller—and never to hear the expression: "That's not my department!"

10. A customer has the right to expect appreciation from everybody in the seller organization with which he or she does business, appreciation for business already given as well as for business to be given in the future . . . provided this Customer's Bill of Rights continues to be observed by the seller organization.

FIGURE 18–2 The Customer Service Institute lived up to its name with the publication of this manifesto, which summarizes what a customer ought to be entitled to. (Courtesy of the Customer Service Institute)

| BETWEEN THE LINES | ## Reconsidering the Recall Policy |

Under President Carter the National Highway Traffic Safety Administration (NHTSA) was the most aggressive of government agencies in exposing suspected car and tire safety problems. Frequently, the NHTSA would issue news releases warning consumers of possible defects in their cars and tires.

When President Reagan took office in 1980, the NHTSA became less aggressive, at least in publicizing its activities. As NHTSA administrator Raymond Peck put it, "The purpose of this agency is not to create publicity and not to excoriate or condemn the manufacturers."*

In August 1981 both the *Washington Post* and the *New York Times* revealed that Ford Motor Company and the Chrysler Corporation had stopped issuing public notices of car recalls for repair of safety defects, choosing instead to notify car owners directly. When questioned about this policy, Ford responded that it would no longer routinely issue press releases on recalls unless significant safety hazards were involved.

The Ford and Chrysler revelations immediately triggered outraged cries from consumer advocates, including Joan Claybrook, President Carter's NHTSA administrator, who said that in the past, manufacturers publicized recalls "because they knew that if they didn't the NHTSA would."

Shortly after the unannounced recall story hit the press, the auto companies reversed themselves. Said Ford, "To avoid any misunderstandings, the company will henceforth make public announcement of safety recalls of vehicles simultaneously with notifying owners."

---

*Peter Behr, "Recalls of Ford's Escort, Lynx Not Announced to the Public," *Washington Post,* 12 August 1981, 1–16.

---

and services. Building such company and product loyalty lies at the heart of a solid consumer relations effort.

- **Expediting complaint handling**   Few companies are free of complaints. Customers protest when appliances don't work, errors are made in billing, or deliveries aren't made on time. Many large firms have established response procedures. Often, a company ombudsman can salvage a customer relationship with a speedy and satisfactory answer to a complaint.
- **Reducing costs**   To most companies an educated consumer is the best consumer. Uninformed buyers cost a company time and money—when goods are returned, service calls are made, and instructions are misunderstood. Many firms have adopted programs to educate customers about many topics: what to look for in choosing fruits and vegetables, how to shop for durable goods, how to use credit wisely, how to conserve electricity. Figure

FIGURE 18–3 Typical of the desire of the nation's oil companies to present a proconsumer image, Shell Oil published a complete set of easy-to-read, illustrated manuals, teaching people how to care for their cars, their homes, and themselves. The free "answer books" were available in Shell stations around the country. (Courtesy of Shell Oil Co.)

18–3 shows booklets from Shell Oil that provided tips to consumers on a variety of topics. Most companies find no value in taking advantage of the customer. In the long run, if customers use products and services wisely and happily, they will return to buy again.

Consumer Programs

Some of the nation's most marketing-oriented firms are leaders in creating innovative consumer relations programs. Most apparently believe that by investing in consumer relations activities, they are safeguarding and ensuring future sales. Here are some of the more novel approaches to consumer relations.

1. The major automobile companies are all engaged actively in consumer relations, although each takes a different tack. The Ford Motor Company es-

tablished a Consumer Affairs Board to meet periodically and mediate unresolved product complaints, rendering binding judgments on the company and its dealers. Ford's initial board consisted of educators, dealers, and motor vehicle officials. At General Motors each car division offered specific consumer relations programs for dealers, introducing them to techniques for handling complaints and getting to the root of customer dissatisfaction. Chrysler Corporation held seminars for its dealers on handling customer complaints and conducted Women on Wheels workshops dealing with basic car repair and maintenance. Chrysler also introduced free, long-term warranties, suggesting confidence in the reliability of its product.

2. Food and pharmaceutical firms have taken the lead in listing product ingredients and nutritional information on their packages. Del Monte was one of the first food processors to list ingredients and nutritional information on its labels and to offer customers further product information on request. Eli Lilly offered a similar product labeling service for its drug items and went one step further by providing label information for immediate antidotal analysis in case of emergencies. Lilly's favorable consumerist record helped it weather an attack against its Darvon product in 1979 and another against its Oraflex product in 1982.

3. Other companies, from appliance sellers (Sears, General Electric, and Whirlpool) to banks (Citibank, Chemical Bank), have translated jargon into easily understandable English on their warranties and loan agreements. Gulf went so far as to publish a booklet called "The Art of Complaining," so its customers would know how and to whom to voice complaints and what to expect in response. All of these companies and many more like them have recognized that in consumer relations, as in many other activities in the public relations field, the best defense is a good offense.

Office of the Ombudsman

One classic research project for the White House Office on Consumer Affairs revealed the following:

- Only four of 100 dissatisfied customers will complain.
- For every complainer there are 24 with the same complaint who never say anything.
- About 13 percent of dissatisfied customers will tell 20 people about it.
- Almost 90 percent of dissatisfied customers don't repurchase from the offending company, compared to 54 to 70 percent who remain loyal when complaints are satisfactorily handled.[4]

At many companies the most immediate response to complaints has been the establishment of ombudsman offices. The term *ombudsman* originally described a government official—in Sweden and New Zealand, for example—appointed to investigate complaints against abuses of public officials. In most firms the office of the ombudsman investigates complaints made against the

A Day in the Life of the Ombudsman

So you want to handle consumer complaints? Here is a random selection of complaints received by the consumer affairs division of Chase Manhattan Bank. How would you have handled them?

1. A businessman, carrying an attaché case, made a deposit at a midtown branch before going to his office. Inadvertently, he left his case on the main banking floor. By the time he discovered that it was missing, the police bomb squad had smashed the innocent case and cordoned off the area. The owner asked the bank for a replacement. Would you have given it to him?
2. After making a deposit and leaving the bank, a woman reported that a huge icicle fell from the bank's roof and nearly hit her. She complained bitterly to consumer affairs. How would you appease her?
3. A young installment loan customer claimed that his car had been removed for reclamation because of delinquent loan payments. He claimed that he had paid the loan on time and objected to the illegal seizure. On checking, it was determined that several loan payments were, in fact, delinquent. Nevertheless, the car was returned, in a very damaged condition. The young man sought reimbursement for repairs. What would you recommend?
4. A customer complained that she had received no response to her numerous letters and memos concerning the hostile treatment accorded her at the local branch. After investigation, it was learned that the woman was a nuisance to branch officers yet kept a very healthy balance in her savings account. Further, all the correspondence to which she referred was written on the backs of checks she submitted in loan payments. How would you handle this problem?
5. The executor of an estate complained that his deceased client, who had been a bank customer, had received a card reading, "Best wishes in your new residence." What remedial action would you recommend?

company and its managers. Such an office generally provides a central location that customers can call to seek redress of grievances.

A five-year study of consumer complaint handling commissioned by the U.S. Office of Consumer Affairs suggested two important caveats for suppliers of consumer goods and services.

1. Consumers who do not complain when they are dissatisfied are often unhappy enough to switch product brands, companies, or both.
2. Since marketing costs are extremely high, it may be less expensive to resolve the complaints of existing customers than to win new ones.[5]

Glass in the Baby Food

For Gerber Products, a company that keeps a stash of teddy bears and cookies to welcome children to the lobby of its Michigan headquarters, the events of February 1986 were unsettling. Specifically, a jar of Gerber's baby food in Schenectady, New York, was reported to have glass in it. Tests at a Gerber laboratory showed that there was no glass in the jar turned in, and the supermarket reporting the incident said it had lost the fragment the customer had turned in and therefore couldn't prove the existence of the glass.

Nonetheless, the action triggered a wave of similar complaints about glass in Gerber baby food across the nation. And Gerber, rejecting the conciliatory posture adopted by other companies in crisis situations, decided to shed its cuddly image and get tough. "We feel strongly we're being had," the company's chief executive officer said. He noted that the Food and Drug Administration tested 40,000 unopened jars of Gerber baby food and concluded there was no public health problem.

The company refused to knuckle under to nationwide consumer groups that urged a recall. It denounced the Brooklyn, New York, district attorney's announcement that she was opening a criminal investigation of the matter. And when the governor of Maryland ordered Gerber's strained peaches off his state's supermarket shelves, the company filed a $150 million lawsuit against Maryland officials, asserting that the action had injured its 58-year reputation for integrity and quality.

Gerber officials argued that it was virtually impossible that the chunks of glass consumers were reporting could have come from its jars. They said each year Gerber produces about a billion jars of baby food under tight technical

---

Some companies—for example, General Motors, American Motors, Chrysler, ITT, and Whirlpool—have installed special telephone lines that allow consumers to call an ombudsman direct and toll-free. An ombudsman also monitors the difficulties customers are having with products. Often, the ombudsman can anticipate product or performance deficiencies. Skillful complaint-handling personnel—who are cheerful, positive, knowledgeable, and genuinely concerned with solving consumer problems—not only can keep customers happy, but also can prevent customer problems in the future.

THE FUTURE OF CONSUMERISM

Despite periodic legislative setbacks and shifting consumerist leadership, the cause of consumerism seems destined to remain strong. Although critics may

controls, using advanced glass-washing equipment and screens designed to fil-
ter out any particle larger than four-thousandths of an inch. The company
added that it kept X-ray machines in factories to check for breakage along the
fast-moving production line.

Gerber officials further noted that in special tests, where chunks of glass
were crammed into its jars, special jar washers successfully flushed out every
last fragment. Said Gerber's director of corporate communications, "We feel
this is a lynch mob," and added that the company's objective was "not to get
panicked." So, in the face of 227 complaints to the Food and Drug Administration about Gerber baby food jars, the nation's largest manufacturer of baby
food continued to hang tough.*

QUESTIONS

1. What do you think of Gerber's public relations strategy?
2. What other public relations options could the company consider?
3. If you were Gerber's public relations director, would you have assumed a
   higher profile?
4. Would you appear on television to defend the company?
5. Would you run 30-second commercials on television to talk about the problem? If so, would you mention the glass problem in the spots?

---

*For further information on the Gerber case, see James Barron, "Gerber Deals Gingerly with Tales
of Tainting," *New York Times,* 8 March 1986, 8; and John Bussey, "Gerber Takes Risky Stance as
Fears Spread About Glass in Baby Food," *Wall Street Journal,* 6 March 1986, 27.

---

argue that nobody uses unit pricing and nobody wears seat belts, the push for
product safety and quality will likely increase in the years ahead. The granddaddy of the consumer movement, Ralph Nader, has suggested that the movement is heading toward more "citizens' groups set up specifically to deal with
new, complicated issues, such as computers, genetic engineering, toxic wastes,
and multinational corporations."[6]

Congress and federal agencies today subject companies to more scrutiny
in their consumer policies. The phrase "Caveat emptor" ("Let the buyer beware") has been replaced by "Caveat venditor" ("Let the seller beware"). For
example, in 1960 there were fewer than 50,000 product liability cases, dealing
with faulty merchandise, warranties, or performance. By 1970 that number
had mushroomed to 500,000 cases. In the 1990s such cases will continue to
increase.

Public interest groups see an opportunity to set the agenda for the nation in the 1990s. However, according to one current activist and former Federal Trade Commission member, the goals for the 1990s don't relate especially to product quality and consumer rights. Among key goals are to "restore excellence and universal opportunity in education and housing, defend the environment, redeem civil rights and liberty, reverse the increase in poverty with a secure net for children and the elderly, and defuse nuclear terror."[7]

The tidal wave of activism can be met only by sophisticated planning on the part of business firms. Companies now audit their programs to assess how well corporate policies protect consumer rights.[8] In essence, the corporate consumerist challenge is to keep one step ahead of legislators and activists by introducing safety, performance, and service standards that show the company's good faith and public interest.

Occasionally, as in the tragic murders from cyanide-laced Tylenol (see the case study in chapter 23), a company cannot avoid the harsh glare of negative publicity about its products. However, in the long run the firm that lives by a proconsumer philosophy should prosper. Conversely, the firm that ignores the push of consumerism may experience difficulty, not only in growing but also in remaining viable.

NOTES

1. "The Consumer Confronts the Businessman," *Across the Board* (November 1977): 83.
2. Willard C. Butcher, president of Chase Manhattan Bank, address at Commonwealth Club of California, San Francisco, CA, 15 September 1978.
3. Grand Union Company, *Corporate Responsibility Report* (pamphlet) (Elmwood Park, NJ: Grand Union Company, 1973).
4. "How Much More Does It Cost to Create A New Customer Compared to Keeping An Existing One," *PR Reporter* (30 May 1988): 1.
5. Robert M. Cosenza and Jerry W. Wilson, "Managing Consumer Dissatisfaction: The Effective Use of the Corporate Written Response to Complaints," *Public Relations Quarterly* (Spring 1982): 17.
6. "Whither Consumerism?" *New York Times*, 23 November 1985, 17.
7. Michael Pertschuk, "The Role of Public Interest Groups in Setting the Public Agenda for the 90s," *Journal of Consumer Affairs* 21 (Winter 1987): 171.
8. Larry J. Rosenberg, John A. Czepiel, and Lester C. Cohen, "Consumer Affairs Audits, Evaluation, and Analysis," *California Management Review* (Spring 1977): 12, 13.

Communications Counselors. *Capital Contacts in Consumerism.* (Available from the author, 1701 K Street, NW, Washington, DC 20006.)

Cosenza, Robert M., and **Jerry W. Wilson.** "Managing Consumer Dissatisfaction: The Effective Use of the Corporate Written Response to Complaints." *Public Relations Quarterly* (Spring 1982): 17–19.

DeCourcy Hinds, Michael. "Seeking Profits in Consumer Complaints." *New York Times,* 26 March 1988. The author points out that competition necessitates keeping customers happy.

Dinsmore, William H. "Please Allow Eight Weeks . . . ." *Public Relations Quarterly* (Winter 1981–82): 28–29.

Harrington, Michael. *The Twilight of Capitalism.* New York: Simon & Schuster, 1976.

Kangun, Norman, Keith K. Cox, James Higginbotham, and **John Burton.** "Consumerism and Marketing Management." *Journal of Marketing* 39, no. 2 (April 1975): 3–10.

Morganstern, Stanley. *Legal Protection for the Consumer.* New York: Oceana, 1973.

Pertschuk, Michael. "The Role of Public Interest Groups in Setting the Public Agenda for the '90s." *Journal of Consumer Affairs* (Winter 1987): 171–182.

Rowat, Donald C. *The Ombudsman Plan: Essay on the Worldwide Spread of an Idea.* Toronto: McClelland & Stewart, 1973.

Rudd, Joel, and **Vicki L. Buttolph.** "Consumer Curriculum Materials: The First Content Analysis." *Journal of Consumer Affairs* (Summer 1987): 108–121. The researchers conclude that business-sponsored curriculum publications have more commercial and advertising content than do nonbusiness materials.

Silk, Leonard, and **David Vogel.** *Ethics and Profits.* New York: Simon & Schuster, 1976.

"Spending to Keep Customers Makes Sense Right on the Bottom Line. . ." *PR Reporter,* 30 May 1988.

Stein, Harry J. "The Muckraking Book in America, 1946–1973." *Journalism Quarterly* 52, no. 2 (Summer 1975): 297–303.

Ways, Max. "Business Needs a Different Political Stance." *Fortune* (September 1975): 97.

SUGGESTED
READINGS

A Tough Turn for the Suzuki Samurai

For the Suzuki Motor Company it was the public relations equivalent of a head-on collision. In June 1988 Consumers Union, publisher of *Consumer Reports,* announced that it had found the Samurai, Suzuki's fast-selling cross between a Jeep and an economy car, "not acceptable" (Figure A). Even more extraordinary, *Consumer Reports* said the vehicle was so unsafe that Suzuki should buy back every one of the 150,000 Samurais sold in the United States since its introduction in 1985.

The watchdog organization said that the Samurai repeatedly toppled after making sharp turns at about 40 miles per hour. Even though the tests involved slightly tighter turns than *Consumer Reports* used with other cars, Consumers Union's technical director said, "The car shouldn't roll over. It's as simple as that. The problem is inherent in its design. The only way to fix it is to make the vehicle longer, wider, and heavier." Consumers Union went on to say that owners should be given refunds.

The *Consumer Reports* announcement, made at an unusual New York City news conference that happened to coincide with the first day of congressional hearings on sport utility vehicles, drew immediate cries of "foul" from Suzuki officials. The company pointed out that for years, so-called consumer advocate groups had been petitioning the National Highway Traffic Safety Administration (NHTSA) for rollover standards for sport utility vehicles. The government had resisted such a move.

FIGURE A The Suzuki Samurai is classified as a sport utility vehicle. (Courtesy of Suzuki)

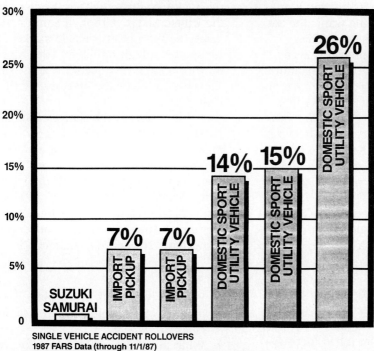

COMPARATIVE INCIDENCE OF ROLLOVER

SINGLE VEHICLE ACCIDENT ROLLOVERS
1987 FARS Data (through 11/1/87)
Compiled by National Highway Traffic Safety Administration

FIGURE B Despite *Consumer Reports'* allegations, the Suzuki Samurai fared better than most other sport utility vehicles and small trucks in terms of the incidence of rollovers, according to the government's 1987 Fatal Accident Reporting System data compiled by the National Highway Traffic Safety Administration.

Suzuki cited government statistics that the Samurai had a lower propensity to turn over than most other similar vehicles (Figure B). The company said *Consumer Reports* had put the Samurai through a second, more difficult maneuvering test after it had passed the test that *Consumer Reports* used with hundreds of other vehicles. In the revised test the course was changed by bringing obstacles closer together, which required sharper turns to avoid them. On the revised test course the Samurai flunked. Three rival utility vehicles passed both tests.

"Suzuki will not allow *Consumer Reports'* statements that result from distorted testing and irresponsible reporting to go unchallenged," said an American Suzuki vice president. "*Consumer Reports* has led the media and consumer to believe that the Samurai was subjected to the same tests done on all of the vehicles it has reviewed in the past 10 years. This is not true. The magazine changed its test for the first time in its history. It appears as though the magazine wants the Samurai to fail," the vice president added.

What made Suzuki's problems even worse was that the NHTSA said the Samurai had been involved in 44 reported rollover incidents, resulting in 16 deaths and 53 injuries. Earlier in the year the Center for Auto Safety, a consumer advocacy group in Washington, had petitioned the NHTSA to recall the Samurai. That petition was being reviewed at the time of the *Consumer Reports* announcement.

Despite all this bad news, Suzuki refused to roll over and play dead. On the contrary, the company responded aggressively, announcing that it would launch its own investigation into Consumers Union and its testing procedure. Suzuki threatened legal action against consumer organizations making "erroneous and inaccurate claims." American Suzuki also announced that it had increased its annual advertising budget by $1.5 million to counter the negative publicity. In its ads it said, "Testing on the Samurai before and since its introduction, combined with Federal government statistics, provides substantial proof that the Samurai is a safe vehicle."

Other automobile observers tended to agree with Suzuki's rebuttal. Said the executive editor of *Car and Driver* magazine, "We thought it was an okay vehicle for what it was. We don't expect off-road vehicles to act like sports cars." To punctuate its argument, Suzuki released an earlier company video of several imported and domestic cars and trucks being rolled over by test drivers as "proof that any vehicle can be rolled over under certain conditions." The tests shown on the video were similar to those done by Consumers Union.

Indeed, it seemed curious that Consumers Union would take off after Suzuki, a relatively new company with just one product in the United States. Although Samurai dominated the sport utility vehicle market and the car sported a high profile on television and in movies, nonetheless Suzuki was the smallest Japanese car company operating in the United States.

The results of the charges and countercharges were inconclusive. Caught in the middle were 150,000 Samurai owners, destined to have difficulty selling or insuring their vehicles, not to mention driving them with confidence. They, beyond all others, could clearly see the gallows humor of the tag line of American Suzuki's advertising campaign: "Never a dull moment."*

QUESTIONS

1. What do you think of Suzuki's aggressive public relations campaign in response to *Consumer Reports*?
2. What other alternative campaigns could the company have launched?
3. Should the company sue Consumers Union?
4. Why did *Consumer Reports* attack Suzuki rather than a competitor like Ford or General Motors?

---

*For further information see Michael deCourcy Hinds, "How Consumers Union Puts Teeth into 'Let the Seller Beware,'" *New York Times*, 11 June 1988, 37; Doron P. Levin, "Test Change Draws Fire from Suzuki," *New York Times*, 10 June 1988, D14; Doron P. Levin, "Consumer Group Asks Recall of Suzuki Samurai as Unsafe," *New York Times*, 3 June 1988, A1; Stewart Troy, "Will Samurai Marketing Work for Suzuki?" *Business Week*, 27 June 1988, 33–34.

19

Investors

Financial relations—or investor relations, or just IR—has been a growth area in public relations since the 1960s. Financial relations generally blends the skills of finance and writing with knowledge of the media, marketing, and, more recently, government, because of its increased role in the capital markets.

Financial relations was born in the mid-1930s, shortly after the passage of the Securities Act of 1933 and the Securities Exchange Act of 1934, which attempted to protect the public from abuses in the issuance and sale of securities. Financial relations remained in relative obscurity, however, until the 1960s, when investors rushed to the stock market to strike their fortunes. Stock prices escalated, and IR enjoyed a heyday.

The euphoria was interrupted in the 1970s, as the investing public grew increasingly disenchanted with stocks. However, the raging bull market of the mid-1980s, prior to the "crash" of 1987, again sent stock prices soaring, and investor relations returned to favor as more individuals invested in shares of publicly owned corporations. In the 1990s the investor relations job will consist basically of three parts.[1]

1. **Compliance** This need results from the increased number of regulations and rule changes promulgated by a wide variety of government agencies, not the least of which is the Securities and Exchange Commission (SEC). IR practitioners must have a comprehensive knowledge of government regulations, particularly SEC reporting requirements.
2. **Institutional investor needs** IR practitioners must be able to satisfy the needs of the institutional investor—the banks, brokers, insurance companies, and mutual funds that oversee the investment of pension funds and other assets managed by institutions.
3. **Individual investor needs** The third element of the IR mix focuses on convincing individuals to invest their savings in common stocks, particularly the common stock the IR professional is marketing.

It's little wonder that chief executives pay good money for IR professionals. Recent salary surveys indicate that IR practitioners are generally paid in the upper range of all public relations salaries, with the better IR pros earning up to $150,000 a year.[2] Not surprisingly, the financial relations field has become a specialized one in which the inexperienced are at a definite disadvantage.

ESSENCE OF INVESTOR RELATIONS

The end of the 1980s was marked by a bustling period of mergers, leveraged buy outs, and other competition for investor capital, all of which stimulated a growing need among companies for people skilled at investor relations. What exactly is investor relations? Basically, IR is the effort to narrow the gap between the perception of a company and the reality; in other words, helping the firm's securities reach their "appropriate" market price. To do this, investor relations professionals must encourage stockholders to hold company shares and persuade Wall Street financial analysts, banks, and mutual funds to take an interest.

A company's stock price is its currency. Premium stock prices allow an organization to acquire others, whereas a low stock price encourages raids from competitors. If shares are fairly priced in relation to current or future expectations, the company has a better chance of raising money for future expansion. In any event, a strong shareholder base is necessary to support management's objectives.

A public company must communicate promptly and candidly any information, both good and bad, that may have an effect on its securities. Practitioners must see that shareholders receive such information fully, fairly, and quickly so that they can decide whether to buy, hold, or sell the company's securities. Chapter 22 expands on this concept.

The institutions and individuals who own the common stock of a company are, in effect, the owners of that corporation. The shareholders, in person or by proxy, elect the board of directors, which in turn selects the officers who run the company. So, in theory at least, shareholders (who own the company) influence the operations of that company. In practice, corporate officers manage companies with relative independence. Nevertheless, shareholders constitute a critical public for any firm.

Why do investors buy a company's shares? The first requisite must be performance. A company that fails to perform can't expect good communications to sell its stock. On the other hand, a thoughtfully planned and executed financial communications program may materially enhance the reputation and therefore the market popularity of a company that performs well.

Organizing the Program

The most effective way to reach the investing public—individuals as well as institutions—is through a systematic program of financial relations, ordinarily managed by an investor relations director. Frequently, programs are bolstered by the involvement of a financial relations counseling firm.

Since most public companies perpetually compete for equity capital, an organized investor relations program is essential. Investor relations has many audiences, including analysts who recommend the purchase and sale of securities, brokers, market makers who specialize in a stock, institutional and individual investors, the media, and even employees. All must receive direct communications but each has different needs.

The IR professional must be a good communicator and a good salesperson, knowledgeable in finance and accounting, conversant in the language of Wall Street, and outgoing. The rapidly changing practice of financial relations also means that the IR director must be up-to-date on recent SEC rulings (see appendix E*).[3]

SOURCES OF INVESTOR INFORMATION

Investors receive corporate information from securities analysts, public media, and corporate communications vehicles, such as annual and quarterly reports, fact books, and annual meetings.

Securities Analysts

Securities analysts greatly influence the buying habits of institutional investors and others. Today, analysts are asked to follow an increasing number of companies, with the average analyst keeping tabs on as many as 40 firms. Frequently analysts aren't able to evaluate a company that does not meet rigid criteria in terms of market value, capitalization, and trading volume. Additionally, many analysts today are young and inexperienced, further complicating the role of the practitioner. Nevertheless, in financial relations analysts are a key public and must be reached.

To reach analysts effectively, credible communications must play a major role. In that effort a firm's management should be accessible; otherwise, a corporate message will likely fall on deaf ears, no matter how good a company's earnings record is.[4] Good practitioners make sure that key analysts are heavily exposed to corporate management. In addition, analyst meetings, presentations, and field trips are most important. A luncheon appearance before the New York Society of Security Analysts, for example, can be a significant platform for reaching Wall Street. Company-sponsored meetings in secondary cities can also serve to broaden interest in a company. Finally, inviting analysts to tour plants, visit headquarters, and meet corporate management on the firm's own turf is another way to introduce and educate analysts about a company and its leadership.

---

*Each year Hill and Knowlton compiles an extensive list of corporate reporting requirements, which it publishes in the *Public Relations Journal*. The list included in Appendix E appeared in Robert W. Taft, "Order Out of Chaos," *Public Relations Journal* (April 1982): 25–37.

Barbara K. Massa

Barbara K. Massa is senior vice president of investor relations and corporate communications for First Union Corporation, one of the nation's fastest-growing bank holding companies. She was a commercial lender for 10 years with First Union National Bank before being drafted to head investor relations. Massa lectures extensively on investor relations and is director and past president of the Bank Investor Relations Association.

What is the essence of good investor relations?
The goal of any investor relations program is to link a company and the investment community in a way that generates a positive perception of the company and its securities. Good programs do this in an active way. They initiate communications with investors and potential investors. They offer information—such as management's goals and strategies—that helps investors form opinions about the company's future. And they provide information about the company in an ongoing way, because investors don't like surprises. It's important to be forthright with information—even bad news—to maintain credibility.

Can investor relations impact the price of a company's stock?
Yes. Stock prices are determined by people's expectations of growth, discounting any risk factor. A good investor relations program provides information that reduces the perceived risks of investors and potential investors. Effective investor relations programs can also influence the price of the company's stock simply by attracting the attention of the investment community. That attention can lead to a broader stock-ownership base, giving more liquidity to a stock and reducing the risk of price fluctuations.

How should an organization handle bad news?
An investor relations team that shares only good news is doing only half its job. Investors want a steady flow of information—good or bad. And it's better for the company if investors hear about any bad news from an

inside source, rather than from the rumor mill. A company can't build loyalty and credibility among its shareholders—and those are very important traits to cultivate—if the investment community believes the company is trying to hide information.

So, a corporation's investor relations team should try to make sure the investment community hears bad news from the corporation first. Investors don't like bad news, but they like uncertainty even less. If they think they know the worst, and they are told what steps management is taking to alleviate the situation, they can make informed decisions about their investments. Investor relations professionals should also make a point of learning about any rumors circulating about the company. Incorrect information can be corrected much more easily if it is detected early. And rumors about bad news can be much more dangerous than the news itself.

How important is the annual report?
It is the most important communications tool a company has for the investment community. It is what investment professionals turn to for basic information about a company. Even people outside the investment community—customers, employees, and suppliers, for instance—rely on annual reports for information about a company.

How important is the small shareholder?
Very important. The degree of importance depends on the particular company—its industry, geographic location, and historical ownership. In general, the individual shareholder is an effective counterbalance to insti-tutional investors. Studies show that a company with a large percentage of individual shareholders often has a more stable stock price than a company with a large percentage of institutional investors. And individual investors tend to be more supportive of the management team and more likely to ride out temporary slowdowns in earnings or other potentially negative situations.

What's the best way to defend oneself from a takeover attempt?
With strong performance. The happier the shareholders are about the way the company is performing, the less the chance of a takeover. If shareholders feel they are getting value from the corporation and increasing their returns in long-term value, the investor relations program has done all it can do to protect the company from a takeover attempt. The company needs the faith of all its constituents—suppliers, customers, and the investment community.

What distinguishes successful investor relations programs from unsuccessful ones?
Successful investor relations programs adhere to one idea: the shareholder is boss. Shareholders' inquiries warrant prompt responses, and their points of view should be considered every time a decision is made. That means getting to know investors and potential investors well. It means learning what their investment objectives are. And it means making sure they stay well informed by taking the initiative to communicate with them.

In the 1980s, surveys indicated that analysts are primarily interested in information that looks ahead.[5] They seek to learn every factor that might affect earnings—from management's long-range plans to prospects for the industry as a whole. They want presentations that go beyond shareholder documents. And, again, they want to see a management team that is forceful and committed to sound corporate growth.

Financial Press

The stock exchanges insist that material corporate announcements must be released by the fastest available means. Ordinarily, this means that such information as top management changes and dividend or earnings announcements must be disseminated by telephone, telegraph, or hand delivery to media outlets. Basically, companies are expected to release material information through the following channels:

1. **Major wire services**—Dow Jones & Company, Reuters Economic Service, Associated Press, or United Press International
2. **Major New York City newspapers**—one or more of the New York City newspapers of general circulation that publish financial news (the *New York Times* and the *Wall Street Journal*)
3. **Statistical services**—particularly Standard & Poor's Corporation and Moody's Investor Service, which keep complete records on all publicly held companies
4. **Private wire services**—services such as PR News Wire and Business Wire, which guarantee, for a fee, that corporate news is carried promptly and reaches newspaper newsrooms and brokerage offices

Achieving broad disclosure for a small company is not easy. A major corporation automatically attracts the attention of the financial community, but the smaller firm, in order to satisfy disclosure requirements, may have to use paid wire services and direct mailings to shareholders. For example, to make the Dow Jones wire, a firm's stock must be listed in the national or supplemental list of the *Wall Street Journal*. The burden of proof in conforming to disclosure requirements, however, rests squarely with the issuer, so a company must take appropriate measures to assure that SEC requirements for prompt disclosure are met.

Positive media stories about a company offer substantial benefits. Investment community professionals read the trade press avidly. Consequently, strategically placed articles discussing technological innovations or effective strategies may boost a company in the eyes of security analysts, stockbrokers, and institutional portfolio managers.

The latest wrinkle in communicating financial information is television. In addition to the recent phenomenon of videotaped annual meetings and annual reports, increased interest in financial matters has prompted an array of investor-related television programs. The nation's top financial show, "Wall

Street Week," reaches millions of viewers each week on the Public Broadcasting System (PBS). Its success influenced the development of another PBS financial program, "The Nightly Business Report," a broad-based, half-hour look at the financial news of the day. In 1982 the nation's first television network devoted to financial news was born, appropriately named the Financial News Network, to give cable viewers an around-the-clock look at everything from commodity prices to leading economic indicators to international news events with potential market impact. With the increased sophistication of narrowcasting—communicating signals to smaller, more targeted, more focused population segments—it is likely that television, particularly cable TV, will play a more significant role in financial news dissemination in the years ahead.

CORPORATE COMMUNICATIONS TOOLS

A company has numerous vehicles for financial communications at its disposal, including an annual report, quarterly reports, an annual meeting, and fact books.

The Annual Report

The annual report is a company's key financial communications tool. Many investor relations professionals swear by it. Others argue that the annual report is exaggerated in importance, contending that the ideal annual report might simply read:

> Dear Shareholder,
> We did well in 1988. Earnings and sales were up. Customers were happy and buying. Your dividend was increased. Thanks for purchasing our stock and not selling it.

Clearly, such brevity is not the trend. Each year annual reports increase from 10 to 40 percent in size and become more complex in nature as well.[6] In addition to providing more detailed data on their individual lines of business, financial structure, and foreign operations, companies also use the reports to promote their views on topics from social responsibility to government regulation. The overriding purpose of the report remains one of marketing, building image and providing product and financial data for analysts, customers, and investors.

In 1987, as a result of lengthy correspondence between the General Motors Corporation and the SEC, it was ruled that companies may reduce their traditional annual report to shareholders, so long as they include all the required disclosure information in an appendix to the proxy statement or in another formal investor document, the 10–K. In making its ruling, the SEC tacitly acknowledged that annual reports were becoming too complex, legalistic, and expensive. Immediately after the SEC's pronouncement, the McKesson Corporation of San Francisco introduced a summary annual report along the lines

YOU MAKE THE CALL

The Adelstein Letter

The following is the letter to shareholders in the current annual report of Adelstein, Inc., a national manufacturer of ball bearings.

Dear Friends:

All things considered, 1988 wasn't a bad year for your company.

Although earnings declined by 10 percent, sales nevertheless reached the $300 million mark last year. We experienced strong demand in most of our domestic markets. However, unexpected environmental difficulties in both our Brazilian and Argentine operations caused a downturn in earnings. Our cut in the dividend for the last quarter was a direct outgrowth of the problems in Brazil and Argentina.

We had great concern once again this year about the rate of domestic inflation in the United States. In order to continue to ensure that our shareholders will receive growth in earnings and dividends, inflation must be kept to a minimum. This is why we feel strongly that it is Adelstein's responsibility to speak out both at the federal and local levels about the evils of inflation. One way Adelstein acts to circumvent the dangers of inflation is through diversification around the world.

Our ball bearing operations in Central America and Canada experienced strong growth last year. Central American operations grew by 6 percent, and Canadian operations, although not growing in percentage terms, nevertheless continued to achieve good operating performance.

Our South American performance, on the other hand, was limited by the problems in Argentina and Brazil. In the year to come, we are confident about the near-term future of Adelstein, Inc. The uncertainty in the economy must be counteracted by strong management controls and rigorous enforcement of expense monitoring. Last year, in an increasingly expansionary inflationary period, Adelstein's expenses increased by 14 percent year to year. This year we plan to do even better.

Clearly, with our plans and strategies firmly in place, we expect Adelstein's operating and financial condition to continue to improve in the coming year.

Todd O. Adelstein
Chairperson of the Board

QUESTIONS

1. As an Adelstein stockholder, would you be pleased with this letter?
2. Did the letter leave out any areas?
3. Did it leave any questions unanswered?
4. From what you read in the letter, how would you assess Adelstein's prospects for improvement next year?

the SEC had suggested. Said McKesson's vice president for corporate relations, "We think we have a tighter, better written, good-looking report that's going to be a more effective communications device and provide users of the information with all, if not more, information than we have in the past."[7] Nonetheless, the summary annual report form was slow to catch on, particularly in the wake of the stock market plunge in October 1987. Most companies produced traditional, lengthy reports as a way to reassure investors that all was well.

Although the individual elements and the general tone of annual reports change gradually over the years and among firms, most reports include a company description, letter to shareholders, financial review, explanation and analysis, management/marketing/issues discussion, and graphics.

- **Company description** This should include the company name, its headquarters address, a description of its overall business, and a summary of its operations in both narrative and numerical form. Many firms begin their annual reports with a one-page, easily readable summary of financial highlights.
- **Letter to shareholders** This letter ordinarily incorporates a photo of the firm's chairperson and president. It covers these key areas: (1) an accounting of last year's achievements; (2) discussion of both the general and the industry environment in which the company operated over the past year and will operate in the future; (3) a discussion of strategies for growth, the general operating philosophy for the future, and new product and capital spending plans; and (4) general targets for increased earnings and returns.

  Optionally, the letter may cite management's major concerns either for the company or for the environment in which it operates. Most of all, the letter to shareholders must be written in simple, understandable language, be short on rhetorical flourishes, and be long on facts. For example, the following excerpt from the 1982 annual report of the Wisconsin Securities Company of Milwaukee includes perhaps the world's most candid letter to shareholders. President George M. Chester wrote:

  > It is surprising so few stockholders sold their Wisconsin Securities stock . . . .
  > In truth it was a difficult year . . . . But George Chester still has a job thanks to his many relatives.[8]

- **Financial review** In light of the SEC's increasing demands for corporate disclosure, many companies have expanded financial reviews to encompass the data historically included in other reports, such as the 10–K. Financial reviews generally include 5- or 10-year summaries of such items as sales, cost of goods, operating costs, operating margin, expenses, capital expenditures, income taxes, and net earnings and such salient shareholder information as price/earnings ratios, debt ratios, return on assets, and return on equity.

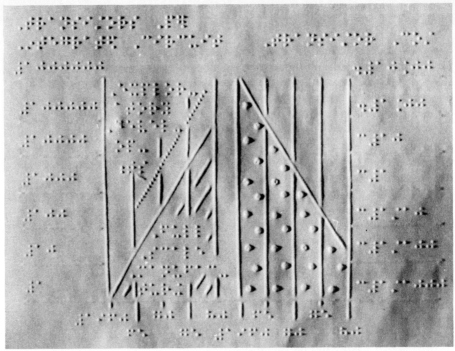

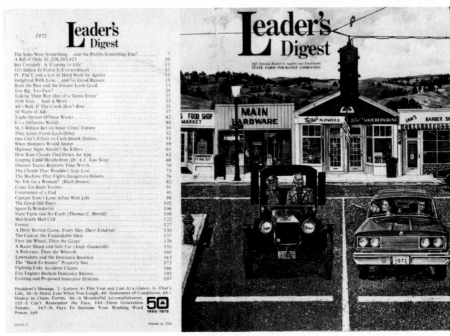

FIGURE 19–1 Annual reports come in all sizes and shapes. AT&T (top) produced a Braille version, complete with a talking-book phonograph record, which went to more than 1,000 blind AT&T investors and required three months to prepare. To celebrate its 50th anniversary, State Farm Insurance Company produced a replica of the familiar *Reader's Digest* as its annual report for agents and employees. (Courtesy of AT&T and State Farm Insurance)

- **Explanation and analysis** This complement to the financial review is a general discussion of the factors influencing the numbers in terms of earnings performance, operating income and expenses, asset growth, and other key financial indicators.

- **Management/marketing/issues discussion** The annual report's narrative section may be devoted to a general profile of key managers, an explanation of the company's markets or products, or essays detailing the company's view on emerging public issues. Many annual report watchers contend that such public issues analysis is even more important than the massive amount of financial data that annual reports include. As Richard A. Lewis, president of Corporate Annual Reports, has said, "Corporations are blunting one of the sharpest communications tools by having to cram them so full of financial data, most of which is incomprehensible to the average shareholder."[9]

- **Graphics** Photographs and charts are critical to the annual report. Most people have limited time to read, but a dynamic chart or striking photo may be enough to draw readers into a report's body. The high prices of freelance annual report photographers (some up to $2,500) give testimony to the importance companies place on good photos. In recent years criticism of the blandness, dullness, and sameness of annual reports has intensified. Some observers charge—often correctly—that annual reports are written by a committee, that they merely serve to bolster the corporate ego, and that few companies ask the most crucial question, Why are we doing all this?[10] What the annual report should do is tell an honest and informative story that serves the needs of its shareholder readers (Figure 19–1). Judging by the current crop of annual reports, this goal, alas, is still elusive.

Responding to pressures to liven up the annual report, companies such as International Paper and Emhart Corporation pioneered in the early 1980s the transfer of the annual report from paper to videotape (Figure 19–2). When surveys indicated that most investors devote an average of just 5 to 15 minutes to printed reports, both firms decided that electronic annual reports might be the answer.[11] Both companies tried to remain true to their printed annual report format by featuring the same elements in the video version, including the chairman in a starring role. Both firms advised stockholders in advance that the televised reports would be cablecast at a particular time on a particular channel, and both seemed pleased with the results. Emhart, in fact, loaned cassettes of the annual report program to interested stockholders. Summarized William F. May, former dean of the New York University Graduate School of Business, "Moving from the hard, cold printed page into the warmth of television serves a tremendous purpose in [educating] the shareholder—current and potential—on the nature of the company. It gives it flesh and blood."[12]

Quarterly Reports

Quarterly reports or interim reports keep shareholders abreast of corporate developments between annual reports. In general, the SEC recommends that the

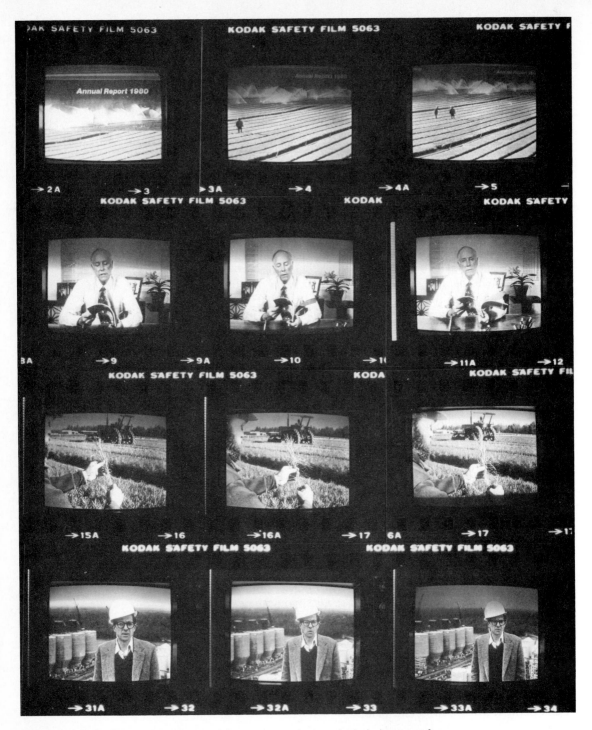

FIGURE 19–2 The International Paper videotape annual report included scenes from IP's seedling nursery, its chairman at his desk, and a report on construction progress at the company's containerboard complex. (Courtesy of International Paper Co.)

quarterly report include comparative financial data for the most recent quarter and year-to-date for the current and preceding year. Such items as net sales, costs and expenses, gross and net income, assets, liabilities, net worth, and earnings per share should always be included. So, too, should a letter to the shareholders, analyzing the important developments during the quarter. In recent years the SEC has been less rigorous in its quarterly report requirements, and some firms have cut back on expenses in producing such reports. McKesson Corporation, following publication of its summary annual report in 1987, went one step further by combining its quarterly report to shareholders with its employee magazine. The company reasoned that since many employees were also shareholders, combining the two publications could save money and be more all-encompassing.

Annual Meeting

Once a year the management of public companies is required to meet with the shareholders in a forum. Occasionally, this annual ''mating dance'' inspires fear and trepidation among managers unused to the glare of public questioning and skepticism. Indeed, several annual meeting gadflies travel from annual meeting to annual meeting, probing management on unpleasant, difficult, and, occasionally, embarrassing subjects. The existence of these gadflies has led some managers to view the meeting with a degree of loathing.

In one celebrated instance in 1982, General Motors (GM) chairman Roger Smith proposed having two annual meetings on the same day. The first meeting, said Smith, would be a short business meeting at which all of GM's top managers would be present but no shareholder questions would be entertained. The second meeting would be held miles away from the first and would feature a designated GM executive to answer shareholder questions. So great was the opposition to Smith's proposition that GM, several days before its meetings, announced that it would hold only one annual meeting after all.

A well-planned and well-executed annual meeting enables corporate managers to communicate effectively with investors (see appendix F for an annual meeting checklist). Here are a few hints for organizing a successful meeting.

- **Management speeches** Beginning with short, punchy speeches from the chairman, president, or both can establish the tone for the meeting. These speeches set an upbeat tempo for the rest of the meeting, emphasizing current developments and perhaps even announcing quarterly earnings or management changes.
- **Stockholder voting** Voting includes choosing directors and auditors and deciding on proposals presented by shareholders. Management's viewpoint on these proposals is spelled out in previously mailed proxy statements.
- **Question-and-answer sessions** The Q & A portion of the meeting is the reason that many stockholders attend. They like to see management in ac-

Handling the Antinuke Shareholders

Associated Nuclear, Inc. (ANI) expects a tough annual meeting because of well-publicized recent problems with nuclear facilities around the country. ANI owns several nuclear plants itself. E. K. Janeway, the dour ANI chairman, pounds the gavel, and the questioning begins.

Questioner: My name is Scotty Margolin, and I own 5 shares. Mr. Janeway, how do you justify the corporation's nuclear activities today?

Janeway: The simple answer is, we don't believe there is a nuclear problem in the country. Such talk is exaggerated, distorted, and generally untrue.

Questioner: My name is Rosie Kierstein, and I own 10 shares. How can you glibly dismiss a question that concerns the possibility of nuclear radiation causing a potential hazard to human life?

Janeway: Very easily—I don't buy the premise. Next question.

Questioner: My name is John Gilbert, and I represent 2,000 shares. How many lawsuits does the company face today, and how many are related to the problems that are being currently reported in the press?

Janeway: We are faced with 30 lawsuits today. Since each is being litigated, I can't comment further.

Questioner: My name is Dhump E. Schultz, 100 shares. How confident are we that the safety procedures we follow at our nuclear plants can avoid the problems that have been recently reported?

Janeway: Our safety requirements are strictly enforced by government regulators. If there's a problem, the government is just as much to blame as private companies.

Questioner: Mark Watson, 5 shares. Could problems like the ones being reported around the country happen at an ANI plant?

Janeway: That's a very hypothetical question. Anything could happen anywhere, but I doubt we'll have trouble.

Questioner: My name is Frank O'Connor, and I own 5 shares. I want to say that I, frankly, am appalled at you, Mr. Janeway, for dismissing these questions with such a blasé and uncaring attitude.

Janeway: Since that is not a question, you are out of order. Please sit down.

QUESTIONS

1. How would you rate Janeway's treatment of the stockholders? his control of the annual meeting?
2. How would you have suggested the questions be answered?
3. If you were an ANI shareholder, what would you think of your management?

tion, answering pertinent questions from the floor. How managers handle questions is thought to reflect their competence in running the company.

Management must be thoroughly briefed in advance about potential questions. Indeed, managers should plan answers before the meeting. Preparing for Q & A sessions may require monitoring other corporate annual meetings, preparing briefing books on potential questions, and even meeting in advance with potential questioners. Some managements, for example, find it worthwhile to lunch with selected gadflies to find out in advance what's on their minds.

Questions should be handled candidly, succinctly, and, whenever possible, in a light, nonthreatening manner. Most stockholders agree that the best meetings are those conducted in a friendly atmosphere. After all, stockholders own the business. A manager's light touch at an annual meeting may win over even the most skeptical stockholders.

The necessity of holding annual meetings has come under question in recent years. Many meetings are dominated by gadflies who care little about the company and lots about generating personal publicity. Attempts have even been made by some managements to propose rule changes that would require shareholder meetings only when a matter of substance is discussed. (Ironically, most of these proposals have been defeated because not enough shareholders return their proxies.) The Investment Company Act of 1940, which calls for regular annual meetings, probably should be reconsidered.

Nonetheless, for now the annual meeting is still a corporate custom. Like any other communications tool, it should be actively managed to promote goodwill and further the positive perception of the company among its shareholders.

Fact Books

Corporate fact books and fact sheets are statistical publications distributed primarily to securities analysts and institutional investors as supplements to the annual report. They unclutter the annual report and turn it into a broad, interpretive document to which the individual shareholder can easily relate.[13]

In general, fact books and fact sheets not only save money but often have significantly greater impact on a busy analyst searching for a quick view of a company's position and prospects. A visually arresting and substantive document, regardless of its size, can serve as an important shareholder relations vehicle (Figure 19–3).

Other Specialized Communications

Periodically, companies complement the traditional array of financial communications with specialized vehicles.

FIGURE 19–3 Fact books and fact sheets come in a variety of sizes and shapes. All, however, have the same objective—to give as clear and as accurate an organizational snapshot in as brief a time as possible.

- **Investors' guides** These mini–fact books give a general corporate description and list leading products, office locations, and financial highlights. Such guides introduce a company and frequently contain tear-out cards for acquiring additional corporate information.
- **Private television packages** In addition to video annual reports and meetings, videocassette packages showing presentations by corporate officers can be shipped directly to portfolio managers and analysts around the country at a comparatively low cost. Video can extend and expand an executive's time and deliver the corporate story to a larger, more targeted financial public over a wider geographic area.[14]
- **Dividend stuffers** Frequently practitioners include management messages in dividend mailings. Shareholders tend to take seriously mailings that include checks; thus, these mailings help greatly in delivering the firm's ideas.
- **Paid advertising space** Periodically, a company can reprint its income statement or balance sheet to encourage a broad audience to find out more about its securities.
- **Special meetings** Some companies have taken the unusual step of organizing special meetings of interested publics, largely to reinspire investors to own the company's stock. The most famous recent gathering of this type

was General Motors' extravagant and extraordinary exhibition in New York City in 1988 at a cost of $20 million. GM attracted 14,000 guests to the Waldorf-Astoria Hotel to show off present and future products. Although the event attracted its share of criticism, many believed that it was a sensible step to restabilize the company's declining image.

TAKEOVER CONTESTS

The hysteria on Wall Street in the late 1980s, caused by an unprecedented wave of outsider attempts to take over bedrock American companies, greatly influenced investor relations. General Electric, DuPont, and American Express were among the acquirers. RCA, Getty Oil, McGraw-Hill, Disney, and Conoco were among the targeted. One venerable company, Texaco, found itself on both sides of the fence, first as acquirer and later as "acquiree," sought by arch raider Carl Icahn. Such takeovers couldn't help leaving bad feelings among the affected. When the Bank of New York attempted to purchase the Irving Trust Company in 1988, Irving spent $40 million of stockholders' money defending itself before caving in. When the Campeau Corporation of Canada took over Federated Department Stores of Cincinnati in 1988, extensive bloodletting was the result. And when the aggressive British company, Beazer PLC, successfully completed its hostile takeover of Koppers Company of Pittsburgh, Beazer's advisor, Shearson Lehman Hutton, was lambasted for its questionable takeover tactics.

Normally, a substantial undervaluation of a company's stock price may precipitate an outsider's attempt to win control of the company in one of two ways.

- A tender offer for shares of stock, in which the raiding party offers shareholders cash, securities, or both
- A proxy contest, in which certain shareholders attempt to oust present management by obtaining sufficient shareholder votes to seize control of the board of directors

In most cases such an unfriendly takeover is inimical to current management, which fights back intensively to ward off the raider. More often than not, as Figure 19–4 graphically illustrates, the public battle gets grimy.

Often, it is the job of the IR professional to establish the preparatory steps to be taken prior to a takeover attempt, including an outline of the moves to resist the actual takeover. Overall strategy must be based on the maintenance of an excellent relationship with stockholders, particularly with those who hold a large amount of stock. Specific IR activities might include the following:

- Appoint a defense committee
- Prepare and update a large-stockholders' list
- Maintain a watch to determine whether company shares are being accumulated rapidly

Chock Full O'Nuts Shareholders

Don't be fooled by Finkelstein

Dear Shareholder:

It appears to me that Jerry Finkelstein has finally reached the end of his rope. I believe that the real issue in the proxy contest is our record at Chock Full O'Nuts v. Jerry Finkelstein's record at his companies. Jerry Finkelstein can't withstand that comparison so he tries to avoid the issue. Several days ago he stooped to a new low:

While I was in the hospital on November 8, under sedation and after a sleepless night, Jerry Finkelstein's lawyers took my deposition. (You should know that I got out of the hospital on November 17 and expect to resume my role in your Company's business shortly.) Out of the 70 pages of testimony I gave, Jerry Finkelstein and his associates selected the fragments they used in their last letter to you. The principal subject matter of that deposition was our Company's acquisition of our vital Butler Street coffee facility. I'd be glad to compare my testimony, given while in the hospital and ill, against Jerry Finkelstein's. As we pointed out to you, the New York State Supreme Court, in denying his try for a preliminary injunction, said:

"[Jerry Finkelstein] manifested a total lack of knowledge with respect to pertinent facts."

Jerry Finkelstein can't withstand that comparison, any more than he can withstand comparison of the record of his companies, Struthers Wells and ABC Industries, with our record at Chock Full.

Don't be fooled by Jerry Finkelstein's "smoke screen."

Compare Chock Full's record for you with the record of Jerry Finkelstein's companies.

Stock Prices	1980	Nov. 18, 1982
Chock Full	$ 3.12—$ 8.00	$14.00
Struthers Wells	$18.00—$28.50	$ 3.00
ABC Industries	$ 1.00—$ 2.00	$ 1.75

Earnings

Chock Full	Year ended July 31, 1982: Income—$5,365,000
Struthers Wells	Nine Months ended August 31, 1982: Loss—($3,746,000)
ABC Industries	Year ended June 30, 1982: Income—$51,000

Dividends

Chock Full	Increased annually since 1980
Struthers Wells	None since 1981
ABC Industries	None ever

Equity per share of common stock

Chock Full	Up approximately 200% from July 31, 1978, to July 31, 1982
Struthers Wells	Down 6% from November 30, 1978, to August 31, 1982
ABC Industries	Down over 75% from June 30, 1978, to June 30, 1982

Don't be fooled by Jerry Finkelstein's "nickel stock" ploy—compare Jerry Finkelstein's compensation ($579,427) with Chock Full's five highest paid officers combined.

Jerry Finkelstein and his associates talk about Chock Full management receiving what they call "nickel stock." They don't tell you that (1) these are restricted shares, designed as compensation tied to continued employment—a practice used by dozens of public companies, (2) the 165,000 shares they complain about represent compensation to a total of 25 Chock Full employees, over a period of three years, or (3) **Jerry Finkelstein got more from his companies last year than Chock Full's five highest paid employees combined, stock compensation included.**

Who is Jerry Finkelstein really out for?

I've told you about Jerry Finkelstein's two-pronged proposal to me for himself and his associates:

—either to have your Company buy them out at a fancy price—they wanted to use the Chock Full treasury to give them what I thought was an unconscionable profit.

—or let them buy me out (they didn't propose to buy your stock, just mine) and take over control of your Company. True, that could have given me a sweet deal. But it would have also given them control of Chock Full's rich balance sheet. And you would have been left holding the bag.

I've told you I turned him down on both counts.

How would you have made out under that proposal?

I ask you to look at the record. If you do, *I believe you will want to support your Company by voting your shares* **FOR** *your Company's Board of Directors.*

Thank you very much.

Sincerely,

John Black

William Black

IMPORTANT INSTRUCTIONS ON VOTING YOUR SHARES

We urge you to vote your shares **FOR** Chock Full O'Nuts Corporation Board of Directors. To assist you in voting your shares, Chock Full O'Nuts Corporation has made arrangements for you to send a Datagram by calling toll free anywhere within the United States.

TO VOTE YOUR SHARES
24 Hour Service
Within the Continental U.S.
800-325-6000

Simply tell the operator you wish to send a toll free Datagram to ID #7041, voting your shares FOR Chock Full O'Nuts Corporation Board of Directors.

Street Name Holders please indicate the name of your broker or bank, number of shares and your account number. If you have any questions or difficulty voting, please call collect:

Morrow & Co.
(212) 255-7400 (collect)

FIGURE 19–4 In late 1982 the Chock Full O' Nuts Company waged a furious takeover defense against the challenge of a dissident group of shareholders led by New York financier Jerry Finkelstein. This ad was typical of the bitterness of the battle, which was ultimately won by management. (Courtesy of Chock Full O' Nuts)

- Step up personal contacts with important stockholders in order to secure their loyalty
- Increase contacts with top-flight securities analysts and investors to improve chances of obtaining intelligence from them
- Prepare envelopes for emergency stockholder mailings
- Retain professional proxy solicitors
- Prepare basic letters and news release forms to be sent immediately to stockholders within hours of learning about the takeover attempt
- Prepare lists of major newspapers in which takeover defense advertisements might appear and prepare the ads themselves
- Organize a public relations campaign to enhance the image of the company both internally and externally

These are but a few of the actions that must be taken in anticipating and warding off a takeover attempt. The key, which many companies under attack fail to recognize until it's too late, is to focus communications strategy on the real worth of the company.[15] A value-oriented emphasis could help wake up the market to the company's true value, force the bidder to up the ante, generate a higher bid from another group, or even price all bidders out of the market. The no-holds-barred takeover phenomenon of the later 1980s put an increased premium on the ability of firms to practice open and honest communications with their shareholders.

CREDIBILITY

The real bottom line in financial communications is improving corporate credibility. Investors show support only when they believe in a firm and its management. Double-talk, fudging, and gobbledygook have no place in communicating with investors, who want to know all the news, the bad as well as the good, quickly and accurately. Because corporate candor is the only path to credibility and respect, these general guidelines should be followed in communicating with the investment community.

1. **Be aggressive.** Aggressive companies don't necessarily acquire the reputation of being stock promoters. Companies today must compete vigorously for visibility. Analysts and investors want to stay informed. Therefore, aggressive communications, truthfully delivered, are the best kind.
2. **Promote success.** The record ordinarily does not speak for itself. Companies must communicate to investors an intelligent evaluation of their securities, competitive position, and market outlook.
3. **Meet despite bad news.** Companies should meet with investors in bad and good times; investors need constant communication. If there are problems within a firm, investors want to know what management is doing to solve them. Most of all, investors hate surprises.
4. **Go to investors; don't make them come to you.** Investors expect to be courted. Firms need to broaden investment ownership. Therefore, a company should volunteer information rather than make investors pry it loose.

WHAT JUDGE CASSEB REALLY SAID

Judge Solomon Casseb, who presided over the Texaco-Pennzoil case, spoke April 2 before the trial lawyers section of the Los Angeles Bar.

There is no official transcript of his remarks. But Texaco's PR people have tried to peddle a Texaco tape and Texaco transcript to selected media. Several major papers turned it down. Others swallowed the bait whole.

What did the Judge actually say? Judith Bloom, vice chair of the trial lawyers section of the Los Angeles County Bar Association, who introduced him, said of the news reports: "The words are probably accurate but that sense was different…the sense was that Judge Casseb didn't feel he was wrong."

Robert Forgnone of Gibson, Dunn and Crutcher, the attorney who chaired the program, wrote us: "I can state that I had no doubts after hearing Judge Casseb's remarks that the Judge believed he would not be reversed on appeal." Judge Casseb himself has repeatedly said he expects to be affirmed on appeal.

So far, the information available on this story is solely what Texaco chose to furnish to selected media. In some cases, they tried to furnish it anonymously. Why? Texaco's management seems to approve of that tactic, judging by the following article.

SATURDAY
APRIL 12, 1986
FINAL
☆☆
San Antonio Light

How Texaco told of Casseb speech
Public relations firm wanted to be silent source on story

By STEVEN H. LEE
Staff Writer

"I don't exist," said the public relations man late Thursday, requesting anonymity as a caveat to what he was about to present to reporters of The Light.

He held in his hands a tape and transcript of a week-old speech delivered by retired District Judge Solomon Casseb Jr., the San Antonio jurist who upheld an $11.1 billion judgment against Texaco Inc. for illegally breaking a merger agreement between Pennzoil Co. and Getty Oil Co.

It was the largest court damage award in history.

Throughout the transcript of the speech, made before the trial lawyers section of the Los Angeles County Bar Association, were excerpts that the public relations executive had highlighted in yellow—statements that he felt either were in error or indicated Casseb had been in Pennzoil's corner.

It was Pennzoil, after all, which had won the suit, having claimed tortuous interference by Texaco in its tentative merger with Getty, after which Texaco snatched Getty for itself. And the public relations man now was working for Texaco—searching for any information that might work to aid Texaco as it appeals that judgment.

"I think this is a story," he said, pointing out a particular passage on page 30 of the transcript.

It had not been part of Casseb's speech, but was taken from an informal question-answer session that followed. The judge had been asked what he thought would happen to the case during appeal.

Although the case was tried in Texas, the issue of whether Pennzoil actually had a binding agreement with Getty was a matter of New York Law—since that was where the alleged agreement took place.

Based on the cases cited as precedent by attorneys in the trial, Casseb made clear that he was confident of his interpretation. But he also held out the possibility that he could have been in error, in the following passage the public relations executive deemed to be particularly damning:

"I feel that there is a good chance that perhaps I may have read the cases wrong, and not have applied it correctly. And as I've said, you know, this is my first experience in trying to analyze New York law after I did 46 years with Texas. So you can see, that can happen to any judge. I mean, none of us are infallible, and that can happen. But if they (the appellate courts) don't (believe I was in error), then I feel that they are going to uphold that verdict and that judgment."

An admission of possible error or a philosophical statement on the fallibility of judges? The public relations executive, as he reviewed the transcript with reporters, pressed the view that Casseb's statement was a significant admission.

However, editors of The Light came to a different conclusion, and decided that the judge's statements were more in the nature of self-deprecating musings.

The editors felt a more significant story was the public relations executive's attempt to use the confidentiality agreement, which is a vital part of the news-gathering relationship, simply to cloak Texaco's attempt to get negative stories about Casseb into print.

Consequently, when the Friday editions of the Houston Chronicle ran the story of Casseb's comments last week, and the wire services distributed the Chronicle piece, The Light chose not to print it.

The Los Angeles Times, which has provided significant coverage of the Texaco-Pennzoil dispute, likewise chose not to print a story about Casseb's comments.

A Times reporter Friday said the paper had sent a reporter to cover Casseb's speech last week, but that a story was not written. Also, she said the Times declined to run Friday's wire story, saying the paper had determined the Casseb quotes to be incidental.

On Friday, Texaco Vice Chairman James W. Kinnear, in a telephone interview, confirmed New York-based Hill & Knowlton Inc. as Texaco's public relations firm of more than 30 years. And he said he assumed that providing information anonymously was "general practice" for the firm.

However, Dr. Frank Walsh, an associate professor of journalism at the University of Texas at Austin, and an authority on public relations issues, disagreed that information of that nature should be presented anonymously. He said the source of the information in this case almost was as significant as what Casseb had to say.

"I think the reader deserves to know that he (the reporter) got the information from Texaco," Walsh said.

Ever since the landmark court decision last November, Texaco has been taking its case to the media. That effort apparently continued Thursday when the public relations executive met with reporters.

When asked why the information provided to The Light Thursday was done so under a cloak of secrecy, Kinnear replied, "I really don't know. As far as I was aware, that meeting (in Los Angeles) was public. And we have made no secret of the fact that Hill & Knowlton has represented us for the past 30 years."

Also, when asked to reply to Casseb's statements, Kinnear said, "I don't think I want to characterize the man said. He said what he said."

Casseb could not be reached for comment Friday.

Anthony Franco, president of the 13,200-member Public Relations Society of America, refused to speak specifically about Hill & Knowlton, or about Texaco. But, when asked, he offered his views on how he would handle a similar situation.

"I wouldn't feel comfortable doing that (anonymously)," Franco said. "I would feel more comfortable saying (to the media), 'I came across this information and thought you'd be interested.'

"Public relations people don't want necessarily to be quoted in front of their client. However, it's usually an either/or situation. A member of the (public relations) society should be prepared to identify himself publicly if he's called upon to do so."

—Reprinted in its entirety with permission of the San Antonio Light.

PENNZOIL COMPANY

FIGURE 19–5 Ooops. Sometimes even the best investor relations counselors make mistakes. (Courtesy of Pennzoil Co.)

5. **Enlist investors in the public policy area**. There are millions of stockholders in the United States today. The implications of even partially mobilizing this vast constituency are awesome. Historically, corporations have not sought out stockholder support for public policy viewpoints, which seems a tragic mistake. To accomplish meaningful legislative and regulatory reforms that favor free enterprise, all concerned parties, shareholders and management alike, must join the fight.

In general, then, the best financial relations policy is an active and open one. Investors need to be informed and want to learn more about the companies whose stock they hold. A firm and its investor relations professionals must work at corporate credibility *all* the time (Figure 19–5).

NOTES

1. Peter G. Osgood, "Investor Relations in the Eighties," *Public Relations Journal* (April 1981): 6.
2. "Higher Pay, Greater Angst Disclosed by Compensation Survey," *Corporate Communications Report* 16, no. 3 (August 1985): 1.
3. Anne F. Hamby, "Structuring a Financial Relations Program," *Public Relations Journal* (April 1978): 21.
4. Brian McBain, "What Motivates an Analyst to Follow a Company?" *Public Relations Journal* (April 1977): 12.
5. Gabriel Werba, "What Analysts Want to Hear," *Public Relations Journal* (April 1982): 19.
6. "The Annual Report 1978: Thick and Innovative," *Business Week*, 16 April 1979, 114.
7. Alan J. Wax, "Firms Adopting New Type of Annual Report," *Newsday*, 5 June 1987.
8. "George M. Chester Thanks Relatives," *Wall Street Journal*, 25 April 1983, 81.
9. Cited in Peg Dardenne, "Emerging Trends in Annual Reports," *Public Relations Journal* (September 1977): 8, 48.
10. Kenneth B. Platnick, "Why Are We Doing All This?" *Communicator's Journal* (November/December 1984): 38–39.
11. Jane Wollman, "Annual Reports Go Video," *Savvy* (August 1982): 21.
12. John F. Budd, Jr., and Bruce Pennington, "Financial Reporting by Television," *Public Relations Journal* (April 1982): 40.
13. "The Hard Facts About Facts Books," *Corporate Communications Report* 5, no. 3 (October 1973): 1–4.
14. Joseph H. Snyder, "Color Video—An Emerging Investor Relations Tool," address at Opinion Research Corporation's second national Financial and Investor Relations Executive Briefing, New York, NY, 12 December 1977.
15. Marvin A. Chatinover, "Communications During a Contested Takeover," *Sorg Says Newsletter* 1, no. 1 (Fall 1985): 1. (Available from Sorg Printing Company, 111 Eighth Avenue, New York, NY 10011.)

SUGGESTED READINGS

Andrew, Gordon G. "Corporate Factsheets." *Public Relations Journal* (April 1982): 43–45.

Berg, Stephen. "DOs & DON'Ts to Attract Investors." *Public Relations Journal* (April 1982): 22–24.

Budd, John F., Jr. "Financial Reporting by Television." *Public Relations Journal* (April 1982): 38–40.

Cannella, Vincent. "Integrated Disclosure: Betwixt and Between." *Public Relations Journal* (August 1981): 8–9.

Casper, P. *The Corporate Annual Report and Corporate Identity Planning Book.* Chicago: AR2 Alexander (212 W. Superior), 1987.

Corporate Annual Report Newsletter (407 S. Dearborn, Chicago, IL 60605).

"Dow Jones Ticket Tape Criteria." *Public Relations Journal* (April 1982): 49.

Dunk, William P., and G. A. Kraut. "Investor Relations: What It Isn't." *Public Relations Journal* (April 1982): 12–14.

Fischer, George, L., and C. R. Davenport. "Are You Telling the Story They Want to Hear?—What Investors Want to Hear." *Public Relations Journal* (April 1981): 14–18.

Fowler, Elizabeth. "The Lure of Investor Relations." *New York Times,* 18 November 1986. The writer sees IR as a growing career path. People are needed to help their employers by encouraging stockholders to hold on to shares and by persuading the financial industry and general public to take an interest in their firms.

Hogan, Bill. "The Asset Test." *Washington Journalism Review* (July 1985): 38–43.

Idea Bank for Annual Reports. New York: Corporate Shareholder Press (271 Madison Ave.), 1987.

Investment Newsletters (Larimi Communications Associates, 5 W. 37th St., New York, NY 10018).

Investor Relations Almanac/Resource Directory (Corporate Shareholder Press, 271 Madison Ave., New York, NY 10016).

"Investor Relations Checklist for the 1980s." *Public Relations Journal* (April 1982): 14.

Lewis, Richard A. *The Annual Report: A Tool to Achieve the CEO's Objectives.* New York: Corporate Annual Reports (112 E. 31st Street), 1987.

Neilson, Winthrop C., and Douglass M. Barnes. "Five Keys to Better PR." *Public Relations Journal* (April 1982): 16–17. Traditional skills, strategies, and programs must be complemented with new ones to meet today's capital market challenges.

Nolan, Joseph. "Protect Your Public Image." *Harvard Business Review* (March/April 1975): 135–142.

Osgood, Peter G. "Investor Relations in the '80s." *Public Relations Journal* (April 1981): 6–8.

Powell, Joanna. "Institutional Investor." *Washington Journalism Review* (July 1985): 44–46.

Roalman, A. R. *Investor Relations Handbook.* New York: Amacon, 1974.

The SEC, The Securities Market and Your Financial Communications. New York: Hill and Knowlton (420 Lexington Ave.).

Shaeffer, Bruce. *Doing Business in America: Guide for the Foreign Investor.* Homewood, IL: Dow Jones-Irwin, 1984.

Taft, Robert W. "Order Out of Chaos." *Public Relations Journal* (April 1982): 25–37.

Taft, Robert W., and Edward O. Raynolds. "Going Public." *Public Relations Journal* (April 1981): 19–24, 32.

Watt, Roop & Co. *Street Talk*. Cleveland, OH: Watt, Roop & Co. Watt, a public relations and marketing counseling firm, prepared this investor-relations planning guide for companies who go public.

Werba, Gabriel. "What Analysts Want to Hear." *Public Relations Journal* (April 1982): 18–20.

What Non–U.S. Companies Need to Know About Financial Disclosure in the United States. New York: Hill and Knowlton (420 Lexington Ave.).

Winter, Elmer L. *A Complete Guide to Preparing a Corporate Annual Report*. New York: Van Nostrand Reinhold Company, 1987.

Crowning Blow at Crown Zellerbach

The takeover mania of the mid-1980s perplexed many a corporate management. The smartest managers used investor relations professionals to organize programs to repel unfriendly takeovers. Such was the thinking in 1984 of William T. Creson, chairman of Crown Zellerbach Corporation. And when the news clattered over the telex at Crown's San Francisco headquarters on the foggy morning of December 12, 1984, Creson didn't like it, but he was ready for it. The tersely worded telex indicated that Sir James Goldsmith, a legendary takeover artist, wanted Crown Zellerbach.

In preparation for just such a moment, Creson had done the following:

- He had retained a high-priced takeover defense team, composed of an investment banker, an attorney, and an investor relations professional.
- The team had updated shareholder lists, all ready for instant access.
- The company had adopted ample shark-repellent rules to frustrate potential raiders. These included a staggered board of directors, a requirement for a two-thirds majority vote on bylaw changes, and a so-called poison pill that granted Crown shareholders the right to buy stock in any merged company at half the market price. The poison pill would go into effect if 100 percent of Crown's shares were acquired.

And so, early in 1985 the battle was joined. In early April Goldsmith offered to buy 70 percent of Crown's outstanding shares at $42.50 per share, almost $15 more than the price at which the stock was selling. It took Creson and company until April 25 to unveil a proposal that, according to analysts, would boost shareholder value to $60 per share, through the gradual liquidation of Crown's valuable timberlands under a partnership arrangement.

Goldsmith answered with a proxy fight to gain board seats and rescind the poison pill. Crown countered and won the proxy battle overwhelmingly.

Flush with its victory, Crown refused to compromise with Goldsmith, who suggested spinning off the timberlands to a separate corporation for tax reasons. When the company refused to compromise, Goldsmith continued buying shares. Crown managers then went on a nationwide tour to persuade shareholders to support their partnership plan. But when they returned to San Francisco, Goldsmith had already acquired 52 percent of Crown's stock.

And then he stopped—well short of the 100 percent ownership that would have activated the poison pill. As one analyst put it, Goldsmith "swallowed Crown and spat out the 'poison pill.'" Three days later Goldsmith became chairman, and the company was his.*

QUESTIONS

1. Why did Crown Zellerbach lose in its attempt to save the company despite its planning?
2. What was fundamentally wrong with Crown's strategy of constructing legal hurdles to block Goldsmith's run for the company?
3. If you were a Crown Zellerbach shareholder, would you have sold out to Goldsmith?
4. If you were Crown's investor relations manager, what strategy would you have recommended the company follow in response to the Goldsmith challenge?

*This case is based largely on Jonathan B. Levine, "Why Crown Zellerbach's Best-Laid Plans Came to Naught," *Business Week,* 23 December 1985, 75.

20

The International Community

In recent years the public relations activities of multinational corporations, religious organizations, the tourist industry, universities, and government have increasingly transcended national boundaries. Ours is an interdependent world, and in order for such activities as trade and commerce to prosper, the problems of communicating verbally and symbolically across national and cultural borders must be overcome. This, in essence, is the challenge of international public relations.

Historically, U.S. business firms were not particularly interested in sales abroad. Until recently, in fact, the U.S. market itself provided enough diversity to fully occupy most companies. However, with the incursion into the U.S. market of the Toyotas, Lufthansas, and Perriers of the world, U.S. companies have looked to expand their reach into overseas markets.

Those companies that have already ventured overseas find that international trade is not at all the same as domestic commerce. International trade is more complicated, conditions of competition abroad are often unfair, and barriers not found in domestic markets confront the potential overseas trader.[1] Indeed, Americans are often surprised to learn that they must sell, design, and package a product differently in Canton, China, from the way they do it in Canton, Ohio.

Public relations has been described as the Achilles heel of the multinational corporation. Despite the fact that a global program can offer optimum benefits to clients in planning, controlling, and assessing worldwide programs, only a few counseling firms are capable of executing projects on a worldwide basis. Consequently, most programs of multinational companies have been carried out in an ad hoc manner.[2]

In many countries—such as Japan, India, and France—the public relations function may take on great significance for an organization. If a company should, through lack of knowledge, run afoul of local customs in the host country, its operations in that country could be hindered. Steeped in customs and the do's and don'ts of doing business in a different country, a practitioner can help steer management past the shoals of trouble. Indeed, the practitioner may fill an important role in helping formulate management policy vis-à-vis the host nation.

One of the most significant international public relations forays was launched in Russia, of all places, in the late 1980s. The Soviet's new leader, Mikhail Gorbachev, initiated his *glasnost* and *perestroika* campaigns to improve the image of the USSR around the world. President Reagan's trip to Moscow in May of 1988 was a public relations master stroke for both countries. Indeed, some argued that improving the public relations image of the two countries was the primary purpose of the 1988 summit.

THE INTERNATIONAL PROFESSIONAL

In addition to possessing the more traditional public relations skills, the overseas practitioner must be a combination marketing tactician, diplomat, troubleshooter, and government relations expert. A skillful professional can help prevent a foreign government from legislating against a company, nationalizing its property, or ordering its removal.

To win acceptance of an idea, product, or person in any community abroad, it is essential to be thoroughly familiar with the customs, beliefs, and history of the area, current economic and political realities, newest fashions, and, of course, the language. At the same time the effective international representative must have a thorough and current knowledge of what is going on back home. A misinformed representative can communicate the wrong message locally because he hasn't been adequately briefed.

In effect, international public relations representatives are the communications link between the host country and the home office. It is essential, therefore, that they convey to the local constituency a fair and accurate portrayal of the organization's positions and, to the home office, a candid climate analysis of the local area (Figure 20–1).

ORGANIZING INTERNATIONAL PUBLIC RELATIONS

In the typical multinational company the international public relations manager usually reports to both the headquarters public relations director and the international department. This latter relationship is extremely important because the international practitioner must be intimately involved with line activities and decisions.

Practitioners are situated in strategic overseas locations. Some U.S. multinationals, for example, position representatives in the Caribbean to cover Latin America, in Hong Kong or Tokyo to cover Asia and the Far East, and in London or Paris to cover Great Britain and Western Europe. In recent years companies have expanded public relations coverage to the Mideast and Africa.

Counseling firms have also expanded their international capabilities. Large agencies (e.g., Hill and Knowlton, Burson-Marsteller, and Shandwick) represent three kinds of clients on the international level.

大通銀行
The Chase Manhattan Bank, N.A.
Chinatown Branch 華埠分行
185 Canal Street
New York, New York 10013
紐約市，堅尼路街，一百八十五號，紐約區號一〇〇一三

NEWS RELEASE

DEC. 7, 1984

中美旅游社提供大通銀行客戶之特別旅遊優待

為使大通銀行華埠分行客戶享有旅遊之特別優待，現在大通銀行華埠分行與中美旅游社已協議一項合作計劃。

凡是大通銀行華埠分行之客戶無論支票帳戶，儲蓄存款帳戶，貨幣市場存款帳戶或六個月以上之優利定期存款帳戶等保持有二千元之存款額一年以上者便可享有中美旅游社之各種旅遊折扣。

合乎上項條件之大通銀行客戶向中美旅遊社訂購機票時可享有百分之五之折扣優待，另外，中美旅游社舉辦之特別旅遊節目大通銀行的客戶還可享有百分之五至百分之十五之折扣優待。

凡在大通銀行申請貸款三千元以上業經批准並在廿四個月以上分期攤還者亦可享有中美旅游社同樣之折扣優待。大通銀行貸款手續方便，快捷，四十八小時內便可知曉。

大通銀行華埠分行曾經理說："大通銀行華埠分行與中美旅游社這次的合作也可增進華埠整個社區之繁榮，大通銀行之客戶不但可以得到高利率之存款收入，又可購到廉價旅遊之機票，真是一舉兩得。"

FIGURE 20–1 American companies with foreign-born customers now living in the United States occasionally attempt to win their hearts, minds, and business by speaking to them in their native tongues, as illustrated by this Chase Manhattan Bank Chinatown branch news release. (Courtesy of Chase Manhattan Bank)

Thomas H. Naylor

T homas H. Naylor is professor of economics at Duke University and managing director of the Naylor Group, an international management consulting firm specializing in strategic management. He has consulted with major corporations in the United States and abroad, including the Soviet Union and Eastern Europe. His articles have appeared in *Business Week,* the *New York Times,* the *Los Angeles Times,* and the *International Herald Tribune.* His most recent book is

The Gorbachev Strategy: Opening the Closed Society.

What is Mikhail Gorbachev's public relations strategy?

If the new chief executive of a major U.S. company such as AT&T or IBM wants to introduce fundamental changes, he must come to grips with the company's culture—the attitudes, values, and customs of the firm's managers and employees. This is precisely the situation in which Gorbachev finds himself as he attempts to de-Stalinize the Soviet Union and open the closed society. His strategy calls for a direct assault on the legacy of Joseph Stalin—the centrally planned economy, the self-serving Communist party, the inflexible government bureaucracy, and the police-state mentality.

If Gorbachev is to succeed, he must confront the culture of the largest risk-free society in the world, a society characterized by full employment, inexpensive housing, free education and medical care, low-cost transportation, the absence of bankruptcy, and cradle-to-grave socialism. But that is exactly what he is doing, and he is doing it very effectively with the aid of a well-honed domestic and international public relations strategy.

How does Gorbachev project his image?

What truly differentiates Gorbachev from previous Soviet leaders, as well as from most American politicians, is the nonconfrontational manner with which he deals with his domestic and foreign adversaries. Gorbachev attempts to co-opt them with a strategy based on mutual gain. He also makes effective use of surprise and suspense to keep his opponents guessing as to the nature of his next move.

How do the Soviets practice press relations today?
Not only do Gorbachev and other Soviet leaders now hold frequent press conferences, but the spokesman for the Soviet Foreign Ministry, Gennadi Gerasimov, makes press statements on an almost daily basis. All of this began at the first summit meeting of Gorbachev and President Reagan in November 1985 and has continued unabated since then. Soviet news commentator Vladimir Posner makes regular appearances before American television audiences, with his perfect English and smooth style. In addition, most of Gorbachev's speeches are published in English in the *Moscow News* and the *Soviet Weekly,* which are distributed in the United States each week. Some have appeared in full-page ads in the *New York Times,* paid for by the Soviet government. Others have been published in full-length books in the United States. Upon writing to the Soviet embassy in Washington for a copy of Gorbachev's Party Congress speech, I received a bound copy with a color photograph of Gorbachev on the cover.

How do the Soviets handle crisis communication?
Although the Soviets were initially subjected to widespread criticism for their two-day delay in reporting the April 26, 1986, nuclear tragedy at Chernobyl, they later displayed a high degree of openness in their explanation of the event to the Soviet people and to the rest of the world. This was in sharp contrast to their blustery response to the international outcry following the invasion of Afghanistan in 1979 and the shooting down of Korean Airlines flight 007 in 1983. Not only did they admit to human error in judgment and to responding too slowly to the crisis, but they openly sought out the advice of Western physicians and nuclear engineers to help them deal with the human and technical problems caused by the accident. Within a month of the accident, the Soviets began releasing an enormous amount of highly detailed information about the cause of the accident as well as its adverse effects. A Soviet diplomat appeared before a congressional committee in Washington and testified about the accident only a few days after it happened.

How did the Soviets respond to the shooting down of the Korean Airlines flight in 1983?
When the Soviets finally responded to the destruction of Korean Airlines flight 007 over their territory in 1983, secrecy, security, and control seemed to have taken precedence over more human concerns such as health, safety, and compassion. As a result, President Reagan was able to turn the disaster into a public relations bonanza for U.S. foreign policy.

What is the state of international public relations practice?
President Ronald Reagan, Pope John Paul II, and Soviet leader Mikhail S. Gorbachev are by far the most successful practitioners of international public relations in the world today.

1. American firms doing business internationally
2. Foreign companies competing for business in the United States
3. Foreign governments seeking to advance the interests of their nations in the United States

Additionally, several public relations networks have developed over the years, linking U.S. counterparts with counselors in other parts of the world to establish quality international standards and take the guesswork out of such relationships.[3]

The key attraction in such networks is the lure of commissioning an established and experienced local presence. Services range from small spot jobs in one country to coordinated worldwide campaigns. The network concept permits smaller agencies to compete with multioffice giants for certain types of business. Among the largest of these networks are the International Public Relations Group of Companies, Local Media, and the Pioneer Group.[4]

PUBLIC RELATIONS ABROAD

International public relations continues to experience healthy growth. The International Public Relations Association (IPRA), established in 1955 "to contribute to the growth and professionalism of public relations practice on a worldwide basis," has more than 800 members in 65 countries. Particularly remarkable was IPRA's 11th PR World Congress in Melbourne, Australia, in 1988. Public relations representatives from China, Hungary, and the Soviet Union were among the more than 700 delegates from 45 countries. During the conference Soviet journalism professor Yassen Zassoursky conceded that the greatest failure of the Chernobyl nuclear accident that claimed hundreds of Soviet lives "was the communications failure." He went on to suggest that "truth is the best way to solve problems." The IPRA Australian conference underscored the growth of public relations practice around the world.

Although the quality of such practice varies from country to country, in virtually every nation the practice of public relations has improved markedly in recent years. Canadian public relations is the rival of American practice in terms of its level of acceptance and management respect for the function and maturity of the profession. Most major Canadian firms have optimum-sized staffs, and the Canadian Public Relations Society, formed in 1948, is extremely active.

In Latin America the scene is more chaotic. In many countries *relaciones publicas* is used interchangeably with the functions of marketing and advertising. Mexican public relations, which began in the 1930s, is more highly developed than that of most other Latin American areas. And Mexican schools of higher learning often teach the subject. One problem in certain countries—such as Argentina, Chile, and Uruguay—is more repressive control of the media by the government.

Public relations has experienced tremendous growth in Great Britain. The largest United Kingdom–based public relations operation—and the world's largest independent agency—is the Shandwick Group, with more than $71 million in public relations fees and almost 700 staff members. No public relations firm in the world has been more aggressive than Shandwick in acquiring other counselors in other countries. London's ''big bang,'' which dropped all barriers to securities market competition in 1987, further enhanced British public relations practice. Although there is only one university, Sterling, that is teaching public relations to a degree level in the United Kingdom, public relations education in the 1990s is sure to expand in Great Britain.

In the rest of Europe the practice is not as well developed. The obvious complication is language—360 million people speaking 12 different languages that are accompanied by varying traditions, cultures, and economies. Public relations in France has developed well since the formation of the first public relations society in 1949, La Maison deVerre, or the Glass House. In West Germany the practice is mixed, wavering under the threat of representing all activities related to sales, stunts, publicity gimmicks, and show business tricks.[5] However, after World War II many German firms began to recognize the importance of organized public relations.

In Africa the field is also growing. The first All-Africa PR Conference was held at Nairobi, Kenya, in 1975. Traditionally, the practice in Africa has been closer to propaganda than to the more open U.S. approach. Obviously, the totalitarian and authoritarian regimes that dominate Africa influence communications.

Although public relations has been slower to develop in the Eastern Bloc and the Soviet Union, the emergence of President and General Secretary Gorbachev augurs well for the practice in the 1990s. At his 1988 summit with President Reagan, Gorbachev was a textbook example of public relations savvy. One afternoon he hosted a meeting of leading media figures. The next afternoon he met with 50 of the most important U.S. industrialists. At the home of the former U.S. ambassador to the Soviet Union, Gorbachev's wife, Raisa, then met for tea with six of the most powerful women in the United States. All these events and many others during the summit were perfectly choreographed as part of Gorbachev's thoughtful public relations strategy.

In much of Asia public relations has evolved slowly. Japan has the most highly developed practice, with more than 100 full-time firms. In Japan the field runs the gamut from press relations to employee communications to management counseling. Elsewhere in Asia, however, the practice is less active, although countries such as India, China, and even Bangladesh have recently experienced progress in the public relations area.

In China the practice is also spreading. In 1986 Hill and Knowlton opened the first Chinese public relations office in Beijing. Little more than a year later, the Chinese Public Relations Society was launched with about 400 practitioners and business people from 16 Chinese provinces, autonomous regions, and municipalities attending the inauguration ceremony. Although for

Toshiba Faces a Trade Ban

In 1987 the huge Toshiba Company of Japan faced the threat of a total ban of its $2.6 billion exports to the United States. The ban was in retaliation for the illegal sale by one of its subsidiaries, Toshiba Machine Company, of sophisticated equipment to the Soviets, which enabled them to make ultraquiet submarine propellers that are difficult for the United States to detect. The sale violated the international agreement of the Coordinating Committee on Export Controls and was condemned in the United States. A significant number of U.S. congressional representatives vowed to single out Toshiba for retribution in the U.S. trade bill being debated.

In the first few months after the sale, Toshiba ignored the situation, going about its business as usual. But when momentum started to build against the company, it adopted an aggressive public relations campaign.

■ First, it retained a Washington law firm under the Foreign Registration Act.
■ Second, it undertook a full-scale independent investigation of its own policies and practices, with the help of the international accounting firm of Price Waterhouse.
■ Third, it formulated a compliance program to make sure that no illegal sales would ever occur in the future.
■ Fourth, it agreed to the resignation of both the chairman and the president of the parent Toshiba Corporation.
■ Fifth, it sent a letter to U.S. congressional representatives, signed by the new Toshiba president, expressing regret and apologizing for the incident.

the Chinese, advertising and public relations are simply tools for product publicity, the popularity of the communications practice in China will mean increasing diversity and quality in the years ahead.

In Australia the 1988 IPRA conference in Melbourne was indicative of the rapid advance of the public relations practice. The Public Relations Institute of Australia is an extremely active organization, and the practice is widespread, particularly in Sydney and Melbourne, Australia's two commercial centers.

THE MEDIA OVERSEAS

In many foreign countries the term *public relations* is a euphemism for *press relations*. Working with the press abroad is not easy; there is often a language barrier, and in many countries the government controls the media. In some foreign nations company developments (sales, earnings, and management changes) are not considered news. In Canada, for example, most management change announcements would have to be paid for to make the newspapers.

- Sixth, it published an ad in U.S. newspapers and magazines bearing the headline "Toshiba Corporation Extends Its Deepest Regrets to the American People."
- Seventh, it enlisted grass roots support from Toshiba's U.S. employees, suppliers, distributors, customers, and others, such as the governors of two states where Toshiba plants already existed or were expected to be located.

The end result of all of this was that the only restrictions in the trade bill a year later were a three-year suspension of the offending subsidiary's products and a three-year ban on government contracts with Toshiba. Toshiba's tardy, yet targeted, public relations campaign had salvaged the bulk of its export business in its most important foreign market.*

QUESTIONS

1. What's your reaction to Toshiba's public relations strategy?
2. Why do you think Toshiba waited before launching its public relations offensive?
3. Why were Toshiba employees and suppliers enlisted in the campaign?
4. If you were the company's public relations counsel, what would your approach be in the United States from here on?

---

*For further information see Damon Darlin, "The Toshiba Case: Japanese Firm's Push to Sell to Soviets Led to Securities Breaches," *Wall Street Journal,* 4 August 1987, 1; and Thane Peterson, "No Tears for Toshiba," *Business Week,* 6 June 1988, 52.

Here are some other idiosyncrasies in dealing with the media in other nations.

- The time-honored U.S. press lunch to introduce products, management changes, or financial information is much less common overseas, where the company frequently meets the press after work at the close of the business day.
- Press conferences in countries such as West Germany, Switzerland, the Netherlands, Norway, and Sweden begin promptly on the appointed hour. Elsewhere, it is customary to wait 15 to 30 minutes.
- Press conference attendees in some countries must include government officials, local bankers, and other dignitaries. In other nations local custom dictates that the company's customers and representatives be included.
- Press kits should usually be composed in both English and the main language of the host country. The press kit should contain (in addition to immediate news and a background on the company) statements on the benefits the company offers the host country.[6]

<table>
<tr><td>

**BETWEEN
THE LINES**

</td><td>

When in Rome . . .

Communicating overseas can be a tricky business. Words, mannerisms, figures of speech, customs—all are different in other countries.

- In Latin America *no* is almost a dirty word in polite society. Not wanting to give a flatly negative answer to a friend or colleague, Latin Americans customarily say "yes" or "of course."
- *Yes* in Japanese means "Yes, I hear what you say," but it doesn't necessarily mean "Yes, I agree."
- In Bulgaria a nod means no and a shake of the head means yes.
- In Italy, if you don't use your hands in an animated fashion in conversation, you are perceived as a big fat bore.
- Arabs point or beckon in summoning dogs, so they don't appreciate that gesture for people.
- The Japanese are overt with humor. Slapstick humor is popular in Japan. So a subtle approach in communications, such as Australia's tourism campaign using the dry-witted Paul Hogan, just doesn't work.

And then there is the minefield of fast-food communications and routines in other countries.

- When Burger King opened its first restaurant in London, employees found the floor littered with pickles. The English, you see, don't care for pickles on their burgers.
- Pizza Hut found that one of the best-selling items in its Far Eastern restaurants was seaweed pizza.
- Employees of the 515 Kentucky Fried Chicken restaurants in Japan take time off to pray for the souls of dead chickens.
- Wendy's International removed the "hot stuffed" baked potato description from its British menu when it found the expression had a most improper connotation in the United Kingdom.

</td></tr>
</table>

DEALING WITH FOREIGN CLIENTS ABROAD

There is nothing magical about providing public relations services in overseas markets. As noted earlier, the key element in dealing effectively overseas lies in the development of a good working knowledge of the language, customs, climate, and people of the particular host area. Other suggestions for dealing effectively in a public relations context overseas include the following:

■ Be innovative, flexible, and prepared to take risks. Stated another way, don't believe what works at home works worldwide.

■ Develop continuing dialogue with consumer, business, and government leaders in the host country.

■ Use the expertise of other local public relations practitioners or agencies.

■ Foster contacts with foreign government and trade offices in the United States, foreign service people, commercial attachés of foreign consulates, and visiting representatives.

■ Introduce philanthropic programs locally.

■ Dismiss the myth that overseas media will never report events unless paid for. If activities are newsworthy, chances are good that local media won't ignore them.[7]

Public relations practitioners operating abroad shouldn't think they have to out-native the natives. No one will expect the local practitioner to be a linguistic expert or to have full knowledge of the country's customs. However, convincing a host of one's willingness to learn about the local country will help immeasurably in ingratiating the public relations practitioner abroad.

FOREIGN PRESS IN THE UNITED STATES

Many foreign publications have bureaus in New York City and Washington, DC. The foreign press represents the single most important source of information about America for hundreds of millions of people throughout the world. There are more than 1,000 active representatives of foreign media in the United States, representing more than 500 news organizations. About 80 percent of the U.S. foreign press corps represents European media; Japan is also broadly represented.

Most foreign correspondents are interested mainly in American politics. Normally, about one-half of a correspondent's time is spent on politics and the other half on such subjects as science, art, business, crime, civil rights, and finance. Foreign bureaus are often one-person operations, and an active international public relations representative can keep foreign journalists constantly serviced with topical and timely information for use in overseas markets.

REPRESENTING FOREIGN CLIENTS IN THE UNITED STATES

One growth area for U.S. public relations firms has been with foreign companies and governments seeking to expand their influence in America. Some firms, in fact, report yearly six-figure retainers on behalf of foreign organizations. Just as U.S. multinational companies need public relations assistance abroad, foreign multinationals need help in doing business in the United States—whether in introducing a product, setting up a subsidiary, opening a new plant, or expanding existing operations. A U.S. consultant can be of tre-

<table>
<tr><td>

BETWEEN THE LINES

</td><td>

Heeeere's Vladimir

The Cold War has officially hit the airwaves, and none of us are likely ever to be the same again. It may have taken certain countries a bit longer to realize the power of media persuasion, but the Soviets, at least, have now recognized the possibilities—with a vengeance.

The emergence of the century's first affable Soviet leader, Mikhail Gorbachev, has ushered in a very aggressive game of Russian media propaganda. Indeed, by 1986 one of the most frequent news analysts on American television was one Vladimir Posner, a Radio Moscow commentator who was born in Paris, learned to speak flawless, accent-free English as a teenager in Manhattan, and moved to Moscow with his Russian father in 1953. So prolific and believable was Posner that when he appeared for eight straight minutes on an ABC-TV analysis of President Reagan's call for increased military spending, the White House had a fit. An incredulous White House communications director Patrick Buchanan questioned how a "trained propagandist" from the Soviet Union could have been allowed to challenge President Reagan's appeals for support. ABC reluctantly agreed with the White House that it had "allowed too much scope to Posner."

Although this was one victory for the Kremlin's public relations offensive, the longer-term persuasion battle was far from over.*

---

*This passage is based on "The War of Words," *U.S. News and World Report,* 7 October 1985, 37.

</td></tr>
</table>

mendous value in working with state and federal legislatures and agencies as well as with the press.

Foreign countries retain the services of public relations counselors to fill a variety of needs.

- Advancing political objectives
- Counseling on the probable U.S. reaction to a government's projected action
- Advancing a country's commercial interests (e.g., sales in the United States, increased private U.S. investment, tourism, etc.)
- Assisting in communications in English
- Counseling and help in winning understanding and support on a specific issue that might undermine the client's standing in the United States and the world community
- Helping modify laws and regulations inhibiting the client's activities in the United States[8]

A foreign government that seeks to hire an American public relations firm often begins by having its embassy in Washington solicit competitive bids. The

Vladimir Posner

winner is expected to provide expertise in disseminating positive news to the media and other public opinion channels. Often it may be necessary to explain to foreign clients—some of whom may totally control the flow of news in their own countries—how an independent press works. Typically, a consultant begins the assignment by identifying potential sources of public opinion and surveying news coverage about the client country. Then, the consultant may suggest activities, such as the following:

1. Selectively contacting influential writers and editors and providing them with background information about the country.
2. Inviting media to visit the client country. Such expense-paid trips (junkets) are often frowned on by responsible media.
3. Checking with foreign policy experts, educators, business leaders, and government officials about current American attitudes toward the country. The results of these surveys, as well as more formal research, are turned over to the client.

YOU MAKE
THE CALL

The Nestle Infant Formula Boycott

In 1977 a coalition of some 40 groups drawn from church, health, and consumer areas met at the University of Minnesota for an organizing conference on infant formula. This group, called INFACT, combined its forces with the New York City–based Interfaith Center on Corporate Responsibility, a coalition of 17 Protestant denominations and about 180 Roman Catholic groups, to attack the Nestle Company and its practices in marketing infant formula to third world nations.

The quarrel between the corporation and the activists had two basic elements: (1) its critics charged that Nestle marketed infant formula too aggressively, thus discouraging breast-feeding, normally nutritionally best for infants; (2) activists pointed to the dangers of improper use of infant formula, such as mixing it with polluted water in third world nations.

By the early 1980s the infant formula topic had become a major aspect of the dialogue between developed and developing nations, with formula makers depicted by their adversaries as corporations interested more in profits than in people. In 1981 the World Health Organization (WHO), a specialized United Nations agency, adopted a code of conduct for the international marketing of infant formula. Essentially, the WHO document eliminated all promotional efforts, leaving Nestle and other infant formula companies to serve as passive order takers rather than marketers. In light of the WHO code, about 20 countries immediately adopted national codes on infant formula.

The gauntlet laid down by the activists posed a major public relations challenge to Nestle. Indeed, when a Nestle subsidiary took over management of Washington's Mayflower Hotel, pickets turned out in great number. Moreover, U.S. retailers were petitioned to stop handling Nestle products. Although Nestle's credibility was badly weakened, it eventually bounced back with an innovative public relations response.

Counselors who work for foreign governments must register with the U.S. Department of Justice and list all their activities on behalf of a foreign principal, including compensation received and expenses incurred. Occasionally, representing a foreign nation, particularly one whose policies differ from those of the United States, is an unpopular task for public relations agencies. Sydney S. Baron & Company, for example, encountered severe criticism for representing the proapartheid government of South Africa. So, too, did Gray & Company, a public relations concern generally regarded as heavily Republican and definitely conservative, when it announced in 1986 that it had a new client, the Marxist government of Angola. Gray quickly resigned from the account when saboteurs advertised Gray's main telephone number as the num-

- In 1981 it opened the Nestle Coordination Center for Nutrition in Washington, DC. The center worked to develop a comprehensive, computerized information system on primary health care and infant and maternal nutrition.
- Nestle's next step, in 1982, was to formally support the WHO code by issuing detailed instructions to its marketing executives around the world and to local authorities in countries where no national code had been adopted. Nestle's directives prohibited mass media advertising, direct sampling for mothers, and participation in trade or consumer promotion in the infant formula area.
- Finally, also in 1982, Nestle established an Infant Formula Audit Commission to review any allegations that the company had violated WHO or national codes. To chair the panel, Nestle named former U.S. Secretary of State Edmund Muskie.

As a postscript to the Nestle imbroglio, the former director of public relations for the Nestle Company, Rafael Pagan, resigned from the company to start his own firm, Pagan International, which was retained by Nestle for ongoing public relations counsel in the infant formula controversy.*

QUESTIONS

1. Had you been Nestle's public relations director, what initial strategy would you have recommended in light of the worldwide infant formula challenge?
2. In addition to the three public relations programs Nestle began, what other alternative responses might the company pursue?

---

*This case was adapted largely from Richard L. Barovick, "Activism on a Global Scale," *Public Relations Journal* (June 1982): 29–31.

---

ber of a local brothel and the lines were flooded. Despite such problems, foreign governments are willing to pay plenty for public relations representation in the United States.

THE OUTLOOK

Multinationals have been under constant attack abroad from a variety of critics, including supranational bodies, national governments, international labor, and consumer and religious groups. This clamor will not soon diminish and is likely to intensify. Since 1980, in fact, at least three major cross-border activist campaigns against major corporations have surfaced.

- One was a brief international boycott of Coca-Cola over allegations that its Guatemalan bottler had used the local army to squash labor unions.
- Another was a campaign against major banks and corporations that maintained trade, investment, and lending relations with South Africa, on the grounds that these operations helped support apartheid. One result of this campaign was a drive by church and university institutional investors to withdraw deposits from banks that participated in South African loans. Another result was the announcement by some major banks that they were discontinuing the practice of lending to South Africa.
- The third campaign, by far the most heralded, was the worldwide boycott of Nestle, the large Swiss multinational that dominated the infant formula business in third world countries. Ironically, the Nestle boycott started in the United States, where the Swiss company has never produced or marketed infant formula.

FIGURE 20–2 One of the most heartening international public relations events took place in December 1985 when the magic of satellite transmission brought together children of comparable ages from Minnesota and the Soviet Union in a live, interactive, musical television show, hosted by American singer John Denver. ''The Children's Summit,'' the brainchild of Minneapolis public relations executive David Speer, was transmitted to 180 stations via the U.S. Public Broadcasting System and to more than 100 million viewers via Gosteleradio, Soviet state television. (Courtesy of Padilla, Speer, Beardsley, Inc.)

The ongoing threat to multinationals lies in the prospect of local regulations imposing widely differing controls, sanctions, and curbs in dozens of different countries. The practice of public relations, therefore, will play a larger role in a corporation's response to local pressures. To survive in an increasingly nationalistic overseas atmosphere, multinationals must tie their policies and practices as closely as possible to the aspirations and goals of their host countries. Multinationals must increase and make known their efforts in upgrading employee job skills, bring more nationals into local and international management, seek out opportunities to improve their public images, and prove themselves honest and sincere residents rather than undesirable aliens.[9] To accomplish all of this, multinational companies abroad will have to rely increasingly on the sound judgment and competent technical skills of international public relations practitioners (Figure 20–2).

NOTES

1. Robert L. Mayall, "Does Anybody Here Know How to Play This Game?" *Public Relations Journal* (June 1981): 33.
2. Ray Josephs, "A Global Approach to Public Relations," *Columbia Journal of World Business* (Fall 1973): 93.
3. Ernest Wittenberg, "Getting It Done Overseas," *Public Relations Journal* (June 1982): 14.
4. "PR Firm Networks Covering the World," *Publicist* (May/June 1977): 1–4.
5. Jules M. Hartogh, "Public Relations in a Changing Europe," *Public Relations Journal* (March 1974): 29.
6. "If You're Planning a Press Conference Abroad," *Practical Public Relations,* 12 August 1974, 1.
7. *Public Relations News* 38, no. 47, 29 November 1982, 1.
8. Carl Levin, "Representing Foreign Interests," *Public Relations Journal* (June 1982): 22.
9. William A. Durbin, "PR at the Multinational Level," *Management Review* (April 1974): 14, 18.

SUGGESTED READINGS

Caruba, Alan. "Pinpointing International Media Contacts." *Public Relations Journal* (August 1984): 23–24.

International Directory of Special Events & Festivals (Available from Special Events Reports, 213 W. Institute Place, Chicago, IL 60610.)

International Library Market Place. New York: R.R. Bowker Co.

IPRA Review (Whiting and Birch Ltd., 90 Dartmouth Road, Forest Hill, London SE2 3HZ). Quarterly.

Nadel, Jack. *Cracking the Global Market: How to Do Business Around the World.* New York: AMACOM (135 W. 50th St.), 1987.

"Public Relations in Japan." *Public Relations Journal* (August 1984): 14–17. This is an interview with Sakae Ohashi, president of Japan's largest public relations firm. Public relations in the United States and Japan are contrasted.

Rautenberg, Steven. "Crisis Public Relations in the Age of Apology: From Chernobyl to Monongahela." Address to American Bankers Association Security and Planning Conference, Orlando, FL, 28 January 1988.

Shaeffer, Bruce. *Doing Business in America: Guide for the Foreign Investor.* Homewood, IL: Dow Jones-Irwin, 1984.

Singer, Joseph. "How to Work with Foreign Clients." *Public Relations Journal* (October 1987): 35–37.

"Special Report: PR in the UK." *PR Week* (30 May–5 June 1988): 8–11.

Wiklund, Erik. *International Marketing Strategies: How to Build Market Share.* New York: McGraw-Hill, 1987.

Bhopal

The worst industrial accident in the history of the world occurred on December 3, 1984, when a poison gas leak at a Union Carbide factory in Bhopal, India, killed more than 2,000 people and injured another 200,000. Thereafter, Union Carbide chairman Warren Anderson and his colleagues confronted perhaps the worst crisis ever faced by an American corporation. Their immediate corporate mission was to strike a difficult balance among the instincts of human compassion, the demands of public relations, and the dictates of corporate survival.

In the days following the Bhopal incident, Carbide executives faced a series of immediate management problems: how best to aid the victims; how to be sure whatever happened at Bhopal wouldn't happen again somewhere else; how to help employees keep up morale; how to assure investors of the corporation's financial stability; how to begin protecting the company from excessive legal liabilities. Each question had to be faced—and answered—at once. And each issue had a public relations side to it.

To complicate matters, Carbide headquarters in Danbury, Connecticut, were besieged by hundreds of reporters who wanted immediate answers. Getting information out of India proved practically impossible, partly because there were only two open phone lines between Bhopal and Bombay, where Union Carbide of India was headquartered. In addition, the Indian government arrested the top company officials in Bhopal and refused to make them available to Carbide executives in the United States. Nonetheless, Carbide officials agreed that, however unreliable, the news from India warranted swift, sweeping, and immediate decisions.

The first decision was to send help to India—medical supplies, respirators, and a doctor with extensive knowledge of methyl isocyanate, the poisonous chemical released from the Carbide plant. Carbide also sent a team of technical experts to examine the plant.

Next, Chairman Anderson, admitting that Bhopal had left him "shattered," decided to hop the company jet and follow the technical team to India to view the situation. As a practical matter, Anderson's journey accomplished nothing. He was arrested on arrival, held briefly, released on $2,500 bail, and told to leave the country. Indian officials refused Anderson's offer of $1 million in immediate aid and use of the company's guest house above Bhopal to house orphans of the victims. Some ridiculed Anderson's trip. Others praised it.

In Connecticut, meanwhile, the company set up a media center at the Danbury Hilton across from Carbide's front gate and refused journalists admission to the headquarters building. The firm chose as its chief spokesman a cautious lawyer and engineer, Carbide's director of safety and environmental affairs. In light of the complexity of the lawsuits it faced, Carbide was circumspect in releasing information. Indeed, it took several months for the company to release its own report about what happened at Bhopal.

Predictably, reporters filled the vacuum by investigating on their own, concluding that many safety rules were routinely ignored in India, that both the staff and nearby residents were largely unaware of how dangerous the chemicals were, that monitoring equipment was often inadequate or poorly understood, and that there was no special si-

UNION CARBIDE

W🌐RLD

JANUARY/FEBRUARY 1985

To Carbiders:

I'm greatly encouraged by recent reports from India that there appears to be virtually no lasting damage to the people injured by the incident at Bhopal. Just before the Christmas holiday, The New York Times reported, and eminent doctors (whom we asked to go to Bhopal and give their independent appraisal of the situation there) confirmed, that almost none of the dire consequences predicted following the catastrophy — permanent blindness, paralysis, severe damage — are, in fact, occuring.

Of course, this in no way diminishes the shock and sadness experienced by Carbiders everywhere.

(continued on page 3)

FIGURE A

On one day, we were working for a company that had one of the best safety records in the industry, which has one of the best records of any in the nation. On the next, every one of us couldn't believe what happened. Why it did is still a mystery; one that we intend to unravel.

One of the reasons I went to India was to help provide immediate relief for the people in Bhopal. Humanitarian efforts are being made by Union Carbide Corporation and Union Carbide India Limited. And I'm particularly gratified by the personal efforts of Carbide employees to establish the relief fund for Bhopal.

We're showing the world that Union Carbide is, indeed, a family, one with a heart and soul in all the countries where we do business. Some observers have also raised questions about our future. Let me put those questions to rest.

The many people who depend on Carbide — employees, investors, customers, and suppliers — may rest assured that we continue to be a strong company, and we resolve to maintain leadership in our various businesses. We are confident that compensation for the Bhopal victims can be arranged in a fair and equitable manner that will not have a material effect on the financial condition of the corporation. Nothing has changed our determination to go forward with the plans and strategies intended to help us reach higher levels of performance.

In December, the corporation faced a crisis, one that will affect us for a long time to come. However, throughout most of our businesses, we're ready to return to the tasks that were in front of us when we entered the month.

Necessary business steps taken in '84 have substantially improved our prospects for 1985. We have important work to do. As difficult as December was for all of us, that work goes forward.

Union Carbide and the chemical industry have been major contributors to the changes that have made this a better century. Our products have improved life for many millions, and chemicals have an enormous contribution yet to make. I'm confident that all of us will be proud to participate in our future efforts.

Warren M. Anderson

FIGURE A   *continued*

ren to warn residents of imminent danger. Until a tour of Carbide's West Virginia pesticide plant was given some weeks after the tragedy, company spokespersons had declined to provide any technical data on the manufacturing and storage of methyl isocyanate. On the other hand, Carbide regularly held press briefings in order to, as one executive put it, "express our sympathy and share with everyone all the information we didn't know."

Internally, to buck up sagging morale, Carbide executives taped video messages for employees around the world and kept a steady stream of encouragement flowing through internal publications (Figure A). Externally, the plunge in Carbide's stock caused the company to begin emphasizing its financial soundness in news releases and briefings. This action tended to give the impression that Carbide was more bottom-line oriented than compassionate. Not helping the situation were the ballyhooed flights to India of publicity-seeking lawyers intent on cashing in on the Bhopal tragedy.

In the months following the crisis, a *Business Week*/Harris poll revealed that fewer than 4 out of 10 Americans who had heard about the Bhopal disaster believed Carbide had done an "excellent" or "good" job. Almost half of those surveyed were able to name Carbide, without prompting, as the company involved in the Bhopal disaster. A year after Bhopal, Carbide faced mounting problems.

- It set up a reserve of nearly $200 million to handle Bhopal-related lawsuits.
- A toxic chemical leak at its West Virginia plant injured more than 100 people, and Carbide was fined $1.37 million for "willful disregard for health and safety."
- The GAF Corporation tried to take it over.
- The company shook up its top management and announced plans to cut more than 5,000 jobs, close several plants, and sell off more than $1 billion in assets, including its Danbury headquarters.

Four years after the Bhopal tragedy, Union Carbide was still mired in legal problems with the government of India. In 1987 it appeared that the company and the Indian government were near a settlement in their bitter legal wrangling over compensation of victims of the poison-gas disaster. The settlement called for Carbide to pay the victims between $500 and $600 million. But as late as 1988 the Indian Supreme Court ruled that the company would have to pay $192 million in interim compensation to victims, and further appeals were scheduled.

Chairman Anderson, having retired from Union Carbide, reflected on the experience that will be linked forever to the company he ran: "I don't look back. If you get mired down, you can't make things happen. If we come out feeling we did the right thing, and the world agrees, then that's the best that could be done."*

QUESTIONS

1. Do you think Warren Anderson made the right decision in flying immediately to Bhopal?
2. How would you assess Union Carbide's public relations posture in the wake of Bhopal?
3. What do you think of the company's reluctance in the first months immediately following the tragedy to announce what specifically had happened?
4. What do you think of the strategy to emphasize the company's financial strength at Bhopal press briefings?
5. Had you been Carbide's public relations director, would you have allowed reporters access to Danbury headquarters and Carbide employees?

---

*For further information on Bhopal see Robert Garfield, "Union Carbide Team: Managing a Crisis," *USA Today*, 7 December 1984, 1B; Michael Isikoff, "Crisis Management: Has Carbide Met the Test?" *Washington Post*, 24 February 1985, G1–20; Stuart Jackson, "Union Carbide's Good Name Takes a Beating," *Business Week*, 31 December 1984, 40; Richard I. Kirkland, Jr., "Union Carbide Coping with Catastrophe," *Fortune*, 7 January 1985, 50–53; Thomas J. Lueck, "Crisis Management at Carbide," *New York Times*, 14 December 1984, D1–2; Barry Meier and James B. Stewart, "A Year After Bhopal, Union Carbide Faces a Slew of Problems," *Wall Street Journal*, 26 November 1985, 1, 56.

PART FOUR

Emerging Trends

21

Managing Public Issues

H elping to manage public issues is the ultimate assignment for a public relations professional. Managements that use public relations properly value public relations advice in developing an organization's response to emerging issues and in helping to influence the perceptions of key constituent publics on these issues. According to W. Howard Chase, who helped coin the phrase "issues management," more than 200 American companies have created executive posts for issues managers.[1] Basically, their task is to help their organizations define and deal with emerging political, economic, and social issues that may affect them.

Organizations have had little choice in recent years but to increase their role in the public policy process. The free enterprise system in general and certain industries and companies in particular have been challenged by the widening role of special interest groups in the policy process and the dramatic growth in public concern about the quality of life, consumerism, and the environment. Large companies, especially, have become increasingly aware that the many external forces surrounding the business world must be scanned, monitored, tracked, and analyzed. Only in that way can the potential effect of those forces on company image and profits be gauged, corporate policy decided, and strategies planned.[2] Such is the domain of issues management.

ISSUES MANAGEMENT DEFINED

W. Howard Chase defined issues management in this way:

> Issues management is the capacity to understand, mobilize, coordinate, and direct all strategic and policy planning functions, and all public affairs/public relations skills, toward achievement of one objective: meaningful participation in creation of public policy that affects personal and institutional destiny.
>
> Issues management is dynamic and proactive. It rejects the hypothesis that any institution must be the pawn of the public policy determined solely by others.

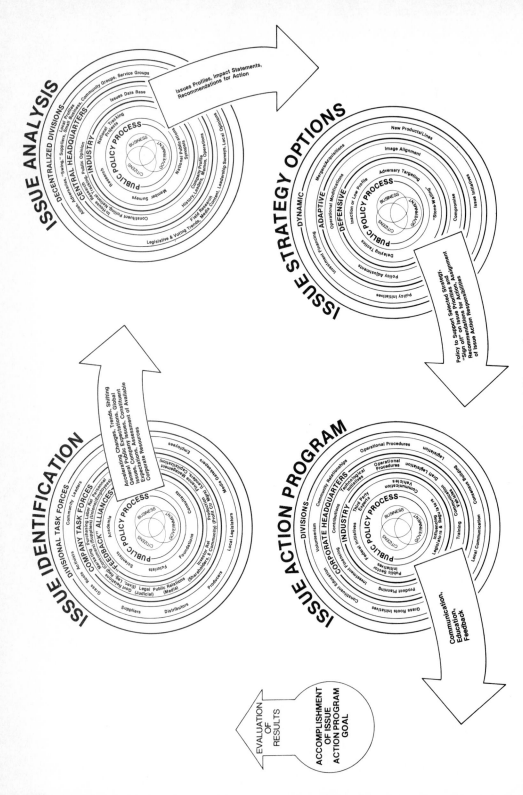

FIGURE 21-1 A pioneer in the field of issues management, W. Howard Chase, along with Barrie L. Jones, developed this tool for predicting the effect of internal and external environmental changes on the performance of the overall corporate system. The model itself assigns decision-making authority and evaluation of issues manager performance. (Courtesy of Issue Action Publications)

The noblest aspect of freedom is that human beings and their institutions have the right to help determine their own destinies. Issues management is the systems process that maximizes self-expression and action programming for most effective participation in public policy formation.

Thus, issues management is the highest form of sound management applied to institutional survival.[3]

Figure 21–1 illustrates the Chase/Jones management process model.

The Public Affairs Council defined issues management in a slightly less grand manner as "a program which a company uses to increase its knowledge of the public policy process and enhance the sophistication and effectiveness of its involvement in that process."[4]

Like public relations itself, there is no precise definition of issues management. Indeed, many suggest that the term *issues management* is another way of saying that the most important public relations skill is counseling management. Even leaders in the issues management movement agree that public relations pioneers such as Ivy Lee, Edward Bernays, Carl Byoir, and John Hill all operated as issues managers when they served as personal advisors to the heads of major organizations. Nonetheless, issues management as a specialized discipline within organizations has developed to the point where the Issues Management Association, founded in the 1980s, already has around 600 members.

APPROACHING ISSUES MANAGEMENT

In approaching issues management, one thing must be clear: no one in our society—not a company, not a chief executive officer, not the president of the United States—can singlehandedly manage issues. The term *issues management* then is something of a misnomer. Like the public relations process itself, issues management breaks down generally into four components.

1. **Issue identification** Urgent issues must first be defined and a tracking mechanism established. Key publics ultimately affected by the issues must also be defined and tracked.
2. **Planning/strategy-setting** A plan to deal with emerging issues must be set. Strategic options and what-if scenarios should be played out. Timetables and budgets should be agreed upon.
3. **Implementation** This is both the tracking and the reporting stage, as well as the action stage to deal with emerging issues. It includes both internal communications to management to keep it abreast of issues development and position-setting as well as external communications to influence perceptions of issues.
4. **Evaluation** After communications have been launched, they must be evaluated to determine whether preset objectives have been met and what refinements are necessary.

In specific terms organizations can manage their own response to issues and therefore influence issues development in the ways that are identified here.

John Scanlon

John Scanlon has pioneered in the field of litigation public relations as senior executive vice president of Daniel J. Edelman, Inc. in New York City. Among his clients Scanlon represented CBS in its suit by General Westmoreland and the *Boston Globe* in its suit by politician John Lakian. In a long and varied career Scanlon has specialized in entertainment public relations, issues management, and politics. He served as deputy commissioner for economic development under New York City Mayor John V. Lindsay and also as press secretary for the city's Municipal Assistance Corporation during New York's fiscal crisis in 1975.

What is public relations?
Public relations is the art of moving target audiences to embrace positions, support ideas, or buy new products.

What is issues management?
Issues management anticipates and prepares organizations, through strategic planning, to predict problems, anticipate threats, minimize surprises, and develop coalitions to effect defined goals and implant solutions.

How important is issues management?

- **Anticipate emerging issues**   Normally, the issues management process anticipates issues 18 months to 3 years away. Therefore, it is neither crisis planning nor postcrisis planning but rather precrisis planning. In other words, issues management deals with an issue that will hit the organization a year down the road, thus distinguishing the practice from the normal crisis planning aspects of public relations.
- **Selectively identify issues**   An organization can influence only a few issues at a time. Therefore, a good issues management process will select several—perhaps 5 to 10—specific priority issues with which to deal. In this way issues management can focus on the most important issues affecting the organization.

Issues management is essential to contemporary business organizations. To remain passive to emerging public disputes and to fail to plan for them ensures that someone else will frame the issue.

Can an organization like CBS really manage issues like the ones involved in the Westmoreland case?
Yes. In the Westmoreland/CBS case the network could have chosen simply to respond to the media. By developing a strategy, CBS recaptured the ability to frame the dispute on its terms.

Do the media today recognize the value of issues management?
It is ironic that the media are remarkably inexperienced in dealing with the media when they are the focus of a story. We have counseled several media clients, and they have indicated a new respect for the PR business as a result of the experiences.

How can an organization keep in front of an emerging issue?
Organizations can keep in front of issues by scanning the "nonprice" [i.e., intangible] environments of the culture. A company futurist, if you will, should follow changing values, political and general trends, and thereby anticipate issues. These issues should then be ranked by impact, probability, and timing. Finally, policies and strategies should be devised prior to implementing programs.

How important are media relationships in managing public issues?
Media relations are extremely important. News unreported is of no impact. Issues tend to be more abstract and less dramatic than breaking news. They are, in short, not "mediagenic." Long-term and credible relationships with media can go far in selling such stories.

What are the basics in helping manage an issue for a client?
The total confidence of the client is important. Full and total access to all the appropriate information is paramount. But accurate and thorough research is and will always be the essential key to proper issues management. In short, a thorough understanding of the issue is critical.

■ **Deal with opportunities and vulnerabilities** Most issues, anticipated well in advance, offer both opportunities and vulnerabilities for organizations. For example, in assessing promised federal budget cuts, an insurance company might anticipate that less money will mean fewer people driving and therefore fewer accident claims. This would mark an opportunity. On the other hand, those cuts might mean that more people are unable to pay their premiums. This, clearly, is a vulnerability that a sharp company should anticipate well in advance.

Assessing such opportunities and vulnerabilities can play a significant role in determining an organization's philanthropic contributions. For instance, if demographic and economic projections indicate the closing of a particular field office, philanthropic contributions in the community in advance of the closing may help cushion the ultimate blow when the firm departs.

- **Plan from the outside-in**   The external environment—not internal strategies—dictates the selection of priority issues. This differs from the normal strategic planning approach, which, to a large degree, is driven by internal strengths and objectives. Issues management is very much driven by external factors.
- **Profit line orientation**   Although many people tend to look at issues management as anticipating crises, its real purpose should be to defend the organization in the light of external factors as well as to enhance the firm's business by seizing imminent opportunities.
- **Action timetable**   Even as the issues management process must identify emerging issues and selectively set them in priority order, it must also propose policy, programs, and an implementation timetable to deal with those issues. Action is the key to an effective issues management process.
- **Dealing from the top**   Just as a public relations department is powerless without the confidence and respect of top management, so, too, must the issues management process operate with the support of the chief executive. The chief executive's personal sanction is critical to the acceptance and conduct of issues management within a firm.

IMPLEMENTING ISSUES MANAGEMENT

Although in many companies issues management is treated as an informal, ad hoc activity, other corporations have formalized the process to regularly involve specific sectors of the organization (Figure 21–2).

PUBLIC POLICY ISSUE MANAGEMENT ORGANIZATION FLOW & PUBLICATIONS

KEY: □ Individuals or Committees
○ Corporate Government and Public Affairs
◇ Publications

FIGURE 21–2   This diagram traces the issues management process at PPG Industries. It pictures the process flow, the principles involved, and the publications used. (Courtesy of the Public Affairs Council)

BETWEEN
THE LINES

The Ideal Issues Manager

According to the executive who manages Dow Chemical's well-reputed issues section, the ideal issues manager ought to have the following 10 qualities:*

1. A natural curiosity, particularly about societal change, technology, the news media, politics, public opinion, and the future
2. An ability and willingness to deal with ambiguous ideas and concepts
3. Ability to see alternative implications in approaches to a given set of data or trends
4. Boldness to suggest, sell, and implement unique approaches to what may appear to be traditional problems
5. Leadership orientation and results motivation that lead to becoming part of the inner circle and moving diverse people into consensus positions
6. A capacity—if not a passion—for sizable workloads and often brutal pressure
7. An ability to write in clear, understandable terms, often creatively synthesizing ideas into policy documents
8. Knowledge about the culture, business, and internal workings of the organization
9. Peripheral vision, which means not getting so wrapped up in the issues you know well that you miss the new issues or new wrinkles that can hit you in the back of the head
10. Awareness of the forces that drive issues

*Richard K. Long, manager of external communications and issues for the Dow Chemical Company, remarks before the 38th National Conference of the Public Relations Society of America, Detroit, MI, 13 November 1985.

In a typical organization the tactical implementation of issues management has tended to fall into four specific job tasks.

1. **Identifying issues and trends**   Issue identification can be accomplished through traditional research techniques as well as more informal methods. Understandably, companies are more concerned with issues that affect them directly. For example, Standard Oil of California organized an extensive campaign to refute criticism of the petroleum industry's use of toxic substances believed to cause cancer. Steel companies, Bethlehem and U.S. Steel, attempted to mobilize public opinion to protest government policies allowing the dumping of low-priced, foreign steel in the United States.

   One way to keep informed about what is being said about a company, industry, or issue is to subscribe to issues-oriented publications of every political persuasion—from *Mother Jones* and *The Village Voice* on the far left to the Liberty Lobby's *Spotlight* on the far right and everything else in between.

2. **Evaluating issue impact and setting priorities**   Evaluation and analysis may be handled by issues committees within an organization. Committees can set priorities for issues management action. At the Upjohn Company, for example, a senior policy committee—composed of managers in each of the firm's major divisions, as well as public affairs and legal staff members—meets quarterly to set issues priorities.

3. **Establishing a company position**   Establishing a position can be a formal process. After the Upjohn senior policy committee has met and decided on issues, Upjohn's public affairs staff prepares policy statements on each topic. At PPG Industries individual issues managers prepare position papers for executive review on topics of direct concern.

4. **Designing company action and response to achieve results**   The best-organized companies for issues management orchestrate integrated responses to achieve results. Typically, companies may coordinate their Washington offices, state lobbying operations, management speeches, advertising messages, and employee communications to forward the firm's point of view (Figures 21–3 and 21–4).

PUBLIC RELATIONS ROLE

The public relations practitioner can successfully manage the public issues process within a company. Public relations is ideally situated between the public and management; its access both to top management and to outside information makes it the logical focus of such a program.

Public relations also has special advantages for gathering information on issues—internal and external contacts, a sensitivity to external forces, and the ability to articulate ideas. Although huge corporations have thus far taken the lead in issues management, one smaller firm, Rexnord, stands out as having formulated a well-developed issues management program. At Rexnord public relations sits in the "issues management catbird seat." Here's Rexnord's checklist for public relations input in the issues management process.

- Identify and list 100 or more issues.
- Seek out the concerns of other managers about particular issues.
- Categorize those issues.
- Start a central issue file. Let people know where it is.
- Determine issues relevant to the corporation and investigate them in depth.
- Assign priorities to these issues.
- Circulate the issues for management input.
- Learn what other institutions are doing.
- List plans to cause action on the issues.
- Begin a speakers' bureau.

We help form public policy.

Corporations are essentially public institutions. The health of the enterprise is largely contingent upon public opinion.

Our role is to serve as counselor, coordinator and catalyst in relations between companies, trade associations and foreign countries and the publics with which they are involved. We clarify the issues. We formulate programs. We communicate the message. And we help form public policy.

In this work we are involved in some of the most important public policy issues of our time.

Our continuing program in the case of landing rights for the supersonic transport Concorde helped to balance questions raised by environmentalists with those who recognize the issues of the speed, efficiency and inevitability of supersonic transport and our traditional close diplomatic ties to England and France. The U.S. Supreme Court decision and the start of service at Kennedy is a gratifying development in this long and difficult campaign.

Our work on behalf of the R.J. Reynolds Tobacco Company is helping assess the potential impact of numerous public issues and concerns.

For the American Seat Belt Council we've helped to position the seat belt and air bag debate in a continuing effort to assure maximum life-saving at minimal cost.

One of the most critical issues of the day is energy conservation. Our efforts in behalf of Dow Chemical Company's Styrofoam brand insulation are helping to educate the public on the need to conserve limited energy resources.

A response to extreme and unfair attacks on sugar and candy with scientific evidence of the nutritional and energy-giving benefits of moderate use of confections is being sought in behalf of the National Confectioners Association.

For client EMI Medical, Inc., we are striving to put into proper perspective the purchase and utilization of the new body and head CAT scanners in the nation's hospitals, weighing the heavy unit costs against the great efficiency, time-saving and pain-saving benefits they provide in comparison to exploratory surgery.

Another continuing public policy problem involves the need for compromise in the area of environmental concerns. We no longer can accept air and water pollution in the name of industrial progress, but at the same time, we cannot sustain a technologically based society if we demand perfection. For Armour-Dial, Division of Greyhound, we interpreted to the community in the area of the company's large soap plant and to media people, government officials and employees the capital equipment program designed to minimize odors and purify discharged waste materials. In the field of nuclear power, for Commonwealth Edison, we interpreted the move toward meeting electricity needs through atomic energy to reduce industrial pollution and at the same time explained the safeguards built into the system.

These examples reflect the scope of our involvement in some of the broad public issues of our times.

EDELMAN

Daniel J. Edelman Inc.
221 N. LaSalle St. Chicago, IL 60601
711 Third Avenue New York, NY 10017
1901 Avenue of the Stars, Los Angeles, CA 90067
703 Market Street San Francisco, CA 94103
1730 Pennsylvania Ave. N.W. Suite 460, Washington, D.C. 20006
Stanhope House, Stanhope Place, London, W22HH, England
Beethovenstrasse 9/6000 Frankfurt, 1 Germany
and DJE International Group affiliates throughout the world.
Brochure available upon request.

FIGURE 21–3 Public relations agencies must move quickly to take advantage of emerging communications opportunities. This public policy issues ad, run by Daniel J. Edelman, emphasizes the firm's role as one of the nation's leading public relations consultants. (Courtesy of Daniel J. Edelman)

Has America become shortsighted?

America once had a vision of its future.

And that vision led us to become the most productive nation on earth, with our citizens enjoying the highest standard of living of any nation in the world.

Today, inflation erodes our economic growth. Inadequate capital investment limits opportunity and undermines our international competitive position. Our companies are hard pressed to keep up with accelerating technological developments. Productivity has been growing much faster in other major industrial nations than it has in the United States.

Why has American economic performance slipped?

Essentially, we seem to have lost sight of what truly drives our economy and what is required to keep our products and ser-vices competitive in world markets. Worse, our vision of the future appears to have narrowed to include only that which is politically fashionable and expedient for the short-term.

It is politically fashionable, for example, to charge that company profits are too high...are a "windfall" ...or are even "obscene." Yet profits constitute the key support for expanding company facilities, financing new research and development, replacing outmoded and inefficient equipment and, ultimately, ensuring greater productivity, higher wages and more jobs.

It's also politically fashionable to demand greater governmental "safeguards," i.e. regulations on the activities of companies. Yet, each year, government regulations cost our society —both companies and individuals—about $100 billion. Much of which could be used instead for new plants, for new products, for new research, for new technology to create new jobs. All of which would make us more competitive in world markets.

It's politically expedient for government—in the interest of "protecting the general welfare"—to spend billions of taxpayer dollars on overregulation without fully weighing costs against benefits. Government overspending, and the resulting federal budget deficit, remains a primary cause of our nation's most serious problem, inflation.

Clearly, we must, as a nation, restore our vision and, with it, our productive capacity.

In the months ahead, we at Chase intend to speak out on the "productive capacity" question: on inflation, on profits, on government regulation, on business investment, on research and development.

Our reason for doing so is quite straightforward. If, as a nation, we are unable to revitalize our productive capacity, Chase's shareholders, customers and employees—together with millions of other Americans —will pay the price. It's a price we need not, and should not, have to pay.

So, we will speak out— as loudly and clearly as we can. We'll do it in our own self interest. And, we believe, in yours.

CHASE

FIGURE 21–4 Companies such as Chase Manhattan Bank are not reluctant to exercise their First Amendment rights on public issues of national and international concern. (Courtesy of Chase Manhattan Bank)

- Determine whether a formal public affairs program is needed to get things rolling.
- Present selected issues at appropriate meetings (e.g., sales meetings, management meetings, and financial meetings).
- Encourage issue-oriented speeches and articles; merchandise them.
- Send letters on the issues to employees, retirees, and shareholders.
- Contact elected officials on the issues.[5]

MANAGING CRISIS

The most significant test for any organization comes when it is hit by a major accident or disaster. How it handles itself in the midst of a crisis may influence how the organization is perceived for years to come. Poor handling of events with the magnitude of NASA's shuttle disaster, Tylenol's capsule poisoning, or Union Carbide's Bhopal tragedy not only can cripple an organization's reputation, but also can cause it enormous monetary loss. It is essential, therefore, that such emergencies be managed intelligently and forthrightly with the news media, employees, and the community at large.

One key to mitigating a disaster lies in crisis planning. Surprisingly, a 1984 study commissioned by Western Union Corporation found that out of 390 of the largest industrial and service companies, only 207—slightly more than half—had plans for informing the public in a crisis.[6] Years ago in the airline industry, crisis planning meant that "one of the PR man's first responsibilities when a crash occurred was to paint over the company's name" on the wreckage before news photographers arrived.[7] Fortunately, times have changed.

Today, organizations from airlines to hospitals prepare for potential crises in a much more thoughtful and deliberate way. One essential principle in dealing with a crisis is not to clam up when disaster strikes. The key to good public relations is to provide prompt, frank, and full information to the media. Invariably, the first inclination of executives is to say, "Let's wait until all the facts are in." But as President Carter's press secretary, Jody Powell, used to say, "Bad news is a lot like fish. It doesn't get better with age." In other words, in saying nothing, an organization is perceived as already having made a decision. That angers the media and compounds the problem. On the other hand, inexperienced spokespersons, speculating nervously or using emotionally charged language, are even worse.

Instead, the story should always be confined to the locale where the incident occurred. The situation should be put into perspective (e.g., "For more than 50 years we've been selling quality, safe cookies"). Messages should be consistent, using a limited number of spokespersons—preferably only one. Comparisons should be avoided; don't give people the opportunity to link your accident with a worse one. Statements should be limited to facts, not speculation or guesswork. Exposure should be limited; the line should be held. But as a senior communications manager for Dow Chemical put it:

Watering Down the Apple Juice

When a company is accused of selling fraudulent products, it is a serious issue. When the fraudulent products are sold to babies, it is even more serious. But that's exactly the issue with which Beech-Nut Nutrition Corporation was faced in late 1986, when the federal government charged that Beech-Nut and other defendants had intentionally shipped adulterated and misbranded apple juice for babies to 20 states, Puerto Rico, the Virgin Islands, and five foreign countries, with the intent to defraud and mislead.

The government's indictment said that the product that Beech-Nut marketed as 100 percent apple juice was really made from beet sugar, cane sugar syrup, corn syrup, and other ingredients, with little if any apple juice in the mixture. The bogus apple juice cost about 20 percent less to make than real apple juice.

After a year of consultation with the Food and Drug Administration, Beech-Nut agreed to pay a $2 million fine, the largest penalty ever paid under the Food, Drug and Cosmetic Act since its enactment in 1938. The corporation also agreed, as part of a plea arrangement with the government, to pay $140,000 in investigative costs to the FDA. The company pleaded guilty to 215 counts charging that it had shipped mislabeled products purporting to be apple juice. Another 145 counts, including charges of conspiracy and mail fraud, were dismissed as part of the plea agreement. Beech-Nut settled the issue a few days before two of its former top officials, including its former president, were to go on trial for conspiracy to distribute adulterated apple juice.

At its announcement Beech-Nut's new president, Dr. Richard Theuer, said that the company had taken measures to improve quality control and prevent similar situations from occurring again. He said that the misrepresented juice, although not pure apple juice, contained only "safe food ingredients"

The public must be fully informed frequently and accurately through the media from the outset . . . by credible senior spokesmen accustomed to dealing with the media in a responsible, respectful manner, who understand and can explain clearly in lay language complex information.[8]

One example of a company that moved quickly to head off a brewing crisis was Rexnord, in the days following a 1979 Chicago DC–10 crash. The crash, which killed 273, was suspected to have been caused by the loss of a bolt that Rexnord feared it had manufactured. The firm issued a statement saying that it was sure that tests would reveal that the bolt was not at fault, and it encouraged questions about the part. Rexnord was eventually exonerated of any blame. When the dust settled, its chief executive explained, "We had no legal obligation to go out in front, but we wanted to do so . . . . I've

and had presented no danger to health. "Under the law Beech-Nut as a corporation is assumed to have the knowledge of the employees about its operation. Rather than engage in a long trial which would not serve the interest of Beech-Nut or its customers, the company chose to plead guilty and put the past behind it," Dr. Theuer said.

In response the U.S. Attorney assigned to the case said, "It is refreshing to see a corporation come to grips with their wrongdoing and agree to an early resolution by the acceptance of today's fine and plea."

One year after the announcement of Beech-Nut's record fine, the case involving its two former employees was settled after five days of deliberations. The verdict: guilty of multiple counts of violating the Food, Drug and Cosmetic Act. The sentence: one year in prison. In the front-page story announcing the guilty verdicts, the assistant U.S. Attorney on the case summarized the findings this way: "This case is a story of corporate greed and irresponsibility."*

QUESTIONS

1. How would you assess Beech-Nut's handling of this issue?
2. What was the public relations strategy Beech-Nut employed relative to the public? relative to its two former employees?
3. If you were Beech-Nut's public relations counsel, what would you do now in terms of Beech-Nut's credibility?

---

*For further information see Leonard Buder, "Beech-Nut Is Fined $2 Million for Sale of Fake Apple Juice," *New York Times,* 14 November 1987, A1; Leonard Buder, "Two Former Executives of Beech-Nut Guilty in Phony Juice Case," *New York Times,* 18 February 1988, A1; Vera Haller, "Beech-Nut Is Fined in Fakery," *The Record,* 14 November 1987, A–3.

---

been talking and writing articles about the public losing faith in business, and this was something we needed to do."[9]

Another firm that adopted this same principle and took it one step further was the Du Pont chemical company, which, in March 1988, announced that it was leaving the chlorofluorocarbon business in light of scientific data that indicated the product was harmful to the earth's protective ozone layer. The decision was completely voluntary, precipitated by no urgent outcries to eliminate a product that dominated its market, and thus caught critics flat-footed. What made the announcement even more remarkable was that for years the company had denied any connection between hydrofluorocarbons and the ozone layer and had battled environmentalists about the ozone layer in full-page advertisements (Figure 21–5).

FIGURE 21–5 Du Pont's issues advertising campaign in the 1970s was a response to criticism of the family of chemicals known as chlorofluorocarbons. In 1988, in a stunning reversal on the issue, Du Pont's management announced that in light of new scientific data it would cease production of the compounds. (Courtesy of Du Pont)

The Employee with AIDS

No issue today is more perplexing than that of acquired immune deficiency syndrome, the fatal disease known as AIDS. As the reported number of AIDS victims increases in our society, organizations are being forced to establish communications policies to help manage the AIDS issue. For a hospital, communicating about the existence of AIDS is a particularly troubling question.

Such were the circumstances when the only hospital in the 30,000-resident community of Madeline Heights learned that its assistant personnel director, Ron Schram, had contracted AIDS. In light of this depressing news, hospital administrator Bob Goldstein had to make several difficult choices.

1. Should Schram, a loyal and valuable hospital employee for 15 years, be fired?
2. Should the hospital's staff be told of Schram's condition?
3. Should the Madeline Heights community be apprised of the employee's condition?
4. Even if nothing is said about its employee with AIDS, what should be the hospital's response if the local media inquire?

QUESTIONS

1. If you were the hospital's public relations director, what general strategy would you suggest that Administrator Goldstein adopt?
2. How would you advise him to answer the four specific questions above?

Although crisis plans differ from organization to organization, the following guidelines should be considered:

1. Develop a written crisis communications plan that defines individual roles and distribute it widely.
2. Identify a single spokesperson for the organization in time of crisis, preferably a public relations officer.
3. Be certain that information released is accurate and precise. Consider the legal ramifications of information released.
4. Let all personnel know the proper procedure for reporting during crisis situations. It's a good idea to designate crisis officers within departments.
5. Share with the news media the institution's plans for releasing information in a crisis situation. Being partners with the media in time of crisis is greatly preferable to being adversaries.
6. Let news people know that information violating an individual's right to privacy or jeopardizing the organization's legal rights may have to be withheld during a crisis.

FIGURE 21–6 In the 1990s no public issue is apt to be more devastating than the life-threatening disease AIDS. To help manage this issue, national ads like this have been blunt, straightforward, and hard-hitting. (Courtesy of the American Foundation for AIDS Research)

7. Coordinate communications plans with the community hospital.
8. Develop a means of notifying families and company officials of serious injuries before releasing the information publicly.
9. Be specific in the guidelines to be followed and be thorough in assigning responsibilities and in carrying out the plan precisely if a crisis should arise.[10]

EMERGING ISSUES OF THE DAY

Issues management has earned a permanent place in the practice of public relations. It is unlikely that the debate will soon diminish on such issues as consumerism, energy and the environment, health and nutrition, corporate social responsibility, minority rights, peace and disarmament, or the proper role of the American enterprise system (Figure 21–6). Conflicts on these and other issues will continue to be resolved in the public arena. Increasingly, business will seek to be represented, loudly and clearly. The debate will require better intellectual resources, better research, and a more sophisticated approach to issues management among organizations and their public relations practitioners.

Business firms, in particular, will have to take the offensive in championing more aggressive positions to deal with unexpected crises and the arguments of critics. Reactive responses will not do; companies must be able to stay in front of emerging issues. In the years ahead, then, few tasks will be greater for America's companies, few challenges more significant for professional public relations practitioners than helping manage public issues.

NOTES

1. "Issues Management, 1976–1982, A Reprise," *Corporate Public Issues* 7, no. 12 (15 June 1982): 2.
2. Paul Cathey, "Industry Has a New Advance Guard—Issue Managers," *Iron Age,* 23 April 1982, 64.
3. "Issues Management Conference—A Special Report," *Corporate Public Issues* 7, no. 23 (1 December 1982): 1–2.
4. Public Affairs Council, *The Fundamentals of Issues Management,* Washington, DC: Public Affairs Council (1220 16th Street, NW), 1978.
5. David L. Shanks, "Ready for the Issues?" *Enterprise* (February 1979): 13–14.
6. "Crisis: Not All Firms Prepared," *USA Today,* 16 August 1984.
7. Thomas Petzinger, Jr., "When Disaster Comes, Public-Relations Men Won't Be Far Behind," *Wall Street Journal,* 23 August 1979, 1.
8. Michael Cooper, "Crisis Public Relations," *Public Relations Journal* (November 1981): 53.
9. Michael A. Verespej, "DC–10 Tragedy Tests Rexnord's Krikorian," *Industry Week,* 6 August 1979, 36.
10. R. Seymour Smith, "How to Plan for a Crisis Communication," *Public Relations Journal* (March 1979): 17–18.

SUGGESTED READINGS

Bergner, Douglas J., ed. *Public Interest Profiles.* 5th ed. Washington, DC: Foundation for Public Affairs (1255 23rd St., NW), 1987.

Chase, Howard. *Issues Management: Origins of the Future.* Stamford, CT: Issue Action Publications (105 Old Long Ridge Rd.), 1984.

Cost Effective Management for Today's Public Affairs. Washington, DC: Public Affairs Council, 1987.

"Crises Can Occur at Anytime, Anywhere, to Any Organization." *PR Reporter* (24 November 1986): 3.

Detwiler, Richard M. "The Myths of Persuasion." *Public Relations Journal* (April 1982): 52–54.

Ewing, Raymond P. *Managing the New Bottom Line: Issues Management for Top Executives.* Homewood, IL: Dow Jones-Irwin, 1987.

Federal Register. (Available from Superintendent of Documents, Government Printing Office, Washington, DC 20402.) The *Federal Register* provides a method of tracking rules and regulations from government agencies and keeping abreast of changes.

Fegley, Robert L. "How Public Relations Can Help the CEO." *Public Relations Journal* (October 1981): 25–26.

The Fundamentals of Issue Management. Monograph. (Available from Public Affairs Council, 1220 16th St., NW, Washington, DC 20036.)

Gollner, Andrew. *Social Change and Corporate Strategy: The Expanding Role of Public Affairs.* Stamford, CT: IAP (105 Old Long Ridge Road), 1984.

Graff, Louis. "The Three Phenomena of Public Relations." *Public Relations Review* (Spring 1981): 17–26.

Griswold, Denny, ed. *PR News.* (Available from *PR News,* 127 E. 80th St., New York, NY 10021.) This weekly newsletter carries industry news and case studies illustrating public relations problems and solutions.

"Guidelines for Public Relations Professionals." *Public Relations Journal* (January 1981): 33.

Heath, Robert, and **Richard A. Nelson.** *Issues Management.* Newbury Park, CA: Sage, 1986.

Issues Management Programs: Why They Fail and How to Make Them Work. Philadelphia, PA: Human Resource Network, 1984.

"It Can Happen to Anyone in a Few Short Seconds." *PR Week* (18–24 April 1988): 10, 11.

Leveraging the Impact of Public Affairs. Philadelphia, PA: Human Resources Network, 1984.

Lukasik, Dr. S. J. "Information for Decision Making." *Public Relations Quarterly* (Fall 1981): 19–22.

Morrison, Catherine. *Forecasting Public Affairs Priorities.* New York: Conference Board (845 Third Ave.), 1987.

O'Dwyer, Jack, ed. *Jack O'Dwyer's Newsletter.* Weekly newsletter. (Available from 271 Madison Ave., New York, NY 10016.)

PR Reporter. Weekly newsletter. (Available from Box 600, Exeter, NH 03833.)

Public Relations Review. Quarterly. (Available from the Foundation for Public Relations Research and Education, University of Maryland College of Journalism, College Park, MD 20742.)

Remmes, Harold. *Lobbying for Your Cause.* Babylon, NY: Pilot Books (103 Cooper St.), 1986.

Simon, David H. "External Pressures on the CEO: Worse Than an Excedrin Headache." *Public Relations Quarterly* (Winter 1981–82): 9–12.

Weaver, Robert A., Jr. "Information Management for the Chief Executive." *Public Relations Quarterly* (Fall 1981): 23–25.

Procter & Gamble's Symbol

In the 1980s the nation's mightiest marketer, Procter & Gamble Company (P&G), was faced with one of the most bizarre public relations problems in modern memory. A whispering campaign, apparently begun by certain fundamentalist religious groups in the South, suddenly erupted nationally, associating the company and its moon-and-stars trademark with Satanism and devil worship. It was an issue that P&G had to manage adroitly or risk forfeiting its corporate trademark.

The rumors first surfaced in 1980 when P&G began getting thousands of phone calls about stories that company officials had confessed on the Phil Donahue and Merv Griffin network-television shows that P&G supported devil worship. Incredibly, no such appearances by P&G executives ever took place on the shows. Nonetheless, the company later found that several pastors had passed on the rumors from their pulpits. Leaflets urging parishioners to boycott the company's well-known products—Crest toothpaste, Ivory soap, Folgers coffee, and the like—began to show up in supermarkets. A typical flyer reported P&G's president as saying "as long as the cults and gays have come out of the closet, he was going to do it too. He said he told Satan that if he would help him prosper, he would give his heart and soul when he died. He gives Satan all the credit for his riches."

Despite the absurdity of the rumor, P&G soon began to realize that many people apparently took the preposterous stories seriously. Wrote one 75-year-old woman, "In the beginning God made the tree. Where did Satan get Charmin?" By 1982 the company was receiving well over 10,000 questions a

month about its relationship with the devil. Clearly, it was time for P&G to blast back. And that's exactly what the company did.

- It armed its Cincinnati headquarters' consumer services division with a full explanation of the symbol that had represented the company since the 1850s. P&G's 15 consumer services staff members patiently explained to caller after caller that the symbol started as simple markings on crates of Star candles, an early P&G product, and evolved over the years into a formal design of a man in the moon, a popular figure of the 1800s, and 13 stars representing the original colonies. A brochure, "Procter & Gamble's Symbol of Quality," was dispatched to anyone who wanted it (Figure A).
- An elaborate tracking system was established to chart the geographical sweep of the rumors as well as the nature of rumor-oriented calls.
- The company notified news outlets about its problem and asked for their help. In response, network news and talk show producers wrote public letters to P&G, confirming the falseness of rumors that company executives had appeared on their programs (Figure B).
- P&G sent out a mailing to 48,000 southern churches and enlisted the aid of religious leaders like Jerry Falwell and Billy Graham in the counterattack. Summarized the Reverend Billy Graham in his public letter, "I urge Christians everywhere to reject these false rumors and to be reminded that it is a sin to 'bear false witness.'"
- Finally, the company announced that it would take legal action to stop the spread

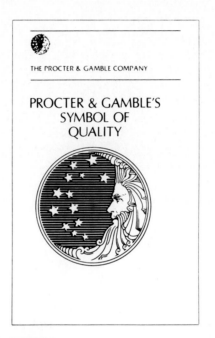

THE PROCTER & GAMBLE COMPANY

PROCTER & GAMBLE'S
SYMBOL OF
QUALITY

FIGURE A

of the rumors. It filed suits in Georgia and Florida, charging several individuals with libeling the character of P&G by circulating "false and malicious" statements about the company and by calling for a boycott of its products. To underscore the seriousness of its case, P&G retained former U.S. Attorney General Griffin Bell to represent it in Atlanta.

Interestingly, all but one of the P&G suit defendants sold products of competing companies, although there was no evidence that the companies themselves were pushing the rumor.

In any event, P&G's tough public relations response stimulated a flurry of publicity, including national newspaper, magazine, and network-television coverage. *Advertising Age* suggested in an article that P&G's vocal public relations campaign itself helped spread the rumor about the symbol, but most thought the P&G offensive was a good idea. After the rumor-deflating publicity, P&G reported that the number of queries to its consumer services department had fallen by half. As the company's public relations manager described the strategy during the crisis, "Sure, it's a hard-nosed approach. But the rumor has gotten so big that we had to do something dramatic to stop it. We want people to know we are taking this very seriously."

As seriously as P&G took the rumor, it couldn't, ultimately, head it off. After squelching the spread of the satanic rumor for several years, the story cropped up again

BILLY GRAHAM

July 31, 1982

Unfounded rumors have been spread that the Procter &
Gamble Company has some connection to devil worship.

Unfortunately, some of these false accusations have
been spread in various churches.

These rumors claim that the Procter & Gamble
100-year-old trademark with its famous moon and 13
stars representing the 13 colonies has something to
do with the supporting of satanism and devil worship.
I have found this to be absolutely false. I urge
Christians everywhere to reject these false rumors
and to be reminded that it is a sin to "bear false
witness."

Billy Graham

CBS NEWS
A Division of CBS Inc.
524 West 57 Street
New York, New York 10019
(212) 975-432

Dear Ms. Gilbert:

In response to viewer inquiries regarding Procter & Gamble
and the erroneous impression that executives of your company
have appeared on 60 MINUTES, we have informed those viewers
that at no time has any executive of P&G appeared on our
broadcast. Further we don't recall the name Procter & Gamble
ever being mentioned by us in any connection.

Sincerely,

Don Hewitt

Don Hewitt
Executive Producer
60 MINUTES

Ms. Kathy Gilbert
Public Affairs Division
The Procter & Gamble Co.
P.O. Box 599
Cincinnati, Ohio 45201

June 10, 1982

ABC News   7 West 66th Street   New York, New York 10023   Telephone 212 887-4002

Av Westin
Vice President
Executive Producer

July 20, 1982

Mr. John G. Smale
President
Proctor & Gamble Co.
6th and Sycamore St.
Cincinnati, Ohio 45201

Dear Mr. Smale:

The ABC News Magazine 20/20 has received numerous
phone calls and letters from the public asking if
Proctor and Gamble representatives, including you,
have been interviewed on 20/20 concerning your company, its trademark and/or satanism/devil worship.
We have advised those viewers that no Proctor and
Gamble representatives have ever discussed those
subjects on our broadcast.

Sincerely,

Av Westin

Av Westin
Vice President
ABC News

AW:bjh

cc: Mr. Patrick J. Hayes
     Section Manager-Public Affairs
     Proctor & Gamble

JERRY FALWELL
& THE OLD-TIME GOSPEL HOUR
LYNCHBURG, VIRGINIA 24514

June 1982

To Whom It May Concern:

It is unfortunate that such false accusations regarding
the Procter & Gamble Company are made in the first place, but
even more concerning that they can be spread as rumor by people
who call themselves Christians.

I have discussed these rumors with the Chairman of the
Board of Procter & Gamble, who happens to be from my home town
in Virginia, and I am certain neither he nor his company is
associated in any way with satanism or devil worship. Christians
have a responsibility to know the truth before spreading stories
and, in this case, the truth is there is no story to tell. I
urge people everywhere to help put an end to these unfortunate
rumors.

Sincerely,

Jerry Falwell

Jerry Falwell

JF:dd

The International Radio and Television Outreach of Thomas Road Baptist Church

FIGURE B

with a vengeance in early 1985. This time it spread like wildfire to the East Coast and wouldn't be denied. After quickly surveying consumers and finding that many didn't even recognize the trademark, P&G announced in April that it would give up its battle and remove the century-old design from all its products.

The next month, still smarting from its decision, the company sued a Virginia minister, a Kansas school teacher, and a Pennsylvania couple, alleging that they had spread "false and malicious" rumors that the company worshiped Satan. Summarized the chief executive of a company that designs corporate logos, "It's certainly one for the books."*

QUESTIONS

1. Do you think P&G could have averted the spread of rumors by immediately changing its corporate symbol?
2. Do you agree with the P&G strategy to escalate the rumor campaign by taking its case to the national media? What alternative public relations strategies might the company have adopted?
3. Do you agree with critics who claimed that the P&G public relations program was an overreaction to an insignificant, special public?
4. Do you agree with the company's strategy to emphasize the corporate name in its counterattack and downplay individual product names?
5. Had you been P&G's public relations manager in 1985, would you have decided to throw in the towel?

---

*For further information on the Procter & Gamble symbol case see Terry Bivens, "Bedeviled by a Wild Rumor, They Fight Back," *Philadelphia Inquirer*, 1 August 1982, 1-D; F. Crain, "New Logo Will Solve P&G Rumor Trouble," *Advertising Age*, 9 May 1985, 50; Marilyn Dillon, "P&G Clings to Trademark Despite Rumors," *Cincinnati Inquirer*, 23 July 1982; Laurie Freeman, "After Devil of Fight, P&G Gives Up," *Advertising Age*, 29 April 1985, 3–10; Bob Greene, "Rumors About P&G Trademark Showed How 'Dumb' People Are," *Columbus Citizen-Journal*, 3 May 1985, 2; Sandra Salmans, "P&G's Battle with Rumors," *New York Times*, 23 July 1982, Dl, D4; and "Man in Moon Loses a Job," *New York Times*, 25 April 1985, 1, D–8.

22

Public Relations and the Law

The legal and public relations professions have always had an uneasy alliance. Public relations practitioners must always understand the legal implications of any issue with which they become involved, and a firm's legal position must always be the first consideration. Lawyers, correctly, must uphold an organization's standing in a court of law. However, public relations professionals are concerned with an organization's standing in another court—the court of public opinion. Whereas a lawyer's job is to tell an organization what it must do, a public relations professional's job is to tell the organization what it should do. And there's a big difference.

From a legal point of view, normally the less an organization says prior to its day in court, the better. In that way the opposition can't gain any new ammunition that will become part of the public record. From a public relations standpoint, though, it may often make sense to go public early on, especially if the organization's integrity or credibility is being called into public question. Such different views often manifest themselves in different advice. A smart general manager carefully weighs both legal and public relations counsel before making a decision.

In this chapter the uneasy alliance between legal and public relations professionals is explored, along with the increasing role that law plays in public relations practice. Such concerns as insider trading, disclosure law, ethics law, privacy law, copyright law, and a host of other legally oriented issues have become much more important for public relations practitioners.

PUBLIC RELATIONS AND INSIDER TRADING

Every public relations professional should know the laws that govern an organization. A practitioner in a hospital should have a general understanding of health care law. A practitioner working for a nonprofit organization should understand the laws that govern donors and recipients. A practitioner who works in a particular industry—chemicals, computers, sports—should understand the laws germane to that particular area.

Nowhere in public relations practice is an understanding of the law more important than in the area of financial disclosure. Every public company has an obligation to deal frankly, comprehensively, and immediately with any information that is considered material in a decision to buy, sell, or even hold the organization's securities. The Securities and Exchange Commission—through a series of court cases, consent decrees, complaints, and comments over the years—has painted a general portrait of disclosure requirements for practitioners (see appendix E), with which all practitioners in public companies should be familiar.

As mentioned in chapter 19, the SEC's overriding concern is that all investors have an opportunity to learn about material information as promptly as possible. Through its general antifraud statute, Rule 10b–5 of the Securities and Exchange Act, the SEC strictly prohibits the dissemination of false or misleading information to investors. It also prohibits insider trading of securities on the basis of material information not disclosed to the public.

In recent years the public has been shocked by a series of celebrated cases involving the use of insider information to amass illegal securities gains. In one of the most notable of these cases, financier Ivan Boesky was fined $100 million in 1988 and sent to the federal penitentiary in Lompoc, California, for weaving a web of complicated insider deals to reap a personal fortune. Several of his accomplices—all millionaire Wall Street securities experts—were also fined, imprisoned, and subjected to public scorn.

In public relations, as noted in chapter 5, the president of the Public Relations Society of America was forced to resign in 1986 when he, too, profited from insider trading. In another case the former public affairs vice president of Beneficial Corporation was accused by the SEC in 1988 of insider violations, when her brothers traded in Beneficial stock a day before a company announcement that investment bankers had been retained to study measures to "maximize shareholder value." The SEC's complaint charged that the public affairs executive had advised her brothers of the company's plan.

Nor have journalists escaped the ignominy of insider trading convictions. The most famous case involved a *Wall Street Journal* reporter, R. Foster Winans, Jr., who was convicted in the summer of 1985 for illegally using his newspaper column in a get-rich-quick stock-trading scheme. Basically, Winans gave favorable opinions about companies in which a couple of his stockbroker friends had already invested heavily. The stocks then generally went up, the brokers and their clients profited handsomely, and Winans was sentenced to prison.

The Supreme Court in 1987 upheld Winans's conviction for securities fraud by the narrowest of votes. In so doing, the court reasoned that by "misappropriating information belonging to the *Journal*," Winans had violated the newspaper's intangible property rights. According to legal experts, this ruling has widespread implications for anyone with access to business information, including public relations professionals. Says one legal scholar,

The ruling could affect reporters who recycle the information they gather by day into freelance articles, novels, or screen plays that they write by night. Silicon Valley engineers who tinker after hours with their own inventions at home, or salesmen who, after years of working for one company, take their experience and years of know-how and go to work for someone in a competitive business could also be affected. All may have used company information in violation of employers' rules. But whereas in the past they might have found themselves reprimanded, fired, or even slapped with a civil suit, they now could face criminal prosecution.[1]

What the Supreme Court ruling means, in effect, is that an employer can adopt work rules or a code of ethics that can carry a criminal penalty. This may create problems for those, like public relations people, who share information with journalists; for whistle blowers, who could be threatened with prosecution for unauthorized disclosure of confidential information; or for anyone involved in the dissemination of sensitive company data.

The court acted forcefully on the question of property rights in the Winans case and, in so doing, left the way open for Congress and the courts to define insider trading as theft. As one victim in the case, the *Wall Street Journal*, summarized it, "Clearly Mr. Winans did wrong, but the law will develop more soundly in the future if everyone understands the nature of the crime: not buying and selling stocks but stealing property."[2]

PUBLIC RELATIONS AND DISCLOSURE LAW

Besides cracking down on insider trading, the SEC has also challenged public relations firms on the accuracy of information they disseminate for clients. In 1971 the SEC charged the public relations counsel for the Pig 'n Whistle Corporation with issuing news releases and other material that "contained false and misleading statements." The SEC's complaint suggested that it was the responsibility of the public relations firm to authenticate the data contained in client news releases.[3]

The responsibility of practitioners in disseminating corporate news fully, fairly, and promptly has expanded in recent years. As a former SEC chairman put it, "There once must have been a time when the role of financial public relations officers was completely enjoyable and not terribly troublesome. Today, everyone who participates in the process of getting information to the public assumes a certain amount of responsibility for its adequacy and accuracy."[4] This reference includes all company counselors—investment bankers, accountants, lawyers, and public relations advisors.

In 1982 the SEC issued a 95-page release, "Adoption of Integrated Disclosure System," which attempted to bring some order to the chaotic SEC requirements. Essentially, the new document tried to make more uniform the instructions governing corporate disclosure of information. Today, in an environment of mergers, takeovers, leveraged buy outs, and the incessant rumors that circulate around them, a knowledge of disclosure law, a sensitivity to dis-

Marjorie M. Scardino

Marjorie M. Scardino is the president of the Economist Newspaper Group, Inc. In addition to the North American operations of a magazine, which has a U.S. circulation of more than 140,000, the Economist Newspaper Group also oversees a growing range of business information publications and services and the Economist diaries. Before taking this position in 1985, Scardino was the managing partner of the Savannah, Georgia, law firm of Brannen, Wessels & Searcy and founder and publisher, with her husband, of the Pulitzer Prize–winning newspaper the *Georgia Gazette*.

How important is the law in communications work today?
Our society continues to favor the courts rather than personal negotiations to settle disputes. As long as that is the case, the law will be a spectre in most of the things we do. But from the journalist's point of view, the law should be only an after-the-fact player. A reporter researches and writes a story, governing himself by the rules of fairness and the public's need for an open discussion of all issues that are of public interest. The law should be merely a framework and process for judging whether the reporter has done his job when there is a dispute. Since the public relations practitioner's role is also as an interpreter, though for more partisan interests, the law should play much the same role for him. And he should not let his positive efforts to

closure requirements, and a bias toward disclosing rather than withholding material information are important attributes of public relations officials.

PUBLIC RELATIONS AND ETHICS LAW

The laws regarding ethical misconduct in society have gotten quite a workout in recent years. Regrettably, public relations practitioners have, in several well-known cases, been at the center of the storm. In 1988 Lyn Nofziger, former White House political director and communications counselor, was sentenced

spread information be curtailed by worrying about lawsuits.

What are the principal legal obligations of public relations people?
I think it is not productive to describe obligations in terms of the law unless you are a lawyer or a policeman. The public relations person's obligation is fairly to represent his client's story to the public (or, conversely, to try to explain to his client his public impact or impression). In doing this, he must take care to present all the truth, without obfuscation. As a practical matter, he must make his story credible, and that means it must include the warts and the beauty marks. Against the truth he must balance his client's privacy, some of which his client must necessarily be prepared to give up if he wants his name in the papers. In the course of his truth-telling, the public relations person might be both providing the disclosure that satisfies the law and making someone (such as his client's competitor) look pretty bad. He can't fear that result, or he'll find himself shying away from the truth.

What are the key elements of disclosure law?
As far as securities laws are concerned, recent insider trading scandals have made them more treacherous. Congress and the SEC are now working to define those principles that only public companies, investors, and traders ever thought about before. In the process they're spreading the law's net to include the media. A reporter or public relations person may receive information in the course of writing a story about a company that could give special insight into the company's value. Probably, if he uses that information for personal gain, or transmits it to another to use for personal gain, he will be in trouble.

In recent years, has press freedom gotten more or less liberalized?
From my perspective press freedom has contracted seriously over the last several years. This is illustrated by events such as the invasion of Grenada (which the press was not allowed to cover firsthand); the Iran-contra scandal (which involved not only misinforming the public through the press, but also misinforming the Congress); restrictions on the Freedom of Information Act (where new rules may be adopted that will both add to the cost of pursuing an information request and require that—in spite of the fact that your right to such material is established in the act—you must justify why you should have the information). Add to this the public's feeling that the press is manipulating,

(Continued, p. 554)

to 90 days in prison and fined $30,000 for violating the Federal Ethics in Government Act, which forbids lobbying former contacts within one year of leaving the government. The clients with which Nofziger was associated included Wedtech Corporation, a New York City–based minority contractor that later became the central focus in another ethics investigation surrounding Attorney General Edwin Meese.

Also in 1988 former White House deputy chief of staff Michael K. Deaver, another well-known public relations professional, was found guilty of perjury—lying to a grand jury—about his lobbying activities. He also faced a

rather than reporting, public opinion and is unduly intrusive and arrogant in the exercise of its power, and you have all the ingredients for a free-speech disaster.

Should there ever be censorship in a democracy?
Not censorship defined and monitored by the government. There is always a place for censorship within a relationship—that of parent to child or corporation to employee, for instance—but those relationships are private. I don't believe there is any social purpose susceptible to enough refinement that government could regulate its attainment by stemming the flow of information.

What is the relationship between ethics and the law?
I think the law should be looked upon as a set of principles that articulates what our society judges to be the citizens' behavior needed to keep order. Ethics often turn out to be more personal, whether to an individual or to a company or institution. What is ethical for you because of your particular professional position or interests may not be ethical for me because I am in a different po-sition. Therefore, the law may not help you when you must decide whether you have a conflict of interest or whether you have fairly dealt with a competitor or a customer.

Many businesses have tried to help their employees make those thorny decisions by creating company codes of conduct. They have done this as much to avoid outside regulation as to ensure that their employees don't transgress moral behavior. One of the problems with writing down the rules, from a legal point of view, is that it provides that many more standards for would-be adversaries to misinterpret. In the past few years we've seen several lawsuits involving media companies having failed to follow written internal policies. *Westmoreland vs. CBS* is one. *Winans vs. The Wall Street Journal* is another.

In my view, it is best if the tenets of ethical behavior—fairness, honesty, and integrity—are part of the corporate culture. That way, ethics will run not only to fair treatment of your client's needs and resources, but also to fair treatment of your own company's. It will make ethics affirmative, not negative.

---

lengthy jail sentence and a serious fine. In response, Deaver railed against the "outrageousness of congressmen saying that I violated the public trust, when they go out and make all the money they want on speaking fees" paid for by special-interest groups.[5]

Deaver has a point. Some of the most powerful representatives in Congress—from House Speaker Jim Wright to Banking Committee chairman Fernand St. Germain to former Bronx representative Mario Biaggi—were also called on the carpet and accused of violating government ethics laws.

The problems of Nofziger and Deaver called into question the role of lobbyists in government. As explained in chapter 16, the activities of lobbyists have been closely watched by Congress since the imposition of the Lobbying Act of 1947. In recent years, however, the practice of lobbying has expanded greatly; the number of registered domestic lobbyists has more than doubled in the last decade. Today, more than 8,800 lobbyists are in action in Washington, DC, and that estimate may be low. Some put the so-called influence-peddling population at about 20,000, or more than 30 lobbyists for every member of Congress.[6]

Complicating the lobbyist issue still further, foreign governments are particularly eager to retain savvy Washington insiders to guide them through the bureaucratic and congressional maze and polish their images in the United States. Public relations counselors are strictly mandated by law to register the foreign entities they represent. However, in recent years a number of representatives of foreign clients have been the subject of scandals and legal investigations. By 1988 there were signs that the public had had enough of international ethics violations. In one jury trial in Kentucky, two former Ashland Oil vice presidents, who had lost their jobs in 1983 because they refused, first, to pay bribes to foreign officials and, then, to lie about the bribes, were awarded $69 million for lost pay and punitive damages against the company. Ashland Oil immediately appealed the landmark verdict.

The increasing number of government officials who resign to become play-for-pay lobbyists—coupled with the lingering legal problems of prominent public relations people like Nofziger and Deaver and the increasing concern in all sectors of society for more ethical behavior—may indicate that those who govern and those who attempt to influence them will in the future be scrutinized more closely for how ethically they do business and how scrupulously they follow the law.

PUBLIC RELATIONS AND PRIVACY LAW

The laws that govern a person's privacy also have implications for the public relations profession. Privacy laws, particularly those that touch on libel and defamation by the media, are curious indeed. When such alleged defamation involves a public figure, the laws get even more curious. Generally, the privacy of an ordinary citizen is protected under the law. A citizen in the limelight, however, has a more difficult problem, especially in proving defamation of character.

To prove such a charge, a public figure must show that the media acted with actual malice in its reporting. "Actual malice" in a public figure defamation case means that statements have been published with the knowledge that they were false or with reckless disregard for whether the statements were false.[7] In a landmark case in 1964, *New York Times v. Sullivan*, the Supreme Court nullified a libel award of $500,000 to an Alabama police official, holding that no damages could be awarded "in actions brought by public officials against critics of their official conduct" unless there was proof of "actual malice." And proving actual malice is difficult.

YOU MAKE THE CALL

Texas Gulf Sulphur

Probably the most far-reaching and widely publicized court case involving financial public relations and SEC disclosure law was that of the Texas Gulf Sulphur (TGS) Company in the 1960s. In late 1963 TGS discovered ore deposits in Canada. Although a potentially spectacular find, the company made no public announcement about the discovery. In subsequent weeks TGS quietly purchased hundreds of acres of surrounding land, and company officers purchased additional shares of TGS stock on the open market. Eventually, as more ore was found in 1964 and officers continued buying TGS stock, rumors circulated concerning the company and its mineral treasure. On April 12, 1964, the company distributed a press release that termed the rumors "unreliable" and stated that test drilling "to date hasn't been conclusive." Despite the negative announcement, TGS officers continued to buy company stock.

Four days later, almost six months after the original discovery, TGS announced that it had "made a major strike of zinc, copper, and silver." The price of TGS stock immediately skyrocketed.

After extensive litigation, the U.S. Court of Appeals ruled that TGS officers had violated SEC disclosure laws. The court said that TGS officials traded on insider information and passed on tips to their friends, who also bought the stock on insider knowledge. The court also ruled that TGS on April 12, 1964, had "issued a false and misleading press release," in violation of Rule 10b–5.

TGS officers, including the director of public relations, and their friends were punished for trading on the information not fully disclosed to the public. The case proved conclusively that a company's failure to make known material information may constitute a violation of the antifraud provision of the Securities and Exchange Act. The TGS case remains today a landmark in the history of public relations law.

QUESTIONS

1. If you had been the public relations director of Texas Gulf Sulphur in 1963, what communications step would you have recommended the company take after it discovered rich ore deposits in Canada?
2. If, as TGS public relations director, you had not been told by management about the ore deposits until April 12, 1964, and then were asked to put out the release denying rumors of a rich ore find, what would you have done?

What has happened in practice is that journalists have often triumphed when sued by public figures. Several libel cases during the 1980s were particularly noteworthy.

- In 1982 the Philadelphia CBS affiliate was hit with a $5.1 million libel suit brought by Mayor William Green when the station aired an erroneous report that Green was the target of a federal grand jury investigation of an alleged $50,000 kickback in return for millions of dollars in sludge-removal contracts.
- CBS-TV itself was hit by a $120 million libel suit filed by Army General William C. Westmoreland, over a 1982 documentary that accused the general of falsifying enemy troop strengths in Vietnam. After the suit was filed, CBS launched its own internal investigation of its program on Westmoreland and found numerous improprieties and biases in the TV production process. But a libel law showdown was not to be. Early in 1985, after 2½ years of litigation, nearly half a million pages of documents, extensive media coverage, and 65 grueling days in court, General Westmoreland settled out of court with CBS, "winning" an eight-sentence joint statement that said the network did not "believe that General Westmoreland was unpatriotic or disloyal in performing his duties as he saw them."

  Even though the case ended with a whimper and proved little, the importance of the public relations profession was boosted when CBS hired a public relations professional, New York counselor John Scanlon, to represent it to the media covering the trial. This may have been the first time that a major media power conceded the value of professional public relations in getting across its story.[8] Several months later Scanlon was retained again, this time by the *Boston Globe* in its trial against politician John Lakian, who had also filed a libel suit.
- Also in 1982 the *Washington Post* initially lost a $2 million suit after a federal jury decided that the newspaper had libeled William P. Tavoulareas when it alleged that he had used his position as president of Mobil Oil to further his son's career in a shipping business (Figure 22–1). The next year a federal judge overturned the verdict against the *Post* because the article in question didn't contain "knowing lies or statements made in reckless disregard of the truth." Following this later ruling, Mobil took out a highly unusual protection policy against media attacks on its executives. Under this defamation insurance policy Mobil executives who believed they had been defamed by the media could be reimbursed for most of the legal expense of bringing their cases to court.

  In 1985 a federal appeals court reinstated the $2 million libel verdict against the *Post*. But later that year the U.S. Court of Appeals of the District of Columbia agreed to reconsider the reinstatement. Finally, in 1988 the Supreme Court ruled in favor of the *Post* by throwing out the Tavoulareas suit for lack of merit. A contrary ruling would have restricted the limits of investigative journalism and broadened the interpretation of defamation of character. Reporters breathed a sigh of relief at the decision.

"It's a great commentary on our times when a jury finds for an oil company against a newspaper."

Frederick Taylor
Executive Editor, The Wall Street Journal, quoted in Newsweek, October 25, 1982

To avoid any misquotation, we wrote Mr. Taylor and asked him if the quote were accurate. His entire reply was the following: "I said it. And you can use it."

For several reasons, we think the statement reflects an astonishing degree of irresponsibility—particularly since Mr. Taylor is the Executive Editor of such a prestigious publication. Specifically—

ONE. The statement was made in reference to a unanimous verdict by a jury which found that *The Washington Post* and two reporters had libeled the President of Mobil. This was a personal suit, brought by him as an individual, which he totally paid for himself, to which Mobil was not a party. The jury did not "find for" Mobil. We seriously doubt that Mr. Taylor was unaware of this distinction. After all, his paper provided coverage of the case and clearly reported its private nature. It was an attempt to substitute a giant oil company as the Goliath attacking the "David-like" *Washington Post*. (Some David!) It was an attempt to erase the fact that the issue in the case involved damage to an individual's reputation. No oil company was involved.

TWO. Even worse, the statement seems to betray a shocking bias. It appears to us that Mr. Taylor thinks oil companies are so venal, so inherently evil that no matter what injustices a newspaper might heap upon them, they should not prevail in a court of law before a jury.

Is Mr. Taylor suggesting that oil companies and their executives be stripped of their civil rights? Or that newspapers should be free to knowingly print false information about them? And, finally, should such behavior be immune from liability?

Mobil

FIGURE 22–1 The initial 1982 libel verdict against the *Washington Post* and in favor of the president of Mobil Oil and his son was chilling to journalists. In a three-column story *Wall Street Journal* executive editor Frederick Taylor blamed the verdict on growing public disenchantment with the press. Mobil, almost immediately, responded to Taylor's charge with this ad. (Courtesy of Mobil Oil Corporation)

- In another celebrated case in 1985, Israeli General Ariel Sharon brought a $50 million libel suit against *Time* magazine. It, too, ended without a libel verdict. However, once again, the jury criticized *Time* for negligent journalism in reporting Sharon's role in a Palestinian refugee camp massacre.
- In 1988 the Supreme Court threw out a suit brought by conservative televangelist/preacher Jerry Falwell against *Hustler* magazine, accusing the sex-oriented periodical with defaming his character in a fictitious liquor advertisement about his mother. Despite the grossness of the ad, the Supreme Court ruled that what was written was clearly a spoof of a public figure and that Falwell, therefore, didn't have a case.

What all these cases illustrate is a growing trend in society to challenge the media for their invasion of personal privacy. Although cases like these tend to confirm the rights of the media to report on public figures, in other cases—particularly those involving gossip-oriented tabloids—the courts have awarded settlements to celebrities who have been wronged.

PUBLIC RELATIONS AND FREE SPEECH LAW

The media, of course, draw their power from the First Amendment, which protects the freedom of the press. Over the years, First Amendment protection has been frequently tested in the courts. One of the most celebrated cases was the Pentagon papers case of 1971, in which the government attempted to stop publication of leaked secret documents about the Vietnam War, claiming a general danger to the national security. The government failed, and newspapers and magazines branded it a victory for the press.[9] In the late 1970s and 1980s political attacks on the media, primarily from conservative camps and big business, focused on the theme that journalists enjoyed too much freedom.

Business, too, has attempted to secure speech freedoms of its own. In one landmark 1978 case the Supreme Court struck down a Massachusetts law that permitted a business corporation to speak only on those issues "which materially affect its business, property, or assets." In the case of *First National Bank of Boston et al. v. Bellotti,* the Court held that companies had the right to spend corporate funds to publicize their opposition to a referendum authorizing the state legislature to enact a graduated personal income tax. That judgment indicated a trend to protect corporations that want to speak out on public issues, and corporations followed up by getting a lot more vocal (Figure 22–2).

PUBLIC RELATIONS AND COPYRIGHT LAW

One body of law that is particularly relevant to public relations professionals is copyright law and the protections it offers writers. Copyright law provides basic, automatic protection for writers, whether or not a manuscript is registered with the Copyright Office or even published. Under the Copyright Act of

Trial by Television

The American system of justice is founded on a simple principle: The accused has the right to be fairly heard in his own defense, and to confront and cross examine his accuser.

This principle, more than any other, defines the difference between freedom and tyranny.

Yet today, here in America, charges are aired before tens of millions of people without fair opportunity for the accused to respond.

They call it "investigative" television journalism. We call it "Trial by Television."

Much of investigative television journalism is solid and responsible reporting—but much is not. Many producers of "news magazine" programs too frequently select story segments with their minds already made up about the points they want to make. Then they proceed to select the facts and quotes which support their case. "Interview" opportunities are sometimes provided the "accused." But the edited "interview" format puts the producer (i.e. the accuser) in full control of deciding what portions, and how much of, the accused's defense the public will be allowed to see.

Rarely does this result in balanced and objective coverage.

The television production team becomes the accuser, judge, and jury. With no real recourse for the accused to get a fair hearing in the court of public opinion. Yet the viewing public is led to believe that the coverage is balanced and objective. This is a deceptive and very dangerous practice.

"Trial by Television," like the kangaroo courts and star chambers of old, needs to be examined. If we decide, as a society, that we are going to try issues, individuals, and institutions on television, then some way must be found to introduce fairness and balance.

Here's what we're doing about it.

Recently, Kaiser Aluminum was the victim of grossly misleading and inaccurate statements on a segment of ABC's "20/20" program. On its "20/20" segment of Thursday, April 3, the announcer accused aluminum house wiring of being unsafe, and Kaiser Aluminum of intentionally marketing an unsafe product. These accusations are blatantly wrong.

Although we were offered an opportunity to be "interviewed," "20/20" reserved the privilege of editing any part of our statement. Any defense we might have made would be subject to their sophisticated editing techniques, and to their commentary. Since it was evident to us that the producers had already formed their opinions, we declined their offer. How can a defense be fair if it is subject to censorship by the accuser?

We have been advised by many to ignore the "20/20" attack on the basis that you can't fight the network, and to prevent further harassment. We will not allow ourselves to be maligned or misrepresented by any group—even television.

Here is what we are doing:
1. We have demanded a satisfactory retraction from ABC-TV.
2. We are asking the Federal Communications Commission, under their "Personal Attack" doctrine, to order ABC-TV to provide us with time and facilities to present our side of the story to the same size audience in a prime time segment.
3. We have asked Congressman Lionel Van Deerlin (D-California), Chairman of the House Sub-Committee on Communications to consider Congressional hearings to examine the implications of this increasingly insidious and dangerous practice.

Here's what you can do about it.

Unfortunately, not all victims of "Trial by Television" have the resources to defend themselves, as we are trying to do. Their only defense is you.

If you believe the rights of the accused to fairly defend themselves are more important than sensational attempts to increase TV ratings; if you believe the right of the public to get balanced and objective information on issues of importance is as important as it has ever been, please speak out and let your elected representatives know.

America was conceived to prevent tyranny by providing checks on the power of any institution. Today, a new power is dispensing its own brand of justice—television. There's only one check against it. You.

If you are upset by the unfairness of "Trial by Television," write your elected representatives, or us at Kaiser Aluminum, Room 1137KB, Lakeside Drive, Oakland, CA 94643.

KAISER ALUMINUM & CHEMICAL CORPORATION

1 One person can make a difference

FIGURE 22–2 Typical of the growing trend of organizations to strike back and speak out, especially when challenged by the media, was this Kaiser Aluminum ad that answered what the company believed were "grossly misleading and inaccurate statements" on a segment of ABC's "20/20" program. (Courtesy of Kaiser Aluminum and Chemical Corporation)

1976, an "original work of authorship" has copyright protection from the moment the work is in fixed form. As soon as an article, short story, or book is put on paper or a computer disk or is spoken into a tape recorder, it is protected by copyright law. You created it, and you own it. What you sell to an editor isn't the article itself, but the right to use the material.

Copyright protection exists for broad categories of works—literary works; musical works, including any accompanying words; dramatic works, including any accompanying music; pantomimes and choreographic works; pictorial, graphic, and sculptural works; motion pictures and other audiovisual works; and sound recordings. Copyright law gives the owner of the copyright the exclusive right to reproduce and authorize others to reproduce the work, prepare derivative works based on the copyrighted material, and perform and/or display the work publicly.[10] That's why Michael Jackson had to pay $47.5 million in 1987 for the rights to the Beatles' compositions to the duly sworn representatives and heirs of John, Paul, George, and Ringo.

Several categories of material are not eligible for copyright protection, such as titles and short slogans; works consisting entirely of information from common sources and public documents, such as calendars, lists, and tables; and speeches and performances that have not been fixed on paper or recorded. Work in the public domain—material that was never covered by copyright or for which the copyright has lapsed, material that lacks sufficient originality, and basic themes and plots—can't be protected by copyright.

Neither can ideas be protected. This means that an old idea, newly packaged, is absolutely permissible, legal, and even recommended. Indeed, there are few truly new ideas in the world, only old ideas put together in new and different ways. So a public relations practitioner shouldn't be overly concerned with violating copyright laws when devising a campaign, program, or manuscript in support of a client's activity.

PUBLIC RELATIONS AND THE LEGAL PROFESSION

What has always been an uneasy alliance between lawyers and public relations professionals has today evolved into a relationship of grudging mutual respect. Lawyers, in fact, are making more use of public relations strategies than ever before. In one 1987 poll 17 percent of lawyers surveyed reported using public relations, up from 14 percent in 1985. And 23 percent said they had used public relations at some point.[11] Nonetheless, four lawyers in five still don't use public relations, reportedly for three basic reasons: (1) it is unprofessional, (2) it is unnecessary, and (3) it creates an undesirable image.[12]

Within the legal profession public relations remains primarily the province of large, big-city firms. For them, using public relations techniques can be quite helpful. Says one partner in a major law firm, "Public relations people are like having a doctor keep you in good health rather than waiting until you're at death's door."[13] Such elite law firms as Milbank, Tweed, Hadley &

McCloy and Fried, Frank, Harris, Shriver & Jacobson have hired public relations counselors to publicize their activities in articles, news releases, and brochures. With the 1984 Supreme Court easing the ban on self-advertisement by lawyers, law firms in the years to come will unquestionably increase their interest in and use of public relations to further their practices.

For their part, public relations counselors have become more open to lawyers and have relaxed the tensions that have existed between the two professions. One public relations practitioner offers these insights into working with lawyers who may be representing a practitioner's organization.

1. **Become an equal partner with legal counsel.** At all times maintain an overview of the legal cases before your organization or industry. Take the initiative with legal counsel to discuss those that you believe may have major public relations implications.
2. **Combat the legal no-comment syndrome.** Research cases in which an organization has publicly discussed issues without damage.
3. **Take the initiative in making announcements.** This will help manage public perception of the issue. If an indictment is pending, consult the legal staff on the advisability of making statements—before you become a target.
4. **Research the background of the jury.** Past lists of jurors in a particular jurisdiction indicate occupations and other important demographic information.
5. **Winning may not be everything.** Outside law firms, trained in an adversarial mode and charging fees that depend on the size of the award, always want to "win." For legal counsel the stakes may also include a winning reputation, which helps to secure future cases. Public relations must bring a long-term perspective to strategic decisions.
6. **Beware of leaving a paper trail.** Any piece of paper that you create may end up in court. That includes desk calendars and notes to yourself. So be careful.[14]

PUBLIC RELATIONS AND THE LAW: THE FUTURE

As our society becomes more contentious, fractious, and litigious, public relations must become more concerned with the law. Indeed, public relations has already become involved with the law in many areas of communications beyond those already cited in this chapter.

■ The Federal Communications Commission in 1987 ruled that the Fairness Doctrine, the subject of years of debate among broadcasters and others, unconstitutionally restricted the First Amendment rights of broadcasters. And the FCC said that broadcasters were no longer obligated to provide equal time for dissenting views. Congressional efforts to turn the doctrine into law were vetoed by President Reagan. But the debate may not be finished.

■ Malpractice suits have proliferated against celebrity spokespersons, who endorse merchandise that ultimately proves faulty, as in the case of legendary

What's in a Letter?

People are curious about the difference between the *R* in a circle and the *C* in a circle when it comes to copyrights. What's the difference? *C* indicates copyright ownership, whereas *R* or *TM* indicates that the word or phrase it accompanies is a registered trademark. Both, in their way, signify ownership—of the right to use the manuscript or word or phrase.

A title can't be copyrighted, yet it can be given trademark protection. *Star Wars,* the movie, for example, was a title that had been granted trademark protection. Thus, when President Reagan's strategic defense initiative was nicknamed "Star Wars" by its critics and nobody sued, they could have—as a violation of trademark law.

quarterback Johnny Unitas and a bankrupt financial services firm that he mistakenly endorsed in 1985.

- The right of publicity has been challenged by the estates of deceased celebrities like Charlie Chaplin, W.C. Fields, Mae West, and the Marx brothers, whose likenesses have been portrayed in product advertisements without the permission of their heirs.

- The decision in 1988 by the Supreme Court that public school officials have broad power to censor school newspapers, plays, and other school-sponsored expressive activities also is sure to be challenged in the years ahead.

- Also in 1988 a federal jury found a cigarette manufacturer, the Liggett Group, liable in the lung-cancer death of a New Jersey woman because the company failed to warn of smoking's health risks before such warnings were required on cigarette packs in 1966. In awarding $400,000 in damages to the late woman's husband, the jury concluded that advertising slogans such as "Just what the doctor ordered" misleadingly suggested that smoking was safe. The verdict was hailed by antismoking advocates as the most important breakthrough since cigarette company advertising was forced off television in 1971. With 110 similar antitobacco cases pending in the United States, it seems quite likely that advertised and publicized corporate claims will come under increased legal scrutiny, not only for cigarette manufacturers but for all those who promote product and service claims.

When coupled with the growing trend by organizations to become more vocal in paid advertisements, issues-oriented publications, employee and shareholder information programs, speakers' bureaus, and the like, it becomes clear that the connection between public relations and the law will intensify dramatically in the 1990s.

NOTES

1. Daniel Lazare, "What's Riding on the Winans Case," *Columbia Journalism Review* (January/February 1988): 5.
2. "We Were Robbed," *Wall Street Journal,* 17 November 1987, 38.
3. Anne F. Hanby, "Structuring a Financial Relations Program," *Public Relations Journal* (April 1978): 21.
4. Ray Garrett, Jr., "The Role of Financial Public Relations," address before the Publicity Club of Chicago, 13 March 1974.
5. Evan Thomas and Thomas M. DeFrank, "Mike Deaver's Rise and Fall," *Newsweek,* 23 March 1987, 23.
6. Evan Thomas, "Peddling Influence," *Time,* 3 March 1986, 27.
7. Howard W. Suckenik, "PR and Legal Issues," *O'Dwyer's PR Services Report* (March 1988): 44.
8. Bill Abrams, "Fierce Public Relations Fight Is Preceding Westmoreland's Court Battle with CBS," *Wall Street Journal,* 31 May 1984, 33.
9. James Boylan, "How Free Is the Press?" *Columbia Journalism Review* (September/October 1987): 32.
10. Jay Stuller, "Your Guide to Copyright," *Writer's Digest* (June 1988): 29.
11. "How Lawyers Use Public Relations," *Public Relations Journal* (January 1988): 30.
12. Ibid.
13. Doug Lavine, "Lawyers Use PR Firms to Buff Their Image," *National Law Journal,* 18 September 1978.
14. Lloyd Newman, "Litigation Public Relations: How to Work with Lawyers," *PR Reporter Tips & Tactics* (23 November 1987): 2.

SUGGESTED READINGS

Cantor, Bill. *Experts in Action: Inside Public Relations.* New York and London: Longman, 1984.

Cheney, Richard. "Dealing with the Press" *National Law Journal* (21 March 1983).

Crisis Management: A Workbook for Survival. Belleville, NJ: Lempert Co. (202 Belleville Ave.), 1987.

Fink, S. *Crisis Management: Planning for the Inevitable.* New York: AMACOM (135 W. 50th St.), 1986.

Hill and Knowlton Executives. *Critical Issues in Public Relations.* Englewood Cliffs, NJ: Prentice-Hall, 1976.

Lavine, Doug. "Lawyers Use PR Firms to Buff Their Image." *National Law Journal* (18 September 1978).

Lerbinger, Otto. *Managing Corporate Crises: Strategies for Executives.* Boston, MA: Barrington Press, 1986.

Lesly, Philip. *Lesly's Public Relations Handbook.* Englewood Cliffs, NJ: Prentice-Hall, 1978.

Meyers, Gerald. *When It Hits the Fan.* Boston, MA: Houghton Mifflin, 1986.

New Principles for Public Companies After the Supreme Court Decision. Englewood Cliffs, NJ: Prentice-Hall, 1988.

Pinsdorf, M. *Communicating When Your Company Is Under Siege.* Lexington, MA: Lexington Books, 1986.

Posner, Ari. "The Culture of Plagiarism." *New Republic* (1988).

Simon, Morton J. *Public Relations Law.* New York: Appleton-Century-Crofts, 1969.

The Screwed Up Odometers

Listen to the lawyers sometimes—yes. But always? No. Public relations advice must be weighed against legal advice when faced with an organizational crisis. The Chrysler Corporation was tested in this regard in 1987, when it and two of its executives were indicted on criminal charges for selling cars driven while their odometers were disconnected.

Although the indictment covered only an 18-month period, the Justice Department asserted that Chrysler odometers had been disconnected for decades and that millions of cars had been sold with inaccurate mileage readings. According to the indictment, executives at Chrysler assembly plants routinely took new cars off the assembly line and drove them as much as 400 miles with the odometers disconnected. In addition, the indictment charged that some cars were damaged in the testing and were only superficially repaired before being shipped to dealers for sale.

Initially, the company, on the advice of its lawyers, responded by arguing that it had done nothing illegal. But its tune quickly changed when it saw that public opinion was running decidedly against it. That's when Chrysler chairman Lee Iacocca, known for his blunt speech, called a news conference at the company's Michigan headquarters and termed the action "dumb" and "unforgivable." "Did we screw up?" Iacocca asked rhetorically. "You bet we did," he answered.

Iacocca said that he had been personally unaware of the disconnecting of odometers until a few months before the indictment. He said that even though disconnecting odometers was standard industry practice, it was still "dumb." Beyond this, however, he said that Chrysler employees had driven 40 cars that had been seriously damaged in accidents, repaired, and then sold as new. "Simply stated," the chairman said, "that's unforgivable, and we've got nobody but ourselves to blame."

At the news conference Chrysler announced that it would give new cars to the 40 owners of the affected models. Other owners, the company said, would be offered longer warranties with broader coverage. "Our big concern is for our customers, the people who had enough faith in Chrysler to buy a vehicle from us," Iacocca said. "These charges and the press reports about them are causing some of those customers to question that faith, and we simply cannot tolerate that."

Apparently the unvarnished, straightforward Iacocca approach, devoid of legalistic posturing, worked splendidly. Four days after the charges had been announced, 55 percent of adult Americans polled in a public opinion survey thought that Chrysler faced a serious problem. In a follow-up survey four days after the news conference, 67 percent of those contacted believed Chrysler had adequateiy dealt with the issue. Chrysler officials added that the company experienced no ill effect on vehicle sales or stock prices.

A few days after the Chrysler news conference, the company was socked with a fine of $1.5 million for alleged health and safety violations at a Newark, Delaware, plant. Or-

> "Testing cars
> is a good idea.
> Disconnecting
> odometers
> is a lousy idea.
> That's a mistake
> we won't make
> again at Chrysler.
> Period."
>
> *Lee Iacocca*

FIGURE A   (Courtesy of Chrysler Corporation)

LET ME SET THE RECORD STRAIGHT.

1. For years, spot checking and road testing new cars and trucks that come off the assembly line with the odometers disengaged was standard industry practice. In our case, the average test mileage was 40 miles.

2. Even though the practice wasn't illegal, some companies began connecting their odometers. We didn't. In retrospect, that was dumb. Since October 1986, however, the odometer of every car and truck we've built has been connected, including those in the test program.

3. A few cars—and I mean a few—were damaged in testing badly enough that they should not have been fixed and sold as new. That was a mistake in an otherwise valid quality assurance program. And now we have to make it right.

WHAT WE'RE DOING TO MAKE THINGS RIGHT.

1. In all instances where our records show a vehicle was damaged in the test program and repaired and sold, *we will offer to replace that vehicle* with a brand new 1987 Chrysler Corporation model of comparable value. No ifs ands or buts.

2. We are sending letters to everyone our records show bought a vehicle that was in the test program and offering a free inspection. If anything is wrong because of a product deficiency, we will make it right.

3. Along with the free inspection, we are extending their present 5-year or 50,000-mile protection plan on engine and powertrain to 7 years or 70,000 miles.

4. And to put their minds completely at ease, we are extending the 7-year or 70,000-mile protection to *all major systems:* brakes, suspension, air conditioning, electrical and steering.

The quality testing program is a good program. But there were mistakes and we were too slow in stopping them. Now they're stopped. Done. Finished. Over.

Personally, I'm proud of our products. Proud of the quality improvements we've made. So we're going to keep right on testing. Because without it we couldn't have given America 5-year 50,000-mile protection five years ahead of everyone else. Or maintained our warranty leadership with 7-year 70,000-mile protection. I'm proud, too, of our leadership in safety-related recalls.

But I'm not proud of this episode. Not at all.

As Harry Truman once said, "The buck stops here." It just stopped. Period.

CHRYSLER MOTORS **7/70** LIMITED WARRANTY
CHRYSLER · PLYMOUTH · DODGE CARS · DODGE TRUCKS

We just want to be the best.

FIGURE A   *continued*

dinarily, this fine, on top of Chrysler's $300,000 fine in the odometer case, would have been more than enough to send public opinion plummeting. But in Chrysler's case top management had been willing to adopt a practical public relations approach rather than an overly legalistic one. As a *Boston Globe* reporter put it, "Iacocca seemed to have patched up the company's image when he did something a corporate chairman rarely does: He apologized for his company, called the odometer tampering 'dumb' and termed the selling of damaged cars 'stupid.' " All of which demonstrates once again that management candor is often preferable to legal pus-syfooting in confronting a major public opinion crisis.

QUESTIONS

1. Why do you think Chrysler originally refused to take the heat on the odometer tampering issue?
2. How would you describe Chairman Iacocca's approach to dealing with bad news?
3. What might have happened if Chrysler had followed its lawyers' advice and remained silent?
4. What else would you suggest that Chrysler consider in addition to the news conference and the national advertising?

23

The Future

Public relations counselor Philip Lesly, who chaired the Task Force on Stature and Role of Public Relations for the Public Relations Society of America, has suggested that the final part of this century will be "dominated by the human climate—the attitudes of people that determine how all segments of society will function."[1] Indeed, the human climate is now a determining factor in the future of every organization, institution, and nation. The emergence of this dominant force in society creates significant opportunities and challenges for public relations.

On the one hand, the field is growing rapidly. Public relations is a significant growth area in universities. More than 160 colleges and universities have a public relations sequence or degree program. Sixty percent of the public relations sequences now rank first or second in sequence enrollments within journalism departments. In 1985, public relations majors constituted about 13 percent of the 82,760 students enrolled in schools of journalism.[2]

The number of continuing education courses in public relations has also increased exponentially. In 1971 New York University's continuing education program in public relations consisted of two classes and 59 students. Today, hundreds of public relations courses are offered by seminar groups, such as the Professional Development Institute in New York City and Ragan Report Workshops in Chicago, each of which offers a variety of practical public relations workshop sessions.

In addition, enrollment in the Public Relations Society of America (PRSA), the field's professional association, is now around 14,000, with another 600 members added annually. The Public Relations Student Society of America is composed of 151 chapters with 5,000 students. In 1968 there were only 6 chapters and 56 students.

The U.S. Department of Labor says that public relations jobs will increase faster than the average for all occupations through the 1980s "because of new spots and replacement of individuals who retire or leave the field for other reasons."[3] However, the most striking testimony to the importance of public relations in society can be seen in the money that people spend on it today. At the end of the 1970s, the 30 largest public relations agencies together produced net fee income of approximately $140 million. By 1988 the net fee income of the top 10 public relations agencies alone totaled close to $450 million.[4] Indisputably, public relations has become very big business.

On the other hand, public relations is faced with all the challenges associated with an increasingly popular field. Many want to enter the profession, and competition for most jobs is fierce. Then, too, as management becomes more aware of the role of public relations, its performance expectations become higher. So the standards to which public relations professionals are held have also increased. Finally, since in most organizations access to top management is a coveted role and public relations is generally granted that access, key public relations positions today are eagerly sought by managers outside the public relations discipline.

A DRAMATICALLY CHANGING SOCIETY

Undeniably, the people who practice public relations today must be better than those who came before them. Institutions today operate in a pressure-cooker environment and must keep several steps ahead of the rapid pace of social, economic, and political change. The environment is being shaped by many factors.

- **Economic globalization** This is affecting all organizations, even nonmultinational companies. Competition will intensify, and so will communications, making it easier to communicate around the world but much more difficult to be heard.
- **Shifting public opinion** Sudden shifts in public opinion are being ignited by instantaneous communications, challenging the ability of communicators to respond to fast-moving events.
- **Aging of society** Households headed by people over 55 are the fastest-growing segment of the consumer market in America, and these "oldsters" control about 30 percent of all personal income.
- **Tenders, mergers, leveraged buy outs** The stock market plunge of October 19, 1987, still reverberates, making American companies more vulnerable to tender offers, mergers, and leveraged buy outs. Increasingly, foreign interests will take over U.S. firms, revising the concept of a domestic marketplace.
- **Downsizing** With this euphemism for firing people, companies are continuing to pare overhead and trim staff to become more competitive. The effect on business and employee morale is profound, and the need for good internal communications is critical.
- **Corporate responsibility** This buzzword of the 1960s and 1970s, quieted by recession and recovery in the 1980s, is apt to surface again in the 1990s, especially as companies fire more people and as legal and ethical questions arise on issues like AIDS.[5]

Coupled with these factors is a society that seems incapable of leashing its voracious appetite for costly litigation. No product or service area is immune from potential suit. And bigness is back in vogue, with mergers not only among huge industrial corporations, but also among hospitals, banks, media companies, and others. Yet, at the same time a growing body of opinion sees big business as a threat, especially because it has become more active politically. Product stewardship, an idea that holds a manufacturer responsible for products in perpetuity, is gaining advocacy.[6] Additionally, consumers are demanding greater accountability from all institutions, as well as higher standards of ethical conduct.

In the face of all these changes, it is understandable that management today is giving greater attention than ever before to the public's opinions of its organization and to public relations professionals who can help deal with those opinions.

RESPONDING TO SOCIETY'S CHANGE

The dramatic changes affecting society in general and its leading institutions in particular hold numerous implications for the future of public relations practice. Public relations generalists, able to coordinate and manage all aspects of the practice—from formulating policy and managing budgets to supervising people and executing programs—will be in demand. But so, too, will be specialists who are expert in dealing with the media, consumers, and investors and who have the sophisticated writing ability that management demands.[7]

Management today regularly scrutinizes public relations budgets and activities to measure results for greater accountability. The wave of merger mania that swept America in the mid-1980s stripped away public relations jobs in many companies. Public relations professionals who remained have been asked to extend their function beyond communications to include strategic planning, issues and analysis, and, most important, assisting top management in solving significant organizational problems. According to Robert L. Fegley, 1979 recipient of the PR Professional of the Year award from *Public Relations News,*

> Chief executives today need people to help them orchestrate their appearances, develop and articulate their themes, build their media connections, research the issues, develop their positions, and express themselves persuasively. They need counsel on trends and problems among their various constituencies. Public relations people, trained to mediate between the institution and its publics in communications, are peculiarly qualified to help our leaders to lead. And this is true for organizations of all kinds—not only business firms, but government agencies, hospitals, universities, not-for-profit organizations, whatever.[8]

Unlike past decades, when top managers were, by necessity, more concerned with the production, marketing, or financial sides of the business, external pressures today necessitate "a much greater need for businessmen to understand the broad environment in which they operate and to communicate to unfamiliar publics what they can do and are doing to meet public de-

Joseph T. Nolan

J oseph T. Nolan, adjunct professor of communications at the University of North Florida, was vice president of public affairs for Monsanto Company. He had overall responsibility for public and government relations, advertising, community affairs, and social responsibility. Before joining Monsanto in 1976, Nolan had been a newspaper editor and correspondent with the *New York Times* and United Press International, a

professor of journalism and public affairs at the University of South Carolina, and a senior communications manager at Chase Manhattan Bank and RCA Corporation. *Business Week* magazine cited him as one of the "top 10 executives in corporate public relations." Nolan has lectured extensively and written articles for numerous major publications on public relations and advertising as well as other business subjects.

What is public relations?
Public relations is the planned effort of individuals and organizations to influence public opinion through a sustained program of actions and communications. *Actions* is the key word. If a public relations practitioner can't influence the actions of his organization, he's not earning his salary.

What are the most significant challenges that confront the public relations profession?
Gaining management's confidence by providing high-quality advice and mature judgment, by focusing on results rather than on activities, and by being able to measure the results with greater precision than is now being done.

What do you see as the future of public relations education?
More emphasis on business management and on the social sciences, such as economics, social psychology, and sociology, and less on developing techniques and understanding gadgetry.

What do you see as the prospects for growth in employment in the public relations profession?
I think that employment will expand steadily, but not explosively, over the next decade or two as more and more enterprises understand what public relations can do to help them.

What parts of the field do you see as growth areas in the 1990s?
Fund-raising and investor and employee relations are likely to increase, but I think that one of the biggest areas of growth will be in dealing with television in all of its aspects. Surveys show that perhaps 80 percent of the public gets its news through television, and yet virtually all public relations departments suffer from a serious print bias.

What parts of the profession do you see as becoming more limited in available opportunities?
I suspect we've reached the saturation point in the placement area and in press-agentry.

What are the greatest threats to the future of public relations?
Inept practitioners—men and women who don't understand thoroughly the enterprise they're trying to represent.

Do you envision that public relations practitioners will be called on to manage organizations in the future?
The best of the public relations practitioners will move up to top management roles just as marketing and financial specialists, engineers, and lawyers have done in the past.

Will public relations ever attain the same stature as the professions of law or accounting?
If public relations keeps working at its accreditation procedure, improving it as it goes along, and does a better job of policing its ranks, it could very well eventually achieve a place alongside accounting, law, and the other professions. This would be an important development, but its importance should not be exaggerated. The only way to get this kind of stature is to merit it, and that must be done every day.

What are the emerging trends you foresee in public relations over the next 20 years?
The most formidable challenge is likely to be managing the new business environment. The decisive issues will be external rather than internal, social and political rather than economic. The pivotal test is making profits for the stockholders and quality products at reasonable prices. The challenge will come primarily from the impact of laws and public opinion.

By the year 2000 what do you predict will be the general state of the practice of public relations?
I predict that major organizations will have a public relations practitioner very near the top and that they will weigh every major decision in light of its public relations impact, just as they do now with respect to its business and financial impact.

mands."[9] To accomplish this, management must rely more heavily on public relations practitioners to better articulate ideas in the never-ending battle to sway public opinion.

Chief executives of the future will have a good grasp of the public relations function and will accept their obligations as communicators-in-chief. They will also take it for granted that their public relations departments have the skills and resources to conduct and manage communications.[10] In return, communications professionals will be paid more and will be expected to do more. The public relations function will be very much in the spotlight.

CHALLENGES FOR PUBLIC RELATIONS IN THE 1990s

As the significance of the practice of public relations intensifies, so, too, will the challenges confronting the public relations profession. The challenges will be worldwide, just as the field itself has become worldwide. The power of communication, especially global communication, will no longer be an American domain. Among the major challenges confronting public relations professionals will be these:

- **Increased need for marketing support** Public relations professionals will be challenged to allocate more of their resources to activities that directly support marketing and sales objectives. Practitioners must better harmonize the communications functions of public relations, advertising, and promotion as the world becomes more competitive.
- **Need for better internal communications** With morale in question as a result of downsizings, mergers, acquisitions, buy outs, and the like, internal communications will become more important. Indeed, as competition increases, so does the necessity for more efficient, higher quality, more innovative organizations. All of this translates into a challenge for better internal communications.
- **Government communications** As government continues its inexorable growth, government public relations, especially at the state and local levels, will grow as a career field to meet the new demands for information of a politically sensitive population. Government relations positions in industry should grow also.
- **Technology** Public relations professionals will be blessed with an expanding array of tools to cope with the speed and impact of rapid, global communications. Practitioners must master this technology if the field is to continue to develop.
- **Measurement** The growth of research to measure and evaluate public relations results will continue. Public relations professionals must find ways to improve their measurement capability.
- **Creativity** Creativity in the 1990s will be at a premium. Management will expect public relations people to demonstrate bright approaches to corporate problems, thoughtful programs for overcoming or avoiding trouble, and

novel ideas for getting attention. The public relations department, in short, must be a storehouse of innovation in the organization.[11]

Added to these challenges must be the task of continuing to develop public relations education, literature, and sophistication so that the field itself continues its trajectory as a profession rather than a craft.

COUNSELING TOP MANAGEMENT

The key challenge for public relations practitioners in the 1990s will be counseling top management. Top managers in corporations, hospitals, associations, government, education, and most other areas are usually very much alone. Few around them challenge their wisdom; many around them are unquestioning sycophants—the last thing a chief executive needs. Top managers, after all, are human beings, too, with all the failings and foibles that go along with that designation. They desperately need advice, and public relations people should be willing and eager to provide it.

The successful public relations counselor in the years ahead will possess the following nine characteristics:

1. **Intimate knowledge of the institution** A public relations professional may be an excellent communicator, but without knowledge of the industry or institution represented, ultimate value will be limited.
2. **Access to and respect of management** The public relations professional who acquires the respect of top management is a powerful force in an organization. Respect comes only from exposure. Thus, it is essential that the public relations professional have ready access to the most senior managers in an organization.
3. **Access to an intelligence network** Public relations professionals need their own intelligence network to give them the unvarnished truth about programs and projects. If the executive vice president is an idiot . . . if the employee incentive program isn't working . . . if the chairman's speech was terrible . . . the public relations professional must be able to tap a team of candid employees who will tell the truth, so that the practitioner can "tell it like it is" to top management—unexpurgated, uncensored, between the eyes.
4. **Familiarity with the reporter on the beat** A public relations professional—no matter how high up in an organization—should keep in touch with the reporters and analysts who follow the organization. Valuable information can be gleaned from such observers and can be most helpful to top management.
5. **Solid skills base** The most competent public relations counselors don't just give orders, they demonstrate skills. They are generally good writers, who don't mind "getting their hands dirty" if it means completing a job competently. In public relations, communications competence is a prerequisite for counseling competence.

The Voluntary Recall

The practice of public relations can materially influence business decisions, especially as organizations become more aware of and responsible to the many publics on which their livelihood depends. A case in point is the Parker Brothers toy company, which, in 1978, suffered a loss of several million dollars almost solely on the basis of public relations advice. And far from being distraught, Parker Brothers management seemed pleased.

Until April 4, 1978, Parker Brothers had no reason to believe that it had anything but a big winner in its new children's toy, Riviton. A construction toy for kids 6 to 12, Riviton was a great success, with more than 900,000 sets sold in less than two years. But on April 4 the 96-year-old company was shaken to learn that an 8-year-old boy in Wisconsin had suffocated from a Riviton rivet in his right lung. The company further learned that the attorney representing the boy's family had contacted the Consumer Product Safety Commission, which, after an investigation, concluded that the incident was an isolated occurrence. Seven months later another youngster suffocated from a Riviton rivet, this time in New Jersey.

Although both these deaths were caused by the product's rivets, Riviton had met all voluntary and industry-set safety standards. Parker Brothers was under no pressure from any government agency to do anything. However, as Parker's president put it, "We never before in 95 years of being in business have heard of a serious accident or fatality resulting from the use or misuse of any of our products." Parker's management saw four alternatives.

1. It could do nothing. Both accidents resulted from product misuse, and any action the firm might take could be overreacting. Nevertheless, the potential for further misuse clearly existed.
2. The company could issue a statement of warning to consumers and put the statement on the product package.
3. The product could be modified to eliminate possible hazards. Modification could take months of research and testing.
4. The company could launch a total recall.

Parker Brothers chose option four. On November 24 Parker's chief counsel notified the Consumer Product Safety Commission of the impending recall.

On the same day Parker Brothers issued the following news release:

> BEVERLY, MA—Parker Brothers today announced the voluntary recall of all Riviton construction toys.
>
> While the Riviton construction toy complies with all safety requirements and does not present a hazard when properly used, Parker Brothers has made the decision to withdraw this product from the market because of two accidental deaths associated with product misuse.
>
> The company reached this decision after the recent death of a 9-year-old child was attributed to choking on a rubber fastening rivet from the Riviton construction toy.

After this announcement Parker hired extra personnel to answer toll-free telephones and offered full rebates. The company contacted its major customers by telegram and telephone to have them start taking returns immediately. The company also hired extra personnel to dispose of the sets as they arrived, through either incineration or burial.

Seven months after Parker's announcement, the toys were still coming in at the rate of 200 a week. In June 1979 the company reported that 420,000 of the 935,000 outstanding sets had been returned. The loss to Parker Brothers was about $10 million, but the company didn't seem to mind. As Parker's president put it, "By demonstrating our concern for the millions of parents who buy and use our products, we have built a more solid relationship with consumers than ever before."

QUESTIONS

1. Do you agree with the president's assessment that Parker's action would ultimately benefit the company?
2. If you were a parent aware of Parker's actions, what would you think of the company? Would you be inclined to purchase Parker Brothers toys for your children?
3. Do you think most companies today, faced with a similar set of circumstances, would have made the same decision that Parker Brothers made?

6. **Propensity toward action** In working for top management, results and performance are all that count. Certainly, planning and setting strategies are critical aspects of public relations. But practitioners, especially those who counsel management, must be inclined toward action. They must be doers. That's what management demands.

7. **Knowledge of the law** Public relations work today confronts legal issues—privacy, copyright, lobbying, and securities laws, broadcasting regulations, and on and on. Although public relations professionals need not be trained lawyers, they must at least be conversant in the general concepts of the law in order to counsel management effectively and also to deal with legal counselors.

8. **Strong sense of integrity and confidence** As noted in chapter 5, public relations professionals must be the ethical conscience of organizations. Their motives and methods must be above reproach. It's also important that public relations counselors demonstrate a confidence in their own positions and abilities. They must surround themselves with the highest caliber performers to enhance the status of the public relations function within the organization.

9. **Contentment with anonymity** Public relations counselors must understand that they are exactly that—counselors to top management. It is the chief who delivers the speeches, charts the strategies, and makes the decisions. And it is the chief, too, who derives the credit. Public relations counselors must remain in the background and should try to stay anonymous. Today, with newspapers demanding the names of spokespersons, with some public relations practitioners attaining national celebrity status, and with the field itself becoming more and more prominent, the challenge of anonymity becomes increasingly more difficult.

EMERGING ISSUES IN PUBLIC RELATIONS

The issues that concern public relations professionals vary from organization to organization and from industry to industry. Nonetheless, several issues concern all practitioners, especially as the field continues to grow in respect and improve its credibility.

Public Relations Education

For public relations to continue to prosper, a solid educational foundation for public relations students must be in place. Today's practitioner has two key stakes in public relations education: one is future employees, and the other is the profession itself.

Over the past few years the Public Relations Society of America and others have focused efforts on the formal education of public relations students. In 1987 a design for undergraduate public relations education was authored by the Public Relations Division of the Association for Education in Journalism and Mass Communication, the Educator's Section of PRSA, and PRSA itself.[12] Among the highlights of the report were these findings and recommendations:

- Two subjects tied for the highest ratings by practitioners and educators: English (within general education) and an internship/practicum/work-study program (within public relations education).
- It is recommended that public relations students, especially those planning to enter the corporate or agency world, give strong consideration to business as the secondary area of concentrated study.
- The traditional arts and sciences remain the solid basis for the undergraduate education of public relations students, essential to their functioning professionally in a complex society.

The report indicated strong agreement between practitioners and educators on what the content of undergraduate public relations education should be. Basically, strong emphasis was placed on communications studies, public relations principles and practices, and ethics. The report further concluded that the growing cooperation and relationships among professionals in the practice of public relations and in education should be nurtured and strengthened to benefit today's students of the field.

Increasing Percentage of Women in Public Relations

Another issue of concern in the field is the impact of the increasing percentage of women in public relations and business communications. In 1980 women accounted for only 10 percent of the public relations population. Today that number is well over 50 percent.[13] Many practitioners express concern that public relations could become a "velvet ghetto," populated almost entirely by women.[14] The expansion of women in public relations is not surprising. Women account for up to 65 percent of all journalism graduates in the United States. According to a study at the University of Maryland, female students are attracted to public relations and advertising because they think these areas are more open to women.[15]

One of the most comprehensive studies of this issue was that launched in 1986 by the International Association of Business Communicators. The results of this study indicated that women are increasingly filling the role of communications technicians rather than managers. As a result, women are being paid less than men, with gender being the strongest predictor of salary. Among its conclusions the report found that the situation does not appear to be improving. Instead, men are turning to other professions or are positioning themselves in certain areas within the field that are highly masculine and highly paid, such as communications management.

All of this may have significant implications for the future. Clearly, more women will enter top management public relations jobs. Competition between the sexes for these jobs will be intense, and counseling fees may decline be-

What's Out? What's In?

Heading into the 1990s, here's how *Business Week* defined and categorized a variety of management concepts.*

What's Out

1. Centralization: Father knows best.
2. Consultants: Company doctors, who still make occasional house calls.
3. Decentralization: Then again, maybe Father doesn't know best.
4. Factory of the future: Robot heaven is not yet available on earth.
5. Management by walking around: The ultimate open-door policy goes perhaps a few steps too far.
6. Quantitative management: The numbers tell it all—except what to do next.
7. Synergy: Genetic engineering for corporations. But when you cross a horse with a donkey, you get a mule.
8. T-groups: Building team spirit. "I am he as you are me, and we are all together." Oh well, at least the Beatles made millions.
9. Theory Y: A form of participatory management. You really do have a say in how things are run. (Sure you do!)
10. Theory Z: The art of Japanese management for those who've forgotten the ABCs of American management.

*Stuart Jackson, "Management Lingo: How to Read Between the Lines," *Business Week*, 20 January 1986, 58.

cause of a perception that women will work for less. A "good old girl" network could form in the public relations field, or, as one practitioner argued, "Women may give public relations a more sensitive appearance instead of the bad name the profession now has."[16]

Licensing

For many years practitioners have argued over the merits of licensing public relations professionals. Among the most outspoken advocates of public relations licensure has been public relations patriarch Edward Bernays. He and others have argued that by licensing public relations people, the quality of those who practice public relations could be protected.

Others, like counselor Philip Lesly, have argued that for public relations people to seek government control "is ludicrously out of step with either logic or the times."[17] Lesly and others have argued that licensing would have a number of damaging effects.

What's In

1. Back to basics: Where you go when your synergistic move into high tech flops.
2. Chapter 11: A new way to break labor contracts or to sidestep liability suits.
3. Corporate culture: Get everybody singing the same song and hope they're in key.
4. Demassing: Slimming down at the top. The latest euphemism for firing people.
5. Intrapreneurship: Discovering the entrepreneurs in your own ranks, which may be easier than keeping the bureaucracy at bay once you do.
6. Niches: Markets your competitors haven't found. Yet.
7. Pay for performance: It used to be known as piecework.
8. Skunk camp: Officially, a management seminar. Unofficially, business boot camp.
9. Touchy-feely managers: The boss is a really nice guy. He's also still the boss.
10. Wellness: Part of the health craze. You'll know it's arrived when they stop serving lemon meringue pie in the company cafeteria.

- Government control by licensure would create real or implied threats to public relations people who might be called on to further a viewpoint that politicians oppose.
- State licensing would stifle out-of-state competition, as it does with lawyers, banks, and others.
- State licensing would lead to a parochial, state-centered view of what public relations is and would create artificial boundaries that would unnecessarily inhibit the practice of public relations across state and even national lines.
- In a day when professionals can't agree on the benefits of being an accredited member of the Public Relations Society of America, licensing would segment the public relations field even more and cause more public confusion.
- The ability to have a license denied or revoked could encourage extremists to demand "delicensing" of anyone who supports an opposing viewpoint.

With no easy answer available on either accreditation or licensing, the debate is likely to continue in the 1990s.

External Challenges

Inevitably, as public relations has enhanced its role in society and increased its respect within organizations, the field itself has attracted others—lawyers, accountants, personnel managers, and general managers of varying backgrounds. Because the public relations executive of an organization is usually close to top management and because access is power in an organization, the role occupied by public relations has become a coveted one. In the 1990s incursions into public relations by others in an organization are apt to intensify, thereby increasing the pressure on practitioners to use their special expertise and unique experience to reinforce their prominent positions in the organizational hierarchy.

IMPLICATIONS FOR BEGINNERS

The reality of a more respected and therefore more competitive public relations profession has numerous implications for persons just starting out in the field. Although competition for public relations positions is stiff, experience is the great equalizer, and smart beginners can optimize their potential for employment by getting a jump on the competition through early experience. How?

- By becoming involved with and active in student public relations organizations
- By securing—through faculty or others—part-time employment that uses the skills important in public relations work
- By attending professional meetings in the community, learning about public relations activities, and meeting public relations practitioners who might prove to be valuable contacts later on
- By seizing every opportunity, from informal internships to voluntary work for nonprofit associations or political candidates to service on the school newspaper to merchandising in-class projects to local merchants

Experience is the key. And full-time student status is an ideal time to begin to acquire working public relations knowledge.

OUTLOOK FOR THE FIELD

Most professions undergo constant change, but few experience more critical or frequent change than public relations. In the 1970s practitioners were introduced to a tidal wave of primary concerns: consumerism, environmentalism, government relations, and public policy forecasting. Areas of public relations opportunity shifted quickly from marketing publicity to financial relations, to employee communications, to public issues management. Steadily through the 1970s the field expanded its horizons and increased its influence.

By the start of the 1980s, the field had significantly increased its role as an active rather than a reactive force in society. One indication of the field's

All Is Not Won . . .

National columnists like James "Scotty" Reston of the *New York Times* and Meg Greenfield of the *Washington Post* complain that the practice of public relations confirms George Orwell's darkest prognostication that a "consummate manipulator of information controls people's thoughts in a systematic and sustained way." Horsefeathers! Much closer to the truth is the wisdom of one Ivan Kershner, administrative assistant for the North Platte, Nebraska, Public Schools, who offers eight guiding principles for public relations.*

1. No matter what you do, it isn't enough.
2. No matter what you do, it will be misinterpreted by somebody.
3. No matter how many copies you distribute, you will have forgotten somebody.
4. Media importance is awarded to an issue in direct opposition to that given the issue by your boss.
5. Never fall prey to the thought that your organization's side of an issue is understood.
6. Assume a total vacuum of comprehension on the part of all parties, and you shall not be disappointed.
7. No matter whom you know, somebody else knows somebody more important.
8. No matter how many people proofread, something is always *mispelled*.

So there, Scotty and Meg!

*"8 Rules for Public Relations," *Communication Briefings* 5, no. 6 (April 1986).

new maturity was the heightened attempt by advertising agencies to buy public relations units. Indeed, in the early 1980s the largest public relations merger in history was consummated with J. Walter Thompson, one of the nation's largest advertising agencies, acquiring Hill and Knowlton, the nation's largest public relations firm.

In the 1990s the U.S. Department of Labor's Bureau of Labor Statistics expects the number of managerial jobs at public relations, marketing, and advertising firms to expand more than 32 percent annually, whereas public relations employment for all industries will grow at a rate of about 39 percent. By the year 2000, say the department's experts, managers with public relations, marketing, and advertising companies will number 427,400.[18] Thus, despite the many challenges it faces, public relations work appears to be on the thresh-

---

BETWEEN
THE LINES

. . . But All Is Not Lost

"The Edsel is the car of the future!" "Dewey elected President!" "There is no market for personal computers!"

Rumors, hearsay, myths—they are all around us. Hardly a week goes by without someone, somewhere emerging with a profound pronouncement that is pithy, novel, and wrong. That's why one week in 1988, when a well-known California public relations counselor (who later claimed he was misquoted) announced to one and all that "PR is dead as a concept," his statement was quickly rebutted by this offering from McGrath/Power West public relations agency.

I rest my case.

MAR/COM MURPHY

The Lighter Side of Marketing Communications, courtesy of McGrath/Power Public Relations, Santa Clara, CA/New York, NY.
© 1988 McGrath/Power.

---

old of its most significant period in history. Never before has society been so vocal in its acknowledgment of and need for the practice of public relations.

As Chrysler chairman Lee Iacocca put it in describing how his company made it back from the brink of bankruptcy,

> Effective public relations was our life support system for awhile. And believe me, I'm not overstating the case. We weren't running on fumes anymore, we were running on faith. The faith of the public that we could make it allowed us to stay in business. And we kept that faith only through our ability to communicate.[19]

Adds practitioner Philip Lesly:

> The future is certain to feel the impact of public relations—by whatever term it is called and by whoever is called on to practice it. The future is there for us in public relations to grow with—if we have the judgment to meet it. It will be up to us to determine whether we sit in on the truly momentous decisions of this generation or merely act as technicians carrying out the initiatives of others.[20]

And that really is the key point. With its responsibilities expanded, its access to management increased, and its importance to the organization more critical than ever before, public relations is poised to command a leadership role in the management of the organizations of the future. Whether the field attains this higher stature depends entirely on the caliber and the competence of the men and the women who engage in the practice of public relations in the 1990s.

NOTES

1. Philip Lesly, "How the Future Will Shape Public Relations—And Vice Versa," *Public Relations Quarterly* (Winter 1981–82): 4.
2. "The Design for Undergraduate Public Relations Education," study co-sponsored by the Public Relations Division of the Association for Education in Journalism and Mass Communication, the Public Relations Society of America, and the Educators Section of PRSA (1987): 1.
3. *The Occupational Outlook Handbook.* Washington, DC: U.S. Department of Labor, 1978–79.
4. Jack O'Dwyer, *Jack O'Dwyer's Newsletter,* period ending 23 March 1988, 4.
5. Bill Cantor, "A Wild Plunge into the Future," *Cantor Commentary* (171 Madison Avenue, New York, NY 10016) (October, 1987): 2.
6. Joseph Nolan, "To Gain a Good Reputation," *Across the Board* (October 1985): 36.
7. "Cantor's Cycle of Corporate Public Relations Staffing," *Cantor Concern* (171 Madison Avenue, New York, NY 10016) (January 1986): 1.
8. Robert L. Fegley, "How Public Relations Can Help the CEO," *Public Relations Journal* (October 1981): 25.
9. "PR: 'The Velvet Ghetto' of Affirmative Action," *Business Week,* 8 May 1978, 122.
10. Edward M. Block, "Strategic Communications: Practicing What We Preach," Foundation for Public Relations Research and Education lecture, 8 November 1987.
11. Robert L. Dilenschneider, "What's Ahead for Public Relations: Problems or Progress?" *Public Relations Quarterly* (Fall 1987): 8.
12. "The Design for Undergraduate Public Relations Education," cited earlier.
13. *The Velvet Ghetto: The Impact of the Increasing Percentage of Women in Public Relations and Business Communications* (San Francisco, CA: IABC Foundation, 1986), 1.
14. "PR: 'The Velvet Ghetto' of Affirmative Action."
15. "Women: The New Majority in Journalism School," *Glamour* (July 1986): 208.
16. Ted Joseph, "The Women Are Coming, the Women Are Coming," *Public Relations Quarterly* (Winter 1985): 22.
17. Philip Lesly, "Analysis of Proposals for Licensing Public Relations," speech delivered before Symposium on Professionalism, Itasca, IL, 5 September 1986.
18. Bill Cantor, "Sixth Annual Review and Forecast of Public Relations Trends," *Cantor Commentary* (January 1988): 5.
19. Lee A. Iacocca, remarks delivered to the PR News Awards Banquet, New York, NY, 20 June 1985.
20. Philip Lesly, "How the Future," 4.

SUGGESTED READINGS

Careers in Public Relations. (Available from the Public Relations Society of America, 845 Third Avenue, New York, NY 10022.)

Carty, **Walter V.** "The Message Before the Medium." *Public Relations Quarterly* (Spring 1977): 20.

"The Corporate Image: PR to the Rescue." *Business Week,* 22 January 1979, 47–50, 54–56.

Design for Public Relations Education. (Available from Public Relations Society of America, 845 Third Avenue, New York, NY 10022.)

Dilenschneider, **Robert L.** "What's Ahead for Public Relations: Problems or Progress?" *Public Relations Quarterly* (Fall 1987): 5–8.

Edelman, Daniel J. "Farley Fellowship Address: Managing the Public Relations Firm in the 21st Century." *Public Relations Review* (Fall 1983): 3–10.

Fewsmith, Phillip, and **Joan Lockwood Finn.** "When You're on the Wrong Side of the Desk." *Public Relations Journal* (February 1982): 28–30. This gives a humorous look at what can—and often does—happen when you are interviewed for a job.

Futurist. (Available from World Future Society, 4916 St. Elmo Avenue, Washington, DC 20014.) This bimonthly journal includes forecasts, trends, and ideas about the future on all topics.

Greyser, Stephen A. "Changing Roles for Public Relations." *Public Relations Journal* (January 1981): 18–25.

Hart, Gary. "Emerging Issues for Public Relations." *Public Relations Journal* (January 1980): 11–14, 27, 30–31.

Jackson, Patrick. "Tomorrow's Public Relations." *Public Relations Journal* (March 1985): 24–25.

Joseph, Ted. "The Women Are Coming, the Women Are Coming." *Public Relations Quarterly* (Winter 1985): 21, 22.

Lesly, Philip. "How the Future Will Shape Public Relations—and Vice Versa." *Public Relations Quarterly* (Winter 1981–82): 4–8.

———. *Lesly's Public Relations Handbook.* 2d ed. Englewood Cliffs, NJ: Prentice-Hall, 1978. See the chapter on "Emerging Principles and Trends."

———. "Report and Recommendations: Task Force on Stature and Role of Public Relations." *Public Relations Journal* (March 1981): 21–44. This overview analyzes the entire public relations profession and indicates the likely course it may take in the years ahead.

———. "The Stature and Role of Public Relations." *Public Relations Journal* (January 1981): 14–17.

Lindenmann, Walter, and **Alison Lapetina.** "Management's View of the Future of Public Relations." *Public Relations Review* (Fall 1981): 3–14.

Martin, Lee. "A Mixed Bag in the Job Market." *Public Relations Journal* (February 1982): 27.

Martinson, David L. "How Future Practitioners Define Public Relations." *Public Relations Quarterly* (Spring 1981): 21–22.

Nolan, Joseph. "To Gain a Good Reputation." *Across the Board* (October 1985): 35–40.

Seifert, Walt. "OSU's Graduates Tackle Diverse Fields, Functions." *Public Relations Journal* (February 1982): 14–15.

"Sixth Annual Review and Forecast of Public Relations Trends." *Cantor Commentary* (171 Madison Ave., New York, NY 10016) (January 1988).

Traub, Doug. "How to Land That First Public Relations Job." *Public Relations Journal* (February 1982): 16–18. Four senior professionals list writing ability, self-discipline, and leadership among qualities needed to make the grade.

Ways, Max. *The Future of Business: Global Issues in the '80s and '90s.* Elmsford, NY: Pergamon Press.

Werle, C. R. "Breaking In: A Different Approach." *Public Relations Journal* (February 1982): 18.

"A Wild Plunge into the Future." *Cantor Commentary* (171 Madison Ave., New York, NY 10016) (October 1987).

The Tylenol Murders

For close to 100 years, Johnson & Johnson Company of New Brunswick, New Jersey, was the epitome of a well-managed, highly profitable, and tight-lipped consumer products manufacturer.

Round I

All that changed on the morning of September 30, 1982, when Johnson & Johnson (J&J) faced as devastating a public relations problem as had confronted any company in history. It was on that morning that Johnson & Johnson management learned that its premier product, extra-strength Tylenol, had been used as a murder weapon to kill three people. In the days that followed, another three people died from swallowing Tylenol capsules loaded with cyanide. And although all the cyanide deaths occurred in Chicago, reports from other parts of the country also implicated extra-strength Tylenol capsules in illnesses of various sorts. These latter reports were later proved to be unfounded, but Johnson & Johnson and its Tylenol-producing subsidiary, McNeil Consumer Products Company, found themselves at the center of a public relations trauma, the likes of which few companies had ever experienced.

Tylenol had been an astoundingly profitable product for Johnson & Johnson. At the time of the Tylenol murders, the product held 35 percent of the $1 billion analgesic market. It contributed an estimated 7 percent to J&J's worldwide sales and almost 20 percent to its profits. Throughout the years Johnson & Johnson had not been—and hadn't needed to be—a particularly high profile company. Its chairman, James E. Burke, who had been with the company almost 30 years, had

never appeared on television and had rarely participated in print interviews.

Johnson & Johnson management, understandably, was caught totally by surprise when the news hit. Initially, Johnson & Johnson had no facts and, indeed, learned much of its information from the media calls that inundated the firm from the beginning. The company recognized that it needed the media to get out as much information to the public as quickly as possible to prevent a panic. Therefore, almost immediately, Johnson & Johnson made a key decision—to open its doors to the media.

The second day of the crisis Johnson & Johnson discovered that an earlier statement that no cyanide was used on its premises was wrong. The company didn't hesitate. Its public relations department quickly announced that the earlier information had been false. Even though the reversal embarrassed the company briefly, Johnson & Johnson's openness was hailed and made up for any damage to its credibility.

Early on in the crisis, the company was largely convinced that the poisonings had not occurred at any of its plants. Nonetheless, Johnson & Johnson recalled an entire lot of 93,000 bottles of extra-strength Tylenol associated with the reported murders. In the process it telegrammed warnings to doctors, hospitals, and distributors at a cost of half a million dollars. McNeil also suspended all Tylenol advertising to reduce attention to the product.

By the second day the company was convinced that the tampering had taken place during Chicago distribution and not in the manufacturing process. Therefore, a total Tylenol recall did not seem obligatory. Chairman Burke himself leaned toward immediately recalling all extra-strength Tylenol capsules, but after consulting with the Federal Bureau of Investigation, the J&J chairman decided not to recall all capsules. The FBI was worried that a precipitous recall would encourage copycat poisoning attempts. Nonetheless, five days later, when a copycat strychnine poisoning occurred in California, Johnson & Johnson did recall all extra-strength Tylenol capsules—31 million bottles—at a cost of over $100 million.

Although the company knew it had done nothing wrong, J&J resisted the temptation to disclaim any possible connection between its product and the murders. Rather, even as it moved quickly to trace the lot numbers of the poisoned packages, it also posted a $100,000 reward for the killer. Through advertisements promising to exchange capsules for tablets, through thousands of letters to the trade, and through statements to the media, the company hoped to put the incident into proper perspective.

At the same time, Johnson & Johnson commissioned a nationwide opinion survey to assess the consumer implications of the Tylenol poisonings. The good news was that 87 percent of Tylenol users surveyed said they realized the maker of Tylenol was not responsible for the deaths. The bad news was that although a high percentage didn't blame Tylenol, 61 percent still said they were not likely to buy extra-strength Tylenol capsules in the future. In other words, even though most consumers knew the deaths weren't Tylenol's fault, they still feared using the product.

But Chairman Burke and Johnson & Johnson weren't about to knuckle under to the deranged saboteurs who poisoned their product. Despite predictions of the imminent demise of extra-strength Tylenol, Johnson & Johnson decided to relaunch the product in a new triple-safety-sealed, tamper-resistant package (Figure A). Many on Wall Street and in the marketing community were stunned by Johnson & Johnson's bold decision.

But so confident was Johnson & Johnson management that it launched an all-out media blitz to make sure that people understood its commitment. Chairman Burke appeared on the widely watched Phil Donahue network television program and skillfully handled 60 minutes of intense public questioning. The investigative news program "60 Minutes"—the scourge of corporate America—was invited by Johnson & Johnson to film its executive strategy sessions to prepare for the new launch. When the program was aired, reporter Mike Wallace concluded that although Wall Street had been ready at first to write off the company, it was now "hedging its bets because of J&J's stunning campaign of facts, money, the media, and truth."

Finally, on November 11, slightly more than two months after the murders, Tylenol management held an elaborate video press conference in New York City, beamed to additional locations around the country, to introduce the new extra-strength Tylenol package. Said Tylenol's chairman to the media,

It is our job at Johnson & Johnson to ensure the survival of Tylenol, and we are pledged to do this. While we consider this crime an assault on society, we are nevertheless ready to fulfill our responsibility, which includes paying the price of this heinous crime. But I urge you not to make Tylenol the scapegoat.

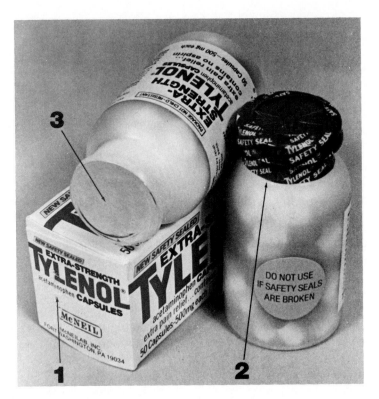

FIGURE A The triple-safety-sealed, tamper-resistant package for Tylenol capsules had (1) glued flaps on the outer box, (2) a tight plastic neck seal, and (3) a strong inner foil seal over the mouth of the bottle. A bright yellow label on the bottle was imprinted with a red warning, "Do not use if safety seals are broken." As it turned out, all these precautions didn't work. (Courtesy of Johnson & Johnson)

In the days and months that followed Burke's news conference, it became clear that Tylenol would not become a scapegoat. In fact, by the beginning of 1983 Tylenol had recaptured an astounding 95 percent of its prior market share. Morale at the company, according to its chairman, was "higher than in years" (Figure B). The euphoria lasted until February 1986, when, unbelievably, tragedy struck again.

Round II

Late in the evening of February 10, 1986, news reports began to circulate that a woman had died in Yonkers, New York, after taking poisoned capsules of extra-strength Tylenol. And the nightmare for Johnson & Johnson began anew.

Once again, the company sprang into action. Chairman Burke addressed reporters at a news conference a day after the incident.

Our Credo

We believe our first responsibility is to the doctors, nurses and patients,
to mothers and all others who use our products and services.
In meeting their needs everything we do must be of high quality.
We must constantly strive to reduce our costs
in order to maintain reasonable prices.
Customers' orders must be serviced promptly and accurately.
Our suppliers and distributors must have an opportunity
to make a fair profit.

We are responsible to our employees,
the men and women who work with us throughout the world.
Everyone must be considered as an individual.
We must respect their dignity and recognize their merit.
They must have a sense of security in their jobs.
Compensation must be fair and adequate,
and working conditions clean, orderly and safe.
Employees must feel free to make suggestions and complaints.
There must be equal opportunity for employment, development
and advancement for those qualified.
We must provide competent management,
and their actions must be just and ethical.

We are responsible to the communities in which we live and work
and to the world community as well.
We must be good citizens — support good works and charities
and bear our fair share of taxes.
We must encourage civic improvements and better health and education.
We must maintain in good order
the property we are privileged to use,
protecting the environment and natural resources.

Our final responsibility is to our stockholders.
Business must make a sound profit.
We must experiment with new ideas.
Research must be carried on, innovative programs developed
and mistakes paid for.
New equipment must be purchased, new facilities provided
and new products launched.
Reserves must be created to provide for adverse times.
When we operate according to these principles,
the stockholders should realize a fair return.

Johnson & Johnson

FIGURE B   (Courtesy of Johnson & Johnson)

A phone survey found that the public didn't blame the company. With discovery of other poisoned Tylenol capsules two days later, the nightmare intensified. The company recorded 15,000 toll-free calls to its Tylenol hotline. And once again, production of Tylenol capsules was halted. "I'm heartsick," Burke told the press. "We didn't believe it could happen again, and nobody else did either."

This time, although Tylenol earned Johnson & Johnson some 13 percent of the company's net profits, the firm decided once and for all to cease production of its over-the-counter medications in capsule form. It offered to replace all unused Tylenol capsules with new Tylenol caplets, a solid form of medication that was less tamper-prone (Figure C). This time the withdrawal of its capsules cost Johnson & Johnson upwards of $150 million after taxes.

And once again, in the face of tragedy, the company and its chairman received high marks. As President Reagan said at a White House reception two weeks after the crisis hit, "Jim Burke of Johnson & Johnson, you have our deepest appreciation for living up to the highest ideals of corporate responsibility and grace under pressure."*

QUESTIONS

1. What might have been the consequences if Johnson & Johnson had decided to "tough out" the first reports of Tylenol-related deaths and not recall the product?

2. What other public relations options did Johnson & Johnson have in responding to the first round of Tylenol murders?

3. Do you think the company made a wise decision by reintroducing extra-strength Tylenol?

4. In light of the response of other companies not to move precipitously when faced with a crisis, do you think Johnson & Johnson should have acted so quickly to remove the Tylenol product when the second round of Tylenol murders occurred in 1986?

5. What specific lessons can be derived from the way in which Johnson & Johnson handled the public relations aspects of these tragedies?

---

*For further information on the first round of Tylenol murders, see Jerry Knight, "Tylenol's Maker Shows How to Respond to Crisis," *Washington Post*, 11 October 1982, 1; Thomas Moore, "The Fight to Save Tylenol," *Fortune*, 29 November 1982, 48; Michael Waldholz, "Tylenol Regains Most of No. 1 Market Share, Amazing Doomsayers," *Wall Street Journal*, 24 December 1982, 1, 19; "60 Minutes," CBS-TV, 19 December 1982. For further information on the second round of Tylenol murders, see Irvin Molotsky, "Tylenol Maker Hopeful on Solving Poisoning Case," *New York Times*, 20 February 1986; Steven Prokesch, "A Leader in a Crisis," *New York Times*, 19 February 1986, B4; Michael Waldholz, "For Tylenol's Manufacturer, The Dilemma Is to Be Aggressive—But Not Appear Pushy," *Wall Street Journal*, 20 February 1986, 27; "Tylenol II: How a Company Responds to a Calamity," *U.S. News & World Report*, 24 February 1986, 49.

FIGURE C (Courtesy of Johnson & Johnson)

Appendices

Appendix A
Code of Professional Standards for the
Practice of Public Relations

PUBLIC RELATIONS SOCIETY OF AMERICA

This Code, adopted by the PRSA Assembly, replaces a Code of Ethics in force since 1950 and revised in 1954. The current Code of Professional Standards, including the previous Statement of Principles, was approved in 1959 and revised in 1963 1977, and 1983.

Declaration of Principles

Members of the Public Relations Society of America base their professional principles on the fundamental value and dignity of the individual, holding that the free exercise of human rights, especially freedom of speech, freedom of assembly, and freedom of the press, is essential to the practice of public relations.

In serving the interests of clients and employers, we dedicate ourselves to the goals of better communication, understanding, and cooperation among the diverse individuals, groups, and institutions of society, and of equal opportunity of employment in the public relations profession.

We pledge:

To conduct ourselves professionally, with truth, accuracy, fairness, and responsibility to the public;

To improve our individual competence and advance the knowledge and proficiency of the profession through continuing research and education;

And to adhere to the articles of the Code of Professional Standards for the Practice of Public Relations as adopted by the governing Assembly of the Society.

Code of Professional Standards for the Practice of Public Relations

These articles have been adopted by the Public Relations Society of America to promote and maintain high standards of public service and ethical conduct among its members.

1. A member shall deal fairly with clients or employers, past, present, or potential, with fellow practitioners, and with the general public.
2. A member shall conduct his or her professional life in accord with the public interest.
3. A member shall adhere to truth and accuracy and to generally accepted standards of good taste.
4. A member shall not represent conflicting or competing interests without the express consent of those involved, given after a full disclosure of the facts; nor place himself or herself in a position where the member's interest is or may be in conflict with a duty to a client, or others, without a full disclosure of such interests to all involved.
5. A member shall safeguard the confidences of present and former clients, as well as those of persons or entities who have disclosed confidences to a member in the context of communications relating to an anticipated professional relationship with such member, and shall not accept retainers or employment that may involve disclosing, using, or offering to use such confidences to the disadvantage or prejudice of such present, former, or potential clients or employers.
6. A member shall not engage in any practice that tends to corrupt the integrity of channels or communication or the processes of government.
7. A member shall not intentionally communicate false or misleading information, and is obligated to use care to avoid communication of false or misleading information.

596

8. A member shall be prepared to identify publicly the name of the client or employer on whose behalf any public communication is made.

9. A member shall not make use of any individual or organization purporting to serve or represent an announced cause, or purporting to be independent or unbiased, but actually serving an undisclosed special or private interest of a member, client, or employer.

10. A member shall not intentionally injure the professional reputation or practice of another practitioner. However, if a member has evidence that another member has been guilty of unethical, illegal, or unfair practices, including those in violation of this Code, the member shall present the information promptly to the proper authorities of the Society for action in accordance with the procedure set forth in Article XII of the Bylaws.

11. A member called as a witness in a proceeding for the enforcement of this Code shall be bound to appear, unless excused for sufficient reason by the judicial panel.

12. A member, in performing services for a client or employer, shall not accept fees, commissions, or any other valuable consideration from anyone other than the client or employer in connection with those services without the express consent of the client or employer, given after a full disclosure of the facts.

13. A member shall not guarantee the achievement of specified results beyond the member's direct control.

14. A member shall, as soon as possible, sever relations with any organization or individual if such relationship requires conduct contrary to the articles of this Code.

Official Interpretations of the Code

Interpretation of Code Paragraph 2, which reads, "A member shall conduct his or her professional life in accord with the public interest."

The public interest is here defined primarily as comprising respect for an enforcement of the rights guaranteed by the Constitution of the United States of America.

Interpretation of Code Paragraph 5, which reads, "A member shall safeguard the confidences of present and former clients, as well as those of persons or entities who have disclosed confidences to a member in the context of communications relating to an anticipated professional relationship with such member, and shall not accept retainers or employment that may involve disclosing, using, or offering to use such confidences to the disadvantage or

prejudice of such present, former, or potential clients or employers."

1. This article does not prohibit a member who has knowledge of client or employer activities that are illegal from making such disclosures to the proper authorities as he or she believes are legally required.

2. Communications between a practitioner and client/employer are deemed to be confidential under Article 5 of the Code of Professional Standards. However, although practitioner/client/employer communications are considered confidential between the parties, such communications are not privileged against disclosure in a court of law.

3. In the absence of any contractual arrangement, the client or employer legally owns the rights to papers or materials created for him.

Interpretation of Code Paragraph 6, which reads, "A member shall not engage in any practice that tends to corrupt the integrity of channels of communication or the processes of government."

1. Practices prohibited by this paragraph are those that tend to place representatives of media or government under any obligation to the member, or the member's employer or client, which is in conflict with their obligations to media or government, such as:
   a. the giving of gifts of more than nominal value;
   b. any form of payment or compensation to a member of the media in order to obtain preferential or guaranteed news or editorial coverage in the medium;
   c. any retainer or fee to a media employee or use of such employee if retained by a client or employer, where the circumstances are not fully disclosed to and accepted by the media employer;
   d. providing trips, for media representatives, that are unrelated to legitimate news interest;
   e. the use by a member of an investment or loan or advertising commitment made by the member, or the member's client or employer, to obtain preferential or guaranteed coverage in the medium.

2. This Code paragraph does not prohibit hosting media or government representatives at meals, cocktails, or news functions and special events that are occasions for the exchange of news information or views, or the furtherance of understanding, which is part of the public relations function. Nor does it prohibit the bona fide press event or tour when media or government representatives are given the opportunity for an on-the-spot viewing of a newsworthy product, process, or event in which the media or government representatives have a legitimate interest. What is customary or reasonable hospitality has to be a matter of particular

judgment in specific situations. In all of these cases, however, it is, or should be, understood that no preferential treatment or guarantees are expected or implied and that complete independence always is left to the media or government representative.

3. This paragraph does not prohibit the reasonable giving or lending of sample products or services to media representatives who have a legitimate interest in the products or services.

4. It is permissible, under Article 6 of the Code, to offer complimentary or discount rates to the media (travel writers, for example) if the rate is for business use and is made available to all writers. Considerable question exists as to the propriety of extending such rates for personal use.

Interpretation of Code Paragraph 10, which reads, ''A member shall not intentionally injure the professional reputation or practice of another practitioner. However, if a member has evidence that another member has been guilty of unethical, illegal, or unfair practices, including those in violation of this Code, the member shall present the information promptly to the proper authorities of the Society for action in accordance with the procedure set forth in Article XII of the Bylaws.''

Blind solicitation, on its face, is not prohibited by the Code. However, if the customer list were improperly obtained, or if the solicitation contained references reflecting adversely on the quality of current services, a complaint might be justified.

Interpretation of Code Paragraph 13, which reads, ''A member shall not guarantee the achievement of specified results beyond the member's direct control.''

This Code paragraph, in effect, prohibits misleading a client or employer as to what professional public relations can accomplish. It does not prohibit guarantees of quality or service. But it does prohibit guaranteeing specific results which, by their very nature, cannot be guaranteed because they are not subject to the member's control. As an example, a guarantee that a news release will appear specifically in a particular publication would be prohibited. This paragraph should not be interpreted as prohibiting contingent fees.

An Official Interpretation of the Code as It Applies to Political Public Relations

Preamble

In the practice of political public relations, a PRSA member must have professional capabilities to offer an employer or client quite apart from any political relationships of value, and members may serve their employer or client without necessarily having attributed to them the character, reputation, or beliefs of those they serve. It is understood that members may choose to serve only those interests with whose political philosophy they are personally comfortable.

Definition

''Political Public Relations'' is defined as those areas of public relations that relate to:

a. the counseling of political organizations, committees, candidates, or potential candidates for public office; and groups constituted for the purpose of influencing the vote on any ballot issue;

b. the counseling of holders of public office;

c. the management, or direction, of a political campaign for or against a candidate for political office; or for or against a ballot issue to be determined by voter approval or rejection;

d. the practice of public relations on behalf of a client or an employer in connection with that client's or employer's relationships with any candidates or holders of public office, with the purpose of influencing legislation or government regulation or treatment of a client or employer, regardless of whether the PRSA member is a recognized lobbyist;

e. the counseling of government bodies, or segments thereof, either domestic or foreign.

Precepts

1. It is the responsibility of PRSA members practicing political public relations, as defined above, to be conversant with the various statutes, local, state, and federal, governing such activities and to adhere to them strictly. This includes, but is not limited to, the various local, state, and federal laws, court decisions, and official interpretations governing lobbying, political contributions, disclosure, elections, libel, slander, and the like. In carrying out this responsibility, members shall seek appropriate counseling whenever necessary.

2. It is also the responsibility of members to abide by PRSA's Code of Professional Standards.

3. Members shall represent clients or employers in good faith, and while partisan advocacy on behalf of a candidate or public issue may be expected, members shall act in accord with the public interest and adhere to truth and accuracy and to generally accepted standards of good taste.

4. Members shall not issue descriptive material or any advertising or publicity information or participate in the preparation or use thereof that is not signed by responsible persons or is false, misleading, or unlabeled as to its source, and are obligated to use care to avoid dissemination of any such material.

5. Members have an obligation to clients to disclose what remuneration beyond their fees they expect to receive as a result of their relationship, such as commissions for media advertising, printing, and the like, and should not accept such extra payment without their client's consent.

6. Members shall not improperly use their positions to encourage additional future employment or compensation. It is understood that successful campaign directors or managers, because of the performance of their duties and the working relationship that develops, may well continue to assist and counsel, for pay, the successful candidate.

7. Members shall voluntarily disclose to employers or clients the identity of other employers or clients with whom they are currently associated, and whose interests might be affected favorably or unfavorably by their political representation.

8. Members shall respect the confidentiality of information pertaining to employers or clients past, present, and potential, even after the relationships cease, avoiding future associations wherein insider information is sought that would give a desired advantage over a member's previous clients.

9. In avoiding practices that might tend to corrupt the processes of government, members shall not make undisclosed gifts of cash or other valuable considerations that are designed to influence specific decisions of voters, legislators, or public officials on public matters. A business lunch or dinner, or other comparable expenditure made in the course of communicating a point of view or public position, would not constitute such a violation. Nor, for example, would a plant visit designed and financed to provide useful background information to an interested legislator or candidate.

10. Nothing herein should be construed as prohibiting members from making legal, properly disclosed contributions to the candidates, party, or referenda issues of their choice.

11. Members shall not, through use of information known to be false or misleading, conveyed directly or through a third party, intentionally injure the public reputation of an opposing interest.

An Official Interpretation of the Code As It Applies to Financial Public Relations

This interpretation of the Society Code as it applies to financial public relations was originally adopted in 1963 and amended in 1972 and 1977 by action of the PRSA Board of Directors. "Financial public relations" is defined as "that area of public relations which relates to the dissemination of information that affects the understanding of stockholders and investors generally concerning the financial position and prospects of a company, and includes among its objectives the improvement of relations between corporations and their stockholders." The interpretation was prepared in 1963 by the Society's Financial Relations Committee, working with the Securities and Exchange Commission and with the advice of the Society's legal counsel. It is rooted directly in the Code with the full force of the Code behind it, and a violation of any of the following paragraphs is subject to the same procedures and penalties as violation of the Code.

1. It is the responsibility of PRSA members who practice financial public relations to be thoroughly familiar with and understand the rules and regulations of the SEC and the laws it administers, as well as other laws, rules, and regulations affecting financial public relations, and to act in accordance with their letter and spirit. In carrying out this responsibility, members shall also seek legal counsel, when appropriate, on matters concerning financial public relations.

2. Members shall adhere to the general policy of making full and timely disclosure of corporate information on behalf of clients or employers. The information disclosed shall be accurate, clear, and understandable. The purpose of such disclosure is to provide the investing public with all material information affecting security values or influencing investment decisions. In complying with the duty of full and timely disclosure, members shall present all material facts, including those adverse to the company. They shall exercise care to ascertain the facts and to disseminate only information they believe to be accurate. They shall not knowingly omit information, the omission of which might make a release false or misleading. Under no circumstances shall members participate in any activity designed to mislead or manipulate the price of a company's securities.

3. Members shall publicly disclose or release information promptly so as to avoid the possibility of any use of the information by any insider or third party. To that end, members shall make every effort to comply with the spirit and intent of the timely-disclosure policies of the stock exchanges, NASD, and the SEC. Material information shall be made available on an equal basis.

4. Members shall not disclose confidential information the disclosure of which might be adverse to a valid corporate purpose or interest and whose disclosure is not required by the timely-disclosure provisions of the law. During any such period of non-disclosure members shall not directly or indirectly (a) communicate the confidential information to any other person or (b) buy or sell or in any other way deal in the

company's securities where the confidential information may materially affect the market for the security when disclosed. Material information shall be disclosed publicly as soon as its confidential status has terminated or the requirement of timely disclosure takes effect.

5. During the registration period, members shall not engage in practices designed to precondition the market for such securities. During registration, the issuance of forecasts, projections, predictions about sales and earnings, or opinions concerning security values or other aspects of the future performance of the company, shall be in accordance with current SEC regulations and statements of policy. In the case of companies whose securities are publicly held, the normal flow of factual information to shareholders and the investing public shall continue during the registration period.

6. Where members have any reason to doubt that projections have an adequate basis in fact, they shall satisfy themselves as to the adequacy of the projections prior to disseminating them.

7. Acting in concert with clients or employers, members shall act promptly to correct false or misleading information or rumors concerning clients' or employers' securities or business whenever they have reason to believe such information or rumors are materially affecting investor attitudes.

8. Members shall not issue descriptive materials designed or written in such a fashion as to appear to be, contrary to fact, an independent third-party endorsement or recommendation of a company or a security. Whenever members issue material for clients or employers, either in their own names or in the name of someone other than the clients or employers, they shall disclose in large type and in a prominent position on the face of the material the source of such material and the existence of the issuer's client or employer relationship.

9. Members shall not use inside information for personal gain. However, this is not intended to prohibit members from making bona fide investments in their company's or client's securities insofar as they can make such investments without the benefit of material inside information.

10. Members shall not accept compensation that would place them in a position of conflict with their duty to a client, employer, or the investing public. Members shall not accept stock options from clients or employers nor accept securities as compensation at a price below market price except as part of an overall plan for corporate employees.

11. Members shall act so as to maintain the integrity of channels of public communication. They shall not pay or permit to be paid to any publication or other communications medium any consideration in exchange for publicizing a company, except through clearly recognizable paid advertising.

12. Members shall in general be guided by the PRSA Declaration of Principles and the PRSA Code of Professional Standards for the Practice of Public Relations of which this Code is an official interpretation.

CONTEMPORARY MARKETING RESEARCH INC. #6-1-107
1270 Broadway   February, 1986
New York, NY 10001

ADVERTISING EFFECTIVENESS TRACKING STUDY   Card 1
MAIN QUESTIONNAIRE   (11-17Z)

RESPONDENT'S NAME: _____

1a. Today, I am interested in obtaining your opinions of financial institutions. To begin with, I'd like you to tell me the names of all the financial institutions you have heard of. (DO NOT READ LIST. RECORD FIRST INSTITUTION MENTIONED SEPARATELY FROM ALL OTHERS UNDER "FIRST MENTION.") (PROBE:) Any others? (RECORD BELOW UNDER "OTHERS.")

1b. Now, thinking only of banks in the New York area, what (other) banks have you heard (RECORD BELOW UNDER "OTHERS.")

2. And what financial institutions, including banks, have you seen or heard advertised within the past 3 months? (DO NOT READ LIST. RECORD BELOW UNDER Q.2.)

3. FOR EACH ASTERISKED INSTITUTION LISTED BELOW AND NOT MENTIONED IN Q.1a/1b OR Q.2, ASK:

Have you ever heard of (NAME)? (RECORD BELOW UNDER Q.3.)

4. FOR EACH ASTERISKED INSTITUTION CIRCLED IN Q.1a/1b OR Q.3 AND NOT CIRCLED IN Q.2, ASK:

Have you seen or heard advertising for (NAME) within the past 3 months? (RECORD BELOW UNDER Q.4.)

| | Q.1a/1b AWARE OF | | Q.2 | Q.3 | Q.4 |
	FIRST MENTION (18)	OTHERS (21)	AWARE ADVTG. (24)	AWARE OF (AIDED)	AWARE ADVTG. (AIDED)
Anchor Savings Bank	1	1	1		
Apple Savings Bank	2	2	2		
Astoria Federal Savings	3	3	3		
Bank Of Commerce	4	4	4		
Bank Of New York	5	5	5		
Bankers Trust	6	6	6		
Barclays Bank	7	7	7		
Bowery Savings Bank	8	8	8		
*Chase Manhattan Bank	9	9	9	9 (27)	9 (29)
*Chemical Bank	0	0	0	0	0
*Citibank	X	X	X	X	X
Crossland Savings Bank	Y	Y	Y		
*Dean Witter	1 (19)	1 (22)	1 (25)	1 (28)	1 (30)
Dime Savings Bank	2	2	2		
Dollar Dry Dock Savings Bank	3	3	3		
*Dreyfus	4	4	4	4	4
Emigrant Savings Bank	5	5	5		
European American Bank	6	6	6		
Fidelity	7	7	7		
Goldome Savings Bank	8	8	8		
*Manufacturer's Hanover Trust	9	9	9	9	9
*Marine Midland Bank	0	0	0	0	0
*Merrill Lynch	X	X	X	X	X
*National Westminster Bank	Y	Y	Y	Y	Y
Prudential Bache	1 (20)	1 (23)	1 (26)		
Shearson-Lehman	2	2	2		
Other (SPECIFY):					
_____	X	X	X		
_____					
_____					

REFER BACK TO Q.2 AND 4. IF RESPONDENT IS AWARE OF ADVERTISING FOR CHASE MANHATTAN BANK
IN Q.2 OR O.4, ASK Q.5a. OTHERWISE, SKIP TO Q.6.

5a. Today we are asking different people about different banks. In your case, we'd like
to talk about Chase Manhattan Bank. You just mentioned that you remember seeing or
hearing advertising for Chase Manhattan Bank. Please tell me everything you remember
seeing or hearing in the advertising. (PROBE FOR SPECIFICS) What else?

_____ (31) _____

_____ (32) _____

_____ (33) _____

_____ (34) _____

_____ (35) _____

5b. And where did you see or hear advertising for Chase Manhattan Bank? (DO NOT READ
LIST) (MORE THAN ONE ANSWER MAY BE GIVEN).
                                            (36)
                      Television.............. 1
                      Radio................... 2
                      Newspaper............... 3
                      Magazine................ 4
                      Billboard............... 5
                      Other (SPECIFY):_____ X

6.   Different banks use different slogans. (START WITH THE X'D QUESTION BELOW AND
CONTINUE UNTIL ALL FOUR QUESTIONS (Q.6a-6d) HAVE BEEN ASKED.)

START:

(√) 6a. What slogan or statement do you associate with Chase Manhattan Bank? (DO NOT
READ LIST)
                                                    (37)
           Chase. The Experience Shows 1
           You Have A Friend At Chase 2
           Ideas You Can Bank On 3
           The Chase Is On 4

           Other (SPECIFY) _____ X

           _____

           _____

( ) 6b. What slogan does Chemical Bank use? (DO NOT READ LIST)
                                                    (38)
           The Chemistry's Just Right At Chemical 1

           Other (SPECIFY) _____ X

           _____

           _____

( ) 6c. What slogan or statement do you associate with Citibank? (DO NOT READ LIST)
                                                    (39)
                      It's Your Citi 1
                      The Citi Never Sleeps 2

           Other (SPECIFY) _____ X

           _____

           _____

( ) 6d. What slogan does Manufacturer's Hanover Trust use? (DO NOT READ LIST)
                                                    (40)
           The Financial Source. Worldwide 1
           We Realize Your Potential 2

           Other (SPECIFY) _____ X

           _____

           _____

7. Now, I'd like to know how likely you, yourself, are to consider banking at several different banks in the future. For each bank I read, please tell me whether you would definitely consider banking there, probably consider banking there, might or might not consider banking there, probably not consider banking there or definitely not consider banking there in the future. Now, how likely are you to consider banking at (READ X'D BANK) in the future? (REPEAT SCALE IF NECESSARY. OBTAIN A RATING FOR EACH BANK.)

	START: ( ) CHASE MANHATTAN BANK	( ) CHEMICAL BANK	( ) CITIBANK	(✓) MANUFACTURER'S HANOVER TRUST
Definitely Consider Banking There	5 (41)	5 (42)	5 (43)	5 (44)
Probably Consider Banking There	4	4	4	4
Might Or Might Not Consider Banking There ..	3	3	3	3
Probably Not Consider Banking There	2	2	2	2
Definitely Not Consider Banking There	1	1	1	1
(DO NOT READ)──>(Currently Bank There).........	X	X	X	X

(45-1)

8a. Now, I'd like you to rate one bank on a series of statements -- Chase Manhattan Bank. If you have never banked there, please base your answers on what you know about this bank and your perceptions of it. After I read each statement, please tell me whether you agree completely, agree somewhat, neither agree nor disagree, disagree somewhat or disagree completely that this statement describes Chase Manhattan Bank. (START WITH X'D STATEMENT AND CONTINUE UNTIL ALL ARE RATED.)

START HERE:	AGREE COMPLETELY	AGREE SOMEWHAT	NEITHER AGREE NOR DISAGREE	DISAGREE SOMEWHAT	DISAGREE COMPLETELY
[ ] Is Responsive To Your Needs	5	4	3	2	1 (46)
[ ] Offers High Quality Accounts And Services	5	4	3	2	1 (47)
[ ] Deals With Its Customers On A Personalized Level	5	4	3	2	1 (48)
[ ] Helps Make Banking Easier	5	4	3	2	1 (49)
[ ] Has Bank Personnel That Are Concerned About You	5	4	3	2	1 (50)
[ ] Designs Accounts To Meet Your Special Needs	5	4	3	2	1 (51)
[ ] Is Responsive To Community Needs	5	4	3	2	1 (52)
[ ] Makes It Easy To Open An IRA Account.	5	4	3	2	1 (53)
[ ] Has A Full Range Of Banking And Investment Services	5	4	3	2	1 (54)
[ ] Is A Bank Where You Want To Have Most Of Your Accounts	5	4	3	2	1 (55)
[ ] Has Bank Personnel That Are Experienced	5	4	3	2	1 (56)
[ ] Has Innovative Accounts And Services.	5	4	3	2	1 (57)
[ ] Understands Your Banking Needs	5	4	3	2	1 (58)
[ ] Has Branches That Are Pleasant To Bank In	5	4	3	2	1 (59)
[ ] Has Accounts To Help People Just Starting Out	5	4	3	2	1 (60)
[ ] Continuously Develops Services To Meet Your Needs	5	4	3	2	1 (61)
[ ] Has Bank Personnel That Are Friendly And Courteous	5	4	3	2	1 (62)
[ ] Has Accounts And Services That Are Right For You	5	4	3	2	1 (63)
[✓] Puts Customers' Needs First	5	4	3	2	1 (64)
[ ] Is A Modern, Up-To-Date Bank	5	4	3	2	1 (65)

END CARD 1

8b. Now, I'd like you to rate one other bank on a series of statements -- <u>Manufacturer's Hanover Trust</u>. If you have never banked there, please base your answers on what you know about this bank and your perceptions of it. After I read each statement, please tell me whether you agree completely, agree somewhat, neither agree nor disagree, disagree somewhat or disagree completely that this statement describes <u>Manufacturer's Hanover Trust</u>. (START WITH X'D STATEMENT AND CONTINUE UNTIL ALL ARE RATED.)

START HERE:	AGREE COMPLETELY	AGREE SOMEWHAT	NEITHER AGREE NOR DISAGREE	DISAGREE SOMEWHAT	DISAGREE COMPLETELY
[ ] Is Responsive To Your Needs	5	4	3	2	1 (7)
[ ] Offers High Quality Accounts And Services	5	4	3	2	1 (8)
[√] Deals With Its Customers On A Personalized Level	5	4	3	2	1 (9)
[ ] Helps Make Banking Easier	5	4	3	2	1 (10)
[ ] Has Bank Personnel That Are Concerned About You	5	4	3	2	1 (11)
[ ] Designs Accounts To Meet Your Special Needs	5	4	3	2	1 (12)
[ ] Is Responsive To Community Needs	5	4	3	2	1 (13)
[ ] Makes It Easy To Open An IRA Account.	5	4	3	2	1 (14)
[ ] Has A Full Range Of Banking And Investment Services	5	4	3	2	1 (15)
[ ] Is A Bank Where You Want To Have Most Of Your Accounts	5	4	3	2	1 (16)
[ ] Has Bank Personnel That Are Experienced	5	4	3	2	1 (17)
[ ] Has Innovative Accounts And Services.	5	4	3	2	1 (18)
[ ] Understands Your Banking Needs	5	4	3	2	1 (19)
[ ] Has Branches That Are Pleasant To Bank In	5	4	3	2	1 (20)
[ ] Has Accounts To Help People Just Starting Out	5	4	3	2	1 (21)
[ ] Continuously Develops Services To Meet Your Needs	5	4	3	2	1 (22)
[ ] Has Bank Personnel That Are Friendly And Courteous	5	4	3	2	1 (23)
[ ] Has Accounts And Services That Are Right For You	5	4	3	2	1 (24)
[ ] Puts Customers' Needs First	5	4	3	2	1 (25)
[ ] Is A Modern, Up-To-Date Bank	5	4	3	2	1 (26)

Now, I'd like to ask you some questions for classification purposes only.

9a. Thinking in terms of <u>all</u> your banking activities, such as checking, savings, CDs, Money Market accounts and any other banking activities, please tell me the name of <u>all</u> the banks you currently use? (DO <u>NOT</u> READ LIST. RECORD ALL ANSWERS UNDER Q.9a BELOW.)

9b. And, what <u>one</u> bank do you consider to be your main bank? (DO <u>NOT</u> READ LIST. RECORD ONE ANSWER BELOW UNDER Q.9b.)

	Q.9a CURRENTLY USE		Q.9b MAIN BANK	
		(27)		(30)
Anchor Savings Bank	1		1	
Apple Savings Bank	2		2	
Astoria Federal Savings	3		3	
Bank Of Commerce	4		4	
Bank Of New York	5		5	
Bankers Trust	6		6	
Barclays Bank	7		7	
Bowery Savings Bank	8		8	
Chase Manhattan Bank	9		9	
Chemical Bank	0		0	
Citibank	X		X	
Crossland Savings Bank	Y		Y	
Dime Savings Bank	1	(28)	1	(31)
Dollar Dry Dock Savings Bank	2		2	
East New York Bank For Savings	3		3	
Emigrant Savings Bank	4		4	
European American Bank	5		5	
Goldome Savings Bank	6		6	
Manhattan Savings Bank	7		7	
Manufacturer's Hanover Trust	8		8	
Marine Midland Bank	9		9	
National Westminster Bank	0		0	
Other (SPECIFY) _____	X		X	
_____		(29)		(32)

9c. What types of accounts or services do you currently have at your main bank? (DO <u>NOT</u> READ LIST. RECORD ALL THAT APPLY BELOW.)

(33)

Savings Account	1
Certificate Of Deposit (CD)	2
Checking Account (Now, Super Now Account)	3
Money Market Account	4
An IRA/Keogh Account	5
A Mortgage	6
A Line Of Credit You Can Draw On By Writing A Check	7
A Regular Visa Card	8
A Premium Visa Card (Gold)	9
A Regular Mastercard	0
A Premium Mastercard	X
Other (SPECIFY):	(34)

_____ 1

_____

_____

9d. And do you ever use an automated teller machine when you visit your main bank?

                                            (35)
                    Yes .... 1 ────────── ⟩ASK Q.9e
                    No .... 2 ────────── ⟩SKIP TO Q.9f

9e. In general, how often do you use an automated teller machine at that bank? (READ LIST)

                                            (36)
            More Than Once A Week 1
            Once A Week 2
            About 2-3 Times A Month 3
            About Once A Month 4
            Less Often Than Once A Month 5

9f. In general, about how often do you visit that bank? That is, how often do you actually go inside the branch? (READ LIST)

                                            (37)
            More Than Once A Week 1
            Once A Week 2
            About 2-3 Times A Month 3
            About Once A Month 4
            Less Often Than Once A Month 5

10a. What is your present marital status? Are you ... (READ LIST)?

                                            (38)
                Married 1
                Divorced Or Separated 2
                Widowed 3
                Single (i.e., Never Married). 4
    (DO NOT READ) ──── (Refused) X

10b. What was the last grade of school you completed? (DO NOT READ LIST.)

                                            (39)
            Some High School or Less 1
            Graduated High School 2
            Some College 3
            Graduated College 4
            Postgraduate Work 5
    (DO NOT READ) ──── (Refused) X

10c. Which of the following describes your employment status outside the home? (READ LIST)

                                            (40)
    Not Employed Outside The Home .... 1 ──────→SKIP TO Q.10e
    Employed Full-Time .... 2 ┐
    Employed Part-Time .... 3 ┘──→ ASK Q.10d

10d. What is your occupation/profession?

    _____ (41)

10e. Thinking now about the liquid assets you have, including CDs, savings, checking and money market accounts, as well as stock, bonds and money market funds at a brokerage house, but not including the house in which you live, would you say the total amount is ... (READ LIST)?

                                            (42)
                Under $5,000 1
                $5,000-$9,999 2
                $10,000-$14,999 3
                $15,000-$24,999 4
                $25,000-$49,999 5
                $50,000 And Over 6
    (DO NOT READ) ──── (Refused) X

606

11. Please stop me when I come to the group that includes your age. (READ LIST)

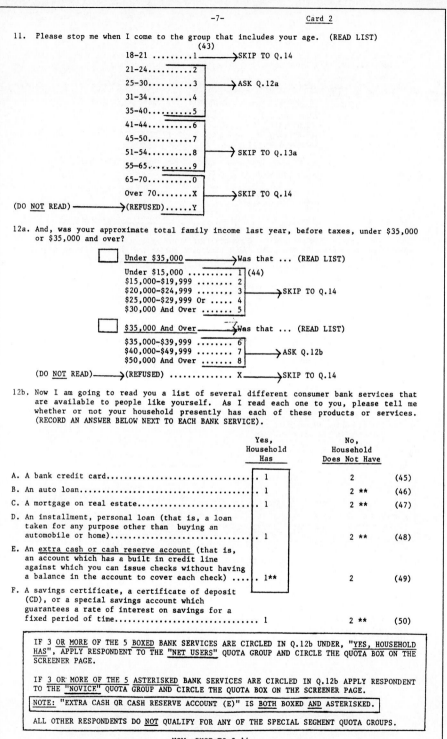

(43)

18-21 ....1 ——→ SKIP TO Q.14

21-24..........2

25-30..........3 ——→ ASK Q.12a

31-34..........4

35-40..........5

41-44..........6

45-50.........7

51-54.........8 ——→ SKIP TO Q.13a

55-65...........9

65-70..........0

Over 70.......X ——→ SKIP TO Q.14

(DO NOT READ) ——→(REFUSED)......Y

12a. And, was your approximate total family income last year, before taxes, under $35,000 or $35,000 and over?

Under $35,000 ————→ Was that ... (READ LIST)

Under $15,000 .... 1 (44)
$15,000-$19,999 2
$20,000-$24,999 .... 3 ——→ SKIP TO Q.14
$25,000-$29,999 Or 4
$30,000 And Over 5

$35,000 And Over ————→ Was that ... (READ LIST)

$35,000-$39,999 6
$40,000-$49,999 .... 7 ——→ ASK Q.12b
$50,000 And Over 8

(DO NOT READ)——→(REFUSED) .... X ——→ SKIP TO Q.14

12b. Now I am going to read you a list of several different consumer bank services that are available to people like yourself. As I read each one to you, please tell me whether or not your household presently has each of these products or services. (RECORD AN ANSWER BELOW NEXT TO EACH BANK SERVICE).

	Yes, Household Has	No, Household Does Not Have	
A. A bank credit card.................................	. 1	2	(45)
B. An auto loan......................................	. 1	2 **	(46)
C. A mortgage on real estate.........................	. 1	2 **	(47)
D. An installment, personal loan (that is, a loan taken for any purpose other than buying an automobile or home)................................	. 1	2 **	(48)
E. An extra cash or cash reserve account (that is, an account which has a built in credit line against which you can issue checks without having a balance in the account to cover each check)	. 1**	2	(49)
F. A savings certificate, a certificate of deposit (CD), or a special savings account which guarantees a rate of interest on savings for a fixed period of time...............................	1	2 **	(50)

IF 3 OR MORE OF THE 5 BOXED BANK SERVICES ARE CIRCLED IN Q.12b UNDER, "YES, HOUSEHOLD HAS", APPLY RESPONDENT TO THE "NET USERS" QUOTA GROUP AND CIRCLE THE QUOTA BOX ON THE SCREENER PAGE.

IF 3 OR MORE OF THE 5 ASTERISKED BANK SERVICES ARE CIRCLED IN Q.12b APPLY RESPONDENT TO THE "NOVICE" QUOTA GROUP AND CIRCLE THE QUOTA BOX ON THE SCREENER PAGE.

NOTE: "EXTRA CASH OR CASH RESERVE ACCOUNT (E)" IS BOTH BOXED AND ASTERISKED.

ALL OTHER RESPONDENTS DO NOT QUALIFY FOR ANY OF THE SPECIAL SEGMENT QUOTA GROUPS.

NOW, SKIP TO Q.14.

13a. And, was your approximate total family income last year, before taxes, under $10,000, $10,000-$29,999, or $30,000 and over?

(51)

☐ Under $10,000 .... 1 ——————→SKIP TO Q.14

☐ $10,000-$29,999 ——→ASK: Was that ... (READ LIST)

Under $15,000 2
$15,000-$19,999 3
$20,000-$24,999, Or .... 4 ——————→ ASK Q.13b
$25,000 And Over 5

☐ $30,000 And Over ——————→ASK: Was that ... (READ LIST)

Under $35,000 6
$35,000-$39,999 7
$40,000-$49,999 .... 8 ——————→ ASK Q.13b
$50,000 And Over 9

(DO NOT READ) ——————→(REFUSED) .... X ——————→SKIP TO Q.14

13b. Now I am going to read you a list of several different products and services that are available to people like yourself. As I read each one to you, please tell me whether or not your household presently has each of these products or services.

	Yes, Household Has	No Household Does Not Have
A. A saving certificate, certificate of deposit (CD), or special savings account which guarantees a rate of interest on savings for a fixed period of time..............................	1	2 (52)
B. A safe deposit box..................	1	2 (53)
C. An investment counselling service or financial planning service to assist you in making investments or in planning estate and household finances...........................	1	2 (54)

REFER TO Q.13A/13B ABOVE:

IF RESPONDENT'S INCOME IS "$30,000 AND OVER" IN Q.13a AND RESPONDENT HAS 2 OR MORE OF THE BOXED BANK SERVICES IN Q.13b, APPLY RESPONDENT TO THE "NET PROVIDER" QUOTA GROUP AND CIRCLE THE QUOTA BOX ON THE SCREENER PAGE.

IF RESPONDENT'S INCOME IS "$10,000-$29,999" IN Q.13a AND RESPONDENT HAS A "SAVINGS CERTIFICATE, CERTIFICATE OF DEPOSIT (CD)" IN Q.13b, APPLY RESPONDENT TO THE "NET PROVIDER" QUOTA GROUP AND CIRCLE THE QUOTA BOX ON THE SCREENER PAGE.

ALL OTHER RESPONDENTS DO NOT QUALIFY FOR ANY OF THE SPECIAL SEGMENT QUOTA GROUPS.

14. CIRCLE AREA YOU ARE INTERVIEWING IN:

New York City   (55)

Bronx 1   Nassau County 6
Brooklyn 2   Rockland County 7
Manhattan 3   Suffolk County 8
Queens 4   Westchester County ..9
Staten Island 5

THANK YOU VERY MUCH FOR YOUR COOPERATION!

COMPLETE ALL RESPONDENT INFORMATION ON FRONT OF SCREENER.

BE SURE TO ATTACH THE PROPER CALL RECORD SHEET(S) TO THE TOP OF THE SCREENER AND STAPLE EVERYTHING TO THIS MAIN QUESTIONNAIRE.

Appendix C
Leading Media Directories

When PR professionals are asked which media directories they use most often, their answers are as varied as the tasks their firms perform. Publishers have carved such precise market niches for their wares that direct comparison of one directory to another is usually inappropriate. A comprehensive list of media directories begins on this page. Directories are listed by category, and then alphabetically. Another list provides complete names and addresses of the publishers cited.

Newspapers

E&P International Yearbook. Annual list of U.S. and Canadian daily newspaper personnel and other data. $60. **Editor & Publisher.**

Family Page Directory. $60 for two editions printed at six-month intervals. Contains information about home, cooking and family interest sections of newspapers. **Public Relations Plus.**

Media Alerts. Data on 200 major dailies as well as 1,900 magazines. $155. **Bacon's.**

National Directory of Community Newspapers. Listings on newspapers serving smaller communities. $35. **American Newspaper Representatives.**

Publicity Checker, Volume 2: Newspapers. $155 when purchased with Volume 1 on magazines. Two volumes list over 7,500 publications. **Bacon's.**

Working Press of the Nation, Volume I: Newspapers. Part of a $260 five-volume set with 25,000 publicity outlets. **National Research Bureau.**

1988 News Bureaus in the U.S. $133. **Larimi.**

Magazines

Media Alerts. Data on 1,900 magazines and 200 major daily newspapers. $155. **Bacon's.**

National Directory of Magazines. Lists basic information on 1,300 magazines in the U.S. and Canada. $125. **Oxbridge.**

Publicity Checker, Vol. I. Part of a two-volume set (for magazines and newspapers) with over 7,500 listings. $155 for both volumes. **Bacon's.**

Standard Periodical Directory. Has 60,000 titles with 50 fields of data per title, divided into 250 subject areas. $295. **Oxbridge.**

Working Press of the Nation, Volume 2: Magazines. Part of a five-volume set with data on 25,000 publicity outlets. $260 for set. **National Research Bureau.**

Television

Cable Contacts Yearbook. Lists all cable systems. $184. **Larimi.**

Radio-TV Directory. Over 1,300 TV stations and 9,000 radio stations. $155. **Bacon's.**

Talk Show Selects. Identifies talk show contacts nationwide for both TV and radio. Emphasizes network and syndication programs. $185. **Broadcast Interview.**

Television Contacts. Updated extensive listings. $233. **Larimi.**

TV News. Guide to news directors and assignment editors. $172. **Larimi.**

TV Publicity Outlets. Two editions are printed at six-month intervals. $159.50. **Public Relations Plus.**

Working Press of the Nation, Volume 3: TV and Radio. Part of a $260 five-volume set with 25,000 publicity outlets. **National Research Bureau.**

Radio

National Radio Publicity Outlets. Two editions are printed at six-month intervals. $159.50 for both. **Public Relations Plus.**

Radio Contacts. Extensive, updated listings. $239. **Larimi.**

Radio-TV Directory. Over 9,000 radio and 1,300 TV stations. $155. **Bacon's.**

Talk Show Selects. Identifies both radio and TV talk show contacts nationwide. Emphasis is on syndicated and network programs. $185. **Broadcast Interview.**

Working Press of the Nation, Volume 3. Includes both radio and TV. Part of a five-volume set that sells for $260 and contains data on 25,000 publicity outlets. **National Research Bureau.**

Newsletters

Directory of Newsletters. Has 13,500 newsletters in U.S. and Canada. Publications are divided into 168 categories. $125. **Oxbridge.**

The Newsletter Yearbook Directory. Lists worldwide newsletters available by subscription. $60. **Newsletter Clearinghouse.**

Newsletters Directory. Guide to more than 8,000 subscription, membership and free newsletters. $140. **Gale Research.**

1988 Investment Newsletters. Lists over 1,000 newsletters. $160. **Larimi.**

Regional

Burrelle's Media Directories. Regional directories for New York State ($85), New Jersey ($70), Pennsylvania ($38), New England ($95), Connecticut ($32), Maine ($25), New Hampshire ($25), Massachusetts ($44), Rhode Island ($25), Vermont ($25) and Greater Boston ($29). **Burrelle's.**

Metro California Media. Detailed listing of California media. $89.50 includes semi-annual revised edition. **Public Relations Plus.**

Minnesota Non-Metro Media Directory. Guide to the media in the Twin Cities region. $90. **Publicity Central.**

New York Publicity Outlets. Media in a 50-mile radius of New York City. $89.50 includes the semi-annual revised edition. **Public Relations Plus.**

New York TV Directory. Lists producers, directors, and others active in the New York market. Published annually. $15. **National Academy.**

Vermont Media Directory. TV, radio, newspaper and magazine listings. $99. **Kelliher.**

Washington News Media. Detailed listings of wire services, newspapers, magazines, radio-TV, and foreign correspondents. $99. **Hudson's.**

1988 Media Guide and Membership Directory. Chicago media outlets. $75. **Publicity Club of Chicago.**

International

International Literary Market Place. $85. **R.R. Bowker.**

International Media Guide. Publishers of Newspapers Worldwide and Consumer Magazines Worldwide. A four-volume set covers business and professional publications for Asia/Pacific; Middle East and Africa; Latin America, and Europe. Each volume sells for $100. **International Media Guide.**

International Publicity Checker. Lists 10,000 western European business, trade and technical magazines, and 1,000 national and regional newspapers. $165. **Bacon's.**

Ulrich's International Periodicals Directory. Lists 70,730 periodicals in 542 subject areas, in two volumes. Over 40,000 entries from the previous edition have been updated. $159.95. **Ulrich's.**

United Kingdom

Editors Media Directories. Series of directories covering journalists, features, profiles. **Editors.**

PIMS United Kingdom Media Directory. Provides detailed access to the total range of UK media. $390 annually, $220 quarterly, or $90 for a single issue. **PIMS U.S.A.**

PIMS United Kingdom Financial Directory. Detailed listings. $300 annually or $90 for a single copy. **PIMS U.S.A.**

Hollis Press and Public Relations Annual. Over 18,000 organizations in the PR industry, with a full range of media. $36. **Hollis.**

Benn's Media Directory. Available in two books, one for the U.K. and the other for international listings. Each is $95; both are $160. Published by Benn Business Information Services. **Nichols.**

Willing's Press Guide. Extensive U.K. media listings. $105 plus $5 shipping. Published by Thomas Skinner Directories. **Business Press International.**

Bowdens Media Directory. Updated three times annually with complete media listings. **Bowdens.**

Canada

Matthews List. Has 3,600 media throughout Canada. Updated three times annually. $130 per year. **Publicorp.**

Australia

Margaret Gee's Media Guide. Lists 2,400 Australian media, updated three times annually. $100. **Margaret Gee.**

Japan

Publishers in English in Japan. Media selection for English-speaking readers. Published by Japan Publications Guide Service. **Pacific Subscription Service.**

Africa

African Book World and Press. Lists over 4,000 publishers. The latest edition is 1983. $78. **K.G. Saur.**

Specialists

Business and Financial News Media. Print, electronic, syndicated columns and individual writers. $85. **Larriston.**

Business and Technical Media. Available on paper and floppy disk, at $200 total for both. **Ron Gold.**

Computer Industry Almanac. Extensive industry data as well as a publications directory. $49.50 hardcover; $29.95 softcover. **Computer Industry Almanac.**

Directory of the College Student Press in America. Has 5,000 student newspapers and magazines on 3,600 campuses. $75. **Oxbridge.**

Encyclopedia of Association Periodicals. Three-volume directory sells for $150, but individual ones sell for $60. Vol. I: business and finance. Vol. II: science and medicine. Vol. III: social sciences and education. **Gale Research.**

Medical and Science News Media. Specialized listings with major news contacts. $85. **Larriston.**

Medical Press List. Available on paper and floppy disk, at a combination price of $125. **Ron Gold.**

Nelson's Directory of Investment Research. Contact information and areas of specialization for over 3,000 security analysts. $259. **W.R. Nelson.**

TIA International Travel News Directory. Comprehensive travel media listings. $35. **Travel Industry Association.**

Travel, Leisure and Entertainment News Media. Major nationwide contacts. $85. **Larriston.**

1988 College/Alumni/Military Publications. Over 1,150 publications in these three fields. $87. **Larimi.**

Working Press of the Nation, Volume 5. Internal Publications Directory. Describes house organs published primarily for distribution inside companies. Part of a five-volume library selling for $260. **National Research Bureau.**

Ethnic

Black Media in America. $50. **Hall Co.**

Burrelle's Special Directories. Directories of Black, Hispanic, and women's media are covered in three volumes at $50 each. **Burrelle's.**

Hispanic Media, U.S.A. Provides a narrative description of Spanish-language media. Includes newspapers, radio, and TV stations. $75 plus $1.50 handling. **The Media Institute.**

General

Business Publications Rates and Data. Monthly directory of magazines and newspapers categorized by field. $398 for 12 monthly issues, or $194 for one copy. **Standard Rate and Data Service.**

Directory of Directories. More than 10,000 entries in two volumes. $195. **Gale Research.**

Gale Directory of Publications. Annual directory to newspapers, magazines, journals and related publications. $135. **Gale.**

Gebbie All-In-One Directory. Comprehensive listings of all media. $79.25. **Gebbie Press.**

Market Guide. Has data on population, income, households, and retail sales for markets around the nation. $70. **E&P.**

Print Media Editorial Calendars. Lists 12-month editorial calendars for 4,200 trades, 1,700 newspapers, 1,500 consumer magazines and 400 farm publications. $195. **Standard Rate and Data Service.**

Experts and Writers

Directory of Experts, Authorities and Spokespersons. Access to over 3,569 experts. $19.95 plus $3.50 shipping. Can be ordered on Rolodex cards for $165. **Broadcast Interview.**

1988 Syndicated Columnists. Over 1,400 columnists listed. $157. **Larimi.**

Syndicate Directory. Lists syndicated features by classification, by-lines, as well as how material is furnished. $6. **E&P.**

Working Press of the Nation, Volume 4: Feature Writer & Photographer Directory. Part of a five-volume set selling for $260. **National Research Bureau.**

Directory Publishers

Publishers of media directories can be found in alphabetical order in the list that follows.

American Newspaper
Representatives
12 South Sixth St., Ste. 520
Minneapolis, MN 55402
612/332-8686
  National Directory of Community
  Newspapers

Bacon's PR and Media Information
Systems
332 S. Michigan Ave.
Chicago, IL 60604
800/621-0561
  Publicity Checker
  Radio-TV Directory
  Media Alerts
  International Publicity Checker

Bowden's Information Services
624 King Street West
Toronto ON M5V 2X9, Canada
416/860-0794
  Bowden's Media Directory

Broadcast Interview Source
2500 Wisconsin Ave., N.W.
Suite 930
Washington, DC 20007
202/333-4904
  Directory of Experts
  Talk Show Selects

Burrelle's Press Clipping Service
75 East Northfield Ave.
Livingston, NJ 07039
201/992-6600
  Regional Media Directories

Computer Industry Almanac
8111 LBJ Freeway, 13th floor
Dallas, TX 75251-1313
214/231-8735
  Computer Industry Almanac

Editor and Publisher
11 West 19th St.
New York, NY 10011
212/675-4380
  E&P International Yearbook
  Market Guide
  Syndicate Directory

Editors Media Directories
9/10 Great Sutton St.
London, EC1VOBX England
  Editors Media Directories

Gale Research
Book Tower
Detroit, MI 48226
313/961-2242
  Directory of Directories
  Directory of Publications
  Encyclopedia of Association
  Periodicals
  Newsletters Directory

Gebbie Press
Box 1000
New Paltz, NY 12561
914/255-7560
  Gebbie All-In-One Directory

Hollis Directories
Contact House
Sunbury-On-Thames
Middlesex TW16 5HG, England
  Hollis Press and Public Relations
  Annual

International Media Guide
Enterprises
22 Elizabeth St.
South Norwalk, CT 06856
203/853-7880
  International Media Guide

Kelliher/Samets
130 South Willard St.
Burlington, VT 05401
802/862-8261
  Vermont Media Directory

Larimi Communications Associates
5 West 37th St.
New York, NY 10018
800/634-4020
212/819-9310
  Cable Contacts Yearbook
  Radio Contacts
  Television Contacts
  TV News
  1988 News Bureaus in the U.S.

Larriston Communications
P.O. Box 20229
New York, NY 10025
212/864-0150
  Business and Financial News
  Media
  Medical and Science News Media
  Travel, Leisure and Entertainment
  News Media

Margaret Gee Media Group
384 Flinders Lane
Melbourne, Victoria 3000 Australia
  Margaret Gee's Media Guide
  Information Australia

The Media Institute
3017 M Street
Washington, DC 20007
202/298-7512
  Hispanic Media, U.S.A.

National Academy of Television
Arts and Sciences
New York Chapter
110 West 57th St.
New York, NY 10019
212/765-2450
  New York TV Directory

National Research Bureau
310 S. Michigan Ave.
Chicago, IL 60604
312/663-5580
  Working Press of the Nation

W.R. Nelson Co.
1 Gateway Plaza
Port Chester, NY 10573
914/937-8400
  Nelson's Directory of Investment
    Research

Newsletter Clearinghouse
44 W. Market St.
P.O. Box 311
Rhinebeck, NY 12572
914/876-2081
  Hudson's Washington News Media
  Newsletter Yearbook Directory

Nichols Publishing
Box 96
New York, NY 10024
212/580-8079
  Benn's Media Directory

Oxbridge Communications
150 Fifth Ave.
New York, NY 10011
212/741-0231
  National Directory of Magazines
  Standard Periodical Directory

Pacific Subscription Service
Box 811
FDR Station
New York, NY 10150
212/929-1629
  Publishers in English in Japan

PIMS U.S.A.
1133 Broadway
New York, NY 10010
212/645-5112
  United Kingdom Financial
    Directory
  United Kingdom Media
    Directory

Public Relations Plus
P.O. Drawer 1197
New Milford, CT 06776
203/354-9361
  All TV Publicity Outlets
  The Family Page Directory
  Metro California Media
  National Radio Publicity Outlets
  New York Publicity Outlets

Publicorp Communications
Box 1029
Pointe Claire PQ
W9S 4H9 Canada
  Matthews List

Publicity Club of Chicago
1441 Shermer Rd. (#110)
Northbrook, IL 60062
  1988 Media Guide
  Publicity Club of Chicago
    Membership Directory

Reed Business Publishing
205 E. 42nd St., Ste. 1705
New York, NY 10017
212/867-2080
  Willing's Press Guide

Ron Gold, N.A.
1341 Ocean Ave. (#366)
Santa Monica, CA 90401
213/399-7938
  Business and Technical Media
  Medical Press List

R.R. Bowker
245 West 17th St.
New York, NY 10011
212/645-9700
  Ulrich's International Periodicals
    Directory

K.G. Saur
175 Fifth Ave.
New York, NY 10010
212/982-1302
  African Book World and Press

Standard Rate and Data Service
3004 Glenview Rd.
Wilmette, IL 60091
312/256-6067
  Print Media Editorial Calendars
  Business Publication Rates and
    Data

Travel Industry Assn. of America
Two Lafayette Center
1133 21st St., N.W.
Washington, DC 20036
202/293-1433
  International Travel News
    Directory

Appendix D
Audiovisual Supports

Material	Advantages	Limitations
Slide series A form of projected audiovisual materials easy to prepare with any 35mm camera	1. Prepared with any 35mm camera for most uses 2. Requires only filming, with processing and mounting by film laboratory 3. Colorful, realistic reproductions of original subjects 4. Easily revised, updated, handled, stored, and rearranged 5. Can be combined with taped narration for greater effectiveness 6. May be played through remote control presentation	1. Requires some skill in photography 2. Requires special equipment for close-up photography and copying 3. Prone to get out of sequence and be projected incorrectly
Filmstrips Closely related to slides, but instead of being mounted as separate pictures, remains uncut as a continuous strip	1. Compact, easily handled, and always in proper sequence 2. Can be supplemented with captions or recordings 3. Inexpensive when quantity reproduction is required 4. Projected with simple, lightweight equipment 5. Projection rate controlled by presenter	1. Relatively difficult to prepare locally 2. Requires film laboratory service to convert slides to filmstrip form 3. In permanent sequence and therefore cannot be rearranged or revised
Overhead transparencies A popular form of locally prepared materials, requiring an overhead projector for presentation	1. Can present information in systematic, developmental sequences 2. Simple-to-operate projector with presentation rate controlled by presenter 3. Requires limited planning 4. Can be prepared by a variety of simple, inexpensive methods.	1. Requires special equipment, facilities, and skills for more advanced preparation methods 2. May be cumbersome and lack finesse of more remote processes

Appendix E
Corporate Reporting Requirements

(Includes SEC's integrated disclosure system, effective May 24, 1982. Prepared by Robert W. Taft, APR, Senior Vice President, Hill and Knowlton, Inc.)

Reporting Required For	Securities and Exchange Commission	New York Stock Exchange	American Stock Exchange	Generally Recommended Publicity Practice, All Companies
Accounting: Change in auditors	8-K; if principal auditor (or auditor for a subsidiary) resigns, declines to be re-elected, or is dismissed or if another is engaged. Disclose date of resignation, details of disagreements, comment letters to SEC by auditor on whether it agrees with reasons stated plus other disclosures detailed in 8-K. See also Regulation S-K, Item 304.	Prompt notice to Exchange, 8-K when filed. The NYSE recommends that the independent audit firm be represented at annual meeting to answer questions.	Same as NYSE.	Press release desirable at time of filing 8-K if differences are major. Consider clear statement in annual report or elsewhere on independence of auditors including their reporting relationship to Board's audit committee.
Accounting: Change in method	Independent public accountant must file letter indicating approval/ disapproval of "improved method of measuring business operations."	Prompt notification to Exchange required.	Notify Exchange before change is made and disclose the impact in succeeding interim and annual reports.	Statement of accounting policies is required in annual report. Give some publicity to accounting changes; illustrate how alternative accounting methods affect earnings. Special problems arise in changing LIFO/FIFO methods of accounting for inventory.
Amendment of charter or bylaws	Report if matter subject to stockholders' approval or if change materially modifies rights of holders of any class of registered securities.	Four copies of any material sent to stockholders in respect to proposed changes. Appropriately certified copy of changes when effective.	Ten copies of any material sent to stockholders must be filed with Exchange when effective with certified copy of (a) charter amendments; (b) directors' resolution as to charter or bylaws.	Recommend immediate publicity if change significantly alters rights or interests of shareholders. "Defensive" provision to make takeovers more difficult likely to receive very wide publicity.
Annual (or special) meeting of stockholders	10-Q following meeting including date of meeting, name of each director elected (if contested), summary of other matters voted on.	Four copies of all proxy material sent to shareholders. Prompt notice of calling of meeting; publicity on material actions at meeting. Ten days advance notice of record date or closing transfer books to Exchange.	Ten copies of all material sent to shareholders. Other requirements same as NYSE.	Press release at time of meeting. Competition for news space minimizes public coverage except on actively contested issues. Check NYSE schedules for competing meetings. Recommend wide distribution of post-meeting report to shareholders.

Reporting Required For	Securities and Exchange Commission	New York Stock Exchange	American Stock Exchange	Generally Recommended Publicity Practice, All Companies
Annual report to shareholders: Contents	Required contents listed under Rule 14a-3 of the '34 Act. SEC still encourages "freedom of management expression."	Requirements are more than satisfied by compliance with SEC requirements.	Requirements are more than satisfied by compliance with SEC requirements.	Check printed annual report and appropriate news release to insure they conform to information reported on Form 10-K. News releases necessary if annual report contains previously undisclosed material information. Trend is to consider report a marketing tool.
Annual report to shareholders: Timing and distribution	Annual report to shareholders must precede or accompany delivery of proxy material. (Proxy material should *arrive* at least 30 days prior to annual meeting.) (Form 10-K must be filed within 90 days of close of year.)	Published and submitted to shareholders at least 15 days before annual meeting but no later than three months after close of fiscal year. PROMPTEST POSSIBLE ISSUANCE URGED. Recommend release of audited figures as soon as available.	Published and submitted to shareholders at least 10 days before meeting but no later than four months after close of fiscal year. PROMPTEST POSSIBLE ISSUANCE URGED. Recommend release of audited figures as soon as available.	Financial information should be released as soon as available; second release at time printed report is issued if report contains other material information. NYSE and Amex urge broad distribution of report to include statistical services so company information is available for "ready public reference."
Annual report: Form 10-K	Required by Section 13 or 15 (d) of Securities Exchange Act of 1934 on Form 10-K. To be filed with SEC no later than 90 days after close of fiscal year. (Some schedules may be filed 120 days thereafter.) Extensive incorporation by reference from annual report to shareholders and from proxy statement now make integration of Form 10-K and report to shareholders more practical. (See general instructions G and H of Form 10-K.)	One signed copy must be filed with Exchange.	Three copies must be filed with Exchange. (See Company Guide, p. 253.)	Publicity usually not necessary unless 10-K contains previously unreported material information.
Bankruptcy or receivership	8-K immediately after appointment of receiver. Identify proceeding, court, date of event, name of receiver and date of appointment. Additional 8-K when order confirming a plan of reorganization is entered by court with information on court, date, details of plan, shares outstanding, assets and liabilities at date of order.	Immediate note to Exchange.	Same as NYSE.	Recommend press release at time of 8-K filing. Purpose is to tell creditors how to secure claims, not to notify stockholders of a material development. Further press releases and disclosures handled by receiver under court jurisdiction. Normally very limited.

Reporting Required For	Securities and Exchange Commission	New York Stock Exchange	American Stock Exchange	Generally Recommended Publicity Practice, All Companies
Compensation	See Regulation S-K, Item 402 for exhaustive discussion of how information on management compensation must be presented in filings with SEC, including issuance of stock options and stock appreciation rights.	Not applicable.	Not applicable.	While not generally "material," information on executive compensation is widely reported when proxy statements issued; public relations issues should be discussed in advance of publication.
Control: Change in	Form 8-K. Disclose name of person acquiring control, amount and source of funds, basis of control, date and description of transaction, percent of voting shares held by new controlling person, identity of person from whom control acquired, terms of loans, terms of agreements with old and new management. Statement on Schedule 13D may be required by new controlling persons.	Prompt written notice to Exchange of any change. Immediate release, if material. Recommends directors be identified in annual report.	Prompt written notice to Exchange. Immediate release, if material.	Recommend immediate announcement of any change in control of company. Normally announced by new controlling party.
Default upon senior securities	10-Q if actual material default in principal, interest, sinking fund installment, arrearage in dividends for preferred, registered or ranking securities not cured within 30 days of any stated grace period and if indebtedness exceeds 5 percent of total assets.	Immediate publicity and notice to the Exchange.	Immediate publicity and notice to the Exchange.	Immediate disclosure probably required at time default condition is known; include amount of default and total arrearage, date of default. Consider discussion of method and timing of curing default.
Directors: Change in	8-K if director resigns or refuses to stand because of disagreement and if resigning director writes and requests disclosure of dispute. New directors and officers must personally file Form 3 upon election. Proxy rules require certain disclosures about votes cast for or withheld from individual directors; disclosure of vote on all directors if one or more directors receive 5 percent plus negative vote.	Prompt written notice to Exchange of any change. Immediate release, if material. Recommends Audit Committee for Board. Recommends directors be identified in annual report.	Prompt written notice to Exchange. Immediate release if material. Recommends that company with no outside directors nominate at least two independent directors.	Recommend immediate announcement of any contemplated change in directors. However, no technical requirement for publicity except where control of company changes or key person is added or lost.

Reporting Required For	Securities and Exchange Commission	New York Stock Exchange	American Stock Exchange	Generally Recommended Publicity Practice, All Companies
Dividends	All issuers of publicly traded securities are required to give notice of dividend declarations pursuant to Rule 10B-17. Over-the-counter companies must provide advance notice of record date for subsequent dissemination to investors, extending comparable stock exchange requirements to OTC market. Failure to comply places issuer in violation of Section 10 (b) of the Securities Exchange Act of 1934.	Prompt notice to Exchange and immediate publicity. "Telephone Alert" to Exchange when the action is unusual and during market hours. "Immediate" means even while directors' meeting is still in progress. Ten days' advance notice of record date. NYSE manual implies announcement of management intention prior to formal board action may be required in case of a "leak" or rumor.	Same as NYSE. Notification to Exchange by telephone or telegram with confirmation by letter.	Prepare publicity in advance and release immediately by a designated officer on word of declaration. Publicity especially important when dividend rate changes. Statement of dividend policy now common in annual reports. Statements of "intention" to take dividend action also becoming common.
Earnings	Form 10-Q required within 45 days of close of each of first three fiscal quarters. Include information outlined in 10-Q, Part I, Instruction 4, plus a narrative management analysis in form outlined in Form S-K, Item 303. Summary of quarterly results for two years in "unaudited" annual report footnote. Form 10-K required to report full year's earnings.	Quarterly. Publicity required. Shareholder mailing recommended. NYSE urges breakout of fourth quarter results for AP and UPI P/E ratio computation.	Quarterly. Should be published within 45 days after end of fiscal quarter for all four quarters.	Immediate publicity; do not hold data until printed quarterly report is published and mailed. Release no later than 10-Q filing; annual results as soon as available. Information in news release must be consistent with 10-Q. Breakout of current quarter results together with year-to-date totals desirable in 2nd, 3rd and 4th quarter releases.
Employee stock purchase and saving plans	Form 11-K may be required under 15 (d) of '34 Act. Form S-8 may also be required.	No specific rules.	No specific rules.	Generally no publicity required or recommended. There is increasing trend to mention such programs in annual report.
Environmental matters	Reg. S-K; Item 103; Instruction 5. Disclosure in Forms 10-Q, 10-K and elsewhere under legal proceedings if a) material; b) involves claim for more than 10 percent of current assets; or c) government agency involved and amount likely to exceed $100,000.	No specific provision.	No specific provision.	SEC increasingly believes extensive environmental disclosure is "meaningless and confusing to investors"; has curtailed pressure for extensive timely press release reporting in favor of orderly filings. Handle conservatively.

Reporting Required For	Securities and Exchange Commission	New York Stock Exchange	American Stock Exchange	Generally Recommended Publicity Practice, All Companies
Extraordinary charge or credit; charge to retained earnings	SEC expects discussion of nature of and reason for charge in "Management Discussion and Analysis."	Disclosure recommended for material provisions for future losses, discontinued operations, foreign operations, future costs. Include detail on amounts reserved, subsequently used and remaining available at year-end. Prior notice to Exchange required for any proposed substantial charge to retained earnings by company or by directly controlled subsidiary.	Same as NYSE for charge.	Generally material. Requires immediate disclosure. Press release should precede SEC filings. There is increasing "enterprise" reporting of impact of extraordinary items on earnings per share.
Float: Increase or decrease in	10-Q if an outstanding "class" of securities is changed more than 5 percent by issuance or purchase of securities, or payment of indebtedness. Include this information in 10-K. New rules specify timing and method for company to tender for own shares. See standard SEC treatment in Regulation S-K, Item 202.	Prompt notice when occasioned by actual or proposed deposit under voting trust agreements, etc., and brought to "official attention" of officers or directors. The NYSE requires prompt announcement of a program to purchase the company's own shares.	Prompt announcement upon establishing program to acquire the company's own shares.	Immediate publicity to extent permitted under registration restraints. Report details of statement of purpose required in 10-Q filing. Normally routine but will attract publicity if announcement signals major corporate repurchase program. Ads and releases where company tenders for own shares must conform with SEC filings. Publicity if there is sharp decrease in floating supply which could affect the market in the company's securities.
Foreign currency translation	New FASB No. 52 requires report of foreign currency translation gains or losses as they occur (quarterly).	No requirement.	No requirement.	Recent adoption of FASB No. 52 should reduce or eliminate need for extended discussion of impact of foreign currency translation outside SEC filings except in extreme cases.
Inflation: Impact of	SEC requires adherence to FASB Statement No. 33. Report in two ways in a footnote: the effect of general inflation (constant dollar); the effect of changes in specific prices of materials (current costs). Discussion is still considered "experimental."	No requirement.	No requirement.	Publicity generally not necessary. However expect considerable shareholder and press interest in this section of annual report during periods of rapid inflation.

Reporting Required For	Securities and Exchange Commission	New York Stock Exchange	American Stock Exchange	Generally Recommended Publicity Practice, All Companies
Legal proceedings	10-Q at start, termination of proceedings and in any quarter when material development occurs (generally damage claims in excess of 10 percent of current assets); also any suit against company by an officer, director or major stockholder. See Regulation S-K, Item 103.	No notice to NYSE required unless proceedings bear on ownership, dividends, interest or principal of listed securities, or start of receivership, bankruptcy, reorganization proceedings.	Public disclosure if material. Prompt notice to Exchange.	Public disclosure recommended if outcome of legal proceedings could have material effect on company and news of proceeding has not already become public. Court filings now commonly distributed to key business media with or without press release.
Listing: Initially or on another exchange	Involved and extensive legal work is required.	See listing requirements which are raised or revised frequently (NYSE Company Manual Section B). Dual listing now permitted.	See listing requirements. Dual listing now permitted.	Bulk of routine publicity handled by exchanges. Amex efforts particularly effective in electronic media. Discuss other special opportunities with legal and public relations counsel.
Management discussion and analysis	See Regulation S-K, Item 303 for complete discussion of presentation for both annual and quarterly financial reports.	Not applicable.	Not applicable.	Generally poorly written. SEC seeks greater discussion of liquidity. When well done, offers major opportunity for superior financial communications.
Market Information: Stock prices; Number of shareholders; Dividend payments; Markets where quoted	See Regulation S-K, Item 201, for standard treatment in all SEC filings.	Not applicable.	Not applicable.	Basic information rarely newsworthy in itself but valuable when presented in proper contexts.
Merger: Acquisition or disposition of assets	8-K if company acquires or disposes of a significant (10 percent of total assets or whole subsidiary) amount of assets or business other than in normal course of business. Proxy soliciting material or registration statement may also be required. Check application of Rule 145(b) to any such transaction involving exchange of stock. (See also Tender Offers.)	8-K filed (where assets acquired). Immediate public disclosure. Prompt notice to Exchange where assets disposed of.	8-K filed, for acquisition or disposition of assets. Immediate public disclosure.	NYSE policy requires immediate announcement as soon as confidential disclosures relating to such important matters are made to "outsiders" (*i.e.*, other than "top management" and their individual confidential "advisors"). Immediate publicity, especially when assets consist of an entire product line, division, operating unit or a "substantial" part of the business.

Reporting Required For	Securities and Exchange Commission	New York Stock Exchange	American Stock Exchange	Generally Recommended Publicity Practice, All Companies
Policy statement on handling inside information	No rule.	No rule.	No rule.	Not specifically required by any regulatory authority. Cases involving insider information have turned on whether company had developed and implemented a written policy on disclosure of material, non-public corporate information. SEC requires submission of such statements as part of consent decree.
Prospectus and registration statement	Prospectus must be filed as part of registration statement. Copies distributed to underwriters and dealers in securities offerings, and in turn to investors. Photos of management, products, maps, other visuals permitted. Forecasts may be included in prospectuses and registration statements. See Regulation S-K, Item 500 for extensive discussion of contents.	Seven copies of final prospectus to Exchange. May be used as part of listing application covering the new securities.	Copy of complete registration filing to Exchange. Recent prospectus may be used as part of listing application covering the new securities.	News release, if issued at time of registration, must state from whom prospectus may be obtained. See SEC Rule 134 for permitted content of release at or after initial filing, and SEC Rule 135 for permitted content of release announcing intention to file.
Projection: Forecast or estimate of earnings	See Reg S-K General Policy (b). SEC policy encourages use of projections of future economic performance that have "a reasonable basis" and are presented in an appropriate format. Obligation to correct promptly when facts change. Should not discontinue or resume projections without clear explanation of action.	Immediate public disclosure when news goes beyond insiders and their confidential advisors.	Public disclosure not required initially, but if earnings forecast released, and later appears to be wrong, issuer must correct promptly and publicly.	Projections should be either avoided altogether or widely circulated with all assumptions stated. Projections by others may require correction by company if wrong but widely believed. Once having made projection, issuer has obligation to "update" it promptly if assumptions prove wrong. Press releases and other communications should include all information necessary to an understanding of the projection. Legal counsel should be consulted.

Reporting Required For	Securities and Exchange Commission	New York Stock Exchange	American Stock Exchange	Generally Recommended Publicity Practice, All Companies
Proxy material	Preliminary copies of proxy form and statement filed with SEC at least 10 days prior to shareholder mailing, finals when sent to holders and to each exchange where listed. SEC has broadened disclosure requirements to include additional information on directors, and has changed form of proxy to provide shareholders greater voice in corporate governance. Issuer must disclose in proxy final date for receipt of shareholder proposals.	Immediate newspaper publicity on controversial issues, especially when there is a contest. Four copies of definitive proxy material to Exchange. Ask for advance review in major matters, e.g., to determine Exchange policy; also whether brokers may vote "street name" shares without instructions from customers.	Same as NYSE. Ten copies of all proxy material are required when sent to shareholders.	Normally publicity not needed on routine matters. Press release at time proxy is mailed becoming more common. Press release may constitute "soliciting" material, so caution is advised. Special rules apply in contests; use caution. Corporate responsibility issues: no requirement to identify shareholder proposals by press release prior to meeting. Expanded information on executive compensation is widely used for round-up stories in spring. Review carefully prior to inquiries.
Questionable or illegal payments	Controversial "voluntary" program requires filing under miscellaneous item of Form 8-K. Guidelines for content published by SEC in May '76. Current policy in dispute.	No requirement.	No requirement.	Recommend press release conforming to 8-K at time 8-K is filed. However, no technical requirement for publicity. Recommend adoption of company policy statement on ethical business practices.
Redemption, repurchase, cancellation, retirement of listed securities	File 10-Q if amount of securities decrease is greater than 5 percent of amount outstanding. File 8-K and full general disclosure if the transaction is material. File Schedule 13E-4 on or prior to date of commencement of repurchase offer. File Schedule 13E-3 if going private.	Immediate press publicity. Fifteen-day advance notice to Exchange prior to redemption. Prompt notice to Exchange of any corporate or other action affecting securities in whole or in part.	Fifteen-day advance notice to Exchange prior to redemption. Prompt notice of corporate action that will result in any of these.	Usually advertisement is required. Written notice to security holders. News release.
Rights to subscribe	Registration under the Securities Act of 1933. Prefiling notice covered by SEC Rule 135. Notice to NASD or exchanges 10 days before record date required under Securities Exchange Act antifraud provisions.	Preliminary discussion necessary. Immediate publicity. Important to work out time schedule with Exchange before any action taken. Notice to shareholders in advance of proposed record date.	Preliminary discussion necessary. Immediate publicity. Important to work out time schedule with Exchange before any action taken. Notice to shareholders in advance of proposed record date. Subscription period must extend at least 14 days after mailing date.	Immediate publicity and mailing to stockholders to give all adequate time "to record their interest and to exercise their rights," according to NYSE.

Reporting Required For	Securities and Exchange Commission	New York Stock Exchange	American Stock Exchange	Generally Recommended Publicity Practice, All Companies
Securities: Change in, change in assets securing	10-Q if rights of holders are materially changed directly or through changes in another class of security. Separate item on Form 10-Q for withdrawal or substitution of assets.	Immediate notice to Exchange.	Immediate notice to Exchange. Timely disclosure if materially significant for investors.	Depends on terms. Occurs infrequently.
Segment reporting: (line of business reporting)	See Regulation S-K, Item 101 for standard treatment in all SEC filings.	No requirement. However, "recommended" for inclusion in annual reports.	Same as NYSE.	SEC requirements have created significant opportunities to describe company in clear and detailed fashion. Evaluate filed information for use in all company presentations.
Stockholder proposals	Rule 14a-8 specifies when and under what circumstances company must include shareholder proposal in proxy materials.	No requirement.	No requirement.	SEC interest in "shareholder democracy" is declining. Current liberal rules may change. Publicity normally limited to special "advocacy" publications. General reporting likely at time of annual meeting only.
Stock split, stock dividend or other change in capitalization	10-Q required for increase or decrease if exceeds 5 percent of amount of securities of the class previously outstanding. Notice to NASD or Exchange 10 days before record date under Securities Exchange Act antifraud provisions.	Immediate public disclosure and Exchange notification. Issuance of new shares requires prior listing approval. "Telephone Alert" procedure should be followed.	Same as NYSE.	Immediate publicity as soon as proposal becomes known to "outsiders" whether formally voted or not. Discuss early whether to describe transaction as "split," "dividend" or both and use terminology consistently.

Reporting Required For	Securities and Exchange Commission	New York Stock Exchange	American Stock Exchange	Generally Recommended Publicity Practice, All Companies
Tender offer	Conduct and published remarks of all parties governed by Sections 13(d), 13(e), 14(d), 14(e) of the '34 Act and regulations thereunder. Schedule 14D-1 disclosure required of raider. Target required to file Schedule 14D-9 for any solicitation or recommendation to security holders. (See also Hart, Scott Rodino requirements.)	Consult Exchange Stock List Department in advance. Immediate publicity and notice to Exchange.	Consult Exchange Securities Division in advance. Immediate publicity and notice to Exchange.	Massive publicity effort required; should not be attempted without thorough familiarity with current rules and constant consultation with counsel. Neither raider nor target should comment publicly until necessary SEC filings have been made. "Stop, look, listen" letter permitted under Rule 14d-9(e).
Treasury stock: Increase or decrease	Check Form 10-Q, items 5 and 6 for possible application. Note: Special rules apply during tender battle.	Notice within 10 days after close of fiscal quarter in which any transaction takes place. Prompt notice of any purchase above prevailing market price.	Same as NYSE. Companies required to notify Exchange on purchase above market price.	Normally no immediate publicity. Reason for action is normally given in annual or quarterly publication before or after event. However, see remarks under "Float," where applicable.

Appendix F
Annual Meeting Checklist

By Frank Widder

The following annual shareholder's meeting checklist can be adapted to serve as a "preflight" for almost any major meeting.

I. Meeting announcement
   A. Shareholder's proxy statement and general notice
   B. Investment houses', major brokers', and institutional investors' notice and invitation
   C. Financial media invitations
   D. Employee notice of meeting
   E. Guests

   Follow-up (by phone or in person)
   A. Investor relations contacts with major shareholders to determine participation, major areas of interest, potential problems
   B. Major investment houses involved with company
   C. Local financial press
   D. Guest relations

II. Management announcement
   A. Notify all key management personnel to make sure they will be there and arrange alternates for those who cannot make it.
   B. Notify all members of the board to determine their ability to make the meeting.
   C. Arrange flight times and book hotel in advance; guarantee arrival if necessary.

III. Management coaching
   A. Draft basic list of shareholder problems and questions.
   B. Arrange meeting with CEO and chairman to prepare answers, with key staff and legal department to run down answers, and practice those answers.
   C. Review and practice management speeches.

IV. Presentation materials
   A. Review orders for graphs and slides, compare with financial review speech.
   B. Screen any films.
   C. Review displays.

V. Agenda: order of presentations with approximate running times (in minutes).
   A. Introduction—chairman calls meeting to order and introduces board and management (4:00)
   B. Opening comments by chairman and review of overall activities of company (6:00)
   C. President's message (with visuals) (15:00)
   D. Financial report by vice president, finance (with slide highlights) (5:00)
   E. Film (20:00)
   F. Present proposals in proxy (limit each shareholder to one statement per issue; hand out ballots to shareholders at beginning) (20:00)
   G. Voting, collect ballots (3:00)
   H. General discussion (limit shareholders to one question each) (30:00)
   I. Announce voting results (3:00)
   J. Present company awards of appreciation (2:00)
   K. Adjournment (1:00)—Total: 1 hour, 49 minutes

Agenda allows 20 minutes additional for discussion or for more questions during presentation of proposals. Final agenda will be printed and passed out by ushers at meeting.

VI. Site preparation
   A. Staff
      1. Electrician, lighting, and sound equipment specialists on hand from 8 A.M. through 5 P.M.
      2. Supervisor of custodial, security, and equipment staff
      3. Walkie-talkie communications network with equipment staff
      4. Waiters for lounge
      5. Caterers for lounge
   B. Parking
      1. Traffic direction displays at parking lot entrances
      2. Parking attendants directing traffic to proper area
      3. Signs pointing to meeting entrance in parking lot
   C. Entrance/reception
      1. Reception tables with pencils and guest roster
      2. Receptionists to staff tables and answer questions about facilities (need to be briefed beforehand)
      3. Well-marked rest areas and signs indicating meeting area
      4. Unarmed security to control crowd and provide protection
      5. Armed security located in discrete areas of meeting room
      6. Name tags for all representatives of company
   D. Display area
      1. Displays set up along walls, not to impede foot traffic, and checked for operation 24 hours in advance
      2. Representatives to staff each booth and be prepared for questions about display
      3. Tables to display necessary financial information—annual report, 10-K, proxy statement, quarterlies
   E. Lounge area
      1. Adequate seating for participants, guests
      2. Breakfast/luncheon tables
   F. Meeting area
      1. Sound, lighting, video checks
      2. Sound mikes for all stage participants
      3. Additional speakers for amplification
      4. Alternate hookup in case of failures—sound, lighting, and video; alternate film in case of breakage
      5. Large screen for slide and film
      6. Slide and film projectors for presentation
      7. Audio and lighting mixers
      8. Portable, remote mikes with long cords for audience questions
      9. Tape recorder hookup to record proceedings

G. Construction
  1. Podium constructed high enough for everyone to have direct view of all participants
  2. Area blocked off for board and management to view film
  3. Area blocked off for lighting and sound equipment
  4. Exits properly marked
  5. Access to podium and all chairs necessary for seating board and management
  6. Logo prominently displayed and lighted above podium
H. Staff
  1. Ushers with flashlights at all entrances for seating
  2. Security at far corners of room
  3. Backstage technicians for sound emergencies
  4. Remote mike monitors on both aisles or front and back of room
  5. Photographer to shoot proceedings, displays, and key presentations
I. Stage seating arrangements
  1. Podium in middle, chairs to either side
  2. Arrange board members in tenure order
  3. Management in hierarchy order
  4. Chairman sits on board side
  5. President on management side
  6. Nameplates for all participants on podium
  7. Glasses, water, ashtrays
J. Shareholder seating
  1. First-come basis
  2. Areas roped off for invited shareholders and guests
  3. Areas roped off for film viewing by participants
  4. Special area for members not represented on stage—public accountants, special staff, guests

VII. Final run-through
  A. Day prior complete mock session of annual report, with key principals and timing of presentation—including possible questions and responses.
  B. Review slide show and cues four hours before meeting.
  C. Check screening room communications to begin film. Make sure time is allowed to clear stage.
  D. Make sure award is ready for presentation.
  E. Hand out scripts to key participants and technical people.

VIII. Day of meeting
  A. Review with supervisor that all technical checks are O.K.
  B. See that all displays are up and working.
  C. Contact board and management people to check for emergencies in transportation. Arrange backup accommodations if necessary.
  D. Sit-down breakfast with key participants to go over agenda and cover any last-minute questions.
  E. Go to convention center, check in with supervisor, security head, parking attendant. Ensure copies of scripts at podium.
  F. Greet participants and guide to lounge.
  G. Wait for shareholders and investors, media. Be available for questions and arrange interviews.
  H. Sit down and wait.
  I. Guide participants, guests to luncheon in lounge. Make sure bar is set up.
  J. Have a drink—and good night.

Appendix G
Official Statement on Public Relations

(Formally adopted by PRSA Assembly, November 6, 1982)
Public relations helps our complex, pluralistic society to reach decisions and function more effectively by contributing to mutual understanding among groups and institutions. It serves to bring private and public policies into harmony.

Public relations serves a wide variety of institutions in society such as businesses, trade unions, government agencies, voluntary associations, foundations, hospitals, and educational and religious institutions. To achieve their goals, these institutions must develop effective relationships with many different aduiences or publics such as employees, members, customers, local communities, shareholders and other institutions, and with society at large.

The managements of institutions need to understand the attitudes and values of their publics in order to achieve institutional goals. The goals themselves are shaped by the external environment. The public relations practitioner acts as a counselor to management, and as a mediator, helping to translate private aims into reasonable, publicly acceptable policy and action.

As a management function, public relations encompasses the following:

- Anticipating, analyzing, and interpreting public opinion, attitudes, and issues which might impact, for good or ill, the operations and plans of the organization.
- Counseling management at all levels in the organization with regard to policy decisions, courses of action, and communication, taking into account their public ramifications and the organization's social or citizenship responsibilities.
- Researching, conducting, and evaluating, on a continuing basis, programs of action and communication to achieve informed public understanding necessary to the success of an organization's aims. These may include marketing, financial, fund-raising, employee, community or government relations, and other programs.
- Planning and implementing the organization's efforts to influence or change public policy.
- Setting objectives, planning, budgeting, recruiting and training staff, developing facilities—in short, *managing* the resources needed to perform all of the above.
- Examples of the knowledge that may be required in the professional practice of public relations include communication arts, psychology, social psychology, sociology, political science, economics, and the principles of management and ethics. Technical knowledge and skills are required for opinion research, public issues analysis, media relations, direct mail, institutional advertising, publications, film/video productions, special events, speeches, and presentations.

In helping to define and implement policy, the public relations practitioner utilizes a variety of professional communication skills and plays an integrative role both within the organization and between the organization and the external environment.

Index